MORALITY IN
PRACTICE

MORALITY IN
PRACTICE

JAMES P. STERBA

University of Notre Dame

WADSWORTH PUBLISHING COMPANY
Belmont, California
A Division of Wadsworth, Inc.

Philosophy Editor Kenneth King
Production Editor Robin Lockwood
Designer Lois Stanfield
Copy Editor John Ehlen

Printed in the United States of America

1 2 3 4 5 6 7 8 9 10—88 87 86 85 84

ISBN 0-534-02745-8

Library of Congress Cataloging in Publication Data

Main entry under title:
Morality in practice.
   1. Social ethics—Addresses, essays, lectures.
I. Sterba, James P.
HM216.M667 1983   170   83–10298
ISBN 0–534–02745–8

DEDICATION

To Sonya,
whose long naps made this book possible.

CONTENTS

PREFACE

The present anthology was born of exasperation. First there were the generous omissions in the available moral problems anthologies—omissions of sufficiently opposing articles on the moral problems covered. Then there were the copy centers that provided the missing articles for student consumption—tardily delivered in one uncollated heap. Then there were the students (only a handful, to be sure) who never seemed to have the $5.82 copying fee the entire month I collected for it in class. The only way out, alas, was to provide a new moral problems anthology that minimized these and other sources of frustration and had other nice features as well. The present book is the result. It has, to recommend it, the following:

Distinctive Features:
1. The anthology contains radically opposing articles defending alternative solutions to six mainline moral problems. Every article included has been published before, edited, and tested for class use.
2. Each section of the anthology begins with an article discussing the basic concepts to be employed and concludes with one or more articles discussing specific practical applications.
3. Introductions are provided which help to set out the framework for the discussion and criticism of the articles in each section.
4. Suggestions for further reading are found at the end of each section.

Innovative Features
1. The Introductions argue that a practical solution to any one of the moral problems considered in the anthology requires solutions to the other moral problems as well. It is argued that this holds irrespective of the ultimate political or moral ideals one happens to endorse.
2. Brief summaries are provided at the beginning of each article to enable students to test and improve their comprehension.

In putting together this anthology I have benefited enormously from the advice and help of many different people. In particular, I would like to thank Ken King and Mary Arbogast of Wadsworth Publishing Co., Robin Lockwood and John Ehlen of Bookman Productions, my wife and colleague Janet Kourany, Lance Leibman of Harvard Law School, Clifton Perry of Auburn University, my colleagues Jorge Garcia and David Solomon, Margaret Battin of the

University of Utah, and Hugh La Follette of East Tennessee State University. I would also like to thank the following reviewers: Bernard Cassidy, Loyola University; Seymour Feldman, Rutgers University; Karen Hanson, Indiana University; David Haslett, University of Delaware; George Lucas, Randolph-Macon College; James Self, University of Florida; Paul Taylor, Iowa State University. Work on this anthology was made possible by financial assistance from Harvard Law School, the Earhart Foundation, and the University of Notre Dame.

James P. Sterba

GENERAL INTRODUCTION

YOU PROBABLY LIKE TO think of yourself as a just and moral person; most of us do. To be truly such, however, you must know something about the demands of justice and how they apply in your own particular circumstances. You must be able to assess, for example, whether your society's economic and legal system is just—that is, whether the ways income and wealth are distributed in your society as well as the methods of enforcing that distribution give people what they deserve. You must also be able to determine whether other institutions in your society—such as the military defense system, the educational system, the foreign aid program—are truly just. Without investigating these things and coming to an informed opinion, none of us has very good reasons for believing that we are just and moral persons and not the perpetrators or the beneficiaries of injustice. For unless we have attained some understanding about such matters, we are like an athlete who claims to be a good player although she is manifestly ignorant of both the rules and the strategies of her sport.

The aim of this anthology is to assist you in acquiring the knowledge you will need to justify a belief that you are a just and moral person. For this purpose, the anthology contains a wide spectrum of readings on six important contemporary moral problems:

1. The problem of the distribution of income and wealth (Who should control what resources within a society?)
2. The problem of distant peoples and future generations (What obligations do we have to distant peoples and future generations?)

3. The problem of abortion and euthanasia (Do fetuses have a right to life and what should we do for the dying?)
4. The problem of discrimination and prejudice (What is the proper response to racial and sexual discrimination and prejudice?)
5. The problem of punishment and responsibility (Who should be punished and in what should their punishment consist?)
6. The problem of war and nuclear deterrence (What are the moral limits to military defense?).

Both theoretical and practical readings about each problem are included. The theoretical selections discuss the options available in each problem area. The practical selections help you face squarely the question of how these options apply to everyday life. By working through these readings you should gain a more informed view about what justice demands of us with respect to each of these moral problems.

You should also come to appreciate why a practical solution to any one of these moral problems requires solutions to the other problems as well. That is to say, the readings on the distribution of wealth and income (in Section I) may have helped you to characterize a morally defensible system for distributing income and wealth within a society; but you would still not know how to apply such a system in a particular society without also inquiring how just that society is with respect to the other problem areas covered by this anthology.

For suppose justice requires us to provide for the basic nutritional needs of distant peoples and future generations as well as for people within our own society. (See the readings in Section II.) Surely such

1

a requirement would at least restrict the use of non-renewable resources to satisfy the nonbasic or luxury needs of persons within our society—a use that might otherwise be permitted by a morally defensible system for distributing income and wealth within our society.

Still further moral restrictions upon the satisfaction of persons' nonbasic or luxury needs could arise from a correct determination of who has a right to life. For example, if fetuses have a right to life, many of us may be morally required to sacrifice the satisfaction of certain nonbasic or luxury needs in order to bring fetuses to term. If, by contrast, euthanasia can be morally justified, scarce resources that are now used to sustain human life could be freed up for other purposes. (See the readings in Section III.)

Justice may also demand that we sacrifice the satisfaction of some nonbasic or luxury needs to remedy past discrimination and prejudice. For example, we may be required to turn away candidates for medical schools and law schools who are otherwise qualified so that other candidates who have suffered from past injustices may be compensated by admission to these schools. (See the readings in Section IV.)

Similarly, the legitimate costs of legal enforcement must ultimately enter into any calculation of who gets what in society. This will require a solution to the problem of punishment and responsibility. (See the readings in Section V.)

A solution to the problem of punishment and responsibility, in turn, itself presupposes solutions to the other moral problems discussed in the anthology. For suppose that, in a society with a just distribution of income and wealth, persons who put forth their best efforts would receive a yearly income of at least $8,000 if the society has the resources. (If you think a just distribution of income would provide some other amount, plug that amount in and make the corresponding adjustments in subsequent figures.) Suppose further that the society in which you and I live has an unjust distribution of income and wealth because, although there are enough resources for a just distribution, many persons who put forth their

best efforts receive no more than $4,000 per year while others receive as much as $400,000. Now let's say that your income is $400,000 and mine is only $4,000 even though I have tried every legal way to increase my income. Assume also that any resort to civil disobedience or armed revolution would be ineffectual and too costly for me personally. If I then rob you of $4,000, thus bringing my yearly income up to the just allotment of $8,000, what would a morally defensible system of punishment and responsibility do to me if I happened to be caught? To require a punishment equal in severity to the $4,000 I took would simply reinforce an unjust distribution of income and wealth. So it seems that only a fairly light punishment or no punishment at all should be required. What this example shows is that the application of a morally defensible solution to the problem of punishment and responsibility depends on a solution to the problem of the distribution of income and wealth in a society. To know, therefore, how to apply a morally defensible system of punishment and responsibility in a particular society, you must know to what degree that society incorporates a morally defensible distribution of income and wealth.

Finally, as we in the United States are painfully aware at the present time, proposed allocations for distributing income and wealth through social welfare programs can come into conflict with proposed allocations for military defense. Many have argued that when this happens we must sacrifice social welfare programs to meet the requirements of military defense, while others have disagreed. Obviously, then, to know exactly how your solutions to the other problem areas treated in this anthology should be applied in a particular society, you also need to know what a morally defensible system of military defense requires for that society. (See the readings in Section VI.)

That the practical solutions to the problem areas covered by the anthology are interconnected can perhaps be usefully represented by means of the following diagram:

A Solution to the Problem of Distant Peoples and Future Generations	←Requires→	A Solution to the Problem of the Distribution of Income and Wealth	←Requires→	A Solution to the Problem of Abortion and Euthanasia
↗ Requires ↙		↑ Requires ↓	↖ Requires ↘	
A Solution to the Problem of Discrimination and Prejudice		A Solution to the Problem of Punishment and Responsibility		A Solution to the Problem of War and Nuclear Deterrence

Put briefly, what is required (or permitted) by a morally defensible solution to the problem of the distribution of income and wealth within a society will depend on what is required (or permitted) by morally defensible solutions to the problems of distant peoples and future generations, abortion and euthanasia, discrimination and prejudice, punishment and responsibility, and war and deterrence. Moreover, as we have seen in the case of the problem of punishment and responsibility, the dependency can run both ways. This means that any solution you might have to one of these moral problems can only be provisional until you are able to determine solutions to the others as well. And even if you are unable at the moment to devise solutions to all of these moral problems, you must still acknowledge that your final solutions will need to be interconnected.

Notice too that acknowledging the interconnectedness of the solutions to these moral problems does not presuppose a commitment to any particular political or moral ideal. For example, whether you tend to be a conservative, a liberal, a libertarian, a socialist, or anything else, the interconnectedness of the solutions to the moral problems we are discussing still obtains. Those who endorse different political and moral ideals will presumably devise different solutions to these practical moral problems; yet in the case of each such ideal the solutions will be interconnected.

Working through the selections of this anthology will not always be an easy task. You will clearly understand some after the first reading; others you may need to read several times. You should also make sure you give each selection a fair hearing, for while some will accord with your current views others will not. It is important that you evaluate these latter with an open mind, allowing for the possibility that after sufficient reflection you may come to view them as the most morally defensible. Indeed, to approach the selections of this anthology in any other way would surely undermine the grounds you have for thinking you are a just and moral person.

THE DISTRIBUTION OF INCOME AND WEALTH

BASIC CONCEPTS

The problem of the distribution of income and wealth within a society has traditionally been referred to as the problem of distributive justice. Less frequently, this problem has been taken to include the distribution of other social goods in addition to income and wealth (e.g., political freedoms such as freedom of speech and freedom of the press), and at times it is expanded to embrace distribution on a worldwide scale rather than being confined to a particular society. The majority of philosophers, however, have tended to agree that the distribution of income and wealth within a specific society is at the heart of the problem of distributive justice.

Just as traditionally, a variety of solutions to this problem have been proposed. As Nicholas Rescher notes in his selection (see pp. 11–16), each of the following has been defended as the ultimate criterion for the distribution of income and wealth: equality, need, ability and/or achievement, effort, productivity, social utility, and supply and demand. Before examining these and other criteria proposed as solutions to the problem of distributive justice, however, it is useful to observe what is common to all such solutions.

First, even though the solutions may differ as to exactly how much income and wealth particular people deserve or should rightfully possess, they all purport to tell us what people deserve or what they have a right to possess. For example, some may think that people deserve to have their needs ful-

filled, others that what people deserve or should rightfully possess is the product of their labor.

Second, all solutions to the problem of distributive justice make a distinction between justice and charity. Justice is what we ought to do as a matter of obligation or duty. By contrast, charity is what we ought to do if we want to choose what is the morally best possible action available to us. Accordingly, the demands of charity go beyond duty. In addition, failure to fulfill the demands of justice is blameworthy, violates someone's rights, and can legitimately be punished. By contrast, failure to fulfill the demands of charity, although not ideal, is not blameworthy, nor does it violate anyone's rights, nor can it legitimately be punished. Of course, certain solutions to the problem of distributive justice will give more scope to justice and less to charity, while others will do just the opposite; but in all such solutions the distinction between justice and charity will still be found to play a role.

Turning from common ground to disputed territory, solutions offered to the problem of distributive justice have tended to take either liberty or equality, or some particular mix of liberty and equality, as the ultimate political ideal. Through the ages different labels have been used for these three positions. With some justification, however, those who take liberty to be the ultimate political ideal can be called libertarians, using the label favored by some of the most ardent contemporary defenders of this ideal. For similar reasons, those who take equality to be the ultimate political ideal may be called socialists, and those who favor a particular mix of liberty and equality can be designated welfare liberals. (As you will see, Ronald Dworkin (see pp. 43–54) objects to this classification, but I will defer consideration of his objection until later.)

LIBERTARIANISM

Libertarians, like John Hospers (see pp. 17–26), who take liberty as the ultimate political ideal, typically define liberty as "the state of being unconstrained by other persons from doing what one wants." This definition limits the scope of liberty in two ways. First, not all constraints, whatever the source, count as a restriction of liberty; the constraints must come from other persons. For example, people who are constrained by natural forces from getting to the top of Mount Everest do not lack liberty in this regard. Second, constraints that have their source in other persons, but that do not run counter to an individual's wants, constrain without restricting that individual's liberty. Thus, for people who do not want to hear Beethoven's Fifth Symphony, the fact that others have effectively proscribed its performance does not restrict their liberty, even though it does constrain what they are able to do.

Of course, libertarians may wish to argue that even such constraints can be seen to restrict a person's liberty once we take into account the fact that people normally want or have a general desire to be unconstrained by others. But other philosophers have thought that the possibility of such constraints points to a serious defect in the libertarian's definition of liberty, which only can be remedied by defining liberty more broadly as "the state of being unconstrained by other persons from doing what one is able to do." Applying this revised definition to the above example, we find that people's liberty to hear Beethoven's Fifth Symphony would be restricted even if they did not want to hear it (and even if, perchance, they did not want to be unconstrained by others), since other people would still be constraining them from doing what they are able to do.

Confident that problems of defining liberty can be overcome in some satisfactory manner, libertarians go on to characterize their political ideal as requiring that each person should have the greatest amount of liberty commensurate with the same liberty for all. From this ideal, libertarians claim to derive a number of more specific requirements, in particular a right to life, a right to freedom of speech, press, and assembly, and a right to property.

Here it is important to observe that the libertarian's right to life is not a right to receive from others the goods and resources necessary for preserving one's life; it is simply a right not to be killed. So understood, the right to life is not a right to welfare. In fact, there are no welfare rights in the libertarian view. Accordingly, the libertarian's understanding of the right to property is not a right to receive from others the goods and resources necessary for one's welfare, but rather a right to acquire goods and resources either by initial acquisition or by voluntary agreement.

Obviously, by defending rights such as these, libertarians can only support a limited role for government. That role is simply to prevent and punish initial acts of coercion—the only wrongful actions for libertarians.

Nevertheless, no libertarian would deny that it is a good thing for people to have sufficient goods and resources to meet at least their basic nutritional needs; what libertarians would deny is that it is the role of government to make provision for such needs. Some good things, like the provision of welfare to the needy, are requirements not of justice but only of charity, libertarians claim. Accordingly, failure to make such provisions is neither blameworthy nor punishable.

A basic difficulty with the libertarian's solution to the problem of distributive justice is the claim that a right to life and a right to property (as the libertarian understands these rights) derive from an ideal of liberty. Why should we think that an ideal of liberty requires a right to life and a right to property that exclude a right to welfare? Surely it would seem that a right to property (as the libertarian understands this right) might well justify a rich person's depriving a poor person of the liberty to acquire the goods and resources necessary for meeting her basic nutritional needs. How could we appeal to an ideal of liberty to justify such a deprivation? Surely we couldn't claim that such a deprivation is justified for the sake of preserving a rich person's liberty to use the goods and resources he possesses to meet his luxury needs. Or could we?

To meet this difficulty, some libertarians have resorted to defining liberty in terms of rights, so that a restriction of liberty is a violation of someone's rights, usually a violation of a right to life or a right to property. But this approach gives rise to a difficulty akin to the one it seeks to resolve. For we could still ask why the libertarian interprets a right to life and a right to property so as to favor a rich person's nonbasic or luxury needs over a poor person's basic nutritional needs rather than so as to favor a poor person's basic nutritional needs over a rich person's nonbasic or luxury needs? Thus whether rights are defined in terms of liberty or liberty is defined in terms of rights, we can still question the justification for the libertarian's interpretation of a right to life and a right to property.

SOCIALISM

Clearly the political ideal that seems furthest removed from the libertarian's ideal of liberty is the socialist's ideal of equality. More specifically, the socialist defends an ideal that calls for equality of need fulfillment. As Karl Marx stated this ideal over a century ago, distribution is to proceed according to the principle, "From each according to his abilities, to each according to his needs."

At first hearing, this ideal might sound simply crazy to someone brought up in a capitalist society. For the obvious objection to such an ideal is, how can you get persons to contribute according to their ability if you are going to distribute income on the basis of persons' needs and not on the basis of their contributions?

The answer, according to a socialist, is to make the work that must be done in a society as much as possible enjoyable in itself. As a result, people will want to do the work they are capable of doing because they find it intrinsically rewarding. For a start, socialists might try to get people to accept presently existing, intrinsically rewarding jobs at lower sala-

ries. For example, they might attempt to have top executives work for $300,000 rather than $600,000 a year. Yet ultimately socialists hope to make all jobs intrinsically as rewarding as possible so that, after people are no longer working primarily for external rewards when making their best contributions to society, distribution can proceed on the basis of need.

Socialists propose to implement their ideal of equality by giving workers democratic control over the work place. This point is stressed by Carl Cohen (see pp. 26–36). Yet Cohen tends to view democratic control of the work place as simply the logical extension of a socialist's commitment to democracy, while most socialists would probably go further and trace their commitment to democracy to their more ultimate ideal calling for equality of need fulfillment. The key idea here is that if workers have more to say about how they do their work, their work itself will be intrinsically more rewarding. As a consequence, they will be more motivated to work, since their work itself will be meeting their needs. Socialists believe that this extension of democracy to the work place will necessarily lead to socialization of the means of production and the end of private property.

Still, even with democratic control of the work place, there will be some jobs that probably can't be made intrinsically rewarding, e.g., garbage collecting or changing bedpans. Now what socialists propose to do with respect to such jobs is to divide them up in some equitable manner. Some people might, for example, collect garbage one day a week and then work at intrinsically rewarding jobs the rest of the work week. Others would change bedpans or do some other slop job one day a week and then work at an intrinsically rewarding job the other days of the work week. By making jobs intrinsically as rewarding as possible, in part through democratic control of the work place and an equitable assignment of unrewarding tasks, socialists think it is possible to have persons contribute according to their ability even when distribution proceeds according to needs.

Finally, it is important to notice that the socialist's ideal of equality does not accord with what exists in countries like the Soviet Union or Albania. Judging the acceptability of the socialist's ideal of equality by what takes place in those countries would be just as unfair as judging the acceptability of a libertarian's ideal of liberty by what takes place in countries like Chile or the Philippines, where as we know, citizens are arrested and imprisoned without cause. By analogy, it would be like judging the merits of college football by the way Vanderbilt's or Northwestern's teams play rather than by the way Alabama's or Notre Dame's teams play. Actually, a fairer comparison would be to judge a socialist's ideal of equality by what takes place in countries like Sweden or Yugoslavia, and to judge a libertarian's ideal of liberty by what takes place in the United States. But even these comparisons are not wholly appropriate since none of these countries fully conforms to those ideals.

A basic difficulty with the socialist's solution to the problem of distributive justice concerns the proclaimed necessity of abolishing private property and socializing the means of production. For it seems perfectly possible to give workers more control over their work place while at the same time the means of production remain privately owned. Of course, private ownership would have a somewhat different character in a society with democratic control of the work place, but it need not cease to be private ownership. After all, private ownership would also have a somewhat different character in a society having a more equal distribution of private holdings, and hence a more equal distribution of bargaining power, than that which is found in most capitalist societies; yet it would not cease to be private ownership. Accordingly, we could imagine a society characterized by private ownership of the means of production in which—because ownership is so widely dispersed throughout the society (e.g., nearly everyone owns 10 shares of major industrial stock and no one more than 20 shares) and because of the degree of democratic control of the work place— many of the valid criticisms socialists make of existing capitalist societies would no longer apply.

WELFARE LIBERALISM

Finding merit in both the libertarian's ideal of liberty and the socialists' ideal of equality, welfare liberals seek to combine the best of both ideals, usually favoring a mix of economic liberty with political equality.

One of the ways this mix of liberty and equality has traditionally been defended is by the argument that the requirements of this mix of liberty and equality can be justified in terms of maximizing total happiness or utility in society. The idea is that if we compare different political ideals with a view to the degree to which they make people happy or maximize utility, a particular mix of liberty and equality will be preferred to all other ideals.

Unfortunately, there is a fundamental problem with this utilitarian defense of welfare liberalism. Consider, for example, a society in which the members are equally divided between the Privileged Rich and the Alienated Poor and suppose that the incomes under two alternative social arrangements for this society are the following:

	Social Arrangement A	Social Arrangement B
Privileged Rich	$100,000	$60,000
Alienated Poor	$ 10,000	$15,000

Given these alternatives, considerations of maximizing utility would appear to favor Social Arrangement A over B. But suppose that welfare liberalism required a high minimum for each person in society. Then it would seem that the welfare liberal would favor Social Arrangement B over A, in apparent conflict with the requirements of social utility. Obviously, the possibility of such a conflict places the utilitarian defense of welfare liberalism in some doubt.

Utilitarians have responded to this problem by appealing to the declining marginal utility of money and other social goods. We all know, for example, that if on a given occasion we ate four apples, the fourth apple would probably not be as enjoyable as the first or second—the utility we experience from eating successive apples would have declined. We also know that such comparisons typically hold across individuals as well—that someone else who likes apples would probably enjoy our third or fourth apple more than we would, on the assumption that we are already quite satiated from the first two. Applied to our earlier example, considerations of the declining marginal utility of income and other social goods would seem to render Social Arrangement B

8

preferable to A from a utilitarian point of view, thus removing the grounds for thinking that welfare liberalism and social utility conflict in this case.

Of course, when such considerations of the declining marginal utility of money and other social goods have been taken into account, the utility values for the two alternatives might end up to be something like this:

Social Arrangement A		Social Arrangement B
Privileged Rich	55	40
Alienated Poor	10	15

And if they did, then there would still presumably remain a conflict between welfare liberalism and social utility, with welfare liberalism favoring Social Arrangement B, and social utility favoring Social Arrangement A . . . unless, of course, additional empirical considerations can be advanced to show that this is not the case.

A possibly more promising defense of welfare liberalism is provided by social contract theory. According to that theory, the requirements of welfare liberalism derive from the free agreement of rational agents. Sometimes, as in the writings of John Locke, this free agreement or "contract" is assumed to be an actual agreement to abide by the requirements of welfare liberalism entered into by rational agents at a particular time and place. But more frequently the "contract" is understood to be a hypothetical agreement; that is, its proponents simply claim that rational agents would freely agree to abide by the requirements of welfare liberalism under certain ideal conditions.

Recently this social contract defense of welfare liberalism has been elaborately set forth by John Rawls. Rawls argues that persons in an "original position" of equality equipped with a "veil of ignorance" that excludes knowledge of particular facts about themselves would favor the ideal of welfare liberalism as expressed by the following two principles:

1. Each person is to have an equal right to the most extensive total system of equal basic liberties that is compatible with a similiar system of liberty for all.
2. Social and economic inequalities are to be arranged so that they are both (a) to the greatest

benefit of the least advantaged, and (b) attached to offices and positions open to all under conditions of fair equality of opportunity.

Rawls argues that persons in the "original position" he described would favor this ideal even when its requirements conflicted with those of social utility. Hence, with regard to our earlier example, Rawls would contend that persons in that original position, ignorant as they are of whether they belong to the Privileged Rich or the Alienated Poor, would play it safe and favor Alternative B over Alternative A, despite the possible loss of social utility involved. In his selection (see pp. 36–43), Rawls attempts to further defend welfare liberalism by showing that his two principles of justice accord with the ideal of a well-ordered society.

Ronald Dworkin defends welfare liberalism in a manner quite similar to that employed by Rawls. In his selection (see pp. 43–54), Dworkin sees the standard social causes endorsed by liberals as rooted in an ideal of equality that requires government to be neutral on the question of what is the good life. This neutrality is very much like that provided by the veil of ignorance in Rawls' "original position." In fact, Rawls specifically requires the veil of ignorance to extend to particular theories of the good life. Dworkin's defense of welfare liberalism, however, does provide a more detailed account of the particular political programs that flow from both his and Rawls' common theoretical framework.

Dworkin also raises a serious objection to any attempt to view welfare liberalism as a particular mix of liberty and equality. He argues that this way of looking at welfare liberalism presupposes that liberty is quantifiable to a degree beyond what we can hope to attain. For example, Dworkin claims that we cannot say traffic regulations interfere less with what most people want to do than would a law forbidding them to speak out in favor of Communism. Dworkin's objection, however, cannot be sustained; all that is actually necessary for conceiving of welfare liberalism as a particular mix of liberty and equality is a rough ranking of liberties and equalities according to their importance. In the context of his example, it suffices if we can reasonably claim that freedom of speech is more important than (say) freedom to run red lights, without claiming anything more precise. Moreover, since Dworkin already sanctions the use of such comparative evaluations with respect to ideals of equality, he really cannot object to their more general use, as is required for this conception of welfare liberalism.

Two basic objections have been raised to the welfare liberal's solution to the problem of distributive justice. The first concerns the practical recommendations of the ideal, the second its ultimate defensibility. According to the first, welfare liberalism does not in fact support the practical recommendations usually associated with it, but rather (and here the critics disagree) it supports either those of socialism or those of libertarianism. For example, some have argued that persons in Rawls' "original position" would in fact choose socialist principles of justice, while others have argued that the welfare liberal's concern for economic liberty can only be fulfilled in a libertarian state. According to the second objection, welfare liberalism does require the practical recommendations usually associated with it, but the ideal fails to provide opponents with any reason to accept it; the ideal simply begs the question with respect to all the important issues.

Of these two objections, the first is by far the more interesting. The second, if valid, would simply show that discussion had reached a regrettable impasse. If the first is valid, it would force consistent welfare liberals to become either socialists or libertarians, at least in their practical recommendations. Accordingly, if we could establish objections of this sort against welfare liberalism (or against libertarianism or socialism), we would be able to build a practical political consensus without necessarily rejecting "opposing" political ideals.

PRACTICAL APPLICATIONS

The application of the ideals of libertarianism, socialism, or welfare liberalism to a particular society obviously has basic and far-reaching effects. These ideals have implications for constitutional structure, the control of industry, taxing policy, social welfare programs, and property law, to name only a few areas affected. The final two selections in this section are from important United States Supreme Court decisions to which our three political ideals can be usefully related.

The U.S. Supreme Court, of course, does not view itself as directly applying one or the other of these political ideals to the laws of the land. Rather the Court views itself as deciding whether particular laws accord with the provisions of the United States Constitution. But these two activities are not unrelated, because for most people, including Supreme Court Justices, one's views about what are the practical applications of the political ideal one takes to be the most morally defensible and one's views about what sort of laws accord with the U.S. Constitution are not clearly separable. Hence it is frequently possible to see how commitment to a political ideal is decisive in judicial decision-making.

Yet beyond coming to appreciate how political ideals and their presumed applications function in judicial decision-making, it is important for you to examine U.S. Supreme Court decisions with a view to determining to what degree the laws of your society accord with the political ideal you take to be the most morally defensible. As was stressed in the general introduction, in order to have good reasons to believe that you are a just and moral person, you need to assess to what degree the laws and institutions of your society are just—in this case, to what degree they accord with the requirements of distributive justice. Examining the two U.S. Supreme Court decisions included in this anthology should serve this purpose quite well.

In the first decision (*Wyman v. James*), the majority of the Court decided that the rights of welfare recipients are limited in various ways, and in particular that recipients are not protected against mandatory visits by caseworkers. Such a decision would surely seem justified if one believed, as libertarians do, that the provision of welfare is, at best, only a requirement of charity. Welfare liberals and socialists, however, would have difficulty accepting this decision, as did the dissenting justices of the Court.

In the second decision (*San Antonio School District v. Rodriguez*), the majority of the Court determined that education is not a right afforded strict protection by the U.S. Constitution, as long as no one is being deprived of an education. Again, this decision seems to agree with the way libertarians would understand the practical applications of their ideal of liberty;

welfare liberals and socialists would probably find themselves persuaded by the arguments of the dissenting justices.

It is important to notice that you can also work backward from your considered judgments about these Supreme Court cases to the political ideal you should favor. Frequently it is only by considering the practical applications of alternative political ideals that we can clarify our views about which ideal is the most morally defensible.

Notice too, as was stressed in the general intro-

duction, that any final solution to the problem of distributive justice within a society presupposes a solution to the other moral problems of this anthology as well. In particular, the problem of distant peoples and future generations, which is discussed in the following section, seems to be clearly connected with the problem of distributive justice. For we cannot know for sure what resources particular persons within a society should receive unless we also know what are the obligations of persons within that society to distant peoples and future generations.

Nicholas Rescher

THE CANONS OF DISTRIBUTIVE JUSTICE

Nicholas Rescher discusses the merits of seven "canons" for the distribution of income and wealth within a society and claims that there are serious objections to regarding any one of these canons as ultimate for all circumstances. As an alternative, Rescher favors a strategy of weighing the merits of each canon in a case by case application.

IN THE COURSE OF the long history of discussions on the subject, distributive justice has been held to consist, wholly or primarily, in the treatment of all people:

1. as equals (except possibly in the case of certain "negative" distributions such as punishments)
2. according to their needs
3. according to their ability or merit or achievements
4. according to their efforts and sacrifices
5. according to their actual productive contribution
6. according to the requirements of the common good, or the public interest, or the welfare of mankind, or the greater good of a greater number
7. according to a valuation of their socially useful services in terms of their scarcity in the essentially economic terms of supply and demand

Correspondingly, seven "canons" of distributive justice result, depending upon which of these factors is taken as the ultimate or primary determinant of individual claims; namely, the canons of equality, need, ability, effort, productivity, public utility, and supply and demand. Brief consideration must be given to each of these proposed conceptions of justice.[1]

THE CANON OF EQUALITY

This canon holds that justice consists in the treatment of people as equals. Here we have the *egalitarian* criterion of (idealistic) democratic theorists. The

From *Distributive Justice* (1966), pp. 73–83. Reprinted by permission of the author.

shortcomings of this canon have already been canvassed in considerable detail . . . to the effect that the principle is oblivious to the reality of differential claims and desert. It is vulnerable to all the same lines of objection which hold against the type of just-wage principle advocated by G. B. Shaw—to let all who contribute to the production of the social-economic product share in it equally.[2] Moreover, the specification of the exact way in which equality is to be understood is by no means so simple and straightforward as it seems on first view. Is one, for example, to think of the type of fixed constant equality that is at issue in a sales tax, or the "equal burden" type of differential equality at issue in a graduated income tax; and more generally, is the "equality" at issue strict equality, equality of sacrifice, equality of opportunity-and-risk, equality of rights, or equality of "consideration," etc.?[3]

A rule of strict equality violates the most elemental requisites of the concept of justice itself: justice not only requires the equal treatment of equals, as the canon at issue would certainly assure, but also under various circumstances requires the converse, the (appropriately measured) unequal treatment of unequals, a requisite which the canon violates blatantly. In any distribution among individuals whose legitimate claims with respect to this distribution are diverse, the treatment of people as equals without reference to their differential claims outrages rather than implements our sense of justice.

THE CANON OF NEED

This canon holds that justice consists in the treatment of people according to their needs. Here we have the *socialistic* principle of the idealistic socialistic and communist theoreticians: "to each according to his needs."[4] Basically this principle is closely allied with the preceding one, and is, like it, one of *rectification*: recognizing that as things stand, men come into the world with different possessions and opportunities as well as differences in natural endowments, the principle professes to treat them, not equally, but so as to *make* them as equal as possible.

Regarding this principle, it has been said:

If the task of distribution were entirely independent of the process of production, this rule would be ideal [from the standpoint of justice]; for it would treat men as equal in those respects in which they are equal; namely, as beings endowed with the dignity and the potencies of personality; and it would treat them as unequal in those respects in which they are unequal; that is, in their desires and capacities.[5]

This limitation of the rule is of itself too narrow. The principle does recognize inequalities, but it recognizes only one sort; it rides roughshod not only over the matter of productive contributions but over all other ways of grounding legitimate claims (e.g., those based on kinship, on [nonproductive] services rendered, on contracts and compacts, etc.) that make for relevant differences, i.e., inequalities, among the potential recipients of a distribution. Nor, for that matter, is the principle as clear-cut as it seems on first view: by the time anything like an adequate analysis of "need" has been provided, the principle covers a wide-ranging area.[6] For example, are we to interpret the "needs" at issue as *real* needs or as *felt* needs?

THE CANON OF ABILITY AND/OR ACHIEVEMENT

This canon holds that justice consists in the treatment of people according to their abilities. Here we have the *meritarian* criterion going back to Aristotle and echoed by the (Jeffersonian) theorists of a "natural aristocracy of ability." Natural ability, however, is a latent quality which subsists in the mode of potentiality. It represents natural endowments that can be cultivated to varying degrees and may or may not become operative and actually put to work. To allocate rewards with reference solely to innate ability, unqualified by considerations of how the abilities in question are used or abused, would be to act in a way that is patently unjust. Moreover, a question can validly be raised as to the propriety of having natural ability—which is, after all, wholly a "gift of the gods" and in no way a matter of desert—count as the sole or even the primary basis of claims.[7]

This objection might be countered by granting that it may hold for *natural* (or innate) ability, but that it fails to be applicable when the "ability" at issue is an *acquired* ability, or perhaps even more aptly, a *demonstrated* ability of the persons at issue, as determined by their achievements. This is the criterion naturally used in giving grades to students and prizes to tennis players (where need, for instance, and effort are deliberately discounted). But in this case the canon becomes transformed, in its essentials, into the Canon of Productivity, which will be dealt with below.

THE CANON OF EFFORT

This canon holds that justice consists in the treatment of people according to their efforts and sacrifices on their own behalves, or perhaps on behalf of their group (family, society, fellowmen). Here we have the *puritanical* principle espoused by theorists of a "Puritan ethic," who hold that God helps (and men should help) those who help themselves. Burke lauded the "natural society" in which "it is an invariable law that a man's acquisitions are in proportion to his labors." Think also of the historic discussions of a just wage and the traditional justification of differential wage scales. On the question of wages, classical socialists such as Fourier and St. Simon argued that the wage should be inversely proportioned to the intrinsic pleasantness (interest, appeal, prestige) of the task. (Presumably, thus, the policeman walking the beat shall receive more than the captain sitting at headquarters.) But the difficulties of this standpoint lie on the surface, e.g., the difficulty of maintaining morale and discipline in a setting in which the claims of ability and responsibility go unrecognized.

Moreover, the principle ignores the fact that effort is of its very nature a many-sided thing: it can be either fruitful or vain, well-directed or misguided, properly applied or misapplied, availing or unavailing, etc. To allocate rewards by effort as such

without reference to its nature and direction is to ignore a key facet of just procedure—to fail to make a distinction that makes a difference. Also, to reward by effort rather than achievement is socially undesirable: it weakens incentive and encourages the inefficient, the untalented, the incompetent.

THE CANON OF PRODUCTIVITY

This canon holds that justice consists in the treatment of people according to their actual productive contribution to their group.[8] Here we have the essentially economic principle of the social-welfare-minded *capitalistic* theoreticians. The claimbases at issue here are primarily those traditionally considered in economics: services rendered, capital advanced, risks run, and the like. Much is to be said on behalf of this principle as a *restricted* rule, governing the division of proceeds and profits resulting from a common productive enterprise; but it is clearly defective as a general principle of distributive justice, simply because it is an overly limited single-factor criterion. The principle is prepared to put aside all considerations not only of unmerited claims in general, but also of merited claims when merited through extra-productive factors such as need and effort.

Yet one cannot fail to be impressed by the appeal to justice of such an argument as the following:

When men of equal productive power are performing the same kind of labour, superior amounts of product do represent superior amounts of effort. . . . If men are unequal in productive power their products are obviously not in proportion to their efforts. Consider two men whose natural physical abilities are so unequal that they can handle with equal effort shovels differing in capacity by fifty per cent. Instances of this kind are innumerable in industry. If these two men are rewarded according to productivity, one will get fifty per cent more compensation than the other. Yet the surplus received by the more fortunate man does not represent any action or quality for which he is personally responsible. It corresponds to no larger output of personal effort, no superior exercise of will, no greater personal desert.

Note here the criticism of a (restricted) purely economic application of the principle by an appeal to one's sense of justice. If such an appeal is to be given but the slightest (even if not ultimately decisive) weight, as I think it must, then the canon in question must *a fortiori* be at once abandoned as an exclusive and exhaustive general principle of distributive justice.

THE CANON OF SOCIAL UTILITY

This canon holds that justice consists in the treatment of people according to the best prospects for advancing the common good, or the public interest, or the welfare of mankind, or the greater good of a greater number. The theory has two basic variants, according as one resorts to a distinction between the common good of men considered *collectively,* as constituting a social group with some sort of life of its own, or merely *distributively,* as an aggregation of separate individuals. In the former case we have the "public interest," expedientialist variant of the canon with roots going back to Hebraic theology, Stoic philosophy, and Roman jurisprudence (*pro bono publico*). In the second case we have *utilitarian* and more modern, individualistic version of the canon.

The same fundamental criticism (already dwelt upon at considerable length in our preceding discussion) can be deployed against both versions of the theory: an individual's *proper share viewed from the angle of the general good* cannot be equated with his *just share* pure and simple, because there is no "pre-established harmony" to guarantee that all of the individual's legitimate claims (the authoritative determinants of his just share) be recognized and acceded to when "the *general* good" becomes the decisive criterion. And insofar as these legitimate claims are disallowed—or *could* be disallowed—in a patently unjust (though socially advantageous) way, the prin-

ciple of the primacy of the general good exhibits a feature which precludes its acceptance as a principle of justice.

THE CANON OF SUPPLY AND DEMAND

This canon holds that justice consists in the treatment of people according to a valuation of their socially useful—or perhaps merely desired—contributions, these being evaluated not on the basis of the value of the product (as with the Canon of Productivity, above), but on the basis of relative scarcity of the service. Here we have the essentially economic principle of the more hard-boiled "play of the market" school of laissez-faire theoreticians. The train dispatcher would thus deserve a larger part of the proceeds of the joint operation than the conductor, the general manager more than the section foreman, the buyer more than the salesgirl, because—while in each case both kinds of contribution are alike essential to the enterprise—the former type of labor calls for skills that are relatively scarcer, being less plentifully diffused throughout the working population. Such valuation then rests not upon the relative extent or intrinsic merit of the contribution made, but upon the fact that that contribution is viewed by the community as necessary or desirable, and can either be made successfully by fewer people, or else involves such expenditures, risks, hardships, or hazards that fewer people are willing to undertake the task. (Throughout recent years successful entertainers have been remunerated more highly than successful physicians—and on this principle, justly so.)

As a criterion of justice, this canon suffers from the same general defects as does the Canon of Productivity which it seeks to qualify. Not only does it put aside any accommodation of unmerited claims, but also any claims based upon factors (such as individual need and expenditure of effort) which have no basis in the making of a productive contribution to felt social needs.

OUR OWN POSITION: THE CANON OF CLAIMS

One and the same shortcoming runs through all of the above canons of distributive justice: they are all *monistic*. They all recognize but one solitary, homogeneous mode of claim production (be it need, effort, productivity, or whatever), to the exclusion of all others. A single specific ground of claim establishment is canonized as uniquely authoritative, and all the others dismissed. As a result, these canons all suffer the aristocratic fault of hyperexclusiveness. As we see it, they err not so much in commission as in omission.

To correct this failing requires that we go from a concept of claim establishment that is monistic and homogeneous to one that is pluralistic and heterogeneous. To do so we put forward, as representing (in essentials) our own position on the issue of distributive justice, the Canon of Claims: Distributive justice consists in the treatment of people *according to their legitimate claims*, positive and negative. This canon shifts the burden to—and thus its implementation hinges crucially upon—the question of the nature of legitimate claims, and of the machinery for their mutual accommodation in cases of plurality, and their reconciliation in cases of conflict. To say this is not a criticism of the principle, but simply the recognition of an inevitable difficulty which must be encountered by any theory of distributive justice at the penalty of showing itself grossly inadequate.

The Canon of Claims plainly avoids the fault of overrestrictiveness: indeed, it reaches out to embrace all the other canons. From its perspective each canon represents one particular sort of ground (need, effort, productivity, etc.) on whose basis certain legitimate claims—upon whose accommodation it insists—can be advanced. The evaluation of these claims in context, and their due recognition under the circumstances, is in our view the key element of distributive justice.

We must be prepared to take such a multifaceted approach to claims because of the propriety of recognizing different kinds of claim-grounds as appropriate types of distribution. Our society inclines to the view that in the case of wages, desert is to be measured according to productivity of contribution qualified by supply-and-demand considerations; in the case of property income, by productivity considerations; in public-welfare distributions, by need qualified to avoid the demoralization inherent in certain types of means-tests; and in the negative distributions of taxation, by ability-to-pay qualified by social-utility considerations. The list could be extended and refined at great length but is already extensive enough to lend support to our pluralistic view of claims.

One important consequence of our canon must be noted. With it, the concept of justice is no solitarily self-sufficient ultimate, but becomes dependent upon the articulation of certain coordinate ideas, namely, those relating to claims and their establishment. The unraveling of the short thesis that distributive justice requires (in general) the accommodation of legitimate claims is but the preface of a long story about claims, a story for which there is neither need nor space here. Moreover, since claims themselves are not (at any rate, not in general) established by considerations of abstract justice, but are in large part grounded in positive law, the heavy dependence of justice upon a body of positive law may be seen. Where abstract justice might countenance various alternative divisions, the law specifies one particular procedure that underwrites a certain specific set of claims. That law shall embody considerations of justice is a trite thesis, but that there is a converse requirement resulting in mutual dependence is less frequently observed.

In espousing the Canon of Claims we may note that the search for a canon of distributive justice is carried back to the Roman jurists' view that the definitive principle of justice is inherent in the dictum *suum cunique tribuens*—"giving each his own." To the question *What is his own?* we have given the answer *What he deserves!*; that is, a share ideally equal—or at any rate generally proportional—to his legitimate claims.

NOTES

1. All of these canons except number 3 (the Canon of Ability) are competently and instructively discussed from an essentially economic point of view—from the special angle of the idea of a just wage or income—in ch. 14 of John A. Ryan, *Distributive Justice* (3rd ed.), New York: Macmillan, 1942.

2. Ryan, *Distributive Justice* (3rd ed.), pp. 180–181: "According to the rule of arithmetical equality, all persons who contribute to the product should receive the same amount of remuneration. With the exception of Bernard Shaw, no important writer defends this rule to-day. It is unjust because it would treat unequals equally. Although men are equal as moral entities, as human persons, they are unequal in desires, capacities, and powers. An income that would fully satisfy the needs of one man would meet only 75 per cent., or 50 per cent., of the capacities of another. To allot them equal amounts of income would be to treat them unequally with regard to the requisites of life and self development. To treat them unequally in these matters would be to treat them unequally as regards the real and only purpose of property rights. That purpose is welfare. Hence the equal moral claims of men which admittedly arise out of their moral equality must be construed as claims to equal degrees of welfare, not to equal amounts of external goods. . . . Moreover, the rule of equal incomes is socially impracticable. It would deter the great majority of the more efficient from putting forth their best efforts and turning out their maximum product. As a consequence, the total volume of product would be so diminished as to render the share of the great majority of persons smaller than it would have been under a rational plan of unequal distribution."

3. Regarding these problems, see S. I. Benn and R. S. Peters, *Social Principles and the Democratic State* (London: Allen & Unwin, 1959), ch. 5, "Justice and Equality."

4. The formula "From each according to his abilities; to each according to his needs" was first advanced by the early French socialists of the Utopian school, and was officially adopted by German socialists in the Gotha Program of 1875.

5. Ryan, *Distributive Justice* (3rd ed.), p. 181.

6. See Benn and Peters, *Social Principles and the Democratic State*, pp. 141–148.

7. "That part of a man's income which he owes to the possession of extraordinary natural abilities is a free boon to him; and from an abstract point of view bears some resemblance to the rent of other free gifts of nature. . . ." A. Marshall, *Principles of Economics* (8th ed., London: Macmillan, 1920), p. 664. The receipt of such "rents" is surely a matter of capitalizing on public necessity rather than one of obtaining the just reward due to individual desert.

8. Two alternative constructions of the principle arise, according as the "productive contribution" at issue is construed as the *total* contribution, or as solely the *net* contribution, i.e., the part that is available for consumption by others after deletion of the producers' own share.

THE LIBERTARIAN MANIFESTO

John Hospers begins by exploring various ways of understanding the basic libertarian thesis that every person is the owner of his or her own life. According to Hospers, such ownership entails rights to life, liberty, and property. Since these rights are violated by an initial use of force, the proper role of government is said to be limited to the retaliatory use of force against those who have initiated its use. All other possible roles for government, such as protecting individuals against themselves or requiring people to help one another, are regarded as illegitimate by the libertarian.

THE POLITICAL PHILOSOPHY THAT is called libertarianism (from the Latin *libertas*, liberty) is the doctrine that every person is the owner of his own life, and that no one is the owner of anyone else's life: and that consequently every human being has the right to act in accordance with his own choices, unless those actions infringe on the equal liberty of other human beings to act in accordance with their choices.

There are several other ways of stating the same libertarian thesis:

1. *No one is anyone else's master, and no one is anyone else's slave.* Since I am the one to decide how my life is to be conducted just as you decide about yours, I have no right (even if I had the power) to make you my slave and be your master, nor have you the right to become the master by enslaving me. Slavery is *forced* servitude, and since no one owns the life of anyone else, no one has the right to enslave another. Political theories past and present have traditionally been concerned with who should be the master (usually the king, the dictator, or government bureaucracy) and who should be the slaves, and what the extent of the slavery should be. Libertarianism holds that no one has the right to use force to enslave the life of another, or any portion or aspect of that life.

2. *Other men's lives are not yours to dispose of.* I enjoy seeing operas; but operas are expensive to produce. Opera-lovers often say, "The state (or the city, etc.) should subsidize opera, so that we can all see it. Also it would be for people's betterment, cultural benefit, etc." But what they are advocating is nothing more or less than legalized plunder. They can't pay for the productions themselves, and yet they want to see opera, which involves a large number of people and their labor; so what they are saying in effect is, "Get the money through legalized force. Take a little bit more out of every worker's paycheck every week to pay for the operas we want to see." But I have no right to take by force from the workers' pockets to pay for what I want.

Perhaps it would be better if he *did* go to see opera—then I should try to convince him to go voluntarily. But to take the money from him forcibly, because in my opinion it would be good for *him*, is still seizure of his earnings, which is plunder.

Besides, if I have the right to force him to help pay for my pet projects, hasn't he equally the right to force me to help pay for his? Perhaps he in turn wants the government to subsidize rock-and-roll, or his new car, or a house in the country? If I have the right to milk him, why hasn't he the right to milk me? If I can be a moral cannibal, why can't he too?

We should beware of the inventors of utopias. They would remake the world according to their vision—with the lives and fruits of the labor of *other* human beings. Is it someone's utopian vision that others should build pyramids to beautify the

From "What Libertarianism Is," in *The Libertarian Alternative* edited by Tibor Machan (1974). Reprinted by permission of the author, the editor, and Nelson-Hall Inc.

landscape? Very well, then other men should provide the labor; and if he is in a position of political power, and he can't get men to do it voluntarily, then he must *compel* them to "cooperate"—i.e. he must enslave them.

A hundred men might gain great pleasure from beating up or killing just one insignificant human being; but other men's lives are not theirs to dispose of. "In order to achieve the worthy goals of the next five-year-plan, we must forcibly collectivize the peasants . . ."; but other men's lives are not theirs to dispose of. Do you want to occupy, rent-free, the mansion that another man has worked for twenty years to buy? But other men's lives are not yours to dispose of. Do you want operas so badly that everyone is forced to work harder to pay for their subsidization through taxes? But other men's lives are not yours to dispose of. Do you want to have free medical care at the expense of other people, whether they wish to provide it or not? But this would require them to work longer for you whether they want to or not, and other men's lives are not yours to dispose of. . . .

3. *No human being should be a nonvoluntary mortgage on the life of another.* I cannot claim your life, your work, or the products of your effort as mine. The fruit of one man's labor should not be fair game for every freeloader who comes along and demands it as his own. The orchard that has been carefully grown, nurtured, and harvested by its owner should not be ripe for the plucking for any bypasser who has a yen for the ripe fruit. The wealth that some men have produced should not be fair game for looting by government, to be used for whatever purposes its representatives determine, no matter what their motives in so doing may be. The theft of your money by a robber is not justified by the fact that he used it to help his injured mother.

It will already be evident that libertarian doctrine is embedded in a view of the rights of man. Each human being has the right to live his life as he chooses, compatibly with the equal right of all other human beings to live their lives as they choose.

All man's rights are implicit in the above statement. Each man has the right to life: any attempt by others to take it away from him, or even to injure him, violates this right, through the use of coercion against him. Each man has the right to liberty: to conduct his life in accordance with the alternatives open to him without coercive action by others. And every man has the right to property: to work to sustain his life (and the lives of whichever others he chooses to sustain, such as his family) and to retain the fruits of his labor.

People often defend the rights of life and liberty but denigrate property rights, and yet the right to property is as basic as the other two: indeed, without property rights no other rights are possible. Depriving you of property is depriving you of the means by which you live. . . .

I have no right to decide how *you* should spend your time or your money. I can make that decision for myself, but not for you, my neighbor. I may deplore your choice of life-style, and I may talk with you about it provided you are willing to listen to me. But I have no right to use force to change it. Nor have I the right to decide how you should spend the money you have earned. I may appeal to you to give it to the Red Cross, and you may prefer to go to prize-fights. But that is your decision, and however much I may chafe about it I do not have the right to interfere forcibly with it, for example by robbing you in order to use the money in accordance with *my* choices. (If I have the right to rob you, have you also the right to rob me?)

When I claim a right, I carve out a niche, as it were, in my life, saying in effect, "This activity I must be able to perform without interference from others. For you and everyone else, this is off limits." And so I put up a "no trespassing" sign, which marks off the area of my right. Each individual's right is his "no trespassing" sign in relation to me and others. I may not encroach upon his domain any more than he upon mine, without my consent. Every right entails a duty, true—but the duty is only that of *forbearance*—that is, of *refraining* from violating the other person's right. If you have a right to life, I have no right to take your life; if you have a right to the products of your labor (property), I have no right to take it from you without your consent. The nonviolation of these rights will not guarantee you protection against natural catastrophes such as floods and earthquakes, but it will protect you against the aggressive activities *of other men*. And rights, after all, have to do with one's relations to other human beings, not with one's relations to physical nature.

Nor were these rights created by government; governments—some governments, obviously not all—*recognize* and *protect* the rights that individuals already have. Governments regularly forbid homicide and theft; and, at a more advanced stage, protect individuals against such things as libel and breach of contract. . . .

The *right to property* is the most misunderstood and unappreciated of human rights, and it is one most constantly violated by governments. "Property" of course does not mean only real estate; it includes anything you can call your own—your clothing, your car, your jewelry, your books and papers.

The right of property is not the right to just *take* it from others, for this would interfere with *their* property rights. It is rather the right to work for it, to obtain non-coercively, the money or services which you can present in voluntary exchange.

The right to property is consistently underplayed by intellectuals today, sometimes even frowned upon, as if we should feel guilty for upholding such a right in view of all the poverty in the world. But the right to property is absolutely basic. It is your hedge against the future. It is your assurance that what you have worked to earn will still be there and be yours, when you wish or need to use it, especially when you are too old to work any longer.

Government has always been the chief enemy of the right to property. The officials of government, wishing to increase their power, and finding an increase of wealth an effective way to bring this about seize some or all of what a person has earned—and since government has a monopoly of physical force within the geographical area of the nation, it has the power (but not the right) to do this. When this happens, of course, every citizen of that country is insecure: he knows that no matter how hard he works the government can swoop down on him at any time and confiscate his earnings and possessions. A person sees his life savings wiped out in a moment when the tax-collectors descend to deprive him of the fruits of his work; or, an industry which has been fifty years in the making and cost millions of dollars and millions of hours of time and planning, is nationalized overnight. Or the government, via infla-

tion, cheapens the currency, so that hard-won dollars aren't worth anything any more. The effect of such actions, of course, is that people lose hope and incentive: if no matter how hard they work the government agents can take it all away, why bother to work at all, for more than today's needs? Depriving people of property is *depriving them of the means by which they live*—the freedom of the individual citizen to do what he wishes with his own life and to plan for the future. Indeed only if property rights are respected is there any point to planning for the future and working to achieve one's goals. *Property rights are what makes long-range planning possible*—the kind of planning which is a distinctively human endeavor, as opposed to the day-by-day activity of the lion who hunts, who depends on the supply of game tomorrow but has no real insurance against starvation in a day or a week. Without the right to property, the right to life itself amounts to little: how can you sustain your life if you cannot plan ahead? and how can you plan ahead if the fruits of your labor can at any moment be confiscated by government? . . .

Indeed, the right to property may well be considered second only to the right to life. Even the freedom of speech is limited by considerations of property. If a person visiting in your home behaves in a way undesired by you, you have every right to evict him; he can scream or agitate elsewhere if he wishes, but not in your home without your consent. Does a person have a right to shout obscenities in a cathedral? No, for the owners of the cathedral (presumably the Church) have not allowed others on their property for that purpose; one may go there to worship or to visit, but not just for any purpose one wishes. Their property right is prior to your or my wish to scream or expectorate or write graffiti on their building. Or, to take the stock example, does a person have a right to shout "Fire!" falsely in a crowded theater? No, for the theater owner has permitted others to enter and use his property only for a specific purpose, that of seeing a film or watching a stage show. If a person heckles or otherwise disturbs other members of the audience, he can be thrown out. (In fact, he can be removed for any reason the owner chooses, provided his admission money is returned). And if he shouts "Fire!" when there is no fire, he may be endangering other lives by causing a panic or a stampede. The right to free speech doesn't give one the right to say anything anywhere; it is circumscribed by property rights.

Again, some people seem to assume that the right to free speech (including written speech) means that they can go to a newspaper publisher and demand that he print in his newspaper some propaganda or policy statement for their political party (or other group). But of course they have no right to the use of his newspaper. Ownership of the newspaper is the product of his labor, and he has a right to put into his newspaper whatever he wants, for whatever reason. If he excludes material which many readers would like to have in, perhaps they can find it in another newspaper or persuade him to print it himself (if there are enough of them, they will usually do just that). Perhaps they can even cause his newspaper to fail. But as long as he owns it, he has the right to put in it what he wishes; what would a property right be if he could not do this? They have no right to place their material in his newspaper without his consent—not for free, nor even for a fee. Perhaps other newspapers will include it, or perhaps they can start their own newspaper (in which case they have a right to put in it what they like). If not, an option open to them would be to mimeograph and distribute some handbills.

In exactly the same way, no one has a right to "free television time" unless the owner of the television station consents to give it; it is his station, he has the property rights over it, and it is for him to decide how to dispose of his time. He may not decide wisely, but it is his right to decide as he wishes. If he makes enough unwise decisions, and courts enough unpopularity with the viewing public or the sponsors, he may have to go out of business; but as he is free to make his own decisions, so is he free to face their consequences. (If the government owns the television station, then government officials will make the decisions, and there is no guarantee of *their* superior wisdom. The difference is that when "the government" owns the station, you are forced to help pay for its upkeep through your taxes, whether the bureaucrat in charge decides to give you television time or not.)

"But why have *individual* property rights? Why not have lands and houses owned by everybody together?" Yes, this involves no violation of individual rights, as long as everybody consents to this arrangement and no one is forced to join it. The parties to it may enjoy the communal living enough (at least for a time) to overcome certain inevitable problems: that some will work and some not, that some will achieve more in an hour than others can do in a day, and still they will all get the same income. The few who do the most will in the end consider themselves "workhorses" who do the work of two or three or twelve, while the others will be "freeloaders" on the efforts of these few. But as long as they can get out of the arrangement if they no longer like it, no violation of rights is involved. They got in voluntarily, and they can get out voluntarily; no one has used force.

"But why not say that everybody owns everything? That we *all* own everything there is?"

To some this may have a pleasant ring—but let us try to analyze what it means. If everybody owns everything, then everyone has an equal right to go everywhere, do what he pleases, take what he likes, destroy if he wishes, grow crops or burn them, trample them under, and so on. Consider what it would be like in practice. Suppose you have saved money to buy a house for yourself and your family. Now suppose that the principle, "everybody owns everything," becomes adopted. Well then, why shouldn't every itinerant hippie just come in and take over, sleeping in your beds and eating in your kitchen and not bothering to replace the food supply or clean up the mess? After all, it belongs to all of us, doesn't it? So we have just as much right to it as you, the buyer, have. What happens if we *all* want to sleep in the bedroom and there's not room for all of us? Is it the strongest who wins?

What would be the result? Since no one would be responsible for anything, the property would soon be destroyed, the food used up, the facilities nonfunctional. Beginning as a house that *one* family could use, it would end up as a house that *no one* could use. And if the principle continued to be adopted, no one would build houses any more—or anything else. What for? They would only be occupied and used by others, without remuneration.

Suppose two men are cast ashore on an island, and they agree that each will cultivate half of it. The first man is industrious and grows crops and builds a shelter, making the most of the situation with which he is confronted. The second man, perhaps thinking that the warm days will last forever, lies in the sun, picks coconuts while they last, and does a minimum of work to sustain himself. At the time of harvest, the second man has nothing to harvest, nor does he assist the first man in his labors. But later when there is a dearth of food on the island, the second man comes to the first man and demands half of the harvest as his right. But of course he has no right to the product of the first man's labors. The first man may freely choose to give part of his harvest to the second out of charity rather than see him starve; but that is just what it is—charity, not the second man's right.

How can any of man's rights be violated? Ultimately, only by the use of force. I can make suggestions to you, I can reason with you, entreat you (if you are willing to listen), but I cannot *force* you without violating your rights; only by forcing you do I cut the cord between your free decisions and your actions. Voluntary relations between individuals involve no deprivation of rights, but murder, assault, and rape do, because in doing these things I make you the unwilling victim of my actions. A man's beating his wife involves no violation of rights if she *wanted* to be beaten. *Force is behavior that requires the unwilling involvement of other persons.*

Thus the use of force need not involve the use of physical violence. If I trespass on your property or dump garbage on it, I am violating your property rights, as indeed I am when I steal your watch; although this is not force in the sense of violence, it *is* a case of your being an unwilling victim of my action. Similarly, if you shout at me so that I cannot be heard when I try to speak, or blow a siren in my ear, or start a factory next door which pollutes my land, you are again violating my rights (to free speech, to property); I am, again, an unwilling victim of your actions. Similarly, if you steal a manuscript of mine and publish it as your own, you are confiscating a piece of my property and thus violating my right to keep what is the product of my labor. Of course, if I give you the manuscript with permission to sign your name to it and keep the proceeds, no violation of rights is involved—any more than if I give you permission to dump garbage on my yard.

According to libertarianism, the role of government should be limited to the retaliatory use of force against those who have initiated its use. It should not enter into any other areas, such as religion, social organization, and economics.

GOVERNMENT

Government is the most dangerous institution known to man. Throughout history it has violated the rights of men more than any individual or group of individuals could do: it has killed people, enslaved them, sent them to forced labor and concentration camps, and regularly robbed and pillaged them of the fruits of their expended labor. Unlike individual criminals, government has the power to arrest and try; unlike individual criminals, it can surround and encompass a person totally, dominating every aspect of one's life, so that one has no recourse from it but to leave the country (and in totalitarian nations even that is prohibited). Government throughout history has a much sorrier record than any individual, even that of a ruthless mass murderer. The signs we see on bumper stickers are chillingly accurate: "Beware: the Government Is Armed and Dangerous."

The only proper role of government, according to libertarians, is that of the protector of the citizen against aggression by other individuals. The government, of course, should never initiate aggression; its proper role is as the embodiment of the *retaliatory* use of force against anyone who initiates its use.

If each individual had constantly to defend himself against possible aggressors, he would have to spend a considerable portion of his life in target practice, karate exercises, and other means of self-defenses, and even so he would probably be helpless against groups of individuals who might try to kill, maim, or rob him. He would have little time for cultivating those qualities which are essential to civilized life, nor would improvements in science, medicine, and the arts be likely to occur. The function of government is to take this responsibility off his shoulders: the government undertakes to defend him against aggressors and to punish them if they attack him. When the government is effective in doing this, it enables the citizen to go about his business unmolested and without constant fear for his life. To do this, of course, government must have physical power—the police, to protect the citizen from aggression within its borders, and the armed forces, to protect him from aggressors outside. Beyond that, the government should not intrude upon his life, either to run his business, or adjust his daily activities, or prescribe his personal moral code.

Government, then, undertakes to be the individual's protector; but historically governments have gone far beyond this function. Since they already have the physical power, they have not hesitated to use it for purposes far beyond that which was entrusted to them in the first place. Undertaking initially to protect its citizens against aggression, it has often itself become an aggressor—a far greater aggressor, indeed, than the criminals against whom it was supposed to protect its citizens. Governments have done what no private citizen can do: arrest and imprison individuals without a trial and send them to slave labor camps. Government must have power in order to be effective—and yet the very means by which alone it can be effective make it vulnerable to the abuse of power, leading to managing the lives of individuals and even inflicting terror upon them.

What then should be the function of government? In a word, the *protection of human rights*.

1. *The right to life:* libertarians support all such legislation as will protect human beings against the use of force by others, for example, laws against killing, attempting killing, maiming, beating, and all kinds of physical violence.
2. *The right to liberty:* there should be no laws compromising in any way freedom of speech, of the press, and peaceable assembly. There should be no censorship of ideas, books, films, or of anything else by government.
3. *The right to property:* libertarians support legislation that protects the property rights of individuals against confiscation, nationalization, eminent domain, robbery, trespass, fraud and misrepresentation, patent and copyright, libel and slander.

Someone has violently assaulted you. Should he be legally liable? Of course. He has violated one of

your rights. He has knowingly injured you and since he has initiated aggression against you he should be made to expiate.

Someone has negligently left his bicycle on the sidewalk where you trip over it in the dark and injure yourself. He didn't do it intentionally; he didn't mean you any harm. Should he be legally liable? Of course; he has, however unwittingly, injured you, and since the injury is caused by him and you are the victim, he should pay.

Someone across the street is unemployed. Should you be taxed extra to pay for his expenses? Not at all. You have not injured him, you are not responsible for the fact that he is unemployed (unless you are a senator or bureaucrat who agitated for further curtailing of business, which legislation passed, with the result that your neighbor was laid off by the curtailed business). You may voluntarily wish to help him out, or better still, try to get him a job to put him on his feet again; but since you have initiated no aggressive act against him, and neither purposely nor accidentally injured him in any way, you should not be legally penalized for the fact of his unemployment. (Actually, it is just such penalties that increase unemployment.)

One man, A, works hard for years and finally earns a high salary as a professional man. A second man, B, prefers not to work at all, and to spend wastefully what money he has (through inheritance), so that after a year or two he has nothing left. At the end of this time he has a long siege of illness and lots of medical bills to pay. He demands that the bills be paid by the government—that is, by the taxpayers of the land, including Mr. A.

But of course B has no such right. He chose to lead his life in a certain way—that was his voluntary decision. One consequence of that choice is that he must depend on charity in case of later need. Mr. A chose not to live that way. (And if everyone lived like Mr. B, on whom would he depend in case of later need?) Each has a right to live in the way he pleases, but each must live with the consequences of his own decision (which, as always, fall primarily on himself). He cannot, in time of need, claim A's beneficence as his right.

If a house-guest of yours starts to carve his initials in your walls and break up your furniture, you have a right to evict him, and call the police if he makes trouble. If someone starts to destroy the machinery in a factory, the factory-owner is also entitled to evict him and call the police. In both cases, persons other than the owner are permitted on the property only under certain conditions, at the pleasure of the owner. If those conditions are violated, the owner is entitled to use force to set things straight. The case is exactly the same on a college or university campus: if a campus demonstrator starts breaking windows, occupying the president's office, and setting fire to a dean, the college authorities are certainly within their rights to evict him forcibly; one is permitted on the college grounds only under specific conditions, set by the administration: study, peaceful student activity, even political activity if those in charge choose to permit it. If they do not choose to permit peaceful political activity on campus, they may be unwise, since a campus is after all a place where all sides of every issue should get discussed, and the college that doesn't permit this may soon lose its reputation and its students. All the same, the college official who does not permit it is quite within his rights; the students do not own the campus, nor do the hired trouble-makers imported from elsewhere. In the case of a privately owned college, the owners, or whoever they have delegated to administer it, have the right to make the decisions as to who shall be permitted on the campus and under what conditions. In the case of a state university or college, the ownership problem is more complex: one could say that the "government" owns the campus or that "the people" do since they are the taxpayers who support it; but in either case, the university administration has the delegated task of keeping order, and until they are removed by the state administration or the taxpayers, it is theirs to decide who shall be permitted on campus, and what non-academic activities will be permitted to their students on the premises.

Property rights can be violated by physical trespass, of course, or by anyone entering on your property for any reason without your consent. (If you *do* consent to having your neighbor dump garbage on your yard, there is no violation of your rights.) But the physical trespass of a person is only a special case of violation of property rights. Property rights can be violated by sound-waves, in the form of a loud noise, or the sounds of your neighbor's hi-fi set while you are trying to sleep. Such violations of property

rights are of course the subject of action in the courts.

But there is another violation of property rights that has not thus far been honored by the courts; this has to do with the effects of *pollution* of the atmosphere.

From the beginnings of modern air pollution, the courts made a conscious decision not to protect, for example, the orchards of farmers from the smoke of nearby factories or locomotives. They said, in effect, to the farmers: yes, your private property is being invaded by this smoke, but we hold that "public policy" is more important than private property, and public policy holds factories and locomotives to be good things. These goods were allowed to override the defense of property rights— with our consequent headlong rush into pollution disaster. The remedy is both "radical" and crystal clear, and it has nothing to do with multi-billion dollar palliative programs at the expense of the taxpayers which do not even meet the real issue. The remedy is simply to enjoin anyone from injecting pollutants into the air, and thereby invading the rights of persons and property. Period. The argument that such an injunction prohibition would add to the costs of industrial production is as reprehensible as the pre-Civil War argument that the abolition of slavery would add to the costs of growing cotton, and therefore should not take place. For this means that the polluters are able to impose the high costs of pollution upon those whose property rights they are allowed to invade with impunity.[1]

What about automobiles, the chief polluters of the air? One can hardly sue every automobile owner. But one can sue the manufacturers of automobiles who do not install anti-smog devices on the cars which they distribute—and later (though this is more difficult), owners of individual automobiles if they discard the equipment or do not keep it functional.

The violation of rights does not apply only to air-pollution. If someone with a factory upstream on a river pollutes the river, anyone living downstream from him, finding his water polluted, should be able to sue the owner of the factory. In this way the price of adding the anti-pollutant devices will be the owner's responsibility, and will probably be added to the cost of the products which the factory produces and thus spread around among all consumers, rather than the entire cost being borne by the users of the river in the form of polluted water, with the consequent impossibility of fishing, swimming, and so on. In each case, pollution would be stopped at the source rather than having its ill effects spread around to numerous members of the population.

What about property which you do not work to earn, but which you *inherit* from someone else? Do you have a right to that? You have no right to it until someone decides to give it to you. Consider the man who willed it to you; it was his, he had the right to use and dispose of it as *he* saw fit; and if he decided to give it to you, this is a windfall for you, but it was only the exercise of *his* right. Had the property been seized by the government at the man's death, or distributed among numerous other people designated by the government, it *would* have been a violation of his rights: for he, who worked to earn and sustain it, would not have been able to dispose of it according to his own judgment. If he doesn't have the right to determine who shall have it, who does?

What about the property status of your intellectual activity, such as inventions you may devise and books you write? These, of course, are your property also; they are the products of your mind; you worked at them, you created them. Prior to that, they did not exist. If you worked five years to write a book, and someone stole it and published it as his own, receiving royalties from its sales, he would have stolen your property just as surely as if he had robbed your home. The same is true if someone used and sold without your permission an invention which was the product of your labor and ingenuity.

The role of government with respect to this issue, at least most governments of the Western world, is a proper one: government protects the products of your labor from the moment they materialize. Copyright law protects your writings from piracy. In the United States, one's writings are protected for a period of twenty-seven years, and another twenty-seven if one applies for renewal of the copyright. In most other countries, they are protected for a period of fifty years after the author's death, permitting both himself and his surviving heirs to reap the fruits of his labor. After that they enter the "public domain"—that is, anyone may reprint them without your or your heirs' permission. Patent law protects your inventions for a limited period, which varies

according to the type of invention. In no case are you forced to avail yourself of this protection; you need not apply for patent or copyright coverage if you do not wish to do so. But the protection of your intellectual property is there, in case you wish to use it.

What about the property status of the airwaves? Here the government's position is far more questionable. The government now claims ownership of the airwaves, leasing them to individuals and corporations. The government renews leases or refuses them depending on whether the programs satisfy authorities in the Federal Communications Commission. The official position is that "we all own the airwaves": but since only one party can broadcast on a certain frequency at a certain time without causing chaos, it is simply a fact of reality that "everyone cannot use it. In fact the government decides who shall use the airwaves and one courts its displeasure only at the price of a revoked license. One can write without government approval, but one cannot use the airwaves without the approval of government.

What policy should have been observed with regard to the airwaves? Much the same as the policy that was followed in the case of the Homestead Act, when the lands of the American West were opening up for settlement. There was a policy of "first come, first served," with the government parcelling out a certain acreage for each individual who wanted to claim the land as his own. There was no charge for the land, but if a man had not used it and built a dwelling during the first two-year period, it was assumed that he was not homesteading and the land was given to the next man in line. The airwaves too could have been given out on a "first come, first served" basis. The first man who used a given frequency would be its owner, and the government would protect him in the use of it against trespassers. If others wanted to use the same frequency, they would have to buy it from the first man, if he was willing to sell, or try to buy another, just as one now does with land.

Laws may be classified into three types: (1) laws protecting individuals against themselves, such as laws against fornication and other sexual behavior, alcohol, and drugs; (2) laws protecting individuals against aggressions by other individuals, such as laws against murder, robbery, and fraud; (3) laws requiring people to help one another; for example, all laws which rob Peter to pay Paul, such as welfare.

Libertarians reject the first class of laws totally. Behavior which harms no one else is strictly the individual's own affair. Thus, there should be no laws against becoming intoxicated, since whether or not to become intoxicated is the individual's own decision: but there should be laws against driving while intoxicated, since the drunken driver is a threat to every other motorist on the highway (drunken driving falls into type 2). Similarly, there should be no laws against drugs (except the prohibition of sale of drugs to minors) as long as the taking of these drugs poses no threat to anyone else. Drug addiction is a psychological problem to which no present solution exists. Most of the social harm caused by addicts, other than to themselves, is the result of thefts which they perform in order to continue their habit—and then the *legal* crime is the theft, not the addiction. The actual cost of heroin is about ten cents a shot; if it were legalized, the enormous traffic in illegal sale and purchase of it would stop, as well as the accompanying proselytization to get new addicts (to make more money for the pusher) and the thefts performed by addicts who often require eighty dollars a day just to keep up the habit. Addiction would not stop, but the crimes would: it is estimated that 75 percent of the burglaries in New York City today are performed by addicts, and all these crimes could be wiped out at one stroke through the legalization of drugs. (Only when the taking of drugs could be shown to constitute a threat to *others*, should it be prohibited by law. It is only laws protecting people against *themselves* that libertarians oppose.)

Laws should be limited to the second class only: aggression by individuals against other individuals. These are laws whose function is to protect human beings against encroachment by others; and this, as we have seen, is (according to libertarianism) the sole function of government.

Libertarians also reject the third class of laws totally: no one should be forced by law to help others, not even to tell them the time of day if requested, and certainly not to give them a portion of one's weekly paycheck. Governments, in the guise of humanitarianism, have given to some by taking from others (charging a "handling fee" in the process, which, because of the government's waste and inefficiency, sometimes is several hundred percent). And in so doing they have decreased incentive, violated

the rights of individuals and lowered the standard of living of almost everyone.

All such laws constitute what libertarians call *moral cannibalism*. A cannibal in the physical sense is a person who lives off the flesh of other human beings. A *moral* cannibal is one who believes he has a right to live off the "spirit" of other human beings—who believes that he has a moral claim on the productive capacity, time, and effort expended by others.

It has become fashionable to claim virtually everything that one needs or desires as one's *right*. Thus, many people claim that they have a right to a job, the right to free medical care, to free food and clothing, to a decent home, and so on. Now if one asks, apart from any specific context, whether it would be desirable if everyone had these things, one might well say yes. But there is a gimmick attached to each of them: *At whose expense?* Jobs, medical care, education, and so on, don't grow on trees. These are goods and services *produced only by men.* Who then is to provide them, and under what conditions?

If you have a right to a job, who is to supply it? Must an employer supply it even if he doesn't want to hire you? What if you are unemployable, or incurably lazy? (If you say "the government must supply it," does that mean that a job must be created for you which no employer needs done, and that you must be kept in it regardless of how much or little you work?) If the employer is forced to supply it at his expense even if he doesn't need you, then isn't *he* being enslaved to that extent? What ever happened to *his* right to conduct his life and his affairs in accordance with his choices?

If you have a right to free medical care, then, since medical care doesn't exist in nature as wild apples do, some people will have to supply it to you for free: that is, they will have to spend their time and money and energy taking care of you whether they want to or not. What ever happened to *their* right to conduct their lives as they see fit? Or do you have a right to violate theirs? Can there be a right to violate rights?

All those who demand this or that as a "free service" are consciously or unconsciously evading the fact that there is in reality no such thing as free services. All man-made goods and services are the result of human expenditure of time and effort. There is no such thing as "something for nothing" in this world. If you demand something free, you are demanding that other men give their time and effort to you without compensation. If they voluntarily choose to do this, there is no problem; but if you demand that they be *forced* to do it, you are interfering with their right not to do it if they so choose. "Swimming in this pool ought to be free!" says the indignant passerby. What he means is that others should build a pool, others should provide the material, and still others should run it and keep it in functioning order, so that *he* can use it without fee. But what right has he to the expenditure of *their* time and effort? To expect something "for free" is to expect it *to be paid for by others* whether they choose to or not.

Many questions, particularly about economic matters, will be generated by the libertarian account of human rights and the role of government. Should government have no role in assisting the needy, in providing social security, in legislating minimum wages, in fixing prices and putting a ceiling on rents,

in curbing monopolies, in erecting tariffs, in guaranteeing jobs, in managing the money supply? To these and all similar questions the libertarian answers with an unequivocal no.

"But then you'd let people go hungry!" comes the rejoinder. This, the libertarian insists, is precisely what would not happen; with the restrictions removed, the economy would flourish as never before. With the controls taken off business, existing enterprises would expand and new ones would spring into existence satisfying more and more consumer needs; millions more people would be gainfully employed instead of subsisting on welfare, and all kinds of research and production, released from the stranglehold of government, would proliferate, fulfilling man's needs and desires as never before. It has always been so whenever government has permitted men to be free traders on a free market. But *why* this is so, and how the free market is the best solution to all problems relating to the material aspect of man's life, is another and far longer story.

NOTES

1. Murray Rothbard, "The Great Ecology Issue," *The Individualist,* 2, no. 2 (Feb. 1970), p. 5.

Carl Cohen

SOCIALIST DEMOCRACY

Socialists, according to Carl Cohen, want to expand the scope of democracy from the political to the economic sphere. To allow the economic sphere to remain under private control is to allow competitive warfare to determine who gets what in society, where victory goes to the strongest rather than to those whose needs are most important. The results of such a system are the well-known evils of unemployment and inflation. The alternative favored by socialists is to require productive property to be publicly owned and publicly planned. This will in effect replace the motive of private profit with one of public service. It will also result in a gain in freedom for most people, since they will thereby acquire more control over the economic aspects of their lives.

DEMOCRACY FULFILLED

WE SOCIALISTS AGREE THAT democracy is necessary and absolutely right. But it is not enough. Democracy is completed, fulfilled, by socialism—which is simply the democratic control of *all* resources in the community by society *as a whole.*

Socialism makes democratic ideals concrete. In it the collective will of the people is put to the service of the people in their daily lives. Through socialism the common interests of all the citizens are protected, their common needs met.

The name "socialism" has—at least to many American ears—a negative, even threatening, connotation. Yet most ordinary people warmly support—under a different name—many activities that are truly socialist in nature. We all know that some things must be done for the community as a whole. And some things can be undertaken *for* the community only *by* the community, acting *as* a community. Constructive collective action in this spirit is socialism.

How, for example, do we "provide for the common defense"? Why, through social action, of course. Armies and warships cannot be maintained by private groups or individuals. National defense undertaken jointly with democratic consent is only one of many socialist enterprises that no one seriously questions.

How do we make and enforce the criminal law? Collectively, of course. Citizens can neither establish criminal codes and courts as individuals, nor punish as individuals. That would be the war of each against all, in which the lives of people would indeed prove nasty, poor, brutish, and short. The adoption of laws, and their enforcement, is an essentially *social* activity. Nothing else would be feasible or sane. Everyone grants that; to this extent we are all socialists.

Is not the same true of national foreign policy? We may differ as individuals, but do we not agree upon the need for one community position? And of health regulations? Do we allow the meat packers or the drug manufacturers to decide for themselves what is fit to eat or prescribe? And everyone now agrees on the need for community policies, collective undertakings to protect the environment, our forests and fish, animals and birds. Shall we not have public parks or seashores? Shall we not join to protect our historical treasures and the beauties of our land? Absurd even to ask. To do these things we must, of course, act as a society, because as individuals we are relatively helpless and ineffective. We will succeed, if we succeed at all, cooperatively, because there is absolutely no other way to have successful armies, just courts, or beautiful parks. All democratic experience teaches the need for collective action. Real democracy *is* social democracy, democratic socialism.

While we all practice socialism in many spheres, its applicability to other spheres in which it is equally necessary is widely denied. Sometimes manipulated by the rich and powerful, sometimes blinded by our own slogans, sometimes dreading unreal philosophical ghosts, we fear to take social action where we ought. We fail to complete our democracy.

How can we complete it? Where would collective action have greatest impact on daily life? In the economy, of course. Action as a society is needed most of all in producing and distributing the necessities and comforts of ordinary human life. Socialism is democracy extended to the world of work and money.

SOCIALISM AND POPULAR WILL

All the wealth of the world—the houses and food, the land and lumber and luxuries—is somehow divided and distributed. How is that done? And how should it be done? We socialists try to rethink such fundamental questions: Who gets what? And Why?

Satisfactory answers to these questions must, of course, prove acceptable to the masses. Being democrats above all, we trust the judgment of the people. Their choices, when fully informed, will be rational and fair. We lay it down as a restriction upon ourselves, therefore, that the great changes socialism requires must come only as the honest expression of the will of the citizens, through action by their freely elected representatives. An organic transformation of society can succeed only when genuinely willed by its members. True socialists—unlike some who falsely parade under that banner—never have and never will force their solutions on an unwilling community. Democracies around the world, from India to Sweden, have enthusiastically applied socialist theory to their problems, devising socialist solutions specially suitable to their circumstances. The same basic theory can be applied successfully, with American ingenuity, to American circumstances. Confident that we can prove this to the satisfaction of the citizens concerned, we commit ourselves without reservations to abide by the judgment of the people after the case has been put farly before them. We compel no one; our socialism is democratic, through and through.

RICH AND POOR

How the wealth of most of the world is now divided is very plain to see. A few people get a great deal, and most people get just barely enough, or a little less than enough, to live decently. Rich and poor are the great classes of society, and everyone knows it well. Early democracies accepted these stark inequities as natural and inevitable. We do not. Some democrats still accept them. Material success (they say) is open to everyone in a system of private enterprise, and rewards properly go to the industrious and the able, those ambitious enough to pull themselves out of poverty by effort and wit. Some succeed, some do not, and most (they conclude) receive their just deserts.

It isn't so. That picture of "free enterprise" is a myth and always has been. In fact, by putting control of industry and finance into private hands, free enterprise results in the ownership of more and more by fewer and fewer, making economic justice unattainable for most. For centuries, wherever capitalism has prevailed, the great body of wealth has rested in the pockets of a tiny fraction of the citizens, while the masses are divided between those who just get by on their wages, and those who are unemployed

and poor, inadequately housed, and often hungry. That great division, between those who have and those who have not, is the leading feature of a private enterprise economy, even when democratic. Those who have get more, because money and property are instruments for the accumulation of more money and more property. Economic freedom in such a system, for the vast majority, is only the freedom to work for another. Working men and women are free to sweat for paychecks, free to look for another job, and maybe—if their needs are desperate—free to go on welfare. These are false freedoms, not deserving the name.

Why does it work out that way? Will the poor always be with us? Ought each person to look out only for himself or herself and devil take the hindmost? We deny that this is the spirit of a decent society. We do not accept the inevitability of poverty; we do not think a democracy need be a cutthroat enterprise, and we know that cooperative action by the members of a society in their joint interests can protect both the essential freedoms of each individual and the economic well-being of all. That rational cooperation is called socialism.

PARKS AND INDUSTRIES

Consider this vivid contrast. No one questions the appropriateness of public parks—places for play and the enjoyment of nature, owned by the people, and operated by their elected representatives (and those they hire) in everyone's interest. Our parks (national, state, and municipal) are among our proudest possessions. Yes, possessions; we own them, each of us, and though some abuse them thoughtlessly, most of us love them and take satisfaction in their beauty. We do not begrudge the need to tax ourselves to maintain them. We could sell the forests and the land, reduce our tax burden thereby, and leave all citizens to take care of their own recreational needs as well as they can. If unable to pay for access to private parks or clubs, or to afford a private lake or a canyon—well, that would be their lookout. Simply to formulate this attitude is to exhibit its absurdity. Natural beauty and opportunity for relaxation and play for ourselves and our children are deep human needs; we fully understand how vital it is that the limited resources of nature, the lakes and forests, streams and wildlife, be preserved, in part at least, for our common and perpetual enjoyment.

Compare with this the condition of the steel industry. Virtually all of the steel in the United States is produced by three companies: U.S. Steel, Republic Steel, Inland Steel. The private owners of these three companies—a tiny fraction of our citizens— literally possess, own as their private property, the foundries, mills, and other facilities that constitute the literal foundation of almost all other industry. Virtually nothing works without steel. Steel mills are not as pretty as parks, true, but are they any less necessary to the well-being of a people? Can any of us do without steel? Not for a day. Cars, trucks, ships, and trains are made of it. Housing and communication depend utterly upon it. Kitchens and radios, elevators and pens—practically all tools and all conveniences require it. Hardly any activity, public or private, goes on without some use of iron or steel. Then why not exhibit the same community concern for steel that we exhibit for our parks? Why let a few capitalists charge us as they please (since we cannot control them) for what we must have? Why suppose that a fair price for steel includes an enormous profit—over and above all the costs of making and shipping the steel—for the private owners of the mills?

What explains so blind an infatuation with "private enterprise"? Under its spell we allow ourselves to be manipulated by the private owners of the steel foundries, gouged (even in our own homes!) by the private owners of the telephone wires. Oil wells and forests, precious resources from our common earth, are exploited by giant corporations whose ultimate object is profit alone. We must wake to see that productive industry, vital to the life of a society, is properly the possession of that society as a whole, not of private individuals or companies. The principles we apply unhesitatingly to parks apply with equal force to factories. Production as well as recreation can be a source of public pride and satisfaction—when socialized. Socialism is nothing more than the *general* application of collective intelligence.

Every democracy, socialist or not, will seek to protect citizens' political rights—but only socialist democracies protect citizens' *economic* rights. Free-

dom of speech and assembly are priceless; are not freedom from unemployment and hunger equally so? We think so. The same collective action needed to defend the citizens against aggression from without is needed to organize production rationally and to distribute wealth justly within our own borders. In the economic sphere as much as any other, cooperation and foresight are central. The public ownership of industry is the only way to achieve them. . . .

THE INHUMANITY OF THE MARKET

Socialism is simply economic good sense. The long-term fruits of capitalism have become too bitter: cycles of boom and bust, unemployment and welfare, personal dissatisfaction and business failure. Inflation steals from everyone (except those who can raise prices and rents quickly); depression demoralizes everyone. Disorder and distress are widespread. Our land itself is abused, our water poisoned, and our air fouled. When everything is left "up for grabs," the grabbing will be vicious and the outcome chaotic. There can be no intelligent planning for future needs, no rational distribution of products or materials in short supply, no reasonable deployment of human energies, in an economy in which the fundamental rule is dog-eat-dog. Legislation designed to blunt the fangs can do no more than reduce the depth of a serious wound.

Capitalism relies upon the so-called "market economy." The prices asked or offered for raw materials and finished products it leaves entirely to private parties, individuals or business firms, who enter a supposedly open market. This free market, it is argued, will be self-regulating; supply and demand will rationalize prices, fairness and productivity will be ensured by competition, enterprise encouraged by the hope of profit.

None of this actually works in the way capitalist mythology depicts it. The system relies upon the wisdom and power of economic fairies that never did exist. Nothing in the market is dependable, since everything within it fluctuates in response to unpredictable and uncontrollable factors: the tastes of buyers, the moods of sellers, the special circumstances of either, accidents causing short supply, or fashions transforming reasonable supply into glut.

Rationality and fairness through competition? No claim could be more fraudulent. In a capitalist market prices depend largely upon the relative strengths (or weaknesses) of the traders. If I own all the orchards, and am therefore the seller of all the cherries in the market, you, dear buyer, will pay my price or eat no cherries. Steel, timber, farm machinery are for sale in the market. Go, dear friend, and bargain with the sellers. Anyone tempted to believe capitalist propaganda about the give and take in the market should put it to the test. Reflect upon your own recent experiences as a shopper: You were told the price of the item you looked at—a TV set or a can of beans—and you paid that price or left without. That is how the market works for ordinary folks. Giant firms, manufacturers or chain retailers, may bargain with suppliers on occasion—but even then the stronger get the better deals. Those who control resources and money control the market, manipulating it in their own interests. Those who enter the market (either as buyer or seller) with great needs but little power are squeezed and exploited. The weak get twisted, the strong do the twisting. That's free enterprise.

Fairness? Markets do not know the meaning of the word. All's fair in war—and market competition is perpetual war, through guile and threat, on a thousand fronts. Rewards go to the aggressive, the keys to victory are accumulation, possession, control. And rules for fair dealing? They will be evaded, broken surreptitiously, even ignored—just like the rules of war—when it profits the combatants. . . .

UNEMPLOYMENT

Two consequences of capitalist disorder deserve special attention.

The first is unemployment. Capitalists speak of unemployment as though it were inevitable, arguing chiefly about what level of unemployment is "acceptable." No level of unemployment is acceptable; it is an intolerable cruelty for which no economic system may be excused. It is entirely possible to eliminate all unemployment—to assure pro-

ductive work to every one—if only we will use our collective intelligence. There are socialist economies in the world, *now*, where unemployment is virtually *nil*—and these are not the communist dictatorships, but socialist democracies. In New Zealand, for example, the number of unemployed workers is reported in the hundreds—in a population of several million—and even those few could probably find some kind of work. Americans tolerate a dreadful unemployment rate in spite of our ability to put an end to it. We can end it promptly—but not in a capitalist system. Capitalists employ workers only when it is profitable to do so. Socialism provides work for all so long as there is beneficial work to be done.

Is there work to be done? There is work unending, here in America and everywhere. Our cities need rebuilding; our vast railway system is decrepit; the majority of our factories are obsolete and in need of replacement; health care is in short supply; our parks deteriorate from over-use and under-care; many of our people hunger for houses not yet built, and so on and on. There is no limit to the work to be done. In the midst of this universal need, with vast resources of human skill and energy, the rate of unemployment remains absurdly large—rising among some groups to 15 percent and 20 percent, and even higher. What clearer exhibition of irrationality can there be than this?

We talk here abstractly about millions of men and women. Each of them is a flesh-and-blood human being, sensitive, anxious to be productive. Without work to do, human beings languish and are warped. Families wrangle and break up. Drug use increases, crime rates rise. Deteriorating cities, dirt, vandalism, and civic neglect are evidence of the underlying economic disorder. Capitalism traps its citizens—though they have the right to self government!—in a web of economic unreason. At work they are exploited; in unemployment, wasted.

INFLATION

If unemployment is the cruelest consequence of capitalism, inflation is the most insidious. It is funny, too, but the humor is sick. The joke is on all of us, busy making money and hoarding money and cherishing money in a system so uncontrolled that the money itself, the blood of the system, steadily declines in value, stealing from all the very essence of their accumulation—their power to buy! To keep the system operative when it falters, the currency that is its idol must be debased. Money is printed recklessly, and achievements measured in earnings turn to ashes. One might think it a fitting punishment, by a vengeful demon, for private greed. But, alas, the masters of the system do not suffer. Owning their property in the form of land and factories (productive wealth that should belong to us all), they endure comfortably. Indeed, they profit both coming *and* going because they operate largely on borrowed money. Their vast loans (from banks, insurance companies, and pension funds) are eventually repaid with inflated dollars worth only a fraction of the useful dollars originally borrowed. The little people (whose amassed savings had been used) discover too late that their nest eggs are shrunken, their retirements insecure. The rich get richer and the poor get children.

PUBLIC OWNERSHIP

Reasonable human beings can end all this. Production and distribution can be designed for human service. Cooperation is the key. Society must be organized with mutual service and mutual benefit as its fundamental theme. That theme is not alien to us; it lies at the core of our highest moral and religious ideals. We must realize these ideals in practice.

Economic cooperation entails two practical principles: (1) productive property must be publicly owned; and (2) production and distribution must be planned for the common good. *Public ownership* and *planning*—acting upon both we can readily achieve the substance of democratic socialism.

Public ownership is the base. Public ownership of what? Of the means by which goods are produced and work is carried on. Private persons are not entitled to own the instruments of our common good. A system enabling some to exact profit from the work of others, to wax rich while the glaring needs of others go unmet, is fundamentally corrupt. We

would end that corruption by bringing all the elements of the productive economy—the electric utilities and the mines, agriculture and transport, the production of metals and paper and drugs, the airlines and the food chains and the telephone system—under public ownership.

We do not propose to confiscate anything. The capital now held by private owners we would have the community pay for, at a fair price. But we would end the surreptitious confiscation by a few of the common wealth. The people have a right to advance their own general welfare through state action. They have that right in the economic sphere as in every other. Individuals will not be deprived of their personal effects, their houses or cars, their books or boots. Indeed, we seek the enlargement of such private goods for individual satisfaction. Individual human beings, after all, are what government is created to serve. But productive property is our common good, our collective concern. We will move it—justly—from private to public hands.

THE ELIMINATION OF PRIVATE PROFIT

The nationalization of all industry will have two consequences. First, *profit* for some from the work of others will be no more. If there is surplus produced by the operation of the utility companies, or the design of computers, or the distribution of any manufactured goods, let that surplus return to the treasury of the entire community. Let all productive systems be used, we say, not for private enrichment but for public benefit, and for continuing investment in the components of public production themselves. Workers should know that they labor each for all, and that any value they produce beyond what they receive in wages will not be taken from them but returned to them in some form of general benefit. One of those benefits will be the reduction of prices; when profits do not need to be squeezed from an enterprise, the consumer need only be charged the actual cost of that product or service. Goods and services will at last be fairly priced.

Telephone networks, natural gas distribution, and electric power supply are good illustrations of the increase in efficiency. These are all virtual monopolies. It makes no sense to have two telephone systems, or two sets of electric power lines, in the same community. Such essential utilities properly belong to all the members of the community served, all of whom need and use them, and must pay for them. That public agencies, even in a capitalist economy, now regulate the utilities is an explicit recognition of our common interest. Why then should *private* parties be permitted to own the lines and generators of a *public* utility? Why should any small group be permitted to *profit* from the necessary use of these instruments by everyone? Of course they should not. In many democracies the public utilities are already completely owned and operated by the public; actual operations change only little; ownership changes entirely. The result is invariably better service at lower cost. Nothing else is fair.

THE RETURN TO PUBLIC SERVICE

By eliminating the need for private profit, the public ownership of industry proves itself not only cheaper but more satisfying for all. A nationalized economy can be guided by one overriding purpose—the *general* welfare. The need for service overrules the need for a good return. Some services yield little profit, or none; yet the self-governed community can nevertheless provide such service widely to its own members.

Take the railroads as an example. The American public is poorly served, when served at all, by privately owned railroads. They would discontinue every service, passenger or freight, that does not maximize financial return on capital investment. While socialist democracies in Western Europe and elsewhere are perfecting their passenger rail services, rebuilding the roadbeds, introducing high-speed, comfortable, and dependable intercity services, the passenger rail network in the United States, because unprofitable, is allowed to rot. Many American cities—even including former great rail centers—no longer have any rail passenger service at all! The private railroads maintain passenger services only where clearly profitable (as between New York and

Washington) or where forced to do so by regulatory agencies—and then they do so grudgingly and poorly. Does the public suffer? "Not our concern," reply the private railroads. "This is a business. A line that loses money regularly must be cut; our primary responsibility is to our stockholders." It is; they are right about that. If the owners of the railroads run them only to make money, they will not run them at all where there is no money to be made. But the fundamental aim of the railroads ought not be to make money; it ought to be to serve the people. It will become that when—but only when—all the people served are stockholders.

When the railroads (and all other vital industries) are nationalized, the task of striking a balance between wide service and reasonable economy will remain. Public ownership does not provide something for nothing; it distributes essential burdens more fairly. The decisions then to be made about what services are worth what burdens will be made by all of us, through elected representatives. Decisions affecting us all will not be reached in closed board rooms by capitalist magnates motivated by selfish interests. All productive enterprise—the railroads are but one illustration—will be conducted for people, and not for profit. . . .

SOCIAL PLANNING

Two practical principles, we said earlier, comprise the substance of democratic socialism. Public ownership is the first, the foundation of socialism. Planning production and distribution for the common good is the second, and the fruit of socialism. When all members of the community have equal voice in the management of the economy, the elected representatives of those voices will naturally seek to deploy productive powers rationally. The community, then fully in command of its own affairs, will deliberate carefully in choosing its economic goals and in devising the means to attain them. It will make plans.

All intelligent humans plan. Preparing for the future is the mark of rational beings. Capitalists plan thoughtfully for their own advancement, plan cautiously for the security of their families, plan assiduously for the growth of their businesses. Yet they bitterly attack us for advocating the same foresight in the larger community! In matters close to them they do not cease to think ahead. But they insist that the community as a whole should entrust its future to an "invisible hand" that is somehow to ensure social health and prosperity. Sophisticated in private affairs, their handling of public affairs is simply immature, primitive.

Critics of socialism (it should be noted in fairness) often do recognize the need to plan in some particular sphere of the economy. Doing so, of course, such critics implicitly abandon their devotion to "free" markets. They plan the supplies of oil or gas, the road system, the storage of grain, and the money supply. But if the use of careful planning is appropriate in any single sphere of the economy, it is no less appropriate for the economy as a whole. Capitalists who plan, but are infuriated by planning, are blinded by an ideology from which they cannot free their own minds.

A few wealthy critics of socialism, on the other hand, are more perceptive but less forthright. They recognize the inconsistencies of capitalism, but they reject large-scale planning in their own interests. They know that in a system without rational direction, the private owners of productive capacity are in the best position when stormy times come. They will be able to capitalize on every fortuitous turn of events. That is how they got rich and will get richer. Economic planning will equalize opportunities in ways they do not like. It will deprive them of opportunities to exploit. Planning—from their selfish perspective—is a threat.

PLANNING WORKS

Two great objections to economic planning must be dealt with. The first is the claim that it does not work. This has been repeatedly proved false.

Every individual, and every community, has experienced successful planning. When we construct a budget for our school or business, for our family or our town, we plan. Ought we to cease budgeting? Bad budgets are sometimes devised, true; our aim then is to improve them, not to discard budgeting

altogether. The same process of improvement through self-correction can take place on a national scale. Community planning need not be always partial, or short-run. What is clearly in our interest to keep under control we need not leave to chance. Department heads who do not plan for their departments, generals who do not adequately plan their battles, we censure and replace. We have learned how essential it is to plan, through zoning, for the growth of our cities, and how we suffer when we fail to do so. The redevelopment of Western Europe, after World War II, was carefully and very successfully planned under American leadership. Military preparedness would be impossible without planning of the most detailed sort. Thorough planning can bring humankind even to the moon. Good planning is the heart of intelligent policy in every sphere, and it always will be. Without a plan there can hardly be any policy at all.

The effectiveness of rational economic planning has been demonstrated again and again. Many socialist countries, maintaining five- and seven-year economic plans under continual adjustment, have met with phenomenal success. Their rates of economic growth have been markedly greater than that of the unplanned American economy over recent decades. True, percentage growth for the American economy is harder than for some others because of our great size. But other economies, almost the size of our own, have been rapidly overtaking us through planning. Economic planning in Japan, for example, has brought stability, full employment, and security for all citizens. The quality of Japanese goods is high, often higher than our own. The quality of their services is very high, often more complete than our own. We cannot hope to compete successfully with them unless we too are prepared to plan thoughtfully for the future.

Planning doomed to failure? Nothing could be further from the truth. The continuing growth of world population absolutely demands the wisest forethought in the use of agricultural resources. Allocation of food supplies will be planned or millions of human beings will starve. Rapidly advancing technology—in the production of energy, in automated manufacture, in the processing of information—will greatly change the appropriate distribution of labor. If we do not plan for that, and develop an economic system that *can* plan for that, we may soon be utterly unable to cope. As a community we must calculate our coming needs—for housing, transport, health care, energy, and food. We must design the capacities to meet these common needs collectively with our collective efforts and intelligence.

Our horizons expand without known limit. With production and distribution jointly owned and jointly managed, there is little we cannot accomplish. But we must use our heads—together.

PLANNING AND DEMOCRACY

The second major objection to economic planning is the claim that it will cost us our freedom. This is as false as the claim that it does not work, and more pernicious.

Here lies the nub of the conflict between democratic socialists and our private enterprise critics. Freedom, says the critic, is the paramount social value. The freedom of each individual as an economic agent must be curtailed, they argue, by any large-scale economic plan. Once the goals are set, and the role of each economic element fixed, every private person must be sharply restricted in the use of his own resources. What can be bought and what can be sold or invested will be determined by the plan. The individual will be forced to work where, and when, and as the socialist bureaucrats have decided. Economic planning, they conclude, is but a pretty name for economic slavery.

The complaint is entirely unfounded. It is plausible only because it supposes, falsely, that economic planning under socialism will be imposed from above, by arbitrary authorities over whom we will have no control. Not so. Democratic socialism brings *democratic* planning. In an economy that is publicly owned and managed, *we* are the planners. Long-range designs for the allocation of resources, decisions about what is to be produced and how it is to be distributed, will come not from a secret, all-powerful elite but from *public* bodies, publicly selected, acting publicly, and answerable to the general public.

This genuine public accountability is absent, we agree, in some countries calling themselves "socialist." We despise that economic czarism as bitterly as do our capitalist friends. That is a false socialism which betrays the democratic spirit to which we are committed. Free citizens, accustomed to governing their own affairs, jealous of their own ultimate authority, will not be fooled by deceitful talk. They—we!—will know when our most important business is truly under our own control, and we will not stand for any other state of affairs. We will give up none of our freedom to do our own planning for our own needs. To the contrary, real freedom of action will be magnified in a truly *democratic* socialism by its increase of economic security for individuals and economic rationality in the whole society.

The critics' picture of socialist planning is a caricature of the real thing. They picture each citizen as a mindless cog in a great machine that grinds on unfeelingly, insensitive to mistakes or changing conditions. But the truly insensitive economy is the *un*-planned one, the economy that cannot respond to human needs because it responds to nothing human at all. In that disordered economy the individual is indeed helpless, a bobbing cork on uncontrolled currents. Those currents are brought under control only by giving each citizen a voice in the control of economic as well as political affairs. Democratic planning ensures that voice. The plans will be ours. We can adjust them as we make errors and learn from them; we can refine them as circumstances change. We can scrap bad plans and devise new ones as we develop new needs or new capacities. A planning economy, *honestly* socialized, will not be our master but our servant. Let our critics not forget that our first principle throughout is *self*-government, democracy.

PLANNING AND LIBERTY

For self-governed citizens liberty is, indeed, a paramount concern. And what is liberty, after all? It consists of the ability and the right of individuals to make choices in determining their own conduct. The greater the range of their choices, the greater their freedom. No one supposes that liberty is absolute, that individuals can be free to do entirely as they please without restriction. Even the best of our laws limit each person's freedom to do some sorts of things in order that all of us may be genuinely free to do many other, more valuable sorts of things. The more complex a society, the more essential are some kinds of self-restriction for the extension of real freedom within it.

We witness this rational trade-off everywhere. Primary education is made compulsory in order that all may enjoy the freedom possible only for those who can read and write. Social security taxation ensures freedom from want in old age. We may resort to a military draft, reluctantly, to keep the country free. And so on. Having to send our children to school, being deprived of some of our income by taxation—these and other sound policies clearly limit us. We accept such limitations in the interest of the greater liberties they promote.

In the economic sphere such trade-offs are essential. Even advocates of "free enterprise" readily admit the necessity of legislation that hinders private monopolies, obliges honest business reports, forbids the sale of untested drugs or spoiled foods, and so on. Such restrictions are justified by their benefits in safeguarding other more essential economic goods.

Limits on the absolute freedom of private economic agents will be entailed by socialized planning; we make no bones about that. Some of these limits—on the freedom to own, buy, and sell productive resources like factories and farms—will be painful to some, just as universal taxation or compulsory schooling are burdensome now to many. The freedoms gained, from economic insecurity and injustice, will be vastly greater than those given up, and vastly more important.

Socialist restrictions will be felt most keenly by a relatively small number of persons who now enjoy luxury and great economic power. Those who never had investment capital at their disposal, who never were the owners of profit-making wealth, are deprived of nothing in losing economic license. Socialist gains, on the other hand, will be felt directly by every citizen, experiencing steady improvement in the quality of his or her own life, and satisfaction in the increased well-being of others. Never was a wiser bargain struck.

DEMOCRACY IN THE WORK PLACE

Democracy calls for participation in the important affairs of one's community. One's community is not only his town, or nation, but also his place of work—the factory or office, the restaurant or construction project. Can we make democracy genuine in such places, in the day-to-day lives of ordinary citizens?

Yes, we can, but only under socialism. Where the ownership of the enterprise is private, and profit-oriented, there must be bosses on the job to represent the owners and protect their profits. The workers are hired, whether by the hour or the month, in the owners' interests; they take orders from the bosses or they are fired. Capitalism inevitably produces authoritarianism in labor-management relations. Collective bargaining, of which capitalists make much, does no more than mitigate the severity of worker subordination.

This authoritarianism can be eliminated, however, if the enterprise is itself community-owned-and-operated. We the people then make the procedural rules, and we can decide to institute democratic processes in the places of work themselves. This dramatic change is not merely utopian; it has already been widely introduced in socialist democracies—in Sweden for example, and even in a few isolated places in the United States. Where it has been thoughtfully designed, work-place democracy has usually proven very successful. It makes for a happier, healthier, and more productive work force. Men and women on the job regain the sense of personal autonomy that traditional hierarchies do not foster and cannot respect. Through collaboration and cooperation, the workers protect one another from abuse, whether deliberate or inadvertent. And everyone is served because day-to-day participation instills pride in the work force, and provides immediate incentives for energetic work of high quality.

Democracy in the work place does not mean disorder. It does not mean that everyone works when and where and how he or she pleases. It means simply that the members of the work force—knowing themselves as owners as well as consumers and workers—participate with community management in setting work rules, production quotas, hours, and procedures. Of all the ways in which democratic ideals can be realized, this is the most concrete, the most immediate, and the most satisfying. It can be achieved under socialism; on a large scale it can be achieved only under socialism. This by itself is a compelling argument for socialist democracy. . . .

John Rawls

A WELL-ORDERED SOCIETY

John Rawls begins by setting forth the ideal of a well-ordered society as a society governed by a public conception of justice whose members view themselves as free and equal moral persons who enjoy a certain degree of social stability. He then defends the importance of the basic structure of society for this ideal and argues that a particular Kantian conception of justice accords well with the ideal.

MY AIM IN THESE remarks is to give a brief account of the conception of equality that underlies the view expressed in *A Theory of Justice* and the principles considered there. I hope to state the fundamental intuitive idea simply and informally; and so I make no attempt to sketch the argument from the original position. In fact, this construction is not mentioned until the end and then only to indicate its role in giving a Kantian interpretation to the conception of equality already presented.

I

When fully articulated, any conception of justice expresses a conception of the person, of the relations between persons, and of the general structure and ends of social cooperation. To accept the principles that represent a conception of justice is at the same time to accept an ideal of the person; and in acting from these principles we realise such an ideal. Let us begin, then, by trying to describe the kind of person we might want to be and the form of society we might wish to live in and to shape our interests and character. In this way we arrive at the notion of a well-ordered society. I shall first describe this notion and then use it to explain a Kantian conception of equality.

First of all, a well-ordered society is effectively regulated by a public conception of justice. That is, it is a society all of whose members accept, and know that the others accept, the same principles (the same conception) of justice. It is also the case that basic social institutions and their arrangement into one scheme (the basic structure) actually satisfy, and are on good grounds believed by everyone to satisfy, these principles. Finally, publicity also implies that the public conception is founded on reasonable beliefs that have been established by generally accepted methods of inquiry; and the same is true of the application of its principles to basic social arrangements. This last aspect of publicity does not mean that everyone holds the same religious, moral, and theoretical beliefs; on the contrary, there are assumed

From "A Kantian Conception of Equality," *Cambridge Review* (1975) pp.94–99. Reprinted by permission of the author and *The Cambridge Review*.

to be sharp and indeed irreconcilable differences on such questions. But at the same time there is a shared understanding that the principles of justice, and their application to the basic structure of society, should be determined by considerations and evidence that are supported by rational procedures commonly recognized.

Secondly, I suppose that the members of a well-ordered society are, and view themselves as, free and equal moral persons. They are moral persons in that, once they have reached the age of reason, each has, and views the others as having, a realised sense of justice; and this sentiment informs their conduct for the most part. That they are equal is expressed by the supposition that they each have, and view themselves as having, a right to equal respect and consideration in determining the principles by which the basic arrangements of their society are to be regulated. Finally, we express their being free by stipulating that they each have, and view themselves as having, fundamental aims and higher-order interests (a conception of their good) in the name of which it is legitimate to make claims on one another in the design of their institutions. At the same time, as free persons they do not think of themselves as inevitably bound to, or as identical with, the pursuit of any particular array of fundamental interests that they may have at any given time; instead, they conceive of themselves as capable of revising and altering these final ends and they give priority to preserving their liberty in this regard.

In addition, I assume that a well-ordered society is stable relative to its conception of justice. This means that social institutions generate an effective supporting sense of justice. Regarding society as a going concern, its members acquire as they grow up an allegiance to the public conception and this allegiance usually overcomes the temptations and strains of social life.

Now we are here concerned with a conception of justice and the idea of equality that belongs to it. Thus, let us suppose that a well-ordered society exists under circumstances of justice. These necessitate some conception of justice and give point to its special role. First, moderate scarcity obtains. This means that although social cooperation is productive and mutually advantageous (one person's or group's gain need not be another's loss), natural resources and the state of technology are such that the fruits of

joint efforts fall short of the claims that people make. And second, persons and associations have contrary conceptions of the good that lead them to make conflicting claims on one another; and they also hold opposing religious, philosophical, and moral convictions (on matters the public conception leaves open) as well as different ways of evaluating arguments and evidence in many important cases. Given these circumstances, the members of a well-ordered society are not indifferent as to how the benefits produced by their cooperation are distributed. A set of principles is required to judge between social arrangements that shape this division of advantages. Thus the role of the principles of justice is to assign the rights and duties in the basic structure of society and to specify the manner in which institutions are to influence the overall distribution of the returns from social cooperation. The basic structure is the primary subject of justice and that to which the principles of justice in the first instance apply.

It is perhaps useful to observe that the notion of a well-ordered society is an extension of the idea of religious toleration. Consider a pluralistic society, divided along religious, ethnic, or cultural, lines in which the various groups have reached a firm understanding on the scheme of principles to regulate their fundamental institutions. While they have deep differences about other things, there is public agreement on this framework of principles and citizens are attached to it. A well-ordered society has not attained social harmony in all things, if indeed that would be desirable; but it has achieved a large measure of justice and established a basis for civic friendship, which makes people's secure association together possible.

II

The notion of a well-ordered society assumes that the basic structure, the fundamental social institutions and their arrangement into one scheme, is the primary subject of justice. What is the reason for this assumption? First of all, any discussion of social justice must take the nature of the basic structure into account. Suppose we begin with the initially attractive idea that the social process should be allowed to develop over time as free agreements fairly arrived at and fully honored require. Straightaway we need an account of when agreements are free and the conditions under which they are reached are fair. In addition, while these conditions may be satisfied at an earlier time, the accumulated results of agreements in conjunction with social and historical contingencies are likely to change institutions and opportunities so that the conditions for free and fair agreements no longer hold. The basic structure specifies the background conditions against which the actions of individuals, groups, and associations take place. Unless this structure is regulated and corrected so as to be just over time, the social process with its procedures and outcomes is no longer just, however free and fair particular transactions may look to us when viewed by themselves. We recognise this principle when we say that the distribution resulting from voluntary market transactions will not in general be fair unless the antecedent distribution of income and wealth and the structure of the market is fair. Thus we seem forced to start with an account of a just basic structure. It's as if the most important agreement is that which establishes the principles to govern this structure. Moreover, these principles must be acknowledged ahead of time, as it were. To agree to them now, when everyone knows their present situation, would enable some to take unfair advantage of social and natural contingencies, and of the results of historical accidents and accumulations.

Other considerations also support taking the basic structure as the primary subject of justice. It has always been recognised that the social system shapes the desires and aspirations of its members; it determines in large part the kind of persons they want to be as well as the kind of persons they are. Thus an economic system is not only an institutional device for satisfying existing wants and desires but a way of fashioning wants and desires in the future. By what principles are we to regulate a scheme of institutions that has such fundamental consequences for our view of ourselves and for our interests and aims? This question becomes all the more crucial when we consider that the basic structure contains social and economic inequalities. I assume that these are necessary, or highly advantageous, for various reasons; they are required to maintain and to run social arrangements, or to serve as incentives; or perhaps they are a way to put resources in the hands of those who can make the best social use of them; and so on. In any case, given these inequalities, individuals' life-prospects are bound to be importantly affected by their family and class origins, by their natural endowments and the chance contingencies of their (particularly early) development, and by other accidents over the course of their lives. The social structure, therefore, limits people's ambitions and hopes in different ways, for they will with reason view themselves in part according to their place in it and take into account the means and opportunities they can realistically expect.

The justice of the basic structure is, then, of predominant importance. The first problem of justice is to determine the principles to regulate inequalities and to adjust the profound and long-lasting effects of social, natural, and historical contingencies, particularly since these contingencies combined with inequalities generate tendencies that, when left to themselves, are sharply at odds with the freedom and equality appropriate for a well-ordered society. In view of the special role of the basic structure, we cannot assume that the principles suitable to it are natural applications, or even extensions, of the familiar principles governing the actions of individuals and associations in everyday life which take place within its framework. Most likely we shall have to loosen ourselves from our ordinary perspective and take a more comprehensive viewpoint.

III

I shall now state and explain two principles of justice, and then discuss the appropriateness of these principles for a well-ordered society. They read as follows:

1. Each person has an equal right to the most extensive scheme of equal basic liberties compatible with a similar scheme of liberties for all.
2. Social and economic inequalities are to meet two conditions: they must be (a) to the greatest expected benefit of the least advantaged; and (b) attached to offices and positions open to all under conditions of fair opportunity.

The first of these principles is to take priority over the second; and the measure of benefit to the least advantaged is specified in terms of an index of social primary goods. These goods I define as rights, liberties, and opportunities, income and wealth, and the social bases of self-respect. Individuals are assumed to want these goods whatever else they want, or whatever their final ends. The least advantaged are defined very roughly, as the overlap between those who are least favored by each of the three main kinds of contingencies. Thus this group includes persons whose family and class origins are more disadvantaged than others, whose natural endowments have permitted them to fare less well, and whose fortune and luck have been relatively less favourable, all within the normal range (as noted below) and with the relevant measures based on social primary goods. Various refinements are no doubt necessary, but this definition of the least advantaged suitably expresses the link with the problem of contingency and should suffice for our purposes here.

I also suppose that everyone has physical needs and psychological capacities within the normal range, so that the problems of special health care and of how to treat the mentally defective do not arise. Besides prematurely introducing difficult questions that may take us beyond the theory of justice, the consideration of these hard cases can distract our moral perception by leading us to think of people distant from us whose fate arouses pity and anxiety. Whereas the first problem of justice concerns the relations among those who in the normal course of things are full and active participants in society and directly or indirectly associated together over the whole course of their life.

Now the members of a well-ordered society are free and equal; so let us first consider the fittingness of the two principles to their freedom, and then to their equality. These principles reflect two aspects of their freedom, namely, liberty and responsibility, which I take up in turn. In regard to liberty, recall that people in a well-ordered society view themselves as having fundamental aims and interests which they must protect, if this is possible. It is partly in the name of these interests that they have a right to equal consideration and respect in the design of their society. A familiar historical example is the religious interest; the interest in the integrity of the person, freedom from psychological oppression and from physical assault and dismemberment is another. The notion of a well-ordered society leaves open what particular expression these interests take; only their general form is specified. But individuals do have interests of the requisite kind and the basic liberties necessary for their protection are guaranteed by the first principle.

It is essential to observe that these liberties are given by a list of liberties; important among these are freedom of thought and liberty of conscience, freedom of the person and political liberty. These liberties have a central range of application within which they can be limited and compromised only when they conflict with other basic liberties. Since they may be limited when they clash with one another, none of these liberties is absolute; but however they are adjusted to form one system, this system is to be the same for all. It is difficult, perhaps impossible, to give a complete definition of these liberties independently from the particular circumstances, social, economic, and technological, of a given well-ordered society. Yet the hypothesis is that the general form of such a list could be devised with sufficient exactness to sustain this conception of justice. Of course, liberties not on the list, for example, the right to own certain kinds of property (e.g., means of production), and freedom of contract as understood by the doctrine of laissez-faire, are not basic; and so they are not protected by the priority of the first principle.[1]

One reason, then, for holding the two principles suitable for a well-ordered society is that they assure the protection of the fundamental interests that members of such a society are presumed to have. Further reasons for this conclusion can be given by describing in more detail the notion of a free person. Thus we may suppose that such persons regard themselves as having a highest-order interest in how all their other interests, including even their fundamental ones, are shaped and regulated by social institutions. As I noted earlier, they do not think of themselves as unavoidably tied to any particular array of fundamental interests; instead they view themselves as capable of revising and changing these final ends. They wish, therefore, to give priority to their liberty to do this, and so their original allegiance and continued devotion to their ends are to be formed and affirmed under conditions that are free. Or, expressed another way, members of a well-ordered society are viewed as responsible for their fundamental interests and ends. While as members of particular associations some may decide in practice to yield much of this responsibility to others, the basic structure cannot be arranged so as to prevent people from developing their capacity to be responsible, or to obstruct their exercise of it once they attain it. Social arrangements must respect their autonomy and this points to the appropriateness of the two principles.

IV

These last remarks about responsibility may be elaborated further in connection with the role of social primary goods. As already stated, these are things that people in a well-ordered society may be presumed to want, whatever their final ends. And the two principles assess the basic structure in terms of certain of these goods: rights, liberties, and opportunities, income and wealth, and the social bases of self-respect. The latter are features of the basic structure that may reasonably be expected to affect people's self-respect and self-esteem (these are not the same) in important ways.[2] Part (a) of the second principle (the difference principle, or as economists prefer to say, the maximin criterion) uses an index of these goods to determine the least advantaged. Now certainly there are difficulties in working out a satisfactory index, but I shall leave these aside. Two points are particularly relevant here: first, social primary goods are certain objective characteristics of social institutions and of people's situation with respect to them; and second, the same index of these goods is used to compare everyone's social circumstances. It is clear, then, that although the index provides a basis for interpersonal comparisons for the purposes of justice, it is not a measure of individuals' overall satisfaction or dissatisfaction. Of course, the precise weights adopted in such an index cannot be laid down ahead of time, for these should be adjusted, to some degree at least, in view of social conditions. What can be settled initially is certain constraints on these weights, as illustrated by the priority of the first principle.

Now, that the responsibility of free persons is implicit in the use of primary goods can be seen in the following way. We are assuming that people are able to control and to revise their wants and desires in the light of circumstances and that they are to have responsibility for doing so, provided that the principles of justice are fulfilled, as they are in a well-ordered society. Persons do not take their wants and desires as determined by happenings beyond their control. We are not, so to speak, assailed by them, as we are perhaps by disease and illness so that wants

and desires fail to support claims to the means of satisfaction in the way that disease and illness support claims to medicine and treatment.

Of course, it is not suggested that people must modify their desires and ends whatever their circumstances. The doctrine of primary goods does not demand the stoic virtues. Society for its part bears the responsibility for upholding the principles of justice and secures for everyone a fair share of primary goods (as determined by the difference principle) within a framework of equal liberty and fair equality of opportunity. It is within the limits of this division of responsibility that individuals and associations are expected to form and moderate their aims and wants. Thus among the members of a well-ordered society there is an understanding that as citizens they will press claims for only certain kinds of things, as allowed for by the principles of justice. Passionate convictions and zealous aspirations do not, as such, give anyone a claim upon social resources or the design of social institutions. For the purposes of justice, the appropriate basis of interpersonal comparisons is the index of primary goods and not strength of feeling or intensity of desire. The theory of primary goods is an extension of the notion of needs, which are distinct from aspirations and desires. One might say, then, that as citizens the members of a well-ordered society collectively take responsibility for dealing justly with one another founded on a public and objective measure of (extended) needs, while as individuals and members of associations they take responsibility for their preferences and devotions.

V

I now take up the appropriateness of the two principles in view of the equality of the members of a well-ordered society. The principles of equal liberty and fair opportunity (part (b) of the second principle) are a natural expression of this equality; and I assume, therefore, that such a society is one in which some form of democracy exists. Thus our question is: by what principle can members of a democratic society permit the tendencies of the basic structure to be deeply affected by social change, and natural and historical contingencies?

Now since we are regarding citizens as free and equal moral persons (the priority of the first principle of equal liberty gives institutional expression to this), the obvious starting point is to suppose that all other social primary goods, and in particular income and wealth, should be equal: everyone should have an equal share. But society must take organizational requirements and economic efficiency into account. So it is unreasonable to stop at equal division. The basic structure should allow inequalities so long as these improve everyone's situation, including that of the least advantaged, provided these inequalities are consistent with equal liberty and fair opportunity. Because we start from equal shares, those who benefit least have, so to speak, a veto; and thus we arrive at the difference principle. Taking equality as the basis of comparison those who have gained more must do so on terms that are justifiable to those who have gained the least.

In explaining this principle, several matters should be kept in mind. First of all, it applies in the first instance to the main public principles and policies that regulate social and economic inequalities. It is used to adjust the system of entitlements and rewards, and the standards and precepts that this system employs. Thus the difference principle holds, for example, for income and property taxation, for fiscal and economic policy; it does not apply to particular transactions or distributions, nor, in general, to small scale and local decisions, but rather to the background against which these take place. No observable pattern is required of actual distributions, nor even any measure of the degree of equality (such as the Gini coefficient) that might be computed from these.[3] What is enjoined is that the inequalities make a functional contribution to those least favoured. Finally, the aim is not to eliminate the various contingencies, for some such contingencies seem inevitable. Thus even if an equal distribution of natural assets seemed more in keeping with the equality of free persons, the question of redistributing these assets (were this conceivable) does not arise, since it is incompatible with the integrity of the person. Nor need we make any specific assumptions about how great these variations are; we only suppose that, as realized in later life, they are influenced by all three kinds of contingencies. The question, then, is by what criterion a democratic society is to organize cooperation and arrange the system of entitlements that encourages and rewards productive efforts? We have a right to our natural abilities and a right to whatever we become entitled to by taking part in a fair social process. The problem is to characterise this process.[4]

At first sight, it may appear that the difference principle is arbitrarily biased towards the least favoured. But suppose, for simplicity, that there are only two groups, one significantly more fortunate than the other. Society could maximise the expectations of either group but not both, since we can maximise with respect to only one aim at a time. It seems plain that society should not do the best it can for those initially more advantaged; so if we reject the difference principle, we must prefer maximising some weighted mean of the two expectations. But how should this weighted mean be specified? Should society proceed as if we had an equal chance of being in either group (in proportion to their size) and determine the mean that maximises this purely hypothetical expectation? Now it is true that we sometimes agree to draw lots but normally only to things that cannot be appropriately divided or else cannot be enjoyed or suffered in common.[5] And we are willing to use the lottery principle even in matters of lasting importance if there is no other way out. (Consider the example of conscription.) But to appeal to it in regulating the basic structure itself would be extraordinary. There is no necessity for society as an enduring system to invoke the lottery principle in this case; nor is there any reason for free and equal persons to allow their relations over the whole course of their life to be significantly affected by contingencies to the greater advantage of those already favored by these accidents. No one had an antecedent claim to be benefited in this way; and so to maximise a weighted mean is, so to speak, to favour the more fortunate twice over. Society can, however, adopt the difference principle to arrange inequalities so that social and natural contingencies are efficiently used to the benefit of all, taking equal division as a benchmark. So while natural assets cannot be divided evenly, or directly enjoyed or suffered in common, the results of their productive efforts can be allocated in ways consistent with an initial equality. Those favoured by social and natural contingencies regard themselves as already compensated, as it were, by advantages to which no one (including themselves) had a prior claim. Thus they think the difference principle appropriate for regulating the system of entitlements and inequalities.

VI

The conception of equality contained in the principles of justice I have described is Kantian. I shall conclude by mentioning very briefly the reasons for this description. Of course, I do not mean that this conception is literally Kant's conception, but rather that it is one of no doubt several conceptions sufficiently similar to essential parts of his doctrine to make the adjective appropriate. Much depends on what one counts as essential. Kant's view is marked by a number of dualisms, in particular, the dualisms between the necessary and the contingent, form and content, reason and desire, and noumena and phenomena. To abandon these dualisms as he meant them is, for many, to abandon what is distinctive in his theory. I believe otherwise. His moral conception has a characteristic structure that is more clearly discernible when these dualisms are not taken in the sense he gave them but reinterpreted and their moral force reformulated within the scope of an empirical theory. One of the aims of *A Theory of Justice* was to indicate how this might be done.

To suggest the main idea, think of the notion of a well-ordered society as an interpretation of the idea of a kingdom of ends thought of as a human society under circumstances of justice. Now the members of such a society are free and equal and so our problem is to find a rendering of freedom and equality that it is natural to describe as Kantian; and since Kant distinguished between positive and negative freedom, we must make room for this contrast. At this point I resorted to the idea of the original position: I supposed that the conception of justice suitable for a well-ordered society is the one that would be agreed to in a hypothetical situation that is fair between individuals conceived as free and equal moral persons, that is, as members of such a society. Fairness of the circumstances under which agreement is reached transfers to the fairness of the principles agreed to. The original position was designed so that the conception of justice that resulted would be appropriate.

Particularly important among the features of the original position for the interpretation of negative freedom are the limits on information, which I called the veil of ignorance. Now there is a stronger and a weaker form of these limits. The weaker supposes that we begin with full information, or else that which we possess in everyday life, and then proceed to eliminate only the information that would lead to partiality and bias. The stronger form has a Kantian explanation: we start from no information at all; for by negative freedom Kant means being able to act independently from the determination of alien causes; to act from natural necessity is to subject oneself to the heteronomy of nature. We interpret this as requiring that the conception of justice that regulates the basic structure, with its deep and long-lasting effects on our common life, should not be adopted on grounds that rest on a knowledge of the various contingencies. Thus when this conception is agreed to, knowledge of our social position, our peculiar desires and interests, or of the various outcomes and configurations of natural and historical accident is excluded. One allows only that information required for a rational agreement. This means that, so far as possible, only the general laws of nature are known together with such particular facts as are implied by the circumstances of justice.

Of course, we must endow the parties with some motivation, otherwise no acknowledgement would be forthcoming. Kant's discussion in the *Groundwork* of the second pair of examples indicates, I believe, that in applying the procedure of the categorical imperative he tacitly relied upon some account of primary goods. In any case, if the two principles would be adopted in the original position with its limits on information, the conception of equality they contain would be Kantian in the sense that by acting from this conception the members of a well-ordered society would express their negative freedom. They would have succeeded in regulating the basic structure and its profound consequences on their persons and mutual relationships by principles the grounds for which are suitably independent from chance and contingency.

In order to provide an interpretation of positive freedom, two things are necessary: first, that the parties are conceived as free and equal moral persons must play a decisive part in their adoption of the conception of justice; and second, the principles of this conception must have a content appropriate to express this determining view of persons and must apply to the controlling institutional subject. Now if correct, the argument from the original position seems to meet these conditions. The assumption that the parties are free and equal moral persons does have an essential role in this argument; and as regards content and application, these principles express, on their public face as it were, the conception of the person that is realised in a well-ordered society. They give priority to the basic liberties, regard individuals as free and responsible masters of their aims and desires, and all are to share equally in the means for the attainment of ends unless the situation of everyone can be improved, taking equal division as the starting point. A society that realised these principles would attain positive freedom, for these principles reflect the features of persons that determined their selection and so express a conception they give to themselves.

NOTES

1. This paragraph confirms H. L. A. Hart's interpretation. See his discussion of liberty and its priority, *Chicago Law Review*, April, 1973, pp. 536–540.

2. I discuss certain problems in interpreting the account of primary goods in 'Fairness to Goodness', to appear in the *Philosophical Review*.

3. For a discussion of such measures, see A. K. Sen, *On Economic Inequality* (Oxford, 1973), chap. 2.

4. The last part of this paragraph alludes to some objections raised by Robert Nozick in his *Anarchy, State, and Utopia* (New York, 1974), esp. pp. 213–229.

5. At this point I adapt some remarks of Hobbes. See *The Leviathan*, Ch. 15, under the thirteenth and fourteenth laws of nature.

Ronald Dworkin

LIBERALISM

Ronald Dworkin examines the question of whether liberalism is a coherent political doctrine or simply an accidental cluster of social "causes." He rejects the idea that liberalism can appropriately be characterized as favoring equality more and liberty less than conservativism does. Instead, he argues that liberalism incorporates an ideal of equality that requires governments to be neutral in regard to theories of the good life. He then shows how liberalism so construed essentially requires the adoption of such liberal social causes as economic redistribution, civil liberties, and judicial safeguards.

I

IN THIS ESSAY I shall propose a theory about what liberalism is; but I face an immediate problem. My project supposes that there is such a thing as liberalism, and the opinion is suddenly popular that there is not. Relatively recently—sometime before the

From "Liberalism," in *Public and Private Morality* edited by Stuart Hampshire (1978) pp. 113–136. Reprinted by permission of Cambridge University Press.

Vietnam War—politicians who called themselves 'liberals' held certain positions that could be identified as a group. Liberals were for greater economic equality, for internationalism, for freedom of speech and against censorship, for greater equality between the races and against segregation, for a sharp separation of church and state, for greater procedural protection for accused criminals, for decriminalization of 'morals' offenses, particularly drug offenses and consensual sexual offenses involving only adults, and for an aggressive use of central government power to achieve all these goals. These were, in the familiar phrase, liberal 'causes', and those who promoted these causes could be distinguished from another large party of political opinion that could usefully be called 'conservative.' Conservatives tended to hold the contrary position to each of the classical liberal causes.

But a series of developments have called into question whether liberalism is in fact a distinct political theory. One of these was the war. Kennedy and his men called themselves liberals; so did Johnson, who retained the Kennedy men and added liberals of his own. But the war was inhumane, and discredited the idea that liberalism was the party of humanity. It would have been possible to argue, of course, that the Bundys and McNamaras and Rostows were false liberals, who sacrificed liberal principles for the sake of personal power, or incompetent liberals who did not understand that liberal principles prohibited what they did. But many critics drew the different conclusion that the war had exposed hidden connections between liberalism and exploitation. Once these supposed connections were exposed, they were seen to include domestic as well as external exploitation, and the line between liberalism and conservatism was then thought to be sham.

Second, politics began to produce issues that seemed no longer to divide into liberal and conservative positions. It is not clear, for example, whether concern for protecting the environment from pollution, even at the cost of economic growth that might reduce unemployment, is a liberal cause or not. Consumer protection appeals equally to consumers who call themselves liberal and those who say they are conservative. Many different groups—not only environmentalists and consumer protectionists—now oppose what is called the growth mentality, that

is, the assumption that it should be an important aim of government to improve the total wealth or product of the country. It is also fashionable to ask for more local control by small groups over political decisions, not so much because decisions made locally are likely to be better, but because personal political relationships of mutual respect and cooperation, generated by local decisions, are desirable for their own sake. Opposition to growth for its own sake, and opposition to the concentration of power, seem liberal in spirit because liberals traditionally opposed the growth of big business and traditionally supported political equality. But these positions nevertheless condemn the strategies of central economic and political organization that have, certainly since the New Deal, been thought to be distinctly liberal strategies.

Third, and in consequence, politicians are less likely than before to identify themselves as 'liberal' or 'conservative', and more likely to combine political positions formerly thought liberal with those formerly thought conservative. President Carter, for example, [professed] what seem to be 'liberal' positions on human rights with 'conservative' positions on the importance of balancing the national budget even at the expense of improved welfare programs, and many commentators attributed his unanticipated nomination to his ability to break through political categories in this way. . . . Citizens, too, seem to have switched positions while retaining labels. Many who now call themselves 'liberal' support causes that used to be conservative: it is now self-identified 'liberals' who want to curtail the regulatory power of the national executive. Politicians and analysts, it is true, continue to use the old categories. . . . But the categories seem to many much more artificial than they did.

I want to argue that a certain conception of equality, which I shall call the liberal conception of equality, is the nerve of liberalism. But that supposes that liberalism is an authentic and coherent political morality, so that it can make sense to speak of 'its' central principle, and these developments may be taken to suggest that that is not. They may seem to support the following sceptical thesis instead. 'The word "liberalism" has been used, since the eighteenth century, to describe various distinct clusters of political positions, but with no important similarity of principle among the different clusters called "liberal" at different times. The explanation of why different clusters formed in various circumstances, or why they were called "liberal", cannot be found by searching for any such principle. It must be found instead in complicated accidents of history, in which the self-interest of certain groups, the prevalence of certain political rhetoric, and many other discrete factors played different parts. One such cluster was formed, for such reasons, in the period of the New Deal: it combined an emphasis on less inequality and greater economic stability with more abundant political and civil liberty for the groups then campaigning for these goals. Our contemporary notion of "liberal" is formed from that particular package of political aims.'

'But the forces that formed and held together that package have now been altered in various ways. Businessmen, for example, have now come to see that various elements in the package—particularly those promoting economic stability—work very much in their favor. White working men have come to see that certain sorts of economic and social equality for racial minorities threaten their own interests. Political liberties have been used, not merely or even mainly by those anxious to achieve the limited economic equality of the New Deal, but also by social rebels who threaten ideals of social order and public decency that the old liberal did not question. The question of Israel, and Soviet violations of the rights of intellectuals, have led the old liberal to withdraw his former tolerance for the Soviet Union and the expansion of its power. So New Deal "liberalism", as a package of political positions, is no longer an important political force. Perhaps a new cluster of positions will form which will be called "liberal" by its supporters and critics. Perhaps not. It does not much matter, because the new cluster, whether it is called liberalism or not, will bear no important connections of principle to the old liberalism. The idea of liberalism, as a fundamental political theory that produced the package of liberal causes, is a myth with no explanatory power whatsoever.'

That is the sceptic's account. There is, however, an alternative account of the break up of the liberal package of ideas. In any coherent political program there are two elements: constitutive political positions that are valued for their own sake, and derivative positions that are valued as strategies, as means

of achieving the constitutive positions. The sceptic believes that the liberal package of ideas had no constitutive political morality at all; it was a package formed by accident and held together by self-interest. The alternate account argues that the package had a constitutive morality, and has come apart, to the extent it has, because it has become less clear which derivative positions best serve that constitutive morality.

On this account, the break up of New Deal liberalism was the consequence, not of any sudden disenchantment with that fundamental political morality, but rather of changes in opinion and circumstance that made it doubtful whether the old strategies for enforcing that morality were right. If this alternate account is correct, then the ideal of liberalism as a fundamental political morality is not only not a myth, but is an idea necessary to any adequate account of modern political history, and to any adequate analysis of contemporary political debate. That conclusion will, of course, appeal to those who continue to think of themselves as liberals. But it must also be the thesis of critics of liberalism; at least of those who suppose that liberalism, in its very nature, is exploitative, or destructive of important values of community, or in some other way malign. For these comprehensive critics, no less than partisans, must deny that the New Deal liberal settlement was a merely accidental coincidence of political positions.

But of course we cannot decide whether the sceptical account or this alternative account is superior until we provide, for the latter, some theory about which elements of the liberal package are to be taken as constitutive and which derivative. Unfortunately liberals and their critics disagree, both between and within the two groups, about that very issue. Critics often say, for example, that liberals are committed to economic growth, to the bureaucratic apparatus of government and industry necessary for economic growth, and to the form of life in which growth is pursued for its own sake, a form of life that emphasises competition, individualism and material satisfactions. It is certainly true that politicians whom we consider paradigmatic liberals, like Hubert Humphrey and Roy Jenkins, emphasized the need for economic growth. But is this emphasis on growth a matter of constitutive principle because liberalism is tied to some form of utilitarianism that makes overall prosperity a good in itself? If so, then the disenchantment of many liberals with the idea of growth argues from the sceptical view that liberalism was a temporary alliance of unrelated political positions that has now been abandoned. Or is it a matter of derivative strategy within liberal theory—a debatable strategy for reducing economic inequality, for example—and therefore a matter on which liberals might disagree without deep schism or crisis? This question cannot be answered simply by pointing out to the conceded fact that many who call themselves liberals once supported economic development more enthusiastically than they do now, any more than it can be shown that there is a connection of principle between imperialism and liberalism simply by naming men who called themselves liberals and were among those responsible for Vietnam. The vital questions here are questions of theoretical connection, and simply pointing at history, without at least some hypothesis about the nature of those connections, is useless.

The same question must be raised about the more general issue of the connection between liberalism and capitalism. It is certainly true that most of those who have called themselves liberals, both in America and Britain, have been anxious to make the market economy more fair in its workings and results, or to mix a market and collective economy, rather than to replace the market economy altogether with a plainly socialist system. That is the basis for the familiar charge that there is no genuine difference, within the context of western politics, between liberals and conservatives. But once again different views about the connection between capitalism and liberalism are possible. It may be that the constitutive positions of New Deal liberalism must include the principle of free enterprise itself, or principles about liberty that can only be satisfied by a market economy for conceptual reasons. If so, then any constraints on the market the liberal might accept, through redistribution or regulation or a mixed economy, would be a compromise with basic liberal principles, perhaps embraced out of practical necessity in order to protect the basic structure from revolution. The charge, that the ideological differences between liberalism and conservatism are relatively unimportant, would be supported by that discovery. If someone was persuaded to abandon capitalism altogether, he would no longer be a liberal; if many former liberals did so, then liberalism would be

crippled as a political force. But perhaps, on the contrary, capitalism is not constitutive but derivative in New Deal liberalism. It might have been popular among liberals because it seemed (rightly or wrongly) the best means of achieving different and more fundamental liberal goals. In that case, liberals can disagree about whether free enterprise is worth preserving under new circumstances, again without theoretical crisis or schism, and the important ideological difference from conservatives may still be preserved. Once again, we must give attention to the theoretical question in order to frame hypotheses with which to confront the political facts.

These two issues—the connection of liberalism with economic growth and capitalism—are especially controversial, but we can locate similar problems of distinguishing what is fundamental from what is strategic in almost every corner of the New Deal liberal settlement. The liberal favors free speech. But is free speech a fundamental value, or is it only a means to some other goal like the discovery of truth (as Mill argued) or the efficient functioning of democracy (as Michaeljohn suggested)? The liberal disapproves of enforcing morality through the criminal law. Does this suggest that liberalism opposes the formation of a shared community sense of decency? Or is liberalism hostile only to using the criminal law to secure that shared community sense? I must say, perhaps out of unnecessary caution, that these questions cannot be answered, at the end of the day, apart from history and developed social theory; but it does not contradict that truism to insist that philosophical analysis of the idea of liberalism is an essential part of that very process.

So my original question—what is liberalism—turns out to be a question that must be answered, at least tentatively, before the more clearly historical questions posed by the sceptical thesis can be confronted. For my question is just the question of what morality is constitutive in particular liberal settlements like the New Deal package.

My project does take a certain view of the role of political theory in politics. It supposes that liberalism consists in some constitutive political morality that has remained roughly the same over some time, and that continues to be influential in politics. It supposes that distinct liberal settlements are formed when, for one reason or another, those moved by that constitutive morality settle on a particular scheme of derivative positions as appropriate to complete a practical liberal political theory, and others, for their own reasons, become allies in promoting that scheme. Such settlements break up, and liberalism is accordingly fragmented, when these derivative positions are discovered to be ineffective, or when economic or social circumstances change so as to make them ineffective, or when the allies necessary to make an effective political force are no longer drawn to the scheme. I do not mean that the constitutive morality of liberalism is the only force at work in forming liberal settlements, or even that it is the most powerful, but only that it is sufficiently distinct and influential to give sense to the idea, shared by liberals and their critics, that liberalism exists, and to give sense to the popular practice of arguing about what it is.

But the argument so far has shown that the claim that a particular position is constitutive rather than derivative in a political theory will be both controversial and complex. How shall I proceed? Any satisfactory description of the constitutive morality of liberalism must meet the following catalogue of conditions. (a) It must state positions that it makes sense to suppose might be constitutive of political programs for people in our culture. I do not claim simply that some set of constitutive principles could explain liberal settlements if people held those principles, but that a particular set does help to explain liberal settlements because people actually have held those principles. (b) It must be sufficiently well tied to the last clear liberal settlement—the political positions I described at the outset as acknowledged liberal 'causes'—so that it can be seen to be constitutive for that entire scheme; so that the remaining positions in the scheme can be seen, that is, to be derivative given that constitutive morality. (c) It must state constitutive principles in sufficient detail so as to discriminate a liberal political morality from other, competing political moralities. If, for example, I say simply that it is constitutive of liberalism that the government must treat its citizens with respect, I have not stated a constitutive principle in sufficient detail, because, although liberals might argue that all their political schemes follow from that principle, conservatives, Marxists and perhaps even fascists would make the same claim for their theories. (d) Once these requirements of authenticity, completeness and distinction are satisfied, then a more

comprehensive and frugal statement of constitutive principles meeting these requirements is to be preferred to a less comprehensive and frugal scheme, because the former will have greater explanatory power, and provide a fairer test of the thesis that these constitutive principles both precede and survive particular settlements.

The second of these four conditions provides a starting point. I must therefore repeat the list of what I take to be the political positions of the last liberal settlement, and I shall, for convenience, speak of 'liberals' as these who support those positions. In economic policy, liberals demand that inequalities of wealth be reduced through welfare and other forms of redistribution financed by progressive taxes. They believe that government should intervene in the economy to promote economic stability, to control inflation, to reduce unemployment, and to provide services that would not otherwise be provided, but they favor a pragmatic and selective intervention over a dramatic change from free enterprise to wholly collective decisions about investment, production, prices and wages. They support racial equality, and approve government intervention to secure it, through constraints on both public and private discrimination in education, housing and employment. But they oppose other forms of collective regulation of individual decision: they oppose regulation of the content of political speech, even when such regulation might secure greater social order, and they oppose regulation of sexual literature and conduct even when such regulation has considerable majoritarian support. They are suspicious of the criminal law and anxious to reduce the extension of its provisions to behavior whose morality is controversial, and they support procedural constraints and devices, like rules against the admissibility of confessions, that make it more difficult to secure criminal convictions.

I do not mean that everyone who holds any of these positions will or did hold them all. Some people who call themselves liberal do not support several elements of this package; some who call themselves conservative support most of them. But these are the positions that we use as a touchstone when we ask how liberal or conservative someone is; and indeed on which we now rely when we say that the line between liberals and conservatives is more blurred than once it was. I have omitted those positions that are only debatably elements of the liberal package, like support for military intervention in Vietnam, or the present campaign in support of human rights in Communist countries, or concern for more local participation in government or for consumer protection against manufacturers, or for the environment. I have also omitted debatable extension of liberal doctrines, like busing and quotas that discriminate in favor of minorities in education and employment. I shall assume that the positions that are uncontroversially liberal positions are the core of the liberal settlement. If my claim is right, that a particular conception of equality can be shown to be constitutive for that core of positions, we shall have, in that conception, a device for stating and testing the claim that some debatable position is also 'really' liberal.

II

Is there a thread of principle that runs through the core liberal positions, and that distinguishes these from the corresponding conservative positions? There is a familiar answer to this question that is mistaken, but mistaken in an illuminating way. The politics of democracies, according to this answer, recognizes several independent constitutive political ideals, the most important of which are the ideals of liberty and equality. Unfortunately, liberty and equality often conflict: sometimes the only effective means to promote equality require some limitation of liberty, and sometimes the consequences of promoting liberty are detrimental to equality. In these cases, good government consists in the best compromise between the competing ideals, but different politicians and citizens will make that compromise differently. Liberals tend relatively to favor equality more and liberty less than conservatives do, and the core set of liberal positions I described is the result of striking the balance that way.

This account offers a theory about what liberalism is. Liberalism shares the same constitutive principles with many other political theories, including conservatism, but is distinguished from these by attaching different relative importance to different principles. The theory therefore leaves room, on the spectrum it describes, for the radical who cares even more for equality and less for liberty than the liberal, and therefore stands even further away from the extreme conservative. The liberal becomes the man in the middle, which explains why liberalism is so

often now considered wish-washy, an untenable compromise between two more forthright positions.

No doubt this description of American politics could be made more sophisticated. It might make room for other independent constitutive ideals shared by liberalism and its opponents, like stability or security, so that the compromises involved in particular decisions are made out to be more complex. But if the nerve of the theory remains the competition between liberty and equality as constitutive ideals, then the theory cannot succeed. In the first place, it does not satisfy condition (b) in the catalogue of conditions I set out. It seems to apply, at best, to only a limited number of the political controversies it tries to explain. It is designed for economic controversies, but is either irrelevant or misleading in the case of censorship and pornography, and indeed, in the criminal law generally.

But there is a much more important defect in this explanation. It assumes that liberty is measurable so that, if two political decisions each invades the liberty of a citizen, we can sensibly say that one decision takes more liberty away from him than the other. That assumption is necessary, because otherwise the postulate, that liberty is a constitutive ideal of both the liberal and conservative political structures, cannot be maintained. Even firm conservatives are content that their liberty to drive as they wish (for example to drive uptown on Lexington Avenue) may be invaded for the sake, not of some important competing political ideal, but only for marginal gains in convenience or orderly traffic patterns. But since traffic regulation plainly involves some loss of liberty, the conservative cannot be said to value liberty as such unless he is able to show that, for some reason, less liberty is lost by traffic regulation than by restrictions on, for example, free speech, or the liberty to sell for prices others are willing to pay, or whatever other liberty he takes to be fundamental.

But that is precisely what he cannot show, because we do not have a concept of liberty that is quantifiable in the way that demonstration would require. He cannot say, for example, that traffic regulations interfere less with what most men and women want to do than would a law forbidding them to speak out in favor of Communism, or a law requiring them not to fix their prices as they think best. Most people care more about driving than speaking for Communism, and have no occasion to fix prices even if they want to. I do not mean that we can make no sense of the idea of fundamental liberties, like freedom of speech. But we cannot argue in their favor by showing that they protect more liberty, taken to be an even roughly measurable commodity, than does the right to drive as we wish; the fundamental liberties are important because we value something else that they protect. But if that is so, then we cannot explain the difference between liberal and conservative political positions by supposing that the latter protect the commodity of liberty, valued for its own sake, more effectively than the former.

It might now be said, however, that the other half of the liberty-equality explanation may be salvaged. Even if we cannot say that conservatives value liberty, as such, more than liberals, we can still say that they value equality less, and that the different political positions may be explained in that way. Conservatives tend to discount the importance of equality when set beside other goals, like general prosperity or even security; while liberals, in contrast, value equality relatively more, and radicals more still. Once again, it is apparent that this explanation is tailored to the economic controversies, and fits poorly with the non-economic controversies. Once again, however, its defects are more general and more important. We must identify more clearly the sense in which equality could be a constitutive ideal for either liberals or conservatives. Once we do so we shall see that it is misleading to say that the conservative values equality, in that sense, less than the liberal. We shall want to say, instead, that he has a different conception of what equality requires.

We must distinguish between two different principles that take equality to be a political ideal. The first requires that the government treat all those in its charge *as equals*, that is, as entitled to its equal concern and respect. That is not an empty requirement: most of us do not suppose that we must, as individuals, treat our neighbor's children with the same concern as our own, or treat everyone we meet with the same respect. It is nevertheless plausible to think that any government should treat all its citizens as equals in that way. The second principle requires that the government treat all those in its charge *equally* in the distribution of some resource of opportunity, or at least work to secure the state of affairs in which they all are equal or more nearly equal in that respect. It is, of course, conceded by

everyone that the government cannot make everyone equal in every respect, but people do disagree about how far government should try to secure equality in some particular resource; for example, in monetary wealth.

If we look only at the economic-political controversies, then we might well be justified in saying that liberals want more equality in the sense of the second principle than conservatives do. But it would be a mistake to conclude that they value equality in the sense of the first and more fundamental principle any more highly. I say that the first principle is more fundamental because I assume that, for both liberals and conservatives, the first is constitutive and the second derivative. Sometimes treating people equally is the only way to treat them as equals; but sometimes not. Suppose a limited amount of emergency relief is available for two equally populous areas injured by floods; treating the citizens of both areas as equals requires giving more aid to the more seriously devastated area rather than splitting the available funds equally. The conservative believes that in many other, less apparent, cases treating citizens equally amounts to not treating them as equals. He might concede, for example, that positive discrimination in university admissions will work to make the two races more nearly equal in wealth, but nevertheless maintain that such programs do not treat black and white university applicants as equals. If he is a utilitarian he will have a similar, though much more general, argument against any redistribution of wealth that reduces economic efficiency. He will say that the only way to treat people as equals is to maximize the average welfare of all members of community, counting gains and losses to all in the same scales, and that a free market is the only, or best, instrument for achieving that goal. This is not (I think) a good argument, but if the conservative who makes it is sincere he cannot be said to have discounted the importance of treating all citizens as equals.

So we must reject the simple idea that liberalism consists in a distinctive weighting between constitutive principles of equality and liberty. But our discussion of the idea of equality suggests a more fruitful line. I assume (as I said) that there is broad agreement within modern politics that the government must treat all its citizens with equal concern and respect. I do not mean to deny the great power of prejudice in, for example, American politics. But few citizens, and even fewer politicians, would now admit to political convictions that contradict the abstract principle of equal concern and respect. Different people hold, however, as our discussion made plain, very different conceptions of what that abstract principle requires in particular cases.

III

What does it mean for the government to treat its citizens as equals? That is, I think, the same question as the question of what it means for the government to treat all its citizens as free, or as independent, or with equal dignity. In any case, it is a question that has been central to political theory at least since Kant.

It may be answered in two fundamentally different ways. The first supposes that government must be neutral on what might be called the question of the good life. The second supposes that government cannot be neutral on that question, because it cannot treat its citizens as equal human beings without a theory of what human beings ought to be. I must explain that distinction further. Each person follows a more-or-less articulate conception of what gives value to life. The scholar who values a life of contemplation has such a conception; so does the television-watching, beer-drinking citizen who is fond of saying 'This is the life', though of course he has thought less about the issue and is less able to describe or defend his conception.

The first theory of equality supposes that political decisions must be, so far as is possible, independent of any particular conception of the good life, or of what gives value to life. Since the citizens of a society differ in their conceptions, the government does not treat them as equals if it prefers one conception to another, either because the officials believe that one is intrinsically superior, or because one is held by the more numerous or more powerful group. The second theory argues, on the contrary, that the content of equal treatment cannot be independent of some theory about the good for man or the good of life, because treating a person as an equal means treating him the way the good or truly wise person would wish to be treated. Good government consists in fostering or at least recognizing good lives; treatment as an equal consists in treating each person

as if he were desirous of leading the life that is in fact good, at least so far as this is possible. . . .

IV

I now define a liberal as someone who holds the first, or liberal, theory of what equality requires. Suppose that a liberal is asked to found a new state. He is required to dictate its constitution and fundamental institutions. He must propose a general theory of political distribution, that is, a theory of how whatever the community has to assign, by way of goods or resources or opportunities, should be assigned. He will arrive initially at something like this principle of rough equality: resources and opportunities should be distributed, so far as possible, equally, so that roughly the same share of whatever is available is devoted to satisfying the ambitions of each. Any other general aim of distribution will assume either that the fate of some people should be of greater concern than that of others, or that the ambitions or talents of some are more worthy, and should be supported more generously on that account.

Someone may object that this principle of rough equality is unfair because it ignores the fact that people have different tastes, and that some of these are more expensive to satisfy than others, so that, for example, the man who prefers champagne will need more funds if he is not to be frustrated than the man satisfied with beer. But the liberal may reply that tastes as to which people differ are, by and large, not afflictions, like diseases, but are rather cultivated, in accordance with each person's theory of what his life should be like. The most effective neutrality, therefore, requires that the same share be devoted to each, so that the choice between expensive and less expensive tastes can be made by each person for himself, with no sense that his overall share will be enlarged by choosing a more expensive life, or that, whatever he chooses, his choice will subsidize those who have chosen more expensively.[1]

But what does the principle of rough equality of distribution require in practice? If all resources were distributed directly by the government through grants of food, housing, and so forth; if every opportunity citizens have were provided directly by the government through the provisions of civil and criminal law; if every citizen had exactly the same talents; if every citizen started his life with no more than what any other citizen had at the start; and if every citizen had exactly the same theory of the good life and hence exactly the same scheme of preferences as every other citizen, including preferences between productive activity of different forms and leisure, then the principle of rough equality of treatment could be satisfied simply by equal distributions of everything to be distributed and by civil and criminal laws of universal application. Government would arrange for production that maximized the mix of goods, including jobs and leisure, that everyone favored, distributing the product equally.

Of course, none of these conditions of similarity holds. But the moral relevance of different sorts of diversity are very different, as may be shown by the following exercise. Suppose all the conditions of similarity I mentioned did hold except the last: citizens have different theories of the good and hence different preferences. They therefore disagree about what product the raw materials and labor and savings of the community should be used to produce, and about which activities should be prohibited or regulated so as to make others possible or easier. The liberal, as lawgiver, now needs mechanisms to satisfy the principles of equal treatment in spite of these disagreements. He will decide that there are no better mechanisms available, as general political institutions, than the two main institutions of our own political economy: the economic market, for decisions about what goods shall be produced and how they shall be distributed, and representative democracy, for collective decisions about what conduct shall be prohibited or regulated so that other conduct might be made possible or convenient. Each of these familiar institutions may be expected to provide a more egalitarian division than any other general arrangement. The market, if it can be made to function efficiently, will determine for each product a price that reflects the cost in resources of material, labor and capital that might have been applied to produce something different that someone else wants. That cost determines, for anyone who consumes that product, how much his account should be charged in computing the egalitarian division of social resources. It provides a measure of how much more his account should be charged for a house than a book, and for one book rather than another. The market will also provide, for the laborer, a measure of how much should be credited to his account for his choice of productive activity over leisure, and for one activity rather than another. It will tell us, through the price it puts on his labor, how much he should gain or lose by his decision to pursue one career rather than another. These measurements make a citizen's own distribution a function of the personal preferences of others as well as of his own, and it is the sum of these personal preferences that fixes the true cost to the community of meeting his own preferences for goods and activities. The egalitarian distribution, which requires that the cost of satisfying one person's preferences should as far as is possible be equal to the cost of satisfying another's, cannot be enforced unless those measurements are made.

We are familiar with the anti-egalitarian consequences of free enterprise in practice; it may therefore seem paradoxical that the liberal as lawgiver should choose a market economy for reasons of equality rather than efficiency. But, under the special condition that people differ only in preferences for goods and activities, the market is more egalitarian than any alternative of comparable generality. The most plausible alternative would be to allow decisions of production, investment, price and wage to be made by elected officials in a socialist economy. But what principles should officials use in making those decisions? The liberal might tell them to mimic the decisions that a market would make if it was working efficiently under proper competition and full knowledge. This mimicry would be, in practice, much less efficient than an actual market would be. In any case, unless the liberal had reason to think it would be much more efficient, he would have good reason to reject it. Any minimally efficient mimicking of an hypothetical market would require invasions of privacy to determine what decisions individuals would make if forced actually to pay for their investment, consumption and employment decisions at market rates, and this information gathering would be, in many other ways, much more expensive than an actual market. Inevitably, moreover, the assumptions officials make about how people would behave in a hypothetical market reflect the officials' own beliefs about how people should behave. So there would be, for the liberal, little to gain and much to lose in a socialist economy in which officials were asked to mimic a hypothetical market.

But any other instructions would be a direct violation of the liberal theory of what equality requires, because if a decision is made to produce and sell goods at a price below the price a market would fix, then those who prefer those goods, are *pro tanto*, receiving more than an equal share of the resources of the community at the expense of those who would prefer some other use of the resources. Suppose the limited demand for books, matched against the demand for competing uses for wood-pulp, would fix the price of books at a point higher than the socialist managers of the economy will charge; those who want books are having less charged to their account than the egalitarian principle would require. It might be said that in a socialist economy books are simply valued more, because they are inherently more worthy uses of social resources, quite apart from the popular demand for books. But the liberal theory of equality rules out that appeal to the inherent value of one theory of what is good in life.

In a society in which people differed only in preferences, then, a market would be favored for its egalitarian consequences. Inequality of monetary wealth would be the consequence only of the fact that some preferences are more expensive than others, including the preference for leisure time rather than the most lucrative productive activity. But we must now return to the real world. In the actual society for which the liberal must construct political institutions, there are all the other differences. Talents are not distributed equally, so the decision of one person to work in a factory rather than a law firm, or not to work at all, will be governed in large part by his abilities rather than his preferences for work or between work and leisure. The institutions of wealth, which allow people to dispose of what they receive by gift, means that children of the successful will start with more wealth than the children of the unsuccessful. Some people have special needs, because they are handicapped; their handicap will not only disable them from the most productive and lucrative employment, but will incapacitate them from using the proceeds of whatever employment they find as efficiently, so that they will need more than those who are not handicapped to satisfy identical ambitions.

These inequalities will have great, often catastrophic, effects on the distribution that a market economy will provide. But, unlike differences in preferences, the differences these inequalities make are indefensible according to the liberal conception of equality. It is obviously obnoxious to the liberal conception, for example, that someone should have more of what the community as a whole has to distribute because he or his father had superior skill or luck. The liberal lawgiver therefore faces a difficult task. His conception of equality requires an economic system that produces certain inequalities (those that reflect the true differential costs of goods and opportunities) but not others (those that follow from differences in ability, inheritance, etc.). The market produces both the required and the forbidden inequalities, and there is no alternative system that can be relied upon to produce the former without the latter.

The liberal must be tempted, therefore, to a reform of the market through a scheme of redistribution that leaves its pricing system relatively intact but sharply limits, at least, the inequalities in welfare that his initial principle prohibits. No solution will seem perfect. The liberal may find the best answer in a scheme of welfare rights financed through redistributive income and inheritance taxes of the conventional sort, which redistributes just to the Rawlsian point, that is, to the point at which the worst-off group would be harmed rather than benefited by further transfers. In that case, he will remain a reluctant capitalist, believing that a market economy so reformed is superior, from the standpoint of his conception of equality, to any practical socialist alternative. Or he may believe that the redistribution that is possible in a capitalist economy will be so inadequate, or will be purchased at the cost of such inefficiency, that it is better to proceed in a more radical way, by substituting socialist for market decisions over a large part of the economy, and then relying on the political process to insure that prices are set in a manner at least roughly consistent with his conception of equality. In that case he will be a reluctant socialist, who acknowledges the egalitarian defects of socialism but counts them as less severe than the practical alternatives. In either case, he chooses a mixed economic system—either redistributive capitalism or limited socialism—not in order to compromise antagonistic ideals of efficiency and equality, but to achieve the best practical realization of the demands of equality itself.

Let us assume that in this manner the liberal either refines or partially retracts his original section of a market economy. He must now consider the second of the two familiar institutions he first selected, which is representative democracy. Democracy is justified because it enforces the right of each person to respect and concern as an individual; but in practice the decisions of a democratic majority may often violate that right, according to the liberal theory of what the right requires. Suppose a legislature elected by a majority decides to make criminal some act (like speaking in favor of an unpopular political position, or participating in eccentric sexual practices) not because the act deprives others of opportunities they want, but because the majority disapproves of those views or that sexual morality. The political decision, in other words, reflects not simply some accommodation of the *personal* preferences of everyone, in such a way as to make the opportunities of all as nearly equal as may be, but the domination of one set of *external* preferences, that is, preferences people have about what others shall do or have. The decision invades rather than enforces the right of citizens to be treated as equals.

How can the liberal protect citizens against that sort of violation of their fundamental right? It will not do for the liberal simply to instruct legislators, in some constitutional exhortation, to disregard the external preferences of their constituents. Citizens will vote these preferences in electing their representatives, and a legislator who chooses to ignore them will not survive. In any case, it is sometimes impossible to distinguish, even by introspection, the external and personal components of a political position: this is the case, for example, with associational preferences, which are the preferences some people have for opportunities, like the opportunity to attend public schools, but only with others of the same 'background'.

The liberal, therefore, needs a scheme of civil rights, whose effect will be to determine those political decisions that are antecedently likely to reflect strong external preferences, and to remove those decisions from majoritarian political institutions altogether. Of course, the scheme of rights necessary to do this will depend on general facts about the prejudices and other external preferences of the ma-

jority at any given time, and different liberals will disagree about what is needed at any particular time. But the rights encoded in the Bill of Rights of the United States Constitution, as interpreted (on the whole) by the Supreme Court, are those that a substantial number of liberals would think reasonably well suited to what the United States now requires (though most would think that the protection of the individual in certain important areas, including sexual publication and practice, are much too weak).

The main parts of the criminal law, however, present a special problem not easily met by a scheme of civil rights that disable the legislature from taking certain political decisions. The liberal knows that many of the most important decisions required by an effective criminal law are not made by legislators at all, but by prosecutors deciding whom to prosecute for what crime, and by juries and judges deciding whom to convict and what sentences to impose. He also knows that these decisions are antecedently very likely to be corrupted by the external preferences of those who make these decisions because those they judge, typically, have attitudes and ways of life very different from their own. The liberal does not have available, as protection against these decisions, any strategy comparable to the strategy of civil rights that simply remove a decision from an institution. Decisions to prosecute, convict and sentence must be made by someone. But he has available, in the notion of procedural rights, a different device to protect equality in a different way. He will insist that criminal procedure be structured to achieve a margin of safety in decisions, so that the process is biased strongly against the conviction of the innocent. It would be a mistake to suppose that the liberal thinks that these procedural rights will improve the *accuracy* of the criminal process, that is, the probability that any particular decision about guilt or innocence will be the right one. Procedural rights intervene in the process, even at the cost of inaccuracy, to compensate in a rough way for the antecedent risk that a criminal process, especially if it is largely administered by one class against another, will be corrupted by the impact of external preferences that cannot be eliminated directly. This is, of course, only the briefest sketch of how various substantive and procedural civil rights follow from the liberal's initial conception of equality; it is meant to suggest, rather than demonstrate, the more precise argument that would be available for more particular rights.

So the liberal, drawn to the economic market and to political democracy for distinctly egalitarian reasons, finds that these institutions will produce inegalitarian results unless he adds to his scheme different sorts of individual rights. These rights will function as trump cards held by individuals; they will enable individuals to resist particular decisions in spite of the fact that these decisions are or would be reached through the normal workings of general institutions that are not themselves challenged. The ultimate justification for these rights is that they are necessary to protect equal concern and respect; but they are not to be understood as representing equality in contrast to some other goal or principle served by democracy or the economic market. The familiar idea, for example, that rights of redistribution are justified by an ideal of equality that overrides the efficiency ideals of the market in certain cases, has no place in liberal theory. For the liberal, rights are justified, not by some principle in competition with an independent justification of the political and economic institutions they qualify, but in order to make more perfect the only justification on which these other institutions may themselves rely. If the liberal arguments for a particular right are sound, then the right is an unqualified improvement in political morality, not a necessary but regrettable compromise of some other independent goal, like economic efficiency. . . .

NOTES

1. A very different objection calls attention to the fact that some people are afflicted with incapacities like blindness or mental disease, so that they require more resources to satisfy the same scheme of preferences. That is a more appealing objection to my principle of rough equality of treatment, but it calls, not for choosing a different basic principle of distribution, but for corrections in the application of the principle like those I consider later.

Supreme Court of the United States

WYMAN, COMMISSIONER OF NEW YORK DEPARTMENT OF SOCIAL SERVICES V. JAMES

The issue before the Supreme Court of the United States was whether the Fourth Amendment prohibition of unreasonable searches applies to visits by welfare caseworkers to recipients of the program for Aid to Families with Dependent Children. The majority of the Court held that the Fourth Amendment does not apply in this case because the visitation is not forced or compelled, and even if it were, the visitation serves the state's overriding interest in the welfare of the dependent children. Dissenting Justices Douglas and Marshall argued that the Fourth Amendment prohibition does apply because the visitation is forced and compelled (although not normally by a threat of a criminal penalty) and because there are other ways of protecting the state's interest in this case. Justices Douglas and Marshall also argued that the decision of the majority is inconsistent with the Supreme Court's rulings with respect to the allocation of benefits in other cases.

MR. JUSTICE BLACKMUN DELIVERED the opinion of the Court.

This appeal presents the issue whether a beneficiary of the program for Aid to Families with Dependent Children (AFDC) may refuse a home visit by the caseworker without risking the termination of benefits.

The New York State and City social services commissioners appeal from a judgment and decree of a divided three-judge District Court. . . .

The District Court majority held that a mother receiving AFDC relief may refuse, without forfeiting her right to that relief, the periodic home visit which the cited New York statutes and regulations prescribe as a condition for the continuance of assistance under the program. The beneficiary's thesis, and that of the District Court majority, is that home visitation is a search and, when not consented to or when not supported by a warrant based on probable cause, violates the beneficiary's Fourth and Fourteenth Amendment rights. . . .

Plaintiff Barbara James is the mother of a son, Maurice, who was born in May 1967. They reside in New York City. Mrs. James first applied for AFDC assistance shortly before Maurice's birth. A caseworker made a visit to her apartment at that time without objection. The assistance was authorized.

Two years later, on May 8, 1969, a caseworker wrote Mrs. James that she would visit her home on May 14. Upon receipt of this advice, Mrs. James telephoned the worker that, although she was willing to supply information "reasonable and relevant" to her need for public assistance, any discussion was not to take place at her home. The worker told Mrs. James that she was required by law to visit in her home and that refusal to permit the visit would result in the termination of assistance. Permission was still denied. . . .

A notice of termination issued on June 2.

Thereupon, without seeking a hearing at the state level, Mrs. James, individually and on behalf of Maurice, and purporting to act on behalf of all other persons similarly situated, instituted the present civil rights suit. . . .

When a case involves a home and some type of official intrusion into that home, as this case appears to do, an immediate and natural reaction is one of concern about Fourth Amendment rights and the protection which that Amendment is intended to

afford. Its emphasis indeed is upon one of the most precious aspects of personal security in the home: "The right of the people to be secure in their persons, houses, papers, and effects. . . ." This Court has characterized that right as "basic to a free society. . . ." And over the years the Court consistently has been most protective of the privacy of the dwelling. . . .

This natural and quite proper protective attitude, however, is not a factor in this case, for the seemingly obvious and simple reason that we are not concerned here with any search by the New York social service agency in the Fourth Amendment meaning of that term. It is true that the governing statute and regulations appear to make mandatory the initial home visit and the subsequent periodic "contacts" (which may include home visits) for the inception and continuance of aid. It is also true that the caseworker's posture in the home visit is perhaps, in a sense, both rehabilitative and investigative. But this latter aspect, we think, is given too broad a character and far more emphasis than it deserves if it is equated with a search in the traditional criminal law context. We note, too, that the visitation in itself is not forced or compelled, and that the beneficiary's denial of permission is not a criminal act. If consent to the visitation is withheld, no visitation takes place. The aid then never begins or merely ceases, as the case may be. There is no entry of the home and there is no search.

If however, we were to assume that a caseworker's home visit, before or subsequent to the beneficiary's initial qualification for benefits, somehow (perhaps because the average beneficiary might feel she is in no position to refuse consent to the visit), and despite its interview nature, does possess some of the characteristics of a search in the traditional sense, we nevertheless conclude that does not fall within the Fourth Amendment's proscription. This is because it does not descend to the level of unreasonableness. It is unreasonableness which is the Fourth Amendment's standard.

There are a number of factors that compel us to conclude that the home visit proposed for Mrs. James is not unreasonable.

The public's interest in this particular segment of the area of assistance to the unfortunate is protection and aid for the dependent child whose family requires such aid for that child. . . . The dependent child's needs are paramount, and only with hesitancy would we relegate those needs, in the scale of comparative values, to a position secondary to what the mother claims as her rights.

The agency, with tax funds provided from federal as well as from state sources, is fulfilling a public trust. The State, working through its qualified welfare agency, has appropriate and paramount interest and concern in seeing and assuring that the intended and proper objects of that tax-produced assistance are the ones who benefit from the aid it dispenses. . . .

One who dispenses purely private charity naturally has an interest in and expects to know how his charitable funds are utilized and put to work. The public, when it is the provider, rightly expects the same. . . .

We therefore conclude that the home visitation as structured by the New York statutes and regulations is a reasonable administrative tool; that it serves a valid and proper administrative purpose for the dispensation of the AFDC program; that it is not an unwarranted invasion of personal privacy; and that it violates no right guaranteed by the Fourth Amendment.

Reversed and remanded with directions to enter a judgment of dismissal.

It is so ordered. . . .

MR. JUSTICE DOUGLAS, dissenting. . . .

In 1969 roughly 127 billion dollars were spent by the federal, state, and local governments on "social welfare." To farmers alone almost four billion dollars were paid, in part for not growing certain crops. . . .

Yet almost every beneficiary whether rich or poor, rural or urban, has a "house"—one of the places protected by the Fourth Amendment against "unreasonable searches and seizures." The question in this case is whether receipt of largesse from the government makes the *home* of the beneficiary subject to access by an inspector of the agency of oversight, even though the beneficiary objects to the intrusion and even though the Fourth Amendment's procedure for access to one's *house* or *home* is not followed. The penalty here is not, of course, invasion of the privacy of Barbara James, only her loss of federal or state largesse. That, however, is merely rephrasing the problem. Whatever the semantics, the central question is whether the government by force of its lar-

gesse has the power to "buy up" rights guaranteed by the Constitution. But for the assertion of her constitutional right, Barbara James in this case would have received the welfare benefit. . . .

The applicable principle, as stated in *Camara* as "justified by history and by current experience" is that "except in certain carefully defined classes of cases, a search of private property without proper consent is 'unreasonable' unless it has been authorized by a valid search warrant."

In *See* we [decided] that the "businessman, like the occupant of a residence, has a constitutional right to go about his business free from unreasonable official entries upon his private commercial property." There is not the slightest hint in *See* that the Government could condition a business license on the "consent" of the licensee to the administrative searches we held violated the Fourth Amendment. It is a strange jurisprudence indeed which safeguards the businessman at his place of work from warrantless searches but will not do the same for a mother in her *home*.

Is a search of her home without a warrant made "reasonable" merely because she is dependent on government largesse?

Judge Skelly Wright has stated the problem succinctly:

"Welfare has long been considered the equivalent of charity and its recipients have been subjected to all kinds of dehumanizing experiences in the government's effort to police its welfare payments. In fact, over half a billion dollars are expended annually for administration and policing in connection with the Aid to Families with Dependent Children program. Why such large sums are necessary for administration and policing has never been adequately explained. No such sums are spent policing the government subsidies granted to farmers, airlines, steamship companies, and junk mail dealers, to name but a few. The truth is that in this subsidy area society has simply adopted a double standard, one for aid to business and the farmer and a different one for welfare." Poverty, Minorities, and Respect for Law, 1970 Duke L. J. 425, 437–438.

If the welfare recipient was not Barbara James but a prominent, affluent cotton or wheat farmer receiving benefit payments for not growing crops, would not the approach be different? Welfare in aid of dependent children, like social security and unemployment benefits, has an aura of suspicion. There doubtless are frauds in every sector of public welfare whether the recipient be a Barbara James or someone who is prominent or influential. But constitutional rights—here the privacy of the *home*—are obviously not dependent on the poverty or on the affluence of the beneficiary. It is the precincts of the *home* that the Fourth Amendment protects; and their privacy is as important to the lowly as to the mighty.

I would sustain the judgment of the three-judge court in the present case.

MR. JUSTICE MARSHALL, whom MR. JUSTICE BRENNAN joins, dissenting.

. . . The record plainly shows . . . that Mrs. James offered to furnish any information that the appellants desired and to be interviewed at any place other than her home. Appellants rejected her offers and terminated her benefits solely on the ground that she refused to permit a home visit. In addition, appellants make no contention that any sort of probable cause exists to suspect appellee of welfare fraud or child abuse.

Simply stated, the issue in this case is whether a state welfare agency can require all recipients of AFDC benefits to submit to warrantless "visitations" of their homes. In answering that question, the majority dodges between constitutional issues to reach a result clearly inconsistent with the decisions of this Court. We are told that there is no such search involved in this case; that even if there were a search, it would not be unreasonable; and that even if this were an unreasonable search, a welfare recipient waives her right to object by accepting benefits. I emphatically disagree with all three conclusions. . . .

. . . In an era of rapidly burgeoning governmental activities and their concomitant inspectors, caseworkers, and researchers, a restriction of the Fourth Amendment to "the traditional criminal law context" tramples the ancient concept that a man's home is his castle. Only last Term, we reaffirmed that this concept has lost none of its vitality. . . .

. . . [I]t is argued that the home visit is justified to protect dependent children from "abuse" and "exploitation." These are heinous crimes, but they are not confined to indigent households. Would the majority sanction, in the absence of probable cause, compulsory visits to all American homes for the purpose of discovering child abuse? Or is this Court prepared to hold as a matter of constitutional law that a mother, merely because she is poor, is substantially more likely to injure or exploit her children? Such a categorical approach to an entire class of citizens would be dangerously at odds with the tenets of our democracy. . . .

Although the Court does not agree with my conclusion that the home visit is an unreasonable search, its opinion suggests that even if the visit were unreasonable, appellee has somehow waived her right to object. Surely the majority cannot believe that valid Fourth Amendment consent can be given under the threat of the loss of one's sole means of support. . . .

In deciding that the homes of AFDC recipients are not entitled to protection from warrantless searches by welfare caseworkers, the Court declines to follow prior case law and employs a rationale that, if applied to the claims of all citizens, would threaten the validity of the Fourth Amendment. . . . Perhaps the majority has explained why a commercial warehouse deserves more protection than does this poor woman's home. I am not convinced; and, therefore, I must respectfully dissent.

SAN ANTONIO INDEPENDENT SCHOOL DISTRICT V. RODRIGUEZ

The issue before the Supreme Court of the United States was whether the Texas School System, by making the availability of funds to school districts a function of the taxable wealth in those districts, is in violation of the Fourteenth Amendment requirement that all citizens receive the "equal protection of the laws." The majority of the Court held that since education is not a right afforded strict protection by the Federal Constitution and since the absolute deprivation of education is not at stake, the Texas School System is not in violation of the Fourteenth Amendment. Dissenting Justices Marshall and Douglas held that since a right to education (although not implicitly or explicitly guaranteed by the Federal Constitution) is a fundamental right from the perspective of the Fourteenth Amendment and since the Texas School System does provide significantly unequal funding to different school districts, the School System is in violation of the Fourteenth Amendment, even though no one has been absolutely deprived of an education.

MR. JUSTICE POWELL DELIVERED the opinion of the Court.

This suit attacking the Texas system of financing public education was initiated by Mexican-American parents whose children attend the elementary and secondary schools in the Edgewood Independent School District, an urban school district in San Antonio, Texas. They brought a class action on behalf of schoolchildren throughout the State who are members of minority groups or who are poor and reside in school districts having a low property tax base. Named as defendants were the State Board of Education, the Commissioner of Education, the State Attorney General, and the Bexar County (San Antonio) Board of Trustees. The complaint was filed in the summer of 1968 and a three-judge court was impaneled in January 1969. In December 1971 the panel rendered its judgment in a *per curiam* opinion holding the Texas school finance system unconstitutional under the Equal Protection Clause of the Fourteenth Amendment. The State appealed, and we noted probable jurisdiction to consider the far-reaching constitutional questions presented. . . . For the reasons stated in this opinion, we reverse the decision of the District Court. . . .

The school district in which appellees reside, the Edgewood Independent School District, has been compared throughout this litigation with the Alamo Heights Independent School District. This comparison between the least and most affluent districts in the San Antonio area serves to illustrate the manner in which the dual system of finance operates and to indicate the extent to which substantial disparities exist despite the State's impressive progress in recent years. Edgewood is one of seven public school districts in the metropolitan area. Approximately 22,000 students are enrolled in its 25 elementary and secondary schools. The district is situated in the core-city sector of San Antonio in a residential neighborhood that has little commercial or industrial property. The residents are predominantly of Mexican-American descent: approximately 90% of the student population is Mexican-American and over 6% is Negro. The average assessed property value per pupil is $5,960—the lowest in the metropolitan area—and the median family income ($4,686) is also the lowest. At an equalized tax rate of $1.05 per $100 of assessed property—the highest in the metropolitan area—the district contributed $26 to the education of each child for the 1967–1968 school year above its Local Fund Assignment for the Minimum Foundation Program. The Foundation Program contributed $222 per pupil for a state-local total of $248. Federal funds added another $108 for a total of $356 per pupil.

Alamo Heights is the most affluent school district in San Antonio. Its six schools, housing approximately 5,000 students, are situated in a residential community quite unlike the Edgewood District. The school population is predominantly "Anglo," having only 18% Mexican-Americans and less than 1% Negroes. The assessed property value per pupil exceeds $49,000, and the median family income is $8,001. In 1967–1968 the local tax rate of $.85 per $100 of valuation yielded $333 per pupil over and above its contribution to the Foundation Program. Coupled with the $225 provided from that Program, the district was able to supply $558 per student. Supplemented by a $36 per-pupil grant from federal sources, Alamo Heights spent $594 per pupil. . . .

. . . [T]hese disparities, largely attributable to differences in the amounts of money collected through local property taxation . . . led the District Court to conclude that Texas' dual system of public school financing violated the Equal Protection Clause. The District Court held that the Texas system discriminates on the basis of wealth in the manner in which education is provided for its people. . . . Finding that *wealth* is a *"suspect"* classification and that *education* is a *"fundamental"* interest, the District Court held that the Texas system could be sustained only if the State could show that it was premised upon some compelling state interest. On this issue the court concluded that "[n]ot only are defendants unable to demonstrate compelling state interests . . . they fail even to establish a reasonable basis for these classifications." . . .

Texas virtually concedes that its historically rooted dual system of financing education could not withstand the strict judicial scrutiny that this Court has found appropriate in reviewing legislative judgments that interfere with fundamental constitutional rights or that involve suspect classifications. If, as previous decisions have indicated, strict scrutiny means that the State's system is not entitled to the usual presumption of validity, that the State rather than the complainants must carry a "heavy burden of justification," that the State must demonstrate that its educational system has been structured with "precision," and is "tailored" narrowly to serve legitimate objectives and that it has selected the "less drastic means" for effectuating its objectives, the Texas financing system and its counterpart in virtually every other State will not pass muster. The State defends the system's rationality with vigor and disputes the District Court's finding that it lacks a "reasonable basis."

This, then, establishes the framework for our analysis. We must decide, first, whether the Texas system of financing public education operates to the disadvantage of some suspect class or impinges upon a fundamental right explicitly or implicitly protected by the Constitution, thereby requiring strict judicial scrutiny. If so, the judgment of the District Court should be affirmed. If not, the Texas scheme must still be examined to determine whether it rationally furthers some legitimate, articulated state purpose and therefore does not constitute an invidious discrimination in violation of the Equal Protection Clause of the Fourteenth Amendment.

The District Court's opinion does not reflect the novelty and complexity of the constitutional questions posed by appellees' challenge to Texas' system of school financing. In concluding that strict judicial scrutiny was required, that court relied on decisions dealing with the rights of indigents to equal treatment in the criminal trial and appellate processes, and on cases disapproving wealth restrictions on the right to vote. Those cases, the District Court concluded, established wealth as a suspect classification. Finding that the local property tax system discriminated on the basis of wealth, it regarded those precedents as controlling. It then reasoned, based on decisions of this Court affirming the undeniable importance of education, that there is a fundamental right to education and that, absent some compelling state justification, the Texas system could not stand.

We are unable to agree that this case, which in significant aspects is *sui generis,* may be so neatly fitted into the conventional mosaic of constitutional analysis under the Equal Protection Clause. Indeed, for the several reasons that follow, we find neither the suspect-classification nor the fundamental interest analysis persuasive.

The wealth discrimination discovered by the District Court in this case, and by several other courts that have recently struck down school-financing laws in other States, is quite unlike any of the forms of wealth discrimination heretofore reviewed by this Court. Rather than focusing on the unique features of the alleged discrimination, the courts in these cases have virtually assumed their findings of a suspect classification through a simplistic process of analysis: since, under the traditional systems of financing public schools, some poorer people receive less expensive educations than other more affluent people, these systems discriminate on the basis of wealth. This approach largely ignores the hard threshold questions, including whether it makes a difference for purposes of consideration under the Constitution that the class of disadvantaged "poor" cannot be identified or defined in customary equal protection terms, and whether the relative—rather than absolute—nature of the asserted deprivation is of significant consequence. Before a State's laws and the justifications for the classifications they create are subjected to strict judicial scrutiny, we think these threshold considerations must be analyzed more closely than they were in the court below. . . .

. . . The individuals, or groups of individuals, who constituted the class discriminated against in our prior cases shared two distinguishing characteristics: because of their impecunity they were completely unable to pay for some desired benefit, and as a consequence, they sustained an absolute deprivation of a meaningful opportunity to enjoy that benefit. . . .

. . . [N]either appellees nor the District Court addressed the fact that, unlike the foregoing cases, lack of personal resources has not occasioned an absolute deprivation of the desired benefit. The argument here is not that the children in districts having relatively low assessable property values are receiving no public education; rather, it is that they are receiving a poorer quality education than that available to children in districts having more assessable wealth. Apart from the unsettled and disputed question whether the quality of education may be determined by the amount of money expended for it, a sufficient answer to appellees' argument is that, at least where wealth is involved, the Equal Protection Clause does not require absolute equality or precisely equal advantages. . . .

. . . [I]n recognition of the fact that this Court has never heretofore held that wealth discrimination alone provides an adequate basis for invoking strict scrutiny, appellees have not relied solely on this contention. They also assert that the State's system impermissibly interferes with the exercise of a "fundamental" right and that accordingly the prior decisions of this Court require the application of the strict standard of judicial review. . . . It is this question—whether education is a fundamental right, in the sense that it is among the rights and liberties protected by the Constitution—which has so consumed the attention of courts and commentators in recent years.

In *Brown v. Board of Education*, . . . a unanimous Court recognized that "education is perhaps the most important function of state and local governments." What was said there in the context of racial discrimination has lost none of its vitality with the passage of time. . . .

"*. . . In these days, it is doubtful that any child may reasonably be expected to succeed in life if he is denied the opportunity of an education. Such an opportunity, where the state has undertaken to provide it, is a right which must be made available to all on equal terms.*"

. . . But the importance of a service performed by the State does not determine whether it must be regarded as fundamental for purposes of examination under the Equal Protection Clause. . . .

. . . It is not the province of this Court to create substantive constitutional rights in the name of guaranteeing equal protection of the laws. Thus, the key to discovering whether education is "fundamental" is not to be found in comparisons of the relative societal significance of education as opposed to subsistence or housing. Nor is it to be found by weighing whether education is as important as the right to travel. Rather, the answer lies in assessing whether there is a right to education explicitly or implicitly guaranteed by the Constitution. . . .

Education, of course, is not among the rights afforded explicit protection under our Federal Constitution. Nor do we find any basis for saying it is implicitly so protected. . . . It is appellees' contention, however, that education is distinguishable from other services and benefits provided by the State because it bears a peculiarly close relationship to other rights and liberties accorded protection under the Constitution. Specifically, they insist that education is itself a fundamental personal right because it is essential to the effective exercise of First Amendment freedoms and to intelligent utilization of the right to vote. In asserting a nexus between speech and education, appellees urge that the right to speak is meaningless unless the speaker is capable of articulating his thoughts intelligently and persuasively. The "marketplace of ideas" is an empty forum for those lacking basic communicative tools. Likewise, they argue that the corollary right to receive information becomes little more than a hollow privilege when the recipient has not been taught to read, assimilate, and utilize available knowledge.

A similar line of reasoning is pursued with respect to the right to vote. Exercise of the franchise, it is contended, cannot be divorced from the educational foundation of the voter. The electoral process, if reality is to conform to the democratic ideal, depends on an informed electorate: a voter cannot cast his ballot intelligently unless his reading skills and thought processes have been adequately developed.

We need not dispute any of these propositions. The Court has long afforded zealous protection against unjustifiable governmental interference with the individual's rights to speak and to vote. Yet we have never presumed to possess either the ability or the authority to guarantee to the citizenry the most *effective* speech or the most *informed* electoral choice. That these may be desirable goals of a system of freedom of expression and of a representative form of government is not to be doubted. These are indeed goals to be pursued by a people whose thoughts and beliefs are freed from governmental interference. But they are not values to be implemented by judicial intrusion into otherwise legitimate state activities.

. . . Whatever merit appellees' argument might have if a State's financing system occasioned an absolute denial of educational opportunities to any of its children, that argument provides no basis for finding an interference with fundamental rights where only relative differences in spending levels are involved and where—as is true in the present case—no charge fairly could be made that the system fails to provide each child with an opportunity to acquire the basic minimal skills necessary for the enjoyment of the rights of speech and of full participation in the political process.

. . . [T]he logical limitations on appellees' nexus theory are difficult to perceive. How, for instance, is education to be distinguished from the significant personal interests in the basics of decent food and shelter? Empirical examination might well buttress an assumption that the ill-fed, ill-clothed, and ill-housed are among the most ineffective participants in the political process, and that they derive the least enjoyment from the benefits of the First Amendment. . . .

We have carefully considered each of the arguments supportive of the District Court's finding that education is a fundamental right or liberty and have found those arguments unpersuasive. . . .

MR. JUSTICE MARSHALL, with whom MR. JUSTICE DOUGLAS concurs, dissenting.

The Court today decides, in effect, that a State may constitutionally vary the quality of education which it offers its children in accordance with the amount of taxable wealth located in the school districts within which they reside. The majority's decision represents an abrupt departure from the mainstream of recent state and federal court decisions concerning the unconstitutionality of state educational financing schemes dependent upon taxable local wealth. More unfortunately, though, the majority's holding can only be seen as a retreat from our historic commitment to equality of educational opportunity and as unsupportable acquiescence in a system which deprives children in their earliest years of the chance to reach their full potential as citizens. The Court does this despite the absence of any substantial justification for a scheme which arbitrarily channels education resources in accordance with the fortuity of the amount of taxable wealth within each district.

In my judgment, the right of every American to an equal start in life, so far as the provision of a state service as important as education is concerned, is far too vital to permit state discrimination on grounds as tenuous as those presented by this record. Nor can I accept the notion that it is sufficient to remit these appellees to the vagaries of the political process which, contrary to the majority's suggestion, has proved singularly unsuited to the task of providing a remedy for this discrimination. I, for one, am unsatisfied with the hope of an ultimate "political" solution sometime in the indefinite future while, in the meantime, countless children unjustifiably receive inferior educations that "may affect their hearts and minds in a way unlikely ever to be undone." *Brown v. Board of Education*, 347 U.S. 483, 494 (1954). I must therefore respectfully dissent. . . .

. . . [T]his Court has never suggested that because some "adequate" level of benefits is provided to all, discrimination in the provision of services is therefore constitutionally excusable. The Equal Protection Clause is not addressed to the minimal sufficiency but rather to the unjustifiable inequalities of state action. It mandates nothing less than that "all persons similarly circumstanced shall be treated alike." . . .

Even if the Equal Protection Clause encompassed

some theory of constitutional adequacy, discrimination in the provision of educational opportunity would certainly seem to be a poor candidate for its application. Neither the majority nor appellants inform us how judicially manageable standards are to be derived for determining how much education is "enough" to excuse constitutional discrimination. One would think that the majority would heed its own fervent affirmation of judicial self-restraint before undertaking the complex task of determining at large what level of education is constitutionally sufficient. . . .

In my view, then, it is inequality—not some notion of gross inadequacy—of educational opportunity that raises a question of denial of equal protection of the laws.

. . . A principled reading of what this Court has done reveals that it has applied a spectrum of standards in reviewing discrimination allegedly violative of the Equal Protection Clause. This spectrum clearly comprehends variations in the degree of care with which the Court will scrutinize particular classifications, depending, I believe, on the constitutional and societal importance of the interest adversely affected and the recognized invidiousness of the basis upon which the particular classification is drawn. . . .

I therefore cannot accept the majority's labored efforts to demonstrate that fundamental interests, which call for strict scrutiny of the challenged classification, encompass only established rights which we are somehow bound to recognize from the text of the Constitution itself. To be sure, some interests which the Court has deemed to be fundamental for purposes of equal protection analysis are themselves constitutionally protected rights. Thus, discrimination against the guaranteed right of freedom of speech has called for strict judicial scrutiny. . . . But it will not do to suggest that the "answer" to whether an interest is fundamental for purposes of equal protection analysis is *always* determined by whether that interest "is a right . . . explicitly or implicitly guaranteed by the Constitution." . . .

I would like to know where the Constitution guarantees the right to procreate . . . or the right to vote in state elections, . . . or the right to an appeal from a criminal conviction. . . . These are instances in which, due to the importance of the interests at stake, the Court has displayed a strong concern with the existence of discriminatory state treatment. But the Court has never said or indicated that these are interests which independently enjoy full-blown constitutional protection. . . .

While ultimately disputing little of this, the majority seeks refuge in the fact that the Court has "never presumed to possess either the ability or the authority to guarantee to the citizenry the most *effective* speech or the most *informed* electoral choice." This serves only to blur what is in fact at stake. With due respect, the issue is neither provision of the most *effective* speech nor of the most *informed* vote. Appellees do not seek the best education Texas might provide. They do seek, however, an end to state discrimination resulting from the unequal distribution of taxable district property wealth that directly impairs the ability of some districts to provide the same educational opportunity that other districts can provide with the same or even substantially less tax effort. The issue is, in other words, one of discrimination that affects the quality of the education which Texas has chosen to provide its children; and, the precise question here is what importance should attach to education for purposes of equal protection analysis of that discrimination.

. . . This Court has frequently recognized that discrimination on the basis of wealth may create a classification of a suspect character and thereby call for exacting judicial scrutiny. The majority, however, considers any wealth classification in this case to lack certain essential characteristics which it contends are common to the instances of wealth discrimination that this Court has heretofore recognized. We are told that in every prior case involving a wealth classification, the members of the disadvantaged class have "shared two distinguishing characteristics: because of their impecunity they were completely unable to pay for some desired benefit, and as a consequence, they sustained an absolute deprivation of a meaningful opportunity to enjoy that benefit." . . . I cannot agree. The Court's distinctions . . . are not in fact consistent with the decisions in *Harper v. Virginia Bd. of Elections*, . . . or *Griffin v. Illinois*, . . . or *Douglas v. California*. . . .

In *Harper*, the Court struck down as violative of the Equal Protection Clause an annual Virginia poll tax of $1.50, payment of which by persons over the age of 21 was a prerequisite to voting in Virginia elections. . . . [T]he Court struck down the poll tax *in toto*; it did not order merely that those too poor to pay the tax be exempted; complete impecunity clearly was not determinative of the limits of the disadvantaged class, nor was it essential to make an equal protection claim.

Similarly, *Griffin* and *Douglas* refute the majority's contention that we have in the past required an absolute deprivation before subjecting wealth classifications to strict scrutiny. The Court characterizes *Griffin* as a case concerned simply with the denial of a transcript or an adequate substitute therefore, and *Douglas* as involving the denial of counsel. But in both cases the question was in fact whether "a State that [grants] *appellate review* can do so in a way that discriminates against some convicted defendants on account of their poverty" (emphasis added). In that regard, the Court concluded that inability to purchase a transcript denies "the poor an adequate *appellate review* accorded to all who have money enough to pay the costs in advance," (emphasis added), and that "the type of an *appeal* a person is afforded . . . hinges upon whether or not he can pay for the assistance of counsel," *Douglas v. California*, . . . (emphasis added). The right of appeal itself was not absolutely denied to those too poor to pay; but because of the cost of a transcript and of counsel, the appeal was a substantially less meaningful right for the poor than for the rich. It was on these terms that the Court found a denial of equal protection, and those terms clearly encompassed degrees of discrimination on the basis of wealth which do not amount to outright denial of the affected right or interest. . . .

Nor can we ignore the extent to which, in contrast to our prior decisions, the State is responsible for the wealth discrimination in this instance. *Griffin*, *Douglas*, *Williams*, *Tate*, and our other prior cases have dealt with discrimination on the basis of individual wealth which was attributable to the operation of the private sector. But we have no such simple *de facto* wealth discrimination here. The means for financing public education in Texas are selected and specified by the State. It is the State that has created local school districts, and tied educational funding to the local property tax and thereby to local district wealth. At the same time, governmentally imposed land use controls have undoubtedly encouraged and rigidified natural trends in the allocation of particular areas for residential or commercial use, and thus determined each district's amount of taxable property wealth. In short, this case, in contrast to the Court's previous wealth discrimination decisions, can only be seen as "unusual in the extent to which governmental action *is* the cause of the wealth classifications."

In the final analysis, then, the invidious characteristics of the group wealth classification present in this case merely serve to emphasize the need for careful judicial scrutiny of the State's justifications for the resulting interdistrict discrimination in the educational opportunity afforded to the schoolchildren of Texas. . . .

The Court seeks solace for its action today in the possibility of legislative reform. The Court's suggestions of legislative redress and experimentation will doubtless be of great comfort to the schoolchildren of Texas' disadvantaged districts, but considering the vested interests of wealthy school districts in the preservation of the status quo, they are worth little more. The possibility of legislative action is, in all events, no answer to this Court's duty under the Constitution to eliminate unjustified state discrimination. . . .

I would therefore affirm the judgment of the District Court.

SUGGESTIONS FOR FURTHER READING

Anthologies

Arthur, John, and Shaw, William. *Justice and Economic Distribution*. Englewood Cliffs: Prentice-Hall, 1978.

Held, Virginia. *Property, Profits and Economic Justice*. Belmont: Wadsworth Publishing Co., 1980.

Sterba, James P. *Justice: Alternative Political Perspectives*. Belmont: Wadsworth Publishing Co., 1980.

Basic Concepts

Plato. *The Republic*. Translated by Francis Cornford. New York: Oxford University Press, 1945.

Aristotle. *Nicomachean Ethics*. Translated by Martin Ostwald. Indianapolis: Bobbs-Merrill, 1962.

Pieper, Joseph. *Justice*. London: Faber and Faber, 1957.

Libertarianism

Hospers, John. *Libertarianism*. Los Angeles: Nash Publishing, 1971.

Nozick, Robert. *Anarchy, State and Utopia*. New York: Basic Books, 1974.

Rothbard, Murray N. *For a New Liberty*. London: Collier Macmillan, 1973.

Practical Applications

Brown, Peter G., and others, eds. *Income Support*. Totowa: Rowman and Littlefield, 1981.

Friedman, David. *The Machinery of Freedom*. New York: Harper and Row, 1973.

Lynd, Straughton, and Alperovitz, Gar. *Strategy and Program*. Boston: Beacon Press, 1973.

Socialism

Marx, Karl. *Critique of the Gotha Program*. Edited by C. P. Dutt. New York: International Publishers, 1966.

Fisk, Milton. *Ethics and Society: A Marxist Interpretation of Value*. New York: New York University Press, 1980.

Harrington, Michael. *Socialism*. New York: Bantam Books, 1970.

Heilbroner, Robert L. *Marxism For and Against*. New York: W. W. Norton & Co., 1980.

Welfare Liberalism

Mill, John Stuart. *On Liberty*. Indianapolis: Bobbs-Merrill Co., 1956.

Ackerman, Bruce A. *Social Justice in The Liberal State*. New Haven: Yale University Press, 1980.

Rawls, John. *A Theory of Justice*. Cambridge: Harvard University Press, 1971.

Sterba, James P. *The Demands of Justice*. Notre Dame: University of Notre Dame Press, 1980.

Singer, Peter. *Practical Ethics*. Cambridge: Cambridge University Press, 1979.

DISTANT PEOPLES AND FUTURE GENERATIONS

BASIC CONCEPTS

The moral problem of distant peoples and future generations has only recently begun to be discussed by professional philosophers. There are many reasons for this neglect, not all of them complimentary to the philosophical profession. Suffice it to say that once the possibility of using modern technology to significantly benefit or harm distant peoples and future generations became widely recognized, philosophers could no longer ignore the importance of this moral problem.

Nevertheless, because the problem has only recently been addressed by philosophers, there has yet to develop a generally acceptable way of even setting out the problem. Unlike the problem of the distribution of income and wealth (see Section I), there is almost no common conceptual framework shared by all solutions to the problem of distant peoples and future generations. Some philosophers have even attempted to "solve" the problem, or at least part of it, by arguing that talk about "the rights of future generations" is conceptually incoherent and thus analogous to talk about "square circles." Accordingly, the key question that must be answered first is: Can we meaningfully speak of distant peoples and future generations as having rights against us or of our having obligations to them?

Answering this question with respect to distant peoples is clearly much easier than answering it with respect to future generations. Very few philosophers have thought that the mere fact people are at a distance from us precludes our having any obligations to them or their having any rights against us. Some philosophers, however, have argued that our ignorance of the specific membership of the class of distant peoples does rule out these moral relationships. Yet this cannot be right, given that in other contexts we recognize obligations to indeterminate classes of people, such as a police officer's obligation to come to the aid of persons in distress or the obligation of food processors not to harm the consumers of their products.

What does, however, seem to be a necessary requirement before distant peoples can be said to have rights against us is that we are capable of acting across the distance that separates us. (This is simply a version of the widely accepted philosophical principle that "ought implies can.") As long as this condition is met—as it typically is for those living in most technologically advanced societies—there seems to be no conceptual obstacle to claiming that distant peoples have rights against us or that we have obligations to them. Of course, showing that it is conceptually possible does not yet prove that these rights and obligations do in fact exist. Such a proof requires a substantial moral argument.

By contrast, answering the above question with respect to future generations is much more difficult and has been the subject of considerable debate among contemporary philosophers.

One issue concerns the question whether it is logically coherent to speak of future generations as having rights *now*. As Annette Baier notes (see pp. 69–73), no one who finds talk about rights to be generally meaningful should question whether we can coherently claim that future generations *will* have rights at some point in the future (specifically, when they come into existence and are no longer *future* generations). But what is questioned, since it is of considerable practical significance, is whether we can coherently claim that future generations have rights *now* when they don't yet exist. Drawing on an analogy with our claims about past generations, Baier claims that we can coherently maintain that future generations have rights *now*.

Others, like Richard T. De George, have argued that such claims are logically incoherent (see pp. 90–96). According to De George, rights logically require the existence of rights-holders and obligations logically require the existence of obligation-recipients. There are, however, at least two difficulties with the view defended by De George beyond the one discussed by Baier.

The first difficulty has to do with the presuppositions said to underlie all talk about rights on the one hand and obligations on the other. The two are treated as if they were similar when they are not. The existence of rights-holders is held to be logically presupposed in any talk about rights, whereas in talk about obligations it is not the existence of obligation--holders but of obligation-*recipients* that is said to be logically presupposed. So it seems perfectly possible to grant that rights-talk presupposes the existence of rights-holders and obligation-talk that of obligation-holders, but then deny that obligation-talk also logically presupposes the existence of obligation-recipients. Instead, one might reasonably hold that what obligation-talk presupposes in this regard is only that there either exists or *will exist* obligation-recipients whose interests can be affected by the obligation-holders.

The second difficulty with this view is that even if it were correct about the existence presuppositions we make when talking about rights and obligations, retaining such usage would still be objectionable because it tends to beg important normative questions. For example, since this usage renders rights-talk and obligation-talk inapplicable to future generations, it tends to favor a negative answer to the following question: Are we morally required to begin *now* to

provide for the welfare of future generations? On this account, it would be preferable to adopt alternative ways of talking about rights and obligations (such as those suggested by Baier and James P. Sterba in their selections) which are more morally neutral and allow the normative and conceptual questions to be more independently addressed.

Still another issue relevant to whether we can meaningfully speak of future generations as having rights against us or our having obligations to them concerns the referent of the term *future generations*. Most philosophers seem to agree that the class of future generations is not "the class of all persons who simply could come into existence." But there is some disagreement concerning whether we should refer to the class of future generations as "the class of persons who will definitely come into existence, assuming that there are such" or as "the class of persons we can reasonably expect to come into existence." The first approach is more "metaphysical," specifying the class of future generations in terms of what will exist; the second approach is more "epistemological," specifying the class of future generations in terms of our knowledge. Fortunately, there does not appear to be any practical moral significance to the choice of either approach.

A final issue that is relevant to whether we can meaningfully speak of future generations as having rights and our having obligations to them concerns whether in a given case the actions of the existing generations that affect future generations can actually benefit or harm those generations. For some philosophers would surely hold that only in cases where future generations can be benefited or harmed by our actions can there be a question of future generations having rights against us or our having obligations to them.

Of course, no one doubts that certain of our actions that affect future generations actually do benefit or harm them. For example, consider an artist who creates a great work of art that will survive for the enjoyment of future generations. Surely such a person will benefit future generations. Just as surely harm will be done to future generations by the careless manner in which many governments and private corporations today dispose of nuclear wastes and other toxic substances.

But suppose some of our actions affect future generations by affecting the membership of the class of future generations. That is, suppose these actions of ours cause different people to be born than otherwise would have been born had we acted differently. For example, imagine that a woman is deciding whether or not to get pregnant, and because of the medication she is taking she will give birth to a defective child if she gets pregnant now. However, if she stops taking her medication and waits three months before getting pregnant she will almost certainly have a normal child. If the woman decides not to wait and gives birth to a defective child, has she harmed that child? If the mother had waited three months, the child she would have then given birth to would certainly have been a different child. So it does not seem that she has harmed the child to which she did give birth, provided that the child's life is worth living. Some people, however, would surely think that the mother was wrong not to wait and give birth to a normal child. But how can such a judgment be supported?

At the level of social choice we can also imagine a similar situation arising. Consider a developing country choosing between a laissez faire population policy and one that restricts population growth. If the restrictive policy is followed, capital accumulation will produce general prosperity within a generation or two. But if the laissez faire policy is followed, low wages and high unemployment will continue indefinitely. Since the choice of either of these will, over time, produce different populations, those born subsequently under the laissez faire policy could hardly claim that they were harmed by the choice of that policy since if the restricted policies had been adopted they would not have been born. Still, some people would surely want to claim that it was wrong for the country to pursue a laissez faire policy. But how could such a claim be supported if no one in subsequent generations is harmed by the choice of that policy?

Contemporary philosophers have sought to deal with the question of whether we can wrong future generations without harming them in three ways. The first is simply to recommend that we "bite the bullet" and claim that "if no one is harmed then no wrong is done." But this approach is not very satisfactory since it flies in the face of our strong intuitions about examples of the above sort. The second

is to claim that regardless of whether one is harmed, we still have an obligation to produce as much happiness or utility as we possibly can. Applied to our examples, this utilitarian approach would probably require the delayed pregnancy; but it would not call for the restricted population policy, since one of the generally recognized problems with this second approach is that it is said to require massive population increases which maximize happiness or utility overall, with little regard for the quality of life. The third approach adopted by contemporary philosophers is to claim that even though we don't have an obligation to produce as much happiness or utility as we possibly can, we do have an obligation to ensure that persons are only brought into existence if they are likely to have lives that are well worth living. Applied to our examples, this obligation would require both the delayed pregnancy and the restricted population policy. Some proponents of this approach, like Sterba (see pp. 97–108), go on to claim that we also have an obligation to bring into existence persons whose lives are well worth living; this however, is not the general view.

Of these three approaches, it is the last that seems to be the most promising. But exactly how to work out the details of this approach (e.g., what constitutes a life well worth living?) is still the subject of considerable debate among contemporary philosophers.

ALTERNATIVE VIEWS

Fortunately, all of the above issues do not have to be fully resolved before we can profitably examine some of the practical solutions that have been proposed to the problem of distant peoples and future generations. In fact, some of the above issues seem to lead us directly to particular solutions for this moral problem.

Not surprisingly most of the solutions that have been proposed are analogous to the solutions we discussed with regard to the problem of the distribution of income and wealth within a society (see Section I).

As before, there is a libertarian solution. Accord-

ing to this view, distant peoples and future generations have no right to receive aid from persons living
in today's affluent societies, but only a right not to
be harmed by them. As before, these requirements
are said to be derived from a political ideal of liberty.
And, as before, we can question whether such an
ideal actually supports these requirements.

Both Garrett Hardin and De George endorse a "no
aid" view in their selections. However, neither Hardin nor De George supports his view on libertarian
grounds. Without denying that there is a general
obligation to help those in need, Hardin argues that
helping those who live in absolute poverty in today's
world would not do any good, and for *that reason* is
not required. Hardin justifies this view on empirical
grounds, claiming that the giving of aid would be
ineffective and even counterproductive for controlling population growth. By contrast, De George supports a "no aid" view for future generations (but not
for distant peoples, who he thinks do have a right
to receive aid) on purely conceptual grounds, claiming that future generations cannot logically have
rights against us or we obligations to them.

We have already noted some of the difficulties with
the view De George defends, as has Baier. Peter
Singer and Sterba both challenge the empirical
grounds on which Hardin's view rests. Singer claims
that Hardin's view accepts the certain evil of unrelieved poverty in today's Third World countries, like
Bangladesh and Somalia, in order to avoid the future possibility of still greater poverty in Third World
countries together with deteriorating conditions in
First and Second World countries. Singer argues,
however, that with a serious commitment to aid from
First World countries, there is a "fair chance" that
Third World countries will bring their population
growth under control, thus avoiding the greater evil
that Hardin feared. Given the likelihood of this result, Singer argues that we have no moral justification for embracing, as Hardin does, the certain evil
of unrelieved poverty in today's Third World countries by denying them aid. Sterba too objects to
Hardin's willingness to sacrifice existing generations
for the sake of a "better future" for subsequent generations. He argues that even if Hardin were right
that providing aid would reduce the "maximal sustainable yield" of the planet's resources, we still
ought to provide that aid. He claims this is so even

if the population level of future generations, once
a rational population policy is in effect, would have
to be smaller than otherwise would have been possible.

The positive solution to the problem of distant
peoples and future generations defended by both
Singer and Sterba can be characterized as a welfare
liberal solution. Singer at some point would want to
defend his "pro aid" view on utilitarian grounds, but
in his selection (pp. 80–89) he tries to base his view
on premises of a more general appeal. The fundamental premise he relies upon is this: If we can prevent something bad without sacrificing anything of
comparable significance we ought to do it. Singer
notes that libertarians, like Robert Nozick, would at
least initially have difficulty accepting this premise.
Nozick would surely claim that the requirement this
premise imposes is at best only one of charity rather
than of justice, so that failing to abide by it is neither
blameworthy nor punishable. Sterba too, although
he is primarily concerned to defend a "pro aid" view
on the basis of a right to life and a right to fair treatment interpreted as positive rights, is sensitive to the
possibility that libertarians might be able to escape
from the conclusion of his argument. Consequently,
he tries to show that the same conclusion follows
when a right to life is interpreted as a negative right,
as libertarians tend to do. But while Sterba may have
secured his view against objections by libertarians,
socialists would certainly not be satisfied with his
defense.

A socialist solution to the problem of distant
peoples and future generations would place considerable stress on the responsibility of First World countries for the situation in Third World countries.
Socialists claim that much of the poverty and unemployment found in Third World countries is the result of the disruptive and exploitative influence of
First World countries. For example, it is claimed that
arms supplied by First World countries enable repressive regimes in Third World countries to remain in
power when they would otherwise be overthrown.
Under these repressive regimes, small groups of
landowners and capitalists are allowed to exploit the
resources in Third World countries for export markets in First World countries. As a result, the majority of people in Third World countries are forced off
the land that their forebears have farmed for genera-

tions and are required to compete for the few, frequently low paying, jobs that have been created to serve the export markets.

Nevertheless, even if socialists are right about the responsibility of First World countries for Third World poverty, it is still a further question whether the socialization of the means of production and the abolition of private property constitutes the only viable moral response to this situation. For it certainly seems possible that some form of restricted private property system that provides for the meeting of everyone's basic needs, justified either on welfare liberal grounds or on libertarian grounds, would serve as well.

PRACTICAL APPLICATIONS

Unlike in the previous section, there does not seem to be as much of a gap between the "alternative views" and the "practical applications" with respect to the problem of distant peoples and future generations. This is because most of the discussions of the alternative views have already taken up the question of practical application (e.g., Singer suggests as a practical application a 10 percent tithe on income in First World countries). The merit of Gus Speth's article, however, is that it is focused squarely on the question of practical application (see pp. 108–113). After reviewing the world situation, Speth sketches a practical program involving conservation, sustainable growth, and equity. Since his program obviously involves substantial aid to Third World countries, you should not endorse such a program unless you have reached the conclusion that arguments such as those presented by Singer and Sterba effectively counter arguments such as those presented by Hardin and De George.

Nevertheless, whatever solution to the problem of distant peoples and future generations you favor, you will still not know how goods and resources should be ultimately distributed in society unless you have a solution to the problem of abortion and euthanasia. For if abortion is morally justified then maybe we should be funding abortions so that every woman, rich or poor, can have an abortion if she wants one. And if euthanasia is morally justified then maybe we should be reallocating resources that are now being used for the purpose of sustaining life. Accordingly, in the next section we will take up the problem of abortion and euthanasia.

Annette Baier

THE RIGHTS OF PAST AND FUTURE PERSONS

Annette Baier argues that there is no conceptual incoherence to thinking of future generations as having rights now. She contends that if we are willing to recognize rights of past persons we should be willing to recognize rights of future persons. Thus, if those who lived in the past can have existing spokespersons pressing their rights, those who will live in the future could have the same. Nor does Baier think that our ignorance of the exact membership of future

From "The Rights of Past and Future Persons," in *Responsibilities to Future Generations*, edited by Ernest Partridge (1981) pp. 171–175. Reprinted by permission of the author, the editor, and Prometheus Books.

generations renders it impossible for future generations to have rights, since such ignorance is also present in other contexts where we do recognize rights. Finally, she claims that the "ontological precariousness" of future generations is not significantly greater than that of the future states of present persons.

NO ONE DOUBTS THAT future generations, once they are present and actual, will have rights, if any of us have rights.[1] What difference is made if we say, not that they *will* have, but that they *do* have rights—*now*? I see two main points of difference—first, that those rights will then give rise to obligations on our part, as well as on their contemporaries' part; and, second, that what they have a right *to* will be different. In addition to whatever political and civil rights they have or will have, they will also each have a right to a fair share of what is then left of the earth's scarce resources. If they *now* have rights, they have rights to share of what is *now* left of those scarce resources. To believe that they have rights is to believe that *we* must safeguard those rights and that, where the right is to a share, that we must share with them, and that the size of our share is affected by their right to share.

Should we believe that future persons not merely *will* have rights, but that they presently *do* have rights? To decide this I shall first consider whether any conceptual incoherence would result. . . .

I turn first to the question of what we are committed to in asserting that a person has a certain right. I take it that this is to assert:

(a). That at least one other person has an obligation to the right-holder. This obligation may be to refrain from interfering with some activity of the right-holder or to take some positive steps to secure for the right-holder what he or she has a right to. These steps may be ones that benefit the right-holder or some third party, as would be the case if I have promised a friend to feed his cat. He thereby has a right to my services that are intended to benefit the cat. Following Feinberg's[2] terminology, I shall say that the obligation is *to* the right-holder and *toward* whomever is the intended beneficiary.

(b). There is, or there should and could in practice be, socially recognized means for the right-holder, or his or her proxy, to take appropriate action should the obligations referred to in *(a)* be neglected. This action will range from securing belated discharge of the obligation, to securing compensation for its neglect, to the initiation of punitive measures against the delinquent obligated person.

I think that this account covers both legally recognized rights and also moral rights that are more than mere "manifesto" rights,[3] since clause *(b)* requires that effective recognition could be given to such rights. Such effective recognition can of course be given only to a set of nonconflicting rights, and so I assume that to claim anything as a right is to claim that its effective recognition is compatible with the effective recognition of the other rights one claims to exist.[4] To claim a moral right to something not effectively recognized as a right is to claim that it could without contradiction to other justifiably recognized rights *be* given recognition, that only inertia, ignorance, greed or ill-will prevents its recognition.

This account of what it is to have a right differs in another sense from the account that is more commonly given. The point of difference lies in the extension of power to claim the right from the right-holder to his spokesman, vicar, or proxy. This extension is required to make sense of the concept of rights of past or future generations. I think we already accept such an extension in empowering executors to claim the rights of the deceased whose wills they execute. The role of executor is distinct from that of trustee for the heirs. We recognize obligations both *to* and *toward* the legal heirs, and *to* the person who made the will. Where the legal heirs are specified only as the "issue" of certain persons known to the will-maker, we already accept the concept of an obligation, owned by the trustees, to look after the interests of such not-yet-determinate persons.

Can those who protect the rights of future persons be properly regarded as their spokesmen, claimants of their rights in the present, when they, unlike executors of wills, cannot be appointed by the original right-holder? The rights of past persons, claimed by their recognized spokesmen, are person-specific rights to have their legally valid powers exercised, while the rights in the present claimed for future persons will be general human rights. No one needs to be privy to the individual wills of future persons to claim their right to clean air. Already recognized spokesmen for known past persons, claiming their particular rights, need knowledge of them, their deeds, and their wishes, and so are sensibly required to have a special tie to the original right-holder, initiated by him. Spokesmen for future persons, claiming general rights, need no such tie.

If future generations have rights, then we, or some of us in some capacity, have obligations to and presumably also toward them, and their spokesman should be empowered to take action to see to it that we discharge those obligations. I see no conceptual incorrectness in attributing such rights. Admittedly we do not now recognize any person as the proper spokesman, guardian, and rights-claimant for future generations. But we could, and perhaps we should.

The fact that future generations are not *now* living persons is irrelevant to the issue, if, as I have argued, we are willing to speak of the rights of those who are no longer living persons. The fact that we do not and cannot have knowledge of the special characteristics and wishes of future generations is, I have claimed, also irrelevant to the recognition of their rights to basic nonspecial human requirements, such as uncontaminated air. Our dependence on fossil fuels may be, compared with the needs of past generations, quite special, and there may be good reasons not to extrapolate that need into the distant future. But there is no reason to think that the need for air will be lessened by technological progress or regress in the future. Our ignorance of precisely *who* future generations will be, and uncertainty of how numerous they will be, may be relevant to the priority of our obligations to them, compared with obligations to the living, should conflicts arise; but it is not relevant to the reality of obligations to future persons, nor to the moral priority of such obligations over our tastes for conspicuous consumption or our demands for luxury and for the freedom to waste or destroy resources.

As lawful heirs of specific past persons, some of us may have a right to what those persons intended us to possess, should there be sufficient moral reason to

recognize the disputed right to pass on private property and to inherit it. By contrast, we all inherit a social order, a cultural tradition, air and water, not as private heirs of private will-makers, but as members of a continuous community. We benefit from the wise planning, or perhaps the thoughtless but fortunate conservation, of past generations. In so far as such inherited public goods as constitutions, civil liberties, universities, parks, and uncontaminated water come to us by the deliberate intention of past generations, we inherit them not as sole beneficiaries but as persons able to share and pass on such goods to an indefinite run of future generations. It was, presumably, not for this generation in particular that public spirited persons in past generations saved or sacrificed.

Rights and obligations are possessed by persons not in virtue of their unique individuality but in virtue of roles they fill, roles that relate to others. For example, children, *qua* children, have obligations to and rights against parents *qua* parents. My obligations as a teacher are owed to my students, whoever they may be. When I discharge obligations to them, such as ordering textbooks, I do not and need not know who those students will be. As long as I believe that determinate actual persons will fill the role of students, will occupy a position involving a moral tie to me, my obligations are real and not lessened by my ignorance of irrelevant details concerning those role-fillers. As long as we believe there will be persons related to us as we are related to past generations, then any obligations and rights this relation engenders will be real. Whether there will be such persons is something about which we can have well-based beliefs, especially as it is to some degree up to us whether to allow such roles to be filled.

The ontological precariousness of future generations that some see as a reason for not recognizing any rights of theirs is not significantly greater than that of the future states of present persons. In neither case does ignorance of details about the future, or the possible nonexistence in that future of those who would benefit from discharge of obligations in the present, affect the reality of our obligations. To make sacrifices *now* so that others may benefit in the future is always to risk wasting that sacrifice. The moral enterprise is intrinsically a matter of risky investment,[5] if we measure the return solely in terms of benefits reaped by those toward whom obligations are

are owed. Only if virtue is its own reward is morality ever a safe investment. The only special feature in a moral tie between us and future generations lies in the inferiority of our knowledge about them, not in the inferiority of their ontological status. They are not merely possible persons, they are whichever possible persons will in the future be actual.

So far I have found no conceptual reason for disallowing talk of the rights of future persons. Neither their nonpresence, nor our ignorance of *who* exactly they are, nor our uncertainty concerning how many of them there are, rules out the appropriateness of recognizing rights on their part. The fact that they cannot now claim their rights from us puts them in a position no different from that of past persons with rights in the present—namely, a position of dependency on some representative in this generation, someone empowered to speak for them. Rights typically are *claimed* by their possessors, so if we are to recognize rights of future persons we must empower some persons to make claims for them.

Another thing that can be done with a right is to waive it. Past persons who leave no will waive the right that they had to determine the heirs of their private property. Since nothing could count as a sign that future generations waive their rights against us, then this dimension of the concept of a right will get no purchase with future generations, unless we empower present persons not merely to claim but also to waive rights of future persons. Waiving rights and alienating them by gift or exchange are both voluntary renunciations of what a right puts in the right-holder's secure possession. However, waiving rights, unlike alienating them, does not involve a transfer of the right. Since the rights that are transferred are always special rights, and the rights of future persons that we are considering are general ones, there can be no question of transferring such rights. But might a proxy waive them? Guardians of present persons (children, incompetents) do have the power to waive some rights on behalf of their wards, but the justification for this practice, and any exercise of it, depends upon the availability of special knowledge of what will and will not benefit the right-holder. It is barely conceivable that we or any official we appointed could have such knowledge of the special needs of some future generations. If we were facing the prospect of a nuclear war and foresaw that any immediate successor generations would live in the ruins of civilization as we have known it, we might judge that there was no point in trying to preserve, say, the Bill of Rights for one's successors, although they had a *prima facie* right to inherit it. One might on their behalf waive that right, in extreme conditions, and bury the Constitution, rather than prolong our agony to fight for it. But such scenarios are bizarre, since it is barely conceivable that those who would bequeath to future generations the effects of a nuclear war would care about the rest of their bequest, about the fragments that might be shored against our ruin. The benefits that might be gained for future generations by empowering any of their ancestors to waive some of their rights seem minimal. Still, this is a question not of the conceptual absurdity of waiving a recognized right of future generations but of the practical wisdom of giving another this power.

I conclude that no conceptual error is involved in speaking of the rights of future generations. The concept of a right includes that of the justified power of the right-holder or his spokesman to press for discharge of obligations affecting his particular interests, or to renounce this power. The concept has already shown itself capable of extension to cover the rights of past persons and could as easily accommodate the rights of future generations if we saw good reason thus to extend it. . . .

NOTES

1. I do not take it for granted that any of us do in any morally significant sense have rights. We do of course have legal rights, but to see them as backed by moral rights is to commit oneself to a particular version of the moral enterprise that may not be the best version. As Hegel and Marx pointed out, the language of rights commits us to questionable assumptions concerning the relation of the individual to the community, and, as Utilitarians have also pointed out, it also commits us more than may be realistic or wise to fixing the details of our moral priorities in advance of relevant knowledge that only history can provide.

2. J. Feinberg, "Duties, Rights and Claims," *American Philosophical Quarterly*, vol. 5, no. 2 (April 1966).

3. J. Feinberg, *Social Philosophy* (Englewood Cliffs, N.J.: Prentice-Hall, 1973), p. 67. The term 'manifesto rights' is from Joel Feinberg, who writes, "[I am] willing to speak of a special 'manifesto sense' of 'right,' in which a right need not be correlated with another's duty. Natural needs are real claims, if only upon hypothetical future beings not yet in existence. I accept the moral principle that to have an unfulfilled need is to have a kind of claim against the world, even if against no one in particular. . . . Such claims, based on need alone, are 'permanent possibilities of rights,' the natural seed from which rights grow." (p. 67)

4. I assume that while it makes sense to speak of *prima facie* and possibly conflicting obligations, statements about rights gave final moral decisions, so there are no *prima facie* or conflicting rights.

5. I have discussed this in "Secular Faith," *Canadian Journal of Philosophy* (March 1979).

Garrett Hardin

LIFEBOAT ETHICS: THE CASE AGAINST HELPING THE POOR

Garrett Hardin argues that our first obligation is to ourselves and our posterity. For that reason, he contends, it would be foolish for rich nations to share their surplus with poor nations, whether through a World Food Bank, the exporting of technology, or unrestricted immigration. In view of the growing populations and improvident behavior of poor nations, such sharing would do no good—it would only overload the environment and lead to demands for still greater assistance in the future.

ENVIRONMENTALISTS USE THE METAPHOR of the earth as a "spaceship" in trying to persuade countries, industries and people to stop wasting and polluting our natural resources. Since we all share life on this planet, they argue, no single person or institution has the right to destroy, waste, or use more than a fair share of its resources.

But does everyone on earth have an equal right to an equal share of its resources? The spaceship metaphor can be dangerous when used by misguided idealists to justify suicidal policies for sharing our resources through uncontrolled immigration and foreign aid. In their enthusiastic but unrealistic generosity, they confuse the ethics of a spaceship with those of a lifeboat.

A true spaceship would have to be under the control of a captain, since no ship could possibly survive if its course were determined by committee. Spaceship Earth certainly has no captain; the United Nations is merely a toothless tiger, with little power to enforce any policy upon its bickering members.

If we divide the world crudely into rich nations and poor nations, two thirds of them are desperately poor, and only one third comparatively rich, with

From "The Case Against Helping the Poor," *Psychology Today* (1974) pp. 38–43, 123–126. Copyright © 1974 Ziff-Davis Publishing Company. Reprinted by permission.

the United States the wealthiest of all. Metaphorically each rich nation can be seen as a lifeboat full of comparatively rich people. In the ocean outside each lifeboat swim the poor of the world, who would like to get in, or at least to share some of the wealth. What should the lifeboat passengers do?

First, we must recognize the limited capacity of any lifeboat. For example, a nation's land has a limited capacity to support a population and as the current energy crisis has shown us, in some ways we have already exceeded the carrying capacity of our land.

ADRIFT IN A MORAL SEA

So here we sit, say fifty people in our lifeboat. To be generous, let us assume it has room for ten more, making a total capacity of sixty. Suppose the fifty of us in the lifeboat see 100 others swimming in the water outside, begging for admission to our boat or for handouts. We have several options: we may be tempted to try to live by the Christian ideal of being "our brother's keeper," or by the Marxist ideal of "to each according to his needs." Since the needs of all in the water are the same, and since they can all be seen as "our brothers," we could take them all into our boat, making a total of 150 in a boat designed for sixty. The boat swamps, everyone drowns. Complete justice, complete catastrophe.

Since the boat has an unused excess capacity of ten more passengers, we could admit just ten more to it. But which ten do we let in? How do we choose? Do we pick the best ten, the neediest ten, "first come, first served"? And what do we say to the ninety we exclude? If we do let an extra ten into our lifeboat, we will have lost our "safety factor," an engineering principle of critical importance. For example, if we don't leave room for excess capacity as a safety factor in our country's agriculture, a new plant disease or a bad change in the weather could have disastrous consequences.

Suppose we decide to preserve our small safety factor and admit no more to the lifeboat. Our survival is then possible, although we shall have to be constantly on guard against boarding parties.

While this last solution clearly offers the only means of our survival, it is morally abhorrent to many people. Some say they feel guilty about their good luck. My reply is simple: "Get out and yield your place to others." This may solve the problem of the guilt-ridden person's conscience, but it does not change the ethics of the lifeboat. The needy person to whom the guilt-ridden person yields his place will not himself feel guilty about his good luck. If he did, he would not climb aboard. The net result of conscience-stricken people giving up their unjustly held seats is the elimination of that sort of conscience from the lifeboat.

This is the basic metaphor within which we must work out our solutions. Let us now enrich the image, step by step, with substantive additions from the real world, a world that must solve real and pressing problems of overpopulation and hunger.

The harsh ethics of the lifeboat become even harsher when we consider the reproductive differences between the rich nations and the poor nations. The people inside the lifeboats are doubling in numbers every eighty-seven years; those swimming around outside are doubling, on the avevage, every thirty-five years, more than twice as fast as the rich. And since the world's resources are dwindling, the difference in prosperity between the rich and the poor can only increase.

As of 1973, the U.S. had a population of 210 million people, who were increasing by 0.8 percent per year. Outside our lifeboat, let us imagine another 210 million people, (say the combined populations of Colombia, Ecuador, Venezuela, Morocco, Pakistan, Thailand, and the Philippines) who are increasing at a rate of 3.3 percent per year. Put differently, the doubling time for this aggregate population if twenty-one years, compared to eighty-seven years for the U.S.

MULTIPLYING THE RICH AND THE POOR

Now suppose the U.S. agreed to pool its resources with those seven countries, with everyone receiving an equal share. Initially the ratio of Americans to non-Americans in this model would be one-to-one. But consider what the ratio would be after eighty-seven years, by which time the Americans would have doubled to a population of 420 million. By then, doubling every twenty-one years, the other group would have swollen to 354 billion. Each American would have to share the available resources with more than eight people.

But, one could argue, this discussion assumes that current population trends will continue, and they may not. Quite so. Most likely the rate of population increase will decline much faster in the U.S. than it will in the other countries, and there does not seem to be much we can do about it. In sharing with "each according to his needs," we must recognize that needs are determined by population size, which is determined by the rate of reproduction, which at present is regarded as a sovereign right of every nation, poor or not. This being so, the philanthropic load created by the sharing ethic of the spaceship can only increase.

THE TRAGEDY OF THE COMMONS

The fundamental error of spaceship ethics, and the sharing it requires, is that it leads to what I call "the tragedy of the commons." Under a system of private property, the men who own property recognize their responsibility to care for it, for if they don't they will eventually suffer. A farmer, for instance, will allow no more cattle in a pasture than its carrying capacity justifies. If he overloads it, erosion sets in, weeds take over, and he loses the use of the pasture.

If a pasture becomes a commons open to all, the right of each to use it may not be matched by a corresponding responsibility to protect it. Asking everyone to use it with discretion will hardly do, for the considerate herdsman who refrains from overloading the commons suffers more than a selfish one who says his needs are greater. If everyone would restrain himself, all would be well; but it takes only one less than everyone to ruin a system of voluntary restraint. In a crowded world of less than perfect hu-

man beings, mutual ruin is inevitable if there are no controls. This is the tragedy of the commons.

One of the major tasks of education today should be the creation of such an acute awareness of the dangers of the commons that people will recognize its many varieties. For example, the air and water have become polluted because they are treated as commons. Further growth in the population or per-capita conversion of natural resources into pollutants will only make the problem worse. The same holds true for the fish of the oceans. Fishing fleets have nearly disappeared in many parts of the world, technological improvements in the art of fishing are hastening the day of complete ruin. Only the replacement of the system of the commons with a responsible system of control will save the land, air, water and oceanic fisheries.

THE WORLD FOOD BANK

In recent years there has been a push to create a new commons called a World Food Bank, an international depository of food reserves to which nations would contribute according to their abilities and from which they would draw according to their needs. This humanitarian proposal has received support from many liberal international groups, and from such prominent citizens as Margaret Mead, U.N. Secretary General Kurt Waldheim, and Senators Edward Kennedy and George McGovern.

A world food bank appeals powerfully to our humanitarian impulses. But before we rush ahead with such a plan, let us recognize where the greatest political push comes from, lest we be disillusioned later. Our experience with the "Food for Peace program," or Public Law 480, gives us the answer. This program moved billions of dollars worth of U.S. surplus grain to food-short, population-long countries during the past two decades. But when P.L. 480 first became law, a headline in the business magazine *Forbes* revealed the real power behind it: "Feeding the World's Hungry Millions: How It Will Mean Billions for U.S. Business."

And indeed it did. In the years 1960 to 1970,

U.S. taxpayers spent a total of $7.9 billion on the Food for Peace program. Between 1948 and 1970, they also paid an additional $50 billion for other economic-aid programs, some of which went for food and food-producing machinery and technology. Though all U.S. taxpayers were forced to contribute to the cost of P.L. 480, certain special interest groups gained handsomely under the program. Farmers did not have to contribute the grain; the Government, or rather the taxpayers, bought it from them at full market prices. The increased demand raised prices of farm products generally. The manufacturers of farm machinery, fertilizers and pesticides benefited by the farmers' extra efforts to grow more food. Grain elevators profited from storing the surplus until it could be shipped. Railroads made money hauling it to ports, and shipping lines profited from carrying it overseas. The implementation of P.L. 480 required the creation of a vast Government bureaucracy, which then acquired its own vested interest in continuing the program regardless of its merits.

EXTRACTING DOLLARS

Those who proposed and defended the Food for Peace program in public rarely mentioned its importance to any of these special interests. The public emphasis was always on its humanitarian effects. The combination of silent selfish interests and highly vocal humanitarian apologists made a powerful and successful lobby for extracting money from taxpayers. We can expect the same lobby to push now for the creation of a World Food Bank.

However great the potential benefit to selfish interests, it should not be a decisive argument against a truly humanitarian program. We must ask if such a program would actually do more good than harm, not only momentarily but also in the long run. Those who propose the food bank usually refer to a current "emergency" or "crisis" in terms of world food supply. But what is an emergency? Although they may be infrequent and sudden, everyone knows that emergencies will occur from time to time. A well-run family, company, organization or country prepares for the likelihood of accidents and emergencies. It expects them, it budgets for them, it saves for them.

LEARNING THE HARD WAY

What happens if some organizations or countries budget for accidents and others do not? If each country is solely responsible for its own well-being, poorly managed ones will suffer. But they can learn from experience. They may mend their ways, and learn to budget for infrequent but certain emergencies. For example, the weather varies from year to year, and periodic crop failures are certain. A wise and competent government saves out of the production of the good years in anticipation of bad years to come. Joseph taught this policy to Pharaoh in Egypt more than 2,000 years ago. Yet the great majority of the governments in the world today do not follow such a policy. They lack either the wisdom or the competence, or both. Should those nations that do manage to put something aside be forced to come to the rescue each time an emergency occurs among the poor nations?

"But it isn't their fault!" some kindhearted liberals argue. "How can we blame the poor people who are caught in an emergency? Why must they suffer for the sins of their governments?" The concept of blame is simply not relevant here. The real question is, what are the operational consequences of establishing a world food bank? If it is open to every country every time a need develops, slovenly rulers will not be motivated to take Joseph's advice. Someone will always come to their aid. Some countries will deposit food in the world food bank, and others will withdraw it. There will be almost no overlap. As a result of such solutions to food shortage emergencies, the poor countries will not learn to mend their ways, and will suffer progressively greater emergencies as their populations grow.

POPULATION CONTROL THE CRUDE WAY

On the average, poor countries undergo a 2.5 percent increase in population each year; rich countries, about 0.8 percent. Only rich countries have anything in the way of food reserves set aside, and even they do not have as much as they should. Poor countries have none. If poor countries received no food from the outside, the rate of their population growth would be periodically checked by crop failures and famines. But if they can always draw on a world food bank in time of need, their population can continue to grow unchecked, and so will their "need" for aid. In the short run, a world food bank may diminish that need, but in the long run it actually increases the need without limit.

Without some system of worldwide food sharing, the proportion of people in the rich and poor nations might eventually stabilize. The overpopulated poor countries would decrease in numbers, while the rich countires that had room for more people would increase. But with a well-meaning system of sharing, such as a world food bank, the growth differential between the rich and the poor countries will not only persist, it will increase. Because of the higher rate of population growth in the poor countries of the world, 88 percent of today's children are born poor, and only 12 percent rich. Year by year the ratio becomes worse, as the fast-reproducing poor outnumber the slow-reproducing rich.

A world food bank is thus a commons in disguise. People will have more motivation to draw from it than to add to any common store. The less provident and less able will multiply at the expense of the abler and more provident, bringing eventual ruin upon all who share in the commons. Besides, any system of "sharing" that amounts to foreign aid from the rich nations to the poor nations will carry the taint of charity, which will contribute little to the world peace so devoutly desired by those who support the idea of a world food bank.

As past U.S. foreign-aid programs have amply and depressingly demonstrated, international charity frequently inspires mistrust and antagonism rather than gratitude on the part of the recipient nation.

CHINESE FISH AND MIRACLE RICE

The modern approach to foreign aid stresses the export of technology and advice, rather than money and food. As an ancient Chinese proverb goes: "Give a man a fish and he will eat for a day; teach him how to fish and he will eat for the rest of his days." Acting on this advice, the Rockefeller and Ford Foundations have financed a number of programs for improving agriculture in the hungry nations. Known as the "Green Revolution," these programs have led to the development of "miracle rice" and "miracle wheat," new strains that offer bigger harvests and greater resistance to crop damage. Norman Borlaug, the Nobel Prize winning agronomist who, supported by the Rockefeller Foundation, developed "miracle wheat," is one of the most prominent advocates of a world food bank.

Whether or not the Green Revolution can increase food production as much as its champions claim is a debatable but possibly irrelevant point. Those who support this well-intended humanitarian effort should first consider some of the fundamentals of human ecology. Ironically, one man who did was the late Alan Gregg, a vice president of the Rockefeller Foundation. Two decades ago he expressed strong doubts about the wisdom of such attempts to increase food production. He likened the growth and spread of humanity over the surface of the earth to the spread of cancer in the human body, remarking that "cancerous growths demand food; but, as far as I know, they have never been cured by getting it."

OVERLOADING THE ENVIRONMENT

Every human born constitutes a draft on all aspects of the environment: food, air, water, forests, beaches, wildlife, scenery and solitude. Food can, perhaps, be significantly increased to meet a growing demand. But what about clean beaches, unspoiled forests, and solitude? If we satisfy a growing population's need for food, we necessarily decrease its per capita supply of the other resources needed by men.

India, for example, now has a population of 600 million, which increases by 15 million each year. This population already puts a huge load on a relatively impoverished environment. The country's forests are now only a small fraction of what they were three centuries ago, and floods and erosion continually destroy the insufficient farmland that remains. Every one of the 15 million new lives added to India's population puts an additional burden on the environment, and increases the economic and social costs of crowding. However humanitarian our intent, every Indian life saved through medical or nutritional assistance from abroad diminishes the quality of life for those who remain, and for subsequent generations. If rich countries make it possible, through foreign aid, for 600 million Indians to swell to 1.2 billion in a mere twenty-eight years, as their current growth rate threatens, will future generations of Indians thank us for hastening the destruction of their environment? Will our good intentions be sufficient excuse for the consequences of our actions?

My final example of a commons in action is one for which the public has the least desire for rational discussion—immigration. Anyone who publicly questions the wisdom of current U.S. immigration policy is promptly charged with bigotry, prejudice, ethnocentrism, chauvinism, isolationism or selfishness. Rather than encounter such accusations, one would rather talk about other matters, leaving immigration policy to wallow in the crosscurrents of special interests that take no account of the good of the whole, or the interests of posterity.

Perhaps we still feel guilty about things we said in the past. Two generations ago the popular press frequently referred to Dagos, Wops, Polacks, Chinks and Krauts, in articles about how America was being "overrun" by foreigners of supposedly inferior genetic stock. But because the implied inferiority of foreigners was used then as justification for keeping them out, people now assume that restrictive policies could only be based on such misguided notions. There are other grounds.

A NATION OF IMMIGRANTS

Just consider the numbers involved. Our Government acknowledges a net inflow of 400,000 immigrants a year. While we have no hard data on the extent of illegal entries, educated guesses put the figure at about 600,000 a year. Since the natural increase (excess of births over deaths) of the resident population now runs about 1.7 million per year, the

yearly gain from immigration amounts to at least 19 percent of the total annual increase, and may be as much as 37 percent if we include the estimate for illegal immigrants. Considering the growing use of birth-control devices, the potential effect of educational campaigns by such organizations as Planned Parenthood Federation of America and Zero Population Growth, and the influence of inflation and the housing shortage, the fertility rate of American women may decline so much that immigration could account for all the yearly increase in population. Should we not at least ask if that is what we want?

For the sake of those who worry about whether the "quality" of the average immigrant compares favorably with the quality of the average resident, let us assume that immigrants and nativeborn citizens are of exactly equal quality, however one defines that term. We will focus here only on quantity; and since our conclusions will depend on nothing else, all charges of bigotry and chauvinism become irrelevant.

IMMIGRATION VS. FOOD SUPPLY

World food banks *move food to the people*, hastening the exhaustion of the environment of the poor countries. Unrestricted immigration, on the other hand, *moves people to the food*, thus speeding up the destruction of the environment of the rich countries. We can easily understand why poor people should want to make this latter transfer, but why should rich hosts encourage it?

As in the case of foreign-aid programs, immigration receives support from selfish interests and humanitarian impulses. The primary selfish interest in unimpeded immigration is the desire of employers for cheap labor, particularly in industries and trades that offer degrading work. In the past, one wave of foreigners after another was brought into the U.S. to work at wretched jobs for wretched wages. In recent years the Cubans, Puerto Ricans and Mexicans have had this dubious honor. The interests of the employers of cheap labor mesh well with the guilty silence of the country's liberal intelligentsia. White

Anglo-Saxon Protestants are particularly reluctant to call for a closing of the doors to immigration for fear of being called bigots.

But not all countries have such reluctant leadership. Most educated Hawaiians, for example, are keenly aware of the limits of their environment, particularly in terms of population growth. There is only so much room on the islands, and the islanders know it. To Hawaiians, immigrants from the other forty-nine states present as great a threat as those from other nations. At a recent meeting of Hawaiian government officials in Honolulu, I had the ironic delight of hearing a speaker, who like most of his audience was of Japanese ancestry, ask how the country might practically and constitutionally close its doors to further immigration. One member of the audience countered: "How can we shut the doors now? We have many friends and relatives in Japan that we'd like to bring here some day so that they can enjoy Hawaii too." The Japanese-American speaker smiled sympathetically and answered: "Yes, but we have children now, and someday we'll have grandchildren too. We can bring more people here from Japan only by giving away some of the land that we hope to pass on to our grandchildren some day. What right do we have to do that?"

At this point, I can hear U.S. liberals asking: "How can you justify slamming the door once you're inside? You say that immigrants should be kept out. But aren't we all immigrants, or the descendants of immigrants? If we insist on staying, must we not admit all others?" Our craving for intellectual order leads us to seek and prefer symmetrical rules and morals: a single rule for me and everybody else; the same rule yesterday, today, and tomorrow. Justice, we feel, should not change with time and place.

We Americans of non-Indian ancestry can look upon ourselves as the descendants of thieves who are guilty morally, if not legally, of stealing this land from its Indian owners. Should we then give back the land to the now living American descendants of those Indians? However morally or logically sound this proposal may be, I, for one, am unwilling to live by it and I know no one else who is. Besides, the logical consequence would be absurd. Suppose that,

intoxicated with a sense of pure justice, we should decide to turn our land over to the Indians. Since all our wealth has also been derived from the land, wouldn't we be morally obliged to give that back to the Indians too?

PURE JUSTICE VS. REALITY

Clearly, the concept of pure justice produces an infinite regression to absurdity. Centuries ago, wise men invented statutes of limitations to justify the rejection of such pure justice, in the interest of preventing continual disorder. The law zealously defends property rights, but only relatively recent property rights. Drawing a line after an arbitrary time has elapsed may be unjust, but the alternatives are worse.

We are all the descendants of thieves, and the world's resources are inequitably distributed. But we must begin the journey to tomorrow from the point where we are today. We cannot remake the past. We cannot safely divide the wealth equitably among all peoples so long as people reproduce at different rates. To do so would guarantee that our grandchildren, and everyone else's grandchildren, would have only a ruined world to inhabit.

To be generous with one's own possessions is quite different from being generous with those of posterity. We should call this point to the attention of those who, from a commendable love of justice and equality, would institute a system of the commons, either in the form of a world food bank, or of unrestricted immigration. We must convince them if we wish to save at least some parts of the world from environmental ruin.

Without a true world government to control reproduction and the use of available resources, the sharing ethic of the spaceship is impossible. For the foreseeable future, our survival demands that we govern our actions by the ethics of a lifeboat, harsh though they may be. Posterity will be satisfied with nothing less.

Peter Singer

THE FAMINE RELIEF ARGUMENT

Peter Singer argues that people in rich countries, by allowing those in poor countries to suffer and die, are actually engaged in reckless homicide. This is because people in rich countries could prevent the deaths of the poor without sacrificing anything of comparable significance. Singer considers a number of objections to his argument and finds them all wanting. Against Hardin's objection that aiding the poor now will lead to disaster in the future, Singer argues that if the right sort of aid is conditionally given, it is possible to avoid a future disaster of the sort Hardin envisions.

SOME FACTS

CONSIDER THESE FACTS: by the most cautious estimates, 400 million people lack the calories, protein, vitamins and minerals needed for a normally healthy life. Millions are constantly hungry; others suffer from deficiency diseases and from infections they would be able to resist on a better diet. Children are worst affected. According to one estimate, 15 million children under five die every year from the combined effects of malnutrition and infection. In some areas, half the children born can be expected to die before their fifth birthday.

Nor is lack of food the only hardship of the poor. To give a broader picture, Robert McNamara, President of the World Bank, has suggested the term 'absolute poverty.' The poverty we are familiar with in industrialized nations is relative poverty—meaning that some citizens are poor, relative to the wealth enjoyed by their neighbours. People living in relative poverty in Australia might be quite comfortably off by comparison with old-age pensioners in Britain, and British old-age pensioners are not poor in comparison with the poverty that exists in Mali or Ethiopia. Absolute poverty, on the other hand, is poverty by any standard. In McNamara's words:

Poverty at the absolute level . . . is life at the very margin of existence.

The absolute poor are severely deprived human beings
struggling to survive in a set of squalid and degraded circumstances almost beyond the power of our sophisticated imaginations and privileged circumstances to conceive.

Compared to those fortunate enough to live in developed countries individuals in the poorest nations have

An infant mortality rate eight times higher
A life expectancy one-third lower
An adult literacy rate 60% less
A nutritional level, for one out of every two in the population, below acceptable standards; and for millions of infants, less protein than is sufficient to permit optimum development of the brain.

And McNamara has summed up absolute poverty as:

a condition of life so characterized by malnutrition, illiteracy, disease, squalid surroundings, high infant mortality and low life expectancy as to be beneath any reasonable definition of human decency.

Absolute poverty is, as McNamara has said, responsible for the loss of countless lives, especially among infants and young children. When absolute poverty does not cause death it still causes misery of a kind not often seen in the affluent nations. Malnutrition in young children stunts both physical and mental development. It has been estimated that the health, growth and learning capacity of nearly half the young children in developing countries are affected by malnutrition. Millions of people on poor diets suffer from deficiency diseases, like goitre, or blindness caused by a lack of vitamin A. The food value

From *Practical Ethics* (1979), pp. 158–181. Reprinted by permission of Cambridge University Press.

of what the poor eat is further reduced by parasites such as hookworm and ringworm, which are endemic in conditions of poor sanitation and health education.

Death and disease apart, absolute poverty remains a miserable condition of life, with inadequate food, shelter, clothing, sanitation, health services and education. According to World Bank estimates which define absolute poverty in terms of income levels insufficient to provide adequate nutrition, something like 800 million people—almost 40% of the people of developing countries—live in absolute poverty. Absolute poverty is probably the principal cause of human misery today.

This is the background situation, the situation that prevails on our planet all the time. It does not make headlines. People died from malnutrition and related diseases yesterday, and more will die tomorrow. The occasional droughts, cyclones, earthquakes and floods that take the lives of tens of thousands in one place and at one time are more newsworthy. They add greatly to the total amount of human suffering; but it is wrong to assume that when there are no major calamities reported, all is well.

The problem is not that the world cannot produce enough to feed and shelter its people. People in the poor countries consume, on average, 400 lbs of grain a year, while North Americans average more than 2000 lbs. The difference is caused by the fact that in the rich countries we feed most of our grain to animals, converting it into meat, milk and eggs. Because this is an inefficient process, wasting up to 95% of the food value of the animal feed, people in rich countries are responsible for the consumption of far more food than those in poor countries who eat few animal products. If we stopped feeding animals on grains, soybeans and fishmeal the amount of food saved would—if distributed to those who need it— be more than enough to end hunger throughout the world.

These facts about animal food do not mean that we can easily solve the world food problem by cutting down on animal products, but they show that the problem is essentially one of distribution rather than production. The world does produce enough food. Moreover the poorer nations themselves could produce far more if they made more use of improved agricultural techniques.

So why are people hungry? Poor people cannot afford to buy grain grown by American farmers. Poor farmers cannot afford to buy improved seeds, or fertilizers, or the machinery needed for drilling wells and pumping water. Only by transferring some of the wealth of the developed nations to the poor of the underdeveloped nations can the situation be changed.

That this wealth exists is clear. Against the picture of absolute poverty that McNamara has painted, one might pose a picture of 'absolute affluence'. Those who are absolutely affluent are not necessarily affluent by comparison with their neighbours, but they are affluent by any reasonable definition of human needs. This means that they have more income than they need to provide themselves adequately with all the basic necessities of life. After buying food, shelter, clothing, necessary health services and education, the absolutely affluent are still able to spend money on luxuries. The absolutely affluent choose their food for the pleasures of the palate, not to stop hunger; they buy new clothes to look fashionable, not to keep warm; they move house to be in a better neighbourhood or have a play room for the children, not to keep out the rain; and after all this there is still money to spend on books and records, colour television, and overseas holidays.

At this stage I am making no ethical judgments about absolute affluence, merely pointing out that it exists. Its defining characteristic is a significant amount of income above the level necessary to provide for the basic human needs of oneself and one's dependents. By this standard Western Europe, North America, Japan, Australia, New Zealand and the oil-rich Middle Eastern states are all absolutely affluent, and so are many, if not all, of their citizens. The USSR and Eastern Europe might also be included on this list. To quote McNamara once more:

The average citizen of a developed country enjoys wealth beyond the wildest dreams of the one billion people in countries with per capita incomes under $200 . . .

These, therefore, are the countries—and individuals—who have wealth which they could, without threatening their own basic welfare, transfer to the absolutely poor.

At present, very little is being transferred. Members of the Organization of Petroleum Exporting Countries lead the way, giving an average of 2.1%

of their Gross National Product. Apart from them, only Sweden, The Netherlands and Norway have reached the modest UN target of 0.7% of GNP. Britain gives 0.38% of its GNP in official development assistance and a small additional amount in unofficial aid from voluntary organizations. The total comes to less than £1 per month per person, and compares with 5.5% of GNP spent on alcohol, and 3% on tobacco. Other, even wealthier nations, give still less: Germany gives 0.27%, the United States 0.22% and Japan 0.21%

The Moral Equivalent of Murder?

If these are the facts, we cannot avoid concluding that by not giving more than we do, people in rich countries are allowing those in poor countries to suffer from absolute poverty, with consequent malnutrition, ill health and death. This is not a conclusion which applies only to governments. It applies to each absolutely affluent individual, for each of us has the opportunity to do something about the situation; for instance, to give our time or money to voluntary organizations like Oxfam, War on Want, Freedom From Hunger, and so on. If, then, allowing someone to die is not intrinsically different from killing someone, it would seem that we are all murderers.

Is this verdict too harsh? Many will reject it as self-evidently absurd. They would sooner take it as showing that allowing to die cannot be equivalent to killing than as showing that living in an affluent style without contributing to Oxfam is ethically equivalent to going over to India and shooting a few peasants. And no doubt, put as bluntly as that, the verdict is too harsh.

These are several significant differences between spending money on luxuries instead of using it to save lives, and deliberately shooting people.

First, the motivation will normally be different. Those who deliberately shoot others go out of their way to kill; they presumably want their victims dead, from malice, sadism, or some equally unpleasant motive. A person who buys a colour television set presumably wants to watch television in colour—not

in itself a terrible thing. At worst, spending money on luxuries instead of giving it away indicates selfishness and indifference to the sufferings of others, characteristics which may be understandable but are not comparable with actual malice or similar motives.

Second, it is not difficult for most of us to act in accordance with a rule against killing people: it is, on the other hand, very difficult to obey a rule which commands us to save all the lives we can. To live a comfortable, or even luxurious life it is not necessary to kill anyone; but it is necessary to allow some to die whom we might have saved, for the money that we need to live comfortably could have been given away. Thus the duty to avoid killing is much easier to discharge completely than the duty to save. Saving every life we could would mean cutting our standard of living down to the bare essentials needed to keep us alive.* To discharge this duty completely would require a degree of moral heroism utterly different from what is required by mere avoidance of killing.

A third difference is the greater certainty of the outcome of shooting when compared with not giving aid. If I point a loaded gun at someone and pull the trigger, it is virtually certain that the person will be injured, if not killed; whereas the money that I could give might be spent on a project than turns out to be unsuccessful and helps no one.

Fourth, when people are shot there are identifiable individuals who have been harmed. We can point to them and to their grieving families. When I buy my colour television, I cannot know who my money would have saved if I had given it away. In a time of famine I may see dead bodies and grieving families on my new television, and I might not doubt that my money would have saved some of them; even then it is impossible to point to a body and say that had I not bought the set, that person would have survived.

Fifth, it might be said that the plight of the hungry is not my doing, and so I cannot be held responsible for it. The starving would have been starving if I had

---

*Strictly, we would need to cut down to the minimum level compatible with earning the income which, after providing for our needs, left us most to give away. Thus if my present position earns me, say, £10,000 a year, but requires me to spend £1,000 a year on dressing respectably and maintaining a car, I cannot save more people by giving away the car and clothes if that will mean taking a job which, although it does not involve me in these expenses, earns me only £5,000.

ever existed. If I kill, however, I am responsible for my victims' deaths, for those people would not have died if I had not killed them. . . .

Do the five differences not only explain, but also justify, our attitudes? Let us consider them one by one:

1. Take the lack of an identifiable victim first. Suppose that I am a travelling salesman, selling tinned food, and I learn that a batch of tins contains a contaminant, the known effect of which when consumed is to double the risk that the consumer will die from stomach cancer. Suppose I continue to sell the tins. My decision may have no identifiable victims. Some of those who eat the food will die from cancer. The proportion of consumers dying in this way will be twice that of the community at large, but which among the consumers died because they ate what I sold, and which would have contracted the disease anyway? It is impossible to tell; but surely this impossibility makes my decision no less reprehensible than it would have been had the contaminant had more readily detectable, though equally fatal, effects.

2. The lack of certainty that by giving money I could save a life does reduce the wrongness of not giving, by comparison with deliberate killing; but it is insufficient to show that not giving is acceptable conduct. The motorist who speeds through pedestrian crossings, heedless of anyone who might be on them, is not a murderer. She may never actually hit a pedestrian; yet what she does is very wrong indeed.

3. The notion of responsibility for acts rather than omissions is more puzzling. On the one hand we feel ourselves to be under a greater obligation to help those whose misfortunes we have caused. (It is for this reason that advocates of overseas aid often argue that Western nations have created the poverty of Third World nations, through forms of economic exploitation which go back to the colonial system.) On the other hand any consequentialist would insist that we are responsible for all the consequences of our actions, and if a consequence of my spending money on a luxury item is that someone dies, I am responsible for that death. It is true that the person would have died even if I had never ex-

isted, but what is the relevance of that? The fact is that I do exist, and the consequentialist will say that our responsibilities derive from the world as it is, not as it might have been.

One way of making sense of the non-consequentialist view of responsibility is by basing it on a theory of rights of the kind proposed by John Locke or, more recently, Robert Nozick. If everyone has a right to life, and this right is a right *against* others who might threaten my life, but not a right *to* assistance from others when my life is in danger, then we can understand the feeling that we are responsible for acting to kill but not for omitting to save. The former violates the rights of others, the latter does not.

Should we accept such a theory of rights? If we build up our theory of rights by imagining, as Locke and Nozick do, individuals living independently from each other in a 'state of nature', it may seem natural to adopt a conception of rights in which as long as each leaves the other alone, no rights are violated. I might, on this view, quite properly have maintained my independent existence if I had wished to do so. So if I do not make you any worse off than you would have been if I had had nothing at all to do with you, how can I have violated your rights? But why start from such an unhistorical, abstract and ultimately inexplicable idea as an independent individual? We now know that our ancestors were social beings long before they were human beings, and could not have developed the abilities and capacities of human beings if they had not been social beings first. In any case we are not, now, isolated individuals. If we consider people living together in a community, it is less easy to assume that rights must be restricted to rights against interference. We might, instead, adopt the view that taking rights to life seriously is incompatible with standing by and watching people die when one could easily save them.

4. What of the difference in motivation? That a person does not positively wish for the death of another lessens the severity of the blame she deserves; but not by as much as our present attitudes to giving aid suggest. The behaviour of the speeding motorist is again comparable, for such motorists usually have no desire at all to kill anyone. They merely enjoy speeding and are in-

different to the consequences. Despite their lack of malice, those who kill with cars deserve not only blame but also severe punishment.

5. Finally, the fact that to avoid killing people is normally not difficult, whereas to save all one possibly could save is heroic, must make an important difference to our attitude to failure to do what the respective principles demand. Not to kill is a minimum standard of acceptable conduct we can require of everyone; to save all one possibly could is not something that can realistically be required, especially not in societies accustomed to giving as little as ours do. Given the generally accepted standards, people who give, say, £100 a year to Oxfam are more aptly praised for above average generosity than blamed for giving less than they might. The appropriateness of praise and blame is, however, a separate issue from the rightness or wrongness of actions. The former evaluates the agent: the latter evaluates the action. Perhaps people who give £100 really ought to give at least £1,000, but to blame them for not giving more could be counterproductive. It might make them feel that what is required is too demanding, and if one is going to be blamed anyway, one might as well not give anything at all.

(That an ethic which put saving all one possibly can on the same footing as not killing would be an ethic for saints or heroes should not lead us to assume that the alternative must be an ethic which makes it obligatory not to kill, but puts us under no obligation to save anyone. There are positions in between these extremes, as we shall soon see.)

To summarize our discussion of the five differences which normally exist between killing and allowing to die, in the context of absolute poverty and overseas aid. The lack of an identifiable victim is of no moral significance, though it may play an important role in explaining our attitudes. The idea that we are directly responsible for those we kill, but not for those we do not help, depends on a questionable notion of responsibility, and may need to be based on a controversial theory of rights. Differences in certainty and motivation are ethically significant, and show that not aiding the poor is not to be con-

demned as murdering them; it could, however, be on a par with killing someone as a result of reckless driving, which is serious enough. Finally the difficulty of completely discharging the duty of saving all one possibly can makes it inappropriate to blame those who fall short of this target as we blame those who kill; but this does not show that the act itself is less serious. Nor does it indicate anything about those who, far from saving all they possibly can, make no effort to save anyone.

These conclusions suggest a new approach. Instead of attempting to deal with the contrast between affluence and poverty by comparing not saving with deliberate killing, let us consider afresh whether we have an obligation to assist those whose lives are in danger, and if so, how this obligation applies to the present world situation.

The Obligation to Assist

The argument for an obligation to assist. The path from the library at my university to the Humanities lecture theatre passes a shallow ornamental pond. Suppose that on my way to give a lecture I notice that a small child has fallen in and is in danger of drowning. Would anyone deny that I ought to wade in and pull the child out? This will mean getting my clothes muddy, and either cancelling my lecture or delaying it until I can find something dry to change into; but compared with the avoidable death of a child this is insignificant.

A plausible principle that would support the judgment that I ought to pull the child out is this: if it is in our power to prevent something very bad happening, without thereby sacrificing anything of comparable moral significance, we ought to do it. This principle seems uncontroversial. It will obviously win the assent of consequentialists; but non-consequentialists should accept it too, because the injunction to prevent what is bad applies only when nothing comparably significant is at stake. Thus the principle cannot lead to the kinds of actions of which non-consequentialists strongly disapprove— serious violations of individual rights, injustice, broken promises, and so on. If a non-consequentialist regards any of these as comparable in moral significance to the bad thing that is to be prevented, he will automatically regard the principle as not applying in those cases in which the bad thing can only be prevented by violating rights, doing injustice, breaking promises, or whatever else is at stake. Most non-consequentialists hold that we ought to prevent what is bad and promote what is good. Their dispute with consequentialists lies in their insistence that this is not the sole ultimate ethical principle: that it is *an* ethical principle is not denied by any plausible ethical theory.

Nevertheless the uncontroversial appearance of the principle that we ought to prevent what is bad when we can do so without sacrificing anything of comparable moral significance is deceptive. If it were taken seriously and acted upon, our lives and our world would be fundamentally changed. For the principle applies, not just to rare situations in which one can save a child from a pond, but to the every-day situation in which we can assist those living in absolute poverty. In saying this I assume that abso-lute poverty, with its hunger and malnutrition, lack of shelter, illiteracy, disease, high infant mortality and low life expectancy, is a bad thing. And I assume that it is within the power of the affluent to reduce absolute poverty, without sacrificing anything of comparable moral significance. If these two assump-tions and the principle we have been discussing are correct, we have an obligation to help those in ab-solute poverty which is no less strong than our obli-gation to rescue a drowning child from a pond. Not to help would be wrong, whether or not it is intrin-sically equivalent to killing. Helping is not, as con-ventionally thought, a charitable act which it is praiseworthy to do, but not wrong to omit; it is something that everyone ought to do.

This is the argument for an obligation to assist. Set out more formally, it would look like this.

First premise:	If we can prevent something bad with-out sacrificing anything of comparable significance, we ought to do it.
Second premise:	Absolute poverty is bad.
Third premise:	There is some absolute poverty we can prevent without sacrificing anything of comparable moral significance.
Conclusion:	We ought to prevent some absolute poverty

The first premise is the substantive moral premise on which the argument rests, and I have tried to show that it can be accepted by people who hold a variety of ethical positions.

The second premise is unlikely to be challenged. Absolute poverty is, as McNamara put it, 'beneath any reasonable definition of human decency' and it would be hard to find a plausible ethical view which did not regard it as a bad thing.

The third premise is more controversial, even though it is cautiously framed. It claims only that some absolute poverty can be prevented without the sacrifice of anything of comparable moral sig-nificance. It thus avoids the objection that any aid I can give is just 'drops in the ocean' for the point is not whether my personal contribution will make any noticeable impression on world poverty as a whole (of course it won't) but whether it will prevent some poverty. This is all the argument needs to sus-tain its conclusion, since the second premise says that any absolute poverty is bad, and not merely the total amount of absolute poverty. If without sacrific-ing anything of comparable moral significance we can provide just one family with the means to raise itself out of absolute poverty, the third premise is vindicated.

I have left the notion of moral significance unex-amined in order to show that the argument does not depend on any specific values or ethical principles. I think the third premise is true for most people liv-ing in industrialized nations, on any defensible view of what is morally significant. Our affluence means that we have income we can dispose of without giv-ing up the basic necessities of life, and we can use this income to reduce absolute poverty. Just how much we will think ourselves obliged to give up will depend on what we consider to be of comparable moral significance to the poverty we could prevent: colour television, stylish clothes, expensive dinners, a sophisticated stereo system, overseas holidays, a (second?) car, a larger house, private schools for our children. . . . For a utilitarian, none of these is likely to be of comparable significance to the reduc-tion of absolute poverty; and those who are not util-itarians surely must, if they subscribe to the principle of universalizability, accept that at least *some* of these things are of far less moral significance than the ab-solute poverty that could be prevented by the money they cost. So the third premise seems to be true on any plausible ethical view—although the precise amount of absolute poverty that can be prevented before anything of moral significance is sacrificed will vary according to the ethical view one accepts. . . .

Objections to the Argument

Property rights. Do people have a right to private property, a right which contradicts the view that they are under an obligation to give some of their wealth away to those in absolute poverty? According to some theories of rights (for instance, Robert Nozick's) provided one has acquired one's property without the use of unjust means like force and fraud, one may be entitled to enormous wealth while others starve. This individualistic conception of rights is in contrast to other views, like the early Christian doctrine to be found in the works of Thomas Aquinas, which holds that since property exists for the satisfaction of human needs, 'whatever a man has in superabundance is owed, of natural right, to the poor for their sustenance'. A socialist would also, of course, see wealth as belonging to the community rather than the individual, while utilitarians, whether socialist or not, would be prepared to override property rights to prevent great evils.

Does the argument for an obligation to assist others therefore presuppose one of these other theories of property rights, and not an individualistic theory like Nozick's? Not necessarily. A theory of property rights can insist on our *right* to retain wealth without pronouncing on whether the rich *ought* to give to the poor. Nozick, for example, rejects the use of compulsory means like taxation to redistribute income, but suggests that we can achieve the ends we deem morally desirable by voluntary means. So Nozick would reject the claim that rich people have an 'obligation' to give to the poor, in so far as this implies that the poor have a right to our aid, but might accept that giving is something we ought to do and failing to give, though within one's rights, is wrong—for rights is not all there is to ethics.

The argument for an obligation to assist can survive, with only minor modifications, even if we accept an individualistic theory of property rights. In any case, however, I do not think we should accept such a theory. It leaves too much to chance to be an acceptable ethical view. For instance, those whose forefathers happened to inhabit some sandy wastes around the Persian Gulf are now fabulously wealthy, because oil lay under those sands; while those whose forefathers settled on better land south of the Sahara live in absolute poverty, because of drought and bad harvests. Can this distribution be acceptable from an impartial point of view? If we imagine ourselves about to begin life as a citizen of either Kuwait or Chad—but we do not know which—would we accept the principle that citizens of Kuwait are under no obligation to assist people living in Chad?

Population and the ethics of triage. Perhaps the most serious objection to the argument that we have an obligation to assist is that since the major cause of absolute poverty is overpopulation, helping those now in poverty will only ensure that yet more people are born to live in poverty in the future.

In its most extreme form, this objection is taken to show that we should adopt a policy of 'triage'. The term comes from medical policies adopted in wartime. With too few doctors to cope with all the casualties, the wounded were divided into three categories: those who would probably survive without medical assistance, those who might survive if they received assistance, but otherwise probably would not, and those who even with medical assistance probably would not survive. Only those in the middle category were given medical assistance. The idea, of course, was to use limited medical resources as effectively as possible. For those in the first category, medical treatment was not strictly necessary; for those in the third category, it was likely to be useless. It has been suggested that we should apply the same policies to countries, according to their prospects of becoming self-sustaining. We would not aid countries which even without our help will soon be able to feed their populations. We would not aid countries which, even with our help, will not be able to limit their population to a level they can feed. We would aid those countries where our help might make the difference between success and failure in bringing food and population into balance.

Advocates of this theory are understandably reluctant to give a complete list of the countries they would place into the 'hopeless' category; but Bangladesh is often cited as an example. Adopting the policy of triage would, then, mean cutting off assistance to Bangladesh and allowing famine, disease and natural disasters to reduce the population of that country (now around 80 million) to the level at which it can provide adequately for all.

In support of this view Garrett Hardin has offered a metaphor: we in the rich nations are like the occupants of a crowded lifeboat adrift in a sea full of drowning people. If we try to save the drowning by bringing them aboard our boat will be overloaded and we shall all drown. Since it is better that some survive than none, we should leave the others to drown. In the world today, according to Hardin, 'lifeboat ethics' apply. The rich should leave the poor to starve, for otherwise the poor will drag the rich down with them.

Against this view, some writers have argued that over-population is a myth. The world produces ample food to feed its population, and could, according to some estimates, feed ten times as many. People are hungry not because there are too many but because of inequitable land distribution, the manipulation of Third World economies by the developed nations, wastage of food in the West, and so on.

Putting aside the controversial issue of the extent to which food production might one day be increased, it is true, as we have already seen, that the world now produces enough to feed its inhabitants—the amount lost by being fed to animals itself being enough to meet existing grain shortages. Nevertheless population growth cannot be ignored. Bangladesh could, with land reform and using better techniques, feed its present population of 80 million; but by the year 2000, according to World Bank estimates, its population will be 146 million. The enormous effort that will have to go into feeding an extra 66 million people, all added to the population within a quarter of a century, means that Bangladesh must develop at full speed to stay where she is. Other low income countries are in similar situations. By the end of the century, Ethiopia's population is expected to rise from 29 to 54 million; Somalia's from 3 to 7 million, India's from 620 to 958 million, Zaire's from 25 to 47 million. What will happen then? Population cannot grow indefinitely. It will be checked by a decline in birth rates or a rise in death rates. Those who advocate triage are proposing that we allow the population growth of some countries to be checked by a rise in death rates—that is, by increased malnutrition, and related diseases; by widespread famines; by increased

infant mortality; and by epidemics of infectious diseases.

The consequences of triage on this scale are so horrible that we are inclined to reject it without further argument. How could we sit by our television sets, watching millions starve while we do nothing? Would not that be the end of all notions of human equality and respect for human life? Don't people have a right to our assistance, irrespective of the consequences?

Anyone whose initial reaction to triage was not one of repugnance would be an unpleasant sort of person. Yet initial reactions based on strong feelings are not always reliable guides. Advocates of triage are rightly concerned with the long-term consequences of our actions. They say that helping the poor and starving now merely ensures more poor and starving in the future. When our capacity to help is finally unable to cope—as one day it must be—the suffering will be greater than it would be if we stopped helping now. If this is correct, there is nothing we can do to prevent absolute starvation and poverty, in the long run, and so we have no obligation to assist. Nor does it seem reasonable to hold that under these circumstances people have a right to our assistance. If we do accept such a right, irrespective of the consequences, we are saying that, in Hardin's metaphor, we would continue to haul the drowning into our lifeboat until the boat sank and we all drowned.

If triage is to be rejected it must be tackled on its own ground, within the framework of consequentialist ethics. Here it is vulnerable. Any consequentialist ethics must take probability of outcome into account. A course of action that will certainly produce some benefit is to be preferred to an alternative course that may lead to a slightly larger benefit, but is equally likely to result in no benefit at all. Only if the greater magnitude of the uncertain benefit outweighs its uncertainty should we choose it. Better one certain unit of benefit than a 10% chance of 5 units; but better a 50% chance of 3 units than a single certain unit. The same principle applies when we are trying to avoid evils.

The policy of triage involves a certain, very great evil: population control by famine and disease. Tens of millions would die slowly. Hundreds of millions would continue to live in absolute poverty, at the very margin of existence. Against this prospect, advocates of the policy place a possible evil which is greater still: the same process of famine and disease, taking place in, say, fifty years time, when the world's population may be three times its present level, and the number who will die from famine, or struggle on in absolute poverty, will be that much greater. The question is: how probable is this forecast that continued assistance now will lead to greater disasters in the future?

Forecasts of population growth are notoriously fallible, and theories about the factors which affect it remain speculative. One theory, at least as plausible as any other, is that countries pass through a 'demographic transition' as their standard of living rises. When people are very poor and have no access to modern medicine their fertility is high, but population is kept in check by high death rates. The introduction of sanitation, modern medical techniques and other improvements reduces the death rate, but initially has little effect on the birth rate. Then population grows rapidly. Most poor countries are now in this phase. If standards of living continue to rise, however, couples begin to realize that to have the same number of children surviving to maturity as in the past, they do not need to give birth to as many children as their parents did. The need for children to provide economic support in old age diminishes. Improved education and the emancipation and employment of women also reduce the birthrate, and so population growth begins to level off. Most rich nations have reached this stage, and their populations are growing only very slowly.

If this theory is right, there is an alternative to the disasters accepted as inevitable by supporters of triage. We can assist poor countries to raise the living standards of the poorest members of their population. We can encourage the governments of these countries to enact land reform measures, improve education, and liberate women from a purely child-bearing role. We can also help other countries to make contraception and sterilization widely available. There is a fair chance that these measures will hasten the onset of the demographic transition and bring population growth down to a manageable level. Success cannot be guaranteed; but the evidence that improved economic security and education reduce population growth is strong enough to make triage ethically unacceptable. We cannot allow millions to die from starvation and disease when there is a reasonable probability that population can be brought under control without such horrors.

Population growth is therefore not a reason against giving overseas aid, although it should make us think about the kind of aid to give. Instead of food handouts, it may be better to give aid that hastens the demographic transition. This may mean agricultural assistance for the rural poor, or assistance with education, or the provision of contraceptive services. Whatever kind of aid proves most effective in specific circumstances, the obligation to assist is not reduced.

One awkward question remains. What should we do about a poor and already overpopulated country which, for religious or nationalistic reasons, restricts the use of contraceptives and refuses to slow its population growth? Should we nevertheless offer development assistance? Or should we make our offer conditional on effective steps being taken to reduce the birthrate? To the latter course, some would object that putting conditions on aid is an attempt to impose our own ideas on independent sovereign nations. So it is—but is this imposition unjustifiable? If the argument for an obligation to assist is sound, we have an obligation to reduce absolute poverty: but we have no obligation to make sacrifices that, to the best of our knowledge, have no prospect of reducing poverty in the long run. Hence we have no obligation to assist countries whose governments have policies which will make our aid ineffective. This could be very harsh on poor citizens of these countries—for they may have no say in the government's policies—but we will help more people in the long run by using our resources where they are most effective. (The same principles may apply, incidentally, to countries that refuse to take other steps that could make assistance effective—like refusing to reform systems of land holding that impose intolerable burdens on poor tenant farmers.) . . .

Too high a standard? The final objection to the argument for an obligation to assist is that it sets a standard so high that none but a saint could attain it. How many people can we really expect to give away everything not comparable in moral significance to the poverty their donation could relieve? For most of us, with commonsense views about what is of moral significance, this would mean a life of real austerity. Might it not be counter-productive to demand so much? Might not people say: 'As I can't do what is morally required anyway, I won't bother to give at all.' If, however, we were to set a more realistic standard, people might make a genuine effort to reach it. Thus setting a lower standard might actually result in more aid being given.

It is important to get the status of this objection clear. Its accuracy as a prediction of human behaviour is quite compatible with the argument that we are obliged to give to the point at which by giving more we sacrifice something of comparable moral significance. What would follow from the objection is that public advocacy of this standard of giving is undesirable. It would mean that in order to do the maximum to reduce absolute poverty, we should advocate a standard lower than the amount we think people really ought to give. Of course we ourselves—those of us who accept the original argument, with its higher standard—would know that we ought to do more than we publicly propose people ought to do, and we might actually give more than we urge others to give. There is no inconsistency here, since in both our private and our public behaviour we are trying to do what will most reduce absolute poverty.

For a consequentialist, this apparent conflict between public and private morality is always a possibility, and not in itself an indication that the underlying principle is wrong. The consequences of a principle are one thing, the consequences of publicly advocating it another.

Is it true that the standard set by our argument is so high as to be counterproductive? There is not much evidence to go by, but discussions of the argument, with students and others have led me to think it might be. On the other hand the conventionally accepted standard—a few coins in a collection tin when one is waved under your nose—is obviously far too low. What level should we advocate? Any figure will be arbitrary, but there may be something to be said for a round percentage of one's income like, say, 10%—more than a token donation, yet not so high as to be beyond all but saints. (This figure has the additional advantage of being reminiscent of the ancient tithe, or tenth, which was traditionally given to the church, whose responsibilities included care of the poor in one's local community. Perhaps the idea can be revived and applied to the global community.) Some families, of course, will find 10% a considerable strain on their finances. Others may be able to give more without difficulty. No figure should be advocated as a rigid minimum or maximum; but it seems safe to advocate that those earning average or above average incomes in affluent societies, unless they have an unusually large number of dependents or other special needs, ought to give a tenth of their income to reducing absolute poverty. By any reasonable ethical standards this is the minimum we ought to do, and we do wrong if we do less.

Richard T. De George

DO WE OWE THE FUTURE ANYTHING?

Richard T. De George argues that, because future generations do not exist, they do not have any rights nor do we have any obligations to them. Still, De George thinks we do have an obligation to promote the continuance of the human race—but an obligation based on considerations of value rather than of rights. At the same time he denies that we have any obligation to produce a continuously increasing standard of living.

THE DESIRE TO AVOID pollution—however defined—involves concern for the duration and quality of human life. Problems dealing with the quality of human life inevitably involve value judgments. And value judgments are notorious candidates for debate and disagreement. Yet in discussions on pollution the desirability of the continuance of the human race is generally taken for granted; most people feel that a continuous rise in the standard of living would be a good thing; and many express a feeling of obligation towards future generations. How well founded are these judgments? The purpose of this paper is to examine the validity and some of the implications of three statements of principles which have a direct bearing on this question and so on the debate concerning pollution and its control. The three principles are the following:

1. Only existing entities have rights.
2. Continuance of the human race is good.
3. Continuous increase in man's standard of living is good.

I

The argument in favor of the principle that only existing entities have rights is straightforward and simple: Non-existent entities by definition do not exist. What does not exist cannot be the subject or bearer of anything. Hence it cannot be the subject or bearer of rights.

Just as non-existent entities have no rights, so it makes no sense to speak about anyone's correlative duty towards non-existent entities. Towards that which does not exist we can have no legal or moral obligation, since there is no subject or term which can be the object of that obligation. Now it is clear that unconceived possible future human beings do not exist, though we can think, e.g., of the class of human beings which will exist two hundred years from now. It follows that since this class does not (yet) exist, we cannot have any obligations to it, nor to any of its possible members. It is a presently empty class.

More generally, then, presently existing human beings have no obligation to any future-and-not-yet existing set or class of human beings. We owe them nothing and they have no legitimate claim on us for the simple reason that they do not exist. No one can legitimately defend their interests or represent their case in court or law or government, because they are not, and so have no interests or rights.

It follows from this that a great deal of contemporary talk about obligations to the future, where this means to some distant future portion of mankind, is simply confused. In dealing with questions of pollution and clean air—as well as with similar issues such as the use of irreplaceable resources—there can be no legitimate question of the **rights** of unconceived future human beings or of any supposedly correlative **obligation** of present-day human beings to them.

Some people may find this to be counterintuitive. That it is not so may perhaps become clearer if we consider what I take to be the feelings of many—if not most people with respect to the past.

Consider the general attitude towards the ancient Greeks and Romans. Did they owe us anything? Did they have any duties or obligations to us? It is clear

From "Do We Owe the Future Anything?" in *Law and the Ecological Challenge* (1978), pp. 180–190. Reprinted by permission of William S. Hein & Co., Inc.

there are no sanctions we can impose on them and no way we can enforce any obligations we may claim they had towards us. But surely even to raise the question of their obligation to us is odd. We may rejoice in what has been saved of the past and handed down to us, and we may regret that some of Plato's dialogues have been lost or that the Library at Alexandria was burned, or that Rome was sacked. But though we may regret such events and though we may judge that they were in some sense ills for mankind or the result of immoral actions, they were not immoral because of any obligation past generations had to us.

The situation is little changed if we come up to more recent—though not too recent—times. The American Founding Fathers had no obligation to us. They could scarcely have envisaged our times or have been expected to calculate the effects of their actions on us. Or consider the unrestrained slaughter of American buffalo for sport. Such action may have been immoral and a waste of a natural resource; but if it was immoral it was not because present-day Americans have any right to have inherited more buffalo than we did.

Since it is not possible to impose sanctions on past generations it makes no sense to speak of legal obligations or even of moral obligations of those generations to us. At best, as some minority groups have been arguing, we might claim that present-day beneficiaries of past injustices are obliged to make restitution to the present descendents of those who in the past suffered injustice. This is a plausible claim, and might serve as a model in the future for some portion of mankind claiming that it has a legal or moral claim against another portion for exploitation or oppression by their forefathers. Whatever the obligation to make restoration for past injustices, however, the injustice was an injustice not primarily against present generations but against those past generations whose rights were violated or whose property or lives were unjustly taken, or who were otherwise oppressed or exploited.

The situation is basically similar today vis-a-vis future generations. Our primary obligation with respect to the control of pollution or to the use of resources is to presently existing human beings rather than to possible future human beings. The best way to protect the interests of future generations—if we

choose to use this language—may be to conserve the environment for ourselves. But my present point is that in dealing with questions of public policy or legislation, the primary values to be considered are those of presently existing people, and not the projected or supposed values of future generations. To argue or act as if we could know the wants or needs of generations hundreds or more years hence is to deceive ourselves, perhaps so as to have an excuse to ignore present-day wants and needs. Hence questions about the amount and kind of pollution to be tolerated, the resources to be rationed or preserved, should not be decided in terms of far distant future needs or requirements but in terms of present and near-future needs and requirements.

It is correct that for the first time in the history of mankind presently living human beings have it within their power to annihilate mankind or to use up irreplaceable resources. But these new capacities do not change the status of our responsibilities or obligations, despite the fact that they are increased. If we do annihilate mankind, it will be no injustice to those who never were and never will be. If we were foolishly to use up vital, irreplaceable resources or disrupt the ecosystem, the reason it would be wrong or bad, unjust or immoral—and so the reason why it might now be something requiring legislation to prevent—is not its effects on those who do not yet exist, but its effects on those who do.

The thrust of the principle we are considering is that present generations or individuals must be considered primary in any calculation of value with respect to either pollution control or the distribution and use of the limited resources of the earth. The rights of presently existing people carry with them the obligation to respect their rights, e.g., to enjoy at least minimal levels of food, shelter, and the like. No one and no generation is required to sacrifice itself for imaginary, non-existent generations of the future. What does have to be considered is the future of presently existing persons—infants as well as adults.

We undoubtedly feel closer to our as yet unconceived descendents—those one removed from the present generation of children—than we do to many people living in places far distant from us, with different customs and values; and if we were to choose between raising the standard of living of these to-us foreign people and preserving our wealth to be shared by our descendents, we might well opt for the latter. To do so is to aggregate to ourselves the right to conserve present resources for those to whom we choose to pass them on at the expense of those presently existing who do not share them. Since, however, presently existing people have rights to the goods of the earth, there seems to be a **prima facie** obligation to attempt to raise the level of living and comfort of presently existing people, wherever they may be, rather than ignoring them and worrying only about our own future heirs. Underfed and impoverished areas of the world may require greater attention and impose greater obligations than non-existent future generations.

Insofar as modern technology is world-significant, so too are some aspects of pollution. Mercury poured into streams finds its way into the ocean and into fish caught in international waters and shipped around the world; fall-out from nuclear blasts circles the globe. If present-day legislative principles in the United States are sufficient to handle the problems posed by pollution in our own country, it is certainly not the case that there are effective means of controlling the problem internationally. The cost of pollution control prevents poorer countries from simultaneously developing their technology in order to raise their living standards and spend the money and resources necessary to curb pollution. It is in cases such as these that it becomes especially important to be conscious of the principle discussed here which emphasizes the overbearing rights of existing persons as opposed to the putative rights of non-existent persons. . . .

Although there is no full fledged obligation to provide, e.g., clean air, for countless future generations, we will have an obligation to provide something for at least those future persons or generations for whom or for which we are rather closely responsible. Generations overlap considerably; but any group in the position to influence and change things, though it cannot be expected to be responsible for generations hundreds, much less thousands of years hence, can be expected to take into account those persons who will be alive within the next fifty or a hundred years. A large number of these people already exist; and if future generations are produced—as barring some global catastrophe they will

be—they **will** have rights and these rights must be considered at least as potential rights. The amount of consideration should be proportional to the probability that they will exist, and should be considered especially by those responsible for bringing them into the world.

Furthermore, if starting from the premise that non-existent entities can have no rights it follows that presently existing persons have no correlative obligations towards them, and so no such obligations to unborn generations, this does not mean that people may not want to consider future possible generations from some point of view other than one of such obligation and take them into account in other ways and for other reasons.

Obviously men are concerned about their own futures and those of their presently existing children and of the presently acknowledged right of their children to have children; it is a claim which must be weighed. Though we cannot assume that the children of present-day children will have exactly the same desires and values as we, there is good reason to believe they will be sufficiently similar to us so that they will need fresh air, that they will not be able to tolerate excessive amounts of mercury or DDT in their food, and that they will probably share a good many of our desires. To speak of the **right** of non-existing future persons to have children in their turn is to treat them as actual. It amounts to saying that if conditions remain more or less the same and if the presently possible entities become actual, then, when they do, they will have the rights we presently attribute to actually existing persons. Our present interest in their happiness, however, is already an actual interest which must be considered and it might impel—though not strictly require—us to leave as many options open to those who will come after us as possible, consistent with taking care of our own needs and wants.

Since most people living now would consider it possible to be living twenty years hence, the conditions of life which the next as yet unborn generation will face is a condition of life which we who presently exist will also face. So with respect to at least one, two, three or perhaps four generations hence, or for roughly fifty to a hundred years hence, it can plausibly be argued that we plan not only for unborn generations but also for ourselves. Our concern for them is equally concern for ourselves. And we do have rights. If this is the case, we can legitimately think and plan and act for the future on the basis of our own concerns, which include **our** hopes and desires for our real or anticipated offspring. But we should be clear about what we are arguing, and not confuse our rights and desires with the supposed rights of non-existent entities.

II

The second principle was: Continuance of the human race is good.

What does this mean and what does it imply?

Can we give any sense to the question: how long should the human race survive? We know that some species have had their span of years on earth and have given way to other species. To ask how long the dinosaur should have survived would be an odd question; for to say that it should have survived for a shorter or longer time than it did would be to speak as if the laws of nature should have been different, or as if the dinosaur's continued existence was a good which it could have done something to prolong beyond the time that it did. It is precisely in this sense—that the survival of the human species is a good in itself and that we should do what we can to keep it going—that we say that the human race should continue to survive. To utter this is to make a value judgment and to express our feelings about the race, despite the fact that we as individuals will die. Some people speak blithely about its being better for the human species to continue for another thousand years than for another five hundred; or for 500,000 rather than 100,000, and so on. But the content which we can give to such statements—other than expressing the judgment that human life is a good in itself, at least under certain circumstances—seems minimal. For we cannot imagine what human life would be like in the far distant future, nor what we can or should do to help make it the case that one of those figures rather than the other is the one that actually becomes the case.

If tomorrow some sort of radiation from the sun were to render all human beings sterile, we could anticipate the demise of the human race as more and more of the present population died off. We could anticipate the difficulties of those who were the rela-

tively last to die. And we could take some solace in the fact that the radiation would have been an act of God and not the result of the acts of men. The demise of the human race would in this case be similar to the extinction of the dinosaur. If a similar occurence was the result of the acts of men, though the result would be the same, it would make more sense in the latter case than in the former to say that man should have continued longer as a species. Just as we consider murder and suicide wrong, so we consider wrong the fouling of the air or water to such an extent that it kills others or ourselves or the whole human race.

Thus, though no injustice is done to those who will never exist because of our actions, and though we do not violate any of their rights—since they have none—we can in some sense say that with the extinction of the human race there would be less value in the world than if it had continued to exist. If we have an obligation to attempt to create and preserve as much value in the world as possible, then we have an obligation to continue the human race, where this does not necessarily mean an obligation to procreate as many people as possible but to achieve as much value as possible, taking into consideration the quality of life of those who will be alive. The basis for the obligation comes not from a consideration of rights, but from a consideration of value.

Such a calculation, obviously, is something which each generation can perform only with respect to the time it is alive and able to act. It can help assure that when it dies those who are still living are in such a condition as to preserve human life and to pass it on at as high a qualitative level as possible. And if that happened consistently each year, each decade, each century, then until there was some act of God presumably man would continue indefinitely—which is a thought we may take some pleasure in contemplating, despite the fact that beyond a rather small number of years we will not be affected by whether the race continues or not.

Thus far, then, though we do not have any obligation **to** non-existent entities, we can legitimately anticipate the future needs and requirements of ourselves and of those who will probably come soon after us; furthermore, since we can make out the case that it would be good for the human race to continue, we have the obligation to do what we can to forestall its demise. This leads us to the third principle.

III

The last of the three principles I proposed at the start of this paper was: Continuous increase in man's standard of living is good. It is a principle which a large number of people seem to subscribe to, one underlying much of our industrial and technological growth and a good deal of the concern for a constantly expanding GNP. As a principle, however, it is both ambiguous and dubious.

There are at least four basic interpretations which can be given to the principle: 1) it can be taken to refer to advancement up the economic ladder by people on an individual basis; 2) it might be understood as a statement about the hopes and aims of each generation for the succeeding generation; 3) it might mean that the standard of living of at least some men should continue to rise, pushing forward the heights to which men can rise; and 4) it can be interpreted to mean that all men in a given society, or throughout the world, should be brought up to a certain constantly rising level of life.

The differences in interpretation are extremely important and both stem from and give rise to different sets of value judgments concerning production, distribution, development of resources, and expenditure of resources on pollution control.

1) The individualistic interpretation puts its emphasis on an individual's ability through work, savings, ingenuity, or other means to advance himself economically. The Horatio Alger ideal, the rise from poverty to wealth, is the model. Increasing one's standard of living became the goal of workers as expressed in the labor union movements, and its results are clearly visible in the high standard of living enjoyed by many large segments of the population in the United States and other industrialized countries. Together with this rise has come the pollution from automobiles and factories and the birth of a small counter-culture which has called into question the necessity, the wisdom, and the value of a constantly rising standard of living.

The hope of a better life expresses an undeniable value when one's life is barely tolerable. It makes less

sense as one's needs are more and more taken care of and the principle becomes dubious once one has achieved a certain standard of living somewhere considerably well above the minimal necessary for survival. There is a point of diminishing returns beyond which the price one has to pay in terms of energy, time, money, and resources expended does not produce correspondingly significant benefits. And if enough people reach that state, then the society's energy and efforts become counter-productive. The result we are seeing is that the attempt to achieve a constantly higher standard of living has resulted in a lower quality of life for all, partially through pollution. This fact, admittedly, is little comfort to those who have not yet arrived at a tolerable level of life and for whom the aspiration to raise their standard of living is a real good; the present point, however, is that at least beyond a certain level the principle cannot be achieved and if acted on may serve to produce more harm than good. (The related problem of inequity in a society will be considered further under the fourth interpretation.)

2) The interpretation of the principle which expresses the hope of parents that their children will have a better life than they suffers the same fate as the preceding interpretation. Where the level of life is already good, the desire that their children's be even better may well be questionable for the reasons we have already seen. Children, of course, have no right to be better off than their parents, although those who are badly off might well wish those they love to enjoy more of the goods of life than they themselves have.

If some generation is to enjoy a higher standard of living than others, however, it is not necessary that it always be some future generation. The desire that some future generation of human beings should be better off than present generations may be the desire of some members of present generations. But it is nothing owed to future generations. Some parents sacrifice themselves and deny themselves for the benefit of their children; some carefully save their wealth only to have their children squander it. In some cases such self-sacrifice is noble and evokes our praise; in others, it is foolish. But any such case of self-sacrifice is above the demands of duty, as is obvious when we see children attempting to demand such sacrifice from their parents as if it were their right. Nor does any parent or group have the right through legislation to demand such sacrifice from others for his own or for other people's children.

3) The view that at least some men should live at constantly higher levels so as to push mankind constantly forward seems hardly defensible for a number of reasons. The first is that it is difficult to describe what a constantly higher standard of living could mean for only a few since their lives are so closely connected to other men and to the energy, pollution, and population problems they all face. Secondly, standard of living is not the same as qualify of life. Simple increase in the standard of living, if measured by the goods one has, simply does not make much sense beyond a certain point. For one's needs beyond that point are artificial, and it is not at all clear that satisfying them makes one happier or more comfortable or any of the other things that an increase in the standard of living is supposed to do, and for which reasons it is desired as a good. Thirdly, it can well be argued that it is unlikely that the constantly higher standard advocated for the few—if sense can be made of it—will help do anything but increase the difference between the level of life of the haves and the have-nots. If taken to mean not that a few men in an advanced industrial society should push mankind forward but that the advanced industrial societies should continue to advance at the expense of the non-industrial societies, then this seems to go clearly against the rights of the latter, and so not be a worthy end at all.

4) The fourth interpretation is the most plausible and has the most vocal defenders today. It maintains that all men in a given society (and ideally throughout the world) should be brought up to a certain constantly rising minimal level of life—at least constantly rising for the foreseeable future, given the wide distance between the level of life of the haves and the have-nots. This is the impetus behind minimum income legislation on the American domestic scene. Globally, it affects the relations between have and have-not countries, between the industrially developed and the underdeveloped countries, and is one of the bases for advocating foreign aid programs of various sorts.

The right of all men to a minimal standard of living is one that I would argue in favor of. But my present concern is to note that the right to a constantly rising minimum is contingent upon the ability of the earth and of society to provide it. If world resources are able to adequately sustain only a limited number of people, and if more than that number are born, the distribution of goods, cannot extend sufficiently far; and those societies which contributed most to the overpopulation of their land and of the earth in general may well have to bear the brunt of the evil consequences.

A continuously rising standard of living therefore is never a right, not always a good, and most often simply one good to be measured against other goods and available resources.

IV

What then, if anything, do we owe future generations? We do not owe them a better life than we enjoy, nor do we owe them resources which we need for ourselves.

When dealing with renewable resources a sound principle might be that, other things being equal, they should not be used up at a faster rate than that at which they can be replaced. But when they are needed at a greater rate than that at which they can be replaced, rationing is insufficient and they raise a problem similar to that raised by non-renewable resources. One can argue that the latter should be used up sufficiently slowly so that there are always reserves; but this may mean using less and less each year or decade, despite increasing demand. An alternative is simply to use what we need, attempting to keep our needs rational, and to face crucially diminished supplies when we are forced to face them, hoping in the meantime that some substitutes will be discovered or developed.

Frequently problems of this type have been approached from a utilitarian point of view, and such an approach is instructive. Let each man count for one, the argument goes, whether he be a present man or a future man. The happiness of each is on a par as far as importance and intrinsic goodness are concerned. But increasing the sum of total happiness is better than its opposite. If by increased growth or unlimited use now of limited resources we increase our happiness by a small amount, but doom those who come after us to struggling along without some important natural resources; and if by conserving our natural resources now our happiness or at least that part which is made up of comfort is somewhat less than it could be, but the happiness of many million or billions who come after us is greater than it would otherwise be, then the moral thing to do is to conserve our resources now and share them with future generations.

This argument presupposes first that there will be the future generations it hypothesizes, that these future generations will want pretty much the same things that we do in order to be happy, that they will not overuse the goods of the earth, and that they will not be able to find any suitable substitutes. If we saved only to have them squander, then no more good might be achieved than if we had spent liberally and they had proportionally less; or if they find, e.g., alternate energy sources, then our penury resulted in less good than there might have been.

In earlier times the ploy of this kind of argument was to trade on the happiness of countless generations in the future as a result of some sacrifice of our happiness now. But there are now a sufficient number of doubts about there being future generations, about their not finding alternative resources, and about our present sacrifices leading to their happiness (since there might be so many of them anyway) as to render the argument less convincing than it might formerly have been.

In any calculus of pleasure or good there is no necessity for future generations to enjoy a higher standard of living at the expense of present generations. If there will be a peak in the standard somewhere along the line, followed by a decline, it might just as well be the present generation which enjoys the peak through the utilization of resources, which, since limited, will be used up sooner or later. There is no greater good served by future generations being the peak since obviously when it comes to their turn, if it is improper for us to enjoy more than our successors, and if this is the proper way to feel, they should feel so also.

Both because of these considerations and because of the large number of unknowables concerning the future, short range considerations are surer and more pertinent than long range considerations. The threshold of pollution has been recently crossed so that it is now obvious that something must be done; legislation consequently is being passed. The amount and kind of pollution to be tolerated, the resources to be rationed or preserved should not be decided in terms of far distant needs or requirements but in terms of present and near-future needs and requirement.

Production involves wastes which have now reached the pollution stage. Its control is costly. The cost must be borne either by the producer (who will pass it on to the consumer) or by society at large through the taxes required, e.g., to purify water. The principle that whoever causes the pollution must pay for cleaning it up, or that no production should be allowed without the mechanism provided to prevent pollution, will make some kinds of production unprofitable. In this case, if such production is considered necessary or desirable, it will have to be subsidized. If society cannot pay for total cleanup it might have to settle for less than it would like; or it might have to give up some of its production or some of the goods to which it had become accustomed; or it might have to forego some of the products it might otherwise produce. Such choices should not be made a priori or by the fiat of government, but by the members of society at large or by as many of them interested and aware and informed enough to help in the decision making process.

There are presently available the means nationally for allocating resources and for controlling use and production through automatic market and natural mechanisms as well as through legislation. Where legislation poses the greatest difficulty is not on the national level but on the international level. For technology has brought us into one closely interdependent world faster than the social and legal mechanisms for solving the world-wide problems of resources, population, and pollution have been able to develop.

The problems posed by the ecological challenge are many and complex. But in dealing with them it should be clear that we owe nothing **to** those who do not yet and may never exist; that nonetheless we do have an obligation to promote the continuance of the human race, and so have an obligation **for** those whom we produce; that though at least minimum standards of living for all are desirable, if some generation is to enjoy the peak it need not be other generations; and that the choice of how to use our resources and continue or control our pollution depends on the price all those concerned wish to pay and the values we wish to espouse and promote.

James P. Sterba

THE WELFARE RIGHTS OF DISTANT PEOPLES AND FUTURE GENERATIONS

James P. Sterba argues that welfare rights of distant peoples and future generations are justified on the basis of a right to life and a right to fair treatment. Sterba contends that whether a right to life is interpreted as a negative right (as libertarians tend to do) or as a positive right (as welfare liberals tend to do) it is possible to show that this right justifies welfare rights which would amply provide for the basic needs of distant peoples and future generations. He also indicates what is required for meeting a person's basic needs and explains how these requirements can vary from society to society and from time to time.

IN ORDER TO FORMULATE social policies to deal with issues like population control, world hunger and energy consumption, we clearly need solutions to many difficult and perplexing problems. Not the least of these problems is the determination of the moral side-constraints we should observe by virtue of our relationship to persons who are separated from us in space (distant peoples) and time (future generations). In this paper I wish, firstly, to show how these side-constraints, which I shall call "the welfare rights of distant peoples and future generations," can be grounded on fundamental moral requirements to which many of us are already committed and, secondly, to determine some of the practical requirements of these side-constraints for the issues of population control and world hunger.

THE WELFARE RIGHTS OF DISTANT PEOPLES

It used to be argued that the welfare rights of distant peoples would eventually be met as a byproduct of the continued economic growth of the technologically developed societies of the world. It was believed that the transfer of investment and technology to the less developed societies of the world would eventually, if not make everyone well off, at least satisfy everyone's basic needs. Now we are not so sure. Presently more and more evidence points to the conclusion that without some substantial sacrifice on the part of the technologically developed societies of the world, many of the less developed societies will never be able to provide their members with even the basic necessities for survival. For example, according to a study prepared by the World Bank in 1979, depending on the growth of world trade, between 470 and 710 million people will be living in conditions of absolute poverty as the 21st century dawns, unless, that is, the technologically developed societies of the world adopt some plausible policy of redistribution.[1] Even those, like Herman Kahn, who argue that an almost utopian world situation will obtain in the distant future, still would have to admit that unless some plausible policy of redistribution is adopted, malnutrition and starvation will continue in the less developed societies for many years to come.[2] Thus, a recognition of the welfare rights of distant peoples would appear to have significant consequences for developed and underdeveloped societies alike.

Of course, there are various senses in which distant peoples can be said to have welfare rights and various moral grounds on which those rights can be justified. First of all, the welfare rights of distant peoples can be understood to be either negative rights or positive rights.[3] A negative right is a right not to be interfered with in some specific manner.

From "The Welfare Rights of Distant Peoples and Future Generations: Moral Side-Constraints on Social Policy," *Social Theory and Practice* (1981), pp. 99–119. Reprinted by permission of *Social Theory and Practice*.

For example, a right to liberty is usually understood to be a negative right; it guarantees each person the right not to have her liberty interfered with provided that she does not unjustifiably interfere with the liberty of any other person. On the other hand, a positive right is a right to receive some specific goods or services. Typical positive rights are the right to have a loan repaid and the right to receive one's just earnings. Secondly, the welfare rights of distant peoples can be understood to be either *in personam* rights or *in rem* rights. *In personam* rights are rights that hold against some specific namable person or persons while *in rem* rights hold against everyone who is in a position to abide by the rights in question. A right to liberty is usually understood to be an *in rem* right while the right to have a loan repaid or the right to receive one's just earnings are typical *in personam* rights. Finally, the rights of distant peoples can be understood to be either legal rights, that is, rights that *are enforced* by coercive sanctions, or moral rights, that is, rights that *ought to be enforced* either simply by noncoercive sanctions (for example, verbal condemnations) or by both coercive and noncoercive sanctions. Accordingly, what distinguishes the moral rights of distant peoples from the requirements of supererogation (the nonfulfillment of which is never blameworthy) is that the former but not the latter can be justifiably enforced either by noncoercive or by coercive and noncoercive sanctions. Since we will be primarily concerned with the moral rights of distant peoples to a certain minimum of welfare, hereafter "right(s)" should be understood as short for "moral right(s)."

Of the various moral grounds for justifying the welfare rights of distant peoples, quite possibly the most evident are those which appeal either to a right to life or a right to fair treatment.[4] Indeed, whether a person's right to life is interpreted as a negative right (as libertarians tend to do)[5] or as a positive right (as welfare liberals tend to do)[6], it is possible to show that the right justifies welfare rights that would amply provide for a person's basic needs. Alternatively, it is possible to justify those same welfare rights on the basis of a person's positive right to fair treatment.

Thus suppose that a person's right to life is a positive right. So understood the person's right to life would most plausibly be interpreted as a right to receive those goods and resources that are necessary for satisfying her basic needs. For a person's basic needs are those which must be satisfied in order not to seriously endanger her health or sanity. Thus receiving the goods and resources that are necessary for satisfying her basic needs would preserve a person's life in the fullest sense. And if a person's positive right to life is to be universal in the sense that it is possessed by every person (as the right to life is generally understood to be) then it must be an *in rem* right. This is because an *in rem* right, unlike an *in personam* right, does not require for its possession the assumption by other persons of any special roles or contractual obligations. Interpreted as a positive *in rem* right, therefore, a person's right to life would clearly justify the welfare rights of distant peoples to have their basic needs satisfied.

Suppose, on the other hand, that a person's right to life is a negative right. Here again, if the right is to be universal in the sense that it is possessed by all persons then it must also be an *in rem* right. So understood the right would require that everyone who is in a position to do so not interfere in certain ways with a person's attempts to meet her basic needs.

But what sort of noninterference would this right to life justify? If one's basic needs have not been met, would a person's right to life require that others not interfere with her taking the goods she needs from the surplus possessions of those who already have satisfied their own basic needs? As it is standardly interpreted, a person's negative right to life would not require such noninterference. Instead, a person's negative right to life is usually understood to be limited in such circumstances by the property rights of those who have more than enough to satisfy their own basic needs.[7] Moreover, those who claim property rights to such surplus goods and resources are usually in a position to effectively prohibit those in need from taking what they require. For surely most underdeveloped nations of the world would be able to sponsor expeditions to the American Midwest or the Australian Plains for the purpose of collecting the grain necessary to satisfy the basic needs of their citizens if they were not effectively prohibited from doing so at almost every stage of the enterprise.

But are persons with such surplus goods and resources normally justified in so prohibiting others from satisfying their basic needs? Admittedly, such persons may have contributed greatly to the value of the surplus goods and resources they possess, but why should that give them power over the life and death of those less fortunate? While their contribution may well justify favoring their nonbasic needs over the nonbasic needs of others, how could it justify favoring their nonbasic needs over the basic needs of others? After all, a person's negative right to life, being an *in rem* right, does not depend on the assumption by other persons of any special roles or contractual obligations. By contrast, property rights that are *in personam* rights require the assumption by other persons of the relevant roles and contractual obligations which constitute a particular system of acquisition and exchange, such as the role of a neighbor and the obligations of a merchant. Consequently, with respect to such property rights, it would seem that a person could not justifiably be kept from acquiring the goods and resources necessary to satisfy her basic needs by the property rights of others to surplus possessions, unless the person herself had voluntarily agreed to be so constrained by those property rights. But obviously few people would voluntarily agree to have such constraints placed upon their ability to acquire the goods and resources necessary to satisfy their basic needs. For most people their right to acquire the goods and resources necessary to satisfy their basic needs would have priority over any other person's property rights to surplus possessions, or alternatively, they would conceive of property rights such that no one could have property rights to any surplus possessions which were required to satisfy their own basic needs.

Even if some property rights could arise, as *in rem* rights by a Lockean process of mixing one's labor with previously unowned goods and resources, there would still be a need for some sort of a restriction on such appropriations. For if these *in rem* property rights are to be *moral rights* then it must be reasonable for every affected party to accept such rights, since the requirements of morality cannot be contrary to reason. Accordingly, in order to give rise to *in rem* property rights, the appropriation of previously unowned goods and resources cannot justifiably limit anyone's ability to acquire the goods and resources necessary to satisfy her basic needs, unless it would be reasonable for the person to voluntarily agree to be so constrained. But obviously it would not be reasonable for many people, particularly those whose basic needs are not being met, to voluntarily agree

to be so constrained by property rights. This means that whether property rights are *in personam* rights and arise by the assumption of the relevant roles and contractual obligations or are *in rem* rights and arise by a Lockean process of mixing one's labor with previously unowned goods and resources, such rights would rarely limit a negative right to life, interpreted as an *in rem* right to noninterference with one's attempts to acquire the goods and resources necessary to satisfy one's basic needs. So interpreted, a negative right to life would clearly justify the welfare rights of distant peoples.

If we turn to a consideration of a person's right to fair treatment, a similar justification of the welfare rights of distant peoples emerges. To determine the requirements of fair treatment, suppose we employ a decision procedure analogous to the one John Rawls developed in *A Theory of Justice*.[8] Suppose, that is to say, that in deciding upon the requirements of fair treatment, we were to discount the knowledge of which particular interests happen to be our own. Since we obviously know what our particular interests are, we would just not be taking that knowledge into account when selecting the requirements for fair treatment. Rather, in selecting these requirements, we would be reasoning from our knowledge of all the particular interests of everyone who would be affected by our decision but not from our knowledge of which particular interests happen to be our own. In employing this decision procedure, therefore, we (like judges who discount prejudicial information in order to reach fair decisions) would be able to give a fair hearing to everyone's particular interests. Assuming further that we are well-informed of the particular interests that would be affected by our decision and are fully capable of rationally deliberating with respect to that information, then our deliberations would culminate in a unanimous decision. This is because each of us would be deliberating in a rationally correct manner with respect to the same information and would be using a decision procedure leading to a uniform evaluation of the alternatives. Consequently, each of us would favor the same requirements for fair treatment.

But what requirements would we select by using this decision procedure? Since by employing this decision procedure we would not be using our knowledge of which particular interests happen to be our own, we would be quite concerned about the pattern according to which goods and resources would be distributed throughout the world. By using this decision procedure, we would reason as though our particular interests might be those of persons with the largest share of goods and resources as well as those of persons with the smallest share of goods and resources. Consequently, we would neither exclusively favor the interests of persons with the largest share of goods by endorsing an unlimited right to accumulate goods and resources nor exclusively favor the interests of persons with the smallest share of goods and resources by endorsing the highest possible minimum for those who are least advantaged. Rather we would compromise by endorsing a right to accumulate goods and resources that was limited by the guarantee of a minimum sufficient to provide each person with the goods and resources necessary to satisfy his or her basic needs.[9] It seems clear, therefore, that a right to fair treatment as captured by this Rawlsian decision procedure would also justify the welfare rights of distant peoples.

What the preceding arguments have shown is that the welfare rights of distant peoples can be firmly grounded either in each person's right to life or each person's right to fair treatment. As a result, it would be impossible for one to deny that distant peoples have welfare rights without also denying that each person has a right to life and a right to fair treatment, unless, that is, one drastically reinterprets the significance of a right to life and a right to fair treatment.[10]

THE WELFARE RIGHTS OF FUTURE GENERATIONS

At first glance, the welfare rights of future generations appear to be just as firmly grounded as the welfare rights of distant peoples. For assuming that there will be future generations, then, they, like generations presently existing, will have their basic needs that must be satisfied. And just as we are now able to make provision for the basic needs of distant peoples, so likewise we are now able to make provision for the basic needs of future generations (for example, through capital investment and the conservation of resources). Consequently, it would seem that there are equally good grounds for taking into account the basic needs of future generations as there are for taking into account the basic needs of distant peoples.

But there is a problem. How can we claim that future generations *now* have rights that we make provision for their basic needs when they don't presently exist? How is it possible for persons who don't yet exist to have rights against those who do? For example, suppose we continue to use up the earth's resources at present or even greater rates, and, as a result, it turns out that the most pessimistic forecasts for the 22nd century are realized.[11] This means that future generations will face widespread famine, depleted resources, insufficient new technology to handle the crisis, and a drastic decline in the quality of life for nearly everyone. If this were to happen, could persons living in the 22nd century legitimately claim that we in the 20th century violated their rights by not restraining our consumption of the world's resources? Surely it would be odd to say that we violated their rights over one hundred years before they existed. But what exactly is the oddness?

Is it that future generations generally have no way of claiming their rights against existing generations? While this does make the recognition and enforcement of rights much more difficult (future generations would need strong advocates in the existing generations), it does not make it impossible for there to be such rights. After all, it is quite obvious that the recognition and enforcement of the rights of distant peoples is a difficult task as well.

Or is it that we don't believe that rights can legitimately exercise their influence over long durations of time? But if we can foresee and control at least some of the effects our actions will have on the ability of future generations to satisfy their basic needs then why should we not be responsible for those same effects? And if we are responsible for them then why should not future generations have a right that we take them into account?

Perhaps what troubles us is that future generations don't exist when their rights are said to demand action. But how else could persons have a right to benefit from the effects our actions will have in the distant future if they did not exist just when those effects would be felt? Those who exist contemporaneously with us could not legitimately make the same demand upon us, for they will not be around to experience those effects. Only future generations could have a right that the effects our actions will have in the distant future contribute to satisfying their basic needs. Nor need we assume that in order for persons to have rights, they must exist when their rights demand action. Thus, to say that future generations have rights against existing generations we can simply mean that there are enforceable requirements upon existing generations that would benefit or prevent harm to future generations.[12]

Yet most likely what really bothers us is that we cannot know for sure what effects our actions will have on future generations. For example, we may at some cost to ourselves conserve resources that will be of little value to future generations who have developed different technologies. Or, because we regard them as useless, we may destroy or deplete resources that future generations will find to be essential to their well-being. However, we should not allow such possibilities to blind us to the necessity for a social policy in this regard. After all, whatever we do will have its effect on future generations. The best approach, therefore, is to use the knowledge that we presently have and assume that future generations will also require those basic resources we now find to be valuable. If it turns out that future generations will require different resources to meet their basic needs from those we were led to expect, then at least we will not be blamable for acting on the basis of the knowledge we had.[13]

As in the case of the welfare rights of distant peoples, we can justify the welfare rights of future generations by appealing either to a right to life or to a right to fair treatment.

Justifying the welfare rights of future generations on the basis of a right to life presents no new problems. As we have seen, a right to life applied to distant peoples is a positive *in rem* right of existing persons to receive the goods and resources necessary to satisfy their basic needs or a negative *in rem* right of existing persons to noninterference with their attempts to acquire the goods and resources necessary to satisfy their basic needs. Accordingly, assuming that by "future generations" we mean "those whom we can reasonably expect to come into existence," then a right to life applied to future generations would be a right of persons whom we can definitely expect to exist to receive the goods and resources necessary to satisfy their basic needs or to noninter-

ference with their attempts to acquire the goods and resources necessary to satisfy their basic needs. Understood in this way, a right to life of future generations would justify the welfare rights of future generations for much the same reasons that a right to life of distant peoples justifies the welfare rights of distant peoples. For future generations clearly have not voluntarily agreed nor would it be reasonable for them to voluntarily agree to have their ability to receive or acquire the goods and resources necessary to satisfy their basic needs limited by the property rights of existing generations to surplus possessions. Thus a right to life of future generations, interpreted either as a positive *in rem* right or a negative *in rem* right, would clearly justify the welfare rights of future generations to have their basic needs satisfied.

To determine the requirements of fair treatment for future generations, suppose we adapt the decision procedure used before to determine the requirements of fair treatment for distant peoples. That procedure required that in reaching decisions we discount our knowledge of which particular interests happen to be our own. Yet discounting such knowledge would not be sufficient to guarantee a fair result for future generations unless we also discounted the knowledge that we are contemporaries. For otherwise, even without using our knowledge of which particular interests happen to be our own, we could unfairly favor existing generations over future generations. Employing this now modified decision procedure, we would find it rational to endorse a right to accumulate goods and resources that was limited so as to provide each generation with a minimum of goods and resources necessary to satisfy the basic needs of the persons belonging to that generation. In this way, a right to fair treatment, as captured by this decision procedure, would justify the welfare rights of future generations.

FUTURE GENERATIONS AND POPULATION CONTROL

The welfare rights of future generations are also closely connected with the population policy of existing generations. For example, under a population policy that places restrictions on the size of families and requires genetic screening, some persons will not be brought into existence who otherwise would have come into existence. Thus, the membership of future generations will surely be affected by whatever population policy existing generations adopt. Given that the size and genetic health of future generations will obviously affect their ability to provide for their basic needs, the welfare rights of future generations would require existing generations to adopt a population policy that takes these factors into account.

But what population policy should existing generations adopt? There are two policies that many philosophers have found attractive.[14] Each policy represents a version of utilitarianism and each has its own difficulties. One policy requires population to increase or decrease so as to produce the largest total net utility possible. The other policy requires population to increase or decrease so as to produce the highest average net utility possible. The main difficulty with the policy of total utility is that it would justify any increase in population—even if, as a result, the lives of most people were not very happy—so long as some increase in total utility were produced. On the other hand, the main difficulty with the policy of average utility is that it would not allow persons to be brought into existence—even if they would be quite happy—unless the utility of their lives were equal or greater than the average. Clearly what is needed is a policy that avoids both of these difficulties.

Peter Singer has recently proposed a population policy designed to do just that—a policy designed to restrict the increase of population more than the policy of total utility but less than the policy of average utility.[15] Singer's policy justifies increasing a population of M members to a population of M + N members only if M of the M + N members would have at least as much utility as the population of M members had initially.

At first it might seem that Singer's population policy provides the desired compromise. For his policy does not require increases in population to meet or surpass the average utility of the original population. Nor does his policy seem to justify every increase in population that increases total utility but only those increases that do not provide less utility to members equal in number to the original population. But the success of Singer's compromise is only apparent. As Derek Parfit has shown, Singer's policy

shares with the policy of total utility the same tendency to increase population in the face of continually declining average utility.[16]

For consider a population with just two members: Abe and Edna. Imagine that Abe and Edna were deliberating whether to have a child and they calculated that if they had a child

1. the utility of the child's life would be somewhat lower than the average utility of their own lives.
2. the child would have no net effect on the total utility of their own lives taken together.

Applied to these circumstances, Singer's population policy would clearly justify bringing the child into existence. But suppose, further, that after the birth of Clyde, their first child, Abe and Edna were deliberating whether to have a second child and they calculated that if they had a second child

1. the utility of the child's life would be somewhat lower than the utility of Clyde's life
2. the child would have no net effect on the total utility of their own lives and Clyde's taken together.

Given these circumstances, Singer's policy would again justify bringing this second child into existence. And if analogous circumstances obtained on each of the next ten occasions that Abe and Edna consider the question of whether to bring additional children into existence, Singer's population policy would continue to justify adding new children irrespective of the general decline in average utility resulting from each new addition to Abe and Edna's family. Thus Singer's policy has the same undesirable result as the policy of total utility. It avoids the severe restriction on population increase of the policy of average utility but fails to restrict existing generations from bringing into existence persons who would not be able to enjoy even a certain minimum of well-being.

Fortunately a policy with the desired restrictions can be grounded on the welfare rights of future generations. As we have seen, the welfare rights of future generations require existing generations to make provision for the basic needs of future generations. As a result, existing generations would have to evaluate their ability to provide both for their own basic needs and for the basic needs of future generations.

Since existing generations by bringing persons into existence would be determining the membership of future generations, they would have to evaluate whether they are able to provide for that membership. Existing generations should not have to sacrifice the satisfaction of their basic needs for the sake of future generations, although they would be required to sacrifice some of their nonbasic needs on this account. Thus, if existing generations believe that were population to increase beyond a certain point, they would lack sufficient resources to make the necessary provision for each person's basic needs, then it would be incumbent upon them to restrict the membership of future generations so as not to exceed their ability to provide for each person's basic needs. For if the rights of future generations were respected, the membership of future generations would never increase beyond the ability of existing generations to make the necessary provision for the basic needs of future generations.

But this is to indicate only the "negative half" of the population policy that is grounded on the welfare rights of future generations, that is, the obligation to limit the size of future generations so as not to exceed the ability of existing generations to provide for the basic needs of future generations. The "positive half" of that population policy, which I have defended elsewhere,[17] is the obligation of existing generations, once their basic needs have been met, to bring into existence additional persons whose basic needs could also be met.

Thus, not only are the welfare rights of future generations clearly justified on the basis of each person's right to life and each person's right to fair treatment, but also these welfare rights in turn justify a population policy that provides an alternative to the policies of average and total utility.

WELFARE RIGHTS AND BASIC NEEDS

It has been argued that the welfare rights of distant peoples and future generations can be justified on the basis of a right to life and a right to fair treatment. Since these welfare rights are understood to be rights to receive or to acquire those goods and resources necessary for satisfying the basic needs of distant peoples and future generations, it is important to get a better understanding of what is necessary for the satisfaction of a person's basic needs in order to more fully appreciate the implications of these welfare rights.

Now a person's basic needs are those which must be satisfied in order not to seriously endanger the person's health and sanity. Thus, the needs a person has for food, shelter, medical care, protection, companionship and self-development are at least in part needs of this sort. Naturally, societies vary in their ability to satisfy a person's basic needs, but the needs themselves would not seem to be similarly subject to variation unless there were a corresponding variation in what constitutes health and sanity in different societies. Consequently, even though the criterion of need would not be an acceptable standard for distributing all social goods because, among other things, of the difficulty of determining both what a person's nonbasic needs are and how they should be arranged according to priority, the criterion does appear to be an acceptable standard for determining the minimum of goods and resources each person has a right to receive or acquire.

Actually, specifying a minimum of this sort seems to be the goal of the poverty index used in the United States since 1964.[18] This poverty index is based on the U.S. Department of Agriculture's Economy Food Plan (for an adequate diet) and on evidence showing that low income families spend about one-third of their income on food. The index is then adjusted from time to time to take into account changing prices. However, in order to accord with the goal of satisfying basic needs, the poverty index would have to be further adjusted to take into account 1) that the Economy Food Plan was developed for "temporary or emergency use" and is inadequate for a permanent diet and 2) that, according to recent evidence, low income families spend one-fourth rather than one-third of their income on food.[19]

Of course, one might think that a minimum should be specified in terms of a standard of living that is purely conventional and varies over time and between societies. Benn and Peters, following this approach, have suggested specifying a minimum in terms of the income received by the most numerous group in a society.[20] For example, in the United

States today the greatest number of household units falls within the $15,000 to $24,999 bracket (in 1979 dollars).[21] Specifying a minimum in this way, however, leads to certain difficulties. Thus, suppose that the most numerous group of household units in society with the wealth of the United States fell within a $500–$999 income bracket (in 1979 dollars). Certainly, it would not thereby follow that a guarantee of $1,000 per household unit would constitute an acceptable minimum for such a society. Or suppose that the income of the most numerous group of household units in such a society fell within the $95,000–$100,000 income bracket (in 1979 dollars). Certainly, a minimum of $100,000 per household unit would not thereby be required. Moreover, there seem to be similar difficulties with any attempt to specify an acceptable minimum in a purely conventional manner.

Nevertheless, it still seems that an acceptable minimum should vary over time and between societies at least to some degree. For example, it could be argued that today a car is almost a necessity in the typical North American household, which was not true fifty years ago nor is it true today in most other areas of the world. Happily, a basic needs approach to specifying an acceptable minimum can account for such variation without introducing any variation into the definition of the basic needs themselves. Instead, variation enters into the cost of satisfying these needs at different times and in different societies.[22] For in the same society at different times and in different societies at the same time, the normal costs of satisfying a person's basic needs can and do vary considerably. These variations are due in large part to the different ways in which the most readily available means for satisfying people's basic needs are produced. For example, in more affluent societies, the most readily available means for satisfying a person's basic needs are usually processed so as to satisfy nonbasic needs at the same time that they satisfy basic needs. This processing is carried out to make the means more attractive to persons in higher income brackets who can easily afford the extra cost. As a result, the most readily available means for satisfying people's basic needs are much more costly in more affluent societies than they are in less affluent societies. This occurs most obviously with respect to the most readily available means for satisfying people's basic needs for food, shelter and transporta-

tion, but it also occurs with respect to the most readily available means for satisfying people's basic needs for companionship, self-esteem and self-development. For a person cannot normally satisfy even these latter needs in more affluent societies without participating in at least some relatively costly educational and social development practices. Accordingly, there will be considerable variation in the normal costs of satisfying a person's basic needs as a society becomes more affluent over time, and considerable variation at the same time in societies at different levels of affluence. Consequently, a basic needs approach to specifying an acceptable minimum would guarantee each person the goods and resources necessary to meet the normal costs of satisfying his basic needs in the society in which he lives.

WELFARE RIGHTS AND WORLD HUNGER

We have seen that the welfare rights of distant peoples and future generations guarantee each person a minimum of goods and resources necessary to meet the normal costs of satisfying her basic needs in the society in which she lives. Let us now determine some of the practical implications of these welfare rights for the issue of world hunger.

At present there is probably a sufficient worldwide supply of goods and resources to meet the normal costs of satisfying the basic nutritional needs of all existing persons in the societies in which they live. According to the former U.S. Secretary of Agriculture, Bob Bergland,

For the past 20 years, if the available world food supply had been evenly divided and distributed, each person would have received more than the minimum number of calories.

In fact, the 4 billion people who inhabited the world in 1978 had available about one-fifth more food per person to eat than the world's 2.7 billion had 25 years ago.[23]

Other authorities have made similar assessments of the available world food supply.[24] In fact, it has been projected that if all arable land were optimally utilized a population of between 38 and 48 billion people could be supported.[25]

Needless to say, the adoption of a policy of meeting the basic nutritional needs of all existing persons would necessitate significant changes, especially in developed societies. For example, the large percentage of the U.S. population whose food consumption clearly exceeds even an adequately adjusted poverty index would have to substantially alter their eating habits. In particular, they would have to reduce their consumption of beef and pork so as to make more grain available for direct human consumption. (Presently the amount of grain fed American livestock is as much as all the people of China and India eat in a year.) Thus, at least the satisfaction of some of the nonbasic needs of the more advantaged in developed societies would have to be foregone so that the basic nutritional needs of all existing persons in developing and underdeveloped societies could be met.

Such changes, however, may still have little effect on the relative costs of satisfying people's basic needs in different societies. For even after the basic nutritional needs of all existing persons have been met, the normal costs of satisfying basic needs would still tend to be greater in developed societies than in developing and underdeveloped societies. This is because the most readily available means for satisfying basic needs in developed societies would still tend to be more processed to satisfy nonbasic needs along with basic needs. Nevertheless, once the basic nutritional needs of future generations are also taken into account, then the satisfaction of the nonbasic needs of the more advantaged in developed societies would have to be further restricted in order to preserve the fertility of cropland and other food-related natural resources for the use of future generations.[26] And once basic needs other than nutritional needs are taken into account as well, still further restrictions would be required. For example, it has been estimated that presently a North American uses fifty times more resources than an Indian. This means that in terms of resource consumption the North American continent's population is the equivalent of 12.5 billion Indians.[27] Obviously, this would have to be radically altered if the basic needs of distant peoples and future generations are to be met. Thus, eventually the practice of utilizing more and more efficient means of satisfying people's basic needs in

developed societies would appear to have the effect of equalizing the normal costs of meeting people's basic needs across societies.[28]

Although the general character of the changes required to meet the basic nutritional needs of distant peoples and future generations seems clear enough, there is still the problem of deciding between alternative strategies for carrying out these changes. Since each of these strategies would impose somewhat different burdens on developed societies and different burdens on different groups within those societies, the fundamental problem is to decide exactly whose nonbasic needs should be sacrificed in order to meet the basic needs of distant peoples and future generations. While there is no easy solution to this problem, alternative strategies for meeting the basic needs of distant peoples and future generations could be fairly evaluated by means of the Rawlsian decision procedure that was used before to justify the welfare rights of distant peoples and future generations. In using this procedure, we would be deciding which particular strategy for meeting the basic needs of distant peoples and future generations would be preferred by persons who discounted the knowledge of the society to which they belonged. Thus, the particular strategies that would be selected by this decision procedure should adequately take into account the competing interests within and between existing generations and future generations.

While the requirements, with respect to world hunger, that the welfare rights of distant peoples and future generations place upon those in developed affluent societies are obviously quite severe, they are not unconditional. For those in developing and underdeveloped societies are under a corresponding obligation to do what they can to meet their own basic nutritional needs, for example, by bringing all arable land under optimal cultivation and by controlling population growth. However, we should not be unreasonable in judging what particular developing and underdeveloping societies have managed to accomplish in this regard. For in the final analysis, such societies should be judged on the basis of what they have managed to accomplish, *given the options available to them*. For example, developing and underdeveloped societies today do not have the option, which Western European societies had during most of the last two centuries, of exporting their excess population to sparsely populated and resource rich continents. In this and other respects, developing and underdeveloped societies today lack many of the options Western European societies were able to utilize in the course of their economic and social development. Consequently, in judging what developing and underdeveloped societies have managed to accomplish we must take into account the options that they actually had available to them in their particular circumstances. In practice, this will mean, for example, that it is not reasonable to expect such societies to reduce their population growth as fast as would ideally be desirable. Nevertheless, at some point, it should be reasonable to expect that all existing persons accept the population policy proposed earlier, according to which the membership of future generations would never be allowed to increase beyond the ability of existing generations to make the necessary provision for the basic needs of future generations. In the meantime, it may be necessary in order to meet the basic needs of at least a temporarily growing world population to utilize renewable resources beyond what would secure their maximal sustainable yield. (Presently, certain renewable resources, such as fishing resources, are being so utilized for far less justifiable ends.) This, of course,

would have the effect of reducing the size of succeeding generations that, according to the proposed population policy, could justifiably be brought into existence. But while such an effect obviously is not ideally desirable, it surely seems morally preferable to allowing existing persons to starve to death in order to increase the size of succeeding generations that could justifiably be brought into existence.[29]

In conclusion, what has been shown is 1) that the welfare rights of distant peoples and future generations, understood as the right of distant peoples and future generations to receive or acquire the goods and resources that are necessary to meet the normal costs of satisfying their basic needs in the society in which they live, can be justified on the basis of a right to life and a right to fair treatment, and 2) that these welfare rights can be used to justify certain requirements for the issues of population control and world hunger. Thus, given the fundamental nature of the moral foundation for these welfare rights, it would be virtually impossible for many of us to consistently reject these welfare rights with their practical requirements for social policies unless we were to reject in its entirety the moral point of view.[30]

NOTES

1. *The Preliminary Report of the Presidential Commission on World Hunger*, December 1979. Section II, Chapter 3.

2. Herman Kahn, William Brown and Leon Martel, *The Next 200 Years* (New York: William Morrow, 1976), Chapter 2.

3. A distinction that is similar to the distinction between positive and negative rights is the distinction between recipient and action rights. Recipient rights, like positive rights, are rights to receive some specific goods or services. However, action rights are a bit more circumscribed than negative rights. Action rights are rights to act in some specific manner, whereas negative rights include both rights of noninterference with actions (and, hence, imply action rights) and rights of noninterference with things or states of affairs (such as a right to one's good name).

   Having previously used the distinction between recipient and action rights (*The Demands of Justice* [Notre Dame: University of Notre Dame Press, 1980, Chapter 6]), in a defense of welfare rights, I now hope to show, in response to critics, particularly Jan Narveson, that the distinction between positive and negative rights can serve as well in the fuller defense of welfare rights which I am presenting in this paper.

4. For other possibilities, see Onora Nell, "Lifeboat Earth," *Philosophy and Public Affairs*, 4 (Spring 1975): 273–92; Peter Singer, "Famine, Affluence and Morality," *Philosophy and Public Affairs*, 1 (1972): 229–43.

5. See, for example, Robert Nozick, *State Anarchy and Utopia* (New York: Basic Books, 1974), p. 179n.

6. See, for example, Ronald Dworkin, "Liberalism," in *Public and Private Morality*, edited by Stuart Hampshire (Cambridge: Cambridge University Press, 1978), pp. 112–43.

7. This is why a negative right to life is usually understood to impose lesser moral requirements than a positive right to life.

8. John Rawls, *A Theory of Justice* (Cambridge: Harvard University Press, 1971). This Rawlsian decision procedure is only designed to secure a fair consideration of everyone's interests. It does not guarantee that *all* will be better off from following the moral requirements that emerge from using the procedure. Thus, some individuals may be required to make significant sacrifices, particularly during the transition to a more favored distribution of goods and resources. On this point, see *The Demands of Justice*, Chapter 4.

9. For further argument, see "Distributive Justice," *American Journal of Jurisprudence*, 55 (1977):55–79 and *The Demands of Justice*, Chapter 2.

10. Notice that even if one interprets a right to life as simply a right not to be killed unjustly, it could still be plausibly argued that a person's right to life would normally be violated when all other legitimate opportunities for preserving his life have been exhausted if he were then *prevented* by others from taking from their surplus goods and resources what he needs to preserve his life.

11. Donella H. Meadows, Dennis L. Meadows, Jorgen Randers and William W. Behrens III, *The Limits to Growth*, second edition (New York: New American Library, 1974), Chapters 3 and 4.

12. Indeed, right claims need not presuppose that there are any rightholders either in the present or in the future, as in the case of a right not to be born and a right to be born. On this point, see my paper "Abortion, Distant Peoples and Future Generations," *The Journal of Philosophy*, 77 (1980): 424–40 and *The Demands of Justice*, Chapter 6.

13. For a somewhat opposing view, see M. P. Golding, "Obligations to Future Generations," *The Monist*, 56 (1972): 85–99.

14. See Henry Sidgwick, *The Methods of Ethics*. 7th edition. (London: Macmillan, 1907), pp. 414–16; Jan Narveson, "Moral Problems of Population," *The Monist*, 57 (1973): 62–86.

15. Peter Singer, "A Utilitarian Population Principle," in *Ethics and Population*, edited by Michael Bayles (Cambridge: Schenkman, 1976), pp. 81–99.

16. Derek Parfit, "On Doing the Best for Our Children," in *Ethics and Population*, edited by Michael Bayles, pp. 100–15.

17. See "Abortion, Distant Peoples and Future Generations," and *The Demands of Justice*, Chapter 6.

18. See *Old Age Insurance* submitted to the Joint Economic Committee of the Congress of the United States in December, 1967, p. 186, and *Statistical Abstracts of the United States for 1979*, p. 434.

19. See Sar Levitan, *Programs in Aid of the Poor* (Baltimore: Johns Hopkins University Press, 1976), pp. 2–4; David Gordon, "Trends in Poverty" in *Problems in Political Economy: An Urban Perspective*, edited by David Gordon, (Lexington, Mass.: C. Heath, 1971), pp. 297–8; Arthur Simon, *Bread for the World* (New York: Paulist Press, 1975), Chapter 8.

20. S. Benn and R. S. Peters, *The Principles of Political Thought* (New York: The Free Press, 1959), p. 167.

21. *Statistical Abstracts*, p. 434.

22. See Bernard Gendron, *Technology and the Human Condition* (New York: St. Martin's Press, 1977), pp. 222–7.

23. Bob Bergland, "Attacking the Problem of World Hunger," *The National Forum* (1979), vol. 69, No. 2, p. 4.

24. Diana Manning, *Society and Food* (Sevenoaks, Ky.: Butterworths, 1977), p. 12; Arthur Simon, *Bread for the World*, p. 14.

25. Roger Revelle, "Food and Population," *Scientific American*, 231 (September, 1974), p. 168.

26. Lester Brown, "Population, Cropland and Food Prices," *The National Forum* (1979), Vol. 69, No. 2, pp. 11–16.

27. Janet Besecker and Phil Elder, "Lifeboat Ethics: A Reply to Hardin," in *Readings in Ecology, Energy and Human Society: Contemporary Perspectives*, edited by William R. Burch, Jr. (New York: Harper and Row, 1977), p. 229.

28. There definitely are numerous possibilities for utilizing more and more efficient means of satisfying people's basic needs in developed societies. For example, the American food industry manufactured for the U.S. Agriculture Department CSM, a product made of corn, soy and dried milk, which supplied all the necessary nutrients and 70 percent of minimum calorie intake for children. Poverty children throughout the world, but not in the United States, received half a million pounds of this product from us in 1967—at a cost of two cents per day per child. See Nick Kotz, *Let Them Eat Promises* (Englewood Cliffs, N.J.: Prentice-Hall, Inc., 1969), p. 125.

29. The rejected option seems to be the one preferred by Garrett Hardin. See his "Lifeboat Ethics: the Case Against Helping the Poor," in this anthology, pp. 73–79.

30. Earlier versions of this paper were presented to a Conference on World Hunger held in Denver, Colorado, to the Economics Department of the University of Nebraska and to the University Seminar on Human Rights, Columbia University. In wish to thank all of those who commented on various versions of the paper, in particular, Robert Audi, Dolores Martin, Arthur Danto, Brian Barry, Jan Narveson, Paul Martin, Mark Rollins, D. Greenberg and the referees for this journal. I also want to thank the University of Notre Dame for a summer grant which enabled me to complete the penultimate draft of this paper.

Gus Speth

PERSPECTIVES FROM THE *GLOBAL 2000 REPORT*

According to Gus Speth, the *Global 2000 Report* echoes a persistent warning sounded by many others in recent years: "Our international efforts to stem the spread of human poverty, hunger and misery are not achieving their goals; the staggering growth of human population, coupled with ever-increasing human demands, are beginning to cause permanent damage to the planet's resource base." Speth argues that we must respond to this warning by getting serious about the conservation of resources and by pursuing a policy of sustainable economic development which is fair to the interests of the poor.

THROUGHOUT THE PAST DECADE, a wide variety of disturbing studies and reports have been issued by the United Nations, the Worldwatch Institute, the World Bank, the International Union for the Con-

From "Resources and Security: Perspectives from the *Global 2000 Report*," *World Future Society Bulletin* (1981), pp. 1–4. Reprinted by permission of *World Future Society Bulletin*.

servation of Nature and Natural Resources, and other organizations. These reports have sounded a persistent warning: our international efforts to stem the spread of human poverty, hunger and misery are not achieving their goals; the staggering growth of human population, coupled with ever-increasing human demands, are beginning to cause permanent damage to the planet's resource base.

The most recent such warning—and the one with which I am most familiar—was issued in July of 1980 by the Council of Environmental Quality and the U.S. State Department. Called *Global 2000 Report to the President*, it is the result of a three-year effort by more than a dozen agencies of the U.S. Government to make long-term projections across the range of population, resource and environmental concerns. Given the obvious limitations of such projections, the *Global 2000 Report* can best be seen as a reconnaissance of the future. And the results of that reconnaissance are disturbing.

I feel very strongly that the *Global 2000 Reports'* findings confront the United States and other nations with one of the most difficult challenges facing our planet during the next two decades—rivaling the global arms race in importance.

The Report's projections point to continued rapid population growth, with world population increasing from 4.5 billion today to more than 6 billion by 2000. More people will be added to the world's population each day in the year 2000 than were born today—about 100 million a year as compared with 75 million in 1980. Most of these additional people will live in the poorest countries, which will contain about four-fifths of the human race by the end of the century.

Unless other factors intervene, this planetary majority will see themselves growing worse off compared with those living in affluent nations. The income gap between rich and poor nations will widen, and the per capita gross national product of the less-developed countries will remain at generally low levels. In some areas—especially in parts of Latin America and East Asia—income per capita is expected to rise substantially. But gross national product in the great populous nations of South Asia—India, Bangladesh and Pakistan—will be less than $200 per capita (in 1975 dollars) by 2000. Today, some 800 million people live in conditions of absolute poverty, their lives dominated by hunger, ill health, and the absence of hope. By 2000, if current policies remain unchanged, their number could grow by 50 percent.

While the Report projects a 90 percent increase in overall world food production in the 30 years from 1970 to 2000, a global per capita increase of less than 15 percent is projected even for the countries that are already comparatively well-fed. In South Asia, the Middle East, and the poorer countries of Africa, per capita food consumption will increase marginally at best, and in some areas may actually decline below present inadequate levels. Real prices of food are expected to double during the same 30-year period.

The pressures of population and growing human needs and expectations will place increasing strains on the Earth's natural systems and resources. The spread of desert-like conditions due to human activities now claims an area about the size of Maine each year. Croplands are lost to production as soils deteriorate because of erosion, compaction, and water-logging and salinization, and as rural land is converted to other uses.

The increases in world food production projected by the Report are based on improvements in crop yields per acre continuing at the same rate as the record-breaking increases of the post-World War II period. These improvements depended heavily on energy-intensive technologies like fertilizer, pesticides, fuel for tractors and power for irrigation. But the Report's projections show no relief from the world's tight energy situation. World oil production is expected to level off by the 1990s. And for the one-quarter of humanity who depend on wood for fuel, the outlook is bleak. Projected needs for wood will exceed available supplies by about 25 percent before the turn of the century.

The conversion of forested land to agricultural use and the demand for fuelwood and forest products are projected to continue to deplete the world's forests. The Report estimates that these forests are now disappearing at rates as high as 18 to 20 million hectares—an area half the size of California—each year. As much as 40 percent of the remaining forests in poor countries may be gone by 2000. Most of the loss will occur in tropical and subtropical areas.

The loss of tropical forests, along with the impact

of pollution and other pressures on habitats, could cause massive destruction of the planet's genetic resource base. Between 500,000 and two million plant and animal species—15 to 20 percent of all species on Earth—could become extinct by the year 2000. One-half to two-thirds of the extinctions will result from the clearing or deterioration of tropical forests. This would be a massive loss of potentially valuable sources of food, pharmaceutical chemicals, building materials, fuel sources and other irreplaceable resources.

Deforestation and other factors will worsen severe regional water shortages and contribute to the deterioration of water quality. Population growth alone will cause demands for water to at least double from 1971 levels in nearly half of the world.

Industrial growth is likely to worsen air quality. Air pollution in some cities in less-developed countries is already far above levels considered safe by the World Health Organization. Increased burning of fossil fuels, especially coal, may contribute to acid rain damage to lakes, plantlife, and the exteriors of buildings. It also contributes to the increasing concentration of carbon dioxide in the Earth's atmosphere, which could possibly lead to climatic changes with highly disruptive effects on world agriculture. Depletion of the stratospheric ozone layer, attributed partly to chlorofluorocarbon emissions from aerosol cans and refrigeration equipment, could also have an adverse effect of food crops and human health.

Disturbing as these findings are, it is important to stress that the *Global 2000 Report*'s conclusions represent not predictions of what will occur, but projections of what could occur if we do not respond. If there was any doubt before, there should be little doubt now—the nations of the world, industrialized and less developed alike, must act urgently and in concert to alter these dangerous trends before the projections of the *Global 2000 Report* become realities.

The warnings, then, are clear. Will we heed them, and will we heed them in time? For if our response is delayed, the costs could be great.

On these matters, I am cautiously optimistic. I like to think that the human race is *not* self-destructive—that it *is* paying, or can be made to pay, attention—that as people throughout the world

come to realize the full dimensions of the challenge before us, we will take the actions needed to meet it.

Our efforts to secure the future must begin with a new appreciation for, and then an application of, three fundamental concepts. They are *conservation*, *sustainable development*, and *equity*. I am convinced that each of them is essential to the development of the kind of long-term global resource strategy we need to deal with the problems I have been discussing.

CONSERVATION

The first thing we must do is to get serious about the conservation of resources—renewable and nonrenewable alike. We can no longer take for granted the renewability of renewable resources. The natural systems—the air and water, the forests, the land—that yield food, shelter and the other necessities of life are susceptible to disruption, contamination and destruction.

Indeed, one of the most troubling of the findings of the *Global 2000 Report* is the effect that rapid population growth and poverty are already having on the productivity of renewable natural resource systems. In some areas, particularly in the less developed countries, the ability of biological systems to support human populations is already being seriously damaged by efforts of present populations to meet desperate immediate needs, such as the needs for grazing land, firewood and building materials.

And these stresses, while most acute in the developing countries, are not confined to them. In recent years, the United States has been losing annually about 3 million acres of rural land—a third of it prime agricultural land—due to the spread of housing developments, highways, shopping malls and the like. We are also losing annually the rough equivalent—in terms of production capability—of another 3 million acres due to soil degradation—erosion and salinization. Other serious resource threats in the United States include those posed by toxic chemicals and other pollutants to groundwater supplies, which provide drinking water for half of the American public, and directly affect both commercial and sport fishing.

Achieving the necessary restraint in the use of renewable resources will require new ways of thinking by the peoples and governments of the world. It will require the widespread adoption of a "Conserver Society" ethic—an approach to resources and environment that, while attuned to the needs of each society, recognizes not only the importance of resources and environment to our own sustenance, well-being and security, but also our obligation to pass this vital legacy along to future generations. Perhaps the most arrogant attitude of which the human spirit is capable is the notion that the riches of the Earth are ours to plunder or carelessly destroy . . . that the needs and the lives of those who will follow us on this tiny and fragile planet are of no concern to us. "Future generations," someone once said "What have they done for us?"

Fortunately, we are beginning to see signs that people in the United States and in other nations *are* becoming aware of the limits to our resources and the importance of conserving them. Energy problems, for example, are pointing the way to a future in which conservation is the password. As energy supplies go down and prices go up, we are learning that conserving—getting more and more out of each barrel of oil or ton of coal—is the cheapest and safest approach. Learning to conserve non-renewable resources like oil and coal is the first step toward building a Conserver Society that values, nurtures, and protects all of its resources. Such a society appreciates economy in design and avoidance of waste. It realizes the limits to low-cost resources and to the environment's carrying capacity. It insists that market prices reflect all costs, social as well as private, so that consumers are fully aware in the most direct way of the real costs of consumption.

The Conserver Society prizes recycling over pollution, durability over absolescence, quality over quantity, diversity over uniformity. It knows that beauty—whether natural or manmade—is too precious to be destroyed and that the Earth's wild creatures demand our conserving restraint not simply for utilitarian reasons but because, as part of the community of life that has evolved here with us, they too call this place home.

In this, the United States must take the lead. We cannot expect the rest of the world to adopt a Conserver Society ethic if we ourselves do not set a strong, successful example.

SUSTAINABLE DEVELOPMENT

But the Conserver Society ethic, by itself, is not enough. It is unrealistic to expect people living at the margin of existence—people fighting desperately for their own survival—to think about the long-term survival of the planet. When people need to burn wood to keep from freezing, they will cut down trees.

We must find a way to break the cycle of poverty, population growth and environmental deterioration. We must find ways to improve the social and economic conditions of the poor nations and poor people of the world—their incomes, their access to productive land, their educational and employment opportunities. It is only through sustainable economic development that real progress can be made in alleviating hunger and poverty and in erasing the conditions that contribute so dangerously to the destruction of our planet's carrying capacity.

One of the most important lessons of the *Global 2000 Report* is that the conflict between development and environmental protection is, in significant part, a myth. Only a concerted attack on the roots of extreme poverty—one that provides people with the opportunity to earn a decent livelihood in a nondestructive manner—will enable us to protect the world's natural systems. It is also clear that development and economic reforms will have no lasting success unless they are suffused with concern for ecological stability and wise management of resources. The key concept here, of course, is *sustainable* development. Economic development, if it is to be successful over the long term, must proceed in a way that enhances the natural resource base of all the developing nations, instead of exploiting those resources for short-term economic or political gain.

Unfortunately, the realities of the current North-South dialogue between the developed and the developing nations suggest that achieving steady, sustainable development will be a difficult process—one that will require great patience and understanding on all sides. For our part here in the United States, we must resist the strong temptation to turn inward—to tune out the rest of the world's problems and to focus exclusively on our own economic difficulties. We must remember that, relatively speaking, we Americans luxuriate in the Earth's abundance, while other nations can barely feed and clothe their people. Unless we act, this disparity between rich and poor will tend to grow, increasing the possibilities for anger and resentment from those on the short end of the wealth equation—the great majority of mankind. One does not have to be particularly farsighted to see that the trends discussed in *Global 2000* heighten the chances for global instability—for exploitation of fears, resentments and frustrations; for incitement to violence; for conflicts based on resources.

The *Global 2000 Report* itself discusses some of the destabilizing prospects that may be in store for us if we do not act decisively:

"The world will be more vulnerable both to natural disaster and to disruptions from human causes . . . Most nations are likely to be still more dependent on foreign sources of energy in 2000 than they are today. Food production will be more vulnerable to disruptions of fossil fuel energy supplies and to weather fluctuations as cultivation expands to more marginal areas. The loss of diverse germ plasm in local strains and wild progenitors of food crops, together with the increase of monoculture, could lead to greater risks of massive crop failures. Larger numbers of people will be vulnerable to higher food prices or even famine when adverse weather occurs. The world will be more vulnerable to the disruptive effects of war. The tensions that could lead to war will have multiplied. The potential for conflict over fresh water alone is underscored by the fact that out of 200 of the world's major river basins, 148 are shared by two countries and 52 are shared by three to ten countries."

The 1980 Report of the Brandt Commission on International Development Issues is eloquent in its plea for action: "War is often thought of in terms of military conflict, or even annihilation. But there is a growing awareness that an equal danger might be chaos—as a result of mass hunger, economic disaster, environmental catastrophes, and terrorism, so we should not think only of reducing the traditional threats to peace, but also of the need for change from chaos to order."

EQUITY

The late Barbara Ward, eminent British scholar, argued that the nations of the world can learn a valuable lesson from the experience of 19th-Century England, where the industrial revolution produced an appalling disparity in the distribution of wealth. It was a time when property owners and industrial managers reaped enormous profits while the laborers and mechanics—and their children—worked themselves into early graves.

Today, Ward observes: "The skew in world income is as great. The already developed peoples—North America, Europe, the Soviet Union, Japan—are the latter-day dukes, commanding over 70 percent of the planet's wealth for less than a quarter of the population. And in all too many developing countries the economic growth of the last two decades has been almost entirely appropriated by the wealthiest ten percent of the people. The comparisons in health, length of life, diet, literacy all work out on the old Victorian patterns of unbelievable injustice."

Ward recommends—and I heartily agree—that the developed nations of today follow the lead of men like Disraeli, who recognized the need to narrow the gap between rich and poor in 19th-Century England and to create a new social order which allowed every citizen a share of the nation's wealth. Without perceptive leaders like Disraeli and other men of conscience who saw the need for reform, Ward argues that the growing pressure for equality and social justice would have torn British society apart. The result would have been similar to that in other nations where far-thinking leadership and compassion were lacking: "social convulsion, violent revolution and an impetus to merciless worldwide war and conquest."

The situation we face in the world today is all too similar. While the humanitarian reasons for acting generously to alleviate global poverty and injustice are compelling enough in themselves, we must also recognize the extent to which global poverty and resource problems can contribute to regional and worldwide political instability—an instability that can threaten the security of nations throughout the world.

Thus, along with conservation and sustainable development, the development of global resource strategy will require a much greater emphasis on *equity*—on a fair sharing of the means to development and the products of growth—not only among nations, but within nations as well.

SUGGESTIONS FOR FURTHER READING

Alternative Views

Amur, Samir. *Unequal Development.* New York: Monthly Review Press, 1976.

Anthologies

Aiken, William, and LaFollette, Hugh. *World Hunger and Moral Obligation.* Englewood Cliffs: Prentice-Hall, 1977.

Brown, Peter, and Shue, Henry. *Boundaries.* Totowa: Rowman and Littlefield, 1981.

Lucas, George R. Jr., and Ogletree, Thomas W. *Lifeboat Ethics.* New York: Harper and Row, 1976.

Partridge, Ernest. *Responsibilities to Future Generations.* Buffalo: Prometheus, 1981.

Sikora, R. I., and Barry, Brian. *Obligation to Future Generations.* Philadelphia: Temple University Press, 1978.

Basic Concepts

Parfit, Derek. "Rights, Interests and Possible People." In *Moral Problems in Medicine,* edited by Samuel Gorovitz, pp. 369–375. Englewood Cliffs: Prentice Hall, 1976.

———. "Future Generations: Further Problems." *Philosophy and Public Affairs* Vol. 11 No. 2 (1982) pp. 113–172.

Bauer, P. T. *Equality, the Third World and Economic Delusion.* Cambridge: Harvard University Press, 1981.

Bayles, Michael D. *Morality and Population Policy.* Birmingham: University of Alabama Press, 1980.

Beitz, Charles R. *Political Theory and International Relations.* Princeton: Princeton University Press, 1979.

Commoner, Barry. *The Closing Circle.* New York: Bantam Books, 1971.

Hardin, Garrett. *Promethean Ethics.* Seattle: University of Washington Press, 1980.

Shue, Henry. *Basic Rights.* Princeton: Princeton University Press, 1980.

Practical Applications

Kahn, Herman; Brown, William; and Martel, Leon. *The Next 200 Years.* New York: William Morrow and Co., 1976.

Schumacher E. F. *Small Is Beautiful.* New York: Harper and Row, 1973.

Wortman, Sterling, and Cummings, Ralph, Jr. *To Feed This World.* Baltimore: Johns Hopkins Press, 1978.

ABORTION AND EUTHANASIA

BASIC CONCEPTS

The problem of abortion and euthanasia has been as thoroughly discussed as any contemporary moral problem. As a result, the conceptual issues have been fairly well laid out, and there have been some interesting attempts to bridge the troublesome normative and practical disagreements that remain.

First of all, almost everyone agrees that the fundamental issue with respect to the justification of abortion is the moral status of the fetus, although considerable disagreement exists as to what the status is.[1] Conservatives on the abortion question, like John Noonan (see pp. 134–144), contend that from conception the fetus has full moral status and hence has a serious right to life. Liberals on the abortion question, like Mary Anne Warren (see pp. 144–154), hold that the fetus at least until birth has almost no moral status whatsoever and hence lacks a serious right to life.[2] Moderates on the abortion question adopt some position in between these two views. And still others, like Judith Jarvis Thomson (see pp. 126–134) and James P. Sterba (see pp. 154–161) adopt for the sake of argument either the conservative or the liberal view on the moral status of the fetus and then try to show that such a view does not lead to the consequences its supporters assume.[3]

Secondly, almost everyone agrees that the position one takes on the moral status of the fetus has a bearing on whether one considers either the distinction between killing and letting die or the doctrine of double effect as relevant to the abortion question. For example, conservatives are quite interested in whether the killing and letting die distinction can be used to show that it is permissible to let the fetus die in certain contexts, even when it would be impermissible to kill the fetus. However, liberals find the use of this distinction in such contexts to be completely unnecessary. Since liberals hold that the fetus has almost no moral status, they do not object to either killing the fetus or letting it die. Similarly, although conservatives are quite interested in whether the doctrine of double effect can be used to permit the death of the fetus as a foreseen but unintended consequence of some legitimate course of action, liberals find no use for the doctrine of double effect in such contexts.

Thirdly, almost everyone agrees that either the killing and letting die distinction or the doctrine of double effect could prove useful in cases of euthanasia. Agreement exists on this point because most of the possible subjects of euthanasia are human beings who, in everyone's view, have full moral status and hence a serious right to life. Accordingly, despite the disagreement as to where it is useful to apply the killing and letting die distinction and the doctrine of double effect, everyone agrees that both of these conceptual tools deserve further examination.

The distinction between killing and letting die, as Terrance C. McConnell points out has both its advocates and its critics. The former maintain that, other things being equal, killing is morally worse than letting die, with the consequence that letting die is justified in cases where killing is not. The critics of this distinction maintain that, other things being equal, killing is not morally worse than letting die, with the consequence that killing is morally justified whenever letting die is. Both its advocates and its critics agree that other things would not be equal if the killing is justified or deserved while the letting die is unwanted and undeserved. They tend to disagree, however, over whether other things would be equal if the killing was in response to a patient's request to die while the letting die involved a prolonged and excruciatingly painful death, or if the killing resulted in the death of just a few individuals while the letting die resulted in the death of many people.

Yet whatever view one adopts as to when other things are equal, it is hard to defend the moral preferability of letting die over killing when both are taken to be intentional acts. As James Rachels so graphically makes the point (see pp. 161–171), it seems impossible to judge the act of A, who intentionally lets Z die while standing ready to finish Z off if that proves necessary, as being morally preferable to the act of B, who with similar motive and intention kills Y. But it is far from clear whether advocates of the killing and letting die distinction are claiming that the distinction holds when the killing and the letting die are both intentional acts, since it is unlikely in such cases that the letting die would be morally justified when the killing is not. Rather, as Bonnie Steinbock argues (see pp. 171–176), advocates of the distinction seem to have in mind a contrast between *intentional* killing and *unintentional* letting die; or more fully stated, a contrast between intentional killing and unintentional letting die when the latter is the foreseen consequence of an otherwise legitimate course of action.

Steinbock maintains that there are at least two types of cases in which letting die, distinguished in this way from killing, seems justified. In the first, a doctor ceases treatment in order to respect the wishes of her patient, foreseeing that the patient will die or will die sooner than otherwise, yet not intending that result. In the second, a doctor's intention is to avoid employing treatment that is extremely painful and has little hope of benefiting the patient, even though she foresees that this may hasten her patient's death. In addition, conservatives have argued that letting die, distinguished in this way from killing, can be justified in cases of ectopic pregnancy and in cases involving cancer of the uterus, since in such cases the fetus's death is the foreseen but unintended consequence of medical treatment that is necessary to preserve the basic well-being of the pregnant woman.

When the killing and letting die distinction is interpreted in this way, it has much in common with the doctrine of double effect. This doctrine places four restrictions on the permissibility of acting when some of the consequences of one's action are evil. These restrictions are the following:

1. the act is good in itself or at least indifferent,
2. only the good consequences of the act are intended,
3. the good consequences are not the effect of the evil, and
4. the good consequences are commensurate with the evil consequences.

The basic idea of the killing and letting die distinction, as we have interpreted it, is expressed by restrictions 2 and 3.

When conservatives apply the doctrine of double effect to a case in which a woman with a cancerous uterus is pregnant, the doctrine is said to justify an abortion because

1. the act of removing the cancerous uterus is good in itself,
2. only the removal of the cancerous uterus is intended,
3. the removal of the cancerous uterus is not a consequence of the abortion, and
4. preserving the life of the mother by removing the cancerous uterus is commensurate with the death of the fetus.

The doctrine is also said to justify unintentionally letting a person die, or "passive euthanasia," at least in the two types of cases described by Steinbock.

In recent moral philosophy, the main objection to the doctrine of double effect has been to question the necessity of its restrictions. Consider the following example. Imagine that a fat person who is leading a party of spelunkers gets herself stuck in the mouth of a cave in which flood waters are rising. The trapped party of spelunkers just happens to have a stick of dynamite with which they can blast the fat person out of the mouth of the cave; either they use the dynamite or they all drown, the fat person with them. Now it would appear that the doctrine of double effect would *not* permit the use of the dynamite in this case because the evil consequences of the act are intended as a means to securing the good consequences in violation of restrictions (2) and (3). Yet it seems plausible to argue in such a case that using the dynamite would be justified on the grounds that (a) the evil to be avoided, i.e., the evil of failing to save the party of spelunkers except for the fat person, is considerably greater than the evil resulting from the means employed, i.e., the evil of intentionally causing the death of the fat person and/or that (b) the greater part of evil resulting from the means employed, i.e., the death of the fat person, would still occur whether or not those means were actually employed.

Now some might want to defend the doctrine of double effect against this line of criticism by maintaining that the spelunkers need not intend the death of the fat person, but only that "she be blown into little pieces" or that "the mouth of the cave be suitably enlarged." But how is the use of the stick of dynamite expected to produce these results except by way of killing the fat person? Thus the death of the fat person would be part of the means employed by the spelunkers to secure their release from the cave, and hence would be impermissible according to the doctrine of double effect. If, however, we think that bringing about the death of the fat person could be morally justified in this case because, for example, (a) and/or (b) obtain, we are then left with a serious objection to the necessity of the restrictions imposed by the doctrine of double effect for acting morally. And, as we shall see when considering the problem of war and nuclear deterrence, still other objections can be raised to the sufficiency of these restrictions.

Given these objections to the doctrine of double effect, it has been suggested by Philippa Foot that we might more profitably deal with the moral questions at issue by distinguishing between negative and positive duties. Negative duties are said to be duties to refrain from doing certain sorts of actions. Typically, these are duties to avoid actions that inflict harm or injury or others. Thus the duties not to kill or not to assault others are negative duties. By contrast, positive duties are duties to do certain actions. Usually, positive duties require actions that aid or benefit others. The duty to repay a debt and the duty to help others in need are positive duties. This distinction is used to resolve practical disputes by

claiming that negative duties have priority over positive duties; accordingly, when negative and positive duties conflict, negative duties always take precedence over positive duties.

Applying this distinction, Foot claims that a doctor is justified in performing an abortion in a situation in which nothing can be done to save the lives of both child and mother, but where the life of the mother can be saved by killing the child. Obviously, this case is quite similar to the example of the fat person stuck in the mouth of the cave. But it is not clear how the distinction between positive and negative duties can help us in either situation. Since both the doctor and the group of spelunkers trapped by the fat person have a negative duty not to kill that takes precedence over any positive duty to help either themselves or others, it would seem that neither aborting the fetus nor blowing up the fat person could be justified on the basis of this distinction. Thus, it would seem that the distinction between negative and positive duties no more justifies the evil consequences in such cases than does the doctrine of double effect. Accordingly, if we want to provide such a justification, we need to find some morally acceptable way of going beyond both of these requirements.

ALTERNATIVE VIEWS

As we mentioned earlier, conservatives hold that the fetus has full moral status and hence a serious right to life. As a consequence, conservatives oppose abortion in a wide range of cases. Hoping to undercut this antiabortion stance, Judith Jarvis Thomson adopts, for the sake of argument, the conservative position on the moral status of the fetus (see pp. 126–134). She then tries to show that abortion is still justified in a wide range of cases. Thomson asks us to imagine that we are kidnapped and connected to an unconscious violinist who now shares the use of our kidneys. The situation is such that if we detach ourselves from the violinist before nine months transpire, the violinist will die. Thomson thinks it is obvious that we have no obligation to share our kidneys with the violinist in such a case, and hence that, in analogous cases, abortion can be justified. Thomson's view has provoked so much discussion that the authors of each of the next three selections all feel compelled to consider her view in the course of developing their own positions.

In his selection, John Noonan objects to Thomson's use of fantasized examples (see pp. 134–144). In place of Thomson's example of an unconscious violinist, Noonan offers a more realistic example found in the law. It is a case in which a family is found to be liable for the frostbite suffered by a dinner guest whom they refused to allow to stay overnight in their home, although it was very cold outside and the guest showed signs of being sick. But although Noonan is surely correct in pointing out the need for realistic examples, there still is an important difference between allowing a person to stay overnight in one's home and allowing a fetus to remain and develop in one's body for approximately nine months.

Mary Anne Warren also objects to Thomson's violinist example, but on grounds quite different from Noonan's (see pp. 144–154). She claims that the example at most justifies abortion in cases of rape, and hence will not provide the desired support for abortion on demand. Thomson, however, did provide additional examples and arguments in an attempt to show that abortion is justified in cases other than rape. Even so, Warren may be right in claiming that the scope of Thomson's defense of abortion falls short of abortion on demand.

James P. Sterba challenges not so much the fantasized examples Thomson employs as the arguments she provides along with those examples (see pp. 154–161). One of these arguments is based on a distinction between what a person can demand as a right and what is required by moral decency. This argument concludes that abortion rarely, if ever, violates anyone's rights. Another argument is based on a restricted interpretation of a right to life. This argument concludes that abortion typically does not violate the fetus's right not to be killed or let die unjustly. Sterba contends that neither of these arguments can be consistently used to support abortion on demand by those who endorse the welfare rights of distant peoples.

Now Thomson might concede that those who endorse the welfare rights of distant peoples cannot avail themselves of her arguments. But then she would most likely argue that libertarians, and political conservatives generally, who do not endorse welfare rights for distant peoples, could make use of her arguments. Sterba, of course, would deny that this is possible since he believes that libertarians, and political conservatives generally, are also required to accept the welfare rights of distant peoples, and hence are required to reject Thomson's arguments for abortion.

Convinced that Thomson's or anyone else's attempt to argue for abortion will prove unsuccessful if the fetus is assumed to have full moral status, Noonan wants to retain and support that assumption. His approach, however, is quite different from that usually adopted by conservatives.

Conservatives typically employ what are called "slippery slope arguments" to show that any attempt to draw a line—whether at implantation, or at quickening, or at viability, or at birth—for the purpose of separating those who do not have full moral status from those who do, fails to be nonarbitrary because of the continuity in the development of the fetus. Conservatives then contend that conception is the only point at which the line can be nonarbitrarily drawn.

By contrast, Noonan proposes to examine various models and methods employed in the debate on abortion, distinguishing those that do not work from those that do. Already we have noted Noonan's objection to fantasized examples. In additon, he objects to any attempt to make exceptions for abortion when the fetus is known to be seriously defective or the result of a rape, arguing that exceptions in such cases would "eat up the rule." Surprisingly, Noonan also objects to the use of special metaphors such as direct and indirect, and in particular rejects the application of the doctrine of double effect to cases of ectopic pregnancy and the removal of a cancerous uterus containing a fetus. In such cases, Noonan claims, the doctor "necessarily intends to perform the abortion, he necessarily intends to kill." What legitimates abortion in such cases, claims Noonan, is not the doctrine of double effect, but rather the principle that whenever the fetus is a danger to the life of the mother, abortion is permissible on grounds of self-defense. But if the mother is justified on grounds of self-defense in aborting the fetus, surely some representative of the fetus would also be justified in defending the fetus against an abortion, given that in Noonan's view the fetus has a serious right to life. Consequently, Noonan has not provided us with a moral solution to such cases. At the same time, it is difficult to see how anyone could ignore the central plea of Noonan's article that we see what otherwise might be overlooked and that we respond to the full range of human experience.

Like Noonan, Warren wants to build a consensus on the abortion question. To achieve this, she proposes a set of criteria for being a person with full moral status that she thinks proabortionists and antiabortionists alike could accept. The criteria are (1) consciousness, (2) developed reasoning, (3) self-motivated activity, (4) a capacity to communicate, and (5) the presence of self-concepts and self-awareness. But while most people would certainly agree that these criteria are met in paradigm cases, conservatives would still reject them as necessary requirements for being a person. Thus, although Warren's view adequately represents the liberal view on abortion, those who hold opposing views would not find it very persuasive.

Hoping to generate some practical consensus on the abortion question, Sterba employs the same sort of tactic against liberals that Thomson employed against conservatives. He assumes for the sake of argument that the fetus has almost no moral status whatsoever, and then tries to show that abortion would still not be justified in a wide range of cases. In particular he argues that, even if the fetus is not a person, those who accept

1. the welfare rights of future generations and
2. an obligation not to bring into existence persons who would lack a reasonable opportunity to lead a good life

are required also to accept

3. an obligation to bring into existence persons who would have a reasonable opportunity to lead a good life;

and (3) severely limits the legitimate use of abortion. According to Sterba, (3) follows from the acceptance of (1) and (2) because any reason we can give for accepting (2) consistent with (1) will suggest an analogous reason for supporting (3). The type of view Sterba defends has been called the "symmetry view" since it argues for a symmetry between the obligation not to procreate and an obligation to pro-

create or, as Sterba puts it, a right not to be born and a right to be born.

In a recently published article, Derek Parfit has challenged the symmetry view. In effect, what Parfit has done is to suggest an interpretation of our duty not to harm others and our duty to benefit others such that, under this interpretation, those who accept (1) and (2) need not accept (3). According to Parfit's interpretation

(a) our duty not to harm others is a duty not to do x if doing x is bad or worse for people who ever exist, and
(b) our duty to benefit others is a duty to do x if not doing x is bad or worse for people who ever exist.

Now assuming that we construe welfare rights of future generations as simply what follows from (a) and (b), Sterba's argument for the symmetry view would surely fail. The reason for this is that (3) is not required by Parfit's interpretation of our duty to benefit others. For although, on Parfit's view, coming into existence can be a benefit, it is not the sort of benefit that is required by our duty to benefit others, because—other things being equal—failing to provide that benefit is not bad or worse for anyone who ever exists.

The principal difficulty with Parfit's challenge to the symmetry view is his restricted interpretation of our duty to benefit others. For how can we accept a duty to do x when not doing x would be bad or worse for people who ever exist without also accepting a duty to do x when doing x would be good or better for people who ever exist? Parfit himself admits that it is hard to accept that

(c) we ought not to increase the sum of suffering without also accepting that
(d) we ought to increase the net sum of happiness.

For similar reasons, it seems hard to accept Parfit's interpretation of our duty to benefit others without also accepting a still broader interpretation of this duty which would justify (3).[4]

Those who find both the conservative and the liberal views on abortion unattractive might be inclined toward the moderate view. This view attempts to draw a line—typically at implantation, or at quickening, or at viability—for the purpose of separating those who do not have full moral status from those who do. The United States Supreme Court in *Wade* v. *Roe* (1973) has frequently been understood as supporting a moderate view on abortion. In this decision, the Court by a majority of 7 to 2 decided that the constitutional right to privacy, protected by the due process clause of the Fourteenth Amendment to the Constitution, entails that (1) no law may restrict the right of a woman to be aborted by a physician during the first three months (trimester) of her pregnancy; (2) during the second trimester abortion may be regulated by law only to the extent that the regulation is reasonably related to the preservation and protection of maternal health; and (3) when the fetus becomes viable (not before the beginning of the third trimester) a law may prohibit abortion, but only subject to an exception permitting abortion wherever necessary to protect the woman's life or health (including any aspects of her physical or mental health). But whether or not the Court's decision was intended to support the moderate view on abortion, the Court's decision has led in practice to abortion on demand, as the authors of the Human Life Bill (see pp. 177–180) indicate.

Now while most of the contemporary discussion of abortion has focused on the moral status of the fetus, most of the discussion of euthanasia has focused on the killing and letting die distinction and the doctrine of double effect. As we noted before, advocates of the killing and letting die distinction and the doctrine of double effect tend to justify only passive euthanasia (i.e., letting a person die as a foreseen but unintended consequence of an otherwise legitimate course of action). In contrast, critics of the killing and letting die distinction and the doctrine of double effect tend to justify also active euthanasia (i.e., intentional killing) on the basis of its consequences. Rachels (pp. 161–170) cites the case of a person suffering from cancer of the throat who has three options: (1) with continued treatment she will have a few more days of pain and then die; (2) if treatment is stopped but nothing else is done, it will be a few more hours; or (3) with a lethal injection she will die at once. In such a case, Rachels thinks, the third option—active euthanasia—is justified on the grounds that the person would be better off dying immediately.

But euthanasia is not only passive or active, it is also voluntary or involuntary. Voluntary euthanasia

has the (informed) consent of the person involved. Involuntary euthanasia lacks such consent, usually but not always because the person involved is incapable of providing it. This means that at least four different types of euthanasia are possible: voluntary passive euthanasia, involuntary passive euthanasia, voluntary active euthanasia and involuntary active euthanasia. Of the four types, voluntary passive euthanasia seems easiest to justify, involuntary active euthanasia the most difficult. But voluntary euthanasia, both passive and active, would seem more justifiable if it could be shown that there is a fundamental moral right to be assisted in bringing about one's own death if one so desires. Even if such a right could be supported, however, it would presumably only have force when one could reasonably be judged to be better off dead.

PRACTICAL APPLICATIONS

It is not at all difficult to see how the various proposed solutions to the problem of abortion and euthanasia would have application in contemporary societies. For example, the Human Life Bill, S. 158 (see pp. 177–180), was designed as the first step toward enforcing a conservative view on abortion. Actually, S. 158 does not claim that the conservative view on abortion is the most morally defensible view; rather, it claims that (1) the Constitution of the United States supports the view that each and every human life has intrinsic worth and equal value, and (2) informed scientific opinion supports the view that human life begins at conception. But (1) and (2) are perfectly consistent with the possibility that the conservative view on abortion is not the most morally defensible view, since even if the U.S. Constitution supports the conservative view of abortion it still may not be the most morally defensible view. Thus S. 185 presupposes rather than in any way establishes the moral legitimacy of the conservative view on abortion. Similarly, in the Karen Quinlan Opinion (see pp. 181–187) the Supreme Court of New Jersey presupposes the moral legitimacy of passive euthanasia and simply affirms that Karen Quinlan's *legal* right to privacy permits passive euthanasia in her case.[5] Accordingly, if you think that different solutions to the problem of abortion and euthanasia are more morally defensible, you should favor other laws and judicial decisions.

But even as you begin to formulate the laws and social institutions, with their demands on social goods and resources, that are needed to enforce what you take to be the most morally defensible solution to the problem of abortion and euthanasia, you will still need to take into account the demands on social goods and resources that derive from solutions to other practical moral problems—such as the problem of discrimination and prejudice, which is taken up in the next section.

NOTES

1. The term "fetus" is understood to refer to any human organism from conception to birth.

2. Note that liberals on the abortion question need not be welfare liberals, although many of them are. Likewise, conservatives on the abortion question need not be libertarians or political conservatives.

3. Henceforth liberals, conservatives, and moderates on the abortion question are simply referred to as liberals, conservatives, and moderates.

4. For further discussion, see James P. Sterba, "Explaining Asymmetry: A Problem for Parfit," *Philosophy and Public Affairs* (1983).

5. The respirator was turned off; as of this writing, however, Karen Quinlan is alive but comatose.

Terrance C. McConnell

THE MORAL STATUS OF THE FETUS, THE KILLING AND LETTING DIE DISTINCTION, AND THE DOCTRINE OF DOUBLE EFFECT

Beginning with a review of the relevant medical terms pertaining to abortion, Terrance C. McConnell distinguishes between disagreements over the moral status of the fetus and disagreements over what reasons (if any) justify abortion, indicating the possible positions to which these disagreements give rise. Next McConnell considers what grounds there are for adopting either the view that killing is always, from a moral point of view, worse than letting die, or the view that there is no morally relevant difference between killing and letting die. He concludes by showing how the doctrine of double effect provides an alternative to accepting either of these two views.

From *Moral Issues in Health Care* (Belmont, CA: Wadsworth Publishing, 1982), pp. 115–118, 120, 122, 159, 162.

THE MORAL STATUS OF THE FETUS

WHEN THE FEMALE REPRODUCTIVE cell, the ovum, is fertilized by the male sex cell, the spermatozoon, the product is called the single-cell zygote. Within the first day of conception the zygote begins to divide. By the third day it consists of sixteen cells. As the zygote continues to grow during the first week, it moves through the fallopian tube into the uterus. At this point, as the zygote is gradually implanted in the uterine wall, the product of conception is called the conceptus. From the second through the eighth week of growth, it is called the embryo. From the third month until birth, it is called the fetus. In ordinary discourse, the term "fetus" is often used to refer to the product of conception at any stage of development. When the fetus is capable of living independently of the womb, it is said to be viable.

When the product of conception is expelled from the uterus prematurely, this is called abortion. When this expulsion is natural rather than intentional, it is called spontaneous abortion (or more commonly, a miscarriage). There are several different methods of performing nonspontaneous (intentional) abortions. One method, called dilation and curettage (D. and C.), involves the following: the womb is dilated and a curette is used to remove the contents of the uterus, either wholly or in pieces. A second method, suction abortion, is when the products of conception are removed from the uterus by a device that sucks the conceptus from the womb. A third method of abortion involves the injection of a saline solution into the sac containing the amniotic fluid that surrounds the conceptus; such an act induces labor. Since nonspontaneous abortion normally ends the life of a creature that is biologically human (that is, it has the same genetic code as any member of the species *Homo sapiens*), many questions have been raised about the permissibility of such a procedure.

THE MORAL ISSUE

At what point of fetal development (if any) and for what reasons (if any) is abortion morally permissible?[1] Putting the question in this way is quite useful because it accurately suggests that there are two basic issues at the heart of the debate about abortion. The first of these two basic issues concerns the stage of fetal development. Many hold that the stage of fetal development is a morally relevant factor in determining the permissibility of abortion. The standard view, of course, is that later abortions are more morally problematic than early abortions. The second basic issue in the debate about abortion concerns the reason the woman expresses for wanting the abortion. Some reasons seem to be more acceptable than others.

Why do people disagree so radically concerning the question of abortion? Opponents in the abortion debate usually disagree about the moral status of the fetus. They disagree about whether the fetus has any rights, and if so, at what stage it has those rights. Conservatives hold that the fetus has full moral rights from the moment of conception. According to the conservative, then, the fetus has the right to life. There is, therefore, a presumption that killing the fetus is wrong. By contrast, liberals contend that the fetus has no moral status. According to this position the fetus has none of the rights that adult human beings possess. The fetus is just another piece of tissue in the woman's body. Thus a person who assents to the liberal position holds that removing the fetus is no more morally objectionable than removing the appendix. Moderates hold a position between these two extremes. They often claim that in the early stages of pregnancy the fetus does not possess full moral rights, but in the later stages it does. Thus at some point in its continuous development the fetus becomes a being with full moral rights. The moral status of the fetus, then, is one of the major sources of controversy in the debate about abortion.

Even among those who agree that abortion is at least sometimes permissible, there is considerable disagreement about what reasons justify an abortion. Let us note the reasons that have been advanced to justify abortion. It will be obvious that some of these reasons are accepted by most, while others have been advanced by only a few. The most common justification for abortion is purely medical: if the fetus is allowed to develop normally and come to term, the woman will die. Only a few would dispute that this is an acceptable reason for a woman to have an abortion. A second and related reason to justify abortion is to protect the woman's physical or mental health. Here, it is not expected that the woman will die, but carrying the fetus to full term will entail a great physical and/or mental sacrifice. That the pregnancy will produce a severely deformed child is a third reason sometimes given to justify abortion. Advocates of this reason appeal to the interests of both the parents and the fetus itself to justify abortion. Abortions performed for any of these first three reasons are often referred to as *therapeutic* abortions. This indicates, of course, that the abortion is done strictly for medical reasons.

Occasionally pregnancy is the result of rape. To force the woman to carry the fetus to full term in this case strikes many as unfair, and this is a fourth reason given to justify abortion. Some regard this as a therapeutic abortion, but since it need not be done for a purely medical reason that term will be reserved to cover only abortions performed for the first three reasons. Of course, in some cases a woman may have a medical reason for seeking an abortion after she has been raped; but many will say that she is justified in having an abortion in such cases even if it is not medically necessary. A fifth reason given to justify abortion is that the pregnancy is unwanted and therefore it saves the would-be child from an unhappy life. This reason is utilitarian in nature, purporting that abortion in certain circumstances will reduce unhappiness in the world. A sixth reason sometimes cited to justify abortion is that another child will place an unbearable financial burden on the woman or her family. This reason appeals to the consequences but is not necessarily utilitarian. It is not claimed that the *overall* unhappiness in the world will be reduced; rather it is asserted that the members of the family will be better off if abortion is performed. A seventh reason cited to justify abortion is a utilitarian one: abortion promotes a goal that is desirable in most societies, birth, or population, control. Population control, it is thought, will reduce significantly the overall suffering and unhappiness in the world. An eighth reason cited to justify abortion is relatively new.[2] Amniocentesis is the process of removing and analyzing the amniotic fluid surrounding the fetus. This process is normally used to test for potential birth defects; however, it will also reveal the sex of the fetus. Some couples want very much to have a child of a particular sex. Thus some have sought abortions because the fetus is not the preferred sex. This is a consequentialist but not a utilitarian reason; it appeals to the happiness of the couple, not to the overall happiness.

Each of the eight reasons just discussed will justify abortion only in certain situations; that is, even if these reasons are accepted, abortion will be justified only if certain conditions obtain. Some people, however, wish to opt for a much more liberal policy. They cite as a justification for abortion a ninth reason: since people have the right to do with their bodies whatever they wish, a woman may have an abortion for any reason. This justification, of course, is acceptable only to a few. It gives a woman a blank check on the question of abortion; she may obtain an abortion any time she wishes. If this justification for abortion is accepted, the other reasons become superfluous. . . .

THE KILLING AND LETTING DIE DISTINCTION

Since the preservation of life is a value of great significance, the factors which might affect the moral status of the act of ending life must be examined. . . . One factor relevant to the moral status of preserving life is the distinction between killing and letting die. Killing a being presumably involves a positive act that is the cause of that being's death. The locution "letting die" is ambiguous. It is sometimes said that a person let another being die when killing that being would also have been a plausible option. Suppose a person encounters a dying animal that is in severe pain and could be killed painlessly by being shot. If this person does not shoot the animal, it is said that he or she let it die. Often, though the phrase "letting die" is used to indicate that a person refrained from saving a being. In this sense it cannot be said that a person let another die unless the following conditions are satisfied: (i) the person had the ability to save or to prolong the life of the one who died; (ii) the person had the opportunity to save or to prolong the life of the one who died; and (iii) the person knew that the first two conditions were satisfied. The reason for including these conditions is clear enough. If I cannot swim and have no other means available to save a drowning person, it is implausible to describe this as a case of my letting the person die. Similarly, if a person has a serious medical problem, which if not attended to will be fatal, it might be said plausibly that a physician present let the person die; but it would be ludicrous to say that a plumber (with no medical knowledge) let that person die. Lack of opportunity will also render the description "letting the person die" inaccurate. Even the best of swimmers cannot be said to have let a person drown if he or she is on the other side of a huge lake. And even if a person has the ability and opportunity to save another, it cannot be said that he or she has let that person die unless the person knew that he or she could have saved the other. Thus if I am a good swimmer and am in my oceanside home reading a philosophy book, I have both the ability and the opportunity to save the person drowning just outside my house. But if I do not know this, I cannot be said to have let the person die.

Not everyone agrees about the importance of the distinction between killing and letting die. With regard to this question there are two extreme theses, each of which has a number of advocates. The first thesis, thesis (I), is this: There is a morally relevant difference between killing and letting die, and that difference is such that killing is always worse, from the moral point of view, than letting die. Thesis (I) is widely accepted in the medical and legal communities, as will be seen when discussing the issue of euthanasia. Why would someone hold this position? Reasons to support the position are rarely articulated, but presumably the following considerations are what advocates of this view have in mind. Killing is a positive act that an agent performs; normally it brings about death sooner than it would otherwise occur. Letting die, by contrast, is merely refraining from acting. And, according to this view, a person is always more responsible for a positive act than for an omission. So bringing about a death by killing is always worse than doing so by letting die. An example might be adduced to support this position. Suppose that you saw a man drowning but were unable (or unwilling) to save him. Wouldn't it be worse, from the moral point of view, for you to shoot the man rather than let him drown? Surely it would. To shoot him would preclude the possibility that he might be saved by someone else or by his

own effort. So, it might be argued, thesis (I) is plausible.

Not all accept thesis (I), however. Some have argued for a second view, thesis (II): There is no morally relevant difference between killing and letting die; one is just as bad as the other. Reasons have been given to support this position. Its defenders argue that the two most important moral features, the result and the motive, are the same in cases of killing and letting die. The result is the death of a person, and the motive is apparently the desire for that death. (Recall that it cannot accurately be said that a person has let another die unless the person could have saved the other and knew this.) What else could be morally relevant? advocates of this view ask. Examples are often cited to lend credence to this position.[3] Suppose that Smith and Jones each stands to inherit a large sum of money from the death of his young son. Each devises a plan to kill his son and to make it look like an accident. Each decides to drown his boy while he is taking a bath. Smith carries out his plan according to schedule and thus can be said to have killed his son. Jones sets about to do the same. But just as he enters the bathroom, his son slips and hits his head, knocking him unconscious. Jones considers himself fortunate, noting that now he will not have to kill his son; he can simply let him die. Is the act of Jones less repugnant than that of Smith?—surely not. From the moral point of view, each has done the wrong thing. And this is so, even though it is true that Smith has killed his son and Jones has merely let his son die. So, the argument goes, there is no morally relevant difference between killing and letting die. . . .

THE DOCTRINE OF DOUBLE EFFECT

The doctrine of double effect is a principle that steers a course between theses (I) and (II) and which purports to provide guidance on these matters. Historically, the doctrine of double effect has its roots in Catholic theology. This doctrine yields judgments on the abortion issue that Catholic theologians find acceptable. But this principle can just as well be viewed as a competitor to theses (I) and (II). Before stating the doctrine, some terms, which are necessary to understand it, will be explained. The doctrine of double effect is based on a distinction between what a person foresees as a result of his or her action and what a person intends by such action. What is it that a person intends when he or she performs a voluntary action? According to this doctrine a person intends in the strictest sense only those things that he or she *aims at as ends* or those things aimed at as *direct means* to such ends. A consequence of a person's action which is known will occur, but which is neither the end sought nor the direct means to that end, is said to be merely foreseen. To illustrate, consider the following example. A patient has cancer. In the judgment of the physician, the treatment most likely to be successful is chemotherapy, and so that is what the physician recommends. The physician realizes that an unfortunate result of the chemotherapy is that the patient will become nauseous and lose hair. The end this doctor is aiming at is to help the patient. The means to this end is to initiate chemotherapy treatments. A foreseen but unintended consequence is that the patient will become nauseous and lose hair. This consequence is unintended in the technical sense because it is neither the end sought nor the direct means to that end. Intuitively it makes sense to say that this consequence is unintended because the physician in no way desires this end; if it were possible to administer the chemotherapy treatments without the accompanying nausea and hair loss, the physician would be delighted.

According to the doctrine of double effect a person is more responsible for what is intended as a result of a voluntary action than for what is merely foreseen will follow from such actions. Given these distinctions, the doctrine of double effect may now be stated as follows: It is permissible to bring about through voluntary actions an evil state of affairs just in case (i) the agent does not intend the evil that results and (ii) performing the action prevents a greater evil or the evil that does occur could only be prevented if the agent were to do evil intentionally. To explain briefly, clause (i) states that it is never permissible for a person, through voluntary actions, to bring about evil if that evil is the end sought or a direct means to that end. Clause (ii) appeals to a kind of proportionality. It states that even when

the evil brought about is foreseen but unintended, it is permissible to allow it to occur only if doing so prevents a greater evil. This principle is called the doctrine of double effect because it distinguishes, for moral reasons, two different effects of an action: those aimed at or intended and those foreseen but in no way desired. The doctrine of double effect forbids a person to do evil intentionally. Bringing about an evil state of affairs is permitted only if the agent does not intend this. . . .

As noted earlier, Catholic theologians have accepted the doctrine of double effect because it, coupled with certain assumptions, supports a very conservative position on the abortion issue. Suppose that a woman is pregnant but that carrying the child full term will be very dangerous to her health; it is judged that she will probably die unless she obtains an abortion. (It must be supposed further, though this is often not pointed out, that ending the life of the fetus is evil in itself.) Abortion, even in this extreme case, is not permitted according to advocates of the doctrine of double effect (who accept the additional assumption). The end sought is to save the life of the woman. The direct means to that end, however, is to kill the fetus, and this is doing evil intentionally (granting that the fetus has the right to life). But isn't allowing the woman to die wrong too? It is not, according to the doctrine of double effect. The end sought is to save the child. The means to that end is to have the woman carry it full term. A foreseen but unintended consequence is that the woman will die. Thus the evil state of affairs brought about is unintended. If it is granted that the fetus has the right to life, then having the woman carry it full term does prevent an evil. And though it is not obvious that the evil it prevents is a greater evil (isn't the death of the woman at least as great an evil?), nevertheless this evil must be tolerated because the other evil—the woman's death—can be prevented only by intentionally doing evil. Thus a very conservative position on the abortion issue is maintained. Of course, this same conclusion might be embraced without adopting the doctrine of double effect. But that is not the point. The point is that one way of defending this position is by appealing to the doctrine of double effect (and the supplementary assumption). . . .

NOTES

1. This way of putting the question is suggested by Roger Wertheimer in "Understanding the Abortion Argument," Joel Feinberg (ed.), *The Problem of Abortion* (Belmont, Calif.: Wadsworth Publishing Company, 1973), p. 33.

2. For a discussion of the topic of abortion for the purpose of sex selection, see "Prenatal Diagnosis for Sex Choice," *The Hastings Center Report*, Vol. 10 (1980), pp. 15–20. See also, Holly S. Goldman, "Amniocentesis for Sex Selection," in Marc D. Basson (ed.), *Ethics, Humanism, and Medicine* (New York: Alan R. Liss, Inc., 1980), pp. 81–93.

3. These examples are borrowed, with slight modifications, from James Rachels, "Active and Passive Euthanasia," *The New England Journal of Medicine*, Vol. 292 (1975), pp. 78–80.

Judith Jarvis Thomson

A DEFENSE OF ABORTION

Judith Jarvis Thomson begins by assuming, for the sake of argument, that the fetus is a person. Using a series of examples, she then argues that even granting this assumption a woman has a right to abortion in cases involving rape, in cases in which the woman's life is endangered, and in cases in which the woman has taken reasonable precautions not to get pregnant. In these cases, Thomson claims, the fetus's assumed right not to be killed unjustly would not be violated by abortion. Thomson further distinguishes between cases in which it would be a good thing for a woman to forego an abortion and cases in which a woman has an obligation to do so.

MOST OPPOSITION TO ABORTION relies on the premise that the fetus is a human being, a person, from the moment of conception. The premise is argued for, but, as I think, not well. Take, for example, the most common argument. We are asked to notice that the development of a human being from conception through birth into childhood is continuous; then it is said that to draw a line, to choose a point in this development and say "before this point the thing is not a person, after this point it is a person" is to make an arbitrary choice, a choice for which in the nature of things no good reason can be given. It is con-cluded that the fetus is, or anyway we had better say it is, a person from the moment of conception. But this conclusion does not follow. Similar things might be said about the development of an acorn into an oak tree, and it does not follow that acorns are oak trees or that we had better say they are. Arguments of this form are sometimes called "slippery slope arguments"—the phrase is perhaps self-explanatory—and it is dismaying that opponents of abortion rely on them so heavily and uncritically.

I am inclined to agree, however, that the prospects for "drawing a line" in the development of the fetus

From "A Defense of Abortion," *Philosophy & Public Affairs*, Vol. 1, no. 1 (Fall, 1971). Copyright © 1971 by Princeton University Press. Excerpts, pp. 47–62, 65–66, reprinted by permission of Princeton University Press.

look dim. I am inclined to think also that we shall probably have to agree that the fetus has already become a human person well before birth. Indeed, it comes as a surprise when one first learns how early in its life it begins to acquire human characteristics. By the tenth week, for example, it already has a face, arms and legs, fingers and toes; it has internal organs, and brain activity is detectable.[1] On the other hand, I think that the premise is false, that the fetus is not a person from the moment of conception. A newly fertilized ovum, a newly implanted clump of cells, is no more a person than an acorn is an oak tree. But I shall not discuss any of this. For it seems to me to be of great interest to ask what happens if, for the sake of argument, we allow the premise. How, precisely, are we supposed to get from there to the conclusion that abortion is morally impermissible? Opponents of abortion commonly spend most of their time establishing that the fetus is a person, and hardly any time explaining the step from there to the impermissibility of abortion. Perhaps they think the step too simple and obvious to require much comment. Or perhaps instead they are simply being economical in argument. Many of those who defend abortion rely on the premise that the fetus is not a person, but only a bit of tissue that will become a person at birth; and why pay out more arguments than you have to? Whatever the explanation, I suggest that the step they take is neither easy nor obvious, that it calls for closer examination than it is commonly given, and that when we do give it this closer examination we shall feel inclined to reject it.

I propose, then, that we grant that the fetus is a person from the moment of conception. How does the argument go from here? Something like this, I take it. Every person has a right to life. So the fetus has a right to life. No doubt the mother has a right to decide what shall happen in and to her body; everyone would grant that. But surely a person's right to life is stronger and more stringent than the mother's right to decide what happens in and to her body, and so outweighs it. So the fetus may not be killed; an abortion may not be performed.

It sounds plausible. But now let me ask you to imagine this. You wake up in the morning and find yourself back to back in bed with an unconscious violinist. A famous unconscious violinist. He has been found to have a fatal kidney ailment, and the Society of Music Lovers has canvassed all the avail-

able medical records and found that you alone have the right blood type to help. They have therefore kidnapped you, and last night the violinist's circulatory system was plugged into yours, so that your kidneys can be used to extract poisons from his blood as well as your own. The director of the hospital now tells you, "Look, we're sorry the Society of Music Lovers did this to you—we would never have permitted it if we had known. But still, they did it, and the violinist now is plugged into you. To unplug you would be to kill him. But never mind, it's only for nine months. By then he will have recovered from his ailment, and can safely be unplugged from you." Is it morally incumbent on you to accede to this situation? No doubt it would be very nice of you if you did, a great kindness. But do you *have* to accede to it? What if it were not nine months, but nine years? Or longer still? What if the director of the hospital says, "Tough luck, I agree, but you've now got to stay in bed, with the violinist plugged into you, for the rest of your life. Because remember this. All persons have a right to life, and violinists are persons. Granted you have a right to decide what happens in and to your body, but a person's right to life outweighs your right to decide what happens in and to your body. So you cannot ever be unplugged from him." I imagine you would regard this as outrageous, which suggests that something really is wrong with that plausible-sounding argument I mentioned a moment ago.

In this case, of course, you were kidnapped; you didn't volunteer for the operation that plugged the violinist into your kidneys. Can those who oppose abortion on the ground I mentioned make an exception for a pregnancy due to rape? Certainly. They can say that persons have a right to life only if they didn't come into existence because of rape; or they can say that all persons have a right to life, but that some have less of a right to life than others, in particular, that those who came into existence because of rape have less. But these statements have a rather unpleasant sound. Surely the question of whether you have a right to life at all, or how much of it you have, shouldn't turn on the question of whether or not you are the product of a rape. And in fact the people who oppose abortion on the ground I mentioned do not make this distinction, and hence do not make an exception in case of rape.

Nor do they make an exception for a case in which

the mother has to spend the nine months of her pregnancy in bed. They would agree that would be a great pity, and hard on the mother; but all the same, all persons have a right to life, the fetus is a person, and so on. I suspect, in fact, that they would not make an exception for a case in which, miraculously enough, the pregnancy went on for nine years, or even the rest of the mother's life.

Some won't even make an exception for a case in which continuation of the pregnancy is likely to shorten the mother's life; they regard abortion as impermissible even to save the mother's life. Such cases are nowadays very rare, and many opponents of abortion do not accept this extreme view. All the same, it is a good place to begin: a number of points of interest come out in respect to it.

1. Let us call the view that abortion is impermissible even to save the mother's life "the extreme view." I want to suggest first that it does not issue from the argument I mentioned earlier without the addition of some fairly powerful premises. Suppose a woman has become pregnant, and now learns that she has a cardiac condition such that she will die if she carries the baby to term. What may be done for her? The fetus, being a person, has a right to life, but as the mother is a person too, so has she a right to life. Presumably they have an equal right to life. How is it supposed to come out that an abortion may not be performed? If mother and child have an equal right to life, shouldn't we perhaps flip a coin? Or should we add to the mother's right to life her right to decide what happens in and to her body, which everybody seems to be ready to grant—the sum of her rights now outweighing the fetus' right to life?

The most familiar argument here is the following. We are told that performing the abortion would be directly killing[2] the child, whereas doing nothing would not be killing the mother, but only letting her die. Moreover, in killing the child, one would be killing an innocent person, for the child has committed no crime, and is not aiming at his mother's death. And then there are a variety of ways in which this might be continued. (1) But as directly killing an innocent person is always and absolutely impermissible, an abortion may not be performed. Or, (2) as directly killing an innocent person is murder, and murder is always and absolutely impermissible, an abortion may not be performed.[3] Or, (3) as one's duty to refrain from directly killing an innocent person

is more stringent than one's duty to keep a person from dying, an abortion may not be performed. Or, (4) if one's only options are directly killing an innocent person or letting a person die, one must prefer letting the person die, and thus an abortion may not be performed.[4]

Some people seem to have thought that these are not further premises which must be added if the conclusion is to be reached, but that they follow from the very fact than an innocent person has a right to life.[5] But this seems to me to be a mistake, and perhaps the simplest way to show this is to bring out that while we must certainly grant that innocent persons have a right to life, the theses in (1) through (4) are all false. Take (2), for example. If directly killing an innocent person is murder, and thus is impermissible, then the mother's directly killing the innocent person inside her is murder, and thus is impermissible. But it cannot seriously be thought to be murder if the mother performs an abortion on herself to save her life. It cannot seriously be said that she *must* refrain, that she *must* sit passively by and wait for her death. Let us look again at the case of you and the violinist. There you are, in bed with the violinist, and the director of the hospital says to you, "It's all most distressing, and I deeply sympathize, but you see this is putting an additional strain on your kidneys, and you'll be dead within the month. But you *have* to stay where you are all the same. Because unplugging you would be directly killing an innocent violinist, and that's murder, and that's impermissible." If anything in the world is true, it is that you do not commit murder, you do not do what is impermissible, if you reach around to your back and unplug yourself from that violinist to save your life.

The main focus of attention in writings on abortion has been on what a third party may or may not do in answer to a request from a woman for an abortion. This is in a way understandable. Things being as they are, there isn't much a woman can safely do to abort herself. So the question asked is what a third party may do, and what the mother may do, if it is mentioned at all, is deduced, almost as an afterthought, from what is concluded that the third parties may do. But it seems to me that to treat the matter in this way is to refuse to grant to the mother that very status of person which is so firmly insisted on for the fetus. For we cannot simply read off what a person may do from what a third party may do. Suppose you find yourself trapped in a tiny house with a growing child. I mean a very tiny house, and a rapidly growing child—you are already up against the wall of the house and in a few minutes you'll be crushed to death. The child on the other hand won't be crushed to death; if nothing is done to stop him from growing he'll be hurt, but in the end he'll simply burst open the house and walk out a free man. Now I could well understand it if a bystander were to say, "There's nothing we can do for you. We cannot choose between your life and his, we cannot be the ones to decide who is to live, we cannot intervene." But it cannot be concluded that you too can do nothing, that you cannot attack it to save your life. However innocent the child may be, you do not have to wait passively while it crushes you to death. Perhaps a pregnant woman is vaguely felt to have the status of a house, to which we don't allow the right of self-defense. But if the woman houses the child, it should be remembered that she is a person who houses it.

I should perhaps stop to say explicitly that I am not claiming that people have a right to do anything whatever to save their lives. I think, rather, that there are drastic limits to the right of self-defense. If someone threatens you with death unless you torture someone else to death, I think you have not the right, even to save your life, to do so. But the case under consideration here is very different. In our case there are only two people involved, one whose life is threatened, and one who threatens it. Both are innocent: the one who is threatened is not threatened because of any fault, the one who threatens does not threaten because of any fault. For this reason we may feel that we bystanders cannot intervene. But the person threatened can.

In sum, a woman surely can defend her life against the threat to it posed by the unborn child, even if doing so involves its death. And this shows not merely that the theses in (1) through (4) are false; it shows also that the extreme view of abortion is false, and so we need not canvass any other possible ways of arriving at it from the argument I mentioned at the outset.

2. The extreme view could of course be weakened to say that while abortion is permissible to save the mother's life, it may not be performed by a third party, but only by the mother herself. But this cannot be right either. For what we have to keep in mind is that the mother and the unborn child are not like two tenants in a small house which has, by an unfortunate mistake, been rented to both: the mother *owns* the house. The fact that she does adds to the offensiveness of deducing that the mother can do nothing from the supposition that third parties can do nothing. But it does more than this: it casts a bright light on the supposition that third parties can do nothing. Certainly it lets us see that a third party who says "I cannot choose between you" is fooling himself if he thinks this is impartiality. If Jones has found and fastened on a certain coat, which he needs to keep him from freezing, but which Smith also needs to keep him from freezing, then it is not impartiality that says "I cannot choose between you" when Smith owns the coat. Women have said again and again "This body is *my* body!" and they have reason to feel angry, reason to feel that it has been like shouting into the wind. Smith, after all, is hardly likely to bless us if we say to him, "Of course it's your coat, anybody would grant that it is. But no one may choose between you and Jones who is to have it. . . ."

3. Where the mother's life is not at stake, the argument I mentioned at the outset seems to have a much stronger pull. "Everyone has a right to life, so the unborn person has a right to life." And isn't the child's right to life weightier than anything other than the mother's own right to life, which she might put forward as ground for an abortion?

This argument treats the right to life as if it were unproblematic. It is not, and this seems to me to be precisely the source of the mistake.

For we should now, at long last, ask what it comes to, to have a right to life. In some views having a right to life includes having a right to be given at least the bare minimum one needs for continued life. But suppose that what in fact *is* the bare minimum a man needs for continued life is something he has no right at all to be given? If I am sick unto death, and the only thing that will save my life is the touch of Henry Fonda's cool hand on my fevered brow, then all the same, I have no right to be given the touch of Henry Fonda's cool hand on my fevered brow. It would be frightfully nice of him to fly in from the West Coast to provide it. It would be less nice, though no doubt well meant, if my friends flew out to the West Coast and carried Henry Fonda back with them. But I have no right at all against anybody that he should do this for me. Or again, to return to the story I told earlier, the fact that for continued life that violinist needs the continued use of your kidneys does not establish that he has a right to be given the continued use of your kidneys. He certainly has no right against you that *you* should give him continued use of your kidneys. For nobody has any right to use your kidneys unless you give him such a right; and nobody has the right against you that you shall give him this right—if you do allow him to go on using your kidneys, this is a kindness on your part, and not something he can claim from you as his due. Nor has he any right against anybody else that *they* should give him continued use of your kidneys. Certainly he had no right against the Society of Music Lovers that they should plug him into you in the first place. And if you now start to unplug yourself, having learned that you will otherwise have to spend nine years in bed with him, there is nobody in the world who must try to prevent you, in order to see to it that he is given something he has a right to be given.

Some people are rather stricter about the right to life. In their view, it does not include the right to be given anything, but amounts to, and only to, the right not to be killed by anybody. But here a related difficulty arises. If everybody is to refrain from killing that violinist, then everybody must refrain from doing a great many different sorts of things. Everybody must refrain from slitting his throat, everybody must refrain from shooting him—and everybody must refrain from unplugging you from him. But does he have a right against everybody that they shall refrain from unplugging you from him? To refrain from doing this is to allow him to continue to use your kidneys. It could be argued that he has a right against us that *we* should allow him to continue to use your kidneys. That is, while he had no right against us that we should give him the use of your kidneys, it might be argued that he anyway has a right against us that we shall not now intervene and deprive him of the use of your kidneys. I shall come back to third-party interventions later. But certainly the violinist has no right against you that *you* shall allow him to continue to use your kidneys. As I said, if you do allow him to use them, it is a kindness on your part, and not something you owe him.

The difficulty I point to here is not peculiar to the right to life. It reappears in connection with all the other natural rights; and it is something which an adequate account of rights must deal with. For present purposes it is enough just to draw attention to it. But I would stress that I am not arguing that people do not have a right to life—quite to the contrary, it seems to me that the primary control we must place on the acceptability of an account of rights is that it should turn out in that account to be a truth that all persons have a right to life. I am arguing only that having a right to life does not guarantee having either a right to be given the use of or a right to be allowed continued use of another person's body—even if one needs it for life itself. So the right to life will not serve the opponents of abortion in the very simple and clear way in which they seem to have thought it would.

4. There is another way to bring out the difficulty. In the most ordinary sort of case, to deprive someone of what he has a right to is to treat him unjustly. Suppose a boy and his small brother are jointly given a box of chocolates for Christmas. If the older boy takes the box and refuses to give his brother any of the chocolates, he is unjust to him, for the brother has been given a right to half of them. But suppose that, having learned that otherwise it means nine years in bed with that violinist, you unplug yourself from him. You surely are not being unjust to him, for you gave him no right to use your kidneys, and no one else can have given him any such right. But we have to notice that in unplugging yourself, you are killing him; and violinists, like everybody else, have a right to life, and thus in the view we were considering just now, the right not to be killed.
So here you do what he supposedly has a right you shall not do, but you do not act unjustly to him in doing it.

The emendation which may be made at this point is this: the right to life consists not in the right not to be killed, but rather in the right not to be killed unjustly. This runs a risk of circularity, but never mind: it would enable us to square the fact that the violinist has a right to life with the fact that you do not act unjustly toward him in unplugging yourself, thereby killing him. For if you do not kill him unjustly, you do not violate his right to life, and so it is no wonder you do him no injustice.

But if this emendation is accepted, the gap in the argument against abortion stares us plainly in the face: it is by no means enough to show that the fetus is a person, and to remind us that all persons have a right to life—we need to be shown also that killing the fetus violates its right to life, i.e., that abortion is unjust killing. And is it?

I suppose we may take it as a datum that in a case of pregnancy due to rape the mother has not given the unborn person a right to the use of her body for food and shelter. Indeed, in what pregnancy could it be supposed that the mother has given the unborn person such a right? It is not as if there were unborn persons drifting about the world, to whom a woman who wants a child says "I invite you in."

But it might be argued that there are other ways one can have acquired a right to the use of another person's body than by having been invited to use it by that person. Suppose a woman voluntarily indulges in intercourse, knowing of the chance it will issue in pregnancy, and then she does become pregnant; is she not in part responsible for the presence, in fact the very existence, of the unborn person inside her? No doubt she did not invite it in. But doesn't her partial responsibility for its being there itself give it a right to the use of her body? If so, then her aborting it would be more like the boy's taking away the chocolates, and less like your unplugging yourself from the violinist—doing so would be depriving it of what it does have a right to, and thus would be doing it an injustice.

And then, too, it might be asked whether or not she can kill it even to save her own life: If she voluntarily called it into existence, how can she now kill it, even in self-defense?

The first thing to be said about this is that it is something new. Opponents of abortion have been so concerned to make out the independence of the fetus, in order to establish that it has a right to life, just as its mother does, that they have tended to overlook the possible support they might gain from making out that the fetus is *dependent* on the mother, in order to establish that she has a special kind of responsibility for it, a responsibility that gives it rights against her which are not possessed by any independent person—such as an ailing violinist who is a stranger to her.

On the other hand, this argument would give the unborn person a right to its mother's body only if her pregnancy resulted from a voluntary act, undertaken in full knowledge of the chance a pregnancy might result from it. It would leave out entirely the unborn person whose existence is due to rape. Pending the availability of some further argument, then, we would be left with the conclusion that unborn persons whose existence is due to rape have no right to the use of their mothers' bodies, and thus that aborting them is not depriving them of anything they have a right to and hence is not unjust killing.

And we should also notice that it is not at all plain that this argument really does go even as far as it purports to. For there are cases and cases, and the details make a difference. If the room is stuffy, and I therefore open a window to air it, and a burglar climbs in, it would be absurd to say, "Ah, now he can stay, she's given him a right to the use of her house—for she is partially responsible for his presence there, having voluntarily done what enabled him to get in, in full knowledge that there are such things as burglars, and that burglars burgle." It would be still more absurd to say this if I had had bars installed outside my windows, precisely to prevent burglars from getting in, and a burglar got in only because of a defect in the bars. It remains equally absurd if we imagine it is not a burglar who climbs in, but an innocent person who blunders or falls in. Again, suppose it were like this: people-seeds drift about in the air like pollen, and if you open your windows, one may drift in and take root in your carpets or upholstery. You don't want children, so you fix up your windows with fine mesh screens, the very best you can buy. As can happen, however, and on very, very rare occasions does happen, one of the screens is defective; and a seed drifts in and takes root. Does the person-plant who now develops have a right to the use of your house? Surely not—despite the fact that you voluntarily opened your windows, you knowingly kept carpets and upholstered furniture, and you knew that screens were sometimes defective. Someone may argue that you are responsible for its rooting, that it does have a right to your house, because after all you *could* have lived out your life with bare floors and furniture, or with sealed windows and doors. But this won't do—for by the same token anyone can avoid a pregnancy due to rape by having a hysterectomy, or anyway by never leaving home without a (reliable!) army.

131

It seems to me that the argument we are looking at can establish at most that there are *some* cases in which the unborn person has a right to the use of its mother's body, and therefore *some* cases in which abortion is unjust killing. There is room for much discussion and argument as to precisely which, if any. But I think we should sidestep this issue and leave it open, for at any rate the argument certainly does not establish that all abortion is unjust killing.

5. There is room for yet another argument here, however. We surely must all grant that there may be cases in which it would be morally indecent to detach a person from your body at the cost of his life. Suppose you learn that what the violinist needs is not nine years of your life, but only one hour: all you need do to save his life is to spend one hour in that bed with him. Suppose also that letting him use your kidneys for that one hour would not affect your health in the slightest. Admittedly you were kidnapped. Admittedly you did not give anyone permission to plug him into you. Nevertheless it seems to me plain you *ought* to allow him to use your kidneys for that hour—it would be indecent to refuse.

Again, suppose pregnancy lasted only an hour, and constituted no threat to life or health. And suppose that a woman becomes pregnant as a result of rape. Admittedly she did not voluntarily do anything to bring about the existence of a child. Admittedly she did nothing at all which would give the unborn person a right to the use of her body. All the same it might well be said, as in the newly emended violinist story, that she *ought* to allow it to remain for that hour—that it would be indecent in her to refuse.

Now some people are inclined to use the term "right" in such a way that it follows from the fact that you ought to allow a person to use your body for the hour he needs, that he has a right to use your body for the hour he needs, even though he has not been given that right by any person or act. They may say that it follows also that if you refuse, you act unjustly toward him. This use of the term is perhaps so common that it cannot be called wrong; nevertheless it seems to me to be an unfortunate loosening of what we would do better to keep a tight rein on. Suppose that box of chocolates I mentioned earlier had not been given to both boys jointly, but was given only to the older boy. There he sits, stolidly eating his way through the box, his small

brother watching enviously. Here we are likely to say "You ought not to be so mean. You ought to give your brother some of those chocolates." My own view is that it just does not follow from the truth of this that the brother has any right to any of the chocolates. If the boy refuses to give his brother any, he is greedy, stingy, callous—but not unjust. I suppose that the people I have in mind will say it does follow that the brother has a right to some of the chocolates, and thus that the boy does act unjustly if he refuses to give his brother any. But the effect of saying this is to obscure what we should keep distinct, namely the difference between the boy's refusal in this case and the boy's refusal in the earlier case, in which the box was given to both boys jointly, and in which the small brother thus had what was from any point of view clear title to half.

A further objection to so using the term "right" that from the fact that A ought to do a thing for B, it follows that B has a right against A that A do it for him, is that it is going to make the question of whether or not a man has a right to a thing turn on how easy it is to provide him with it; and this seems not merely unfortunate, but morally unacceptable. Take the case of Henry Fonda again. I said earlier that I had no right to the touch of his cool hand on my fevered brow, even though I needed it to save my life. I said it would be frightfully nice of him to fly in from the West Coast to provide me with it, but that I had no right against him that he should do so. But suppose he isn't on the West Coast. Suppose he has only to walk across the room, place a hand briefly on my brow—and lo, my life is saved. Then surely he ought to do it, it would be indecent to refuse. Is it to be said "Ah, well, it follows that in this case she has a right to the touch of his hand on her brow, and so it would be an injustice in him to refuse"? So that I have a right to it when it is easy for him to provide it, though no right when it's hard? It's rather a shocking idea that anyone's rights should fade away and disappear as it gets harder and harder to accord them to him.

So my own view is that even though you ought to let the violinist use your kidneys for the one hour he needs, we should not conclude that he has a right to do so—we should say that if you refuse, you are, like the boy who owns all the chocolates and will give none away, self-centered and callous, indecent in fact, but not unjust. And similarly, that even supposing a case in which a woman pregnant due to rape ought to allow the unborn person to use her body for the hour he needs, we should not conclude that he has a right to do so; we should conclude that she is self-centered, callous, indecent, but not unjust, if she refuses. The complaints are no less grave; they are just different. However, there is no need to insist on this point. If anyone does wish to deduce "he has a right" from "you ought," then all the same he must surely grant that there are cases in which it is not morally required of you that you allow that violinist to use your kidneys, and in which he does not have a right to use them, and in which you do not do him an injustice if you refuse. And so also for mother and unborn child. Except in such cases as the unborn person has a right to demand it—and we were leaving open the possibility that there may be such cases—nobody is morally *required* to make large sacrifices, of health, of all other interests and concerns, of all other duties and commitments, for nine years, or even for nine months, in order to keep another person alive. . . .

8. My argument will be found unsatisfactory on two counts by many of those who want to regard abortion as morally permissible. First, while I do argue that abortion is not impermissible, I do not argue that it is always permissible. I am inclined to think it a merit of my account precisely that it does *not* give a general yes or a general no. It allows for and supports our sense that, for example, a sick and desperately frightened fourteen-year-old schoolgirl, pregnant due to rape, may *of course* choose abortion, and that any law which rules this out is an insane law. And it also allows for and supports our sense that in other cases resort to abortion is even positively indecent. It would be indecent in the woman to request an abortion, and indecent in a doctor to perform it, if she is in her seventh month, and wants the abortion just to avoid the nuisance of postponing a trip abroad. The very fact that the ar-

guments I have been drawing attention to treat all cases of abortion, or even all cases of abortion in which the mother's life is not at stake, as morally on a par ought to have made them suspect at the outset.

Secondly, while I am arguing for the permissibility of abortion in some cases, I am not arguing for the right to secure the death of the unborn child. It is easy to confuse these two things in that up to a certain point in the life of the fetus it is not able to survive outside the mother's body; hence removing it from her body guarantees its death. But they are importantly different. I have argued that you are not morally required to spend nine months in bed, sustaining the life of that violinist; but to say this is by no means to say that if, when you unplug yourself, there is a miracle and he survives, you then have a right to turn round and slit his throat. You may detach yourself even if this costs him his life; you have no right to be guaranteed his death, by some other means, if unplugging yourself does not kill him. There are some people who will feel dissatisfied by this feature of my argument. A woman may be utterly devastated by the thought of a child, a bit of herself, put out for adoption and never seen or heard of again. She may therefore want not merely that the child be detached from her, but more, that it die. Some opponents of abortion are inclined to regard this as beneath contempt—thereby showing insensitivity to what is surely a powerful source of despair. All the same, I agree that the desire for the child's death is not one which anybody may gratify, should it turn out to be possible to detach the child alive.

At this place, however, it should be remembered that we have only been pretending throughout that the fetus is a human being from the moment of conception. A very early abortion is surely not the killing of a person, and so is not dealt with by anything I have said here.

NOTES

1. Daniel Callahan, *Abortion: Law, Choice and Morality* (New York, 1970), p. 373. This book gives a fascinating survey of the available information on abortion. The Jewish tradition is surveyed in David M. Feldman, *Birth Control in Jewish Law* (New York, 1968), Part 5, the Catholic tradition in John T. Noonan, Jr., "An Almost Absolute Value in History," in *The Morality of Abortion*, ed. John T. Noonan, Jr. (Cambridge, Mass., 1970).

2. The term "direct" in the arguments I refer to is a technical one. Roughly, what is meant by "direct killing" is either killing as an end in itself, or killing as a means to some end, for example, the end of saving someone else's life. See note 5, below, for an example of its use.

3. Cf. *Encyclical Letter of Pope Pius XI on Christian Marriage*, St. Paul Editions (Boston, n.d.), p. 32: "however much we may pity the mother whose health and even life is gravely imperiled in the performance of the duty allotted to her by nature, nevertheless what could ever be a sufficient reason for excusing in any way the direct murder of the innocent? This is precisely what we are dealing with here." Noonan (*The Morality of Abortion*, p. 43) reads this as follows: "What cause can ever avail to excuse in any way the direct killing of the innocent? For it is a question of that."

4. The thesis in (4) is in an interesting way weaker than those in (1), (2), and (3): they rule out abortion even in cases in which both mother *and* child will die if the abortion is not performed. By contrast, one who held the view expressed in (4) could consistently say that one needn't prefer letting two persons die to killing one.

5. Cf. the following passage from Pius XII, *Address to the Italian Catholic Society of Midwives*: "The baby in the maternal breast has the right to life immediately from God.—Hence there is no man, no human authority, no science, no medical, eugenic, social, economic or moral 'indication' which can establish or grant a valid juridical ground for a direct deliberate disposition of an innocent human life, that is a disposition which looks to its destruction either as an end or as a means to another end perhaps in itself not illicit.—The baby, still not born, is a man in the same degree and for the same reason as the mother" (quoted in Noonan, *The Morality of Abortion*, p. 45).

John Noonan

HOW TO ARGUE ABOUT ABORTION

John Noonan examines various models and methods used in the debate on abortion, distinguishing those that do not work from those that do. According to Noonan, those that do not work involve (1) fantasized examples, such as Thomson's unconscious violinist, (2) hard cases which are resolved in ways that ignore the child's interests, and (3) spatial metaphors, such as "direct" and "indirect," which obscure the moral distinctions involved. Those that do work are (1) balancing values in a nonquantitative manner, (2) seeing what might be otherwise overlooked, and (3) responding to the full range of human experience.

AT THE HEART OF the debate about abortion is the relation of person to person in social contexts. Analogies, metaphors, and methods of debate which do not focus on persons and which do not attend to the central contexts are mischievous. Their use arises from a failure to appreciate the distinctive character of moral argument—its requirement that values be organically related and balanced, its dependence on

From "Responding to Persons: Methods of Moral Argument in Debate over Abortion," *Theology Digest* (1973), pp. 291–307. Reprinted by permission of *Theology Digest*.

personal vision, and its rootedness in social experience. I propose here to examine various models and methods used in the debate on abortion distinguishing those such as fantasized situations, hard cases, and linear metaphors, all of which do not work, from the balancing, seeing, and appeal to human experience which I believe to be essential. I shall move from models and metaphors which take the rule against abortion as the expression of a single value to the consideration of ways of argument intended to suggest the variety of values which have converged in the formulation of the rule. The values embodied in the rule are various because abortion is an aspect of the relation of person to person, and persons are larger than single values; and abortion is an act in a social context which cannot be reduced to a single value. I write as a critic of abortion, with no doubt a sharper eye for the weaknesses of its friends than of its foes, but my chief aim is to suggest what arguments count.

ARTIFICIAL CASES

One way of reaching the nub of a moral issue is to construct a hypothetical situation endowed with precisely the characteristics you believe are crucial in the real issue you are seeking to resolve. Isolated from the clutter of detail in the real situation, these characteristics point to the proper solution. The risk is that the features you believe crucial you will enlarge to the point of creating a caricature. The pedagogy of your illustration will be blunted by the uneasiness caused by the lack of correspondence between the fantasized situation and the real situation to be judged. Such is the case with recent efforts by philosopher, Judith Jarvis Thomson to construct arguments justifying abortion.

Suppose, says Thomson, a violinist whose continued existence depends on acquiring new kidneys. Without the violinist's knowledge—he remains innocent—a healthy person is kidnapped and connected to him so that the violinist now shares the use of healthy kidneys. May the victim of the kidnapping break the connection and thereby kill the violinist? Thomson intuits that the normal judgment will be Yes. The healthy person should not be imposed upon by a lifelong physical connection with the violinist. This construct, Thomson contends, bears upon abortion by establishing that being human does not carry with it a right to life which must be respected by another at the cost of serious inconvenience.

This ingenious attempt to make up a parallel to pregnancy imagines a kidnapping; a serious operation performed on the victim of the kidnapping; and a continuing interference with many of the activities of the victim. It supposes that violinist and victim were unrelated. It supposed nothing by which the victim's initial aversion to his yoke-mate might be mitigated or compensated. It supposes no degree of voluntariness. The similitude to pregnancy is grotesque. It is difficult to think of another age or society in which a caricature of this sort could be seriously put forward as a paradigm illustrating the moral choice to be made by a mother.

While Thomson focuses on this fantasy, she ignores a real case from which American tort law has generalized. On a January night in Minnesota, a cattle buyer, Orlando Depue, asked a family of farmers, the Flateaus, with whom he had dined, if he could remain overnight at their house. The Flateaus refused and, although Depue was sick and had fainted, put him out of the house into the cold night. Imposing liability on the Flateaus for Depue's loss of his frostbitten fingers the court said, "In the case at bar defendants were under no contract obligation to minister to plaintiff in his distress; but humanity demanded they do so, if they understood and appreciated his condition . . . The law as well as humanity required that he not be exposed in his helpless condition to the merciless elements." Depue was a guest for supper although not a guest after supper. The American Law Institute, generalizing, has said that it makes no difference whether the helpless person is a guest or a trespasser. He has the privilege of staying. His host has the duty not to injure him or put him into an environment where he becomes nonviable. The obligation arises when one person "understands and appreciates" the condition of the other. Although the analogy is not exact, the case seems closer to the mother's situation than the case imagined by Thomson; and the emotional response of the Minnesota judges seems to be a truer reflection of what humanity requires. . . .

HARD CASES AND
EXCEPTIONS

In the presentation of permissive abortion to the American public, major emphasis has been put on situations of great pathos—the child deformed by thalidomide, the child affected by rubella, the child known to suffer from Tay-Sachs disease or Downs syndrome, the raped adolescent, the exhausted mother of small children. These situations are not imagined, and the cases described are not analogies to those where abortion might be sought; they are themselves cases to which abortion is a solution. Who could deny the poignancy of their appeal?

Hard cases make bad law, runs the venerable legal adage, but it seems to be worse law if the distress experienced in situations such as these is not taken into account. If persons are to be given preeminence over abstract principle, should not exceptions for these cases be made in the most rigid rule against abortion? Does not the human experience of such exceptions point to a more sweeping conclusion— the necessity of abandoning any uniform prohibition of abortion, so that all the elements of a particular situation may be weighted by the woman in question and her doctor?

So far, fault can scarcely be found with this method of argumentation, this appeal to common experience. But the cases are oversimplified if focus is directed solely on the parents of a physically defective child or on the mother in the cases of rape or psychic exhaustion. The situations are very hard for the parents or the mother; they are still harder for the fetus who is threatened with death. If the fetus is a person as the opponents of abortion contend, its destruction is not the sparing of suffering by the sacrifice of a principle but by the sacrifice of a life. Emotion is a proper element in moral response, but to the extent that the emotion generated by these cases obscures the claims of the fetus, this kind of argumentation fosters erroneous judgment.

In three of the cases—the child deformed by drugs, disease, or genetic defect—the neglect of the child's point of view seems stained by hypocrisy. Abortion is here justified as putting the child out of the misery of living a less than normal life. The child is not consulted as to the choice. Experience, which

teaches that even the most seriously incapacitated prefer living to dying, is ignored. The feelings of the parents are the actual consideration, and these feelings are treated with greater tenderness than the fetal desire to live. The common unwillingness to say frankly that the abortion is sought for the parents' benefit is testimony, unwillingly given, to the intuition that such self-preference by the parents is difficult for society or for the parents themselves to accept.

The other kind of hard case does not mask preference for the parent by a pretense of concern for the fetus. The simplest situation is that of a pregnancy due to rape—in presentations to some legislatures it was usual to add a racist fillip by supposing a white woman and a black rapist—but this gratuitous pandering to bias is not essential. The fetus, unwanted in the most unequivocal way, is analogized to an invader of the mother's body—is it even appropriate to call her a mother when she did nothing to assume the special fiduciary cares of motherhood? If she is prevented from having an abortion, she is being compelled for nine months to be reminded of a traumatic assault. Do not her feelings override the right to life of her unwanted tenant?

Rape arouses fear and a desire for revenge, and reference to rape evokes emotion. The emotion has been enough for the state to take the life of the rapist. Horror of the crime is easily extended to horror of the product, so that the fetal life becomes forfeit too. If horror is overcome, adoption appears to be a more humane solution than abortion. If the rape case is not being used as a stalking horse by proponents of abortion—if there is a desire to deal with it in itself—the solution is to assure the destruction of the sperm in the one to three days elapsing between insemination and impregnation.

Generally, however, the rape case is presented as a way of suggesting a general principle, a principle which could be formulated as follows: Every unintended pregnancy may be interrupted if its continuation will cause emotional distress to the mother. Pregnancies due to bad planning or bad luck are analogized to pregnancies due to rape; they are all involuntary. Indeed many pregnancies can without great difficulty be assimilated to the hard case, for how often do persons undertake an act of sexual intercourse consciously intending that a child be the fruit of that act? Many pregnancies are unspecified by a particular intent, are unplanned, are in this sense involuntary. Many pregnancies become open to termination if only the baby consciously sought has immunity.

This result is unacceptable to those who believe that the fetus is human. It is acceptable to those who do not believe the fetus is human, but to reach it they do not need the argument based on the hard case. The result would follow immediately from the mother's dominion over a portion of her body. Opponents of abortion who out of consideration for the emotional distress caused by rape will grant the rape exception must see that the exception can be generalized to destroy the rule. If, on other grounds they believe the rule good, they must deny the exception which eats it up.

DIRECT AND INDIRECT

From the paradigmatic arguments, I turn to metaphors and especially those which, based on some spatial image, are misleading. I shall begin with "direct" and "indirect" and their cousins, "affirmative" and "negative." In the abortion argument "direct" and "indirect," "affirmative" and "negative" occur more frequently in these kinds of questions: If one denies that a fetus may be killed directly, but admits that indirect abortion is permissible, is he guilty of inconsistency? If one maintains that there is a negative duty not to kill fetuses, does he thereby commit himself to an affirmative obligation of assuring safe delivery of every fetus? If one agrees that there is no affirmative duty to actualize as many spermatic, ovoid, embryonic, or fetal potentialities as possible, does one thereby concede that it is generally permissible to take steps to destroy fertilized ova? The argumentative implications of these questions can be best unravelled by looking at the force of the metaphors invoked.

"Direct" and "indirect" appeal to our experience of linedrawing and of travel. You reach a place on a piece of paper by drawing a straight or crooked line—the line is direct or indirect. You go to a place without detours or you go in a roundabout fashion—your route is direct or indirect. In each instance, whether your path is direct or indirect your

destination is the same. The root experience is that you can reach the same spot in ways distinguished by their immediacy and the amount of ground covered. "Indirectly" says you proceed more circuitously and cover more ground. It does not, however, say anything of the reason why you go circuitously. You may go indirectly because you want to cover more ground or because you want to disguise your destination.

The ambiguity in the reason for indirectness—an ambiguity present in the primary usage of the term—carries over when "indirect" is applied metaphorically to human intentions. There may be a reason for doing something indirectly—you want to achieve another objective besides the indirect action. You may also act indirectly to conceal from another or from yourself what is your true destination. Because of this ambiguity in the reason for indirection, "indirect" is apt to cause confusion when applied in moral analysis.

Defenders of an absolute prohibition of abortion have excepted the removal of a fertilized ovum in an ectopic pregnancy and the removal of a cancerous uterus containing an embryo. They have characterized the abortion involved as "indirect." They have meant that the surgeon's attention is focused on correcting a pathological condition dangerous to the mother and he only performs the operation because there is no alternative way of correcting it. But the physician has to intend to achieve not only the improvement of the mother but the performance of action by which the fertilized ovum becomes nonviable. He necessarily intends to perform an abortion, he necessarily intends to kill. To say that he acts indirectly is to conceal what is being done. It is a confusing and improper use of the metaphor.

A clearer presentation of the cases of the cancerous uterus and the ectopic pregnancy would acknowledge them to be true exceptions to the absolute inviolability of the fetus. Why are they not exceptions which would eat up the rule? It depends on what the rule is considered to be. The principle that can be discerned in them is, whenever the embryo is a danger to the life of the mother, an abortion is permissible. At the level of reason nothing more can be asked of the mother. The exceptions do eat up any rule of preferring the fetus to the mother—any rule of fetus first. They do not destroy the rule that the life of the fetus has precedence over other interests of the mother. The exceptions of the ectopic pregnancy and the cancerous uterus are special cases of the general exception to the rule against killing, which permits one to kill in self-defense. Characterization of this kind of killing as "indirect" does not aid analysis.

It is a basic intuition that one is not responsible for all the consequences of one's acts. By living at all one excludes others from the air one breathes, the food one eats. One cannot foresee all the results which will flow from any given action. It is imperative for moral discourse to be able to distinguish between injury foreseeably inflicted on another, and the harm which one may unknowingly bring about. "Direct" and "indirect" are sometimes used to distinguish the foreseen consequence from the unconsidered or unknown consequence. This usage does not justify terming abortion to save a mother's life "indirect." In the case of terminating the ectopic pregnancy, the cancerous uterus, the life-threatening fetus generally, one considers precisely the consequence, the taking of the fetal life.

Just as one intuits that one is not responsible for all the consequences, so one intuits that one is not called to right all wrongs. No one is bound to the impossible. There is, therefore, an intuitive difference between the duty to refrain from doing harm to anyone and the duty to help everyone in distress. The duty to refrain is possible of fulfillment if it refers only to conscious infliction of harm. The duty to help is impossible if one is going to develop as a human being, getting educated, earning a living, marrying, raising a family, and so forth. The needs of other human beings are subordinated or postponed by everyone to the fulfillment of many of one's own needs, and rightly so. The distinction between affirmative and negative duties, another linear metaphor, rests on this universal experience. The terms do have a basis in moral life. Their usefulness in moral analysis, however, is not great. The crucial distinction is not between negative and affirmative, but between limited and unlimited duty.

It is possible to state the duty not to kill the fetus as the duty to care for the fetus. Opponents of abortion, however, do not commit thereby themselves to the position that all fertilized ova must be born. A pregnant woman may, for example, take the chance of killing the baby by going for a walk or a drive instead of staying safely in bed. She is not responsible

for all the consequences of her acts. She is not called to help the fetus in every possible way. The negative duty or the convertible affirmative duty excludes acts which have a high probability of death for the fetus, but not those with a low probability of death. Similarly, one has a duty not to kill one's older children, and a duty to care for them, but no duty to keep them free from all risk of harm. No inconsistency exists in not equating a limited negative duty with an unlimited affirmative duty; no inconsistency exists in rejecting high risk acts and approving low risks acts.

LINEDRAWING

The prime linear metaphor is, of course, linedrawing. It is late in the history of moral thought for anyone to suppose that an effective moral retort is, "Yes, but where do you draw the line?" or to make the inference that, because any drawing of a line requires a decision, all linedrawing is arbitrary. One variant or another of these old ploys is, however, frequently used in the present controversy. From living cell to dying corpse a continuum exists. Proponents of abortion are said to be committed to murder, to euthanasia, or, at a minimum, to infanticide. Opponents are alleged to be bound to condemn contraception—after all, spermatazoa are living human cells. Even if contraception is admitted and infanticide rejected, the range of choice is still large enough for the line drawn to be challenged—is it to be at nidation, at formation of the embryo, at quickening, at viability, at birth? Whoever adopts one point is asked why he does not move forward or backward by one stage of development. The difficulty of presenting apodictic reasons for preferring one position is made to serve as proof that the choice may be made as best suits the convenience of an individual or the state.

The metaphor of linedrawing distracts attention from the nature of the moral decision. The metaphor suggests an empty room composed of indistinguishable grey blocks. In whatever way the room is divided, there are grey blocks on either side of the line. Or if the metaphor is taken more mathematically, it suggests a series of points, which, wherever bisected, are fungible with each other. What is obscured in the spatial or mathematical model is the variety of values whose comparison enters into any moral decision. The model appeals chiefly to those novices in moral reasoning who believe that moral judgment is a matter of pursuing a principle to its logical limit. Single-mindedly looking at a single value, they ask, if this is good, why not more of it? In practice, however, no one can be so single-hearted. Insistence of this kind of logical consistency becomes the preserve of fanatics or of controversialists eager to convict their adversaries of inconsistency. If more than one good is sought by a human being, he must bring the goods he seeks into relationship with each other; he must limit one to maintain another; he must mix them.

The process of choosing multiple goods occurs in many particular contexts—in eating, in studying, in painting. No one supposes that those who take the first course must forego dessert, that the election of English means History shall not be studied, that the use of blue excludes red. Linear models for understanding choice in these matters are readily perceived as inappropriate. The commitment to values, the cutting off of values, and the mixing of values accompany each other.

Is, however, the choice of the stage of development which should not be destroyed by abortion a choice requiring the mixing of multiple goods? Is not the linear model appropriate when picking a point on the continuum of life? Are not the moral choices which require commitment and mixing made only after the selection of the stage at which a being becomes a person? To these related questions the answers must all be negative. To recognize a person is a moral decision; it depends on objective data but it also depends on the perceptions and inclinations and ends of the decision makers; it cannot be made without commitment and without consideration of alternative values. Who is a person? This is not a question asked abstractly, in the air, with no purpose in mind. To disguise the personal involvement in the response to personhood is to misconceive the issue of abortion from the start.

Those who identify the rational with the geometrical, the algebraic, the logical may insist that, if the fundamental recognition of personhood depends upon the person who asks, then the arbitrariness of any position on abortion is conceded. If values must

be mixed even in identifying the human, who can object to another's mixture? The issue becomes like decisions in eating, studying, and painting, a matter of discretion. A narrow rationalism of this kind uses "taste" as the ultimate epithet for the non-rational. It does not acknowledge that each art has its own rules. It claims for itself alone the honorable term "reason."

As this sort of monopoly has become unacceptable in general philosophy, so it is unnecessary to accept it here. Taste, that is perceptiveness, is basic; and if it cannot be disputed, it can be improved by experience. Enology, painting, or moral reasoning all require basic aptitude, afford wide ranges of options, have limits beyond which a choice can be counterproductive, and are better done by the experienced than by amateurs. Some persons may lack almost any capacity for undertaking one or another of them. Although all men are moral beings, not all are proficient at moral judgment, so that morality is not a democratic business. Selecting multiple goods, those who are capable of the art perceive, test, mix and judge. The process has little in common with linedrawing. In the case of abortion, it is the contention of its opponents that in such a process the right response to the data is that the fetus is a human being.

BALANCING

The process of decisionmaking just described is better caught by the term "balancing." In contrast to linedrawing, balancing is a metaphor helpful in understanding moral judgment. Biologically understood, balancing is the fundamental metaphor for moral reasoning. A biological system is in balance when its parts are in the equilibrium necessary for it to live. To achieve such equilibrium, some parts—the heart, for example—must be preserved at all costs; others may be sacrificed to maintain the whole. Balance in the biological sense does not demand an egalitarian concern for every part, but an ordering and subordination which permit the whole to function. So in moral reasoning the reasoner balances values.

The mistaken common reading of this metaphor

is to treat it as equivalent to weighing, so that balancing is understood as an act of quantitative comparison analogous to that performed by an assayer or a butcher. This view tacitly supposes that values are weights which are tangible and commensurate. One puts so many units on one pan of the scales and matches them with so many units on the other to reach a "balanced" judgment. To give a personal example, Daniel Callahan has questioned my position that the value of innocent life cannot be sacrificed to achieve the other values which abortion might secure. The "force of the rule," he writes, "is absolutist, displaying no 'balance' at all." He takes balancing in the sense of weighing and wonders how one value can be so heavy.

That justice often consists in the fair distribution or exchange of goods as in the familiar Aristotelian examples has no doubt worked to confirm a quantitative approach. Scales as the symbol of justice seem to suggest the antiquity of the quantitative meaning of balance. But the original sense of the scales was otherwise. In Egypt where the symbol was first used, a feather, the Egyptian hieroglyphic for truth, turned the balance. As put by David Daube in his illuminating analysis of the ancient symbolism, "The slightest turning of the scales—'but in the estimation of a hair'—will decide the issue, and the choice is between salvation and annihilation." Not a matching of weights, but a response to reality was what justice was seen to require, and what was at stake was not a slight overweighing in one direction or the other, but salvation. Moral choice, generally, has this character of a hair separating good from evil.

A fortiori then, in moral judgement, where more values are in play than in any system of strict law or commutative justice, balancing is a misleading metaphor if it suggests a matching of weights. It is an indispensable metaphor if it stands for the equilibrium of a living organism making the choices necessary for its preservation. A single value cannot be pursued to the point of excluding all other values. This is the caricature of moral argument I have already touched on in connection with the metaphor of linedrawing. But some values are more vital than others, as the heart is more vital to the body than the hand. A balanced moral judgment requires a sense of the limits, interrelations, and priority of values. It is the position of those generally opposed

to abortion that a judgment preferring interests less than human life to human life is unbalanced, that a judgment denying a mother's fiduciary responsibility to her child is unbalanced, that a judgment making killing a principal part of the profession of a physician is unbalanced, that a judgment permitting agencies of the state to procure and pay for the destruction of the offspring of the poor or underprivileged is unbalanced. They contend that such judgments expand the right limits of a mother's responsibility for herself, destroy the fiduciary relation which is a central paradigm for the social bond, fail to relate to the physician's service to life and the state's care for its citizens. At stake in the acceptance of abortion is not a single value, life, against which the suffering of the mother or parents may be balanced. The values to be considered are the child's life, the mother's faithfulness to her dependent, the physician's commitment to preserving life; and in the United States today abortion cannot be discussed without awareness that if law does not prohibit it, the state will fund it, so that the value of the state's abstention from the taking of life is also at issue. The judgment which accepts abortion, it is contended, is unbalanced in subordinating these values to the personal autonomy of the mother and the social interest in population control.

SEEING

The metaphor of balancing points to the process of combining values. But we do not combine values like watercolors. We respond to values situated in subjects. "Balancing" is an inadequate metaphor for moral thinking in leaving out of account the central moral transaction—the response of human beings to other human beings. In making moral judgments we respond to those human beings whom we see.

The mataphor of sight is a way of emphasizing the need for perception, whether by eyes or ears or touch, of those we take as subjects to whom we respond. Seeing in any case is more than the registration of a surface. It is a penetration yielding some sense of the other's structure, so that the experiencing of another is never merely visual or auditory or tactile. We see the features and comprehend the humanity at the same time. Look at the fetus, say the anti-abortionists, and you will see humanity. How long, they ask, can a man turn his head and pretend that he just doesn't see?

An accusation of blindness, however, does not seem to advance moral argument. A claim to see where others do not see is a usual claim of charlatans. "Illumination" or "enlightenment" appear to transcend experience and make moral disputation impossible. "Visionary" is often properly a term of disparagement. Is not an appeal to sight the end of rational debate?

In morals, as in epistemology, there is nonetheless no substitute for perception. Are animals within the range of beings with a right to life, and babies not, as Michael Tooley has recently suggested? Should trees be persons, as Christopher Stone has recently maintained? Questions of this kind are fundamentally frivolous for they point to the possibility of moral argument while attempting to deny the foundation of moral argument, our ability to recognize human persons. If a person could in no way perceive another person to be like himself, he would be incapable of moral response. If a person cannot perceive a cat or a tree as different from himself, he cuts off the possibility of argument. Debate should not end with pointing, but it must begin there.

Is there a contradiction in the opponents of abortion appealing to perception when fetuses are normally invisible? Should one not hold that until beings are seen they have not entered the ranks of society? Falling below the threshold of sight, do not fetuses fall below the threshold of humanity? If the central moral transaction is response to the other person, are not fetuses peculiarly weak subjects to elicit our response? These questions pinpoint the principal task of the defenders of the fetus—to make the fetus visible. The task is different only in degree from that assumed by defenders of other persons who have been or are "overlooked." For centuries, color acted as a psychological block to perception, and the blindness induced by color provided a sturdy basis for discrimination. Minorities of various kinds exist today who are "invisible" and therefore unlikely to be "heard" in the democratic process. Persons literally out of sight of society in prisons and mental insitutions are often not "recognized" as fellow humans by the world with which they have "lost touch." In each of these instances those who seek to vindicate the rights of the unseen must begin by calling attention to their existence. "Look" is the exhortation they address to the callous and the negligent.

Perception of fetuses is possible with not substantially greater effort than that required to pierce the physical or psychological barriers to recognizing other human beings. The main difficulty is everone's reluctance to accept the extra burdens of care imposed by an expansion of the numbers in whom humanity is recognized. It is generally more convenient to have to consider only one's kin, one's peers, one's country, one's race. Seeing requires personal attention and personal response. The emotion generated by identification with a human form is necessary to overcome the inertia which is protected by a vision restricted to a convenient group. If one is willing to undertake the risk that more will be required in one's action, fetuses may be seen in multiple ways—circumstantially, by the observation of a pregnant woman; photographically, by pictures of life in the womb; scientifically, in accounts written by investigators of prenatal life and child psychologists; visually, by observing a blood transfusion or an abortion while the fetus is alive or by examination of a fetal corpse after death. The proponent of abortion is invited to consider the organism kicking the mother, swimming peacefully in amniotic fluid, responding to the prick of an instrument, being extracted from the womb, sleeping in death. Is the kicker or swimmer similar to him or to her? Is the response to pain like his or hers? Will his or her own face look much different in death?

RESPONSE

Response to the fetus begins with grasp of the data which yield the fetus' structure. That structure is not merely anatomical form; it is dynamic—we apprehend the fetus' origin and end. It is this apprehension which makes response to the nameless fetus different from the conscious analogizing that goes on when we name a cat. Seeing, we are linked to the being in the womb by more than an inventory of shared physical characteristics and by more than a number of made-up psychological characteristics.

The weakness of the being as potential recalls our own potential state, the helplessness of the being evokes the human condition of contingency. We meet another human subject.

Seeing is impossible apart from experience, but experience is the most imprecise of terms. What kind of experience counts, and whose? There are experiences which only women and usually only those within the ages of 14 to 46 who are fertile can have: conceiving a child, carrying a child, having an abortion, being denied an abortion, giving birth. There are experiences only a fetus can have: being carried, being aborted, being born. There is the experience of obstetricians who regularly deliver children and occasionally abort them; there is the differently-textured experience of the professional abortionist. There is the experience of nurses who prepare the mother for abortion, care for her after the abortion, and dispose of the aborted fetus. There is the experience of physicians, social workers, and ministers, who advise a woman to have an abortion or not to have one. There is the experience of those who enforce a law against abortion, and those who stealthily or openly, for profit or for conscience's sake, defy it. There is the experience of those who have sexual intercourse knowing that abortion is or is not a remedy if an accidental pregnancy should result. There is the experience of society at large of a pattern of uncontrolled abortion or of its regulation.

Some arguments are unduly exclusivist in the experience they will admit. Those who suggest that abortion is peculiarly a matter for women disqualify men because the unique experience of pregnancy is beyond their achievement. Yet such champions of abortion do not regularly disqualify sterile women whose experience of pregnancy must be as vicarious as a man's. Tertullian taught that only those who have known motherhood themselves have a right to speak from experience on the choices presented by abortion. Yet even Tertullian did not go so far as to say that only mothers who had both given birth and had had abortions were qualified to speak. Efforts of this sort to restrict those who are competent rest on a confusion between the relevant and the personal. You do not have to be a judge to know that bribery is evil or a slave to know that slavery is wrong. Vicarious experience, in this as in other moral matters, is a proper basis for judgment.

Vicarious experience appears strained to the outer limit when one is asked to consider the experience of the fetus. No one remembers being born, no one knows what it is like to die. Empathy may, however, supply for memory, as it does in other instances when we refer to the experience of infants who cannot speak or to the experience of death by those who cannot speak again. The experience of the fetus is no more beyond our knowledge than the experience of the baby and the experience of dying.

Participation in an abortion is another sort of experience relevant to moral judgment. Generals are not thought of as the best judges of the morality of war, nor is their experience thought to be unaffected by their profession, but they should be heard, when the permissibility of war is urged. Obstetricians are in an analogous position, their testimony subject to a discount. The testimony of professional abortionists is also relevant, although subject to an even greater discount. Nurses are normally more disinterested witnesses. They speak as ones who have empathized with the female patient, disposed of the fetal remains, and, like the Red Cross in wartime, have known what the action meant by seeing the immediate consequences.

The experience of individuals becomes a datum of argument through autobiography and testimony, inference and empathy. The experience of a society has to be captured by the effort of sociologists and novelists, historians and lawyers, psychologists and moralists; and it is strongly affected by the prism of the medium used. Typically the proponents of abortion have put emphasis on quantitative evidence— for example, on the number of abortions performed in the United States or in the world at large. The assumption underlying this appeal to experience is that what is done by a great many persons cannot be bad, is indeed normal. This assumption, often employed when sexual behavior is studied, is rarely favored when racial discrimination or war are considered. It is a species of natural law, identifying the usual with the natural. The experience appealed to counts as argument only for those who accept this identification and consider the usual the good.

Psychological evidence has been called upon by the opponents of abortion. Trauma and guilt have been found associated with the election of abortion. The inference is made that abortion is the cause of this unhappiness. As in many arguments based on social consequences, however, the difficulty is to isolate the cause. Do persons undergoing abortion have character pre-dispositions which would in any event manifest themselves in psychic disturbance? Do they react as they do because of social conditioning which could be changed to encourage a positive attitude to abortion? Is the act of abortion at the root of their problems or the way in which the process is carried out? None of these questions is settled; the evidence is most likely to be convincing to those already inclined to believe that abortion is an evil.

Another kind of experience is that embedded in law. In Roman law where children generally had little status independent of their parents, the fetus was "a portion of the mother or her viscera." This view persisted in nineteenth century American tort law, Justice Holmes in a leading case describing the fetus as "a part of the body of the mother." In recent years, however, the tort cases have asked, in Justice Bok's phrase, if the fetus is a person; and many courts have replied affirmatively. The change, a striking revolution in torts law, came from the courts incorporating into their thought new biological data on the fetus as a living organism. Evidence on how the fetus is now perceived is also provided by another kind of case where abortion itself is not involved—the interpretation in wills and trusts of gifts to "children" or "issue." In these cases a basic question is, "What is the common understanding of people when they speak of children?" The answer, given repeatedly by American courts, is that "the average testator" speaking of children means to include a being who has been conceived but not born. Free from the distorting pressures of the conflict over abortion, this evidence of the common understanding suggests that social experience has found the fetus to be within the family of man.

The most powerful expression of common experience is that given by art and literature. Birth has almost everywhere been celebrated in painting. The Nativity has been a symbol of gladness not only because of its sacral significance, but because of its human meaning—"joy that a man is born into the world." Abortion, in contrast, has rarely been the subject of art. Unlike other forms of death, abortion has not been seen by painters as a release, a sacrifice, or a victory. Characteristically it has stood for sterility, futility, and absurdity. Consider, for example, Orozco's mural, "Gods of the Modern World" in the Baker Library at Dartmouth College. Academia is savagely satirized by portraying professors as impotent attendants in an operating room in which truth is stillborn. Bottled fetuses in the foreground attest the professors' habitual failure. The entire force of the criticism of academic achievement comes from the painter's knowledge that everyone will recognize abortion as a grave defeat and the bottling of dead fetuses as a travesty of healthy birth. Whoever sees such a painting sees how mankind has commonly experienced abortion.

In contemporary American literature, John Updike's *Couples* comments directly upon abortion, using it at a crucial turn as both event and symbol. Piet Hanema, married to Angela, has promiscuously pursued other married women, among them Foxy Whitman, who is now pregnant by him. They have this exchange:

All I know is what I honestly want. I want this damn thing to stop growing inside me.

Don't cry.

Nature is so stupid. It has all my maternal glands working, do you know what that means, Piet? You know what the great thing about being pregnant I found out was? It's something I just couldn't have imagined. You're never alone. When you have a baby inside you you are not alone. It's a person.

To procure the abortion it becomes necessary for Piet to surrender his own wife Angela to Freddy who has access to the abortionist. Embarked upon his course Piet does not stop at this act which destroys his own marriage irretrievably. Foxy's feelings at the time of the abortion are then described through Piet:

Not until days later, after Foxy had survived the forty-eight hours alone in the house with Toby and the test of Ken's return from Chicago, did Piet learn, not from Freddy but from her as told by Freddy, that at the moment of anesthesia she had panicked; she had tried to strike the Negress pressing the sweet, sweet mask to her face and through the first waves of ether had continued to cry that she should go home, that she was supposed to have this baby, that the child's father was coming to smash the door down with a hammer and would stop them.

Updike's only comment as an author is given as Piet then goes to Foxy's house: "Death, once invited in, leaves his muddy bootprints everywhere." The elements of the experience of abortion are here: the hatred of the depersonalized burden growing, willy-nilly, in the womb; the sense of a baby, a person, one's own child; the desperate desire to be rid of the burden extinguishing all other considerations; the ineffectual hope of delivery the moment before the child's death. A mask covers the human face of the mother. Symbolically the abortion seals a course of infidelity. Conclusively it becomes death personified. . . .

Mary Anne Warren

ON THE MORAL AND LEGAL STATUS OF ABORTION

Mary Anne Warren argues that if we assume the fetus to be a person, there is a wide range of cases in which we cannot provide a defense of abortion. To provide such a defense, Warren sets out five criteria for being a person which she thinks should be acceptable to antiabortion-ists and proabortionists alike. Appealing to these criteria, she contends that fetuses, even when their potentiality is taken into account, do not sufficiently resemble persons to have a significant right to life.

In a "Postscript" to her article, she defends her view against the objection that it would justify infanticide. Although by her criteria newborn infants would not have a significant right to life, she claims that infanticide would still not be permissible, so long as there are people willing to care and provide for the well-being of such infants.

WE WILL BE CONCERNED with both the moral status of abortion, which for our purposes we may define as the act which a woman performs in voluntarily terminating, or allowing another person to terminate, her pregnancy, and the legal status which is appropriate for this act. I will argue that, while it is not possible to produce a satisfactory defense of a woman's right to obtain an abortion without showing that a fetus is not a human being, in the morally relevant sense of that term, we ought not to conclude that the difficulties involved in determining whether or not a fetus is human make it impossible to produce any satisfactory solution to the problem of the moral status of abortion. For it is possible to show that, on the basis of intuitions which we may expect even the opponents of abortion to share, a fetus is not a person, and hence not the sort of entity to which it is proper to ascribe full moral rights.

Of course, while some philosophers would deny the possibility of any such proof,[1] others will deny that there is any need for it, since the moral permissibility of abortion appears to them to be too obvious to require proof. But the inadequacy of this attitude should be evident from the fact that both the friends and the foes of abortion consider their position to be morally self-evident. Because proabortionists have never adequately come to grips with the conceptual issues surrounding abortion, most if not all, of the arguments which they advance in opposition to laws restricting access to abortion fail to refute or even weaken the traditional anti-abortion argument, i.e., that a fetus is a human being, and therefore abortion is murder.

These arguments are typically of one of two sorts. Either they point to the terrible side effects of the restrictive laws, e.g., the deaths due to illegal abortions, and the fact that it is poor women who suffer the most as a result of these laws, or else they state that to deny a woman access to abortion is to deprive her of her right to control her own body. Unfortunately, however, the fact that restricting access to abortion has tragic side effects does not, in itself, show that the restrictions are unjustified, since murder is wrong regardless of the consequences of prohibiting it; and the appeal to the right to control one's body, which is generally construed as a property right, is at best a rather feeble argument for the permissibility of abortion. Mere ownership does not give me the right to kill innocent people whom I find on my property, and indeed I am apt to be held responsible if such people injure themselves while on my property. It is equally unclear that I have any moral right to expel an innocent person from my property when I know that doing so will result in his death.

Furthermore, it is probably inappropriate to describe a woman's body as her property, since it seems natural to hold that a person is something distinct from her property, but not from her body. Even those who would object to the identification of a person with his body, or with the conjunction of his body and his mind, must admit that it would be very odd to describe, say, breaking a leg, as damaging one's property, and much more appropriate to describe it as injuring one*self*. Thus it is probably a mistake to argue that the right to obtain an abortion is in any way derived from the right to own and regulate property.

But however we wish to construe the right to abortion, we cannot hope to convince those who consider abortion a form of murder of the existence of any such right unless we are able to produce a clear and convincing refutation of the traditional antiabortion argument, and this has not, to my knowledge, been done. With respect to the two most vital issues which that argument involves, i.e., the

humanity of the fetus and its implication for the moral status of abortion, confusion has prevailed on both sides of the dispute.

Thus, both proabortionists and antiabortionists have tended to abstract the question of whether abortion is wrong to that of whether it is wrong to destroy a fetus, just as though the rights of another person were not necessarily involved. This mistaken abstraction has led to the almost universal assumption that if a fetus is a human being, with a right to life, then it follows immediately that abortion is wrong (except perhaps when necessary to save the woman's life), and that it ought to be prohibited. It has also been generally assumed that unless the question about the status of the fetus is answered, the moral status of abortion cannot possibly be determined. . . . John Noonan is correct in saying that "the fundamental question in the long history of abortion is, How do you determine the humanity of a being?"[2] He summarizes his own antiabortion argument, which is a version of the official position of the Catholic Church, as follows:

. . . *it is wrong to kill humans, however poor, weak, defenseless, and lacking in opportunity to develop their potential they may be. It is therefore morally wrong to kill Biafrans. Similarly, it is morally wrong to kill embryos.*[3]

Noonan bases his claim that fetuses are human upon what he calls the theologians' criterion of humanity: that whoever is conceived of human beings is human. But although he argues at length for the appropriateness of this criterion, he never questions the assumption that if a fetus is human then abortion is wrong for exactly the same reason that murder is wrong.

Judith Thomson is, in fact, the only writer I am aware of who has seriously questioned this assumption; she has argued that, even if we grant the antiabortionist his claim that a fetus is a human being, with the same right to life as any other human being, we can still demonstrate that, in at least some and perhaps most cases, a woman is under no moral obligation to complete an unwanted pregnancy.[4] Her argument is worth examining, since if it holds up it may enable us to establish the moral permissibility of abortion without becoming involved in problems about what entitles an entity to be considered human, and accorded full moral rights. To be able to do this would be a great gain in the power and simplicity of the proabortion position, since, although I will argue that these problems can be solved at least as decisively as can any other moral problem, we should certainly be pleased to be able to avoid having to solve them as part of the justification of abortion.

On the other hand, even if Thomson's argument does not hold up, her insight, i.e., that it requires *argument* to show that if fetuses are human then abortion is properly classified as murder, is an extremely valuable one. The assumption she attacks is particularly invidious, for it amounts to the decision that it is appropriate, in deciding the moral status of abortion, to leave the rights of the pregnant woman out of consideration entirely, except possibly when her life is threatened. Obviously, this will not do; determining what moral rights, if any, a fetus possesses is only the first step in determining the moral status of abortion. Step two, which is at least equally essential, is finding a just solution to the conflict between whatever rights the fetus may have, and the rights of the woman who is unwillingly pregnant. While the historical error has been to pay far too little attention to the second step, Ms. Thomson's suggestion is that if we look at the second step first we may find that a woman has a right to obtain an abortion *regardless* of what rights the fetus has.

Our own inquiry will also have two stages. In Section I, we will consider whether or not it is possible to establish that abortion is morally permissible even on the assumption that a fetus is an entity with a full-fledged right to life. I will argue that in fact this cannot be established, at least not with the conclusiveness which is essential to our hopes of convincing those who are skeptical about the morality of abortion, and that we therefore cannot avoid dealing with the question of whether or not a fetus really does have the same right to life as a (more fully developed) human being.

In Section II, I will propose an answer to this question, namely, that a fetus cannot be considered a member of the moral community, the set of beings with full and equal moral rights, for the simple reason that it is not a person, and that it is personhood, and not genetic humanity, i.e., humanity as defined by Noonan, which is the basis for membership in this community. I will argue that a fetus, whatever

its stage of development, satisfies none of the basic criteria of personhood, and is not even enough *like* a person to be accorded even some of the same rights on the basis of this resemblance. Nor, as we will see, is a fetus's *potential* personhood a threat to the morality of abortion, since, whatever the rights of potential people may be, they are invariably overridden in any conflict with the moral rights of actual people.

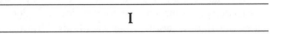

I

We turn now to Professor Thomson's case for the claim that even if a fetus has full moral rights, abortion is still morally permissible, at least sometimes, and for some reasons other than to save the woman's life. Her argument is based upon a clever, but I think faulty, analogy. She asks us to picture ourselves waking up one day, in bed with a famous violinist. Imagine that you have been kidnapped, and your bloodstream hooked up to that of the violinist, who happens to have an ailment which will certainly kill him unless he is permitted to share your kidneys for a period of nine months. No one else can save him, since you alone have the right type of blood. He will be unconscious all that time, and you will have to stay in bed with him, but after the nine months are over he may be unplugged, completely cured, that is provided that you have cooperated.

Now then, she continues, what are your obligations in this situation? The antiabortionist, if he is consistent, will have to say that you are obligated to stay in bed with the violinist: for all people have a right to life, and violinists are people, and therefore it would be murder for you to disconnect yourself from him and let him die. But this is outrageous, and so there must be something wrong with the same argument when it is applied to abortion. It would certainly be commendable of you to agree to save the violinist, but it is absurd to suggest that your refusal to do so would be murder. His right to life does not obligate you to do whatever is required to keep him alive; nor does it justify anyone else in forcing you to do so. A law which required you to stay in bed with the violinist would clearly be an unjust law, since it is no proper function of the law to force un-

146

willing people to make huge sacrifices for the sake of other people toward whom they have no such prior obligation.

Thomson concludes that, if this analogy is an apt one, then we can grant the antiabortionist his claim that a fetus is a human being, and still hold that it is at least sometimes the case that a pregnant woman has the right to refuse to be a Good Samaritan towards the fetus, i.e., to obtain an abortion. For there is a great gap between the claim that *x* has a right to life, and the claim that *y* is obligated to do whatever is necessary to keep *x* alive, let alone that he ought to be forced to do so. It is *y*'s duty to keep *x* alive only if he has somehow contracted a *special* obligation to do so; and a woman who is unwillingly pregnant, e.g., who was raped, has done nothing which obligates her to make the enormous sacrifice which is necessary to preserve the conceptus.

This argument is initially quite plausible, and in the extreme case of pregnancy due to rape is probably conclusive. Difficulties arise, however, when we try to specify more exactly the range of cases in which abortion is clearly justifiable even on the assumption that the fetus is human. Professor Thomson considers it a virtue of her argument that it does not enable us to conclude that abortion is *always* permissible. It would, she says, be "indecent" for a woman in her seventh month to obtain an abortion just to avoid having to postpone a trip to Europe. On the other hand, her argument enables us to see that "a sick and desperately frightened schoolgirl pregnant due to rape may *of course* choose abortion, and that any law which rules this out is an insane law" (p. 65). So far, so good; but what are we to say about the woman who becomes pregnant not through rape but as a result of her own carelessness, or because of contraceptive failure, or who gets pregnant intentionally and then changes her mind about wanting a child? With respect to such cases, the violinist analogy is of much less use to the defender of the woman's right to obtain an abortion.

Indeed, the choice of a pregnancy due to rape, as an example of a case in which abortion is permissible even if a fetus is considered a human being, is extremely significant; for it is only in the case of pregnancy due to rape that the woman's situation is adequately analogous to the violinist case for our intuitions about the latter to transfer convincingly. The crucial difference between a pregnancy due to rape and the *normal* case of an unwanted pregnancy is that in the normal case we cannot claim that the woman is in no way responsible for her predicament; she could have remained chaste, or taken her pills more faithfully, or abstained on dangerous days, and so on. If, on the other hand, you are kidnapped by strangers, and hooked up to a strange violinist, then you are free of any shred of responsibility for the situation, on the basis of which it could be argued that you are obligated to keep the violinist alive. Only when her pregnancy is due to rape is a woman clearly just as nonresponsible.[5]

Consequently, there is room for the antiabortionist to argue that in the normal case of unwanted pregnancy a woman has, by her own actions, assumed responsibility for the fetus. For if *x* behaves in a way which he could have avoided, and which he knows involves, let us say, a 1 percent chance of bringing into existence a human being, with a right to life, and does so knowing that if this should happen then that human being will perish unless *x* does certain things to keep him alive, then it is by no means clear that when it does happen *x* is free of any obligation to what he knew in advance would be required to keep that human being alive.

The plausibility of such an argument is enough to show that the Thomson analogy can provide a clear and persuasive defense of a woman's right to obtain an abortion only with respect to those cases in which the woman is in no way responsible for her pregnancy, e.g., where it is due to rape. In all other cases, we would almost certainly conclude that it was necessary to look carefully at the particular circumstances in order to determine the extent of the woman's responsibility, and hence the extent of her obligation. This is an extremely unsatisfactory outcome, from the viewpoint of the opponents of restrictive abortion laws, most of whom are convinced that a woman has a right to obtain an abortion regardless of how and why she got pregnant.

Of course a supporter of the violinist analogy might point out that it is absurd to suggest that forgetting her pill one day might be sufficient to obligate a woman to complete an unwanted pregnancy. And indeed it *is* absurd to suggest this. As we will see, the moral right to obtain an abortion is not in the least dependent upon the extent to which the woman is responsible for her pregnancy. But unfortunately, once we allow the assumption that a fetus has full moral rights, we cannot avoid taking this absurd suggestion seriously. Perhaps we can make this point more clear by altering the violinist story just enough to make it more analogous to a normal unwanted pregnancy and less to a pregnancy due to rape, and then seeing whether it is still obvious that you are not obligated to stay in bed with the fellow.

Suppose, then, that violinists are peculiarly prone to the sort of illness the only cure for which is the use of someone else's bloodstream for nine months, and that because of this there has been formed a society of music lovers who agree that whenever a violinist is stricken they will draw lots and the loser will, by some means, be made the one and only person capable of saving him. Now then, would you be obligated to cooperate in curing the violinist if you had voluntarily joined this society, knowing the possible consequences, and then your name had been drawn and you had been kidnapped? Admittedly, you did not promise ahead of time that you would, but you did deliberately place yourself in a position in which it might happen that a human life would be lost if you did not. Surely this is at least a prima facie reason for supposing that you have an obligation to stay in bed with the violinist. Suppose that you had gotten your name drawn deliberately; surely *that* would be quite a strong reason for thinking that you had such an obligation.

It might be suggested that there is one important disanalogy between the modified violinist case and the case of an unwanted pregnancy, which makes the woman's responsibility significantly less, namely, the fact that the fetus *comes into existence* as the result of the result of the woman's actions. This fact might give her a right to refuse to keep it alive, whereas she would not have had this right had it existed previously, independently, and then as a result of her actions become dependent upon her for its survival.

My own intuition, however, is that x has no more right to bring into existence, either deliberately or as a foreseeable result of actions he could have avoided, a being with full moral rights (y), and then refuse to do what he knew beforehand would be required to keep that being alive, than he has to enter into an agreement with an existing person, whereby he may be called upon to save that person's life, and then refuse to do so when so called upon. Thus, x's responsibility for y's existence does not seem to lessen his obligation to keep y alive, if he is also respon-

sible for y's being in a situation in which only he can save him.

Whether or not this intuition is entirely correct, it brings us back once again to the conclusion that once we allow the assumption that a fetus has full moral rights it becomes an extremely complex and difficult question whether and when abortion is justifiable. Thus the Thomson analogy cannot help us produce a clear and persuasive proof of the moral permissibility of abortion. Nor will the opponents of the restrictive laws thank us for anything less; for their conviction (for the most part) is that abortion is obviously *not* a morally serious and extremely unfortunate, even though sometimes justified act, comparable to killing in self-defense or to letting the violinist die, but rather is closer to being a morally neutral act, like cutting one's hair.

The basis of this conviction, I believe, is the realization that a fetus is not a person, and thus does not have a full-fledged right to life. Perhaps the reason why this claim has been so inadequately defended is that it seems self-evident to those who accept it. And so it is, insofar as it follows from what I take to be perfectly obvious claims about the nature of personhood, and about the proper grounds for ascribing moral rights, claims which ought, indeed, to be obvious to both the friends and foes of abortion. Nevertheless, it is worth examining these claims, and showing how they demonstrate the moral innocuousness of abortion, since this apparently has not been adequately done before.

II

The question which we must answer in order to produce a satisfactory solution to the problem of the moral status of abortion is this: How are we to define the moral community, the set of beings with full and equal moral rights, such that we can decide whether a human fetus is a member of this community or not? What sort of entity, exactly, has the inalienable rights to life, liberty, and the pursuit of happiness? Jefferson attributed these rights to all *men*, and it may or may not be fair to suggest that he intended to attribute them *only* to men. Perhaps he ought to have attributed them to all human beings. If so, then we arrive, first, at Noonan's problem of defining what makes a being human, and, second, at the equally vital question which Noonan does not consider, namely, What reason is there for identifying the moral community with the set of all human beings, in whatever way we have chosen to define that term?

1. On the Definition of 'Human'

One reason why this vital second question is so frequently overlooked in the debate over the moral status of abortion is that the term 'human' has two distinct, but not often distinguished, senses. This fact results in a slide of meaning, which serves to conceal the fallaciousness of the traditional argument that since (1) it is wrong to kill innocent human beings, and (2) fetuses are innocent human beings, then (3) it is wrong to kill fetuses. For if 'human' is used in the same sense in both (1) and (2) then, whichever of the two senses is meant, one of these premises is question-begging. And if it is used in two different senses then of course the conclusion doesn't follow.

Thus, (1) is a self-evident moral truth,[6] and avoids begging the question about abortion, only if 'human being' is used to mean something like "a full-fledged member of the moral community." (It may or may not also be meant to refer exclusively to members of the species *Homo sapiens.*) *We may call this the moral* sense of 'human'. It is not to be confused with what we will call the *genetic* sense, i.e., the sense in which *any* member of the species is a human being, and no member of any other species could be. If (1) is acceptable only if the moral sense is intended, (2) is non-question-begging only if what is intended is the genetic sense.

In "Deciding Who is Human," Noonan argues for the classification of fetuses with human beings by pointing to the presence of the full genetic code, and the potential capacity for rational thought (p. 135). It is clear that what he needs to show, for his version of the traditional argument to be valid, is that fetuses are human in the moral sense, the sense in which it is analytically true that all human beings have full moral rights. But, in the absence of any argument showing that whatever is genetically human is also morally human, and he gives none, nothing more than genetic humanity can be demonstrated by the presence of the human genetic code. And, as we will see, the *potential* capacity for rational

thought can at most show that an entity has the potential for *becoming* human in the moral sense.

2. Defining the Moral Community

Can it be established that genetic humanity is sufficient for moral humanity? I think that there are very good reasons for not defining the moral community in this way. I would like to suggest an alternative way of defining the moral community, which I will argue for only to the extent of explaining why it is, or should be, self-evident. The suggestion is simply that the moral community consists of all and only *people*, rather than all and only human beings;[7] and probably the best way of demonstrating its self-evidence is by considering the concept of personhood, to see what sorts of entity are and are not persons, and what the decision that a being is or is not a person implies about its moral rights.

What characteristics entitle an entity to be considered a person? This is obviously not the place to attempt a complete analysis of the concept of personhood, but we do not need such a fully adequate analysis just to determine whether and why a fetus is or isn't a person. All we need is a rough and approximate list of the most basic criteria of personhood, and some idea of which, or how many, of these an entity must satisfy in order to properly be considered a person.

In searching for such criteria, it is useful to look beyond the set of people with whom we are acquainted, and ask how we would decide whether a totally alien being was a person or not. (For we have no right to assume that genetic humanity is necessary for personhood.) Imagine a space traveler who lands on an unknown planet and encounters a race of beings utterly unlike any he has ever seen or heard of. It he wants to be sure of behaving morally toward these beings, he has to somehow decide whether they are people, and hence have full moral rights, or whether they are the sort of thing which he need not feel guilty about treating as, for example, a source of food.

How should he go about making this decision? If he has some anthropological background, he might look for such things as religion, art, and the manufacturing of tools, weapons, or shelters, since these factors have been used to distinguish our human from our prehuman ancestors, in what seems to be closer to the moral than the genetic sense of 'human'. And no doubt he would be right to consider the presence of such factors as good evidence that the alien beings were people, and morally human. It would, however, be overly anthropocentric of him to take the absence of these things as adequate evidence that they were not, since we can imagine people who have progressed beyond, or evolved without ever developing, these cultural characteristics.

I suggest that the traits which are most central to the concept of personhood, or humanity in the moral sense, are, very roughly, the following:

1. consciousness (of objects and events external and/or internal to the being), and in particular the capacity to feel pain;
2. reasoning (the *developed* capacity to solve new and relatively complex problems);
3. self-motivated activity (activity which is relatively independent of either genetic or direct external control);
4. the capacity to communicate, by whatever means, messages of an indefinite variety of types, that is, not just with an indefinite number of possible contents, but on indefinitely many possible topics;
5. the presence of self-concepts, and self-awareness, either individual or racial, or both.

Admittedly, there are apt to be a great many problems involved in formulating precise definitions of these criteria, let alone in developing universally valid behavioral criteria for deciding when they apply. But I will assume that both we and our explorer know approximately what (1)–(5) mean, and that he is also able to determine whether or not they apply. How, then, should he use his findings to decide whether or not the alien beings are people? We needn't suppose that an entity must have *all* of these attributes to be properly considered a person; (1) and (2) alone may well be sufficient for personhood, and quite probably (1)–(3) are sufficient. Neither do we need to insist that any one of these criteria is *necessary* for personhood, although once again (1) and (2) look like fairly good candidates for necessary conditions, as does (3), if 'activity' is construed so as to include the activity of reasoning.

All we need to claim, to demonstrate that a fetus is not a person, is that any being which satisfies *none* of (1)–(5) is certainly not a person. I consider this

claim to be so obvious that I think anyone who denied it, and claimed that a being which satisfied none of (1)–(5) was a person all the same, would thereby demonstrate that he had no notion at all of what a person is—perhaps because he had confused the concept of a person with that of genetic humanity. If the opponents of abortion were to deny the appropriateness of these five criteria, I do not know what further arguments would convince them. We would probably have to admit that our conceptual schemes were indeed irreconcilably different, and that our dispute could not be settled objectively.

I do not expect this to happen, however, since I think that the concept of a person is one which is very nearly universal (to people), and that it is common to both proabortionists and antiabortionists, even though neither group has fully realized the relevance of this concept to the resolution of their dispute. Furthermore, I think that on reflection even the antiabortionists ought to agree not only that (1)–(5) are central to the concept of personhood, but also that it is a part of this concept that all and only people have full moral rights. The concept of a person is in part a moral concept; once we have admitted that x is a person we have recognized, even if we have not agreed to respect, x's right to be treated as a member of the moral community. It is true that the claim that x is a *human being* is more commonly voiced as part of an appeal to treat x decently than is the claim that x is a person, but this is either because 'human being' is here used in the sense which implies personhood, or because the genetic and moral senses of 'human' have been confused.

Now if (1)–(5) are indeed the primary criteria of personhood, then it is clear that genetic humanity is neither necessary nor sufficient for establishing that an entity is a person. Some human beings are not people, and there may well be people who are not human beings. A man or woman whose consciousness has been permanently obliterated but who remains alive is a human being which is no longer a person; defective human beings, with no appreciable mental capacity, are not and presumably never will be people; and a fetus is a human being which is not yet a person, and which therefore cannot coherently be said to have full moral rights. Citizens of the next century should be prepared to recognize highly advanced, self-aware robots or computers, should such be developed, and intelligent inhabitants of other worlds, should such be found, as people in the fullest sense, and to respect their moral rights. But to ascribe full moral rights to an entity which is not a person is as absurd as to ascribe moral obligations and responsibilities to such an entity.

3. Fetal Development and the Right to Life

Two problems arise in the application of these suggestions for the definition of the moral community to the determination of the precise moral status of a human fetus. Given that the paradigm example of a person is a normal adult human being, then (1) How like this paradigm, in particular how far advanced since conception, does a human being need to be before it begins to have a right to life by virtue, not of being fully a person as of yet, but of being *like* a person? and (2) To what extent, if any, does the fact that a fetus has the *potential* for becoming a person endow it with some of the same rights? Each of these questions requires some comment.

In answering the first question, we need not attempt a detailed consideration of the moral rights of organisms which are not developed enough, aware enough, intelligent enough, etc., to be considered people, but which resemble people in some respects. It does seem reasonable to suggest that the more like a person, in the relevant respects, a being is, the stronger is the case for regarding it as having a right to life, and indeed the stronger its right to life is. Thus we ought to take seriously the suggestion that, insofar as "the human individual develops biologically in a continuous fashion . . . the rights of a human person might develop in the same way."[8] But we must keep in mind that the attributes which are relevant in determining whether or not an entity is enough like a person to be regarded as having some of the same moral rights are no different from those which are relevant to determining whether or not it is fully a person—i.e., are no different from (1)–(5)—and that being genetically human, or having recognizably human facial and other physical features, or detectable brain activity, or the capacity to survive outside the uterus, are simply not among these relevant attributes.

Thus it is clear that even though a seven- or eight-month fetus has features which make it apt to arouse in us almost the same powerful protective instinct as is commonly aroused by a small infant, neverthe-less it is not significantly more personlike than is a very small embryo. It is *somewhat* more personlike; it can apparently feel and respond to pain, and it may even have a rudimentary form of consciousness, insofar as its brain is quite active. Nevertheless, it seems safe to say that it is not fully conscious, in the way that an infant of a few months is, and that it cannot reason, or communicate messages of indefinitely many sorts, does not engage in self-motivated activity, and has no self-awareness. Thus, in the *relevant* respects, a fetus, even a fully developed one, is considerably less personlike than is the average mature mammal, indeed the average fish. And I think that a rational person must conclude that if the right to life of a fetus is to be based upon its resemblance to a person, then it cannot be said to have any more right to life than, let us say, a newborn guppy (which also seems to be capable of feeling pain), and that a right of that magnitude could never override a woman's right to obtain an abortion, at any stage of her pregnancy.

There may, of course, be other arguments in favor of placing legal limits upon the stage of pregnancy in which an abortion may be performed. Given the relative safety of the new techniques of artificially inducing labor during the third trimester, the danger to the woman's life or health is no longer such an argument. Neither is the fact that people tend to respond to the thought of abortion in the later stages of pregnancy with emotional repulsion, since mere emotional responses cannot take the place of moral reasoning in determining what ought to be permitted. Nor, finally, is the frequently heard argument that legalizing abortion, especially late in the pregnancy, may erode the level of respect for human life, leading, perhaps, to an increase in unjustified euthanasia and other crimes. For this threat, if it is a threat, can be better met by educating people to the kinds of moral distinctions which we are making here than by limiting access to abortion (which limitation may, in its disregard for the rights of women, be just as damaging to the level of respect for human rights).

Thus, since the fact that even a fully developed fetus is not personlike enough to have any significant right to life on the basis of its personlikeness shows that no legal restrictions upon the stage of pregnancy in which an abortion may be performed can be justified on the grounds that we should protect the rights of the older fetus; and since there is no other apparent justification for such restrictions, we may conclude that they are entirely unjustified. Whether or not it would be *indecent* (whatever that means) for a woman in her seventh month to obtain an abortion just to avoid having to postpone a trip to Europe, it would not, in itself, be *immoral*, and therefore it ought to be permitted.

4. Potential Personhood and the Right to Life

We have seen that a fetus does not resemble a person in any way which can support the claim that it has even some of the same rights. But what about its *potential*, the fact that if nurtured and allowed to develop naturally it will very probably become a person? Doesn't that alone give it at least some right to life? It is hard to deny that the fact that an entity is a potential person is a strong prima facie reason for not destroying it; but we need not conclude from this that a potential person has a right to life, by virtue of that potential. It may be that our feeling that it is better, other things being equal, not to destroy a potential person is better explained by the fact that potential people are still (felt to be) an invaluable resource, not to be lightly squandered. Surely, if every speck of dust were a potential person, we would be much less apt to conclude that every potential person has a right to become actual.

Still, we do not need to insist that a potential person has no right to life whatever. There may well be something immoral, and not just imprudent, about wantonly destroying potential people, when doing so isn't necessary to protect anyone's rights. But even if a potential person does have some prima facie right to life, such a right could not possibly outweigh the right of a woman to obtain an abortion, since the rights of any actual person invariably outweigh those of any potential person, whenever the two conflict. Since this may not be immediately obvious in the case of a human fetus, let us look at another case.

Suppose that our space explorer falls into the hands of an alien culture, whose scientists decide to create a few hundred thousand or more human beings, by breaking his body into its component cells, and using these to create fully developed human beings, with, of course, his genetic code. We may imagine that each of these newly created men

will have all of the original man's abilities, skills, knowledge, and so on, and also have an individual self-concept, in short that each of them will be a bona fide (though hardly unique) person. Imagine that the whole project will take only seconds, and that its chances of success are extremely high, and that our explorer knows all of this, and also knows that these people will be treated fairly. I maintain that in such a situation he would have every right to escape if he could, and thus to deprive all of these potential people of their potential lives; for his right to life outweighs all of theirs together, in spite of the fact that they are all genetically human, all innocent, and all have a very high probability of becoming people very soon, if only he refrains from acting.

Indeed, I think he would have a right to escape even if it were not his life which the alien scientists planned to take, but only a year of his freedom, or, indeed, only a day. Nor would he be obligated to stay if he had gotten captured (thus bringing all these people-potentials into existence) because of his own carelessness, or even if he had done so deliberately, knowing the consequences. Regardless of how he got captured, he is not morally obligated to remain in captivity for *any* period of time for the sake of permitting any number of potential people to come into actuality, so great is the margin by which one actual person's right to liberty outweighs whatever right to life even a hundred thousand potential people have. And it seems reasonable to conclude that the rights of a woman will outweigh by a similar margin whatever right to life a fetus may have by virtue of its potential personhood.

Thus, neither a fetus's resemblance to a person, nor its potential for becoming a person provides any basis whatever for the claim that it has any significant right to life. Consequently, a woman's right to protect her health, happiness, freedom, and even her life,[9] by terminating an unwanted pregnancy, will always override whatever right to life it may be appropriate to ascribe to a fetus, even a fully developed one. And thus, in the absence of any overwhelming social need for every possible child, the laws which restrict the right to obtain an abortion, or limit the period of pregnancy during which an abortion may be performed, are a wholly unjustified violation of a woman's most basic moral and constitutional rights.[10] . . .

POSTSCRIPT ON INFANTICIDE

Since the publication of this article, many people have written to point out that my argument appears to justify not only abortion, but infanticide as well. For a new-born infant is not significantly more person-like than an advanced fetus, and consequently it would seem that if the destruction of the latter is permissible so too must be that of the former. Inasmuch as most people, regardless of how they feel about the morality of abortion, consider infanticide a form of murder, this might appear to represent a serious flaw in my argument.

Now, if I am right in holding that it is only people who have a full-fledged right to life, and who can be murdered, and if the criteria of personhood are as I have described them, then it obviously follows that killing a new-born infant isn't murder. It does *not* follow, however, that infanticide is permissible, for two reasons. In the first place, it would be wrong, at least in this country and in this period of history, and other things being equal, to kill a new-born infant, because even if its parents do not want it and would not suffer from its destruction, there are other people who would like to have it, and would, in all probability, be deprived of a great deal of pleasure by its destruction. Thus, infanticide is wrong for reasons analogous to those which make it wrong to wantonly destroy natural resources, or great works of art.

Secondly, most people, at least in this country, value infants and would much prefer that they be preserved, even if foster parents are not immediately available. Most of us would rather be taxed to support orphanages than allow unwanted infants to be destroyed. So long as there are people who want an infant preserved, and who are willing and able to provide the means of caring for it, under reasonably humane conditions, it is, *ceteris parabis*, wrong to destroy it.

But, it might be replied, if this argument shows that infanticide is wrong, at least at this time and in this country, doesn't it also show that abortion is wrong? After all, many people value fetuses, are disturbed by their destruction, and would much prefer that they be preserved, even at some cost to themselves. Furthermore, as a potential source of pleasure to some foster family, a fetus is just as valuable as an infant. There is, however, a crucial difference between the two cases: so long as the fetus is unborn, its preservation, contrary to the wishes of the pregnant woman, violates her rights to freedom, happiness, and self-determination. Her rights override the rights of those who would like the fetus preserved, just as if someone's life or limb is threatened by a wild animal, his right to protect himself by destroying the animal overrides the rights of those who would prefer that the animal not be harmed.

The minute the infant is born, however, its preservation no longer violates any of its mother's rights, even if she wants it destroyed, because she is free to put it up for adoption. Consequently, while the moment of birth does not mark any sharp discontinuity in the degree to which an infant possesses the right to life, it does mark the end of its mother's right to determine its fate. Indeed, if abortion could be performed without killing the fetus, she would never possess the right to have the fetus destroyed, for the same reasons that she has no right to have an infant destroyed.

On the other hand, it follows from my argument that when an unwanted or defective infant is born into a society which cannot afford and/or is not willing to care for it, then its destruction is permissible. This conclusion will, no doubt, strike many people as heartless and immoral; but remember that the very existence of people who feel this way, and who are willing and able to provide care for unwanted infants, is reason enough to conclude that they should be preserved.

NOTES

1. For example, Roger Wertheimer, who in "Understanding the Abortion Argument" (*Philosophy and Public Affairs*, 1, No. 1 [Fall, 1971], 67–95), argues that the problem of the moral status of abortion is insoluble, in that the dispute over the status of the fetus is not a question of fact at all, but only a question of how one responds to the facts.

2. John Noonan, "Abortion and the Catholic Church: A Summary History," *Natural Law Forum*, 12 (1967), 125.

3. John Noonan, "Deciding Who Is Human," *Natural Law Forum*, 13 (1968), 134.

4. "A Defense of Abortion."

5. We may safely ignore the fact that she might have avoided getting raped, e.g., by carrying a gun, since by similar means you might likewise have avoided getting kidnapped, and in neither case does the victim's failure to take all possible precautions against a highly unlikely event (as opposed to reasonable precautions against a rather likely event) mean that he is morally responsible for what happens.

6. Of course, the principle that it is (always) wrong to kill innocent human beings is in need of many other modifications, e.g., that it may be permissible to do so to save a greater number of other innocent human beings, but we may safely ignore these complications here.

7. From here on, we will use 'human' to mean genetically human, since the moral sense seems closely connected to, and perhaps derived from, the assumption that genetic humanity is sufficient for membership in the moral community.

8. Thomas L. Hayes, "A Biological View," *Commonweal*, 85 (March 17, 1967), 677–78; quoted by Daniel Callahan, in *Abortion, Law, Choice, and Morality* (London: Macmillan & Co., 1970).

9. That is, insofar as the death rate, for the woman, is higher for childbirth than for early abortion.

10. My thanks to the following people, who were kind enough to read and criticize an earlier version of this paper: Herbert Gold, Gene Glass, Anne Lauterbach, Judith Thomson, Mary Mothersill, and Timothy Binkley.

James P. Sterba

ABORTION, DISTANT PEOPLES, AND FUTURE GENERATIONS

James P. Sterba contends that, with or without the assumption that the fetus is a person, liberals on the abortion issue who are also committed to the welfare rights of distant peoples and future generations cannot consistently endorse abortion on demand. For if we assume, on the one hand, that the fetus is a person, then a distinction between what a person can demand as a right and what is required by moral decency cannot be used by liberals who support the welfare rights of distant peoples to justify abortion on demand. The same holds true, Sterba claims, for a restricted interpretation of a right to life. If we assume, on the other hand, that the fetus is not a person and hold that we have an obligation not to bring into existence persons who would lack a reasonable opportunity to lead a good life, then liberals who support the welfare rights of future generations would in consistency be committed to

From "Abortion, Distant Peoples, and Future Generations," *The Journal of Philosophy* (1980) pp. 424–440. Reprinted by permission of *The Journal of Philosophy*.

endorsing an obligation to bring into existence persons who would have a reasonable opportunity to lead a good life. This obligation, Sterba contends, would severely limit the use of both abortion and contraception.

THOSE WHO FAVOR A liberal view on abortion and thus tend to support abortion on demand are just as likely to support the rights of distant peoples to basic economic assistance and the rights of future generations to a fair share of the world's resources.[1] Yet, as I shall argue, many of the arguments offered in support of abortion on demand by those who favor a liberal view on abortion are actually inconsistent with a workable defense of these other social goals. If I am right, many of those who favor a liberal view on abortion (whom I shall henceforth refer to as "liberals") will have to make an unwelcome choice: either moderate their support for abortion or moderate their commitment to the rights of distant peoples and future generations. I shall argue that the most promising way for liberals to make this choice is to moderate their support for abortion. . . .

THE WELFARE RIGHTS OF DISTANT PEOPLES

Of the various moral grounds for justifying the welfare rights of distant peoples, quite possibly the most evident are those which appeal either to a right to life or a right to fair treatment.[2] Indeed, whether one interprets a person's right to life as a negative right (as libertarians tend to do) or as a positive right (as welfare liberals tend to do), it is possible to show that the right justifies welfare rights that would amply provide for a person's basic needs.[3] Alternatively, it is possible to justify those same welfare rights on the basis of a person's positive right to fair treatment. In what follows, however, I do not propose to work out these moral justifications for the welfare rights of distant peoples.[4] Rather I wish to show that if one affirms welfare rights of distant peoples, as liberals tend to do, then there are certain arguments for abortion that one in consistency should reject. These arguments for abortion all begin with the assump-

tion that the fetus is a person and then attempt to show that abortion can still be justified in many cases.

Distant Peoples and Abortion

One such argument is based on a distinction between what a person can demand as a right and what is required by moral decency. Abortion, it is said, may offend against the requirements of moral decency, but it rarely, if ever, violates anyone's rights. Judith Jarvis Thomson[5] illustrates this view as follows:

. . . even supposing a case in which a woman pregnant due to rape ought to allow the unborn person to use her body for the hour he needs, we should not conclude that he has a right to do so; we should conclude that she is self-centered, callous, indecent, but not unjust if she refuses (132–133).

In Thomson's example, the sacrifice the pregnant woman would have to make to save the innocent fetus-person's life is certainly quite minimal.[6] Yet Thomson and other defenders of abortion contend that this minimal sacrifice is simply a requirement of moral decency and that neither justice nor the rights of the fetus-person requires the woman to contribute the use of her womb even for one hour! But if such a minimal life-sustaining sacrifice is required neither by justice nor by the rights of the fetus-person, then how could one maintain that distant peoples have a right to have their basic needs satisfied? Obviously to satisfy the basic needs of distant peoples would require a considerable sacrifice from many people in the technologically developed nations of the world. Taken individually, such sacrifices would be far greater than the sacrifice of Thomson's pregnant woman. Consequently, if the sacrifice of Thomson's pregnant woman is merely a requirement of moral decency, then the far greater sacrifices necessary to meet the basic needs of distant peoples, if required at all, could only be requirements of moral decency.

Thus liberals who want to support the welfare rights of distant peoples would in consistency have to reject this first argument for abortion.

Another argument for abortion that is also inconsistent with the welfare rights of distant peoples grants that the fetus-person has a right to life and then attempts to show that her right to life often does not entitle her to the means of survival. Thomson again illustrates this view:

If I am sick unto death, and the only thing that will save my life is the touch of Henry Fonda's cool hand on my fevered brow, then all the same, I have no right to be given the touch of Henry Fonda's cool hand on my fevered brow. It would be frightfully nice of him to fly in from the West Coast to provide it. It would be less nice, though no doubt well meant, if my friends flew out to the West Coast and carried Henry Fonda back with them. But I have no right at all against anybody that he should do this for me (129–130).

According to Thomson, what a person's right to life explicitly entitles her to is not the right to receive or acquire the means of survival, but only the right not to be killed or let die unjustly.

To understand what this right not to be killed or let die unjustly amounts to, consider the following example:

Tom, Dick, and Gertrude are adrift on a lifeboat. Dick managed to bring aboard provisions that are just sufficient for his own survival. Gertrude managed to do the same. But Tom brought no provisions at all. So Gertrude, who is by far the strongest, is faced with a choice. She can either kill Dick to provide Tom with the provisions he needs or she can refrain from killing Dick, thus letting Tom die.

Now, as Thomson understands the right not to be killed or let die unjustly, Gertrude's killing Dick would be unjust, but her letting Tom die would not be unjust because Dick has a greater right to his life and provisions than either Tom or Gertrude.[7] Thus killing or letting die unjustly always involves depriving a person of something to which she has a greater right—typically either her functioning body or property the person has which she needs to maintain her life. Consequently, a person's right to life would entitle her to her functioning body and whatever property she has which she needs to maintain her life.

Yet Thomson's view allows that some persons may not have property rights to goods that are necessary to meet their own basic needs whereas others may have property rights to more than enough goods to meet their own basic needs. It follows that if persons with property rights to surplus goods choose not to share their surplus with anyone else, then, according to Thomson's account, they would still not be violating anyone's right to life. For although, by their decision not to share, they would be killing or letting die those who lack the means of survival, they would not be doing so unjustly, because they would not be depriving anyone of her property.

Unfortunately, Thomson never explains how some persons could justifiably acquire property rights to surplus goods that would restrict others from acquiring or receiving the goods necessary to satisfy their basic needs. And Thomson's argument for abortion crucially depends on the justification of just such restrictive property rights. For otherwise the fetus-person's right to life would presumably entail a right to receive the means of survival.

It is also unclear how such restrictive property rights would be compatible with each person's right to fair treatment. Apparently, one would have to reinterpret the right to fair treatment so that it had nothing to do with receiving the necessary means of survival. A difficult task indeed.

But most importantly, accepting this defense of abortion with its unsupported assumption of restrictive property rights would undermine the justification for the welfare rights of distant peoples. For the same sort of rights that would restrict the fetus-person from receiving what she needs for survival would also restrict distant people from receiving or acquiring what they need for survival. Thus liberals who support the welfare rights of distant peoples would have an additional reason to reject this argument for abortion.[8]

Of course, many liberals cannot but be unhappy with the rejection of the two arguments for abortion which we have considered. For although they would not want to give up their support for the welfare rights of distant peoples, they are still inclined to support abortion on demand.

Searching for an acceptable resolution of this conflict, liberals might claim that what is wrong with the preceding arguments for abortion is that they both make the generous assumption that the fetus is a person. Once that assumption is dropped, liberals might claim, arguments for abortion on demand can be constructed which are perfectly consistent with the welfare rights of distant peoples. Although this line of argument initially seems quite promising, on closer examination it turns out that even accepting arguments for abortion on demand that do not assume that the fetus is a person raises a problem of consistency for the liberal. This is most clearly brought out in connection with the liberal's support for the welfare rights of future generations.

The Welfare Rights of Future Generations

At first glance the welfare rights of future generations appear to be on a par with the welfare rights of distant peoples. For, assuming that there will be future generations, then, they, like generations presently existing, will have their basic needs that must be satisfied. And, just as we are now able to take action to provide for the basic needs of distant peoples, so likewise we are now able to take action to provide for the basic needs of future generations (e.g., through capital investment and the conservation of resources). Thus, it should be possible to justify welfare rights for future generations by appealing either to a right to life or a right to fair treatment, but here again, as in the case of the welfare rights of distant peoples, I shall simply assume that such justifications can be worked out.

The welfare rights of future generations are also closely connected with the population policy of existing generations. For example, under a population policy that places restrictions on the size of families and requires genetic screening, some persons will not be brought into existence who otherwise would come into existence under a less restrictive population policy. Thus, the membership of future generations will surely be affected by whatever population policy existing generations adopt. Given that the size and genetic health of future generations will obviously affect their ability to provide for their basic needs, the welfare rights of future generations would require existing generations to adopt a population policy that takes these factors into account. . . .

Fortunately, a policy with the desired restrictions can be grounded on the welfare rights of future generations. Given that the welfare rights of future generations require existing generations to make provision for the basic needs of future generations,

existing generations would have to evaluate their ability to provide both for their own basic needs and for the basic needs of future generations. Since existing generations by bringing persons into existence would be determining the membership of future generations, they would have to evaluate whether they are able to provide for that membership. And if existing generations discover that, were population to increase beyond a certain point, they would lack sufficient resources to make the necessary provision for each person's basic needs, then it would be incumbent upon them to restrict the membership of future generations so as not to exceed their ability to provide for each person's basic needs. Thus, if the rights of future generations are respected, the membership of future generations would never increase beyond the ability of existing generations to make the necessary provision for the basic needs of future generations. . . .

Future Generations and Abortion

Now the population policy that the welfare rights of future generations justify suggests an argument for abortion that liberals would be inclined to accept. The argument assumes that the fetus is not a person and then attempts to show that aborting the fetus is either justified or required if the fetus will develop into a person who lacks a reasonable opportunity to lead a good life. Most versions of the argument even go so far as to maintain that the person who would otherwise be brought into existence in these unfavorable circumstances has in fact a right not to be born, i.e., a right to be aborted. Joel Feinberg puts the argument as follows:

. . . if, before the child has been born, we know that the conditions for the fulfillment of his most basic interests have already been destroyed, and we permit him nevertheless to be born, we become a party to the violation of his rights.

In such circumstances, therefore, a proxy for the fetus might plausibly claim on its behalf, a right not to be born. That right is based on his future rather than his present interests (he has no actual present interests); but of course it is not contingent on his birth because he has it before birth, from the very moment that satisfaction of his most basic future interests is rendered impossible ("Is There a Right to Be Born?" 354).

The argument is obviously analogous to arguments

for euthanasia. For, as in arguments for euthanasia, it is the nonfulfillment of a person's basic interests which is said to provide the legitimate basis for the person's right to have her life terminated.

However, in order for this argument to function as part of a defense for abortion on demand, it is necessary to show that no similar justification can be given for a right to be born. And it is here that the assumption that the fetus is not a person becomes important. For if the fetus were a person and if, moreover, this fetus-person had a reasonable opportunity to lead a good life, then, it could be argued, this fetus-person would have a right to be born. Thus, proceeding from the assumption that the fetus is not a person, various arguments have been offered to show that a similar justification cannot be given for a right to be born.[9]

One such argument bases the asymmetry on a failure of reference in the case of the fetus that would develop into a person with a reasonable opportunity for a good life. The argument can be summarized as follows:

If I bring into existence a person who lacks a reasonable opportunity to lead a good life, there will be a person who can reproach me that I did not prevent his leading an unfortunate existence. But if I do not bring into existence a person who would have a reasonable opportunity to lead a good life, there will be no person who can reproach me for preventing his leading a fortunate existence. Hence, only the person who lacks a reasonable opportunity to lead a good life can claim a right not to be born.

But notice that, if I do not bring into existence a person who would lack a reasonable opportunity to lead a good life, there will be no person who can thank me for preventing her leading an unfortunate existence. And, if I do bring into existence a person who had a reasonable opportunity to lead a good life, there will be a person who can thank me for not preventing her leading a fortunate existence. Thus, whatever failure of reference there is, it occurs in both cases, and therefore, cannot be the basis for any asymmetry between them.[10]

A second argument designed to establish the asymmetry between the two cases begins with the assumption that a person's life cannot be compared with her nonexistence unless the person already exists. This means that, if one allows a fetus to develop into a person who has a reasonable opportunity to lead a good life, one does not make that person better off than if she never existed. And it also means that if one allows a fetus to develop into a person who lacks a reasonable opportunity to lead a good life one does not make that person worse off than if she never existed. But what then justifies a right not to be born in the latter case? According to the argument, it is simply the fact that unless the fetus is aborted a person will come into existence who lacks a reasonable opportunity to lead a good life. But if this fact justifies a right not to be born, why, in the former case, would not the fact that unless the fetus is aborted a person will come into existence who has a reasonable opportunity to lead a good life suffice to justify a right to be born? Clearly, no reason has been given to distinguish the cases.

Furthermore, consider the grounds for aborting a fetus that would develop into a person who lacks a reasonable opportunity to lead a good life. It is not simply that the person is sure to experience some unhappiness in her life because in every person's life there is some unhappiness. Rather it is because the amount of expected unhappiness in this person's life would render her life not worth living. This implies that the justification for aborting in this case is based on a comparison of the value of the person's life with the value of her nonexistence. For how else can we say that the fact that a fetus would develop into a person who lacks a reasonable opportunity to lead a good life justifies our preventing the person's very existence? Consequently, this argument depends upon a denial of the very assumption with which it began, namely that the person's life cannot be compared with his nonexistence unless that person already exists.

Nevertheless, it might still be argued that an analogous justification cannot be given for a right to be born on the grounds that there is a difference in strength between one's duty to prevent a fetus from developing into a person who lacks a reasonable opportunity to lead a good life and one's duty not to prevent a fetus from developing into a person who has a reasonable opportunity to lead a good life. For example, it might be argued that the former duty is a relatively strong duty to prevent harm, whereas the latter duty is a relatively weak duty to promote well-being, and that only the relatively strong duty justifies a correlative right—in this case, a right not to

158

be born. But, even granting that our duty to prevent harm is stronger than our duty to promote well-being, in the case at issue we are dealing not just with a duty to promote well-being but with a duty to promote *basic* well-being. And, as liberals who are committed to the welfare rights of future generations would be the first to admit, our duty to prevent basic harm and our duty to promote basic well-being are not that distinct from a moral point of view. From which it follows that, if our duty to prevent basic harm justifies a right not to be born in the one case, then our duty to promote basic well-being would justify a right to be born in the other.

Nor will it do to reject the notion of a right to be born on the grounds that if the fetus is not a person then the bearer of such a right, especially when we violate that right by performing an abortion, would *seem* to be a potential or possible person. For the same would hold true of the right not to be born which is endorsed by liberals such as Feinberg and Narveson: the bearer of such a right, especially when we respect that right by performing an abortion, would also *seem* to be a potential or possible person. In fact, however, neither notion necessarily entails any metaphysical commitment to possible persons who "are" whether they exist or not. For to say that a person into whom a particular fetus would develop has a right not to be born is to say that there is an enforceable requirement upon certain persons the violation of which would fundamentally harm the person who would thereby come into existence. Similarly, to say that a person into whom a particular fetus would develop has a right to be born is to say that there is an enforceable requirement upon certain persons the respecting of which would fundamentally benefit the person who would thereby come into existence. So understood, neither the notion of a right to be born nor that of a right not to be born entails any metaphysical commitment to possible persons as bearers of rights.

Of course, recognizing a right to be born may require considerable personal sacrifice, and some people may want to reject any morality that requires such sacrifice. This option, however, is not open to liberals who are committed to the welfare rights of future generations. For such liberals are already committed to making whatever personal sacrifice is necessary to provide for the basic needs of future generations. Consequently, liberals committed to the welfare rights of future generations cannot consistently reject a prohibition of abortion in cases involving a right to be born simply on the grounds that it would require considerable personal sacrifice.

But there is an even more basic inconsistency in being committed both to the welfare rights of future generations and to abortion on demand. For, as we have seen, commitment to the welfare rights of future generations requires the acceptance of a population policy according to which existing generations must ensure that the membership of future generations does not exceed the ability of existing generations to provide for the basic needs of future generations. Thus for liberals who assume that the fetus is not a person, this population policy would have the same implications as the argument we considered which justifies abortion in certain cases on the basis of a person's right not to be born. For if existing generations violate this population policy by bringing into existence persons whose basic needs they cannot fulfill, they would also thereby be violating the right not to be born of those same persons, since such persons would not have a reasonable opportunity to lead a good life. But, as we have also seen, accepting this argument which justifies abortion in certain cases on the basis of a person's right not to be born commits one to accepting also a parallel argument for prohibiting abortion in certain other cases on the basis of a person's right to be born. Consequently, commitment to the population policy demanded by the welfare rights of future generations will likewise commit liberals to accepting this parallel argument for prohibiting abortion in certain cases. Therefore, even assuming that the fetus is not a person, liberals cannot consistently uphold the welfare rights of future generations while endorsing abortion on demand.

There remains the further question of whether liberals who are committed to the welfare rights of distant peoples and future generations can make a moral distinction between contraception and abortion—assuming, that is, that the fetus is not a person. In support of such a distinction, it might be argued that, in cases where abortion is at issue, we can roughly identify the particular person into whom a fetus would develop and ask whether that person would be fundamentally benefited or fundamentally harmed by being brought into existence, whereas we cannot do anything comparable in cases where contraception is at issue. Yet, though this difference does exist, it does not suffice for morally distinguishing abortion from contraception. For notice that if persons do not practice contraception when conditions are known to be suitable for bringing persons into existence who would have a reasonable opportunity to lead a good life, then there will normally come into existence persons who have thereby benefited. Similarly, if persons do not practice contraception when conditions are known to be unsuitable for bringing persons into existence who would have a reasonable opportunity to lead a good life (e.g., when persons who would be brought into existence would very likely have seriously debilitating and ultimately fatal genetic defects), then there will normally come into existence persons who have thereby been harmed. On grounds such as these, therefore, we could certainly defend a "right not to be conceived" and a "right to be conceived" which are analogous to our previously defended "right not to be born" and "right to be born." Hence, it would follow that liberals who are committed to the welfare rights of distant peoples and future generations can no more consistently support "contraception on demand" than they can consistently support abortion on demand.

Needless to say, considerably more sacrifice would normally be required of existing generations in order to fulfill a person's right to be born or right to be conceived than would be required to fulfill a person's right not to be born or right not to be conceived. For example, fulfilling a person's right to be born may ultimately require caring for the needs of a child for many years whereas fulfilling a person's right not to be born may require only an early abortion. Therefore, because of the greater sacrifice that would normally be required to fulfill a person's right to be born, that right might often be overridden in particular circumstances by the rights of existing persons to have their own basic needs satisfied. The existing persons whose welfare would have priority over a person's right to be born are not only those who would be directly involved in bringing the person into existence but also those distant persons whose welfare rights would otherwise be neglected if goods and resources were diverted to bringing additional persons into existence. This would, of course, place severe restrictions on any population increase in technologically developed nations so long as persons in technologically underdeveloped nations still fail to have their basic needs satisfied. But for persons committed to the welfare rights of distant peoples as well as to the welfare rights of future generations, no other policy would be acceptable.

Obviously these results cannot but be embarrassing for many liberals. For what has been shown is that, with or without the assumption that the fetus is a person, liberals who are committed to the welfare rights of distant peoples and future generations cannot consistently endorse abortion on demand. Thus, assuming that the welfare rights of distant peoples and future generations can be firmly grounded on a right to life and a right to fair treatment, the only morally acceptable way for liberals to avoid this inconsistency is to moderate their support for abortion on demand.

NOTES

1. It is not difficult to find philosophers who not only favor a liberal view on abortion and thus tend to support abortion on demand, but also favor these other social goals as well. See Jan Narveson, "Moral Problems of Population," *Monist*, LVII, 1 (January 1973): 62–86, and "Aesthetics, Charity, Utility and Distributive Justice," *ibid.*, LVI, 4 (October 1972): 527–551; Joel Feinberg, "Is There a Right to Be Born?" in James Rachels, ed., *Understanding Moral Philosophy* (Encino, Calif.: Dickenson, 1976), pp. 346–357, and "The Rights of Animals and Future Generations," in William Blackstone, *Philosophy and Environmental Crisis* (Athens: Univ. of Georgia Press, 1972), pp. 41–68; Michael Tooley, "Abortion and Infanticide," *Philosophy & Public Affairs*, II, 1 (Fall 1972): 37–65, and "Michael Tooley Replies," *ibid.*, II, 4 (Summer 1973): 419–432; Mary Anne Warren, "Do Potential People Have Moral Rights?", *Canadian Journal of Philosophy*, VII, 2 (June 1977): 275–289.

2. For other possibilities, see Onora Nell, "Lifeboat Earth," *Philosophy & Public Affairs*, IV, 3 (Spring 1975): 273–292; Peter Singer, "Famine, Affluence and Morality," *ibid.*, I, 3 (Spring 1972): 229–243.

3. A person's basic needs are those which must be satisfied if the person's health and sanity are not to be seriously endangered.

4. For an attempt to work out these justifications, see this anthology, page 97.

5. See pages 126–134.

6. Hereafter the term 'fetus-person' will be used to indicate the assumption that the fetus is a person. The term 'fetus' is also understood to refer to any human organism from conception to birth.

7. See her "Killing, Letting Die, and the Trolley Problem," *Monist*, LIX, 2 (April 1976): 204–217.

8. Notice that my critique of Thomson's arguments for abortion on demand differs from critiques that attempt to find an *internal* defect in Thomson's arguments. [For example, see Richard Werner's "Abortion: the Moral Status of the Unborn," *Social Theory and Practice*, III, 2 (Fall 1974): 210–216.] My approach has been to show that Thomson's arguments are *externally* defective in that a liberal who is committed to the welfare rights of distant peoples cannot consistently accept those arguments. Thus, Jan Narveson's telling objections to Werner's internalist critique of Thomson's arguments [see his "Semantics, Future Generations and the Abortion Problem," *ibid.*, III, 4 (Fall 1975): 464–466] happily do not apply to my own critique.

9. See Narveson, "Utilitarianism and New Generations," *Mind*, LXXVI, 301 (January 1967): 62–72, and "Moral Problems of Population," *op. cit.*

10. For a similar argument, see Timothy Sprigge "Professor Narveson's Utilitarianism," *Inquiry*, XI, 3 (Autumn 1968: 332–346), p. 338.

James Rachels
EUTHANASIA, KILLING, AND LETTING DIE

James Rachels criticizes a recent policy statement of the American Medical Association on the grounds that it endorses the doctrine that there is an important moral difference between active and passive euthanasia. Rachels denies that there is any moral difference between the two. He argues that once we judge a patient would be better off dead, it should not matter much whether we kill her or let her die. He points out that both killing and letting die can be intentional and deliberate and can proceed from the same motives; further, that when killing and letting die are similar in these and other relevant respects, our moral assessment of these acts is also similar. Rachels concludes by considering a number of counterarguments to his view and finds them all wanting. In particular, Rachels rejects the idea that the killing and letting die distinction can be supported on the grounds that our duty to refrain from harming people is much stronger than our duty to help people in need. Rather he contends that, when conditions are similar, our duty to refrain from harming people and our duty to help people in need have a similar moral force.

DR F. J. INGELFINGER, former editor of the *The New England Journal of Medicine*, observes that

This is the heyday of the ethicist in medicine. He delineates the rights of patients, of experimental subjects, of fetuses, of mothers, of animals, and even of doctors. (And what a far cry it is from the days when medical "ethics" consisted of condemning economic improprieties such as fee splitting and advertising!) With impeccable logic—once certain basic assumptions are granted—and with graceful prose, the ethicist develops his arguments. . . . Yet his precepts are essentially the products of armchair exercise and remain abstract and idealistic until they have been tested in the laboratory of experience.[1]

One problem with such armchair exercises, he complains, is that in spite of the impeccable logic and the graceful prose, the result is often an absolutist ethic which is unsatisfactory when applied to particular cases, and which is therefore of little use to the practicing physician. Unlike some absolutist philosophers, "the practitioner appears to prefer the principles of individualism. As there are few atheists in fox holes, there tend to be few absolutists at the bedside."[2]

I must concede at the outset that this chapter is another exercise in "armchair ethics" in the sense that I am not a physician but a philosopher. Yet I am no absolutist; and my purpose is to examine a doctrine that *is* held in an absolute form by many doctors. The doctrine is that there is an important moral difference between active and passive euthanasia, such that even though the latter is sometimes permissible, the former is always forbidden. This is an absolute which doctors hold "at the bedside" as well as in the seminar room, and the "principles of individualism" make little headway against it. But I will argue that this is an irrational dogma, and that there is no sound moral basis for it.

I will not argue, simply, that active euthanasia is all right. Rather, I will be concerned with the *relation* between active euthanasia and passive euthanasia: I will argue that there is no moral difference between them. By this I mean that there is no reason to prefer one over the other as a matter of principle—the fact that one case of euthanasia is active, while another is passive, is not *itself* a reason to think one morally better than the other. If you already think that pas-

sive euthanasia is all right, and you are convinced by my arguments, then you may conclude that active euthanasia must be all right, too. On the other hand, if you believe that active euthanasia is immoral, you may want to conclude that passive euthanasia must be immoral, too. Although I prefer the former alternative, I will not argue for it here. I will only argue that the two forms of euthanasia are morally equivalent—either both are acceptable or both are unacceptable.

I am aware that this will at first seem incredible to many readers, but I hope that this impression will be dispelled as the discussion proceeds. The discussion will be guided by two methodological considerations, both of which are touched on in the editorial quoted above. The first has to do with my "basic assumptions." My arguments are intended to appeal to all reasonable people, and not merely to those who already share my philosophical preconceptions. Therefore, I will try not to rely on any assumptions that cannot be accepted by any reasonable person. None of my arguments will depend on morally eccentric premises. Second, Dr. Ingelfinger is surely correct when he says that we must be as concerned with the realities of medical practice as with the more abstract issues of moral theory. As he notes, the philosopher's precepts "remain abstract and idealistic until they are tested in the laboratory of experience." Part of my argument will be precisely that, when "tested in the laboratory of experience," the doctrine in question has terrible results. I believe that if this doctrine were to be recognized as irrational, and rejected by the medical profession, the benefit to both doctors and patients would be enormous. In this sense, my paper is not intended as an "armchair exercise" at all.

THE AMERICAN MEDICAL ASSOCIATION POLICY STATEMENT

"Active euthanasia," as the term is used, means taking some positive action designed to kill the patient; for example, giving him a lethal injection of potassium chloride. "Passive euthanasia," on the other hand, means simply refraining from doing anything to keep the patient alive. In passive euthanasia we withhold medication or other life-sustaining therapy, or we refuse to perform surgery, etc., and let the patient die "naturally" of whatever ills already afflict him.

Many doctors and theologians prefer to use the term "euthanasia" only in connection with active euthanasia, and they use other words to refer to what I am calling "passive euthanasia"—for example, instead of "passive euthanasia" they may speak of "the right to death with dignity." One reason for this choice of terms is the emotional impact of the words: it *sounds* so much better to defend "death with dignity" than to advocate "euthanasia" of any sort. And of course if one believes that there is a great moral difference between active and passive euthanasia— as most doctors and religious writers do—then one may prefer a terminology which puts as much psychological distance as possible between them. However, I do not want to become involved in a pointless dispute about terminology, because nothing of substance depends on which label is used. I will stay with the terms "active euthanasia" and "passive euthanasia" because they are the most convenient; but if the reader prefers a different terminology he may substitute his own throughout, and my arguments will be unaffected.

The belief that there is an important moral difference between active and passive euthanasia obviously has important consequences for medical practice. It makes a difference to what doctors are willing to do. Consider, for example, the following familiar situation. A patient who is dying from incurable cancer of the throat is in terrible pain that we can no longer satisfactorily alleviate. He is certain to die within a few days, but he decides that he does not want to go on living for those days since the pain is unbearable. So he asks the doctor to end his life now; and his family joins in the request. One way that the doctor might comply with this request is simply by killing the patient with a lethal injection. Most doctors would not do that, not only because of the possible legal consequences, but because they think such a course would be immoral. And this is understandable: the idea of killing someone goes against very deep moral feelings; and besides, as we are often reminded, it is the special business of doctors to save and protect life, not to destroy it. Yet, even so, the physician may sympathize with the

dying patient's request and feel that it is entirely reasonable for him to prefer death now rather than after a few more days of agony. The doctrine that we are considering tells the doctor what to do: it says that although he may not administer the lethal injection—that would be "active euthanasia," which is forbidden—he *may* withhold treatment and let the patient die sooner than he otherwise would.

It is no wonder that this simple idea is so widely accepted, for it seems to give the doctor a way out of his dilemma without having to kill the patient, and without having to prolong the patient's agony. The idea is not a new one. What *is* new is that the idea is now being incorporated into official ments of medical ethics. What was once unofficially done is now becoming official policy. The idea is expressed, for example, in a 1973 policy statement of the American Medical Association, which says (in its entirety):

> *The intentional termination of the life of one human being by another—mercy killing—is contrary to that for which the medical profession stands and is contrary to the policy of the American Medical Association.*
>
> *The cessation of the employment of extraordinary means to prolong the life of the body when there is irrefutable evidence that biological death is imminent is the decision of the patient and/or his immediate family. The advice and judgment of the physician should be freely available to the patient and/or his immediate family.*[3]

This is a cautiously worded statement, and it is not clear *exactly* what is being affirmed. I take it, however, that at least these three propositions are intended:

1. Killing patients is absolutely forbidden; however, it is sometimes permissible to allow patients to die.
2. It is permissible to allow a patient to die if
   a. there is irrefutable evidence that he will die soon anyway;
   b. "extraordinary" measures would be required to keep him alive; and
   c. the patient and/or his immediate family requests it.
3. Doctors should make their own advice and judgments available to the patient and/or his immediate family when the latter are deciding whether to request that the patient be allowed to die.

The first proposition expresses the doctrine which is the main subject of this paper. As for the third, it seems obvious enough, provided that 1 and 2 are accepted, so I shall say nothing further about it.

I do want to say a few things about 2. Physicians often allow patients to die; however, they do *not* always keep to the guidelines set out in 2. For example, a doctor may leave instructions that if a hopeless, comatose patient suffers cardiac arrest, nothing be done to start his heart beating again. "No-coding" is the name given to this practice, and the consent of the patient and/or his immediate family is not commonly sought. This is thought to be a medical decision (in reality, of course, it is a moral one) which is the doctor's affair. To take a different sort of example, when a Down's infant (a mongoloid) is born with an intestinal blockage, the doctor and parents may agree that there will be no operation to remove the blockage, so that the baby will die.[4] (If the same infant were born without the obstruction, it certainly would not be killed. This is a clear application of the idea that "letting die" is all right even though killing is forbidden.) But in such cases it is clear that the baby is *not* going to die soon anyway. If the surgery were performed, the baby would proceed to a "normal" infancy—normal, that is, for a mongoloid. Moreover, the treatment required to save the baby—abdominal surgery—can hardly be called "extraordinary" by today's medical standards.

Therefore, all three conditions which the AMA statement places on the decision to let die are commonly violated. It is beyond the scope of this paper to determine whether doctors are right to violate those conditions. But I firmly believe that the second requirement—2b—is not acceptable. Only a little reflection is needed to show that the distinction between ordinary and extraordinary means is not important. Even a very conservative, religiously-oriented writer such as Paul Ramsey stresses this. Ramsey gives these examples:

Suppose that a diabetic patient long accustomed to self-administration of insulin falls victim to terminal cancer, or suppose that a terminal cancer patient suddenly develops diabetes. Is he in the first case obliged to continue, and in the second case obliged to begin, insulin treatment and die painfully of cancer, or in either or both cases

may the patient choose rather to pass into diabetic coma and an earlier death? . . . Or an old man slowly deteriorating who from simply being inactive and recumbent gets pneumonia: are we to use antibiotics in a likely successful attack upon this disease which from time immemorial has been called "the old man's friend"?[5]

I agree with Ramsey, and with many other writers, that in such cases treatment may be withheld even though it is not "extraordinary" by any reasonable standard. Contrary to what is implied by the AMA statement, the distinction between heroic and non-heroic means of treatment can *not* be used to determine when treatment is or is not mandatory.

Killing and Letting Die

I return now to the distinction between active and passive euthanasia. Of course, not every doctor believes that this distinction is morally important. Over twenty years ago Dr. D.C.S. Cameron of the American Cancer Society said that "Actually the difference between euthanasia [i.e., killing] and letting the patient die by omitting life-sustaining treatment is a moral quibble."[6] I argue that Cameron was right.

The initial thought can be expressed quite simply. In any case in which euthanasia seems desirable, it is because we think that the patient would literally be better off dead—or at least, no worse off dead—than continuing the kind of life available to him. (Without this assumption, even *passive* euthanasia would be unthinkable.) But, as far as the main question of ending the patient's life is concerned, it does not matter whether the euthanasia is active or passive: *in either case,* he ends up dead sooner than he otherwise would. And if the results are the same, why should it matter so much which method is used?

Moreover, we need to remember that, in cases such as that of the terminal cancer-patient, the justification for allowing him to die, rather than prolonging his life for a few more hopeless days, is that he is in horrible pain. But if we simply withhold treatment, it may take him *longer* to die, and so he will suffer *more* than he would if we were to administer the lethal injection. This fact provides strong reason for thinking that, once we have made the initial decision not to prolong his agony, active euthanasia is actually preferable to passive euthanasia rather than the reverse. It also shows a kind of incoherence in the conventional view: to say that passive euthanasia is preferable is to endorse the option which leads to more suffering rather than less, and is contrary to the humanitarian impulse which prompts the decision not to prolong his life in the first place.

But many people are convinced that there is an important moral difference between active and passive euthanasia because they think that, in passive euthanasia, the doctor does not really *do* anything. No action whatever is taken; the doctor simply does nothing, and the patient dies of whatever ills already afflict him. In active euthanasia, however, we *do something* to bring about the patient's death. We kill him. Thus, the difference between active and passive euthanasia is thought to be the difference between doing something to bring about someone's death, and not doing anything to bring about anyone's death. And of course if we conceive the matter in *this* way, passive euthanasia seems preferable. Ramsey, who denounces the view I am defending as "extremist" and who regards the active/passive distinction as one of the "flexibly wise categories of traditional medical ethics," takes just this view of the matter. He says that the choice between active and passive euthanasia "is not a choice between directly and indirectly willing and doing something. *It is rather the important choice between doing something and doing nothing,* or (better said) ceasing to do something that was begun in order to do something that is better because now more fitting."[7]

This is a very misleading way of thinking, for it ignores the fact that in passive euthanasia the doctor *does* do one thing which is very important: namely, he lets the patient die. We may overlook this obvious fact—or at least, we may put it out of our minds—if we concentrate only on a very restricted way of describing what happens: "The doctor does not administer medication or any other therapy; he does not instruct the nurses to administer any such medication; he does not perform any surgery"; and so on. And of course this description of what happens is correct, as far as it goes—these are all things that the doctor does not do. But the point is that the doctor *does* let the patient die when he could save him, and this must be included in the description, too.

There is another reason why we might fall into this error. We might confuse *not saving* someone with *letting him die*. Suppose a patient is dying, and Dr. X could prolong his life. But he decides not to do so and the patient dies. Now it is true of everyone on earth that he did not save the patient. Dr. X did not save him, and neither did you, and neither did I. So we might be tempted to think that all of us are in the same moral position, reasoning that since neither you nor I are responsible for the patient's death, neither is Dr. X. None of us did anything. This, however, is a mistake, for even though it is true that none of us saved the patient, it is *not* true that we all let him die. In order to let someone die, one must be *in a position* to save him. You and I were not in a position to save the patient, so we did not let him die. Dr. X, on the other hand, was in a position to save him, and did let him die. Thus the doctor is in a special moral position which not just everyone is in.

Here we must remember some elementary points, which are so obvious that they would not be worth mentioning except for the fact that overlooking them is a source of so much confusion in this area. The act of letting someone die may be intentional and deliberate, just as the act of killing someone may be intentional and deliberate. Moreover, the doctor is *responsible* for his decision to let the patient die, just as he would be responsible for giving the patient a lethal injection. The decision to let a patient die is subject to moral appraisal in the same way that a decision to kill is subject to moral appraisal: it may be assessed as wise or unwise, compassionate or sadistic, right or wrong. If a doctor deliberately let a patient die who was suffering from a routinely curable illness, then he would be to blame for what he did, just as he would be to blame if he had needlessly killed the patient. It would be no defense at all for him to insist that, *really*, he didn't "do anything" but just stand there. We would all know that he did do something very serious indeed, for he let the patient die.

These considerations show how misleading it is to characterize the difference between active and passive euthanasia as a difference between doing something (killing), for which the doctor may be morally culpable; and doing nothing (just standing there while the patient dies), for which the doctor is not culpable. The real difference between them is, rather, the difference between *killing* and letting die, both of which are actions for which a doctor, or anyone else, will be morally responsible.

Now we can formulate our problem more precisely. If there is an important moral difference between active and passive euthanasia, it must be because *killing someone is morally worse than letting someone die.* But is it? Is killing, in itself, worse than letting die? In order to investigate this issue, we may consider two cases which are exactly alike except that one involves killing where the other involves letting someone die. Then we can ask whether this difference makes any difference to our moral assessments. It is important that the cases be *exactly* alike except for this one difference, since otherwise we cannot be confident that it is *this* difference which accounts for any variation in our assessments.

1. Smith stands to gain a large inheritance if anything should happen to his six-year-old cousin. One evening while the child is taking his bath, Smith sneaks into the bathroom and drowns the child, and then arranges things so that it will look like an accident.
2. Jones also stands to gain if anything should happen to his six-year-old cousin. Like Smith, Jones sneaks in planning to drown the child in his bath. However, just as he enters the bathroom Jones sees the child slip, hit his head, and fall face down in the water. Jones is delighted; he stands by, ready to push the child's head back under if it is necessary, but it is not necessary. With only a little thrashing about, the child drowns all by himself, "accidentally," as Jones watches and does nothing.

Now Smith killed the child, while Jones "merely" let the child die. That is the only difference between them. Did either man behave better, from a moral point of view? Is there a moral difference between them? *If the difference between killing and letting die were itself a morally important matter, then we should say that Jones's behavior was less reprehensible than Smith's.* But do we actually want to say that? I think not, for several reasons. In the first place, both men acted from the same motive, personal gain, and both had exactly the same end in view when they acted.

We may infer from Smith's conduct that he is a bad man, although we may withdraw or modify that judgment if we learn certain further facts about him; for example, that he is mentally deranged. But would we not also infer the very same thing about Jones from his conduct? And would not the same further considerations also be relevant to any modification of that judgment? Moreover, suppose Jones pleaded in his defense, "After all, I didn't kill the child. I only stood there and let him die." Again, if letting die were in itself less bad than killing, this defense should have some weight. But—morally, at least—it does not. Such a "defense" can only be regarded as a grotesque perversion of moral reasoning.

Thus, it seems that when we are careful not to smuggle in any further differences which prejudice the issue, the mere difference between killing and letting die does not itself make any difference to the morality of actions concerning life and death.[8]

Now it may be pointed out, quite properly, that the cases of euthanasia with which doctors are concerned are not like this at all. They do not involve personal gain or the destruction of normal, healthy children. Doctors are concerned only with cases in which the patient's life is of no further use to him, or in which the patient's life has become or soon will become a positive burden. However, the point is the same in those cases: the difference between killing or letting die does not, *in itself*, make a difference, from the point of view of morality. If a doctor lets a patient die, for humane reasons, he is in the same moral position as if he had given the patient a lethal injection for humane reasons. If his decision was wrong—if, for example, the patient's illness was in fact curable—then the decision would be equally regrettable no matter which method was used to carry it out. And if the doctor's decision was the right one, then the method he used is not itself important.

The AMA statement isolates the crucial issue very well: "the intentional termination of the life of one human being by another." But then the statement goes on to deny that the cessation of treatment *is* the intentional termination of a life. This is where the mistake comes in, for what is the cessation of treatment, in those circumstances, if it is not "the intentional termination of the life of one human being by another"? Of course it is exactly that; if it were not, there would be no point to it.

COUNTER-ARGUMENTS

Our argument has now brought us to this point: we cannot draw any moral distinction between active and passive euthanasia on the grounds that one involves killing while the other only involves letting someone die, because that is a difference that does not make a difference, from a moral point of view. Some people will find this hard to accept. One reason, I think, is that they fail to distinguish the question of whether killing is, in itself, worse than letting die, from the very different question of whether most actual cases of killing are more reprehensible than most actual cases of letting die. Most actual cases of killing are clearly terrible—think of the murders reported in the newspapers—and we hear of such cases almost every day. On the other hand, we hardly ever hear of a case of letting die, except for the actions of doctors who are motivated by humanitarian reasons. So we learn to think of killing in a much worse light than letting die; and we conclude, invalidly, that there must be something about killing which makes it *in itself* worse than letting die. But this does not follow for it is not the bare difference between killing and letting die that makes the difference in these cases. Rather, it is the other factors—the murderer's motive of personal gain, for example, contrasted with the doctor's humanitarian motivation, or the fact that the murderer kills a healthy person while the doctor lets die a terminal patient racked with disease—that account for our different reactions to the different cases.

There are, however, some substantial arguments that may be advanced to oppose my conclusion. Here are two of them:

The first counter-argument focuses specifically on the concept of *being the cause of someone's death*. If we kill someone, then we are the cause of his death. But if we merely let someone die, we are not the cause; rather, he dies of whatever condition he already has. The doctor who gives the cancer patient a lethal injection will have caused his patient's

death, and will have this on his conscience; whereas if he merely ceases treatment, the cancer and not the doctor is the cause of death. This is supposed to make a moral difference. This argument has been advanced many times. Ramsey, for example, urges us to remember that "In omission no human agent causes the patient's death, directly or indirectly."[9] And, writing in the *Villanova Law Review* for 1968, Dr. J. Russell Elkinton said that what makes the active/passive distinction important is that in passive euthanasia, "the patient does not die from the act [e.g. the act of turning off the respirator] but from the underlying disease or injury."[10]

This argument will not do, for two reasons. First, just as there is a distinction to be drawn between being and not being the cause of someone's death, there is also a distinction to be drawn between letting someone die and not letting anyone die. It is certainly desirable, in general, not to be the cause of anyone's death; but it is also desirable, in general, not to let anyone die when we can save them. (Doctors act on this precept every day.) Therefore, we cannot draw any special conclusion about the relative desirability of passive euthanasia just on these grounds. Second, the reason why we think it is bad to be the cause of someone's death is that we think that death is a great evil—and so it is. However, if we have decided that euthanasia, even passive euthanasia, is desirable in a given case, then we have decided that in *this* instance death is no greater an evil than the patient's continued existence. And if this is true, then the usual reason for not wanting to be the cause of someone's death simply does not apply. To put the point just a bit differently: There is nothing wrong with being the cause of someone's death if his death is, all things considered, a good thing. And if his death is *not* a good thing, then *no* form of euthanasia, active or passive, is justified. So once again we see that the two kinds of euthanasia stand or fall together.

The second counter-argument appeals to a favorite idea of philosophers, namely that our duty not to harm people is generally more stringent than our duty to help them. The law affirms this when it forbids us to kill people, or steal their goods, but does not require us in general to save people's lives or give them charity. And this is said to be not merely a point about the law, but about morality as well. We do not have a strict moral duty to help some poor man in Ethiopa—although it might be kind and generous of us if we did—but we *do* have a strict moral duty to refrain from doing anything to harm him. Killing someone is a violation of our duty not to harm, whereas letting someone die is merely a failure to give help. Therefore, the former is a more serious breach of morality than the latter; and so, contrary to what was said above, there is a morally significant difference between killing and letting die.

This argument has a certain superficial plausibility, but it cannot be used to show that there is a morally important difference between active and passive euthanasia. For one thing, it only seems that our duty to help people is less stringent than our duty not to harm them when we concentrate on certain sorts of cases: cases in which the people we could help are very far away, and are strangers to us; or cases in which it would be very difficult for us to help them, or in which helping would require a substantial sacrifice on our part. Many people feel that, in *these* types of cases, it may be kind and generous of us to give help, but we are not morally required to do so. Thus it is felt that when we give money for famine relief we are being especially big-hearted, and we deserve special praise—even if it would be immodest of us to seek such praise—because we are doing more than, strictly speaking, we are required to do.[11]

However, if we think of cases in which it would be very easy for us to help someone who is close at hand and in which no great personal sacrifice is required, things look very different. Think again of the child drowning in the bathtub: *of course* a man standing next to the tub would have a strict moral duty to help the child. Here the alleged asymmetry between the duty to help and the duty not to do harm vanishes. Since most of the cases of euthanasia with which we are concerned are of this latter type—the patient is close at hand, it is well within the professional skills of the physician to keep him alive—the alleged asymmetry has little relevance.

It should also be remembered, in considering this argument, that the duty of doctors toward their patients *is* precisely to help them; that is what doctors are supposed to do. Therefore, even if there were a general asymmetry between the duty to help and the duty not to harm—which I deny—it would not apply in the special case of the relation between doctors and their patients. Finally, it is not clear that killing such a patient *is* harming him, even though in other cases it certainly is a great harm to someone to kill him, for as I said before, we are going under the assumption that the patient would be no worse off dead than he is now; if this is so, then killing him is not harming him. For the same reason we should not classify letting such a patient die as failing to help him. Therefore, even if we grant that our duty to help people is less stringent than our duty not to harm them, nothing follows about our duties with respect to killing and letting die in the special case of euthanasia.

PRACTICAL CONSEQUENCES

This is enough, I think, to show that the doctrine underlying the AMA statement is false. There is no general moral difference between active and passive euthanasia; if one is permissible, so is the other. Now if this were merely an intellectuual mistake, having no significant consequences for medical practice, the whole matter would not be very important. But the opposite is true: the doctrine has terrible consequences for, as I have already mentioned—and as doctors know very well—the process of being "allowed to die" can be relatively slow and painful, while being given a lethal injection is relatively quick and painless. Dr. Anthony Shaw describes what happens when the decision has been made not to perform the surgery necessary to "save" a mongoloid infant:

When surgery is denied [the doctor] must try to keep the infant from suffering while natural forces sap the baby's life away. As a surgeon whose natural inclination is to use the scalpel to fight off death, standing by and watching a salvageable baby die is the most emotionally exhausting experience I know. It is easy at a conference, in a theoretical discussion, to decide that such infants should be allowed to die. It is altogether different to stand by in the nursery and watch as dehydration and infection wither a tiny being over hours and days. This is a terrible ordeal for me and the hospital staff—much more so than for the parents who never set foot in the nursery.[12]

Why must the hospital staff "stand by in the nursery

and watch as dehydration and infection wither a tiny being over hours and days"? Why must they merely "try" to reduce the infant's suffering? The doctrine which says that the baby may be allowed to dehydrate and wither, but not be given an injection which would end its life without suffering, is not only irrational but cruel.

The same goes for the case of the man with cancer of the throat. Here there are three options: with continued treatment, he will have a few more days of pain, and then die; if treatment is stopped, but nothing else is done, it will be a few more hours; and with a lethal injection, he will die at once. Those who oppose euthanasia in all its forms say that we must take the first option, and keep the patient alive for as long as possible. This view is so patently inhumane that few defend it; nevertheless, it does have a certain kind of integrity. It is at least consistent. The third option is the one I think best. But the *middle* position—that, although the patient need not suffer for days before dying, he must nevertheless suffer for a few more hours—is a "moderate" view which incorporates the worst, and not the best, features of both extremes.

Let me mention one other practice that we would be well rid of if we stopped thinking that the distinction between active and passive euthanasia is important. About one in six hundred babies born in the United States is mongoloid. Most of these babies are otherwise healthy—that is, with only the usual pediatric care, they will proceed to a "normal" infancy. Some, however, are born with other congenital defects such as intestinal obstructions which require surgery if the baby is to live. As I have already mentioned, sometimes the surgery is withheld and the baby dies. But when there is no defect requiring surgery, the baby lives on.[13] Now surgery to remove an intestinal obstruction is not difficult; the reason why it is not performed in such cases is, clearly, that the child is mongoloid and the parents and doctor judge that because of *this* it is better for the child to die.

But notice that this situation is absurd, no matter what view one takes of the lives and potentials of such babies. If you think that the life of such an infant is worth preserving, then what does it matter if it needs a simple operation? Or, if you think it better that such a baby not live on, then what difference does it make if its intestinal tract is *not*

blocked? In either case, the matter of life or death is being decided on irrelevant grounds. It is the mongolism, and not the intestine, that is the issue. The matter should be decided, if at all, on *that* basis, and not be allowed to depend on the essentially irrelevant question of whether the intestinal tract is blocked.

What makes this situation possible, of course, is the idea that when there is an intestinal obstruction we can "let the baby die," but when there is no such defect there is nothing we can do, for we must not "kill" it. The fact that this idea leads to such results as deciding life or death on irrelevant grounds is another good reason why it should be rejected.

Doctors may think that all of this is only of academic interest, the sort of thing which philosophers may worry about but which has no practical bearing on their own work. After all, doctors must be concerned about the legal consequences of what they do, and active euthanasia is clearly forbidden by the law. They are right to be concerned about this. There have not been many prosecutions of doctors in the United States for active euthanasia, but there have been some. Prosecutions for passive euthanasia, on the other hand, are virtually nonexistent, even though there are laws under which charges could be brought, and even though this practice is much more wide-spread. Passive euthanasia, unlike active euthanasia, is by and large tolerated by the law. The law may sometimes compel a doctor to take action which he might not otherwise take to keep a patient alive,[14] but of course this is very different from bringing criminal charges against him after the patient is dead.

Even so, doctors should be concerned with the fact that the law and public opinion are forcing upon them an indefensible moral position, which has a considerable effect on their practices. Of course, most doctors are not now in the position of being coerced in this matter, for they do not regard themselves as merely going along with what the law requires. Rather, in statements such as the AMA statement that I quoted, they are endorsing the doctrine as a central point of medical ethics. In that statement, active euthanasia is condemned not merely as illegal but as "contrary to that for which the medical profession stands," while passive euthanasia is approved. However, if my arguments have been sound, there really is no intrinsic moral difference between them (although there may be morally important differences in their consequences, varying from case to case); so while doctors may have to discriminate between them to satisfy the law, they should not do any *more* than that. In particular, they should not give the distinction any added authority and weight by writing it into official statements of medical ethics.

NOTES

1. F. J. Ingelfinger, "Bedside Ethics for the Hopeless Case," *The New England Journal of Medicine* 289 (25 October 1973), p. 914.

2. Ibid.

3. This statement was approved by the House of Delegates of the AMA on December 4, 1973. It is worth noting that some state medical societies have advised *patients* to take a similar attitude toward the termination of their lives. In 1973 the Connecticut State Medical Society approved a "background statement" to be signed by terminal patients which includes this sentence: "I value life and the dignity of life, so that I am not asking that my life be directly taken, but that my life not be unreasonably prolonged or the dignity of life be destroyed." Other state medical societies have followed suit.

4. A discussion of this type of case can be found in Anthony Shaw, "'Doctor, Do We Have a Choice?'" *The New York Times Magazine*, 30 January 1972, pp. 44–54. Also see Shaw's "Dilemmas of 'Informed Consent' in Children," *The New England Journal of Medicine* 289 (25 October 1973), pp. 885–90.

5. Paul Ramsey, *The Patient as Person* (New Haven, Conn.: Yale University Press, 1970), pp. 115–16.

6. D.C.S. Cameron, *The Truth About Cancer* (Englewood Cliffs, N.J.: Prentice-Hall, 1956), p. 116.

7. Ramsey, *The Patient as Person*, p. 151.

8. Judith Jarvis Thomson has argued that this line of reasoning is unsound. Consider, she says, this argument which is parallel to the one involving Smith and Jones:

Alfrieda knows that if she cuts off Alfred's head he will die, and wanting him to die, cuts it off; Bertha knows that if she punches Bert in the nose he will die—Bert is in peculiar physical condition—and, wanting him to die, punches him in the nose. But what Bertha does is surely every bit as bad as what Alfrieda does. So cutting off a man's head isn't worse than punching a man in the nose. ["Killing, Letting Die, and the Trolley Problem," The Monist 59 (1976), p. 204.]

She concludes that, since this absurd argument doesn't prove anything, the Smith/Jones argument doesn't prove anything either.

However, I think that the Alfrieda/Bertha argument is not absurd, as strange as it is. A little analysis shows that it is a sound argument and that its conclusion is true. We need to notice first that the reason why it is wrong to chop someone's head off is, obviously, that this causes death. The act is objectionable because of its consequences. Thus, a different act with the same consequences may be equally objectionable. In Thomson's example, punching Bert in the nose has the same consequences as chopping off Alfred's head; and, indeed, the two actions are equally bad.

Now the Alfrieda/Bertha argument presupposes a distinction between the act of chopping off someone's head, and the results of this act, the victim's death. (It is stipulated that, except for the fact that Alfrieda chops off someone's head, while Bertha punches someone in the nose, the two acts are "in all other respects alike." The "*other*" respects include the act's consequence, the victim's death.) This is not a distinction we would normally think to make, since we cannot in fact cut off someone's head without killing him. Yet in thought the distinction can be drawn. The question raised in the argument, then, is whether, *considered apart from their consequences*, head-chopping is worse than nose-punching. And the answer to *this* strange question is No, just as the argument says it should be.

The conclusion of the argument should be construed like this: The bare fact that one act is an act of head-chopping, while another act is an act of nose-punching, is not a reason for judging the former to be worse than the latter. At the same time—and this is perfectly compatible with the argument—the fact that one act causes death, while another does not, *is* a reason for judging the former to be worse. The parallel construal of my conclusion is: The bare fact that one act is an act of killing, while another act is an act of letting die, is not a reason for judging the former to be worse than the latter. At the same time—and this is perfectly compatible with my argument—the fact that an act (of killing, for example) prevents suffering, while another act (of letting die, for example) does not, *is* a reason for preferring one over the other. So once we see exactly how the Alfrieda/Bertha argument *is* parallel to the Smith/Jones argument, we find that Thomson's argument is, surprisingly, quite all right.

9. Ramsey, *The Patient as Person*, p. 151.

10. J. Russell Elkinton, "The Dying Patient, the Doctor, and the Law," *Villanova Law Review* 13 (Summer 1968), p. 743.

11. For the purposes of this essay we do not need to consider whether this way of thinking about "charity" is justified. There are, however, strong arguments that it is morally indefensible: see Peter Singer, "Famine, Affluence, and Morality," *Philosophy and Public Affairs* 1 (Spring 1972), pp. 229–43. Also see James Rachels, "Killing and Letting People Die of Starvation," forthcoming in *Philosophy*, for a discussion of the killing/letting die distinction in the context of world hunger, as well as further arguments that the distinction is morally unimportant.

12. Shaw, "'Doctor, Do We Have a Choice?'" p. 54.

13. See the articles by Shaw cited in note 4.

14. For example, in February 1974 a Superior Court judge in Maine ordered a doctor to proceed with an operation to repair a hole in the esophagus of a baby with multiple deformities. Otherwise the operation would not have been performed. The baby died anyway a few days later. "Deformed Baby Dies Amid Controversy," *The Miami Herald*, 25 February 1974, p. 4-B.

Bonnie Steinbock

THE INTENTIONAL TERMINATION OF LIFE

Bonnie Steinbock defends the policy statement of the American Medical Association on euthanasia against James Rachels's critique. She argues that the statement does not rest on the belief that there is a moral difference between active and passive euthanasia. Rather she contends that the statement rejects both active and passive euthanasia but permits "the cessation of the employment of extraordinary means," which she claims is not the same as passive euthanasia. She points out that doctors can cease to employ extraordinary means to respect the wishes of the patient or because continued treatment is painful and has little chance of success, without intending to let the patient die. She allows, however, that in some cases ceasing to employ extraordinary means does amount to intending to let the patient die, and also that in other cases killing may even be morally preferable to letting die.

Reprinted with permission from *Ethics in Science and Medicine*, pp. 59–64, Bonnie Steinbock, "The Intentional Termination of Life." Copyright 1979, Pergamon Press, Ltd.

ACCORDING TO JAMES RACHELS[1] a common mistake in medical ethics is the belief that there is a moral difference between active and passive euthanasia. This is a mistake, [he] argues, because the rationale underlying the distinction between active and passive euthanasia is the idea that there is a significant moral difference between intentionally killing and letting die. . . . Whether the belief that there is a significant moral difference (between intentionally killing and intentionally letting die) is mistaken is not my concern here. For it is far from clear that this distinction *is* the basis of the doctrine of the American Medical Association which Rachels attacks. And if the killing/letting die distinction is not the basis of the AMA doctrine, then arguments showing that the distinction has no moral force do not, in themselves, reveal in the doctrine's adherents either "confused thinking" or "a moral point of view unrelated to the interests of individuals". Indeed, as we examine the AMA doctrine, I think it will become clear that it appeals to and makes use of a number of overlapping distinctions, which may have moral significance in particular cases, such as the distinction between intending and foreseeing, or between ordinary and extraordinary care. Let us then turn to the statement, from the House of Delegates of the American Medical Association, which Rachels cites:

The intentional termination of the life of one human being by another—mercy-killing—is contrary to that for which the medical profession stands and is contrary to the policy of the American Medical Association.

The cessation of the employment of extraordinary means to prolong the life of the body when there is irrefutable evidence that biological death is imminent is the decision of the patient and/or his immediate family. The advice and judgment of the physician should be freely available to the patient and/or his immediate family.[2]

Rachels attacks this statement because he believes that it contains a moral distinction between active and passive euthanasia. . . .

I intend to show that the AMA statement does not imply support of the active/passive euthanasia distinction. In forbidding the intentional termination of life, the statement rejects both active and passive euthanasia. It does allow for ". . . the cessation of the employment of extraordinary means . . ." to prolong life. The mistake Rachels makes is in identifying the cessation of life-prolonging treatment with passive euthanasia, or intentionally letting die. If it were right to equate the two, then the AMA statement would be self-contradictory, for it would begin by condemning, and end by allowing, the intentional termination of life. But if the cessation of life-prolonging treatment is not always or necessarily passive euthanasia, then there is no confusion and no contradiction.

Why does Rachels think that the cessation of life-prolonging treatment is the intentional termination of life? He says:

The AMA policy statement isolates the crucial issue very well: the crucial issue is "the intentional termination of the life of one human being by another". But after identifying this issue, and forbidding "mercy-killing", the statement goes on to deny that the cessation of treatment is the intentional termination of a life. This is where the mistake comes in, for what is the cessation of treatment, in these circumstances, if it is not "the intentional termination of the life of one human being of another"? Of course it is exactly that, and if it were not, there would be no point to it.[3]

However, there *can* be a point (to the cessation of life-prolonging treatment) other than an endeavor to bring about the patient's death, and so the blanket identification of cessation of treatment with the intentional termination of a life is inaccurate. There are at least two situations in which the termination of life-prolonging treatment cannot be identified with the intentional termination of the life of one human being by another.

The first situation concerns the patient's right to refuse treatment. Rachels gives the example of a patient dying of an incurable disease, accompanied by unrelievable pain, who wants to end the treatment which cannot cure him but can only prolong his miserable existence. Why, they ask, may a doctor accede to the patient's request to stop treatment, but not provide a patient in a similar situation with a lethal dose? The answer lies in the patient's right to refuse treatment. In general, a competent adult has the right to refuse treatment, even where such treatment is necessary to prolong life. Indeed, the right to refuse treatment has been upheld even when the patient's reason for refusing treatment is generally agreed to be inadequate.[4] This right can be over-ridden (if, for example, the patient has dependent children) but, in general, no one may legally compel you to undergo treatment to which you have not consented. "Historically, surgical intrusion has always been considered a technical battery upon the person and one to be excused or justified by consent of the patient or justified by necessity created by the circumstances of the moment. . . . "[5]

At this point, it might be objected that if one has the right to refuse life-prolonging treatment, then consistency demands that one have the right to decide to end his life, and to obtain help in doing so. The idea is that the right to refuse treatment somehow implies a right to voluntary euthanasia, and we need to see why someone might think this. The right to refuse treatment has been considered by legal writers as an example of the right to privacy or, better, the right to bodily self-determination. You have the right to decide what happens to your own body, and the right to refuse treatment is an instance of that more general right. But if you have the right to determine what happens to your body, then should you not have the right to choose to end your life, and even a right to get help in doing so?

However, it is important to see that the right to refuse treatment is not the same as, nor does it entail, a right to voluntary euthanasia, even if both can be derived from the right to bodily self-determination. The right to refuse treatment is not itself a "right to die"; that one may choose to exercise this right even at the risk of death, or even *in order to die*, is irrelevant. The purpose of the right to refuse medical treatment is not to give persons a right to decide whether to live or die, but to protect them from the unwanted interferences of others. Perhaps we ought to interpret the right to bodily self-determination more broadly so as to include a right to die: but this would be a substantial extension of our present understanding of the right to bodily self-determination, and not a consequence of it. Should we recognize a right to voluntary euthanasia, we would have to agree that people have the right not merely to be left alone, but also the right to be killed. I leave to one side that substantive moral issue. My claim is simply that there can be a reason for terminating life-prolonging treatment other than "to bring about the patient's death".

The second case in which termination of treat-ment cannot be identified with intentional termination of life is where continued treatment has little chance of improving the patient's condition and brings greater discomfort than relief.

The question here is what treatment is appropriate to the particular case. A cancer specialist describes it in this way:

My general rule is to administer therapy as long as a patient responds well and has the potential for a reasonably good quality of life. But when all feasible therapies have been administered and a patient shows signs of rapid deterioration, the continuation of therapy can cause more discomfort than the cancer. From that time I recommend surgery, radiotherapy, or chemotherapy only as a means of relieving pain. But if a patient's condition should once again stabilize after the withdrawal of active therapy and if it should appear that he could still gain some good time, I would immediately reinstitute active therapy. The decision to cease anticancer treatment is never irrevocable, and often the desire to live will push a patient to try for another remission, or even a few more days of life.[6]

The decision here to cease anticancer treatment cannot be construed as a decision that the patient die, or as the intentional termination of life. It is a decision to provide the most appropriate treatment for that patient at that time. Rachels suggests that the point of the cessation of treatment is the intentional termination of life. But here the point of discontinuing treatment is not to bring about the patient's death but to avoid treatment that will cause more discomfort than the cancer and has little hope of benefiting the patient. Treatment that meets this description is often called "extraordinary".[7] The concept is flexible, and what might be considered "extraordinary" in one situation might be ordinary in another. The use of a respirator to sustain a patient through a severe bout with a respiratory disease would be considered ordinary; its use to sustain the life of a severely brain damaged person in an irreversible coma would be considered extraordinary.

Contrasted with extraordinary treatment is ordinary treatment, the care a doctor would normally be expected to provide. Failure to provide ordinary care constitutes neglect, and can even be construed as the intentional infliction of harm, where there is a legal obligation to provide care. The importance of the ordinary/extraordinary care distinction lies partly in its connection to the doctor's intention. The withholding of extraordinary care should be seen as a decision not to inflict painful treatment on a patient without reasonable hope of success. The withholding of ordinary care, by contrast, must be seen as neglect. Thus, one doctor says, "We have to draw a distinction between ordinary and extraordinary means. We never withdraw what's needed to make a baby comfortable, we would never withdraw the care a parent would provide. We never kill a baby. . . . But we may decide certain heroic intervention is not worthwhile."[8]

We should keep in mind the ordinary/extraordinary care distinction when considering an example given by Rachels to show the irrationality of the active/passive distinction with regard to infanticide. The example is this: a child is born with Down's syndrome and also has an intestinal obstruction which requires corrective surgery. If the surgery is not performed, the infant will starve to death, since it cannot take food orally. This may take days or even weeks, as dehydration and infection set in. Commenting on this situation, Rachels says:

I can understand why some people are opposed to all euthanasia, and insist that such infants must be allowed to live. I think I can also understand why other people favor destroying these babies quickly and painlessly. But why should anyone favor letting "dehydration and infection wither a tiny being over hours and days"? The doctrine that says that a baby may be allowed to dehydrate and wither, but may not be given an injection that would end its life without suffering, seems so patently cruel as to require no further refutation.[9]

Such a doctrine perhaps does not need further refutation; but this is not the AMA doctrine. For the AMA statement criticized by Rachels allows only for the cessation of extraordinary means to prolong life when death is imminent. Neither of these conditions is satisfied in this example. Death is not imminent in this situation, any more than it would be if a normal child had an attack of appendicitis. Neither the corrective surgery to remove the intestinal obstruction, nor the intravenous feeding required to keep the infant alive until such surgery is performed, can be regarded as extraordinary means, for neither is particularly expensive, nor does either place an

overwhelming burden on the patient or others. (The continued existence of the child might be thought to place an overwhelming burden on its parents, but that has nothing to do with the characterization of the means to prolong its life as extraordinary. If it had, then *feeding* a severely defective child who required a great deal of care could be regarded as extraordinary.) The chances of success if the operation is undertaken are quite good, though there is always a risk in operating on infants. Though the Down's syndrome will not be alleviated, the child will proceed to an otherwise normal infancy.

It cannot be argued that the treatment is withheld for the infant's sake, unless one is prepared to argue that all mentally retarded babies are better off dead. This is particularly implausible in the case of Down's syndrome babies who generally do not suffer and are capable of giving and receiving love, of learning and playing, to varying degrees.

In a film on this subject entitled, "Who Should Survive?", a doctor defended a decision not to operate, saying that since the parents did not consent to the operation, the doctors' hands were tied. As we have seen, surgical intrusion requires consent, and in the case of infants, consent would normally come from the parents. But, as their legal guardians, parents are required to provide medical care for their children, and failure to do so can constitute criminal neglect or even homicide. In general, courts have been understandably reluctant to recognize a parental right to terminate life-prolonging treatment.[10] Although prosecution is unlikely, physicians who comply with invalid instructions from the parents and permit the infant's death could be liable for aiding and abetting, failure to report child neglect, or even homicide. So it is not true that, in this situation, doctors are legally bound to do as the parents wish.

To sum up, I think that Rachels is right to regard the decision not to operate in the Down's syndrome example as the intentional termination of life. But there is no reason to believe that either the law or the AMA would regard it otherwise. Certainly the decision to withhold treatment is not justified by the AMA statement. That such infants have been allowed to die cannot be denied; but this, I think, is the result of doctors misunderstanding the law and the AMA position.

Withholding treatment in this case is the intentional termination of life because the infant is deliberately allowed to die; that is the point of not operating. But there are other cases in which that is not the point. If the point is to avoid inflicting painful treatment on a patient with little or no reasonable hope of success, this is not the intentional termination of life. The permissibility of such withholding of treatment, then, would have no implications for the permissibility of euthanasia, active or passive.

The decision whether or not to operate, or to institute vigorous treatment, is particularly agonizing in the case of children born with spina bifida, an opening in the base of the spine usually accompanied by hydrocephalus and mental retardation. If left unoperated, these children usually die of meningitis or kidney failure within the first few years of life. Even if they survive, all affected children face a lifetime of illness, operations and varying degrees of disability. The policy used to be to save as many as possible, but the trend now is toward selective treatment, based on the physician's estimate of the chances of success. If operating is not likely to improve significantly the child's condition, parents and doctors may agree not to operate. This is not the intentional termination of life, for again the purpose is not the termination of the child's life but the avoidance of painful and pointless treatment. Thus, the fact that withholding treatment is justified does not imply that killing the child would be equally justified.

Throughout the discussion, I have claimed that intentionally ceasing life-prolonging treatment is not the intentional termination of life unless the doctor has, as his or her purpose in stopping treatment, the patient's death.

It may be objected that I have incorrectly characterized the conditions for the intentional termination of life. Perhaps it is enough that the doctor intentionally ceases treatment, foreseeing that the patient will die; perhaps the reason for ceasing treatment is irrelevant to its characterization as the intentional termination of life. I find this suggestion implausible, but am willing to consider arguments for it. Rachels has provided no such arguments: indeed, he apparently shares my view about the intentional termination of life. For when he claims that

the cessation of life-prolonging treatment *is* the intentional termination of life, his reason for making the claim is that "if it were not, there would be no point to it". Rachels believes that the point of ceasing treatment, "in these cases", is to bring about the patient's death. If that were not the point, he suggests, why would the doctor cease treatment? I have shown, however, that there can be a point to ceasing treatment which is not the death of the patient. In showing this, I have refuted Rachels' reason for identifying the cessation of life-prolonging treatment with the intentional termination of life, and thus his argument against the AMA doctrine.

Here someone might say: Even if the withholding of treatment is not the intentional termination of life, does that make a difference, morally speaking? If life-prolonging treatment may be withheld, for the sake of the child, may not an easy death be provided, for the sake of the child, as well? The unoperated child with spina bifida may take months or even years to die. Distressed by the spectacle of children "lying around waiting to die", one doctor has written, "It is time that society and medicine stopped perpetuating the fiction that withholding treatment is ethically different from terminating a life. It is time that society began to discuss mechanisms by which we can alleviate the pain and suffering for those individuals whom we cannot help."[11]

I do not deny that there may be cases in which death is in the best interests of the patient. In such cases, a quick and painless death may be the best thing. However, I do not think that, once active or vigorous treatment is stopped, a quick death is always preferable to a lingering one. We must be cautious about attributing to defective children *our* distress at seeing them linger. Waiting for them to die may be tough on parents, doctors and nurses—it isn't necessarily tough on the child. The decision not to operate need not mean a decision to neglect, and it may be possible to make the remaining months of the child's life comfortable, pleasant and filled with love. If this alternative is possible, surely it is more decent and humane than killing the child. In such a situation, withholding treatment, foreseeing the child's death, is not ethically equivalent to killing the child, and we cannot move from the permissibility of the former to that of the latter. I am worried that there will be a tendency to do precisely that if active euthanasia is regarded as morally equivalent to the withholding of life-prolonging treatment.

CONCLUSION

The AMA statement does not make the distinction Rachels wishes to attack, i.e. that between active and passive euthanasia. Instead, the statement draws a distinction between the intentional termination of life, on the other hand, and the cessation of the employment of extraordinary means to prolong life, on the other. Nothing said by Rachels shows that this distinction is confused. It may be that doctors have misinterpreted the AMA statement, and that this had led, for example, to decisions to allow defective infants slowly to starve to death. I quite agree with Rachels that the decisions to which they allude were cruel and made on irrelevant grounds.

Certainly it is worth pointing out that allowing someone to die can be the intentional termination of life, and that it can be just as bad as, or worse than, killing someone. However, the withholding of life-prolonging treatment is not necessarily the intentional termination of life, so that if it is permissible to withhold life-prolonging treatment, it does not follow that, other things being equal, it is permissible to kill. Furthermore, most of the time, other things are not equal. In many of the cases in which it would be right to cease treatment, I do not think that it would also be right to kill.

Acknowledgements

I would like to express my thanks to Jonathan Bennett, Josiah Gould, Deborah Johnson, David Pratt, Bruce Russell, and David Zimmerman, all of whom provided helpful criticism and suggestions.

NOTES

1. James Rachels. Active and passive euthanasia. *New Engl. J. Med.*, **292**, 78–80, 1975.

2. Rachels, p. 78.

3. Rachels, p. 79–80.

4. For example, *In re Yetter*, 62 Pa. D. & C. 2d 619, C.P., Northampton County Ct., 1974.

5. David W. Meyers, Legal aspects of voluntary euthanasia, *Dilemmas of Euthanasia*, (Edited by John Behnke and Sissela Bok), p. 56. Anchor Books, New York, 1975.

6. Ernest H. Rosenbaum, Md., *Living with Cancer*, p. 27. Praeger, New York, 1975.

7. Cf. Tristam Engelhardt, Jr., Ethical issues in aiding the death of young children, *Beneficent Euthanasia* (Edited by Marvin Kohl), Prometheus Books, Buffalo, N.Y. 1975.

8. B. D. Colen, *Karen Ann Quinlan: Living and Dying in the Age of Eternal Life*, p. 115. Nash, 1976.

9. Rachels, p. 79.

10. Cf. Norman L. Cantor, Law and the termination of an incompetent patient's life-preserving care. *Dilemmas of Euthanasia. op. cit.*, pp. 69–105.

11. John Freeman, Is there a right to die—quickly?, *J. Pediat.* **80**. p. 905.

THE HUMAN LIFE BILL

The Human Life Bill, S. 158, purports to fill the need for a branch of the federal government of the United States to answer both the scientific question of whether unborn children are human beings and the value question of whether the law should accord equal worth to every human being. Neither of these questions was answered by the Supreme Court in *Roe v. Wade*. In answer to the scientific question, S. 158 affirms that human life begins at conception. Opponents of this view are said to be confusing the scientific question with the value question. In answer to the value question, S. 158 affirms that the values embodied in the U.S. Constitution require a sanctity-of-life ethic rather than a quality-of-life ethic. This means that every human life has intrinsic worth and equal value under the U.S. Constitution.

THE SUBCOMMITTEE ON SEPARATION of Powers of the Senate Committee on the Judiciary, to which was referred the bill, S. 158, to recognize that the life of each human being begins at conception and to enforce the fourteenth amendment by extending its protection to the life of every human being, having considered the same, reports favorably thereon with an amendment in the nature of a substitute and recommends that the bill as amended do pass.

I. AMENDMENT IN THE NATURE OF A SUBSTITUTE

Strike out the enacting clause and all after the enacting clause and substitute in lieu thereof the following:

Be it enacted by the Senate and House of Representatives of the United States of America in Congress assembled, *That title 42 of the United States Code shall be amended at the end thereof by adding the following new chapter:*

CHAPTER 101

SECTION 1. (a) The Congress finds that the life of each human being begins at conception.

(b) The Congress further finds that the fourteenth amendment to the Constitution of the United States protects all human beings.

II. PURPOSE OF THE PROPOSED ACT

The purpose of S. 158 is first, to recognize the biological fact that the life of each human being begins at conception; second, to affirm that every human life has intrinsic worth and equal value regardless of its stage or condition; and third, to enforce the fourteenth amendment by ensuring that its protection of life extends to all human beings.

III. NEED FOR THIS LEGISLATION

To protect the lives of human beings is the highest duty of government. Our nation's laws are founded on respect for the life of each and every human being. The Declaration of Independence holds that the right to life is a self-evident, inalienable right of every human being. Embodied in the statement that "all men are created equal" is the idea of the intrinsic worth and equal value of every human life. The author of the Declaration, Thomas Jefferson, explained in later years that "[t]he care of human life and happiness, and not their destruction, is the first and only legitimate object of good government."

Today there is a strong concern among many citizens that government is not fulfilling its duty to protect the lives of all human beings. Since 1973 abortion has been available on demand nationwide, resulting in more than one and one-half million abortions per year. Yet this abrupt and fundamental shift in policy occurred without any prior inquiry by any branch of the federal government to determine whether the unborn children being aborted are living human beings. Nor has any branch of the federal government forthrightly faced the question whether our law should continue to affirm the sanctity of human life—the intrinsic worth and equal value of all human life—or whether our law should now reject the sanctity of life in favor of some competing ethic. Only by determining whether unborn children are human beings, and deciding whether our law should and does accord intrinsic worth and equal value to their lives, can our government rationally address the issue of abortion.

The Subcommittee has taken pains to separate its consideration of the two questions. In this report we shall often refer to the "scientific question" and the "value question" as a convenient shorthand. We have analyzed the testimony of various witnesses and sources of public record as they relate to each question separately. And we report separately our conclusions on each question.

We emphasize that both questions must be answered by some branch of government before the abortion issue can be fully and rationally resolved. The need for Congress to investigate both questions stems partly from the self-professed institutional limitations of our federal judiciary. The Supreme Court, in its 1973 abortion decision, declared itself unable to resolve when the life of a human being begins: "When those trained in the respective disciplines of medicine, philosophy, and theology are unable to arrive at any consensus, the judiciary, at this point in the development of man's knowledge, is not in a position to speculate as to the answer." *Roe* v. *Wade*, (1973). The Court went on to explain that a "wide divergence of thinking" exists on the "sensitive and difficult" question of when a human life begins; hence, the judiciary is not competent to resolve the question.

As a result of its self-professed inability to decide when the life of a human being begins, the Supreme Court rendered its 1973 abortion decision without considering whether unborn children are living human beings. And because the Court did not consider whether unborn children are living human beings, it was able to avoid an explicit decision on whether our law accords intrinsic worth and equal value to the life of every human being regardless of stage or condition. The Court thus declined to address either of the crucial questions relevant to protecting unborn children under the law: the Court addressed neither the scientific question nor the value question. The Court's entire 1973 opinion concerning the power of states to protect unborn children—including the Court's ruling on personhood of the unborn—must be read in light of this failure to resolve the two fundamental questions concerning the existence and value of unborn human life.

That a judicial decision addressing neither of these fundamental questions has led to a national policy of abortion on demand throughout the term of pregnancy is a great anomaly in our constitutional system. It is important to examine the judicial reasoning that led to this result. The Court held that "the right of personal privacy includes the abortion decision," but added that "this right is not unqualified and must be considered against important state interests in regulation." . . . Because it did not resolve whether unborn children are human beings, the Court could not make an informed decision on whether abortions implicate the interest and duty of the states to protect living human beings. Still, without purporting to know whether unborn children are living human beings, the Court stated by fiat that they are not protected as persons under the fourteenth amendment.

Then the Court created judge-made rules governing abortions. During the first three months of an unborn child's life, the states may do nothing to regulate or prohibit the aborting of the child. In the next three months of the unborn child's life, the state may regulate only the manner in which the child is aborted; but abortion remains available on demand. In the final three months before the child is born, the states may prohibit abortions except when necessary to preserve the "life or health of the mother." . . .

The apparently restrictive standard for the third trimester has in fact proved no different from the standard of abortion on demand expressly allowed during the first six months of the unborn child's life. The exception for maternal health has been so broad in practice as to swallow the rule. The Supreme

Court has defined "health" in this context to include "all factors—physical, emotional, psychological, familial, and the woman's age—relevant to the well-being of the patient." *Doe* v. *Bolton*, (1973). Since there is nothing to stop an abortionist from certifying that a third-trimester abortion is beneficial to the health of the mother—in this broad sense—the Supreme Court's decision has in fact made abortion available on demand throughout the pre-natal life of the child, from conception to birth. . . .

A congressional determination that unborn children are human beings and that their lives have intrinsic worth and equal value will encourage the Court to reexamine the results and the reasoning of *Roe* v. *Wade*. In *Roe* the Court expressed a desire to decide the abortion issue "consistent with the relative weights of the respective interests involved. . . . " The Court's view of the relative weight of the interests of the unborn child was necessarily influenced by the Court's professed inability to determine whether the unborn child was a living human being. It is difficult to believe that the Court would again balance the respective interests in such a way as to allow abortion on demand, if the Court were to recognize that one interest involved was the life of a human being.

IV. THE SCIENTIFIC QUESTION: WHEN DOES A HUMAN LIFE BEGIN

During the course of eight days of hearings, fifty-seven witnesses testified on S. 158 before the Subcommittee. Of these witnesses, twenty-two, including world-renowned geneticists, biologists, and practicing physicians, addressed the medical and biological questions raised by the bill. Eleven testified in support of the bill and eleven in opposition.

The testimony of these witnesses and the voluminous submissions received by the Subcommittee demonstrate that contemporary scientific evidence points to a clear conclusion: the life of a human being begins at conception, the time when the process of fertilization is complete. Until the early nineteenth century science had not advanced sufficiently to be able to know that conception is the beginning of a human life; but today the facts are beyond dispute. . . .

It may at first seem difficult to reconcile the existence of such a broad consensus with the testimony of some witnesses opposing S. 158 before this subcommittee who emphatically denied that it is possible to determine when a human life begins. If the facts are so clear, it is crucial to understand how, for example, one noted professor of genetics from Yale University School of Medicine could say that he knows of no scientific evidence that shows when actual human life exists.

Such statements appear on the surface to present a direct contradiction to the biological evidence discussed above. The explanation of this apparent contradiction lies in the existence of the two distinct questions identified above, the scientific question and the value question. We must consider not only whether unborn children are human beings but also whether to accord their lives intrinsic worth and value equal to those of other human beings. The two questions are separate and distinct. It is a scientific question whether an unborn child is a human being, in the sense of a living member of the human species. It is a value question whether the life of an unborn child has intrinsic worth and equal value with other human beings.

Those witnesses who testified that science cannot say whether unborn children are human beings were speaking in every instance to the value question rather than the scientific question. No witness raised any evidence to refute the biological fact that from the moment of human conception there exists a distinct individual being who is alive and is of the human species. No witness challenged the scientific consensus that unborn children are "human beings," insofar as the term is used to mean living beings of the human species. . . .

V. THE VALUE QUESTION: SHOULD WE VALUE ALL HUMAN LIVES EQUALLY?

The answer to the scientific question casts the value question in clear relief. Unborn children are human beings. But should our nation value all human lives

179

equally? Scientific evidence is not relevant to this question. The answer is a matter of ethical judgement.

Deeply engrained in American society and American constitutional history is the ethic of the sanctity of innocent human life. The sanctity-of-life ethic recognizes each human life as having intrinsic worth simply by virtue of its being human. If, as a society, we reject this ethic, we must inevitably adopt some other standard for deciding which human lives are of value and are worthy of protection. Because the standards some use to make such decisions turn on various qualities by which they define which lives are worthy of protection, the alternative to the sancity-of-life ethic is often termed the "quality-of-life ethic." A sharp division exists today between those who affirm the sanctity-of-life ethic and those who reject it in favor of the quality-of-life ethic. The Supreme Court has never purported to decide which ethic our Constitution mandates for valuing the lives of human beings before birth. Nevertheless, deciding which ethic should apply is fundamental to resolving the abortion issue under the Constitution. . . .

Advocates of a quality-of-life ethic vary in the qualities they choose as a standard for which human lives to value. The common element of every "quality of life" view, however, is a denial of the intrinsic worth of all human life, along with an attempt to define what qualities must be present in a human being before its life is to be valued.

Our constitutional history leaves no doubt which ethic is written into our fundamental law. The Declaration of Independence expressly affirms the sanctity of human life:

We hold these truths to be self-evident, that all men are created equal, that they are endowed by their Creator with certain unalienable rights, that among these are life, liberty, and the pursuit of happiness.

The proponents of the fourteenth amendment argued for the amendment on the basis of these principles. Congressman John A. Bingham of Ohio, who drafted the first section of the fourteenth amendment, stated after the adoption of the Joint Resolution of Congress proposing this amendment:

Before that great law [of the United States,] the only question to be asked of the creature claiming its protection is this: Is he a man? Every man is entitled to the protection of American law, because its divine spirit of equality declares that all men are created equal.

It is instructive to note that the highest court of West Germany accorded constitutional protection to unborn children precisely because the court affirmed the principle of the sanctity of human life. The "Basic Law," or the Bonn constitution, of West Germany guarantees the "right to life." The court explained this guarantee as a reaction against the Nazi regime's idea of "Destruction of Life Unworthy to Live" and as an "affirmation of the fundamental value of human life. . . . "

Because it affirms the Constitution, the Subcommittee cannot accept any legal rule that would allow judges, scientists, or medical professors to decide that some human lives are not worth living. We must instead affirm the intrinsic worth of *all* human life. We find that the fourteeenth amendment embodies the sanctity of human life and that today the government must affirm this ethic by recognizing the "personhood" of all human beings. Earlier we found, based upon scientific examination, that the life of each human being begins at conception. Now, basing our decision not upon science but upon the values embodied in our Constitution, we affirm the sanctity of all human life. Science can tell us whether a being is alive and a member of the human species. It cannot tell us whether to accord value to that being. The government of any society that accords intrinsic worth to all human life must make *both* a factual determination recognizing the existence of all human beings *and* a value decision affirming the worth of human life.

180

THE KAREN QUINLAN OPINION

After being examined by a number of physicians, Karen Quinlan was found to be in a "chronic, persistent vegetative state," although not "brain dead" by the ordinary medical standard. It was judged that no form of treatment could restore her to cognitive or sapient life. At the time, she was being sustained by a respirator. Her father, Joseph Quinlan, asked to be appointed her legal guardian with the expressed purpose of discontinuing the use of the respirator. A lower court refused this request. The Supreme Court of New Jersey, however, granted the request on the condition that (1) attending physicians of Joseph Quinlan's choice conclude that there is no reasonable possibility of Karen's ever being restored to cognitive, sapient life and that the use of the respirator should be discontinued; and on the further condition that (2) the "Ethics Committee" of the institution where Karen is hospitalized concur in the physicians' judgment.

THE FACTUAL BASE

ON THE NIGHT OF April 15, 1975, for reasons still unclear, Karen Quinlan ceased breathing for at least two 15 minute periods. She received some ineffectual mouth-to-mouth resuscitation from friends. She was taken by ambulance to Newton Memorial Hospital. There she had a temperature of 100 degrees, her pupils were unreactive and she was unresponsive even to deep pain. The history at the time of her admission to that hospital was essentially incomplete and uninformative. . . .

Dr. Morse and other expert physicians who examined her characterized Karen as being in a "chronic persistent vegetative state." Dr. Fred Plum, one of such expert witnesses, defined this as a "subject who remains with the capacity to maintain the vegetative parts of neurological function but who no longer has any cognitive function."

Dr. Morse, as well as the several other medical and neurological experts who testified in this case, believed with certainty that Karen Quinlan is not "brain dead." They identified the Ad Hoc Committee of Harvard Medical School report (*infra*) as the ordinary medical standard for determining brain death, and all of them were satisfied that Karen met

none of the criteria specified in that report and was therefore not "brain dead" within its contemplation.

In this respect it was indicated by Dr. Plum that the brain works in essentially two ways, the vegetative and the sapient. He testified

We have an internal vegetative regulation which controls body temperature which controls breathing, which controls to a considerable degree blood pressure, which controls to some degree heart rate, which controls chewing, swallowing and which controls sleeping and waking. We have a more highly developed brain which is uniquely human which controls our relation to the outside world, our capacity to talk, to see, to feel, to sing, to think. Brain death necessarily must mean the death of both of these functions of the brain, vegetative and the sapient. Therefore, the presence of any function which is regulated or governed or controlled by the deeper parts of the brain which in laymen's terms might be considered purely vegetative would mean that the brain is not biologically dead.

Because Karen's neurological condition affects her respiratory ability (the respiratory system being a brain stem function) she requires a respirator to assist her breathing. From the time of her admission to Saint Clare's Hospital Karen has been assisted by an MA-1 respirator, a sophisticated machine which de-

From "In the Matter of Karen Quinlan, An Alleged Incompetent," Supreme Court of New Jersey 355A 2d 647.

livers a given volume of air at a certain rate and periodically provides a "sigh" volume, a relatively large measured volume of air designed to purge the lungs of excretions. Attempts to "wean" her from the respirator were unsuccessful and have been abandoned.

The experts believe that Karen cannot now survive without the assistance of the respirator; that exactly how long she would live without it is unknown; that the strong likelihood is that death would follow soon after its removal, and that removal would also risk further brain damage and would curtail the assistance the respirator presently provides in warding off infection.

It seemed to be the consensus not only of the treating physicians but also of the several qualified experts who testified in the case, that removal from the respirator would not conform to medical practices, standards and traditions.

The further medical consensus was that Karen in addition to being comatose is in a chronic and persistent "vegetative" state, having no awareness of anything or anyone around her and existing at a primitive reflex level. Although she does have some brain stem function (ineffective for respiration) and has other reactions one normally associates with being alive, such as moving, reacting to light, sound and noxious stimuli, blinking her eyes, and the like, the quality of her feeling impulses is unknown. She grimaces, makes stereotyped cries and sounds and has chewing motions. Her blood pressure is normal.

Karen remains in the intensive care unit at Saint Clare's Hospital, receiving 24-hour care by a team of four nurses characterized, as was the medical attention, as "excellent." She is nourished by feeding by way of a nasal-gastro tube and is routinely examined for infection, which under these circumstances is a serious life threat. The result is that her condition is considered remarkable under the unhappy circumstances involved.

Karen is described as emaciated, having suffered a weight loss of at least 40 pounds, and undergoing a continuing deteriorative process. Her posture is described as fetal-like and grotesque; there is extreme flexion-rigidity of the arms, legs and related muscles and her joints are severely rigid and deformed.

From all of this evidence, and including the whole testimonial record, several basic findings in the physical area are mandated. Severe brain and associated damage, albeit of uncertain etiology, has left Karen in a chronic and persistent vegetative state. No form of treatment which can cure or improve that condition is known or available. As nearly as may be determined, considering the guarded area of remote uncertainties characteristic of most medical science predictions, she can *never* be restored to cognitive or sapient life. Even with regard to the vegetative level and improvement therein (if such it may be called) the prognosis is extremely poor and the extent unknown if it should in fact occur.

She is debilitated and moribund and although fairly stable at the time of argument before us (no new information having been filed in the meanwhile in expansion of the record), no physician risked the opinion that she could live more than a year and indeed she may die much earlier. Excellent medical and nursing care so far has been able to ward off the constant threat of infection, to which she is peculiarly susceptible because of the respirator, the tracheal tube and other incidents of care in her vulnerable condition. Her life accordingly is sustained by the respirator and tubal feeding, and removal from the respirator would cause her death soon, although the time cannot be stated with more precision.

The determination of the fact and time of death in past years of medical science was keyed to the action of the heart and blood circulation, in turn dependent upon pulmonary activity, and hence cessation of these functions spelled out the reality of death.

Developments in medical technology have obfuscated the use of the traditional definition of death. Efforts have been made to define irreversible coma as a new criterion for death, such as by the 1968 report of the Ad Hoc Committee of the Harvard Medical School (the Committee comprising ten physicians, an historian, a lawyer and a theologian), which asserted that:

From ancient times down to the recent past it was clear that, when the respiration and heart stopped, the brain would die in a few minutes; so the obvious criterion of no heart beat as synonymous with death was sufficiently accurate. In those times the heart was considered to be the central organ of the body; it is not surprising that its failure marked the onset of death. This is no longer valid when modern resuscitative and supportive measures are used. These improved activities can now restore "life" as judged by the ancient standards of persistent respiration and continuing heart beat. This can be the case even when there is not the remotest possibility of an individual recovering consciousness following massive brain damage.

The Ad Hoc standards, carefully delineated, included absence of response to pain or other stimuli, pupilary reflexes, corneal, pharyngeal and other reflexes, blood pressure, spontaneous respiration, as well as "flat" or isoelectric electroencephalograms and the like, with all tests repeated "at least 24 hours later with no change." In such circumstances, where all of such criteria have been met as showing "brain death," the Committee recommends with regard to the respirator:

The patient's condition can be determined only by a physician. When the patient is hopelessly damaged as defined above, the family and all colleagues who have participated in major decisions concerning the patient, and all nurses involved, should be so informed. Death is to be declared and then the respirator turned off. The decision to do this and the responsibility for it are to be taken by the physician-in-charge, in consultation with one or more physicians who have been directly involved in the case. It is unsound and undesirable to force the family to make the decision. . . . (emphasis in original).

But, as indicated, it was the consensus of medical testimony in the instant case that Karen, for all her disability, met none of these criteria, nor indeed any comparable criteria extant in the medical world and representing, as does the Ad Hoc Committee report, according to the testimony in this case, prevailing and accepted medical standards.

We have adverted to the "brain death" concept and Karen's disassociation with any of its criteria, to emphasize the basis of the medical decision made by Dr. Morse. When plaintiff and his family, finally reconciled to the certainty of Karen's impending death, requested the withdrawal of life support mechanisms, he demurred. His refusal was based upon his conception of medical standards, practice and ethics described in the medical testimony, such as in the evidence given by another neurologist, Dr. Sidney Diamond, a witness for the State. Dr. Diamond asserted that no physician would have failed to provide respirator support at the outset, and none

would interrupt its life-saving course thereafter, except in the case of cerebral death. In the latter case, he thought the respirator would in effect be disconnected from one already dead, entitling the physician under medical standards and, he thought, legal concepts, to terminate the supportive measures. We note Dr. Diamond's distinction of major surgical or transfusion procedures in a terminal case not involving cerebral death, such as here:

The subject has lost human qualities. It would be incredible, and I think unlikely, that any physician would respond to a sudden hemorrhage, massive hemorrhage, or a loss of all her defensive blood cells, by giving her large quantities of blood. I think that *** *major surgical procedures would be out of the question even if they were known to be essential for continued physical existence.*

This distinction is adverted to also in the testimony of Dr. Julius Korein, a neurologist called by plaintiff. Dr. Korein described a medical practice concept of "judicious neglect" under which the physician will say:

Don't treat this patient anymore, *** *it does not serve either the patient, the family, or society in any meaningful way to continue treatment with this patient.*

Dr. Korein also told of the unwritten and unspoken standard of medical practice implied in the foreboding initials DNR (do not resuscitate), as applied to the extraordinary terminal case:

Cancer, metastatic cancer, involving the lungs, the liver, the brain, multiple involvements, the physician may or may not write: Do not resuscitate. *** *[I]t could be said to the nurse: if this man stops breathing don't resuscitate him.* *** *No physician that I know personally is going to try and resuscitate a man riddled with cancer and in agony and he stops breathing. They are not going to put him on a respirator.* *** *I think that would be the height of misuse of technology.*

While the thread of logic in such distinctions may be elusive to the non-medical lay mind, in relation to the supposed imperative to sustain life at all costs, they nevertheless relate to medical decisions, such as the decision of Dr. Morse in the present case. We agree with the trial court that that decision was in accord with Dr. Morse's conception of medical standards and practice.

We turn to that branch of the factual case pertaining to the application for guardianship, as distinguished from the nature of the authorization sought by the applicant. The character and general suitability of Joseph Quinlan as guardian for his daughter, in ordinary circumstances, could not be doubted. The record bespeaks the high degree of familial love which pervaded the home of Joseph Quinlan and reached out fully to embrace Karen, although she was living elsewhere at the time of her collapse. The proofs showed him to be deeply religious, imbued with a morality so sensitive that months of tortured indecision preceded his belated conclusion (despite earlier moral judgments reached by the other family members, but unexpressed to him in order not to influence him) to seek the termination of life-supportive measures sustaining Karen. A communicant of the Roman Catholic Church, as were other family members, he first sought solace in private prayer looking with confidence, as he says, to the Creator, first for the recovery of Karen and then, if that were not possible, for guidance with respect to the awesome decision confronting him.

To confirm the moral rightness of the decision he was about to make he consulted with his parish priest and later with the Catholic chaplain of Saint Clare's Hospital. He would not, he testified, have sought termination if that act were to be morally wrong or in conflict with the tenets of the religion he so profoundly respects. He was disabused of doubt, however, when the position of the Roman Catholic Church was made known to him as it reflected in the record in this case. While it is not usual for matters of religious dogma or concepts to enter a civil litigation (except as they may bear upon constitutional rights, or sometimes, familial matters) they were rightly admitted in evidence here. The judge was bound to measure the character and motivations in all respects of Joseph Quinlan as prospective guardian; and insofar as these religious matters bore upon them, they were properly scrutinized and considered by the court.

Thus germane, we note the position of that Church as illuminated by the record before us. We have no reason to believe that it would be at all discordant with the whole of Judeo-Christian tradition, considering its central respect and reverence for the sanctity of human life. It was in this sense of relevance that we admitted as *amicus curiae* the New Jersey Catholic Conference, essentially the spokesman for the various Catholic bishops of New Jersey, organized to give witness to spiritual values in public affairs in the statewide community. The position statement of Bishop Lawrence B. Casey, reproduced in the *amicus* brief, projects these views:

(a) The verification of the fact of death in a particular case cannot be deduced from any religious or moral principle and, under this aspect, does not fall within the competence of the church;—that dependence must be had upon traditional and medical standards, and by these standards Karen Ann Quinlan is assumed to be alive.

(b) The request of plaintiff for authority to terminate a medical procedure characterized as "an extraordinary means of treatment" would not involve euthanasia. This upon the reasoning expressed by Pope Pius XII in his *allocutio* (address) to anesthesiologists on November 24, 1957, when he dealt with the question:

Does the anesthesiologist have the right, or is he bound, in all cases of deep unconsciousness, even in those that are completely hopeless in the opinion of the competent doctor, to use modern artificial respiration apparatus, even against the will of the family?

His answer made the following points:

1. In ordinary cases the doctor has the right to act in this manner, but is not bound to do so unless this is the only way of fulfilling another certain moral duty.
2. The doctor, however, has no right independent of the patient. He can act only if the patient explicitly or implicitly, directly or indirectly, gives him the permission.
3. The treatment as described in the question constitutes extraordinary means of preserving life and so there is no obligation to use them nor to give the doctor permission to use them.
4. The rights and the duties of the family depend on the presumed will of the unconscious patient if he or she is of legal age, and the family, too, is bound to use only ordinary means.
5. This case is not to be considered euthanasia in any way; that would never be licit. The interruption of attempts at resuscitation, even when it causes the arrest of circulation, is not more than

an indirect cause of the cessation of life, and we must apply in this case the principle of double effect.

So it was that the Bishop Casey statement validated the decision of Joseph Quinlan:

Competent medical testimony has established that Karen Ann Quinlan has no reasonable hope of recovery from her comatose state by the use of any available medical procedures. The continuance of mechanical (cardiorespiratory) supportive measures to sustain continuance of her body functions and her life constitute extraordinary means of treatment. Therefore, the decision of Joseph • • • Quinlan to request the discontinuance of this treatment is, according to the teachings of the Catholic Church, a morally correct decision. (Emphasis in original.). . .

It is from this factual base that the Court confronts and responds to three basic issues:

1. Was the trial court correct in denying the specific relief requested by plaintiff, *i.e.*, authorization for termination of the life-supporting apparatus, on the case presented to him? Our determination on that question is in the affirmative.
2. Was the court correct in withholding letters of guardianship from the plaintiff and appointing in his stead a stranger? On that issue our determination is in the negative.
3. Should this Court, in the light of the foregoing conclusions, grant declaratory relief to the plaintiff? On that question our Court's determination is in the affirmative.

This brings us to a consideration of the constitutional and legal issues underlying the foregoing determinations.

CONSTITUTIONAL AND LEGAL ISSUES

The claimed interests of the State in this case are essentially the preservation and sanctity of human life and defense to the right of the physician to administer medical treatment according to his best judgment. In this case the doctors say that removing Karen from the respirator will conflict with their professional judgment. The plaintiff answers that Karen's present treatment serves only a maintenance function; that the respirator cannot cure or improve her condition but at best can only prolong her inevitable slow deterioration and death; and that the interests of the patient, as seen by her surrogate, the guardian, must be evaluated by the court as predominant, even in the face of an option *contra* by the present attending physicians. Plaintiff's distinction is significant. The nature of Karen's care and the realistic chances of her recovery are quite unlike those of the patients discussed in many of the cases where treatments were ordered. In many of those cases the medical procedure required (usually a transfusion) constituted a minimal bodily invasion and the chances of recovery and return to functioning life were very good. We think that the State's interest *contra* weakens and the individual's right to privacy grows as the degree of bodily invasion increases and the prognosis dims. Ultimately there comes a point at which the individual's rights overcome the State interest. It is for that reason that we believe Karen's choice, if she were competent to make it, would be vindicated by the law. Her prognosis is extremely poor,—she will never resume cognitive life. And the bodily invasion is very great,—she requires 24-hour intensive nursing care, antibiotics, and the assistance of a respirator, a catheter and feeding tube.

Our affirmance of Karen's independent right of choice, however, would ordinarily be based upon her competency to assert it. The sad truth, however, is that she is grossly incompetent and we cannot discern her supposed choice based on the testimony of her previous conversations with friends, where such testimony is without sufficient probative weight. Nevertheless we have concluded that Karen's right of privacy may be asserted on her behalf by her guardian under the peculiar circumstances here present.

If a putative decision by Karen to permit this noncognitive, vegetative existence to terminate by natural forces is regarded as a valuable incident of her right of privacy, as we believe it to be, then it should not be discarded solely on the basis that her condition prevents her conscious exercise of the choice. The only practical way to prevent destruction of the right is to permit the guardian and family of Karen to render their best judgment, subject to the qualifications hereinafter stated, as to whether she would exercise it in these circumstances. If their conclusion is in the affirmative this decision should be accepted by a society the overwhelming majority of whose members would, we think, in similar circumstances, exercise such a choice in the same way for themselves or for those closest to them. It is for this reason that we determine that Karen's right of privacy may be asserted in her behalf, in this respect, by her guardian and family under the particular circumstances presented by this record. . . .

Having concluded that there is a right of privacy that might permit termination of treatment in the circumstances of this case, we turn to consider the relationship of the exercise of that right to the criminal law. We are aware that such termination of treatment would accelerate Karen's death. The County Prosecutor and the Attorney General stoutly maintain that there would be criminal liability for such acceleration. Under the statutes of this State, the unlawful killing of another human being is criminal homicide. We conclude that there would be no criminal homicide in the circumstances of this case. We believe, first, that the ensuing death would not be homicide but rather expiration from existing natural causes. Secondly, even if it were to be regarded as homicide, it would not be unlawful. . . .

DECLARATORY RELIEF

We thus arrive at the formulation of the declaratory relief which we have concluded is appropriate to this case. Some time has passed since Karen's physical and mental condition was described to the Court. At that time her continuing deterioration was plainly projected. Since the record has not been expanded we assume that she is now even more fragile and nearer to death than she was then. Since her present treating physicians may give reconsideration to her present posture in the light of this opinion, and since we are transferring to the plaintiff as guardian the choice of the attending physician and therefor other physicians may be in charge of the case who may take a different view from that of the present attending physicians, we herewith declare the fol-

lowing affirmative relief on behalf of the plaintiff. Upon the concurrence of the guardian and family of Karen, should the responsible attending physicians conclude that there is no reasonable possibility of Karen's ever emerging from her present comatose condition to a cognitive, sapient state and that the life-support apparatus now being administered to Karen should be discontinued, they shall consult with the hospital "Ethics Committee" or like body of the institution in which Karen is then hospitalized. If that consultative body agrees that there is no reasonable possibility of Karen's ever emerging from her present comatose condition to a cognitive, sapient state, the present life-support system may be withdrawn and said action shall be without any civil or criminal liability therefor on the part of any participant, whether guardian, physician, hospital or others. We herewith specifically so hold.

CONCLUSION

We therefore remand this record to the trial court to implement (without further testimonial hearing) the following decisions:

1. To discharge, with the thanks of the Court for his service, the present guardian of the person of Karen Quinlan, Thomas R. Curtin, Esquire, a member of the Bar and an officer of the court.
2. To appoint Joseph Quinlan as guardian of the person of Karen Quinlan with full power to make decisions with regard to the identity of her treating physicians.

We repeat for the sake of emphasis and clarity that upon the concurrence of the guardian and family of Karen, should the responsible attending physicians conclude that there is no reasonable possibility of Karen's ever emerging from her present comatose condition to a cognitive, sapient state and that the life-support apparatus now being administered to Karen should be discontinued, they shall consult with the hospital "Ethics Committee" or like body of the institution in which Karen is then hospitalized. If that consultative body agrees that there is no reasonable possibility of Karen's ever emerging from her present comatose condition to a cognitive, sapient state, the present life-support system may be withdrawn and said action shall be without any civil or criminal liability therefor, on the part of any participant, whether guardian, physician, hospital or others.

By the above ruling we do not intend to be

understood as implying that a proceeding for judicial declaratory relief is necessarily required for the implementation of comparable decisions in the field of medical practice.

Modified and remanded.

SUGGESTIONS FOR FURTHER READING

Alternative Views

Callahan, Daniel. *Abortion: Law, Choice and Morality.* New York: Macmillan, 1970.

Grisez, Germain. *Abortion.* New York: Corpus, 1970.

Grisez, Germain, and Boyle, Joseph. *Life and Death with Liberty and Justice.* Notre Dame: University of Notre Dame Press, 1979.

Kluge, Eike-Henner. *The Practice of Death.* New Haven: Yale University Press, 1975.

Nicholson, Susan. *Abortion and The Roman Catholic Church.* Knoxville: Religious Ethics, 1978.

Ramsey, Paul. *The Patient as Person.* New Haven: Yale University Press, 1970.

Summer, L. W. *Abortion and Moral Theory.* Princeton: Princeton University Press, 1981.

Anthologies

Cohen, Marshall, and others. *The Rights and Wrongs of Abortion.* Princeton: Princeton University Press, 1974.

Feinberg, Joel. *The Problem of Abortion.* Belmont: Wadsworth Publishing Co., 1973.

Kohl, Marvin. *Beneficent Euthanasia.* Buffalo: Prometheus, 1975.

Ladd, John. *Ethical Issues Relating to Life and Death.* New York: Oxford University Press, 1979.

Munson, Ronald. *Interventions and Reflections.* Belmont: Wadsworth Publishing Co., 1979.

Noonan, John. *The Morality of Abortion.* Cambridge: Harvard University Press, 1970.

Basic Concepts

Devine, Philip. *The Ethics of Homicide.* Ithaca: Cornell University Press, 1978.

Glover, Jonathan. *Causing Death and Saving Lives.* New York: Penguin Books, 1977.

Steinbock, Bonnie, editor. *Killing and Letting Die.* Englewood Cliffs: Prentice-Hall, 1980.

Practical Applications

Denes, Magda. *In Necessity and Sorrow: Life and Death in an Abortion Hospital.* New York: Penguin Books, 1977.

Manier, Edward, and others, eds. *Abortion: New Directions for Policy Studies.* Notre Dame: University of Notre Dame Press, 1977.

Law Reform Commission of Canada. *Euthanasia, Aiding Suicide and Cessation of Treatment.* Working Paper 28, 1982.

BASIC CONCEPTS

Solutions to the problem of discrimination and prejudice tend to be either backward-looking or forward-looking. Backward-looking solutions seek to rectify and compensate for past injustices caused by discrimination or prejudice. Forward-looking solutions seek to realize an ideal of a society free from discrimination and prejudice. In order to justify a backward-looking solution to the problem of discrimination and prejudice, it is necessary to determine (1) who has committed or benefited from a wrongful act of discrimination or prejudice and (2) who deserves compensation for that act. In order to justify a forward-looking solution to the problem, it is necessary to determine (1) what a society free from discrimination and prejudice would be like and (2) how we might best attempt to realize such a society. Solutions of both types have been proposed to deal with racism and sexism, the dominant forms of discrimination and prejudice in our times.

In this section, Richard Wasserstrom sketches three possible forward-looking ideals of a society free from racism or sexism (see pp. 194–199). First is the assimilationist ideal. According to this ideal, race or sex would have no more significance than eye color does in existing societies. Next is the pluralist ideal, according to which race or sex would have no more significance than religion does in existing societies with freedom of religion. Last is the diversity ideal with respect to sex, according to which sex would have roughly the same role it has within existing societies.

In addition to describing these three forward-looking solutions to the problem of discrimination and prejudice, Wasserstrom also distinguishes four questions that generally arise in discussions of this problem with respect to race and sex. First is the question of social realities: What is the correct description of the existing social arrangements with respect to race and sex? Second is the the question of causation: What is the explanation for those social arrangments and by what mechanisms are they perpetuated or changed? Third is the question of ideals: What would a society free from racism and sexism be like? Fourth is the question of instrumentalities: How might a society most effectively and fairly move from the existing state of affairs to a closer approximation of the ideal? Wasserstrom contends that confusions abound in discussions of matters concerning race and sex because these four questions are not always kept distinct.

Another useful way of approaching the topic of discrimination and prejudice is to note what particular solutions to the problem are favored by the political ideals of libertarianism, welfare liberalism, and socialism (see Section I).

Libertarians, for whom liberty is the ultimate political ideal, are not likely to recognize any need to correct for acts of discrimination and prejudice. Bad as these acts may be, they usually do not—according to libertarians—violate anyone's rights, and hence do not demand rectification. In particular, since no one can demand a right to equal basic educational opportunities (a person's educational opportunities being simply a function of the property the person controls), no one can justify affirmative action or preferential treatment on the basis of an earlier failure to recognize such a right.

Socialists, for whom equality is the ultimate political ideal, recognize a need to correct for discrimination and prejudice. However, the correctives socialists support are not limited to affirmative action or preferential treatment; ultimately, socialists want to bring about the socialization of the means of production and the end of private property.

Finally, welfare liberals, for whom the ultimate political ideal is a particular mix of liberty and equality, favor affirmative action or preferential treatment as a central requirement of their political program.

Yet irrespective of how we approach the topic of discrimination and prejudice, one factor we all must consider is the differences in natural talents and capabilities shown by members of different races, sexes, and ethnic groups. Some have claimed that such differences support different assignments of rights and duties in a society. Accordingly, there is a need to consider to what degree the natural talents and capabilities shown by members of different races, sexes, and ethnic groups are different, and whether the differences, such as they are, actually support different assignments of rights and duties in a society.

Proposed solutions to the problem of discrimination and prejudice usually involve favoring or compensating those who are less qualified now because they were denied equal basic opportunities in the past. This practice is called "affirmative action" and "preferential treatment" (basically forward-looking terminology, usually employed by those who favor the practice), but is also described as "reverse discrimination" (basically backward-looking terminology, usually employed by those who do not favor the practice). Such proposed solutions to the problem of discrimination and prejudice usually presuppose a right of equal opportunity or a standard of hiring by competence.

ALTERNATIVE VIEWS

On pages 200–208, Alan H. Goldman takes up two central objections to the standard of hiring by com-

petence. The first is the libertarian objection that employers have a right to hire whomever they please; the second is the egalitarian objection that hiring by competence rewards undeserved advantages and purely native talents.

Goldman's initial response to the libertarian objection is that the right of equal opportunity supports the standard of hiring by competence. Goldman admits that libertarians have rarely recognized such a right. Nevertheless, he argues that if libertarians wish to be understood as taking a moral stance they must endorse such a right, because morality requires that practices "operate to the good of all."

Now libertarians might indeed agree that morality requires practices which "operate to the good of all," yet deny that this necessitates a right to equal opportunity. They might, for example, claim that this requirement can be met simply by respecting each person's rights to life and property (rights which libertarians take to be grounded in an ideal of liberty).

Anticipating this line of defense, Goldman argues that hiring by competence is also supported by considerations of social utility which specifically involve certain fundamental liberties. Unfortunately, it is not clear from Goldman's discussion whether the liberties in question are of the sort that would require libertarians to pay them heed. For liberties can be of two sorts, negative and positive. Both negative and positive liberties are states in which one is unconstrained by other persons from doing what one wants; the two kinds of liberty differ as to what counts as a constraint. In the definition of negative liberties, the constraints that would prevent people from doing what they want to do are always acts of commission. When speaking of positive liberties, on the other hand, the constraints envisioned are acts of either commission or omission.

It seems clear enough that an ideal of positive liberty does indeed support a right to equal opportunity, since lack of opportunity will frequently be due to the failure of others to provide it (an act of omission). But libertarians interpret their ideal to be one of negative liberty (prohibiting only constraints that are acts of commission). Hence a quite different defense is needed to show that the libertarian ideal supports a right of equal opportunity. And it is not clear that Goldman has provided such a defense.[1]

A different problem arises when Goldman attempts to answer the egalitarian objection to a standard of hiring by competence. Goldman argues that the alternative suggested by egalitarians, a random allocation of the desirable positions in society, is "the worst of all possible worlds." But while Goldman may be right about the merits of this suggested alternative, he is wrong in thinking that it is an alternative egalitarians usually endorse. For example, egalitarians who follow Marx favor a two-stage approach to realizing their ideal.[2] In the first stage, the principle of distribution is from each according to her ability, to each according to her contribution. In the second stage, when a society has become sufficiently productive and jobs have been redesigned so as to be generally enjoyable in themselves, the principle of distribution is from each according to her ability, to each according to her need. At both stages, however, a standard of hiring by competence rather than a system of random allocation seems to be the appropriate method for assigning positions. For if people are to be rewarded on the basis of their contributions, as they are at the first stage, then it makes sense to hire them on the basis of their competences. Even at the second stage, hiring by competence still seems to be appropriate, especially since at this stage the egalitarian objection that hiring by competence rewards undeserved advantages and native talents no longer applies. Accordingly, egalitarians who follow Marx would have little reason to reject a standard of hiring by competence, although they would, of course, want to link such a standard with a program of restructuring jobs and socializing the means of production.

Acknowledging that gross violations of the standard of hiring by competence as well as the right of equal opportunity have occurred in the past, many have argued that affirmative action is required either to remedy these past violations or to help realize a society free from the evils of racism and sexism. In opposition, others have argued that affirmative action embodies injustices of its own.

In the next selection, Bernard R. Boxill examines this opposition to affirmative action (see pp. 208–217). Some have contended that affirmative action benefits just those from among the groups that have suffered discrimination who do not deserve compensation. Against this Boxill argues that even if those who benefit from affirmative action are less deserving of compensation than others, they do still deserve to receive the compensation of affirmative action. Boxill's defense, however, seems to assume that we can compensate virtually all those who are deserving of compensation for past injustices. But this is not always possible, due to limited resources or limited political power. Under such circumstances, might it not be more appropriate to use our resources and power to benefit those most deserving of compensation? This might lead us to fund remedial educational programs or job training programs rather than affirmative action programs. It may not be possible, of course, to institute the programs that would effectively compensate for the most serious injustices of the past. In that case, adopting affirmative action programs may be the best that we can do. But even when that is the case, it is still important to distinguish what ideally we should do, when circumstances permit it, from what is the best we can do given the nonideal circumstances in which we live.

As we noted before, at some point we must consider the differences in natural talents and capabilities of the members of different races, sexes, and ethnic groups, and their relevance to the problem of discrimination and prejudice. Now no one disputes that there are such differences. What people disagree about is exactly what these differences are and what is their moral significance.

To determine exactly what these differences are, we would need to distinguish natural talents and capabilities from socially produced talents and capabilities. For example, everyone agrees that blacks, as a group, presently score lower on standard IQ tests than whites; but some have claimed that this difference is significantly due to native endowment, while others have claimed that it is socially produced, and still others have questioned the reliability of the IQ test itself as a measure of intellectual ability.[3] Similarly, no one denies that outside the family there are far more men in high-status roles in contemporary societies than women, yet disagreement still abounds as to whether this state of affairs is primarily due to differences in native endowment or differences that are socially produced. Also in this section, Steven Goldberg argues that the presence of the hormone testosterone in men, causing them to be aggressive, suffices to explain the greater number of men in high-status roles (see pp. 217–221). However, Evelyn Reed argues that this effect can be traced to the appearance of class-divided societies, with their institutions of patriarchal family, private property, and the state (see pp. 222–228).

But how are we to deal with these questions? Since the evidence relevant to determining which differences among the members of different races, sexes, and ethnic groups are the effect of natural talents and capabilities and which are socially produced seems inconclusive at best, it might be useful to consider what such a determination would show.

Suppose we were able to conclusively establish, by the most appropriate standard for assessing natural talent and capability, that women, as a group, were slightly more intelligent than men. Would we then be required to rearrange the distribution of desirable positions, goods, and resources in society so that they effectively favored women over men? Not at all. For even if women were superior to men in this important respect, we could still argue that because of the fundamental equality of women and men, we should bring it about that both sexes shared the same percentage of desirable positions and incomes in society. To bring this about, of course, we may have to compensate men for their slightly lower intellectual endowment, possibly by providing them with some additional educational advantages. But we may judge that this is the best way for a society to recognize the fundamental equality of women and men.

Nevertheless, some might object that if women as a group actually have slightly more native intelligence than men, then their educational and their other social advantages should also be slightly better than those of men. But this can be denied on the grounds that the fundamental equality of women and men is a more basic moral consideration, requiring us to compensate for the intellectual differences between women and men rather than emphasizing them.[4]

Accordingly, even without a fully adequate determination of what differences among the members of different races, sexes, and ethnic groups are the effect of natural talents and capabilities and which are socially produced, it should be possible to reach a morally defensible solution to the problem of discrimination and prejudice, provided that we accept the basic equality of members of different races, sexes, and ethnic groups.

PRACTICAL APPLICATIONS

Assuming that we accept the need for affirmative action programs to compensate for past injustices, there remains the question of what form such programs should take. In *University of California v. Bakke* (see pp. 228–241) a majority of the Supreme Court of the United States agreed with the goals of the affirmative action program of the Medical School of the University of California at Davis, which were

1. to reduce the historic deficit of traditionally disfavored minorities in medical schools and the medical profession;
2. to counter the effects of societal discrimination;
3. to increase the number of physicians who practice in communities currently underserved; and
4. to obtain an ethnically diverse student body.

While accepting these goals, a majority of the Court found that the means employed by the Davis program (reserving 16 of 100 openings for adequately qualified minorities) violated the equal protection clause of the Fourteenth Amendment of the U.S. Constitution. What was constitutionally unacceptable about the Davis program was its use of a "quota" with respect to admitting minorities. What would have been constitutionally acceptable, according to the Court, was the use of race or ethnic origin as a "factor" in admitting minorities. When used as a factor, "race or ethnic background may be deemed a 'plus' in a particular applicant's file, yet it does not insulate the individual from comparison with all other candidates for the available seats."

In attempting to assess the moral defensibility of the Court's decision, it is hard to determine what distinguishes a quota affirmative action program from a factor affirmative action program. If a quota is to be filled only by applicants who are judged to be adequately qualified (although not as qualified as those who are accepted through the regular admissions program), it is difficult to see how employing a quota in an affirmative action program does not involve the same sort of calculation as would employing race or ethnicity as a factor in such a program. That very point was made by the justices who dissented from this portion of the Court's opinion. Later, in *Weber* v. *United States* (1979), a majority of the Court did allow that quotas could be used in affirmative action programs, but only when such quotas have been agreed to by representatives of the parties involved.

No less important than the *Bakke* decision, in helping you determine what is the most morally defensible solution to the problem of discrimination and prejudice, is the rejection of the Equal Rights Amendment (ERA). On June 30, 1982 the extended deadline for the ERA expired, three states short of the 38 required for ratification. The United States Commission on Civil Rights and more than 450 national organizations endorsed the amendment, claiming that is was needed to eliminate discriminatory practices against women and especially to provide equal pay for equal work. Opponents of the ERA claimed that it would lead to unisex toilets and to women being drafted for combat duty. Since many of the opponents of the ERA also oppose the practices the amendment was intended to eliminate, there still seems to be a need for an amendment of the appropriate sort. But if this is to be achieved in the next phase of the political struggle, greater attention must be paid to how the generally acknowledged political ideals of liberty and equality apply to the relationship between women and men.

Obviously many of the proposed solutions to the problem of discrimination and prejudice require costly redistributive programs, the funding of which would affect the availability of goods and resources for implementing solutions to the other moral problems considered in this anthology. Again, this shows the interdependence of the solutions to all these moral problems. The next section takes up the problem of punishment and responsibility, the solution to which will likewise put demands on the available goods and resources, and will also presuppose the implementation of morally defensible solutions to the other moral problems considered in this anthology.

NOTES

1. For an account of what such a defense might look like, see James P. Sterba, "Neo-Libertarianism," in *Justice: Alternative Political Perspectives*, edited by James P. Sterba (Belmont: Wadsworth, 1980).

2. Karl Marx, *Critique of the Gotha Program*, edited by C. P. Dutt (New York: International Publishers, 1966).

3. For a review of the relevant literature, see N. J. Block and Gerald Dworkin, "IQ, Heritability and Equality," *Philosophy and Public Affairs*, vol. 3, no. 4 and vol. 4, no. 1 (1974).

4. See also Richard Wasserstrom, *Philosophy and Social Issues* (Notre Dame: University of Notre Dame Press, 1980), chapters 2 and 3.

Richard Wasserstrom

RACISM AND SEXISM

Richard Wasserstrom claims that much of the confusion in thinking and arguing about matters concerning race and sex stems from a failure to keep separate the following questions:

1. What is the correct description of the existing social arrangements with respect to either race or sex?
2. What is the explanation for those social arrangements and by what mechanisms are they perpetuated or changed?
3. How would things be arranged in a good or just society with respect to race or sex?
4. How might a society most effectively and fairly move from the existing state of affairs to a closer approximation of the ideal?

Wasserstrom then goes on to answer question (1) and sketch three possible answers to question (3).

RACISM AND SEXISM ARE two central issues that engage the attention of many persons living within the United States today. But while there is relatively little disagreement about their importance as topics, there is substantial, vehement, and apparently intractable disagreement about what individuals, practices, ideas, and institutions are either racist or sexist and for what reasons. In dispute are a number of related questions concerning how individuals and institutions ought to regard and respond to matters relating to race or sex.

Much of the confusion in thinking and arguing about matters concerning race and sex and in trying to determine which institutions, practices, attitudes, or beliefs are either racist or sexist results, I believe, from a failure to see that there are different domains of inquiry within which any of these matters can be examined. As a result, any inquiry concerned with the question of racism or sexism, or the question of the relevance of persons' race or sex, can most profitably begin by distinguishing these domains and getting clear about which questions one is or is not seeking to answer. What I offer in this essay is, first, a general theory about the proper places or contexts

within which to discuss and assess the varieties of issues and arguments which arise within this general topic, and second, a rather detailed examination of the primary questions that arise within several of these contexts. To call the overall structure a general theory is to use a somewhat pretentious phrase for marking what seem to me to be the essentially different and distinct questions that can be asked about such things as the relevance of race or sex and the defensibility or indefensibility of programs, practices, attitudes, or beliefs which take into account or concern a person's race or sex. I call it a general theory chiefly because it provides an analytic framework within which to investigate a large number of issues concerning any characteristic, like race or sex. That is to say, while this inquiry is concerned solely with issues relating to race ar sex, it is my belief that this same schema—this same way of marking off questions and contexts—works just as well and in just the same manner for a consideration of comparable issues that might be addressed in respect to socioeconomic class, or religion, or any other comparable characteristic of individuals.

There are four questions, or domains of inquiry,

From *Philosophy and Social Issues* (1980) pp. 11–17, 23–29. Reprinted by permission of the University of Notre Dame Press.

that I think it essential to distinguish and keep separate. The first is what I call the question of the social realities. Within this domain, one is concerned with asking what is the correct, complete description of the existing social arrangements in respect to either the characteristic of race or sex. Under the category of social arrangements I mean to include such things as the existing institutional structures, laws, practices, places in society, attitudes, and ideologies—and within the idea of an ideology I include both beliefs about the facts and beliefs about the appropriateness of the existing set of arrangements.

The second question is devoted to the task of explanation. Given a description of what the social reality at any given time and place is, one can certainly ask how things got that way and by what mechanisms they tend to be perpetuated or changed. There can be, and typically is, an array of competing explanatory theories concerning the causes of the social reality and the determinants of social change and stability. For example, much of the literature about the social relations between men and women is focused upon this question of explanation. Complex and sophisticated theories utilizing the ideas of Freud, Levi-Strauss, and Marx have been developed to explain the past and present oppression of women.[1] Alternative theories, drawing upon such things as the behavior of animals, the nature of early human societies, and the psychological and physiological differences between men and women, have also been offered to explain the dominance of males.[2]

The third question is what I call the question of ideals. Within this domain one is concerned with asking the question of how things ought to be arranged: if we had the good or the just society in respect to race or sex, if the social reality were changed so that it in fact conformed to our vision of what the social arrangments ought to be as to these characteristics, what would that society's institutions, practices, and ideology be in respect to matters of racial and sexual differentiation? In other words, what, if anything, would be the social significance of race or sex in a society which got things right as to these two characteristics; when, if at all, would either individuals or institutions ever care about and make social decisions concerning the race or sex of the individuals in that society?

The fourth and final question is that of instru-

mentalities. Once one has developed the correct account of the social realities, and the most defensible conception of the nature of the good society, and the most adequate theory of how the social realities came about and are maintained, then the remaining question is the broadly instrumental one of the appropriate vehicle of social change. How, given all of this, might a society most effectively and fairly move from the existing state of affairs to a closer approximation of the ideal?

It is a central part of my thesis that many of the debates over matters pertaining to race or sex are less illuminating than they otherwise would be because they neglect to take into account these four different domains, each of which is important and deserving of separate consideration, and to identify clearly which of these four questions is in fact being addressed. While I do not claim that all the significant normative and conceptual questions concerning race and sex can be made to disappear or be rendered uncontroversial once these distinctions are fully grasped, I do believe that an awareness and use of these distinctions can produce valuable insights that contribute to their resolution. In particular, it can, for example, be seen quite readily that the often-asked question of whether race or sex is relevant is not as straightforward or unambiguous as may appear at first. The question may be about social realities, about how the categories of race or sex in fact function in the culture and to what effect. Or the question may be about explanations, about the theory which most adequately explains what has caused the social realities in respect to race or sex, or about the theory which most accurately identifies the features, if any, which underlie the social realities in respect to race or sex. Or the question may be about ideals, about what the good society would make of race or sex. Or the question may be about instrumentalities, about how to achieve a closer approximation of the ideal, given the social realities and the most adequate explanatory theories. When the issues are properly disentangled, one thing that is possible is that what might be an impermissible way to take race or sex into account in the ideal society, may nonetheless be a desirable and appropriate way to take race or sex into account, given the social realities. . . .

One way to think and talk about race and sex is,

as I have indicated, to concentrate upon the domain of the social realities. Here one must begin by insisting that to talk about either is to talk about a particular social and cultural context.

In our own culture the first thing to observe is that race and sex are socially important categories. They are so in virtue of the fact that we live in a culture which has, throughout its existence, made race and sex extremely important characteristics of and for all the people living in the culture.[3]

It is surely possible to imagine a culture, for instance, in which race would be an unimportant, insignificant characteristic of individuals. In such a culture race would be largely if not exclusively a matter of superficial physiology; a matter, we might say, simply of the way one looked. And if it were, then any analysis of race and racism would necessarily assume very different dimensions from what they do in our society. In such a culture, the meaning of the term "race" would itself have to change substantially. This can be seen by the fact that in such a culture it would literally make no sense to say of a person that he or she was "passing."[4] This is something that can be said and understood in our own culture and it shows at least that to talk of race is to talk of more than the way one looks.[5] . . .

The point can be put another way: Race does not function in our culture in the way eye color does. Eye color is an irrelevant category; nobody cares what color people's eyes are; it is not an important cultural fact; nothing turns on what eye color you have. It is essential to see that race is not like that at all. This truth affects, among other things, what will and will not count as cases of racism. In our culture to be nonwhite—and especially to be black—is to be treated as and seen to be a member of a group that is different from and inferior to the group of standard, fully developed persons, the adult white males.

In our society, to be black is to be at a disadvantage in terms of virtually every conceivable measure of success or satisfaction—be it economic, vocational, political, or social. To see that this is so one need only conduct a simple thought experiment. If one wanted to maximize one's chances of being wealthy, satisfied with one's employment, politically powerful, secure from arbitrary treatment within the social institutions, and able to pursue one's own goals and develop one's own talents to the fullest, and if one could choose to be born either white or black, which race would one choose to be born? . . .

It is even clearer in the case of sex than in the case of race that one's sexual identity is a centrally important, crucially relevant category within our culture. If anything, it seems even more important and more fundamental than one's race. It is evident that there are substantially different role expectations and role assignments to persons in accordance with their sexual physiology, and that the positions of the two sexes in the culture are distinct. We have a patriarchal society of sorts in which it matters enormously whether one is a male or a female.[6] Just as with the case of race, by almost all important measures it is more advantageous to be a male rather than a female.

The roles, status, and opportunities of men and women are different. We learn very early and forcefully that we are either males or females and that much turns upon which sex we are. A woman's success or failure in life is still defined largely in terms of her activities within the family. It is important for her that she marry, and when she does she is expected to take responsibility for the wifely tasks: the housework, the child care, and the general emotional welfare of the husband and children. Her status in society is determined in substantial measure by the vocation and success of her husband. Economically, women are substantially worse off than men. They do not receive pay for the work that is done in the home. As members of the labor force their wages are significantly lower than those paid to men, even when they are engaged in similar work and have similar educational backgrounds. The higher the prestige or the salary of the job, the less likely it is that a woman will fill that job. And, of course, women are conspicuously absent from most positions of authority and power in the major political institutions of our society. . . .

Just as we can and must ask what is involved in our or any other culture in being of one race or one sex rather than the other, and how individuals are in fact viewed and treated, we can also ask a different question, namely, what would the good or just society make of an individual's race or sex, and to what degree, if at all, would racial and sexual distinctions ever properly be taken into account there? Indeed, it could plausibly be argued that we could not have a wholly adequate idea of whether a society was racist or sexist unless we had some conception of what a thoroughly nonracist or nonsexist society would look like. This question is an extremely instructive as well as an often neglected one. Comparatively little theoretical literature that deals with either racism or sexism has concerned itself in a systematic way with this issue, but as will be seen it is in some respects both a more important and a more complicated one where sex is concerned than where race is involved. Moreover, as I shall argue, many discussions of sexual differences which touch upon this question do so inappropriately by concentrating upon the relatively irrelevant question of whether the differences between males and females are biological rather than social in origin. . . .

In order to ask more precisely what some of the possible ideals are of desirable racial or sexual differentiation, it is necessary to ask: Differentiation in respect to what? And one way to do this is to distinguish in a crude way among three levels or areas of social and political arrangements and activities. First, there is the area of basic political rights and obligations, including such things as the rights to vote and to travel, and the obligation to pay taxes. Second, there is the area of important, but perhaps less primary institutional benefits and burdens of both governmental and nongovernmental types. Examples are access to and employment in the significant economic markets, the opportunity to acquire and enjoy housing in the setting of one's choice, the right of persons who want to marry each other to do so, and the duties (nonlegal as well as legal) that persons acquire in getting married. And third, there is the area of individual, social interaction, including such matters as whom one will marry, have as friends, and, perhaps, what aesthetic preferences one will cultivate and enjoy.

As to each of these three areas we can ask, for example, whether in a nonracist or a nonsexist society it would be thought appropriate ever to take the race or sex of an individual into account. It is, for instance, a widely held, but by no means unanimously accepted, view that we would have the good society in respect to race if race were to be a wholly unimportant characteristic of individuals—if, that is, race were to function in the lives of indi-

viduals in the way in which eye color now does.

Thus, one conception of a nonracist society is that which is captured by what I shall call the assimilationist ideal: a nonracist society would be one in which the race of an individual would be the functional equivalent of the eye color of individuals in our society today.[7] In our society no basic political rights and obligations are determined on the basis of eye color. No important institutional benefits and burdens are connected with eye color. Indeed, except for the mildest sort of aesthetic preferences, a person would be thought odd who even made private, social decisions by taking eye color into account. It would, of course, be unintelligible, and not just odd, were a person to say today that while he or she looked blue-eyed, he or she regarded himself or herself as really a brown-eyed person. Because eye color functions differently in our culture than does race, there is no analogue to passing for eye color. Were the assimilationist ideal to become a reality, the same would be true of one's race. In short, according to the assimilationist ideal, a nonracist society would be one in which an individual's race was of no more significance in any of these three areas than is eye color today.

What is a good deal less familiar is an analogous conception of the good society in respect to sexual differentiation—one in which an individual's sex were to become a comparably unimportant characteristic. An assimilationist society in respect to sex would be one in which an individual's sex was of no more significance in any of the three areas than is eye color today. There would be no analogue to transsexuality, and, while physiological or anatomical sex differences would remain, they would possess only the kind and degree of significance that today attaches to the physiologically distinct eye colors persons possess.

It is apparent that the assimilationist ideal in respect to sex does not seem to be as readily plausible and obviously attractive here as it is in the case of race. In fact, many persons invoke the possible realization of the assimilationist ideal as a reason for rejecting the Equal Rights Amendment and indeed the idea of women's liberation itself. The assimilationist ideal may be just as good and just as important an ideal in respect to sex as it is in respect to race, but it is important to realize at the outset that this appears to be a more far-reaching proposal when applied to sex rather than race and that many more persons think there are good reasons why an assimilationist society in respect to sex would not be desirable than is true for the comparable racial ideal. . . .

There is . . . another [ideal] that is closely related to, but distinguishable from that of the assimilationist ideal. It can be understood by considering how religion rather than eye color tends to be thought about in our culture today and incorporated within social life today. If the good society were to match the present state of affairs in respect to one's religious identity, rather than the present state of affairs in respect to one's eye color, the two societies would be different, but not very greatly so. In neither would we find that the allocation of basic political rights and duties ever took an individual's religion into account. And there would be a comparable indifference to religion even in respect to most important institutional benefits and burdens—for example, access to employment in the desirable vocations, the opportunity to live where one wished to live, and the like. Nonetheless, in the good society in which religious differences were to some degree socially relevant, it would be deemed appropriate to have some institutions (typically those which are connected in an intimate way with these religions) which did in a variety of ways properly take the religion of members of the society into account. For example, it would be thought both permissible and appropriate for members of a religious group to join together in collective associations which have religious, educational, and social dimensions, and when it came to the employment of persons who were to be centrally engaged in the operation of those religious institutions (priests, rabbis and ministers, for example), it would be unobjectionable and appropriate explicitly to take the religion of job applicants into account. On the individual, interpersonal level, it might also be thought natural and possibly even admirable, were persons to some significant degree to select their associates, friends, and mates on the basis of their religious orientation. So there is another possible and plausible ideal of what the good society would look like in respect to a particular characteristic in which differences based upon that characteristic would be to some degree maintained in some aspects of institutional and interpersonal life. The diversity of the religious beliefs of individuals would be

reflected in the society's institutional and ideological fabric in a way in which the diversity of eye color would not be in the assimilationist society. The picture is a more complex, somewhat less easily describable one than that of the assimilationist ideal. . . .

Nor do I even mean to suggest that all persons who reject the assimilationist ideal in respect to sex would necessarily embrace something like the kind of pluralistic ideal I have described as matching something like our present arrangements and ideas concerning the relevance of religious identity—although these do seem to exhaust the plausible ideals in respect to race. Some persons might think the right ideal was one in which substantially greater sexual differentiation and sex-role identification were retained than would be the case within a good society of that general type. Thus, someone might believe, for instance, that the good society was, perhaps, essentially like the one they think we now have in respect to sex: equality of basic political rights, such as the right to vote, but all of the sexual differentiation in both legal and nonlegal, formal and informal institutions, all of the sex-role socialization and all of the differences in matters of temperament that are characteristic of the way in which our society has been and still is ordered. And someone might also believe that the prevailing ideological concomitants of these arrangements are the correct and appropriate ones to perpetuate.[8]

This could, of course, be regarded as a version of the pluralistic ideal described above, with the emphasis upon the extensive character of the institutional, normative, and personal differences connected with sexual identity. Whether it is a form of this pluralistic ideal or a different ideal altogether turns, I think, upon two things: first, how pervasive the sexual differentiation is in terms of the number, importance, and systemic interconnectedness of the institutions and role expectations connected with being of one sex or the other, and, second, whether the ideal contains within it a conception of the appropriateness of significant institutional and interpersonal inequality, e.g., that the woman's job is in large measure to serve and be dominated by the male. The more either or both of these features is present, the clearer is the case for regarding this as an ideal, distinctively different from either of the other two described so far. . . .

NOTES

1. For an example of this kind of theory see Rubin, "The Traffic in Women" in Reiter (ed.), *Toward an Anthropology of Women* (New York: Monthly Review Press, 1975), pp. 157–210.

2. For an example of this kind of theory see Tiger, *Men in Groups* (New York : Random House, 1969).

3. In asserting the importance of one's race and sex in our culture, I do not mean to deny the importance of other characteristics, in particular, socioeconomic class. I do think that in our culture race and sex are two very important facts about a person, and I am skeptical of theories which "reduce" the importance of these features to a single, more basic one, *e.g.*, class. But apart from this one bit of skepticism I think that all of what I have to say is compatible with several different theories concerning why race and sex are so important, including, for instance, most versions of Marxism. *See, e.g.*, the account provided in Mitchell, *Woman's Estate* (New York: Pantheon Books, 1971).

4. Passing is the phenomenon in which a person who in some sense knows himself or herself to be black "passes" as white because he or she looks white. A version of this is described in Sinclair Lewis' novel, *Kingsblood Royal* (New York: Random House, 1947), where the protagonist discovers when he is an adult that he, his father, and his father's mother are black (or, in the idiom of the late 1940s, Negro) in virtue of the fact that his great grandfather was black. His grandmother knew this and was consciously passing. When he learns about his ancestry, one decision he has to make is whether to continue to pass or to acknowledge to the world that he is in fact "Negro."

5. That looking black is not in our culture a necessary condition for being black can be seen from the phenomenon of passing. That it is not a sufficient condition can be seen from the book *Black Like Me* (Boston: Houghton Mifflin, 1961) by John Howard Griffin, where "looking black" is easily understood by the reader to be different from being black. I suspect that the concept of being black is, in our culture, one which combines both physiological and ancestral criteria in some fairly complex, yet imprecise fashion.

6. One very good general account of the structure of patriarchy and of its major dimensions and attributes is that found in the chapter, "Theory of Sexual Politics," in Millett, *Sexual Politics* (Garden City, N. Y., Doubleday & Co., 1970), pp. 23–58. The essay seems to me to be a major contribution to an understanding of the subject. I draw upon Millett's analytic scheme in my description of the social realities of sex.

7. There is a danger in calling this ideal the "assimilationist" ideal. That term often suggests the idea of incorporating oneself, one's values, and the like into the dominant group and its practices and values. No part of that idea is meant to be captured by my use of the term. Mine is a stipulative definition.

8. Thus, for example, a column appeared a few years ago in the *Washington Star* concerning the decision of the Cosmos Club to continue to refuse to permit women to be members. The author of the column (and a member of the club) defended the decision on the ground that women appropriately had a different status in the society. Their true distinction was to be achieved by being faithful spouses and devoted mothers. The column closed with this paragraph:

"In these days of broken homes, derision of marriage, reluctance to bear children, contempt for the institution of the family—a phase in our national life when it seems more honorable to be a police-woman, or a model, or an accountant than to be a wife or mother—there is a need to reassert a traditional scale of values in which the vocation of homemaker is as honorable and distinguished as any in political or professional life. Such women, as wives and widows of members, now enjoy in the club the privileges of their status, which includes [sic] their own drawing rooms, and it is of interest that they have been among the most outspoken opponents of the proposed changes in club structure." Groseclose, "Now—Shall We Join the Ladies?" *Washington Star*, Mar. 13, 1975.

Alan H. Goldman

JUSTICE AND HIRING BY COMPETENCE

Alan H. Goldman defends the standard of hiring by competence against the libertarian objection that employers have no obligation to hire the most competent as well as the egalitarian objection that hiring the most competent rewards undeserved advantages and purely native talents. Against the libertarian objection, Goldman argues that the standard of hiring by competence is supported by considerations of equality of opportunity and social utility. Against the egalitarian objection, Goldman argues that justice and morality support the standard of hiring by competence over a random allocation of the desirable positions in society.

THE ISSUE TO BE settled in this paper regards a general rule for hiring or awarding scarce desirable positions in society. In recent political debates on the subject of reverse discrimination or preferential hiring, the principle of hiring by competence has seemed to remain sacrosanct, at least if one can judge by the lip-service paid to it by all sides of the discussion. Proponents of affirmative action go to great lengths to distinguish minority "goals" from quotas. While strict quotas for raising percentages of blacks and women employed by a fixed date, which would result in strong reverse discrimination, are acknowledged to be incompatible with the maintenance of strict competence standards, percentage goals for minorities toward which good faith efforts are made are held to encourage minority hiring while maintaining existing standards. Opponents of the policy on the other hand seem to feel that by demonstrating how academic standards of excellence suffer and most qualified individuals fail to get positions through pressure for reverse discrimination, they thereby show affirmative action programs in universities to be unjust.

But despite apparent unanimity regarding the principle in the context of this public debate, it has recently come under attack in more sophisticated philosophical circles from both the left and the right. Libertarians argue or imply that corporations or organizations with positions to fill can give them to whomever they choose, that society has no right to interfere in this free process. Corporations like individuals have the right to control their legitimately

acquired assets and to disburse them to whom they choose, and the right to freely hire is part of this more general right. Egalitarians on the other hand hold the principle of hiring by competence unjust in rewarding initial undeserved advantages and purely native talents. Individuals do not deserve those initial advantages for which they can claim no responsibility, and hiring by competence alone often rewards just such chance talents and advantageous initial social positions. I will argue here against these attacks. I will be concerned with two central questions: (1) Does society have the right to impose and enforce any rule of hiring against corporations with positions to fill? (2) If the answer to (1) is affirmative, which principle of hiring ought to be adopted from the point of view of justice? I will argue against libertarians in this area that society does have the right and duty to enforce a principle, and against egalitarians that hiring by competence is just, that with several qualifications it is as just as human nature allows, and that even without them it is more just than seemingly egalitarian alternatives.

I. THE LIBERTARIAN POSITION

The first question to be faced here is why one system of hiring can be judged more just than another at all, i.e. why the award of jobs by private corporations

From "Justice and Hiring by Competence," *American Philosophical Quarterly* (1977) pp. 17–26. Reprinted by permission of the *American Philosophical Quarterly*.

as opposed to the award of other benefits by private individuals involves considerations of justice rather than simply questions of right and wrong. There are situations in which individuals or corporations can make wrong, even overall morally wrong decisions, without treating anyone unjustly or unfairly. To say that principles of hiring are a matter of distributive social justice is to imply that certain individuals acquire distributive *rights* to certain positions, and that to refuse them these positions is to refuse to grant them what is legitimately due them. The libertarian denies that any such rights exist. He argues that just as Mary has the right to marry whom she pleases, so a private corporation with benefits in the form of jobs to award has the right to hire whom it pleases without interference.

No one acquires a right to marry Mary, and similarly, argues the libertarian, no one acquires a right to a benefit from a private corporation which it has not contracted away. It will be useful in criticizing this position to see how far this analogy can be pressed. The difference between the case of Mary and that of the corporation cannot lie in the fact that a person's vital interests are affected by the job he works at, since his vital interests appear equally affected by his spouse, and yet as we said no one acquires a right to marry Mary—she can choose as capriciously as she wants. Thus we cannot argue simply from the fact that it makes a great deal of difference to people what jobs they get to the conclusion that society has a right to enforce a certain rule of hiring against private corporations. Nor does the converse seem to create a distinction, for if Mary's right to choose derives from the fact that her vital interests are involved as well, the same holds true of the corporation's vital interests in its personnel. Since a corporation's welfare and even continued existence depends upon who occupies its various positions, it can be argued that these choices should be left to it. It seems then that just as Mary has the right to choose a husband who will make her unhappy in the long run, i.e. she treats no one unjustly in doing so even if some other suitor would make a perfect spouse, so a corporation has the right to hire total incompetents if it chooses to act so unwisely. Nor can we argue simply that a corporation has no right to hire whom it pleases since the consequences of such freedom are bad (given present biases against minorities). For we perhaps can think

of more scientific (or traditional?) ways to match spouses in comparison to which free choice has bad long range consequences for happiness, yet we would not want to deny Mary that right, nor contract it away ourselves. Even gains to her own interest or happiness do not justify interference with Mary's free choice, so that her right to choose derives from more than calculation of interests in particular cases. So in the case of a corporation, while it is difficult to see how hiring the most competent could damage its long range interests, perhaps it has a right to ignore those interests if it so chooses.

Are the cases then really totally analogous in relevant ways? First, although interests seem parallel as seen above, are the basic rights involved indeed similar? In Mary's case the general rights underlying her particular freedom in this case include a right over her own body and the freedom to control her life as she sees fit. That these rights, especially the first, have wide scope and absolute priority within their domains is in the interest of all to recognize. In the case of the corporation, the rights presumably involved are at most weaker versions or narrower cases of these: namely the right to property and that of free association. A corporation may be said to have a property right in the positions it chooses to fill in virtue of having legitimately acquired the assets with which to fund the positions. A corporation like an individual has a right to control those goods or assets which it has legitimately acquired. And the right to control its own assets is empty unless it is free to disburse them as or to whom it chooses. Since present members of the corporation must associate with new appointees, the freedom to associate with whom one pleases may also be cited in support of the libertarian position here. An enforced rule for hiring may force present members to work closely with others against their will, making their work unpleasant for them. And the friction created by this forced close association may be detrimental to the continued smooth operation of the company or organization.

Clearly the right over one's body, which applies in the case of Mary's marriage, is more basic than the right to external property, which applies in the hiring case . . . and the freedom to control one's life broader and more precious in total than that of free association. It can nevertheless be argued that just as the former rights constitute the paramount considerations in Mary's case, so do the latter in the case of the corporation. The corporation's property rights to control the disbursement of its assets and the right of free association of its members can be held to imply a specific right to hire whom it pleases without interference from society. In relation to the analogy with Mary's specific right to choose a spouse following from her rights over her own body and to control her life plan, the central questions here are first, whether Mary's rights always entail that she cannot treat others unjustly in choosing a spouse (i.e. whether these rights are absolute in this sphere), and second, whether there might be other rights involved in the case of the corporation, but not in Mary's case, which limit or override those to which it can appeal in support of free choice. To the extent that Mary's specific right to marry whom she pleases is not absolute, and to the extent that the two cases are disanalogous regarding the rights and interests involved, we cannot argue from Mary's case to an absolute right to hire freely of the corporation.

It should first be noticed regarding the question of the scope of Mary's right that she can treat Dick unfairly or unjustly despite her right to choose, if she has led him on and then rejected him in favor of another at the altar. There are situations in which someone might acquire a legitimate expectation to marry Mary and be treated unjustly or unfairly by her subsequently. This might lead us to suspect that injustice in hiring as well has to do with thwarting legitimate expectations arising from previous efforts. But what could render expectations of individuals to jobs legitimate, given the corporation members' rights of property and free association? It might be held that the only parallel would be a corporation's refusing a job to an individual promised that position, but there are contract laws to prevent that from occurring, and the libertarian acknowledges the state's duty to enforce contracts freely made. (At least the rights in question, as in Mary's case, are already shown to be somewhat limited in scope.)

But there is a difference from the average case of whom one chooses to marry in that whether corporations have competent people or not affects the goods they produce for the rest of society, while whom one marries affects basically only oneself. If Mary happened to be a seventeenth century queen of England and her marriage affected how the country was ruled, she would lose her right to choose whom

she pleased, and her subjects could complain of a choice being unfair to them. Similarly it seems society can complain if it fails to get necessary goods and services because of incompetents in positions of responsibility. If one corporation hires incompetents or relative incompetents because of discriminatory practices, it will soon be driven out of business in a competitive situation, but if there is such a practice generally in a whole sector of the economy, the public can complain for the price it pays for such lack of efficiency. To assume that competition will root out all such practices is to oversimplify motives and knowledge of both producers and consumers, and this assumption has proved empirically false.

It may be asked, however, how a social interest in more material goods and services can override recognized rights of individuals or private corporations within the society, like the rights of property and free association here. To determine a social interest is not necessarily to demonstrate the right of society or the state to further that interest, especially when individual or private corporation rights are apparently ignored in the process. For one principal purpose of recognizing individual rights within a system of social justice is to protect individuals from losses whenever utilitarian calculations run against them in particular cases. The recognition of the right to property, for example, means that a person will not be dispossessed whenever another is in greater need, although such forced transfer would raise total or average utility in particular cases. Therefore the rights to property and free association, it could be argued by analogy, should not be overridden here by the social interest in maximizing goods and services. A private corporation with assets to disburse for jobs should be free to hire whom it pleases, even when this results in lower efficiency in its production of goods and services. Efficiency cannot be permitted to override recognized rights, or our rights and freedoms would be fragile indeed. Thus while it may be in the interest of all, even of those in power in corporations, to have the most competent hired, there may exist rights to ignore the maximization of interest satisfaction, as in the case of marriage choices.

While I accept the above account of rights as far as it goes, it presents an oversimplified picture when used only in conjunction with appeal to property and free association rights in the context of this libertarian argument for freedom in hiring. What is ignored is the fact that recognition of particular rights, like that of property, is established in the first place in relation to a set of varied social values including welfare, and that such rights are therefore rarely (never?) unlimited in scope, but include exception clauses recognizing rights established in relation to other values. My right to dispose of my property as I please does not include a right to dispose of my knife in an editor's chest; my right to use my property according to my own wishes does not include a right to play my stereo at deafening volumes; and my right to spend my assets as I like does not allow me to buy nerve gas, even if I keep it sealed in my basement vault. The above examples represent restrictions of freedom to prevent harm, annoyance or potential harm, but these are not the only possible cases. In the initial formulation of rules and rights the value of freedom may be weighed against those of equality or equity, and welfare, for example. This is compatible with the fact that welfare or utility considerations are no longer applied once the rights have been established and their scopes defined. Thus while it may be in the interest of all to recognize a right to personal property, this right may include an exception clause regarding filling jobs by corporations, again in the interest of all. This does not mean that property rights are to be overriden in specific cases for net gains in social welfare—property would be too precarious in that case—but general exception clauses of narrower scope (than any net gain in welfare) are compatible with the existence and protection of specific rights like that of property.

We have not yet won the argument with the libertarian, however. For his position is precisely that freedoms, including those of disbursing property and associating with those of one's choice, may only be limited to prevent harm. And a defender of this position would undoubtedly want to press the distinction here between the interests of individuals in maximizing available goods and services and any potential harm to them from the exercise of these freedoms on the part of corporations in hiring. I am not sure, however, that the distinction between harm and utility can be drawn at all in relation to many positions of responsibility in society, such as pilots, surgeons, police and even automobile, home or toy manufacturers. Relative incompetents in these positions represent not only losses in efficiency, but

serious potential harm. Thus the harm principle itself, if it allows prevention of unnecessary risk or potential harm, which it must to be at all plausible, may require enforcement of a rule for hiring the most competent in many positions. On a deeper level it may be questioned whether considerations of freedom can be so sharply differentiated from considerations of equality and welfare when designing basic institutions or establishing rules and recognizing rights. To approach this question in this present context, we must first examine how considerations of equality or equity figure in the issue of hiring by competence, for this is somewhat less obvious than the relevance of social welfare or utility.

There is in fact another right involved in this issue which libertarians ignore—what is generally recognized as the right to equality of opportunity. To allow jobs to be awarded capriciously, especially given deep-seated prejudices known to exist in our society, is to deny equal opportunity for goods in a most blatant fashion. An equal opportunity for jobs is the necessary condition for an equal chance to all other basic goods. Thus the right of equal opportunity, if recognized at all, must also be acknowledged to figure more prominently in the issue of a social rule for hiring than the right to property or free association. The reason for this unequal weight is that the right to property as well as that of free association continue to exist although limited by exception clauses regarding corporations' doling out jobs, as they continue to exist with clauses involving limited redistributive taxation or open housing in the name of equality. But equal opportunity for social goods does not exist at all without equal opportunity for jobs. While redistributive taxation, open housing, and integrated schools are advocated in the name of this right, they amount to little when jobs can be denied to those who have managed to acquire superior qualifications with their help. The enforcement of some rule for hiring stipulating criteria not based purely upon inborn or initial chance factors is the first prerequisite for equality of opportunity, since decent jobs are not only of highest value in themselves, but means to most other valuable things.

This admittedly may not bother the thoroughgoing libertarian. For he will most likely recognize no such right as that to equal opportunity, nor give it any weight at all against the maximization of individual freedoms in regard to property and association. He holds that people have a right (short of harm) to what they have freely and legitimately acquired, and that no general right like that of equal opportunity should be recognized which involves repeated violations of individuals' rights to their acquired property. Have we then finally reached in regard to this issue an impasse in moral argument, uncovered an ultimate clash in moral attitude? Rather than admit this we can plausibly continue the argument by accusing the libertarian first of failing to assume a moral attitude on this issue at all, and second of inconsistency in his appeal to the absolute value of freedom over equality.

We can first point out then that part of what it means to assume a moral attitude is to recognize the moral equality of others (implied in a recognition of their subjectivity, i.e. feelings, points of view, etc.)—to accept rules which could be willed from their positions in the social context, or at least by neutral agents. If this recognition of moral equality or moral community within a system of social rules is to be given content as well as form, it means that the rules must not only apply to all, but as far as possible operate to the good of all. It also means that there is a presumption of equality not only in worth but in material conditions, which must be weighed against other values such as that of freedom in the formulation of more specific moral rules. A minimal moral outcome of this balancing (too minimal for egalitarians) is to formulate rules which result not in equality of goods, but in something approaching an equal chance to acquire goods through effort. Hence the recognition and protection of this right in social rules, such as a rule for hiring, seem a minimal condition for a moral social system. To bring this argument down to the specific issue at hand, its upshot is that rules protecting equality of opportunity, and specifically the recognition that society has the right to enforce some fair rule for hiring against private corporations, are necessary if distributions of property and other goods are to be just.

I have been speaking thus far as if freedom here is to be balanced against equality and welfare, but also indicated above that absolute liberty with respect to property and association may not result in the overall maximization of freedom desired by the libertarian. For poverty and the lack of satisfaction of basic needs which poverty entails constitute an impediment to freedom as well, to the basic freedom to

formulate and pursue a meaningful life plan and control one's life as one desires. This is perhaps the most essential liberty of all, and if it is denied through the operation of a social or economic system which leaves some in need so that others may totally control their property, we can view this as an unwarranted conventional constraint upon liberty (property is only protected in the first place by the social system). It follows that any rule of hiring which results in more goods and services, as long as some of these trickle down to those whose freedom is compromised by want, can be adopted not only in the name of welfare or utility, but to increase freedom as well. This does not mean in general that every increase in welfare is to be counted as an increase in freedom as well, or that despotic states with higher GNP's are to be preferred, but only that no social system can be justified in the name of freedom which leaves those at the bottom constrained within the circle of dire poverty. A society with severe racial biases and no rule for hiring results in that situation. Thus we again arrive at the conclusion that society has the right to impose some rule for hiring against private corporations, this time in the name of freedom. Restrictions upon the freedom of corporations to choose capriciously or invidiously in hiring are necessary to protect or create freedom for those for whom equality of opportunity is its necessary condition.

If rules for hiring are then justified through considerations of utility or welfare and equality of opportunity, why not equal opportunity to marry Mary, or the adoption of mating rules which can be shown to maximize happiness or compatibility in the long run? Do the above arguments apply equally to this case, and if so mustn't they be dismissed in light of our intuitions against social rules for marriage choices? In answer to the first part of the first question, equal opportunity to marry Mary would amount only to an equal opportunity to win her favor, for that is the only relevant qualification we can presently think of for marrying her (we have no independent reliable criteria for what will make her happy in the long run). We might say that equality of opportunity for passing this purely subjective test exists already (Mary's favor might be won by one who could not have been predicted in terms of knowledge of her prior preferences), or given that Mary has certain relatively fixed prejudices, we might deny the possibility of enforcing any rule (except education against such biases) to create equal opportunity for passing this purely subjective test. In answer to the second part of the question, even if we had independent criteria for happiness in marriage as we do for successful job performance, since whom Mary marries affects herself far more than others, others having at most a peripheral interest, we can leave the choice and its consequences to her. Regarding the consideration of social welfare, the welfare of others is not involved in the average marriage cases as it is in who occupies various productive positions. Regarding the consideration of equal opportunity for those applying for jobs versus marriage consents, equality of opportunity in the latter case is not a necessary condition for equal chances at other goods, hence not a necessary condition for basic freedoms or a just social system overall, as it is in the case of jobs. For all these reasons none of my above arguments imply by analogy that society has the right to enforce a rule for mating against Mary.

These last points of difference apply as well to the more important and difficult cases of an individual hiring someone for temporary help, or the small businessman who gives a job to his son. Must we to be consistent apply our rule to all such cases and deny these freedoms as well? The first distinction between the case of the small business or private individual and the large corporation is the interest of the public in their products and services. If a small business is the only source of a vital service or product in a given area, it may be reasonable to demand competents in positions of responsibility. Otherwise it may be unreasonable to demand the proprietor to take the time and bear the cost to advertise the position, etc. (this is especially clear in the case of my hiring someone to unload my rented truck, or similar cases). The right of free association is also more central in the case of a small business, and this ws part of the reasoning of Congress in applying nondiscriminatory regulations only to businesses with more than twenty-five employees. Since these differences are real, and since equality of opportunity and social welfare do not require that literally every position in society be open to all, but only a certain proportion of them, we may in applying these rationales establish a rule for hiring only for corporations over a certain size, recognizing that the drawing of a precise line will be somewhat arbitrary.

Thus my argument to the effect that certain individuals acquire rights to certain jobs and that corporations treat them unjustly if they are denied those positions involves two steps; first, society has the right in the name of social utility and equality of opportunity to establish a rule for hiring and enforce it against private as well as public corporations and organizations; second, by satisfying this social rule through effort an individual comes to deserve the position in question. The second step is dependent upon the first, which has been established in this section (the second step will be more prominent in the next). I have now provided criteria for the acceptability of a rule for hiring, i.e. social utility and protection of equal opportunity, without having completely shown how a single rule could meet both. In demonstrating that hiring by competence is the correct rule, we must consider the counterarguments of the egalitarian.

II. THE EGALITARIAN POSITION

If the argument of the last section is correct, that is if a rule for hiring is to be justified in terms of social utility and equality of opportunity, it seems easy to show that hiring by competence qualifies as a just distributive principle. Many major theories of distributive justice, especially liberal theories, agree that practices are to be preferred which result in Pareto improvements, i.e. in benefits to some without loss to others. In regard to social utility, it can be argued that hiring by competence results not only in improvements over alternatives of this sort, but in the production of more goods for everyone in society (strong Pareto improvements). Hiring the most competent analytically entails increased goods and services, for competence is defined in terms of the ability to perform in a job by satisfying social demand. (I assume here the ability to judge competence according to qualifications, a difficulty which does not in any case affect the argument that we should *aim at* competence.)

The egalitarian attempts to refute the above justification by arguing that those abilities relevant to awarding jobs on the basis of efficiency, which is the basis for hiring in a pure market economy with only profit motives operating, are irrelevant from the point of view of justice; that in rewarding native talent, intelligence and social position (which even if acquired required an ability for acquisition for which the agent can claim no responsibility), the practice of hiring by competence involves rewards which are arbitrary from a moral point of view. Individuals deserve only those benefits which they have earned. They do not deserve their native advantages and so do not deserve those benefits, including good jobs, which flow from them throughout their lives. A child born rich and intelligent stands a far better chance than do other children of acquiring competence qualifications for desirable positions later in life, yet he cannot be said to deserve that better chance from the point of view of justice, nor thus the job which he eventually gets. Thus increments to social welfare from hiring by competence are a matter of social utility from which questions of justice must be separated. The egalitarian appears to have uncovered a conflict between the two criteria for a just rule advanced in the first section, i.e. maximization of utility through hiring by competence seems inconsistent with equality of opportunity in the present social context, and he claims the moral predominance of considerations of equality over those of social utility.

I do not think that any such radical separation of analyses of justice and efficiency could accord with our intuitions regarding the former, as these are aroused by specific examples. Although we may not all be Utilitarians, it seems we must grant that welfare does at least count as a positive consideration, and certainly at the extreme involved in this issue. Following Nicholas Rescher, I would argue that a practice or rule which generates a sum total of goods of 15 units to be distributed in a hypothetical society of 4 individuals in shares of 4, 4, 4, 3 is preferable from the point of view of justice to one which generates 8 units to be distributed in shares of 2, 2, 2, 2, despite its greater inequality. In other words, those who could have received 4 units under the first plan could legitimately claim injustice at being reduced so as to equal the lowest share under the second, other things being equal. If a claim of injustice or unfairness at being so reduced in moving from the first socio-economic plan to the second is justified, then aggregate utility in itself must be a considera-

tion of distributive justice, and plans must be prima facie preferable which result in larger aggregates. To deny this is perhaps to grant too large a moral force to the feelings of envy and pride. For even the person with the lowest share in our hypothetical case is better off under the first plan than the second, except for the fact that he sees others around him with more. There may seem to be a complication here in that those with less relative income (even though more absolute) may be in a worse position to bid for scarce goods. But these alternatives in relation to choices between hiring by competence or other rules for hiring may be taken to refer to goods available, and not simply income. The argument is that more goods will be available to all if competents occupy productive positions, and this is what the egalitarian wrongly claims to be irrelevant to the choice of a just rule for hiring.

Even if we continue to insist upon a radical separation of justice (in a narrow sense) from efficiency, it seems we must admit that the latter can override the former from a moral point of view when it comes to hiring or filling positions of responsibility. It may be, for example, that those best qualified to be brain surgeons do not most deserve the benefits of those positions from a radically egalitarian view of justice, but surely egalitarians would want them to have the jobs anyway (even if they are not the ones on the operating tables). We pointed out in the last section other jobs as well in which incompetents represent not only losses in goods and services, but potential harm of a serious sort. When we think of all the cases of severe harm such as bodily injury or death which occur from defective products or incompetents conducting vital services, it is clear that lowering ranges of competence further would be something to avoid even if at the expense of equality or fairness in the narrowest of senses to job applicants. Since jobs carry responsibilities as well as benefits, society can legitimately complain if its welfare is sacrificed by a policy which leaves those responsibilities unfulfilled. And victims of avoidable irresponsibility (avoidable through a different system of distributive justice or alternative rule for hiring) can complain not only of incompetence or inconvenience, but of injustice. Another way of expressing this is to say, as we said in the last section, that the public has a right to be spared such avoidable harm. . . .

That the egalitarian argument fails becomes more

clear if we seriously consider its alternative to hiring by competence, for the central question in this section is whether randomization is more just as claimed, given the present educational system and pay scales. Is a job lottery, which equalizes chances for desirable positions, the ideal of distributive justice in this area, given present inequalities as frozen into education and pay scales? The general principle, . . . which does seem sound in general, is that when shares are unalterably unequal, it is fair, other things being equal, to equalize chances for unequal shares; but of course the crucial issue here, which is generally the case in debates on equality, is whether other things are equal, here regarding job applicants. The central problem for establishing any rule of hiring is the stipulation of criteria regarding which characteristics of individuals are to be considered relevant in awarding the positions. Is winning a lottery to be the only relevant characteristic? It seems at first glance (but I believe at first glance only) the most truly egalitarian.

The central complaint against hiring by competence without sufficient compensatory mechanisms in the educational system was that it tended to reward initial differences for which the agents could claim no responsibility. But certainly a process of random selection in the job market, aside from losses in efficiency, comes out worse on this score. It can be admitted that differences in competence for various positions constitute reasonable barometers of prior efforts to acquire competence only where the educational system has attempted to correct for initial inequalities. But even when such remedial efforts are lacking, the acquisition of competence still represents the expenditure of some effort in a socially desirable way, although the effort is not strictly proportional to the degree of competence acquired. The question is whether it is more just to ignore socially productive effort altogether and make all reward a matter of pure chance, which seems implausible or inconsistent if the only complaint against hiring by competence was that it rewarded chance factors to some degree. The effect of a lottery at any level is to negate differences in previous efforts, and if the cost of negating initial social differences (which can be equalized otherwise) is to render all effort meaningless as a measure of desert as well, it hardly seems worth it from the point of view of distributive justice.

The argument in favor of randomization now becomes that although it awards jobs on the basis of pure chance, at least it equalizes the chances—if benefits are to be doled out according to rolls of the dice, at least the dice should not be loaded. While the dice are loaded at present in favor of the rich, the talented and the intelligent, randomizing the process of hiring restores the balance which should have been restored by the neglectful educational and economic systems. In reply it could be argued first that in the original Book of Life all had equal chances at intelligence, etc., which is just a colourful way of saying that how intelligent you are or who your parents happen to be *is* a matter of chance from your point of view: it is simply a matter of chance operating further in the past. It makes a difference whether the chance factor operated in the past or in the present in the form of a job lottery, however, since in the interim have occurred the efforts of those who have attained requisite skills. Second, there is an important difference ignored in the above argument between correcting for inequalities in the educational or tax systems and annihilating them at the final bell in the hiring process. For there is a limit to the justifiable neglect of those with superior talents, motivation and monetary assets, and their efforts should be ignored no more than those less fortunate once reasonable attempts have been made to motivate the latter and make their success possible.

The real contrast still reduces to that between rewarding chance versus rewarding effort and past and potential social contribution, and it still seems that a random lottery for hiring is the worst of all possible worlds by these criteria. Where there is no ulterior social purpose in the reward of some benefit than the distribution of some windfall good, and where furthermore no previous actions of the individuals in question can be seen to create differential rights or deserts to the goods, a random process of choosing is fairest. This follows from the presumption of equality of persons deduced in the first section. But when positions are assigned for socially productive purposes, and when individuals are therefore encouraged to direct their efforts towards fulfilling these purposes, past and potential productivity achieved through these efforts cannot be justly ignored. The same points apply to a lesser extent to randomization for those above a certain minimal level of competence, and in any case the egalitarian's reasoning must lead him to suggest this only for reasons of efficiency and not justice, which he takes to be distinct. Total randomization functions as the

ideal of egalitarian justice in this area (given that jobs and their rewards must be unequal), and it is therefore relevant to argue as I have that it is a misconceived ideal. . . .

Bernard R. Boxill

THE MORALITY OF PREFERENTIAL HIRING

Bernard R. Boxill seeks to rebut two objections to preferential hiring. The first is that preferential hiring benefits just those from among the groups that have suffered discrimination who do not deserve compensation. The second objection is that preferential hiring is unfair to young white men. Against the first objection, Boxill argues that even if those who benefit from preferential hiring are less deserving of compensation than others, they still do deserve to receive the compensation of preferential hiring. Against the second objection, Boxill argues that even if white males have not individually wronged blacks and women, they have unfairly benefited from such wrongs. Accordingly, it is not unfair to require white males to compensate blacks and women to the degree that they have unfairly benefited.

MANY PHILOSOPHERS HAVE HELD that preferential hiring is morally objectionable. They do not object to the compensation of those who have suffered from various forms of discrimination, but hold, rather, that preferential hiring is not, for a number of reasons, an appropriate method of compensation.[1] In this essay I rebut two of the principal arguments raised against preferential hiring, namely (1) that preferential hiring benefits just those from among the groups that have suffered discrimination who do not deserve compensation, and (2) that preferential hiring is unfair to young white men.

I

The most common version of the first argument, always dragged out with an air of having played a

trump, is that since those of discriminated groups who benefit from preferential hiring must be minimally qualified, they are not those of the group who deserve compensation. Alan Goldman, for example, argues this way: "Since hiring within the preferred group still depends upon relative qualifications and hence upon past opportunities for acquiring qualifications, there is in fact a reverse ratio established between past discriminations and present benefits, so that those who most benefit from the program, those who actually get jobs, are those who least deserve to." But surely to argue from the above to the conclusion that preferential hiring is unjustified is a non sequitur. Let us grant, that qualified blacks, for example, are less deserving of compensation than unqualified blacks, that those who most deserve

---

compensation should be compensated first, and finally that preferential hiring is a form of compensation. How does it follow that preferential hiring of qualified blacks is unjustified? Surely, the assumption that unqualified blacks are more deserving of compensation than qualified blacks does not require us to conclude that qualified blacks deserve no compensation. Because I have lost only one leg, I may be less deserving of compensation than another who has lost two legs, but it does not follow that I deserve no compensation at all.

Much the same can be said of Simon's somewhat less contentious argument that "preferential hiring policies award compensation to . . . those who have the ability and qualifications to be seriously considered for the jobs available. Surely it is far more plausible to think that collective compensation ought to be equally available to all group members." But again, from the fact that preferential hiring does not award compensation to "all group members" how does it follow that preferential hiring is unjustified compensation to those of the group who "have the ability and qualifications"? It is easy to turn Simon's argument against him. If "all group members" should be compensated, then why insinuate that the qualified ones should be left out? And, if they should not be left out, why not compensate them in the manner best suited to their situation and aspirations—with good jobs—and compensate the unqualified in the manner best suited to their situation—cash settlements, remedial training, and so on.

The premise which would make the above argument less objectionable and which these critics of preferential hiring have not appeared to notice is that compensation can be made to only one section of the group—either the qualified or the unqualified, but not both. Given that the unqualified are most deserving of compensation, then a case should be mounted for claiming that, in the circumstances, preferential hiring should not be instituted because it takes from those who are most deserving of compensation (the unqualified) to give to those who are less deserving (the qualified). But it should be noted that even with the above premise, the argument does not quite yield what the critics want. For they want to show that preferential hiring of qualified minorities is unjustified *tout court*. And that is much more than showing that it is impracticable.

Now suppose the critics say that they meant that qualified blacks, for example, are not simply less deserving of compensation than unqualified blacks but that they deserve no compensation at all, just because they are qualified. The previous argument was that the ground for compensation is wrongful injury, so that if qualified blacks are generally less wronged they are therefore less deserving of compensation than unqualified blacks. The present argument is that the ground for compensation is not wrongful injury but, rather, lack of qualifications. In other words, though qualified blacks are discriminated against or suffer wrongful injury, their qualifications exclude them from consideration for compensation. Thus, James W. Nickel, who is one of the very few to have noticed the complication that discriminated persons can overcome the handicap of discrimination, adopts this last view. Allowing that it is perhaps only the least "problematic approach," he determines that "the ones who have a right to compensation are those who have personally been injured by discrimination and who have not been able to overcome this injury."

But why should this be so? I am not questioning that on practical grounds we may be unable to compensate the qualified members of a generally discriminated group. I am questioning that just because a person has overcome his injury, he no longer has a right to compensation. Nickel himself gives no argument, but it may be that he mistakenly narrows the grounds for compensation.

Certainly the unqualified person is hurt and probably harmed. He is hurt in the sense that he will lose out to the qualified in the competition for jobs. And he is harmed too, if his lack of qualification involves a stunting of his intellectual and moral development. But though these are grounds for saying that he deserves compensation, they are not the only ones. For, as I have argued in an earlier essay, there are at least two very different grounds for compensation or reparation. One ground looks forward; it evaluates present harms and, disregarding whether or not they are due to wrong, seeks to remedy them to secure some future good. The other looks backward; it seeks to rectify past injustices and can ignore whether or not the victims are *now* in a sorry state. Thus, I do not dispute that the unqualified have a claim to compensation—whether or not they have been wronged. What I do dispute is that just because they have overcome their injuries the qualified have no claim to compensation. For if they have overcome their injuries, they have borne the costs of compensation that should be borne by those who inflicted the injuries. If I am swindled and by time and effort retrieve my money, shouldn't I be compensated for my time and effort? Or if I have plenty of money and hire a good lawyer, shouldn't I also claim from my swindlers the money I paid the lawyer?

The costs, in time and effort, of overcoming an injury have results other than overcoming the injury. A person who has worked hard and long to overcome an injury is not what he would have been had he never been injured. He may be better, or he may be worse. Adversity can strengthen or it can merely harden. Thus middle-class blacks are alternately praised for their toughness and deprecated for their insensitivity. But these side-effects of the cost of overcoming wrongful injury are not the main issue. In particular, though I may be a better person for prevailing over unfair obstacles, this does not absolve my injurers from the obligation to compensate me.

Consequently, being harmed is not the only ground for deserving compensation. There is also the ground of simply having been wronged. Goldman, for example, has overlooked this. Repeatedly he stresses that qualified blacks are the least harmed of blacks, while ignoring that this does not entail they have not been wronged. "Do we want a policy which inverts the ratio of past harm to present benefit . . . ?" he asks, pointing to the "inconsistency of compensating past harm with benefits to those harmed least . . ." and to the fact that "the beneficiaries of affirmative action, with the exception of certain blue collar workers, are generally not economically depressed." But this view overlooks that being unqualified and economically depressed are not the only grounds for compensation.

This does not affect the proposition that unqualified blacks are more deserving of compensation than qualified blacks. Irving Thalberg, for example, asks us to consider two groups of persons K' and K''. K' consists of persons who, despite "dreadful persecution," now manage to hold their own in the larger society, and K'' consists of persons who, though "never oppressed," now are at the "bottom of the socioeconomic-political pecking order." Which of

these groups, he asks us, "most deserve special treatment?" It is clear that, though they are admittedly not at all the victims of injustice, he is himself inclined to choose K''. But though Thalberg takes this position, he does not at all commit himself to the claim that K' deserves nothing. On the contrary, by stressing that "our resources are enough for one group only" he clearly implies that he would allow that K' has a claim too, though K'' has a stronger claim. Now as it happens, I agree with Thalberg, though the case I have in mind is easier than his. My case is that when we have one group, say K, whose members are equally oppressed because they are K's, those K's who nevertheless manage to qualify themselves are less deserving of compensation than those K's who fail to qualify themselves. This case is easier than Thalberg's because the people to whom he would give preference are not victims but only unqualified, while the people to whom I would give preference are both victims and unqualified.

So far I have agreed that qualified blacks are less deserving of compensation than unqualified blacks. And I have agreed that this is because they may be less harmed and perhaps less wronged than unqualified blacks. What I reject is the facile assumption that this in any way implies or suggests that preferential hiring is unjustified. My premise—which at first seemed to be allowed by critics of preferential hiring—is that qualified blacks, though perhaps less harmed or wronged than unqualified blacks, are still harmed and wronged or, at least, still wronged. But it is just this premise that now seems to be denied. Thus Goldman first makes the claim (which I can allow) that in the preferential hiring of qualified minority candidates, there is "an inverse ratio established between past discrimination and present benefits." But then, on the next page, he makes the very much stronger claim—which does not at all follow from the first—that preferential hiring "singles out for benefits within a generally unjustly treated minority just that minority that has not been unjustly treated."

This confusion between being the *least* wronged and harmed of a group and being only *slightly*, or not at all, harmed or wronged is essential to the present objection to preferential hiring. Thus, since preferential hiring has been proposed as giving the edge to persons characterized by some group quality—for example, being black—the question has been raised about how high the correlation is between being black and being harmed or wronged. We may agree, I trust, that it must be very high. Goldman, for example, does not deny this. It is only perfect correlation, that "every member of the group has suffered from unjust denial of a job or of a decent education" that he labels a "drastic claim." But if so, then the serious objection to preferential hiring as a practice cannot be that a tiny fraction of qualified blacks will get breaks they do not deserve. Surely, if this is the only practical way to help a group, the vast majority of which fully deserves compensation, that objection would be only grudging. But I contend that it is not the serious objection. The serious objection is that no qualified blacks deserve compensation. And that, I submit, can seem plausible only if we confuse being less harmed and wronged than others of their group with being only slightly, or not at all, harmed and wronged.

Suppose, however, that there is not a high correlation between being harmed or wronged and being black. This is an important possibility for, if true, it undoes the argument in the preceding paragraph. Blackstone, for example, after noting the unexceptional proposition that there is "no invariable connection between a person's being black or female and suffering from past invidious discrimination," leaps to the conclusion that there are lots of blacks who have suffered from no invidious discrimination. Thus, he writes, "there are many blacks . . . who are highly advantaged, who are the sons and daughters of well educated and affluent lawyers, doctors and industrialists. A policy of reverse discrimination would mean that such highly advantaged individuals would receive preferential treatment over the sons and daughters of disadvantaged whites . . . I submit that such a situation is not social justice." Now this may seem like a commendable effort to define the groups deserving compensation in socioeconomic, rather than racial, terms. But it raises troubling questions. Why does Blackstone assume so easily, for example, that "reverse discrimination" would mean that the "highly advantaged" blacks he speaks of would be getting preferred treatment over disadvantaged whites? I would have thought that being so advantaged they would likely be vying with their peers—the highly advantaged sons and daughters of white doctors, lawyers, and industrialists—leaving the sons and daughters of disadvantaged blacks to

get preferential treatment over the children of disadvantaged whites. If, with all their advantages, the black people Blackstone describes are still reduced to competing against disadvantaged whites then all the more would it seem that they have been harmed most deeply and grievously.

Taken at its best, Blackstone's objection may be that preferential hiring gives an unfair edge to advantaged blacks who have lost out in the competition for jobs and places. Unquestionably, preferential hiring gives such blacks an edge over disadvantaged blacks. Since, however, this is the edge the middle-class has over the lower class, to make his objection stick, Blackstone should recommend sweeping changes in the class structure. But Blackstone makes no such recommendation. Preferential hiring would give an unfair edge to advantaged blacks over disadvantaged whites, if the positions and places it serves them would otherwise go to disadvantaged whites. But this would be so only if the competition they have "lost out" in were fair. Since the small number of blacks gaining desirable positions and places shows the competition is not fair, the edge advantaged blacks gain is over advantaged whites.

In arriving at the above claim, I have left several assumptions unstated. The most obvious is that the black and white groups are roughly equal in native talent and intelligence. If they are not, then unless differences in native ability between the groups are remediable and justice requires that they be removed, it is not at all clear that the lower qualifications of blacks are any indication that they had been wronged. Fortunately, this difficulty can be avoided. The weight of informed opinion is against Jensen, but even if it is ultimately shown to have some merit, his theory that as a group blacks have less native intellectual talent than whites is, for now, extremely controversial. Jensen himself, though regrettably not chary enough in proposing policies based on this theory, is tentative enough in stating it. Consequently, given its present uncertainty and the great injustice that would be wreaked on a people if it proved false and educational policies were based on it, I submit that we are not warranted now in basing any policies on it.

A more serious attempt to explain the group differences in qualifications between blacks and whites is to attribute them to cultural differences. This is a complex issue. Though controversial, it cannot be swept aside in the manner of the last objection. For it has several different versions which must be considered separately. The first, with which we are all by now familiar, is that the tests administered for admission to colleges and professional schools are culturally biased, giving an unfair advantage to white applicants. This version is irrelevant. It explains, perhaps, why blacks are underrepresented in positions of responsibility and wealth, but it does not purport to show that underrepresentation is just. The second version, more to the point, is that blacks simply are not as interested as whites in society's positions of affluence and prestige. Barry Gross suggests this line in his argument that underrepresentation is no clear indication of discrimination: "The members of a group might simply lack interest in certain jobs (for example, Italians in the public school system are in short supply)." But this analogy fails, though Gross does not appear to notice it, when applied to the case of blacks. For it isn't as if blacks are underrepresented in the public school system or in law or in banking or in the professions. It is that they are underrepresented in all of these. Consequently, though Gross may be right that "sociologically, groups are simply not represented in various jobs and at various levels in percentages closely approximating their percentage of the population," he fails to see that the case of blacks presents a matter of an altogether different order. Lack of interest in this or in that area—presumably culturally determined—may explain away underrepresentation of a cultural group in this or in that area. Unless, however, we assume that some cultures have no interest in any of the traditional areas, we cannot explain a group's general underrepresentation in all desirable positions in society by citing cultural differences.

The more common version of the argument that cultural differences explain black underrepresentation in desirable positions is not that blacks lack an interest in these positions but that they lack the discipline for them. This argument is a non sequitur. Even if the traits which inhibit the success of blacks are cultural traits—supposedly a lack of appropriate work habits and discipline—it does not follow that they are not wrongful injuries. In order to survive and retain their sanity and equilibrium in impossibly unjust situations, people may have to resort to patterns of behavior and consequently may develop habits or cultural traits which are debilitating and unproductive in a more humane environment. I see no reason why these cultural traits—which may be deeply ingrained and extremely difficult to eradicate—should not be classed as unjust injuries. It is admittedly unusual to think of cultural traits as injuries because we think of cultures as, in an important sense, self-imposed. This is true of most cultures in the traditional sense of national and ethnic cultures. Such cultures come with built-in philosophical self-justifications. In the sense that participants in them necessarily have elaborate resources with which to justify themselves, they may be viewed as self-imposed. Consequently, though such cultures may encourage development of traits which inhibit advancement in modern society, it would be hazardous to call the traits injuries. At most, they would be self-imposed injuries. But not all cultures are, in that important sense, self-imposed. Certain cultures contain none of the elaborate philosophical self-justification of ordinary cultures. Thus, in describing what he called the "culture of poverty" for example, Oscar Lewis notes that though it is a genuine culture in the traditional anthropological sense, in that it provides human beings with a "design for living" it "does not provide much support . . . poverty of culture is one of the crucial traits of the culture of poverty."

But the idea that blacks form a cultural group is not notably advantageous for the critics of preferential hiring. For it can be argued that since blacks have been discriminated against as a group, they deserve compensation as a group. Further, individual blacks—in particular qualified ones—should not have to prove specific cases of discrimination against them in order to qualify for preferential treatment. But the critics claim that blacks do not comprise a group in the sense required by the argument. Goldman, for example, objects to treating blacks as a legitimate group eligible for compensatory treatment because they "do not qualify as genuine groups or social organizations in the sense in which sociologists generally use these terms." He goes on to point out that in genuine groups there is "actual interaction among members, each of whom occupies a certain position or plays a certain role in the group reciprocal to other roles, roles being reciprocal when their performances are mutually dependent." But I submit, on that very account, that cultural groups do qualify as genuine groups. There is, for example, "actual interaction" among the members of a cultural group. That interaction is, of course, not specifically economic or political. Members of a cultural group do not, for example, necessarily buy from each other or employ each other or rule each other. Still they *do* interact and that interaction is just as important as the activities already mentioned.

Members of a cultural group share basic values and ideals—that is what we mean by calling them members of the same cultural group—and they interact intellectually by exchanging ideas about these values and ideals, by clarifying, criticizing, and extending them and by severing and drawing connections between them. In this way they come better to understand themselves. All prosperous and progressive peoples engage in this bustling process of self-clarification. Some call it the cause of all progress, others the reward of progress. In either case, it is a great good. If then it is objected that blacks are underrepresented in positions of wealth and prestige because of cultural differences, then if they have been wronged as a group, preferential hiring of qualified blacks is justified as a way of compensating the group. For it needs no argument to show that the intellectually most active and advanced of a cultural group play a crucial role in the above-mentioned process of self-clarification. If then, as seems likely, they will be among those qualified, and preferential hiring will give them the opportunity to play their crucial role in the group, then it is a way of compensating the group. And it will not do to object that if blacks form a cultural group, then the qualified among them should seek employment within that group. Though cultural groups may have originally been economic units, this is no longer the case in today's world of mass migrations. There is no reason why distinct cultural groups cannot be economically integrated.

But even if blacks do not form a cultural group, then preferential hiring is still justified. For if blacks have the same basic goals, aspirations, dreams, and hopes as whites and would, if given real opportunities, work assiduously to realize them, then—given the unjustness of assuming at this stage that blacks as a group have less native intelligence than whites and given the existence of independent evidence of widespread and pervasive discrimination against

blacks—it is a reasonable assumption that the lesser merit of qualified blacks relative to qualified whites is due to injustice. . . .

II

Even if the force of all the preceding arguments is acknowledged, however, the case for preferential hiring is still not established at this point. For, while I have shown that the qualified members of groups which have been generally discriminated against deserve some compensation, I have not shown that the compensation they deserve is preferential hiring.

This issue raises two different questions. First, given that qualified minorities do deserve some compensation, why is preferential hiring the best form of compensation for them? Second, even if preferential hiring of qualified minorities is best for them, is it best or even justifiable overall? What, for example, about the costs to general productivity? Or to excellence? Most of all, perhaps, what about the costs to the young white males who will be displaced in favor of minorities? Why should the burden of compensation be placed on their shoulders slone?

Professor Thomson has already given, I think, the main answer to the first difficulty. She argues persuasively that "what blacks and women were denied was full membership in the community; and nothing can more appropriately make amends for that wrong than precisely what will make them feel they now finally have it. And that means jobs. Financial compensation . . . slips through the fingers; having a job, and discovering you do it well, yield—perhaps better than anything else—that very self-respect which blacks and women have had to do without." It is only necessary to add perhaps that particularly in the case of the qualified is it appropriate that their compensation be jobs. For by the very fact that they have taken the trouble to become qualified they show that what they want is jobs, or at least, that they are fully prepared and anxious to get jobs. Though it may be generally true that jobs will make those previously excluded finally feel that they are "part of it," it need not be generally true, that all those previously excluded will want jobs. Some may prefer "financial compensation."

But, even though it may be admitted that getting and keeping a job is an excellent thing for the self-respect and self-esteem of qualified members of minority groups—for having a job helps a person to feel he is contributing his "fair share" and, if he discovers that he does it well, also helps him to recognize and appreciate his powers—the question has been raised whether getting and keeping a job *because of preferential hiring* may not undermine self-respect. Thus Barry Gross writes that the beneficiary of preferential hiring "may come to feel himself inferior." Thomas Nagel warns that preferential hiring "cannot do much for the self-esteem of those who know they have benefited from it, and it may threaten the self-esteem of those in the favored group who would in fact have gained their positions even in the absence of the discriminatory policy, but who cannot be sure that they are not among its beneficiaries." Thomas Sowell cautions that though "here and there, this program has undoubtedly caused some individuals to be hired who would otherwise not have been hired . . . even that is a doubtful gain in the larger context of attaining self-respect and the respect of others."

Though evidently closely related, these objections are not all quite the same. Gross' objection, for example, seems to be that a person preferentially hired for a job for which he is incompetent or who is outclassed by his colleagues will come to feel inferior. This is true but irrelevant, for preferential hiring does not require that incompetents be hired or that a candidate be hired who will be outclassed by his colleagues. The points made by Nagel and Sowell overlap but raise two distinct difficulties. On the one hand, the difficulty may be that the beneficiary of preferential hiring may lose self-respect because he may fear that he is getting what he does not deserve. I admit that a person who accepts what he knows he does not deserve (or have a right to) and knows he is taking away from someone more deserving acts in opposition to his self-respect and in trying to rationalize his act, may come to compromise and lose his self-respect. But I deny that this is relevant here. For the major conclusion of all the preceding arguments is that though the preferred candidate may be less excellently qualified than another candidate, he must still overall be the most deserving. Given this, the present difficulty does not arise. On the other hand, the difficulty may be that though the preferred candidate knows that he is overall the most deserving, he may still feel uneasy

and compromised because he knows he is not the most qualified or, at least, he does not know that he is the most qualified. This difficulty is quite different from the previous one. Here, the preferred candidate knows his deserts and that he is the most deserving. What he would like to be reassured about are his qualifications. This does not, however, argue against preferential hiring. For suppose preferential hiring is not instituted and that as a result more qualified but perhaps less deserving candidates are routinely hired. What about their self-respect and self-esteem? Shouldn't *they* feel their self-respect jeopardized for filling jobs others deserve more? Since this is evidently a more serious worry than the more deserving person's worry, on this point too, preferential hiring is not unjustified.

Having shown that there is every reason to believe that preferential hiring is the best form of compensatory treatment for qualified minorities and that they would suffer no severe penalties to self-respect and self-esteem from it, I turn to the question whether it is best or justifiable overall. But I shall not spend much time on the question of its costs to efficiency or excellence. I shall concentrate instead on the objection that preferential hiring is unjustified because it puts all the burden of compensation on the white male applicant.

Here again I think that Professor Thomson has proceeded in the right way. She admits first that there is no reason why the young white male applicants should bear the major costs of compensating, but then argues that though few of these have "themselves individually, done any wrongs to blacks and women . . . ," because "they have profited from the wrongs the community did" there is reason why they should bear some of the costs of compensation. In opposing the second part of her argument, Simon objects to her "assumption that if someone gains from an unjust practice for which he is not responsible and even opposes, the gain is not his and can be taken from him without injustice." What he fails to notice, however, is that if his objection stands, it just may turn out that no one should have to bear the costs of compensation and thus no compensation should be given. For though it is probably not true of actual societies, it is quite possible to conceive of a society some of whose members have gained at the expense of others because of earlier unjust practices, but none of whose members now have any responsibility for these practices. In such a society all of the beneficiaries of injustice would be analogous to the young white male applicants, and if Simon is right, those who have suffered losses because of the earlier injustice have no claim to compensation. It is important therefore to consider carefully the claim that the innocent beneficiaries of injustice owe no obligation of compensation to those from whose unfair losses they have profited.

Few of its proponents, however, have offered a sustained argument for it. Blackstone, for example, says simply that the fact that the white male applicant has profited from past injustice is "inadequate" ground to exact compensation from him, and Simon seems to argue mainly for the minor point that if the white male applicant has himself suffered from some unjust social practice then it is "questionable" whether he owes anyone compensation. Fullinwider, however, has attempted a more thorough treatment. Conceding first what he calls the compensation principle—"he who wrongs another shall pay for the wrong"—he accuses Professor Thomson of confusing it with the "suspect" principle—"he who benefits from a wrong shall pay for the wrong." To clinch the point, Fullinwider asks us to consider the following ingenious example. A neighbor pays a construction company to pave his driveway, but someone maliciously directs the workmen to pave Fullinwider's driveway instead. Fullinwider admits that his neighbor has been "wronged and damaged" and that he himself has "benefited from the wrong." However, since he is not responsible for the wrong, he denies that he is "morally required to compensate" his neighbor by "paying" him for it.

This example makes us see that not all cases where compensation may be due are straightforward, though one kind of case clearly is. If John steals Jeff's bicycle and "gives" it to me, however innocent I may be, I have no right to it and must return it to Jeff as soon as I discover the theft. Given that this kind of example is unproblematic, in what way does it differ from Fullinwider's, which is problematic?

One difference is that whereas I can simply hand over Jeff's bicycle to him, Fullinwider cannot simply hand over the pavement in his driveway. It will be objected that the proposal was not that Fullinwider should hand over the pavement, but that

he should pay his neighbor for it. But now the case has been changed. I did not say that I had a duty to pay Jeff the cost of his bicycle. I said that I had a duty to return the bicycle to Jeff. If Jeff told me to keep the bicycle but pay him for it, I do not admit that I would have a duty to do so. I could fairly object that when I accepted the bicycle I did not believe that I would have to pay for it, and if I had thought that I would have to, I might not have accepted it. Paying for the bicycle now would impose a cost on me because I might have preferred to spend my money in a different way and, being innocent of any wrongdoing, I see no reason why I should be penalized. The point is that though the beneficiary of an injustice has no right to his advantage, if he is innocent of the injustice, he does not deserve to be penalized. Thus, where compensation is concerned, the obligations of the innocent beneficiary of injustice and of the person responsible for the injustice are quite different. Though the former has no right to his benefits, the obligation of compensation cannot impose any losses on him over and above the loss of his unfair benefits. If compensation is impossible without such loss, it is unjustified. On the other hand, in the case of the person responsible for injustice, even if compensation requires him to give up more than he has unfairly gained, it is still justified.

But though Fullinwider's example is cogent as far as it goes, it is irrelevant as an argument against preferential hiring. It is cogent as far as it goes because, as the above analysis shows, requiring young white males to pay women and minorities all the unfair advantages they enjoyed would indeed be unfair. The advantages cannot simply be transferred from their hands into those of the preferred group as in my example of the bicycle. Compensation of this form would impose on young white males costs in time and effort over and above the costs of the unfair advantages they are required to return. They could with justice protest that they are being penalized because they might not have accepted the advantages had they known what it would cost them—now they are "out" both the advantages plus their time and effort. But though cogent, this argument is irrelevant to preferential hiring. Preferential hiring does not require young white males to pay over, at additional costs to themselves, the price of their advantages. It proposes instead to compensate the injured with goods no one yet has established a right to and in a way, therefore, which imposes no unfair losses on anyone. And these goods are, of course, jobs.

To that it may be objected that although a white male applicant may not have established a right to this or that job, he has a right to a fair competition for it, and preferential hiring violates that right. But on the contrary, by refusing to allow him to get the job because of an unfair advantage, preferential hiring makes the competition fairer. The white male applicant can still complain, of course, that had he known that preferential hiring would be instituted, he would not have accepted his advantages in the first place. Since, if he knew that preferential hiring would be instituted, he would necessarily also have known that his advantages were unfair, his complaint amounts to his saying that had he known his advantages were unfair, he would not have accepted them. But then, if he is so concerned with fairness, and if preferential hiring makes the competition fairer, he should have no objections to it. Or somewhat less contentiously, preferential hiring imposes no unfair losses on him.

Thus, a fairer application of Fullinwider's example of the driveway to preferential hiring would go as follows: Suppose an "improve your neighborhood group" offered a valuable prize for the best driveway on the block. Would Fullinwider, though he is totally innocent of his unfair advantage, be justified in insisting that he deserves to get the prize over his neighbor who has, at further cost to himself, built another somewhat inferior driveway? If someone objects that jobs are not analogous to prizes, suppose a visitor wants to rent a driveway on the block to park his car, would Fullinwider be justified in insisting that he most *deserves* to have his driveway chosen? Of course, Fullinwider can still truly point out that his driveway is the best, and perhaps if efficiency alone were the consideration, it ought to be chosen. But laying aside efficiency as I have, it is clear that it is the neighbor who most deserves that his driveway be chosen.

III

In Part I, I considered one set of objections to preferential hiring: that it compensates those who do not deserve it. At bottom these objects failed, because those who proposed them focused their attentions too exclusively on how much more fortunately placed the black middle class is than the black lower class. This made it seem as if members of the black middle class were absolutely advantaged. From being least harmed of blacks, it came to seem as if they were not appreciably harmed or not harmed at all. For balance, why not compare the black middle class with the white middle class?

Why shouldn't the black community have a vigorous and prosperous middle class as does the white community? Certainly it is a great tradition in western political philosophy that the stability and progress of a community depends on its having such a class. On the other hand, it may be, of course, as another tradition in western political philosophy has it, that there should be no classes at all. But that is another debate.

In Part II, I took up the objections against preferential hiring as a form of compensation, the most troubling of which was that young white men are compelled to bear the major costs of compensation. I admitted this point but argued that preferential hiring does not require it. What preferential hiring requires is that young white males bear some of the costs of compensation. Here I showed that though they may be innocent of wrongdoing against women and blacks, because they have had the advantage of such wrongdoing, it is not unjustified that they bear some of the costs. I conclude that no telling argument has been raised against preferential hiring.

I am indebted to Gregory Kavka, Thomas Hill, Sidney Trivus, and Jan Boxill for comments on an earlier draft of this paper.

NOTES

1. See for example, Alan H. Goldman, "Reparations to Individuals or Groups?" *Reverse Discrimination*, ed. Barry Gross (New York: Prometheus Books, 1977); Goldman, "Justice and Hiring by Competence,"

American Philosophical Quarterly 14, no. 1 (1977); Goldman "Affirmative Action," *Equality and Preferential Treatment*, ed. Marshall Cohen, Thomas Nagel, Thomas Scanlon (Princeton: Princeton University Press, 1977), pp. 192–209; Robert Simon, "Preferential Hiring: A Reply to Judith Jarvis Thomson," *Equality and Preferential Treatment*.

Steven Goldberg

THE INEVITABILITY OF PATRIARCHY

Steven Goldberg argues that the male hormonal system alone is sufficient to explain patriarchy, male dominance, and male attainment of high-status roles. This hormonal system gives males a significant "head start" toward the attainment of high-status roles. While admitting that women have been socialized away from competing with men for such roles, Goldberg argues that this is for their own good since, in a competitive struggle, most women would lose out to men because of the aggression factor. Conceding that the resulting unequal status of women amounts to "discrimination of a sort," Goldberg defends this inequality as biologically inevitable.

IF MALE AGGRESSION WERE THE ONLY DIFFERENCE . . .

AGGRESSION IS THE ONLY sexual difference that we can explain with direct (as opposed to convincing, but hypothetical) biological evidence. . .

Therefore, *we are assuming throughout this chapter that there are no differences between men and women except in the hormonal system that renders the man more aggressive.* This alone would explain patriarchy, male dominance, and male attainment of high-status roles; for the male hormonal system gives men an insuperable "head start" toward attaining those roles which any society associates with leadership or high status as long as the roles are not ones that males are biologically incapable of filling.

AGGRESSION AND ATTAINMENT

In other words, I believe that in the past we have been looking in the wrong direction for the answer to the question of why every society rewards male roles with higher status than it does female roles (even when the male tasks in one society are the female tasks in another). While it is true that men are always in the positions of authority from which status tends to be defined, male roles are not given high status primarily *because* men fill these roles; men fill these roles because their biological aggression "advantage" can be manifested *in any non-child related area rewarded by high status in any society.* (Again: the line of reasoning used in this book demonstrates only that the biological factors we discuss would make the social institutions we discuss inevitable and does not preclude the existence of other forces also leading in the same direction; there may be a biologically based tendency for women to prefer male leadership, but there need not be for male attainment of leadership and high-status roles to be inevitable.) As we shall see, this aggression "advantage" can be most manifested and can most enable men to reap status rewards *not* in those relatively homogeneous, collectivist primitive societies in which both male and female must play similar economic roles if the society is to survive or in the monarchy (which guarantees an occasional female leader); this biological factor will be given freest play in the complex, relatively individualistic, bureaucratic, democratic society which, of necessity, must emphasize organizational authority and in which social mobility is relatively free of traditional barriers to advancement. There were more female heads of state in the first two-thirds of the sixteenth century than in the first two-thirds of the twentieth.

The mechanisms involved here are easily seen if we examine any roles that males have attained by channeling their aggression toward such attainment. We will assume for now that equivalent women could *perform* the tasks of roles as well as men if they could attain the roles. Here we can speak of the corporation president, the union leader, the governor, the chairman of an association, or any other role or position for which aggression is a precondition for attainment. Now the environmentalist and the feminist will say that the fact that all such roles are nearly always filled by men is attributable not to male aggression but to the fact that women have not been allowed to enter the competitive race to attain these positions, that they have been told that these positions are in male areas, and that girls are socialized away from competing with boys in general. Women *are* socialized in this way, but again we must ask why. If innate male aggression has nothing to do with male attainment of positions of authority and status in the political, academic, scientific, or financial spheres, if aggression has nothing to do with the reasons why *every* society socializes girls away from those areas which are given high status and away from competition in general, then why is it never the *girls* in any society who are socialized toward these areas, why is it never the nonbiological roles

played by women that have high status, why is it always boys who are told to compete, and why do women never "force" men into the low-status, nonmaternal roles that women play in every society?

These questions pose no problem if we acknowledge a male aggression that enables men to attain any nonbiological role given high status by any society. For one need merely consider the result of a society's *not* socializing women away from competitions with men, from its *not* directing girls toward roles women are more capable of playing than are men or roles with status low enough that men will not strive for them. No doubt some women would be aggressive enough to succeed in competitions with men and there would be considerably more women in high-status positions than there are now. But most women would lose in such competitive struggles with men (because men have the aggression advantage) and so most women would be forced to live adult lives as failures in areas in which society had *wanted them to succeed*. It is women, far more than men, who would never allow a situation in which girls were socialized in such a way that the vast majority of them were doomed to adult lifetimes of failure to live up to their own expectations. Now I have no doubt that there is a biological factor that gives women the desire to emphasize maternal and nurturance roles, but the point here is that we can accept the feminist assumption that there is no female propensity of this sort and still see that a society must socialize women away from roles that men will attain through their aggression. For if women did not develop an alternative set of criteria for success their sense of their own competence would suffer intolerably. It is undeniable that the resulting different values and expectations that are attached to men and women will tend to work against the aggressive woman while they work for the man who is no more aggressive. But this is the unavoidable result of the fact that most men are more aggressive than most women so that this woman, who is as aggressive as the average man, but more aggressive than most women, is an exception. Furthermore, even if the sense of competence of each sex did not necessitate society's attaching to each sex values and expectations based on those qualities possessed by each sex, observation of the majority of each sex by the population would "automatically" lead to these values and expectations being attached to men and women.

SOCIALIZATION'S CONFORMATION TO BIOLOGICAL REALITY

Socialization is the process by which society prepares children for adulthood. The way in which its goals conform to the reality of biology is seen quite clearly when we consider the method in which testosterone generates male aggression (testosterone's serially developing nature). Preadolescent boys and girls have roughly equal testosterone levels, yet young boys are far more aggressive than young girls. Eva Figes has used this observation to dismiss incorrectly the possibility of a hormone-aggression association. Now it is quite probable that the boy is more aggressive than the girl for a purely biological reason. We have seen that it is simplistic to speak simply in terms of hormone levels and that there is evidence of male-female differences in the behavior of infants shortly after birth (when differential socialization is not a plausible explanation of such differences). The fetal alteration of the boy's brain by the testosterone that was generated by his testes has probably left him far more sensitive to the aggression-related properties of the testosterone that is present during boyhood than the girl, who did not receive such alteration. But let us for the moment assume that this is not the case. This does not at all reduce the importance of the hormonal factor. For even if the boy is more aggressive than the girl only because the society allows him to be, the boy's socialization still flows from society's acknowledging biological reality. Let us consider what would happen if girls have the same innate aggression as boys and if a society did not socialize girls away from aggressive competitions. Perhaps half of the third-grade baseball team would be female. As many girls as boys would frame their expectations in masculine values and girls would develop not their feminine abilities but their masculine ones. During adolescence, however, the same assertion of the male chromosomal program that causes the boys to grow beards raises their testosterone level, and their potential for aggression, to a level far above that of the adolescent woman. If society did not teach young girls that beating boys at competitions was unfeminine (behavior inappropriate for a woman), if it did not socialize them away from

the political and economic areas in which aggression leads to attainment, these girls would grow into adulthood with self-images based not on succeeding in areas for which biology has left them better prepared than men, but on competitions that most women could not win. If women did not develop feminine qualities as girls (assuming that such qualities do not spring automatically from female biology) then they would be forced to deal with the world in the aggressive terms of men. They would lose every source of power their feminine abilities now give them and they would gain nothing. . . .

DISCRIMINATION OF A SORT

If one is convinced that sexual biology gives the male an advantage in aggression, competitiveness, and dominance, but he does not believe that it engenders in men and women different propensities, cognitive aptitudes, and modes of perception, and if he considers it discrimination when male aggression leads to attainment of position even when aggression is not relevant to the task to be performed, then the unavoidable conclusion is that discrimination so defined is unavoidable. Even if one is convinced from the discussion in the following sections that the differing biological substrates that underlie the mental apparatus of men and women *do* engender different propensities, cognitive aptitudes, and modes of perception, he will probably agree that the relevance of this to male attainment of male roles is small when compared to the importance of male biological aggression to attainment. Innate tendencies to specific aptitudes *would* indicate that at any given level of competence there will be more men than women or vice versa (depending on the qualities relevant to the task) and that the very best will, in all probability, come from the sex whose potentials are relevant to the task. Nonetheless, drastic sexual differences in occupational and authority roles reflect male aggression and society's acknowledgment of it far more than they do differences in aptitudes, yet they are still inevitable.

In addition, even if artificial means were used to place large numbers of women in authority positions, it is doubtful that stability could be maintained.

Even in our present male bureaucracies problems arise whenever a subordinate is more aggressive than his superior and, if the more aggressive executive is not allowed to rise in the bureaucracy, delicate psychological adjustments must be made. Such adjustments are also necessary when a male bureaucrat has a female superior. When such situations are rare exceptions adjustments can be made without any great instability occurring, particularly if the woman in the superior position complements her aggression with sensitivity and femininity. It would seem likely, however, that if women shared equally in power at each level of the bureaucracy, chaos would result for two reasons. Even if we consider the bureaucracy as a closed system, the excess of male aggression would soon manifest itself either in men moving quickly up the hierarchy or in a male refusal to acknowledge female authority. But a bureaucracy is not a closed system, and the discrepancy between male dominance in private life and bureaucratic female dominance (from the point of view of the male whose superior is a woman) would soon engender chaos. Consider that even the present minute minority of women in high authority positions expend enormous amounts of energy trying *not* to project the commanding authority that is seen as the mark of a good male executive. It is true that the manner in which aggression is manifested will be affected by the values of the society in general and the nature of the field of competition in particular; aggression in an academic environment is camouflaged far more than in the executive arena. While a desire for control and power and a single-mindedness of purpose are no doubt relevant, here aggression is not easily defined. One might inject the theoretical argument that women could attain positions of authority and leadership by countering the male's advantage in aggression with feminine abilities. Perhaps, but the equivalents of the executive positions in every area of suprafamilial life in every society have been attained by men, and there seems no reason to believe that, suddenly, feminine means will be capable of neutralizing male aggression in these areas. And, in any case, an emphasis on feminine abilities is hardly what the feminists desire. All of this can be seen in a considerably more optimistic light, from the point of view of most women, if one considers that the biological abilities possessed only by women are complemented by biologically generated propensities directing women to roles that can be filled only by women. But it is still the same picture.

FIFTY-ONE PERCENT OF THE VOTE

Likewise, one who predicates political action on a belief that a society is oppressive until half of the positions of authority are filled by women faces the insuperable task of overcoming a male dominance that has forced every political and economic system to conform to it and that may be maintained as much by the refusal of women to elect widespread female leadership as by male aggression and ability. No doubt an exceptional configuration of factors will someday result in a woman's being elected president, but if one considers a society "sexist" until it no longer associates authority primarily with men and until a woman leader is no longer an exception, then he must resign himself to the certainty that all societies will be "sexist" forever. Feminists make much of the fact that women constitute a slight majority of voters but in doing so make the assumption that it is possible to convince the women who constitute this majority to elect equal female leadership. This is a dubious assumption since the members of a society will inevitably associate authority with males if patriarchy and male dominance are biologically inevitable. It would be even more dubious if there is an innate tendency for women to favor men who "take the lead." However, proceeding from this assumption and assuming that the feminists were successful, it is a sure bet that democracy—which obviously is not biologically inevitable (not patriarchy, which is)—would be eliminated as large numbers of males battled for the relatively small numbers of positions of power from which the rules that govern the battle are made. In any real society, of course, women can have the crucial effect of mobilizing political power to achieve particular goals and of electing those men who are motivated by relatively more life-sustaining values than other men just as mothers have the crucial effect of coloring and humanizing the values of future male leaders.

"OPPRESSION"

All of this indicates that the theoretical model that conceives of male success in attaining positions of status, authority, and leadership as *oppression* of the female is incorrect if only because it sees male aggressive energies as *directed toward* females and sees the institutional mechanisms that flow from the fact of male aggression as *directed toward* "oppressing" women. In reality these male energies are directed toward attainment of desired positions and toward succeeding in whatever areas a particular society considers important. The fact that women lose out in these competitions, so that the sex-role expectations of a society would have to become different for men and women even if they were not different for other reasons, is an inevitable byproduct of the reality of the male's aggression advantage and not the cause, purpose, or primary function of it. In other words, men who attain the more desired roles and positions do so because they channel their aggression advantage toward such attainment; whether the losers in such competitions are other men or women is important only in that—because so few women succeed in these competitions—the society will attach different expectations to men and women (making it more difficult for the exceptional, aggressive, woman to attain such positions even when her aggression is equal to that of the average man). Perhaps one could at least begin to defend a model that stressed "oppression" if he dealt only with male dominance in dyadic relationships; here male energies are directed toward the female, but to call that which is inevitable "oppression" would seem to confuse more than clarify and, if one feels that male dominance is "oppressive," this model offers an illusory hope of change where there is no possibility of change. Male dominance is the emotional resolution (felt by both the man and the woman) of the difference between a man and a woman in the biological factors relevant to aggression; male authority in dyadic relationships, and the socialization of boys and girls toward this male authority, is societal conformation to this biological difference and a result of society's attempting to most smoothly and effectively utilize this difference. Note that all that I say in this paragraph—indeed, in this book—accepts the feminist assumption that women do not follow their own biologically generated imperatives, which are eternally different from those of men. I do this in an attempt to show the inadequacy of the feminist model and not because it is less than ludicrous to suppose that women do not hear their own drummer. This book does not pretend to explain female behavior, but merely to show that women would have to behave as they do if they were nothing more than less aggressive men. If one reversed the feminist model he could view the desire of the vast majority of women to have children as oppressing men by succeeding in an area in which men are doomed by their biology to fail. Such a theoretical model leaves much to be desired.

Evelyn Reed

WOMEN: CASTE, CLASS OR OPPRESSED SEX?

Evelyn Reed argues that the inferior status of women did not result from any biological deficiency as a sex. Rather, its origins can be traced to the appearance of class-divided societies with their institutions of the patriarchal family, private property, and state power. Against those who claim that the oppression of women derives from their belonging to a separate caste or class, Reed points out that women have always belonged to both superior and inferior castes and classes. Thus Reed concludes that full female liberation can only come as part of a social revolution which liberates the entire working class.

THE NEW STAGE IN the struggle for women's liberation already stands on a higher ideological level than did the feminist movement of the last century. Many of the participants today respect the Marxist analysis of capitalism and subscribe to Engels's classic explanation of the origins of women's oppression. It came about through the development of class society, founded upon the family, private property, and the state.

But there still remain considerable misunderstandings and misinterpretations of Marxist positions, which have led some women who consider themselves radicals or socialists to go off course and become theoretically disoriented. Influenced by the myth that women have always been handicapped by their childbearing functions, they tend to attribute the roots of women's oppression, at least in part, to biological sexual differences. In actuality its causes are exclusively historical and social in character.

Some of these theorists maintain that women constitute a special class or caste. Such definitions are not only alien to the views of Marxism but lead to the false conclusion that it is not the capitalist system but men who are the prime enemy of women. I propose to challenge this contention.

The findings of the Marxist method, which have laid the groundwork for explaining the genesis of woman's degradation, can be summed up in the following propositions:

First, women were not always the oppressed or "sec- *ond" sex. Anthropology, or the study of prehistory, tells us the contrary. Throughout primitive society, which was the epoch of tribal collectivism, women were the equals of men and recognized by man as such.*

Second, the downfall of women coincided with the breakup of the matriarchal clan commune and its replacement by class-divided society with its institutions of the patriarchal family, private property and state power.

The key factors which brought about this reversal in woman's social status came out of the transition from a hunting and food-gathering economy to a far higher mode of production based upon agriculture, stock raising and urban crafts. The primitive division of labor between the sexes was replaced by a more complex social division of labor. The greater efficiency of labor gave rise to a sizable surplus product, which led first to differentiations and then to deepgoing divisions among the various segments of society.

By virtue of the directing roles played by men in large-scale agriculture, irrigation and construction projects, as well as in stock raising, this surplus wealth was gradually appropriated by a hierarchy of men as their private property. This, in turn, required the institution of marriage and the family to fix the legal ownership and inheritance of a man's property. Through monogamous marriage the wife was brought under the complete control of her husband who was thereby assured of legitimate sons to inherit his wealth.

As men took over most of the activities of social

From "Women: Caste, Class or Oppressed Sex?" in *Problems of Women's Liberation* (1970) pp. 64–76. © 1970 by International Socialist Review. Reprinted by permission of Pathfinder Press, Inc.

production, and with the rise of the family institution, women became relegated to the home to serve their husbands and families. The state apparatus came into existence to fortify and legalize the institutions of private property, male dominion and the father-family, which later were sanctified by religion.

This, briefly, is the Marxist approach to the origins of woman's oppression. Her subordination did not come about through any biological deficiency as a sex. It was the result of the revolutionary social changes which destroyed the equalitarian society of the matriarchal gens or clan and replaced it with a patriarchal class society which, from its birth, was stamped with discriminations and inequalities of many kinds, including the inequality of the sexes. The growth of this inherently oppressive type of socioeconomic organization was responsible for the historic downfall of women.

But the downfall of women cannot be fully understood, nor can a correct social and political solution be worked out for their liberation, without seeing what happened at the same time to men. It is too often overlooked that the patriarchal class system which crushed the matriarchy and its communal social relations also shattered its male counterpart, the fratriarchy—or tribal brotherhood of men. Woman's overthrow went hand in hand with the subjugation of the mass of toiling men to the master class of men.

The import of these developments can be more clearly seen if we examine the basic character of the tribal structure which Morgan, Engels and others described as a system of "primitive communism." The clan commune was both a sisterhood of women and a brotherhood of men. The sisterhood of women, which was the essence of the matriarchy, denoted its collectivist character. The women worked together as a community of sisters: their social labors largely sustained the whole community. They also raised their children in common. An individual mother did not draw distinctions between her own and her clan sisters' progeny, and the children in turn regarded all the older sisters as their mutual mothers. In other words, communal production and communal possessions were accompanied by communal child-raising.

The male counterpart of this sisterhood was the brotherhood, which was molded in the same communal pattern as the sisterhood. Each clan or phratry of clans comprising the tribe was regarded as a

"brotherhood" from the male standpoint just as it was viewed as a "sisterhood" or "motherhood" from the female standpoint. In this matriarchal-brotherhood the adults of both sexes not only produced the necessities of life together but also provided for and protected the children of the community. These features made the sisterhood and brotherhood a system of "primitive communism."

Thus, before the family that had the individual father standing at its head came into existence, the functions of fatherhood were a *social*, not a *family* function of men. More than this, the earliest men who performed the services of fatherhood were not the mates or "husbands" of the clan sisters but rather their clan brothers. This was not simply because the processes of physiological paternity were unknown in ancient society. More decisively, this fact was irrelevant in a society founded upon collectivist relations of production and communal child-raising.

However odd it may seem to people today, who are so accustomed to the family form of child-raising, it was perfectly natural in the primitive commune for the clan brothers, or "mothers' brothers," to perform the paternal functions for their sisters' children that were later taken over by the individual father for his wife's children.

The first change in this sister-brother clan system came with the growing tendency for pairing couples, or "pairing families" as Morgan and Engels called them, to live together in the same community and household. However, this simple cohabitation did not substantially alter the former collectivist relations or the productive role of the women in the community. The sexual division of labor which had formerly been allotted between clan sisters and brothers became gradually transformed into a sexual division of labor between husbands and wives.

But so long as collectivist relations prevailed and women continued to participate in social production, the original equality between the sexes more or less persisted. The whole community continued to sustain the pairing units, just as each individual member of these units made his and her contribution to the labor activities.

Consequently, the pairing family, which appeared at the dawn of the family system, differed radically from the nuclear family of our times. In our ruthless competitive capitalist system every tiny family must sink or swim through its own efforts—it cannot count on assistance from outside sources. The wife is dependent upon the husband while the children must look to the parents for their subsistence, even if the wage earners who support them are stricken by unemployment, sickness or death. In the period of the pairing family, however, there was no such system of dependency upon "family economics," since the whole community took care of each individual's basic needs from the cradle to the grave.

This was the material basis for the absence, in the primitive commune, of those social oppressions and family antagonisms with which we are so familiar.

It is sometimes said or implied that male domination has always existed and that women have always been brutally treated by men. Contrariwise, it is also widely believed that the relations between the sexes in matriarchal society were merely the reverse of our own—with women dominating men. Neither of these propositions is borne out by the anthropological evidence.

It is not my intention to glorify the epoch of savagery nor advocate a romantic return to some past "golden age." An economy founded upon hunting and food-gathering is the lowliest stage in human development, and its living conditions were rude, crude and harsh. Nevertheless, we must recognize that male and female relations in that kind of society were fundamentally different from ours.

Under the clan system of the sisterhood of women and the brotherhood of men there was no more possibility for one sex to dominate the other than there was for one class to exploit another. Women occupied the most eminent position because they were the chief producers of the necessities of life as well as the procreators of new life. But this did not make them the oppressors of men. Their communal society excluded class, racial or sexual tyranny.

As Engels pointed out, with the rise of private property, monogamous marriage and the patriarchal family, new social forces came into play in both society at large and the family setup which destroyed the rights exercised by earliest womankind. From simple cohabitation of pairing couples there arose the rigidly fixed, legal system of monogamous marriage. This brought the wife and children under the complete control of the husband and father who gave the family his name and determined their conditions of life and destiny.

Women, who had once lived and worked together

as a community of sisters and raised their children in common, now became dispersed as wives of individual men serving their lords and masters in individual households. The former equalitarian sexual division of labor between the men and women of the commune gave way to a family division of labor in which the woman was more and more removed from social production to serve as a household drudge for husband, home and family. Thus women, once "governesses" of society, were degraded under the class formations to become the governesses of a man's children and his chief housemaid.

This abasement of women has been a permanent feature of all three stages of class society, from slavery through feudalism to capitalism. So long as women led or participated in the productive work of the whole community, they commanded respect and esteem. But once they were dismembered into separate family units and occupied a servile position in home and family, they lost their prestige along with their influence and power.

Is it any wonder that such social changes should bring about intense and long-enduring antagonism between the sexes? As Engels says:

Monogamy then does by no means enter history as a reconciliation of man and wife, and still less as the highest form of marriage. On the contrary, it enters as the subjugation of one sex by the other, as the proclamation of an antagonism between the sexes unknown in all preceding history. . . . The first class antagonism appearing in history coincides with the development of the antagonism of man and wife in monogamy, and the first class oppression with that of the female by the male sex (Origin of the Family, Private Property, and the State).

Here it is necessary to note a distinction between two degrees of women's oppression in monogamous family life under the system of private property. In the productive farm family of the preindustrial age, women held a higher status and were accorded more respect than they receive in the consumer family of our own city life, the nuclear family.

So long as agriculture and craft industry remained dominant in the economy, the farm family, which was a large or "extended" family, remained a viable productive unit. All its members had vital functions to perform according to sex and age. The women in the family helped cultivate the ground and engaged in home industries as well as bearing children, while the children and older folks produced their share according to ability.

This changed with the rise of industrial and monopoly capitalism and the nuclear family. Once masses of men were dispossessed from the land and small businesses to become wage earners in factories, they had nothing but their labor power to sell to the capitalist bosses for their means of subsistence. The wives of these wage earners, ousted from their former productive farm and homecraft labors, became utterly dependent upon their husbands for the support of themselves and their children. As men became dependent upon their bosses, the wives became more dependent upon their husbands.

By degrees, therefore, as women were stripped of their economic self-dependence, they fell ever lower in social esteem. At the beginning of class society they had been removed from *social* production and social leadership to become farm-family producers, working through their husbands for home and family. But with the displacement of the productive farm family by the nuclear family of industrial city life, they were driven from their last foothold on solid ground.

Women were then given two dismal alternatives. They could either seek a husband as provider and be penned up thereafter as housewives in city tenements or apartments to raise the next generation of wage slaves. Or the poorest and most unfortunate could go as marginal workers into the mills and factories (along with the children) and be sweated as the most downtrodden and underpaid section of the labor force.

Over the past generations women wage workers have conducted their own labor struggles or fought along with men for improvements in their wages and working conditions. But women as dependent housewives have had no such means of social struggle. They could only resort to complaints or wrangles with husband and children over the miseries of their lives. The friction between the sexes became deeper and sharper with the abject dependency of women and their subservience to men.

Despite the hypocritical homage paid to womankind as the "sacred mother" and devoted homemaker, the *worth* of women sank to its lowest point under capitalism. Since housewives do not produce commodities for the market nor create any

surplus value for the profiteers, they are not central to the operations of capitalism. Only three justifications for their existence remain under this system: as breeders, as household janitors, and as buyers of consumer goods for the family.

While wealthy women can hire servants to do the dull chores for them, poor women are riveted to an endless grind for their whole lives. Their condition of servitude is compounded when they are obliged to take an outside job to help sustain the family. Shouldering two responsibilities instead of one, they are the "doubly oppressed."

Even middle-class housewives in the Western world, despite their economic advantages, are victimized by capitalism. The isolated, monotonous, trivial circumstances of their lives lead them to "living through" their children—a relationship which fosters many of the neuroses that afflict family life today. Seeking to allay their boredom, they can be played upon and preyed upon by the profiteers in the consumer goods fields. This exploitation of women as consumers is part and parcel of a system that grew up in the first place for the exploitation of men as producers.

The capitalists have ample reason for glorifying the nuclear family. Its petty household is a goldmine for all sorts of hucksters from real estate agents to the manufacturers of detergents and cosmetics. Just as automobiles are produced for individual use instead of developing adequate mass transportation, so the big corporations can make more money by selling small homes on private lots to be equipped with individual washing machines, refrigerators, and other such items. They find this more profitable than building large-scale housing at low rentals or developing community services and child-care centers.

In the second place, the isolation of women, each enclosed in a private home and tied to the same kitchen and nursery chores, hinders them from banding together and becoming a strong social force or a serious political threat to the Establishment.

What is the most instructive lesson to be drawn from this highly condensed survey of the long imprisonment of womankind in the home and family of class society—which stands in such marked contrast to their stronger, more independent position in pre-class society? It shows that the inferior status of the female sex is not the result of their biological makeup or the fact that they are the childbearers.

Childbearing was no handicap in the primitive commune; it *became* a handicap, above all, in the nuclear family of our times. Poor women are torn apart by the conflicting obligations of taking care of their children at home while at the same time working outside to help sustain the family. Women, then, have been condemned to their oppressed status by the same social forces and relations which have brought about the oppression of one class by another, one race by another, and one nation by another. It is the capitalist system—the ultimate stage in the development of class society—which is the fundamental source of the degradation and oppression of women.

Some women in the liberation movement dispute these fundamental theses of Marxism. They say that the female sex represents a separate caste or class. Ti-Grace Atkinson, for example, takes the position that women are a separate *class*: Roxanne Dunbar says that they comprise a separate *caste*. Let us examine these two theoretical positions and the conclusions that flow from them.

First, are women a caste? The caste hierarchy came first in history and was the prototype and predecessor of the class system. It arose after the breakup of the tribal commune with the emergence of the first marked differentiations of segments of society according to the new divisions of labor and social functions. Membership in a superior or inferior station was established by being born into that caste.

It is important to note, however, that the caste system was also inherently and at birth a class system. Furthermore, while the caste system reached its fullest development only in certain regions of the world, such as India, the class system evolved far beyond it to become a world system, which engulfed the caste system.

This can be clearly seen in India itself, where each of the four chief castes—the Brahmans or priests, the soldiers, the farmers and merchants, and the laborers, along with the "out-castes" or pariahs—had their appropriate places in an exploitative society. In India today, where the ancient caste system survives in decadent forms, capitalist relations and power prevail over all the inherited precapitalist institutions, including the caste relics.

However, those regions of the world which advanced fastest and farthest on the road to civilization bypassed or overleaped the caste system altogether.

Western civilization, which started with ancient Greece and Rome, developed from slavery through feudalism to the maturest stage of class society, capitalism.

Neither in the caste system nor the class system—nor in their combinations—have women comprised a separate caste or class. Women themselves have been separated into the various castes and classes which made up these social formations.

The fact that women occupy an inferior status as a *sex* does not *ipso facto* make women either an inferior caste or class. Even in ancient India women belonged to different castes, just as they belong to different classes in contemporary capitalist society. In the one case their social status was determined by birth into a caste; in the other it is determined by their own or their husband's wealth. But the two can be fused—for women as for men. Both sexes can belong to a superior caste and possess superior wealth, power and status. . . .

Turning to the other position, it is even more incorrect to characterize women as a special "class." In Marxist sociology a class is defined in two interrelated ways: by the role it plays in the processes of production and by the stake it has in the ownership of property. Thus the capitalists are the major power in our society because they own the means of production and thereby control the state and direct the economy. The wage workers who create the wealth own nothing but their labor power, which they have to sell to the bosses to stay alive.

Where do women stand in relation to these polar class forces? They belong to all strata of the social pyramid. The few at the top are part of the plutocratic class: more among us belong to the middle class: most of us belong to the proletarian layers of the population. There is an enormous spread from the few wealthy women of the Rockefeller, Morgan and Ford families to the millions of poor women who subsist on welfare dole. *In short, women, like men, are a multiclass sex.*

This is not an attempt to divide women from one another but simply to recognize the actual divisions that exist. The notion that all women as a sex have more in common than do members of the same class with one another is false. Upper-class women are not simply bedmates of their wealthy husbands. As a rule they have more compelling ties which bind them together. They are economic, social and political bedmates, united in defense of private property, profiteering, militarism, racism—and the exploitation of other women.

To be sure, there can be individual exceptions to this rule, especially among young women today. We remember that Mrs. Frank Leslie, for example, left a $2 million bequest to further the cause of women's suffrage, and other upper-class women have devoted their means to secure civil rights for our sex. But it is quite another matter to expect any large number of wealthy women to endorse or support a revolutionary struggle which threatens their capitalist interests and privileges. Most of them scorn the liberation movement, saying openly or implicitly, "What do we need to be liberated from?". . .

It is true that all forms of class society have been male-dominated and that men are trained from the cradle on to be chauvinistic. But it is not true that men as such represent the main enemy of women. This crosses out the multitudes of downtrodden, exploited men who are themselves oppressed by the main enemy of women, which is the capitalist system. These men likewise have a stake in the liberation struggle of the women: they can and will become our allies.

Although the struggle against male chauvinism is an essential part of the tasks that women must carry out through their liberation movement, it is incorrect to make that the central issue. This tends to conceal or overlook the role of the ruling powers who not only breed and benefit from all forms of discrimination and oppression but are also responsible for breeding and sustaining male chauvinism. Let us remember that male supremacy did not exist in the primitive commune, founded upon sisterhood and brotherhood. Sexism, like racism, has its roots in the private property system.

A false theoretical position easily leads to a false strategy in the struggle for women's liberation. Such is the case with a segment of the Redstockings who state in their *Manifesto* that "women are an oppressed *class.*" If all women compose a class then all men must form a counterclass—the oppressor class. What conclusion flows from this premise? That there are no men in the oppressed class? Where does this leave the millions of oppressed white working men who, like the oppressed blacks, Chicanos and other minorities, are exploited by the monopolists? Don't they have a central place in the struggle for social revolution? At what point and under what banner do these oppressed peoples of all races and both sexes join together for common action against their common enemy? To oppose women as a class against men as a class can only result in a diversion of the real class struggle.

Isn't there a suggestion of this same line in Roxanne Dunbar's assertion that female liberation is the basis for social revolution? This is far from Marxist strategy since it turns the real situation on its head. Marxists say that social revolution is the basis for full female liberation—just as it is the basis for the liberation of the whole working class. In the last analysis the real allies of women's liberation are all those forces which are impelled for their own reasons to struggle against and throw off the shackles of the imperialist masters.

The underlying source of women's oppression, which is capitalism, cannot be abolished by women alone, nor by a coalition of women drawn from all classes. It will require a worldwide struggle for socialism by the working masses, female and male alike, together with every other section of the oppressed, to overthrow the power of capitalism, which is centered today in the United States.

In conclusion, we must ask, what are the connections between the struggle for women's liberation and the struggle for socialism?

First, even though the full goal of women's liberation cannot be achieved short of the socialist revolution, this does not mean that the struggle to secure reforms must be postponed until then. It is imperative for Marxist women to fight shoulder to shoulder with all our embattled sisters in organized actions for specific objectives from now on. This has been our policy ever since the new phase of the women's liberation movement surfaced a year or so ago, and even before.

The women's movement begins, like other movements for liberation, by putting forward elementary demands. These are: equal opportunities with men in education and jobs; equal pay for equal work; free abortions on demand; and child-care centers financed by the government but controlled by the community. Mobilizing women behind these issues not only gives us the possibility of securing some improvements but also exposes, curbs and modifies the worst aspects of our subordination in this society.

Second, why do women have to lead their own

struggles for liberation, even though in the end the combined anticapitalist offensive of the whole working class will be required for the victory of the socialist revolution? The reason is that no segment of society which has been subjected to oppression, whether it consists of Third World people or of women, can delegate the leadership and promotion of their fight for freedom to other forces—even though other forces can act as their allies. We reject the attitude of some political tendencies that say they are Marxists but refuse to acknowledge that women have to lead and organize their own independent struggle for emancipation, just as they cannot understand why blacks must do the same.

The maxim of the Irish revolutionists—"who would be free themselves must strike the blow"— fully applies to the cause of women's liberation. Women must themselves strike the blows to gain their freedom. And this holds true after the anticapitalist revolution triumphs as well as before.

In the course of our struggle, and as part of it, we will reeducate men who have been brainwashed into believing that women are naturally the inferior sex due to some flaws in their biological makeup. Men will have to learn that, in the hierarchy of oppressions created by capitalism, their chauvinism and dominance is another weapon in the hands of the master class for maintaining its rule. The exploited

worker, confronted by the even worse plight of his dependent housewife, cannot be complacent about it—he must be made to see the source of the oppressive power that has degraded them both.

Finally, to say that women form a separate caste or class must logically lead to extremely pessimistic conclusions with regard to the antagonism between the sexes in contrast with the revolutionary optimism of the Marxists. For unless the two sexes are to be totally separated, or the men liquidated, it would seem that they will have to remain forever at war with each other.

As Marxists we have a more realistic and hopeful message. We deny that women's inferiority was predestined by her biological makeup or has always existed. Far from being eternal, woman's subjugation and the bitter hostility between the sexes are no more than a few thousand years old. They were produced by the drastic social changes which brought the family, private property and the state into existence.

This view of history points up the necessity for a no less thoroughgoing revolution in socioeconomic relations to uproot the causes of inequality and achieve full emancipation for our sex. This is the purpose and promise of the socialist program, and this is what we are fighting for.

United States Supreme Court

UNIVERSITY OF CALIFORNIA V. BAKKE

The issue before the Supreme Court of the United States was whether the special admissions program of the Medical School of the University of California at Davis violated the equal protection clause of the Fourteenth Amendment. A majority of the Court decided that the "quota system" employed by the Medical School was not necessary in order to accomplish the legitimate goals of the program, and hence was in violation of the equal protection clause. A different majority of the Court (with only Justice Powell as the common member) allowed that taking race and ethnicity into account as a factor in an admission program does not violate the equal protection clause of the Fourteenth Amendment. Dissenting in part, Justice Brennan and others argued that in practice there is no real difference between a "quota" admission system and a "factor" admission system.

MR. JUSTICE POWELL ANNOUNCED the judgment of the Court.

The Medical School of the University of California at Davis opened in 1968 with an entering class of 50 students. In 1971, the size of the entering class was increased to 100 students, a level at which it remains. No admissions program for disadvantaged or minority students existed when the school opened, and the first class contained three Asians but no blacks, no Mexican-Americans, and no American Indians. Over the next two years, the faculty devised a special admissions program to increase the representation of "disadvantaged" students in each medical school class. The special program consisted of a separate admissions system operating in coordination with the regular admissions process.

Under the regular admissions procedure, a candidate could submit his application to the medical school beginning in July of the year preceding the academic year for which admission was sought. Because of the large number of applications, the admissions committee screened each one to select candidates for further consideration. Candidates whose overall undergraduate grade point averages fell below 2.5 on a scale of 4.0 were summarily rejected. About one out of six applicants was invited for a personal interview. Following the interviews, each candidate was rated on a scale of 1 to 100 by his interviewers and four other members of the admissions committee. The rating embraced the interviewers' summaries, the candidate's overall grade point average, grade point average in science courses, and scores on the Medical College Admissions Test (MCAT), letters of recommendation, extracurricular activities, and other biographical data. The ratings were added together to arrive at each candidate's "benchmark" score. Since five committee members rated each candidate in 1973, a perfect score was 500; in 1974, six members rated each candidate, so that a perfect score was 600. The full committee then reviewed the file and scores of each applicant and made offers of admission on a

"rolling" basis. The chairman was responsible for placing names on the waiting list. They were not placed in strict numerical order; instead, the chairman had discretion to include persons with "special skills."

The special admissions program operated with a separate committee, a majority of whom were members of minority groups. On the 1973 application form, candidates were asked to indicate whether they wished to be considered as "economically and/or educationally disadvantaged" applicants; on the 1974 form the question was whether they wished to be considered as members of a "minority group," which the medical school apparently viewed as "Blacks," "Chicanos," "Asians," and "American Indians." If these questions were answered affirmatively, the application was forwarded to the special admissions committee. No formal definition of "disadvantage" was ever produced, but the chairman of the special committee screened each application to see whether it reflected economic or educational deprivation. Having passed this initial hurdle, the applications then were rated by the special committee in a fashion similar to that used by the general admissions committee, except that special candidates did not have to meet the 2.5 grade point average cut-off applied to regular applicants. About one-fifth of the total number of special applicants were invited for interviews in 1973 and 1974. Following each interview, the special committee assigned each special applicant a benchmark score. The special committee then presented its top choices to the general admissions committee. The latter did not rate or compare the special candidates against the general applicants, but could reject recommended special candidates for failure to meet course requirements or other specific deficiencies. The special committee continued to recommend special applicants until a number prescribed by faculty vote were admitted. While the overall class size was still 50, the prescribed number was eight; in 1973 and 1974, when the class size had doubled to 100, the prescribed number of special admissions also doubled, to 16.

From the year of the increase in class size— 1971—through 1974, the special program resulted in the admission of 21 black students, 30 Mexican-Americans, and 12 Asians, for a total of 63 minority students. Over the same period the regular admissions program produced one black, six Mexican-Americans, and 37 Asians, for a total of 44 minority students. Although disadvantaged whites applied to the special program in large numbers, none received an offer of admission through that process. Indeed, in 1974, at least, the special committee explicitly considered only "disadvantaged" special applicants who were members of one of the designated minority groups.

Allan Bakke is a white male who applied to the Davis Medical School in both 1973 and 1974. In both years Bakke's application was considered by the general admissions program, and he received an interview. His 1973 interview was with Dr. Theodore H. West, who considered Bakke "a very desirable applicant to [the] medical school." Despite a strong benchmark score of 468 out of 500, Bakke was rejected. His application had come late in the year, and no applicants in the general admissions process with scores below 470 were accepted after Bakke's application was completed. There were four special admissions slots unfilled at that time, however, for which Bakke was not considered. After his 1973 rejection, Bakke wrote to Dr. George H. Lowrey, Associate Dean and Chairman of the Admissions Committee, protesting that the special admissions program operated as a racial and ethnic quota.

Bakke's 1974 application was completed early in the year. His student interviewer gave him an overall rating of 94, finding him "friendly, well tempered, conscientious and delightful to speak with." His faculty interviewer was, by coincidence, the same Dr. Lowrey to whom he had written in protest of the special admissions program. Dr. Lowrey found Bakke "rather limited in his approach" to the problems of the medical profession and found disturbing Bakke's "very definite opinions which were based more on his personal viewpoints than upon a study of the total problem." Dr. Lowrey gave Bakke the lowest of his six ratings, an 86; his total was 549 out of 600. Again, Bakke's application was rejected. In neither year did the chairman of the admissions committee,

Dr. Lowrey, exercise his discretion to place Bakke on the waiting list. In both years, applicants were admitted under the special program with grade point averages, MCAT scores, and bench mark scores significantly lower than Bakke's.

After the second rejection, Bakke filed the instant suit in the Superior Court of California. He sought mandatory, injunctive, and declaratory relief compelling his admission to the Medical School. He alleged that the Medical School's special admissions program operated to exclude him from the school on the basis of his race, in violation of his rights under the Equal Protection Clause of the Fourteenth Amendment, Art. I, § 21 of the California Constitution, and § 601 of Title VI of the Civil Rights Act of 1964. The University cross-complained for a declaration that its special admissions program was lawful. The trial court found that the special program operated as a racial quota, because minority applicants in the special program were rated only against one another, and 16 places in the class of 100 were reserved for them. Declaring that the University could not take race into account in making admissions decisions, the trial court held the challenged program violative of the Federal Constitution, the state constitution and Title VI. The court refused to order Bakke's admission, however, holding that he had failed to carry his burden of proving that he would have been admitted but for the existence of the special program.

Bakke appealed from the portion of the trial court judgment denying him admission, and the University appealed from the decision that its special admissions program was unlawful and the order enjoining it from considering race in the processing of applications. The Supreme Court of California transferred the case directly from the trial court, "because of the importance of the issues involved." The California court accepted the findings of the trial court with respect to the University's program. Because the special admissions program involved a racial classification, the supreme court held itself bound to apply strict scrutiny. It then turned to the goals the University presented as justifying the special program. Although the court agreed that the goals of integrating the medical profession and increasing the number of physicians willing to serve members of minority groups were compelling state interests, it concluded that the special admissions program was not the least intrusive means of achieving those goals. Without passing on the state constitutional or the federal statutory grounds cited in the trial court's judgment, the California court held that the Equal Protection Clause of the Fourteenth Amendment required that "no applicant may be rejected because of his race, in favor of another who is less qualified, as measured by standards applied without regard to race."

Turning to Bakke's appeal, the court ruled that since Bakke had established that the University had discriminated against him on the basis of his race, the burden of proof shifted to the University to demonstrate that he would not have been admitted even in the absence of the special admissions program. . . . The court initially ordered a remand for the purpose of determining whether, under the newly allocated burden of proof, Bakke would have been admitted to either the 1973 or the 1974 entering class in the absence of the special admissions program. In its petition for rehearing below, however, the University conceded its inability to carry that burden. The California court thereupon amended its opinion to direct that the trial court enter judgment ordering Bakke's admission to the medical school. That order was stayed pending review of this Court. . . .

Over the past 30 years, this Court has embarked upon the crucial mission of interpreting the Equal Protection Clause with the view of assuring to all persons "the protection of equal laws," in a Nation confronting a legacy of slavery and racial discrimination. Because the landmark decisions in this area arose in response to the continued exclusion of Negroes from the mainstream of American society, they could be characterized as involving discrimination by the "majority" white race against the Negro minority. But they need not be read as depending upon that characterization for their results. It suffices to say that "[o]ver the years, this Court consistently repudiated '[d]istinctions between citizens solely because of their ancestry' as being 'odious to a free people whose institutions are founded upon the doctrine of equality.' "

Petitioner urges us to adopt for the first time a more restrictive view of the Equal Protection Clause and hold that discrimination against members of the white "majority" cannot be suspect if its purpose can be characterized as "benign." The clock of our liberties, however, cannot be turned back to 1868. It is far too late to argue that the guarantee of equal protection to *all* persons permits the recognition of special wards entitled to a degree of protection greater than that accorded others. "The Fourteenth Amendment is not directed solely against discrimination due to a 'two-class theory'—that is, based upon differences between 'white' and Negro."

Once the artificial line of a "two-class theory" of the Fourteenth Amendment is put aside, the difficulties entailed in varying the level of judicial review according to a perceived "preferred status of a particular racial or ethnic minority are intractable. The concepts of "majority" and "minority" necessarily reflect temporary arrangements and political judgments. As observed above, the white "majority" itself is composed of various minority groups, most of which can lay claim to a history of prior discrimination at the hands of the state and private individuals. Not all of these groups can receive preferential treatment and corresponding judicial tolerance of distinctions drawn in terms of race and nationality, for then the only "majority" left would be a new minority of White Anglo-Saxon Protestants. There is no principled basis for deciding which groups would merit "heightened judicial solicitude" and which would not. Courts would be asked to evaluate the extent of the prejudice and consequent harm suffered by various minority groups. Those whose societal injury is thought to exceed some arbitrary level of tolerability then would be entitled to preferential classifications at the expense of individuals belonging to other groups. Those classifications would be free from exacting judicial scrutiny. As these preferences began to have their desired effect, and the consequences of past discrimination were undone, new judicial rankings would be necessary. The kind of variable sociological and political analysis necessary to produce such rankings simply does not lie within the judicial competence—even if they otherwise were politically feasible and socially desirable.

Moreover, there are serious problems of justice connected with the idea of preference itself. First, it may not always be clear that a so-called preference is in fact benign. Courts may be asked to validate burdens imposed upon individual members of particular groups in order to advance the group's general interest. Nothing in the Constitution supports the notion that individuals may be asked to suffer otherwise impermissible burdens in order to enhance the societal standing of their ethnic groups. Second, preferential programs may only reinforce common stereotypes holding that certain groups are unable to achieve success without special protection based on a factor having no relationship to individual worth. Third, there is a measure of inequity in forcing innocent persons in respondent's position to bear the burdens of redressing grievances not of their making.

By hitching the meaning of the Equal Protection Clause to these transitory considerations, we would be holding, as a constitutional principle, that judicial scrutiny of classifications touching on racial and ethnic background may vary with the ebb and flow of political forces. Disparate constitutional tolerance of such classifications well may serve to exacerbate racial and ethnic antagonisms rather than alleviate them. Also, the mutability of a constitutional principle, based upon shifting political and social judgments, undermines the chances for consistent application of the Constitution from one generation to the next, a critical feature of its coherent interpretation. In expounding the Constitution, the Court's role is to discern "principles sufficiently absolute to give them roots throughout the community and continuity over significant periods of time, and to lift them above the level of the pragmatic political judgments of a particular time and place." . . .

We have held that in "order to justify the use of a suspect classification, a State must show that its purpose or interest is both constitutionally permissible and substantial, and that its use of the classification is 'necessary . . . to the accomplishment' of its purpose or the safeguarding of its interest." The special admissions program purports to serve the purposes of: (i) "reducing the historic deficit of traditionally disfavored minorities in medical schools and the medical profession," (ii) countering the effects of societal discrimination; (iii) increasing the number of physicians who will practice in communities currently underserved; and (iv) obtaining the educational benefits that flow from an ethnically diverse student body. It is necessary to decide which, if any, of these purposes is substantial enough to support the use of a suspect classification.

(i) If petitioner's purpose is to assure within its student body some specified percentage of a particular

group merely because of its race or ethnic origin, such a preferential purpose must be rejected not as insubstantial but as facially invalid. Preferring members of any one group for no reason other than race or ethnic origin is discrimination for its own sake. This the Constitution forbids.

(ii) The State certainly has a legitimate and substantial interest in ameliorating, or eliminating where feasible, the disabling effects of identified discrimination. The line of school desegregation cases, commencing with *Brown*, attests to the importance of this state goal and the commitment of the judiciary to affirm all lawful means towards its attainment. In the school cases, the States were required by court order to redress the wrongs worked by specific instances of racial discrimination. That goal was far more focused than the remedying of the effects of "societal discrimination," an amorphous concept of injury that may be ageless in its reach into the past.

We have never approved a classification that aids persons perceived as members of relatively victimized groups at the expense of other innocent individuals in the absence of judicial, legislative, or administrative findings of constitutional or statutory violations. After such findings have been made, the governmental interest in preferring members of the injured groups at the expense of others is substantial, since the legal rights of the victims must be vindicated. In such a case, the extent of the injury and the consequent remedy will have been judicially, legislatively, or administratively defined. Also, the remedial action usually remains subject to continuing oversight to assure that it will work the least harm possible to other innocent persons competing for the benefit. Without such findings of constitutional or statutory violations, it cannot be said that the government has any greater interest in helping one individual than in refraining from harming another. Thus, the government has no compelling justification for inflicting such harm. . . .

The purpose of helping certain groups whom the faculty of the Davis Medical School perceived as victims of "societal discrimination" does not justify a classification that imposes disadvantages upon persons like respondent, who bear no responsibility for whatever harm the beneficiaries of the special admissions program are thought to have suffered. To hold otherwise would be to convert a remedy heretofore reserved for violations of legal rights into a privilege that all institutions throughout the Nation could grant at their pleasure to whatever groups are perceived as victims of societal discrimination. That is a step we have never approved.

(iii) Petitioner identifies, as another purpose of its program, improving the delivery of health care services to communities currently underserved. It may be assumed that in some situations a State's interest in facilitating the health care of its citizens is sufficiently compelling to support the use of a suspect classification. But there is virtually no evidence in the record indicating that petitioner's special admissions program is either needed or geared to promote that goal. The court below addressed this failure of proof:

"The University concedes it cannot assure that minority doctors who entered under the program, all of whom express an 'interest' in participating in a disadvantaged community, will actually do so. It may be correct to assume that some of them will carry out this intention, and that it is more likely they will practice in minority communities than the average white doctor. Nevertheless, there are more precise and reliable ways to identify applicants who are genuinely interested in the medical problems of minorities than by race. An applicant of whatever race who has demonstrated his concern for disadvantaged minorities in the past and who declares that practice in such a community is his primary professional goal would be more likely to contribute to alleviation of the medical shortage than one who is chosen entirely on the basis of race and disadvantage. In short, there is [sic] no empirical data to demonstrate that any one race is more selflessly socially oriented or by contrast that another is more selfishly acquisitive."

Petitioner simply has not carried its burden of demonstrating that it must prefer members of particular ethnic groups over all other individuals in order to promote better health care delivery to deprived citizens. Indeed, petitioner has not shown that its preferential classification is likely to have any significant effect on the problem.

(iv) The fourth goal asserted by petitioner is the attainment of a diverse student body. This clearly is a constitutionally permissible goal for an institution of higher education. Academic freedom, though not a specifically enumerated constitutional right, long has been viewed as a special concern of the First Amendment. The freedom of a university to make its own judgments as to education includes the selection of its student body. . . .

Thus, in arguing that its universities must be accorded the right to select those students who will contribute the most to the "robust exchange of ideas," petitioner invokes a countervailing constitutional interest, that of the First Amendment. In this light, petitioner must be viewed as seeking to achieve a goal that is of paramount importance in the fulfillment of its mission. . . .

Physicians serve a heterogenous population. An otherwise qualified medical student with a particular background—whether it be ethnic, geographic, culturally advantaged or disadvantaged—may bring to a professional school of medicine experiences, outlooks and ideas that enrich the training of its student body and better equip its graduates to render with understanding their vital service to humanity.

Ethnic diversity, however, is only one element in a range of factors a university properly may consider in attaining the goal of a heterogeneous student body. Although a university must have wide discretion in making the sensitive judgments as to who should be admitted, constitutional limitations protecting individual rights may not be disregarded. Respondent urges—and the courts below have held—that petitioner's dual admissions program is a racial classification that impermissibly infringes his rights under the Fourteenth Amendment. As the interest of diversity is compelling in the context of a university's admissions program, the question remains whether the program's racial classification is necessary to promote this interest.

It may be assumed that the reservation of a specified number of seats in each class for individuals from the preferred ethnic groups would contribute to the attainment of considerable ethnic diversity in the student body. But petitioner's argument that this is the only effective means of serving the interest of diversity is seriously flawed. In a most fundamental sense the argument misconceives the nature of the state interest that would justify consideration of race or ethnic background. It is not an interest in simple ethnic diversity, in which a specified percentage of the student body is in effect guaranteed to be members of selected ethnic groups, with the remaining percentage an undifferentiated aggregation of students. The diversity that furthers a compelling state interest encompasses a far broader array of qualifications and characteristics of which racial or ethnic origin is but a single though important element. Petitioner's special admissions program, focused *solely* on ethnic diversity, would hinder rather than further attainment of genuine diversity. . . .

The experience of other university admissions programs, which take race into account in achieving the educational diversity valued by the First Amendment, demonstrates that the assignment of a fixed number of places to a minority group is not a necessary means toward that end. An illuminating example is found in the Harvard College program:

"In recent years Harvard College has expanded the concept of diversity to include students from disadvantaged economic, racial and ethnic groups. Harvard College now recruits not only Californians or Louisianans but also blacks and Chicanos and other minority students.

"In practice, this new definition of diversity has meant that race has been a factor in some admission decisions. When the Committee on Admissions reviews the large middle group of applicants who are 'admissible' and deemed capable of doing good work in their courses, the race of an applicant may tip the balance in his favor just as geographic origin or a life spent on a farm may tip the balance in other candidates' cases. A farm boy from Idaho can bring something to Harvard College that a Bostonian cannot offer. Similarly, a black student can usually bring something that a white person cannot offer."

"In Harvard college admissions the Committee has not set target-quotas for the number of blacks, or of musicians, football players, physicists or Californians to be admitted in a given year. . . . But that awareness [of the necessity of including more than a token number of black students] does not mean that the Committee sets the minimum number of blacks or of people from west of the Mississippi who are to be admitted. It means only that in choosing among thousands of applicants who are not only 'admissible' academically but have other strong qualities, the Committee, with a number of criteria in mind, pays some attention to distribution among many types and categories of students."

In such an admissions program, race or ethnic

background may be deemed a "plus" in a particular applicant's file, yet it does not insulate the individual from comparison with all other candidates for the available seats. The file of a particular black applicant may be examined for his potential contribution to diversity without the factor of race being decisive when compared, for example, with that of an applicant identified as an Italian-American if the latter is thought to exhibit qualities more likely to promote beneficial educational pluralism. Such qualities could include exceptional personal talents, unique work or service experience, leadership potential, maturity, demonstrated compassion, a history of overcoming disadvantage, ability to communicate with the poor, or other qualifications deemed important. In short, an admissions program operated in this way is flexible enough to consider all pertinent elements of diversity in light of the particular qualifications of each applicant, and to place them on the same footing for consideration, although not necessarily according them the same weight. Indeed, the weight attributed to a particular quality may vary from year to year depending upon the "mix" both of the student body and the applicants for the incoming class.

This kind of program treats each applicant as an individual in the admissions process. The applicant who loses out on the last available seat to another candidate receiving a "plus" on the basis of ethnic background will not have been foreclosed from all consideration for that seat simply because he was not the right color or had the wrong surname. It would mean only that his combined qualifications, which may have included similar nonobjective factors, did not outweigh those of the other applicant. His qualifications would have been weighed fairly and competitively, and he would have no basis to complain of unequal treatment under the Fourteenth Amendment.

In summary, it is evident that the Davis special admission program involves the use of an explicit racial classification never before countenanced by this Court. It tells applicants who are not Negro, Asian, or "Chicano" that they are totally excluded from a specific percentage of the seats in an entering class. No matter how strong their qualifications, quantitative and extracurricular, including their own potential for contribution to educational diversity, they are never afforded the chance to compete with applicants from the preferred groups for the special admission seats. At the same time, the preferred applicants have the opportunity to compete for every seat in the class.

The fatal flaw in petitioner's preferential program is its disregard of indiviual rights as guaranteed by the Fourteenth Amendment. Such rights are not absolute. But when a State's distribution of benefits or imposition of burdens hinges on the color of a person's skin or ancestry, that individual is entitled to a demonstration that the challenged classification is necessary to promote a substantial state interest. Petitioner has failed to carry this burden. For this reason, that portion of the California court's judgment holding petitioner's special admissions program invalid under the Fourteenth Amendment must be affirmed.

In enjoining petitioner from ever considering the race of any applicant, however, the courts below failed to recognize that the State has a substantial interest that legitimately may be served by a properly devised admissions program involving the competitive consideration of race and ethnic origin. For this reason, so much of the California court's judgment as enjoins petitioner from any consideration of the race of any applicant must be reversed.

With respect to respondent's entitlement to an injunction directing his admission to the Medical School, petitioner has conceded that it could not carry its burden of proving that, but for the existence of its unlawful special admissions program, respondent still would not have been admitted. Hence, respondent is entitled to the injunction, and that portion of the judgment must be affirmed.

Opinion of Mr. Justice Brennan, Mr. Justice White, Mr. Justice Marshall, and Mr. Justice Blackmun, concurring in the judgment in part and dissenting.

Davis' articulated purpose of remedying the effects of past societal discrimination is, under our cases, sufficiently important to justify the use of race-conscious admissions programs where there is a sound basis for concluding that minority underrepresentation is substantial and chronic, and that the handicap of past discrimination is impeding access of minorities to the medical school.

. . . . A state government may adopt race-conscious programs if the purpose of such programs is to remove the disparate racial impact its actions might otherwise have and if there is reason to believe that the disparate impact is itself the product of past discrimination, whether its own or that of society at large. There is no question that Davis' program is valid under this test.

Certainly, on the basis of the undisputed factual submissions before this Court, Davis had a sound basis for believing that the problem of underrepresentation of minorities was substantial and chronic and that the problem was attributable to handicaps imposed on minority applicants by past and present racial discrimination. Until at least 1973, the practice of medicine in this country was, in fact, if not in law, largely the prerogative of whites. In 1950, for example, while Negroes comprised 10% of the total population, Negro physicians constituted only 2.2% of the total number of physicians. The overwhelming majority of these, moreover, were educated in two predominantly Negro medical schools, Howard and Meharry. By 1970, the gap between the proportion of Negros in medicine and their proportion in the population had widened: The number of Negroes employed in medicine remained frozen at 2.2% while the Negro population had increased to 11.1%. The number of Negro admittees to predominantly white medical schools, moreover, had declined in absolute numbers during the years 1955 to 1964.

Moreover, Davis had very good reason to believe that the national pattern of underrepresentation of minorities in medicine would be perpetuated if it retained a single admissions standard. For example, the entering classes in 1968 and 1969, the years in which such a standard was used, included only one Chicano and two Negroes out of 100 admittees. Nor is there any relief from this pattern of underrepresentation in the statistics for the regular admissions program in later years.

Davis clearly could conclude that the serious and persistent underrepresentation of minorities in medicine depicted by these statistics is the result of handicaps under which minority applicants labor as a consequence of a background of deliberate, purposeful discrimination against minorities in education and in society generally, as well as in the medical profession. From the inception of our national life, Negroes have been subjected to unique legal disabilities impairing access to equal educational opportunity. Under slavery, penal sanctions were imposed upon anyone attempting to educate Negroes. After enactment of the Fourteenth Amendment the States continued to deny Negroes equal educational opportunity, enforcing a strict policy of segregation that itself stamped Negroes as inferior, which relegated minorities to inferior educational institutions, and which denied them intercourse in the mainstream of professional life necessary to advancment. Segregation was not limited to public facilities, moreover, but was enforced by criminal penalties against private action as well. Thus, as late as 1908, this Court enforced a state criminal conviction against a private college for teaching Negroes together with whites.

Green v. *County School Board* gave explicit recognition to the fact that the habit of discrimination and the cultural tradition of race prejudice cultivated by centuries of legal slavery and segregation were not immediately dissipated when *Brown I* announced the constitutional principle that equal educational opportunity and participation in all aspects of American life could not be denied on the basis of race. Rather, massive official and private resistance prevented, and to a lesser extent still prevents, attainment of equal opportunity in education at all levels and in the professions. The generation of minority students applying to Davis Medical School since it opened in 1968—most of whom were born before or about the time *Brown I* was decided—clearly have been victims of this discrimination. Judicial decrees recognizing discrimination in public education in California testify to the fact of widespread discrimination suffered by California-born minority applicants; many minority group members living in California, moreover, were born and reared in school districts in southern States segregated by law. Since separation of school children by race "generates a feeling of inferiority as to their status in the community that may affect their hearts and minds in a way unlikely ever to be undone," the conclusion is inescapable that applicants to medical school must be few indeed who endured the effects of *de jure* segregation, the resistance to *Brown I*, or the equally debilitating pervasive private discrimination fostered by our long history of official discrimination, and yet come to the starting line with an education equal to whites.

Moreover, we need not rest solely on our own conclusion that Davis had sound reason to believe that the effects of past discrimination were handicapping minority applicants to the Medical School, because the Department of Health, Education, and Welfare, the expert agency charged by Congress with promulgating regulations enforcing Title VI of the Civil Rights Act of 1964, has also reached the conclusion that race may be taken into account in situations where a failure to do so would limit participation by minorities in federally funded programs, and regulations promulgated by the Department expressly contemplate that appropriate race-conscious programs may be adopted by universities to remedy unequal access to university programs caused by their own or by past societal discrimination. It cannot be questioned that, in the absence of the special admissions program, access of minority students to the Medical School would be severely limited and, accordingly, race-conscious admissions would be deemed an appropriate response under these federal regulations. . . .

The second prong of our test—whether the Davis program stigmatizes any discrete group or individual and whether race is reasonably used in light of the program's objectives—is clearly satisfied by the Davis program.

It is not even claimed that Davis' program in any way operates to stigmatize or single out any discrete and insular, or even any identifiable, nonminority group. Nor will harm comparable to that imposed upon racial minorities by exclusion or separation on grounds of race be the likely result of the program. It does not, for example, establish an exclusive preserve for minority students apart from and exclusive of whites. Rather, its purpose is to overcome the effects of segregation by bringing the races together. True, whites are excluded from participation in the special admissions program, but this fact only operates to reduce the number of whites to be admitted in the regular admissions program in order to permit admission of a reasonable percentage—less than their proportion of the California population—of otherwise underrepresented qualified minority applicants.

Nor was Bakke in any sense stamped as inferior by the Medical School's rejection of him. Indeed, it is conceded by all that he satisfied those criteria regarded by the School as generally relevant to academic performance better than most of the minority members who were admitted. Moreover, there is absolutely no basis for concluding that Bakke's rejection as a result of Davis' use of racial preference will affect him throughout his life in the same way as the segregation of the Negro school children in *Brown I* would have affected them. Unlike discrimination against racial minorities, the use of racial preferences for remedial purposes does not inflict a pervasive injury upon individual whites in the sense that wherever they go or whatever they do there is a significant likelihood that they will be treated as second-class citizens because of their color. This distinction does not mean that the exclusion of a white resulting from the preferential use of race is not sufficiently serious to require justification; but it does mean that the injury inflicted by such a policy is not distinguishable from disadvantages caused by a wide range of government actions, none of which has ever been thought impermissible for that reason alone.

In addition, there is simply no evidence that the Davis program discriminates intentionally or unintentionally against any minority group which it purports to benefit. The program does not establish a quota in the invidious sense of a ceiling on the number of minority applicants to be admitted. Nor can the program reasonably be regarded as stigmatizing the program's beneficiaries or their race as inferior. The Davis program does not simply advance less qualified applicants; rather, it compensates applicants, whom it is uncontested are fully qualified to study medicine, for educational disadvantage which it was reasonable to conclude was a product of state-fostered discrimination. Once admitted, these students must satisfy the same degree requirements as regularly admitted students; they are taught by the same faculty in the same classes; and their performance is evaluated by the same standards by which regularly admitted students are judged. Under these circumstances, their performance and degrees must be regarded equally with the regularly admitted students with whom they compete for standing. Since minority graduates cannot justifiably be regarded as less well qualified than nonminority graduates by virtue of the special admissions program, there is no reasonable basis to conclude that minority graduates at schools using such programs would

be stigmatized as inferior by the existence of such programs.

Finally, Davis' special admissions program cannot be said to violate the Constitution simply because it has set aside a predetermined number of places for qualified minority applicants rather than using minority status as a positive factor to be considered in evaluating the applications of disadvantaged minority applicants. For purposes of constitutional adjudication, there is no difference between the two approaches. In any admissions program which accords special consideration to disadvantaged racial minorities, a determination of the degree of preference to be given is unavoidable, and any given preference that results in the exclusion of a white candidate is no more or less constitutionally acceptable than a program such as that at Davis. Furthermore, the extent of the preference inevitably depends on how many minority applicants the particular school is seeking to admit in any particular year so long as the number of qualified minority applicants exceeds that number. There is no sensible, and certainly no constitutional, distinction between, for example, adding a set number of points to the admissions rating of disadvantaged minority applicants as an expression of the preference with the expectation that this will result in the admission of an approximately determined number of qualified minority applicants and setting a fixed number of places for such applicants as was done here.

The "Harvard" program, as those employing it readily concede, openly and successfully employs a racial criterion for the purpose of ensuring that some of the scarce places in institutions of higher education are allocated to disadvantaged minority students. That the Harvard approach does not also make public the extent of the preference and the precise workings of the system while the Davis program employs a specific, openly stated number, does not condemn the latter plan for purposes of Fourteenth Amendment adjudication. It may be that the Harvard plan is more acceptable to the public than is the Davis "quota." If it is, any State, including California, is free to adopt it in preference to a less acceptable alternative, just as it is generally free, as far as the Constitution is concerned, to abjure granting any racial preferences in its admissions program. But there is no basis for preferring a particular preference program simply because in achieving the same goals that the Davis Medical School is pursuing, it proceeds in a manner that is not immediately apparent to the public.

Accordingly, we would reverse the judgment of the Supreme Court of California holding the Medical School's special admissions program unconstitutional and directing respondent's admission, as well as that portion of the judgment enjoining the Medical School from according any consideration to race in the admissions process.

United States Commission on Civil Rights

THE EQUAL RIGHTS AMENDMENT

The proposed Equal Rights Amendment reads as follows:

Resolved by the Senate and House of Representatives of the United States of America in Congress assembled (two-thirds of each House concurring therein), That the following article is proposed as an amendment to the Constitution of the United States, which shall be valid to all intents and purposes as part of the Constitution when ratified by the legislatures of three-fourths of the several States within seven years from the date of its submission by the Congress:

"ARTICLE—

"SECTION 1. Equality of rights under the law shall not be denied or abridged by the United States or by any State on account of sex.

"SEC. 2. The Congress shall have the power to enforce, by appropriate legislation, the provisions of this article.

"SEC. 3. This amendment shall take effect two years after the date of ratification."

Family Law

A WOMAN'S RIGHTS DURING marriage, as well as after—whether the marriage ends as a result of death or divorce—have traditionally be those of a second-class citizen. Many State laws still reflect their roots in the English common law view of the married woman as the property of her husband.

Some of the more oppressive aspects of this discrimination have been removed over the past century, so that a married woman can now own property, enter into contracts, be granted custody of her children, and, in most cases, keep her own earnings.

However, laws covering marriage continue to deny women equal rights.

Marital property laws illustrate the persistence of sex bias against women. In Georgia, for example, a married couple's home belongs only to the husband, even when it has been paid for by the wife. In other States, the husband is given the right to manage and control marital property without the wife's consent, again, even if it was purchased with the wife's earnings. In Wisconsin, the earnings of a married woman "accruing from labor performed for her husband, or in his employ, or payable by him" are

From Senate Report No. 92–689 and the *Statement on the Equal Rights Amendment,* United States Commission on Civil Rights (1978) pp. 5–7.

not considered her separate property and are subject to her husband's control.

The same bias is evident in laws that deny a woman the right to sue a third party who has injured her husband and thereby deprived her of his services. A husband, similarly deprived, can sue.

The married woman who chooses to be a full-time homemaker has the least legal and economic protection of all, since many States do not recognize her labor as having economic value. This is repugnant to the view of marriage as a partnership between the husband and the wife, with both performing different but equally important roles, each having economic significance.

The lack of economic value accorded a woman's contributions to a marriage is demonstrated in the case of a Nebraska farm couple who worked the land together for 33 years. When the husband died in 1974, his wife learned that in the Federal Government's eyes the farm belonged entirely to him. Unless she could prove that she helped to pay for its purchase or improvement, she would be liable for a $25,000 inheritance tax. Her years of work, even the joint title, was no proof. Had the wife died first, her husband would have had to pay no tax.

In most States, when a marriage ends, distribution of the marital property follows a similar rule. Until a recent successful challenge under the Pennsylvania State ERA, a woman in that State was faced with the legal presumption that all the household articles acquired during the marriage—such as the stove, the TV, and even her jewelry—belonged to her husband, unless she could prove that she paid for them. While States like New York do not have such an explicit presumption, the result is often the same because one's legal rights to property generally are determined by proof of actual economic contribution or of receipt as gift. Most homemakers who earn no wages cannot establish such proof.

Sex-based roles and presumptions also affect a married woman's ability to get credit. This is true even under the Federal Equal Credit Opportunity Act (enacted to make credit available without discrimination on the basis of sex or marital status), since creditors may consider State marital property laws in determining creditworthiness.

Similar hardships face the homemaker under the social security program. Since she has no independent entitlement to benefits, if she becomes disabled, she and her dependents have no right to social security, even though her services are lost to her family. Because the program does not recognize the economic value of her contribution to the family, she will not receive benefits under her husband's coverage if she is widowed before the age of 50 unless she has minor or disabled children in her care. This is true even if she is disabled and cannot work.

The only economic "right" the married woman has traditionally had is the theoretical "right to support during a marriage." The significance of this "right" and the potential effect of the ERA on it have been primary targets of distortion by ERA opponents trying to argue that the amendment will strip away women's rights. In fact, the legal duty of a husband to support his wife is largely unenforceable. It is little more than myth, since courts will not interfere in an ongoing marriage to ensure adequate support either for the wife or for the children.

Laws governing support and alimony during separation and after divorce are similarly illusory in the benefits they appear to confer upon women. The reality is that only 14 percent of divorced wives were awarded alimony in 1975 and that fewer than half were able to collect their payments regularly. Similar enforcement problems exist for collecting child support. A study tracing child support payments over 10 years showed that 62 percent of male parents failed to comply fully with court-ordered child support payments in the first year after the order, and 42 percent did not make even a single payment. By the 10th year, 79 percent were making no payments at all.

Support laws are so poorly enforced that most separated and divorced women have no choice but to work outside the home or turn to welfare. A study in Jefferson County, Alabama, revealed that the average amount of support ordered for a woman and two children was $80 per month, substantially less than the amount she would receive under welfare. In Rhode Island, because support payments are so erratic, they are not counted as income when applying for credit. . . .

Women in the Labor Force

Women who work outside the home continue to be disadvantaged by sex-role stereotypes and gender lines that affect employment opportunities and achievements. These women, too, stand to gain under the Equal Rights Amendment. Despite recent legislative reform and efforts to enforce Federal and State antidiscrimination laws, sex bias in employment persists.

While the labor market has provided increased job opportunities for women in recent years, most of the openings have been in clerical and service areas traditionally dominated by women. Indeed, occupational segregation by sex increased substantially between 1970 and 1976. Not only are the jobs held by women different from those held by men, but the evidence is that they are valued less by society.

In professional and technical fields, women are overrepresented in jobs that are lower on the career ladder than men in the same industries: women are teachers more often than principals, bookkeepers more often than comptrollers. Even within a traditional woman's field, clerical occupations, women are more likely to be employed in lower paying positions as typists, stenographers, secretaries, and file clerks, while men tend to be employed as administrative assistants, a higher paying clerical occupation. In general, the jobs in which women are concentrated pay lower salaries than those paid in traditionally male-dominated positions, even when these positions involve equivalent skill, effort, and responsibility.

Even when adjustments are made for education and occupation, women earn less than men. In 1976 a woman who attended 4 years of college was earning about as much as a man with 8 years of elementary school education. On the average, in 1976 women clerical workers earned $4,200 less than male clerical workers, and saleswomen earned $6,900 less than salesmen. In public employment, the median income for women working full time was $9,215 in 1975, while the median income for men was $13,118.

Criminal Law

Criminal law is another area in which women and men are treated differently because of their sex. This treatment has most often been disadvantageous to women, as both victims and offenders.

In some jurisdictions, definitions of criminal behavior and legal defenses, reflect sex-based notions.

In Alabama, for example, if a husband finds his wife in the act of adultery and immediately kills her, he is not guilty of murder, but of the lesser crime of manslaughter. However, the same defense is not available to a wife.

This view that husbands have a special prerogative when it comes to their wives also is reflected in the laws of those States that do not recognize a charge of forcible rape as a crime when committed by a husband against his wife, regardless of the circumstances and degree of coercion involved.

Explicit sex lines similarly are found in prostitution laws. Traditionally, prostitution was defined as a "woman's act," with no attempt to penalize the men who paid or were paid for it. Although many jurisdictions have revised these laws to cover men as well as women, "less than half explicitly penalize the patrons of prostitution, and many of those that do impose less stringent penalties against patrons than prostitutes."

Sex-based definitions of criminal behavior also permeate the juvenile justice system, which often subjects girls and boys to differing definitions of delinquent behavior and to different sentences. In general, more girls are detained for "status" offenses such as promiscuity or truancy, while boys are arrested for delinquent acts such as theft. On the average, girls are institutionalized for less serious conduct than boys and for longer periods of time.

Sentencing and parole statutes and practices further illustrate the persistent sex-based discrimination in criminal law. In some States, laws still mandate indeterminate sentences for women, while men receive set minimum and maximum terms. This disparate treatment stems from the sex-based presumption that "women, including women offenders, are more malleable than men and thus more amenable to reform and rehabilitation. In practice, this means that a woman offender remains in custody until the prison administration finds she has been 'corrected' while a man who has been imprisoned 'does time' for some set period. . . ." The result may be that the female offender is incarcerated far longer or far shorter than a man convicted of the same offense; in either case, the comparative time in prison may bear no relationship either to the crime or to rehabilitation. . . .

SUGGESTIONS FOR FURTHER READING

Anthologies

Bishop, Sharon, and Weinzweig, Marjorie. *Philosophy and Women*. Belmont: Wadsworth Publishing Co., 1979.

Blackstone, William, and Heslep, Robert. *Social Justice and Preferential Treatment*. Athens: University of Georgia Press, 1977.

Cohen, M.; Nagel, T.; and Scanlon, T. *Equality and Preferential Treatment*. Princeton: Princeton University Press, 1977.

Freeman, Jo. *Women: A Feminist Perspective*. Palo Alto: Mayfield Publishing Co., 1975.

Gould, Carol C., and Wartofsky, Marx W. *Women and Philosophy*. New York: G. P. Putnam & Sons, 1976.

Gross, Barry. *Reverse Discrimination*. Buffalo: Prometheus, 1976.

Jaggar, Alison, and Struhl, Paula Rothenberg. *Feminist Frameworks*. New York: McGraw-Hill Co., 1978.

Vetterling-Braggin, Mary; Elliston, Frederick; and English, Jane. *Feminism and Philosophy*. Totowa: Littlefield, Adams, 1977.

Alternative Views

Bittker, Boris. *The Case for Black Reparations*. New York: Random House, 1973.

DeCrow, Karen. *Sexist Justice*. New York: Vintage, 1975.

Friedan, Betty. *The Feminine Mystique*. New York: W. W. Norton & Co., 1963.

Jencks, Christopher, et. al. *Inequality: A Reassessment of the Effect of Family and Schooling in America*. New York: Basic Books, 1972.

Livingston, John. *Fair Game*. San Francisco: W. H. Freeman & Co., 1979.

Millet, Kate. *Sexist Politics*. Garden City: Doubleday & Co., 1970.

Sowell, Thomas. *Black Education: Myths and Tragedies*. New York: McKay, 1972.

Practical Applications

Irving, John. *The World According to Garp*. New York: Dutton, 1978.

Sindles, Allan P. *Bakke, De Funio and Minority Admissions*. New York: Youngman, 1978.

United States Commission on Civil Rights. *Statement on the Equal Rights Amendment*. Washington D.C.: U.S. Government Printing Office, 1978.

PUNISHMENT AND RESPONSIBILITY

BASIC CONCEPTS

The problem of punishment and responsibility is the problem of who should be punished and in what their punishment should consist. It is a problem of punishment *and* responsibility, since determining who should be punished and in what their punishment should consist involves an assessment of responsibility. However, before discussing alternative justifications for assigning punishment, it is important to first get clear about the concepts of punishment and responsibility.

Let us begin with the concept of punishment. Consider the following definition:

(a) Punishment is hardship inflicted on an offender by someone entitled to do so.

This definition certainly seems adequate to many standard cases of punishment. For example, suppose you pursue and capture a young man who has just robbed a drug store. The police then arrive and arrest the fellow. He is tried, convicted, and sentenced to two years in prison. Surely it would seem that a sentence of two years in prison in this case would constitute punishment, and obviously the sentence meets the conditions of (a).

But suppose we vary the example a bit. Suppose that, as before, you pursue the robber, but this time he gets away and in the process drops the money he took from the drug store, which you then retrieve. Suppose further that two eyewitnesses identify you as the robber, and you are arrested by the police, tried,

and sentenced to two years in prison. Surely we would like to say that in this example it is you who are being punished, although unjustly so; but according to (a) this is not the case. For according to this definition, punishment can only be inflicted on offenders, and you are not an offender. But this simply shows that (a) is too narrow a definition of punishment. There clearly are cases like our modified example, in which we can truly say that nonoffenders, i.e., innocent people, are being punished. Accordingly, an acceptable definition of punishment should allow for such cases.

Let us consider then the following definition of punishment, which does allow for the possibility that nonoffenders can be punished:

(b) Punishment is hardship inflicted on a person by someone entitled to do so.

Although (b) clearly represents an advance over (a) in that it allows for the possibility that innocent people can be punished, serious difficulties remain. For according to (b) paying taxes is punishment, as is the civil commitment of mentally ill persons who have not committed any offense. And even though we may have good reasons for opposing taxation and even good reasons for opposing civil commitment, it is usually not because we regard such impositions as punishments. Clearly then a definition of punishment which classifies paying taxes and civil commitment as punishments is simply too broad; what is needed is a definition that is narrower than (b) but broader than (a).

Consider the following possibility:

(c) Punishment is hardship inflicted on a person who is found guilty of an offense by someone entitled to do so.

This definition, like (b), allows that innocent people can be punished, since it is possible that a person can be found guilty by some procedure or other without really being guilty. Yet (c), unlike (b), does not allow that just any hardship imposed by someone entitled to do so is punishment. Rather, only a hardship imposed *for an offense* can be a punishment. This definition is also quite similar to the definition that Kurt Baier sets out (see pp. 247–255), according to which a deprivation suffered by a recipient at the hands of an imponent is punishment if the recipient suffers the deprivation on account of a wrong, a crime, or an offense. In fact, if we assume that hardships are deprivations and that offenses include wrongs and crimes, these two definitions turn out to be identical. But are they adequate?

It would seem they are not. For, according to (c), paying a $5 parking ticket or suffering a 15 yard penalty in a football game are both punishments. Yet in both cases the hardship imposed lacks the moral condemnation and denunciation that is characteristic of punishment. This suggests the following definition:

(d) Punishment is hardship involving moral condemnation and denunciation inflicted on a person who is found guilty of an offense by someone entitled to do so.

Baier agrees that his definition needs to be modified to resemble (d). Examples like the $5 parking ticket and the 15 yard penalty indicate that we need to distinguish between punishments proper, which satisfy the conditions of (d), and mere penalties, which only satisfy the conditions of (c). When we impose mere penalties, we are claiming that a person has done something wrong, maybe even something morally wrong; but, because of the insignificant nature of the offense, we don't attempt to determine whether the person we claim to have committed the offense is morally blameworthy for so acting. Since we don't make this determination, we don't go on to morally condemn and denounce those we penalize. By contrast, when we impose punishments

proper we do make such a determination and, as a consequence, we do condemn and denounce those we penalize.

Baier goes on to draw attention to a number of interesting implications of the concept of punishment. For instance, he notes that a deprivation cannot be punishment if everyone believes that the person suffering the deprivation is being victimized. He also points out that A may be punished by B even when B does not intend to punish A, but only intends to victimize her.

Turning to the concept of responsibility, we find that this concept is employed in a variety of different but related contexts. Roughly, the underlying idea seems to be the following:

1. X is responsible for y if and only if X is related to y in such a way that either (a) it is appropriate to grade X with respect to y or (b) it is appropriate to praise or blame X with respect to y on the basis of a grade that has already been determined.

In the second part of his selection, Kurt Baier helps to clarify further the concept of responsibility by distinguishing and defining accountability, task-responsibility, answerability, culpability, and liability. Baier defines these varieties of responsibility along the following lines:

2. X is accountable if and only if X has the powers and capabilities required to be guided by promulgated social rules.
3. X is task-responsible if and only if there is an obligatory social requirement that X discharge a particular task.
4. X is answerable if and only if X has failed to satisfy an obligatory social requirement.
5. X is culpable if and only if X has failed to discharge an obligatory social requirement without an adequate excuse.
6. X is liable if and only if X is subject to punishment, condemnation, or payment of compensation.

Relating Baier's definitions to our general definition of responsibility, we find that if X is either accountable, task-responsible, or answerable then (1a) is satisfied, and if X is culpable or liable then (1b) is satisfied.

Notice that when we ask whether X is answerable, culpable, or liable, our ultimate aim in attempting to assign responsibility is usually either to blame or to excuse X with respect to y. If, on the other hand, our ultimate aim in attempting to assign responsibility is to praise X with respect to y, somewhat different yet analogous questions have to be asked.

Of course, when the law becomes concerned with assigning responsibility, its ultimate aim is usually to either blame or excuse X, but not to praise. Moreover, when X is found to be culpable or liable in such legal contexts, X is said to have *mens rea*, that is, foresight of consequences, knowledge of circumstances, and voluntariness. By contrast, in everyday contexts we might assess responsibility by simply asking the more general question of whether X could have acted otherwise than she did—which is to say, did X have the opportunity and/or ability to act otherwise?

With a clear understanding of the concepts of punishment and responsibility, we should be in a better position to examine alternative justifications for assigning punishment in society.

FORWARD-LOOKING AND BACKWARD-LOOKING VIEWS

There are basically two kinds of justifications for punishment: forward-looking and backward-looking. Forward-looking justifications maintain that punishment is justified because of its relationship to what *will occur*. Backward-looking justifications maintain that punishment is justified because of its relationship to what *has occurred*. An example of a forward-looking justification would be the claim that punishment is justified because it deters or reforms persons from crime. An example of a backward-looking justification would be the claim that punishment is justified because it fits or is proportionate to a crime or because it is applied to a person who is responsible for a crime. Those who adopt forward-looking justifications for punishment view punishment from the point of view of a social engineer who is seeking to produce certain good consequences in society. By contrast, those who adopt backward-looking justifications view punishment from the point of view of

a stern balancer who is seeking to achieve a moral balance between punishment and the crime.

Karl Menninger provides us with a forceful example of a forward-looking justification for punishment—one that is directed at the reform of the offender (see pp. 255–262). Menninger criticizes the existing criminal justice system as ineffective at preventing crime, grounded as it is on a theory of human motivation that fails to recognize the similarities between the motives of offenders and nonoffenders. In its place, Menninger would have us put a therapeutic treatment program which would detain offenders, and possibly potential offenders, until they are reformed. Thus Menninger would replace vengeful punishment—which he regards as itself a crime—with humanitarian reform.

One prerequisite for the justification of Menninger's system of humanitarian reform which is not generally recognized is that the opportunities open to offenders for leading a good life must be reasonably adequate, or at least arguably just and fair. If this is not the case, there would be little justification for asking criminal offenders to live their lives within the bounds of the legal system. Nor for that matter could we expect any attempt at implementing a system of reform like Menninger's to be generally effective in a society characterized by basic social and economic injustices. For in such a society, criminal offenders who perceive these injustices in their society will have a strong moral reason to resist any attempt to turn them into law-abiding citizens.

Yet even if a system of punishment does not succeed very well at reforming criminal offenders, some have claimed that it can still be justified if it provides general deterrence, that is, if it deters the general public from committing crime. In fact, we may presume that supporters of a forward-looking view would ideally want a system of punishment that secures the good consequences of *both* reform and general deterrence. However, C. S. Lewis (see pp 262–266) claims that the goals of both reform and deterrence are opposed to a fundamental requirement of justice—that of giving people what they deserve. Obviously, if Lewis's critique is sound, it presents a serious difficulty for Menninger's approach, as well as for any other forward-looking view.

Needless to say, raising difficulties for forward-looking justifications for punishment is not the same as directly defending backward-looking justifications. Hence the importance of the attempt by Edmund L. Pincoffs (see pp. 266–275) to provide us with such a defense. Pincoffs begins by setting out the following three principles which, he claims, are characteristic of a traditional backward-looking justification for punishment:

1. The only acceptable reason for punishing a person is that she has committed a crime.
2. The only acceptable reason for punishing a person in a given manner and degree is that the punishment is equal to the crime.
3. Whoever commits a crime must be punished in accordance with her desert.

Pincoffs claims that the underlying rationale for these principles can be expressed as follows:

(a) A proper justification for punishment is one that justifies it to the criminal.
(b) Punishment is justified because the criminal has willed the punishment she now suffers.

But how can criminals be said to will their own punishment if normally they do not like or want to be punished? One possible answer, which seems consistent with Pincoffs's analysis, is that criminals by deliberately violating the rights of others (e.g., by harming others in some way) imply that they think it is reasonable for them to do so. But if this were the case, it would be reasonable for anyone else in similar circumstances to do the same. As a result, criminals would be implicitly allowing that it is all right for others to violate their rights by inflicting punishment on them, and in this sense they could be said to will their own punishment.

In response to such a defense of a backward-looking justification for punishment, supporters of the forward-looking view might claim that the above principles and their underlying rationale are only proximate answers to the question of why punishment is justified, the ultimate answer to which is still given by the forward-looking view. Since Pincoffs's principles and their underlying rationale do not seem to be compatible with Menninger's system of humanitarian reform, such a response does imply that the ultimate forward-looking justification for punishment is to be found more in general deterrence than in humanitarian reform. But even if this

were the case, the ultimate justification for punishment would still be forward-looking.

To meet this response, supporters of a backward-looking view need to show why Pincoffs's principles and their underlying rationale cannot be subsumed under a forward-looking justification. One way this might be done is by showing that Pincoffs's principles and their underlying rationale can be grounded in a social contract theory of corrective justice analogous to the social contract theory of distributive justice discussed in Section I. Since many are convinced that a social contract theory of distributive justice conflicts with forward-looking goals, it should be possible to argue that a social contract theory of corrective justice does the same.[1]

PRACTICAL APPLICATION

Obviously, a crucial area for the application of forward-looking and backward-looking views is that of capital punishment. Ernest van den Haag and Louis Schwartz state briefly some of the main arguments for and against capital punishment (see pp. 276–278). Sometimes van den Haag and Schwartz present their arguments simply by way of example, in which case we must ask ourselves about the generality of the examples they give.

In 1976 the Supreme Court of the United States (see pp. 279–285) examined the question of whether capital punishment violates the Eighth Amendment prohibition of cruel and unusual punishment. The majority of the Court held that it does not violate that prohibition. In support of its ruling, the majority of the Court maintained that capital punishment does not offend against contemporary standards of decency as shown by recent legislation in this area. But with regard to the harder question of whether capital punishment is contrary to human dignity and so lacks either a forward-looking or a backward-looking justification, the Court simply deferred to state legislatures. That left the Court with the easier task of deciding whether the procedures for imposing capital punishment, as provided by the Georgia statute which was under review, were capricious and arbitrary. On this score the Court found no reason to fault the Georgia statute.

In more recent cases, however, the Court has gone beyond this purely procedural issue and ruled that the imposition of capital punishment for rape (*Coker* v. *Georgia*) and the imposition of capital punishment on anyone who did not fire the fatal shot or intend the death of the victim (*Locket* v. *Ohio*) would be unconstitutional. Given that the Court has not seen fit to defer to the judgment of state legislatures in these matters, it is not clear why the Court should continue to defer to their judgment with regard to the question of whether capital punishment can be supported by an adequate forward-looking or backward-looking justification.

In any case, once you have faced that question yourself and worked out a theory of corrective justice, you will still not know exactly how to apply that theory unless you also know how just the distribution of goods and resources is in your society. This is because whether you adopt an essentially forward-looking or an essentially backward-looking theory of corrective justice, you will need to know what

economic crimes—that is, crimes against property—should be punished according to your theory; and in order to know that, you will need to know what demands are placed on the available goods and resources by solutions to the other moral problems discussed in this anthology. Of course, some crimes (e.g., many cases of murder and rape) are not crimes against property but crimes against persons. And presumably these crimes would be proscribed by your theory of corrective justice independently of the solutions to other contemporary moral problems. Nevertheless, since most crimes that are committed are crimes against property, the primary application of your theory will still depend on solutions to the other moral problems discussed in this anthology. In particular, you will need to know to what extent goods and resources can be legitimately expended for military defense—which just happens to be the moral problem taken up next, in the final section of this anthology.

NOTE

1. James P. Sterba, "Retributive Justice," *Political Theory* (1977); "Social Contract Theory and Ordinary Justice," *Political Theory* (1981).

Kurt Baier

THE CONCEPTS OF PUNISHMENT AND RESPONSIBILITY

Kurt Baier claims that a deprivation suffered by a recipient at the hands of an imponent is punishment if the recipient suffers the deprivation on account of a wrong, a crime, or an offense. Baier goes on to comment on various aspects of this definition. He notes that for the

From "The Strengths and Limits of the Retributive Theory of Punishment," *Philosophic Exchange* (1977) pp. 38–42; and "Responsibility and Action," *Nature of Human Actions*, edited by Myles Brand (1970) pp. 103–108. Reprinted by permission of Kurt Baier and The Center for Philosophic Exchange.

imposition of deprivation to be punishment it must express moral disapproval or condemnation. He also notes that a deprivation cannot be punishment if everyone believes that the person suffering the deprivation is being victimized. Baier next tries to clarify the concept of responsibility by distinguishing and defining accountability, task-responsibility, answerability, culpability, and liability. Baier illustrates these distinctions with an example of a sea captain who is accountable for his action, task-responsible for the safety of his passengers, answerable for any loss of life and property, culpable in that he lacks a valid excuse, and hence liable to punishment for those losses.

Punishment

What, then, is punishment? Punishment involves two main roles, recipient and imponent, and something, a deprivation, which the recipient suffers normally at the hands of the imponent. Finally, there is some condition (e.g., the commission of a wrong, a crime, or an offense) such that the deprivation suffered by the recipient amounts to punishment if and only if he suffers it *on account* of such a condition. It must also be mentioned that given cases of punishment may be flawless, (deserved, just, effective, justified) or flawed, and that if we attempt to state the necessary and sufficient conditions of something being punishment, we must distinguish between those of flawless punishment and those of punishment whether flawed or flawless.

Let me now say a few words about each of these points. . . .

(i) *The core*: Being punished *consists in* undergoing something normally unwanted. Receiving money could not therefore count as being punished, even if one hated it. Conversely, the fact that, let us say, imprisonment happens not to be unwanted by the person on whom it is inflicted, does not *ipso facto* disqualify it from being punishment. Of course, we may want to say that it is then flawed: perhaps unsuitable, perhaps ineffective, and so on.

Punishing someone *consists in* imposing on him something normally unwanted. What is imposed must be *intended* as something unwanted: one cannot unintentionally or accidentally punish someone, but it would be unintentional *punishment* if what is inflicted were not intended as something normally unwanted. Punishment is a deliberate *punitive* measure and so must be intended as something deprivatory and so normally unwanted.

(ii) *The relation between the two roles*: Suffering something normally unwanted cannot be suffering

punishment unless it is suffered at the hands of someone who inflicts it as something unwanted. The fact that someone deserves his suffering, does not by itself make that suffering punishment. Even if the suffering is "his own doing" and he deserves it—if as we say "he had it coming to him"—this is at best punishment in an extended or loose sense; as when a judge decides not to punish for larceny,—on the grounds that "the culprit *has been punished enough* already",—someone who as a consequence of an affair with his boss' daughter has lost his job, his wife, and his self-respect, and has been forced to steal to keep alive.

(iii) *The social context*: Punishment consists in something, deliberately depriving someone, which is prima facie wrong, but yet the word 'punishment' implies that it is something which is not prima facie wrong. Wherever the imposition of a deprivation is exhibited as punishment we take it to be prima facie justified, unless it is flawed (unjust) punishment. This means that those of the punished person's rights must be suspended which would otherwise be violated by the deprivation. In primitive societies, the suspension of rights is the only thing the society can manage to organize: the actual deprivation is left to individual initiative. When a person is outlawed, any other person may kill him and none of the duties of mutual aid apply to him. In more highly organized societies, the suspension of the individual's rights is only relative to the organs of punishment. The fact that a person has been condemned to death does not give anyone (except the executioner) the right to kill him.

This suspension of rights is always for a specific time; only in extreme cases is it permanent. The notion of expiation or atonement which is traditionally attached to the concept of punishment implies that during the time the punishment (the suspension of rights) lasts, the recipient is not a member in good standing, but when the punishment has been "served", he is received back into society as a member in good standing. This is true not only of legal punishment, but also of all other forms. The child under punishment is not a member in good standing in his family and, in so far as the society at large approves of the punishment of children by their parents, the child is not a member in good standing while he serves his punishment also in the larger social context.

(iv) *Moral disapproval:* Joel Feinberg has recently revived the idea, for some time ignored under the influence of Legal Positivism, that for the imposition of deprivation to be punishment it must express the moral disapproval or condemnation by the imponent of the conduct *for which* the deprivation is imposed. A system which attaches penalties to breaches of rules and then imposes those penalties on all and only on people whom it has found guilty of a breach of the rules, looks like a system of punishment but is not unless the imposition of penalties at the same time *signifies* moral condemnation by the imponent. If this is sound, as I think it is, then it shows that the idea of punishment is essentially at home in morality rather than in law, even if it is true that the law is among other things the enforcement of morality. This point is important, as we shall see more clearly below.

Both punishment and penalization must be distinguished from the social imposition of some burden, such as the heavy excise many states impose on smoking and drinking. These impositions differ from punishment and penalization in that they leave the individual *morally free to choose* between the course which carries certain pay offs as well as state-imposed burdens and the course which carries neither the pay offs nor the burdens. It would be wrong to think of this tax as a punishment or penalty *for* smoking or drinking (though someone opposed to smoking and drinking may well say that the penalty *of*, not *for* smoking, is lung cancer, of drinking, cirrhosis; this is a *prudential warning* against these practices, not a threat of reprisals) since most states count on people going on smoking and drinking as sources of state revenue. To speak of some imposition as a punishment or the imposition of a penalty is to imply that people are not (or generally are thought not to be) morally free to make such a choice, though of

course they normally *can* choose what they are not morally free to do. Punishment expresses permissive moral condemnation of the conduct punished and is therefore inconsistent with a positive attitude of the imponent towards its recurrence or continuation, while taxation is perfectly compatible with it.

(v) *"For" something:* There is fairly general agreement that if someone's suffering of a deprivation at the hands of another is to be punishment, then there must be something *on account of which* the deprivation is imposed, something it is for. Some have taken this to be merely a point about the meaning of the word 'punishment', others interpret it to mean that punishment cannot be just and therefore not justified, unless it is inflicted *for* something which is capable of providing such a justification.

The definitional point is settled comparatively easily. We can say that no deprivation can *be* punishment unless it is imposed on someone *only after* he has been properly *found* to satisfy the condition for which the system of punishment imposes it. This does not mean that the punitive system, say the parental one, must have spelled out in detail what these conditions are, but there must be some understanding on the part of the recipients of what these conditions are. The system is flawed to the extent to which this is not true. In a crude "common law" system, the only developed legal function is that of judge, i.e., of the official who "finds" (authoritatively determines) whether or not someone has broken the law. But this does not mean then because there is no legislator who has spelled out the rules, the people do not know, at least roughly, what these rules are.

From this it plainly does not follow that a person suffers punishment only if he actually satisfies these conditions. What does follow is that it is *not deserved* punishment if he does not. If the imponent made a mistake in judging that the accused did satisfy the condition, then there was a miscarriage of justice. Nevertheless, the imponent meted out punishment and the recipient suffered it.

It also follows that if the accused is *found* not guilty, that is, if the judge's or jury's verdict is 'Not guilty', then an imposition of deprivation after that cannot be punishment. It is not even a miscarriage of justice, but *naked, blatant, shameless,* mistreatment or victimization or something of the sort.

But what about the imponent's state of mind? Can

the imposition *be* punishment if the imponent does *not believe* that the recipient is guilty (or believes that *he is not*) but pretends to believe it? I think it is punishment if the other conditions are satisfied. But it is punishment so seriously flawed that it amounts to victimization: victimization by deliberately wrongful punishment, though its being victimization is now concealed from the public. Thus, K.B. Armstrong in a much-quoted article which was one of the first in the Retributivist revival, says that this is a mistake because it would include cases such as those of an innocent man who had been found guilty by a court that had meticulously observed formal court procedures, been sentenced to death and been executed, hence such impositions were cases not of punishment but of something else, perhaps victimization. Similarly, John Kleinig, says "deliberately to impose unpleasant treatment on a person knowing full well that he has not committed any offense (even though he may have been 'alleged' to have committed an offense or may even have been formally 'found guilty' of an offense) *is not to punish him*, but to victimize, take advantage of, bully, persecute, tyrannize, or oppress him (and perhaps others) for various ends, and to cover this up *by making it look as though he is being punished*." It seems that both of them must think that nothing can be *both* punishment and victimization, for otherwise the fact that these are cases of victimization would not show that they are *not* cases of punishment. But this is a mistake.

It may perhaps be thought that punishment and victimization must be incompatible, for this reason: if it is *known* that the imposition is victimization, then it cannot be punishment, hence no one who knows or believes that it is victimization can consistently believe that it is punishment, hence those who are ignorant of its being victimization merely believe, wrongly, that it is punishment until they discover that it is victimization. But the analogous case of a miscarriage of justice should make us suspicious of this argument. The fact that someone discovers that an imposition is a miscarriage of justice does not show that it was or is not punishment. Plainly the crucial question is who can know what and when.

The imposition may be punishment even if at the time the whole moral community (except the court) knows that it is a miscarriage of justice, but not if they know it is victimization. And it can be punish-

ment in both cases if they find out only later: then it was and of course always will be a case of a miscarriage of justice or victimization as well as a case of (flawed) punishment.

That this can be so is explained by what should by now have become obvious, namely, that what makes the imposition punishment is that it is a "branding" of the recipient as one who satisfies the conditions of punishment (commission of an offense, crime, or wrong), on account of which he deserves the community's moral condemnation and the deprivation of certain rights. This "stigma" can, of course, be put on wrongly, whether by mistake (miscarriage of justice) or deliberately (victimization). But this is beside the point: it is punishment if he has been branded. If everybody knows at the time that he is innocent and that the court knows this too, then, there is only the unsuccessful attempt at "branding" him. If the community discovers the fraud only later, then the attempt was successful. The unmasking of the fraud does not undo the punishment, it merely reveals it to have been wrongful. If he is "branded" by a miscarriage of justice, then he has been punished even though everybody (except, of course, the court) knows that he was "branded" by mistake.

The "branding" is thus a rather complex one. Success is not simply a matter of *convincing* the moral community that the recipient really was guilty, for he can get branded even if they know he is innocent (the case of miscarriage of justice). Nor is it simply the uttering in the appropriate context, of the magic formula "we *find* you guilty" for he does not get "branded" when the whole community knows he is innocent (the case of victimization or travesty of justice). I think the pronouncement of the magic formula in the appropriate context *normally* suffices to "brand" the recipient but it can fail to do so, namely, in the abnormal case when the whole community knows (or for good reason believes) that the court proceedings have been a travesty of justice, that the formula "we find you guilty" was fradulently applied.

There is, however, a further question, namely, whether what the imponent of the deprivation is doing to the recipient *amounts to punishing him* if the imponent himself knows or believes the recipient innocent. It is natural to think that if the imposition amounts to punishment, then it must amount to punis*hing*. But this need not be so. One of the reasons why this is overlooked is a confusion between two things. The first is that no one can suffer punishment unless his deprivation is deliberately imposed by someone (as I said above, under (ii), hence no one can suffer punishment unless he is punished by someone, i.e., deliberately has imposed on him by that person a deprivation amounting to punish*ment*. The second is that under certain conditions, someone's deliberately imposing a deprivation on someone amounts to his punis*hing* him. The two may be logically unconnected. It may be the case that even though Jones *is being punished by* Smith, Smith is not *ipso facto* punishing Jones, just as (perhaps) Jones may be *lying to* Smith (if in order to deceive him he tells him something he thinks untrue) without Smith's *being lied to* by Jones (if what Jones tells him is in fact true). Whether or not the two are logically connected, depends on whether a person (logically) can punish another when he believes him not guilty. Consider the case of Jones who believes that his favorite daughter has broken the window, but then inflicts (what he had said would be, or now says is) the penalty for breaking windows on his stepson whom he dislikes but, mistakenly, thinks innocent of the misdeed. We might then want to say that the stepson suffers deserved punishment at the hands of his stepfather (because Jones is deliberately imposing the deprivation on the pretense that his stepson has broken the window) but might nevertheless insist that Jones has not punished him for breaking the window (or anything else) since he does not believe him guilty. We might want to insist that when Jones says "I am punishing you for breaking the window" this is false as well as being a lie, but also that if he had said "You are being punished for breaking the window", it would have been true, though even then Jones' remark would be dishonest or even lying.

Finally, it should be noted that in the case of legal punishment, where there is a division of labor between prosecutor, jury, judge, and actual administrator of the deprivation (executioner, prison warden, etc.), there is no longer a single punisher and so the simple question of what the punisher must believe if his imposition is to count as his punishing the recipient is no longer applicable. We can no longer find a straightforward answer to the question, 'Who punished him?'. The punishing is a cooperative enterprise involving the playing of many parts, any of which may be performed faultily without necessarily preventing the recipient from getting punished, i.e., getting the stigma of guilt attached to him. . . .

Responsibility

In a recent paper, Hart constructs the following story to illustrate the most important types of ascription of responsibility:

> *As captain of the ship, X was responsible for the safety of his passengers and crew. But on his last voyage he got drunk every night and was responsible for the loss of the ship with all aboard. It was rumored that he was insane, but the doctors considered that he was responsible for his actions. Throughout the voyage he behaved quite irresponsibly and various incidents in his career showed that he was not a responsible person. He always maintained that the exceptional winter storms were responsible for the loss of the ship, but in the legal proceedings brought against him he was found criminally responsible for his negligent conduct, and in separate civil proceedings he was held legally responsible for the loss of life and property. He is still alive and he is morally responsible for the deaths of many women and children.*

2.1) Accountability. In Hart's story the doctors considered the captain responsible for his actions. They ascribed to him responsibility in the sense of "accountability," being fit to be brought to account (the German *Zurechnungsfähigheit*), because of the possession of all those psychological powers which are necessary and sufficient for the ability to be guided by promulgated social rules. Minors and madmen lack these powers. They cannot be guided by social rules any more than the blind can be guided by traffic lights. They are therefore unfit to be brought to account; they are not accountable. Certain mental disorders may not altogether destroy these psychological powers but merely significantly reduce or impair them. We then speak of "diminished or impaired responsibility" (i.e., accountability).

Accountability may be a necessary condition of the proper imposition of any of the types of unwanted treatment. For even if the imposition of such treatment on nonaccountable persons did have the effect of raising the level of conformity with the social rules, this could not (ex hypothesi) be due to their greater willingness to be guided by the promulgated rules. Bringing them to account would not, therefore, be a practice auxiliary to that of rule-promulgation. Such a practice would lack an important safeguard and would therefore require additional and possibly less plausible assumptions for its justification.

2.2) Task-responsibility and other obligatory social requirements.

In Hart's story, X as the captain of the ship was responsible for the safety of the passengers and the crew. Let us call this sense of "responsibility" "task-responsibility." Unlike accountability, task-responsibility is always *for* something specific. A person simply is or is not accountable; or if we insist that he must be accountable for something, he is accountable for *anything* and *everything* for which one could be brought to account, i.e., "responsible for his actions." However, he is not task-responsible for any and all of his actions, but only for certain specific tasks. Unlike accountability, task-responsibility can be deliberately assumed or refused.

We indicate what he is task-responsible for in two different ways. We can indicate it by specifying a state of affairs: "for the safety of the crew," "for getting the dogs fed." Or we can indicate it by the identification of creatures capable of a good or interest, such as humans or dogs: "for Mary" or "for his dobermans." Such specifications may mean two quite different things. If I am task-responsible for Mary or the dobermans, I am task-responsible either for their well-being or for their not doing anything which would constitute the violation of a social rule.

A task-responsibility is a certain sort of obligatory social requirement. Other sorts are moral rules, duties, obligations, and commitments. There are no sharp lines between these sorts, for they are not sorts based on the same principle of classification. Roughly, moral rules mark out the things that are wrong for anyone ("Killing is wrong"); duties, the recurring tasks attacned to a social role or position ("One of the duties of a parent is to look after his children"); obligations, the specific tasks a given person is required to perform as a consequence of his dealings with others ("You have an obligation to pay for the car repairs since the accident was your fault"); and commitments, the specific tasks he has undertaken to perform ("I am afraid summer teaching is one of my commitments for next summer. I promised

the chairman some time ago"); and responsibilities, those requirements whose fulfillment involves forethought, care, intelligence, and initiative. Cooking her husband's meals, but not obedience to him, may be one of a wife's responsibility. But since these classifications are cross-classifications, there is no reason why one and the same task, say, providing for a certain woman, should not be among someone's duties (as her husband), his obligations (because in saving his life she had suffered injuries making her incapable of earning her own living), his commitments (since he had undertaken to do so in the marriage contract), and a responsibility (since it involves care, foresight, and initiative).

2.3) Answerability.

If a person is accountable and has failed to satisfy one of the obligatory social requirements, not necessarily a task-responsiblity, then another type of ascription of responsibility is applicable. I shall call it ascription of "answerability." I call it that because to be held responsible in this sense is to be required, by the rules of the practice of bringing people to account, to answer the question why one failed to conform to the obligatory social rule or directive in question. Much depends on what sort of true explanation of his failure is available to him, as we shall see shortly.

It will be helpful to make clear the differences between task-responsibility and answerability. Since one may conscientiously perform all one's tasks, one may be task-responsible for many things without being answerable for any; and vice versa, when the obligatory requirement one fails to perform is not a task-responsibility. What one is answerable for, can be indicated in the same ways as what one is task-responsible for. Thus, prior to the catastrophe the captain was (task-)responsible for the safety of the passengers and the crew and, therefore, after the catastrophe, became responsible = answerable for the loss of their lives. And if Jones is (task-)responsible for his daughter Joan, then is answerable for any harm or hurt she suffers, and/or for any breach by her of an obligatory social rule.

Unlike task-responsibility, answerability cannot be assumed, but is incurred. One becomes task-responsible when an obligatory social rule or directive comes to apply to one, but answerable when one fails to conform to it. One ceases to be task-responsible if that rule no longer applies to one, but one ceases to be answerable only when he has provided the appropriate answer.

2.4) Culpability. In Hart's story, the remarks "He was found criminally responsible for his negligent conduct," "He was held legally responsible for the loss of life and property," and "He is morally responsible for the deaths of many women and children" report the ascription to the captain of responsibility in yet another sense, which I shall call "culpability." To say that someone is responsible for something in this sense is to say that he failed to discharge an obligatory social requirement without adequate excuse. It is, in other words, to claim that he is answerable for something and that he has no exculpatory answer.

It should not be thought, however, that "responsible" and "culpable" mean exactly the same or are used in exactly the same way. All that can be said is that they can be used to ask and answer similar questions, all appropriate at the third stage or phase of the activity of bringing someone to account. Thus, the question "Is Jones responsible for this?" can be rendered either as "Was Jones' conduct culpable?" or "Was Jones culpable in doing this?" There are three linguistic differences between the two expressions. The first is that whereas only persons can be responsible in this sense, either persons or conduct can be culpable, and persons are culpable simply because their conduct is. But this seemingly important difference is purely verbal since the ground for saying that a person is responsible or that conduct is culpable is the absence of an excuse. A second difference is that whereas, typically, the object of responsibility, what a person is responsible *for*, is a state of affairs or a person, the corresponding object of culpability is conduct, someone's failing to obey a rule. But here again the difference is more apparent than real. For the states of affairs a person is responsible for are those states of affairs which a rule requires him either to prevent or at any rate not to bring about, such as harm to another, and which he has failed to keep, whence he is responsible. The third difference is more substantial. A person can only be responsible or not responsible; he cannot be more or less so, but he can be more or less culpable. Of course, he can be solely or partly (i.e., jointly) responsible, but that only means that he may either be or not be solely or jointly responsible for some-

thing, but he cannot be more or less so. Whether someone is responsible for something is the question of whether he lacks an *exculpatory* explanation. Although this does not itself allow of degrees, it indirectly refers to something that does, namely, the weight of the excuse contained in the explanation, a weight which may suffice to exculpate or may merely extenuate.

Again, similar questions can be asked by means of "Who (if anyone) is (responsible) = *to blame* for this?" and "Is he *guilty* of this?" The first question arises only in cases where something undesirable has happened, but the answer "He is to blame" ("It is his fault") can be given only if that undesirable event or state of affairs has come about because someone broke a social rule and did so without exculpatory explanation. The second question is asked in reference to an actual accusation, which is formulated in such a way that the degree of culpability is already built into it. The accusation determines how extenuating the explanation must be to amount to exculpation.

And what is an exculpatory, what an inculpatory explanation? The ground of this distinction is derivable from the object of the practice of bringing people to account. As we have seen, that object is by unobjectionable methods to eliminate or reduce in number those cases of rule-breaking which result from people's inadequate resolve to do what is obligatorily required. If there is no call to strengthen someone's resolve, then he need not be brought to account. The goal of the practice is just a stiffening of that resolve where necessary. Therefore those who have transgressed an obligatory social rule in conditions under which a person "with the best will in the world" would have done the same thing, need not be brought to account. Persons whose transgression has such an explanation, have an exculpatory explanation why they failed to conform. It may be true that the willingness of others to obey the social rules could be increased by inflicting undesirable treatment on all those who have transgressed them whether they have an excuse or not. The justification of this safeguard for the individual of goodwill then depends on whether the loss through greater rule-violation or the loss through reduced protection for persons of goodwill is the greater. The existence of so-called "strict liability" expresses the judgment that in those cases conformity to the rule is more important than the protection of the nonculpable individual. Exculpatory explanations are those which show that a person's failure to conform was not due to an inadequacy of his will, but occurred or would have occurred *despite its adequacy*. Such explanations fall into three main categories: i) inability, ii) compulsion, iii) and ignorance.

i) A person failed to accomplish what he was required to do, although he was set on doing it. The main cases are opposition by irresistible force (a policeman, a cramp in the leg); opposition by someone with superior gamesmanship (a more aggressive driver); prevention by circumstances from doing what is required (no vacant parking lot, a flat tire). In these cases, a man failing to keep an appointment has the exculpatory explanation that with the best will in the world he could not make it.

ii) A person fails to do what is required because he was set on something else, but was so set because of excessive pressure on his will. In these cases, although the failure is due to a misdirected will, it is not due to lack of goodwill because in the absence of the excessive pressure, the person's will would not have been set in the wrong direction. The explanation is exculpatory because it shows that what is needed is not the redirection of Jones' will but the elimination of the excessive pressure on it. The main cases are coercion (threat of death or pain or loss), compulsion by circumstances ("The storm compelled him to jettison the cargo"), and inner compulsion ("He was too frightened to do it"). In all these cases, the question of what constitutes excessive pressure on the will depends on how much pressure the person is (or can legitimately be) required to resist. It is conceivable that a soldier on active duty who under torture gives away military information cannot offer the torture as an exculpatory explanation since he may be required to withstand such torture. A bank clerk, on the other hand, may be able to claim that he was coerced to hand over the money if the holdup man threatened to shoot him.

iii) A person failed to do (accomplish) what he was required to do through ignorance. This, too, typically is not, though it may be, a case of lack of goodwill, because the person would do what is required of him if he were not ignorant. However, this may be a case of lack of goodwill, namely, if the ignorance itself is due to lack of goodwill in failing

to make the required effort to acquire the relevant knowledge. The main cases are ignorance of the requirement ("He did not know there was a law against it"), ignorance of some necessary conditions of success ("He did not know it was not loaded," "He did not know it was rat poison"). In all these cases what he knew he was doing (pulling the trigger, pouring the liquid) had a feature he did not know it had, on account of which what he did constituted his failure to conform and would not have been done had he known that it had that feature.

If the explanation of a person's behavior does not belong to one of these exculpatory types, it is inculpatory. In that case, the person who is answerable has failed to answer, and therefore must be said to be responsible, in the sense of culpable. He is to blame for what happened. It is his fault. He is guilty of something, i.e., he culpably failed to conform to a relevant social directive.

2.5) Liability. When a person has been found culpable, then he becomes liable to one or more of the three types of unwanted treatment (punishment, condemnation, payment of compensation). It must be recalled that what we are giving is a rational reconstruction of actual practices. In fact not all culpable men are punished, and some are liable to punishment although not culpable. Nevertheless it should be clear that the point of the whole procedure would be lost if culpability did not entail prima facie liability to punishment, that is to entail such liability unless the particular case can be shown to be exceptional in a way for which the rules of the procedure could not allow.

Bearing in mind the stages of the process of bringing people to account we can now sum up the various senses of "responsible," taking the final cumulative sense, where responsible = prima facie liable, as the main sense. Ascriptions of accountability and task-responsibility (as well as other forms of obligatory requirements, e.g., duty) state that the *presuppositions* of responsibility in the main sense are satisfied; ascriptions of answerability that a *presumption* of responsibility in the main sense is satisfied, a presumption which may, however, be rebutted by providing an excuse; ascriptions of culpability that the sufficient conditions of responsibility in the main sense are satisfied, that is the sense in which it means the satisfaction of the sufficient conditions of prima facie liability (i.e., liability unless there is something exceptional about the case).

Thus, that our captain was responsible-for-his-actions = accountable, and that he was responsible = task-responsible for the safety of the passengers, means that the presuppositions of responsibility in the main sense are satisfied: the question of his responsibility in the main sense does not even arise unless both these preliminary claims are established. When we say that it is the captain who is responsible = answerable for the loss of life and property,

we mean that there is a presumption that he is responsible in the main sense and that he is responsible in the main sense unless he has an excuse (or in cases of strict answerability, even if he has an excuse). Finally, that the captain is legally and morally responsible = to blame, for the deaths of many women and children, is to ascribe to him responsibility in the main sense, i.e., that prima facie he is liable to some form of undesirable treatment. To say that someone is responsible in the main sense is thus to say that all the conditions for saying that he is prima facie liable are satisfied.

Karl Menninger

THE CRIME OF PUNISHMENT

Karl Menninger argues that the reason crime is so difficult to eradicate is that it serves the needs of offenders and nonoffenders alike. In fact, according to Menninger, the motives of offenders and nonoffenders are quite similar; what distinguishes serious offenders is simply a greater sense of helplessness and hopelessness in the pursuit of their goals. Menninger concludes that we must find better ways to enable people to realize their goals. Menninger also argues that punishment as a vengeful response to crime does not work, because crime is an illness requiring treatment by psychiatrists and psychologists. Thus Menninger finds vengeful punishment itself to be a crime.

FEW WORDS IN OUR language arrest our attention as do "crime," "violence," "revenge," and "injustice." We abhor crime; we adore justice; we boast that we live by the rule of law. Violence and vengefulness we repudiate as unworthy of our civilization, and we assume this sentiment to be unanimous among all human beings.

Yet crime continues to be a national disgrace and a world-wide problem. It is threatening, alarming,

wasteful, expensive, abundant, and apparently increasing! In actuality it is decreasing in frequency of occurrence, but it is certainly increasing in visibility and the reactions of the public to it.

Our system for controlling crime is ineffective, unjust, expensive. Prisons seem to operate with revolving doors—the same people going in and out and in and out. *Who cares?*

Our city jails and inhuman reformatories and

wretched prisons are jammed. They are known to be unhealthy, dangerous, immoral, indecent, crime-breeding dens of iniquity. Not everyone has smelled them, as some of us have. Not many have heard the groans and the curses. Not everyone has seen the hate and despair in a thousand blank, hollow faces. But, in a way, we all know how miserable prisons are. *We want them to be that way.* And they are. *Who cares?*

Professional and big-time criminals prosper as never before. Gambling syndicates flourish. White-collar crime may even exceed all others, but goes undetected in the majority of cases. We are all being robbed and we know who the robbers are. They live nearby. *Who cares?*

The public filches millions of dollars worth of food and clothing from stores, towels and sheets from hotels, jewelry and knick-knacks from shops. The public steals, and the same public pays it back in higher prices. *Who cares?*

Time and time again somebody shouts about this state of affairs, just as I am shouting now. The magazines shout. The newspapers shout. The television and radio commentators shout (or at least they "deplore"). Psychologists, sociologists, leading jurists, wardens, and intelligent police chiefs join the chorus. Governors and mayors and Congressmen are sometimes heard. They shout that the situation is bad, bad, bad, and getting worse. Some suggest that we immediately replace obsolete procedures with scientific methods. A few shout contrary sentiments. Do the clear indications derived from scientific discovery for appropriate changes continue to fall on deaf ears? Why is the public so long-suffering, so apathetic and thereby so continuingly self-destructive? How many Presidents (and other citizens) do we have to lose before we do something?

The public behaves as a sick patient does when a dreaded treatment is proposed for his ailment. We all know how the aching tooth may suddenly quiet down in the dentist's office, or the abdominal pain disappear in the surgeon's examining room. Why should a sufferer seek relief and shun it? Is it merely the fear of pain of the treatment? Is it the fear of unknown complications? Is it distrust of the doctor's ability? All of these, no doubt.

But, as Freud made so incontestably clear, the sufferer is always somewhat deterred by a kind of subversive, internal opposition to the work of cure. He suffers on the one hand from the pains of his affliction and yearns to get well. But he suffers at the same time from traitorous impulses that fight against the accomplishment of any change in himself, even recovery! Like Hamlet, he wonders whether it may be better after all to suffer the familiar pains and aches associated with the old method than to face the complications of a new and strange, even though possibly better way of handling things.

The inescapable conclusion is that society secretly *wants* crime, *needs* crime, and gains definite satisfactions from the present mishandling of it! We condemn crime; we punish offenders for it; but we need it. The crime and punishment ritual is a part of our lives. We need crimes to wonder at, to enjoy vicariously, to discuss and speculate about, and to publicly deplore. We need criminals to identify ourselves with, to envy secretly, and to punish stoutly. They do for us the forbidden, illegal things we *wish* to do and, like scapegoats of old, they bear the burdens of our displaced guilt and punishment—"the iniquities of us all."

We have to confess that there is something fascinating for us all about violence. That most crime is not violent we know but we forget, because crime is a breaking, a rupturing, a tearing—even when it is quietly done. To all of us crime seems like violence.

The very word "violence" has a disturbing, menacing quality. . . . In meaning it implies something dreaded, powerful, destructive, or eruptive. It is something we abhor—or do we? Its first effect is to startle, frighten—even to horrify us. But we do not always run away from it. For violence also intrigues us. It is exciting. It is dramatic. Observing it and sometimes even participating in it gives us acute pleasure.

The newspapers constantly supply us with tidbits of violence going on in the world. They exploit its dramatic essence often to the neglect of conservative reporting of more extensive but less violent damage—the flood disaster in Florence, Italy, for example. Such words as crash, explosion, wreck, assault, raid, murder, avalanche, rape, and seizure evoke pictures of eruptive devastation from which we cannot turn away. The headlines often impute violence metaphorically even to peaceful activities. Relations are "ruptured," a tie is "broken," arbitration "collapses," a proposal is "killed."

Meanwhile on the television and movie screens there constantly appear for our amusement scenes of fighting, slugging, beating, torturing, clubbing, shooting, and the like which surpass in effect anything that the newspapers can describe. Much of this violence is portrayed dishonestly; the scenes are only semirealistic; they are "faked" and romanticized.

Pain cannot be photographed; grimaces indicate but do not convey its intensity. And wounds—unlike violence—are rarely shown. This phony quality of television violence in its mentally unhealthy aspect encourages irrationality by giving the impression to the observer that being beaten, kicked, cut, and stomped, while very unpleasant, are not very painful or serious. For after being slugged and beaten the hero rolls over, opens his eyes, hops up, rubs his cheek, grins, and staggers on. The *suffering* of violence is a part both the TV and movie producers *and* their audience tend to repress.

Although most of us *say* we deplore cruelty and destructiveness, we are partially deceiving ourselves. We disown violence, ascribing the love of it to other people. But the facts speak for themselves. We do love violence, all of us, and we all feel secretly guilty for it, which is another clue to public resistance to crime-control reform.

The great sin by which we all are tempted is the wish to hurt others, and this sin must be avoided if we are to live and let live. If our destructive energies can be mastered, directed, and sublimated, we can survive. If we can love, we can live. Our destructive energies, if they cannot be controlled, may destroy our best friends, as in the case of Alexander the Great, or they may destroy supposed "enemies" or innocent strangers. Worst of all—from the standpoint of the individual—they may destroy us.

Over the centuries of man's existence, many devices have been employed in the effort to control these innate suicidal and criminal propensities. The earliest of these undoubtedly depended upon fear— fear of the unknown, fear of magical retribution, fear of social retaliation. These external devices were replaced gradually with the law and all its machinery, religion and its rituals, and the conventions of the social order.

The routine of life formerly required every individual to direct much of his aggressive energy against the environment. There were trees to cut down, wild animals to fend off, heavy obstacles to remove, great burdens to lift. But the machine has gradually changed all of this. Today, the routine of life, for most people, requires no violence, no fighting, no killing, no life-risking, no sudden supreme exertion: occasionally, perhaps, a hard pull or a strong push, but no tearing, crushing, breaking, forcing.

And because violence no longer has legitimate and useful vents or purposes, it must *all* be controlled today. In earlier times its expression was often a virtue, today its control is the virtue. The control involves symbolic, vicarious expressions of our violence—violence modified; "sublimated," as Freud called it; "neutralized," as Hartmann described it. Civilized substitutes for direct violence are the objects of daily search by all of us. The common law and the Ten Commandments, traffic signals and property deeds, fences and front doors, sermons and concerts, Christmas trees and jazz bands—these and a thousand other things exist today to help in the control of violence.

My colleague, Bruno Bettelheim, thinks we do not properly educate our youth to deal with their violent urges. He reminds us that nothing fascinated our forefathers more. The *Iliad* is a poem of violence. Much of the Bible is a record of violence. One penal system and many methods of child-rearing express violence—"violence to suppress violence." And, he concludes [in the article "Violence: A Neglected Mode of Behavior"]: "We shall not be able to deal intelligently with violence unless we are first ready to see it as a part of human nature, and then we shall come to realize the chances of discharging violent tendencies are now so severely curtailed that their regular and safe draining-off is not possible anymore."

Why aren't we all criminals? We all have the impulses; we all have the provocations. But becoming civilized, which is repeated ontologically in the process of social education, teaches us what we may do with impunity. What then evokes or permits the breakthrough? Why is it necessary for some to bribe their consciences and do what they do not approve of doing? Why does all sublimation sometimes fail and overt breakdown occur in the controlling and managing machinery of the personality? Why do we sometimes lose self-control? Why do we "go to pieces"? Why do we explode?

These questions point up a central problem in psychiatry. Why do some people do things they do

257

not want to do? Or things we do not want them to do? Sometimes crimes are motivated by a desperate need to act, to do *something* to break out of a state of passivity, frustration, and helplessness too long endured, like a child who shoots a parent or a teacher after some apparently reasonable act. Granting the universal presence of violence within us all, controlled by will power, conscience, fear of punishment, and other devices, granting the tensions and the temptations that are also common to us all, why do the mechanisms of self-control fail so completely in some individuals? Is there not some pre-existing defect, some moral or cerebral weakness, some gross deficiency of common sense that lets some people tumble or kick or strike or explode, while the rest of us just stagger or sway?

When a psychiatrist examines many prisoners, writes [Seymour] Halleck [in *Psychiatry and the Dilemmas of Crime*], he soon discovers how important in the genesis of the criminal outbreak is the offender's previous *sense of helplessness or hopelessness.* All of us suffer more or less from infringement of our personal freedom. We fuss about it all the time; we strive to correct it, extend it, and free ourselves from various oppressive or retentive forces. We do not want others to push us around, to control us, to dominate us. We realize this is bound to happen to some extent in an interlocking, interrelated society such as ours. No one truly has complete freedom. But restriction irks us.

The offender feels this way, too. He does not want to be pushed around, controlled, or dominated. And because he often feels that he is thus oppressed (and actually is) and because he does lack facility in improving his situation without violence, he suffers more intensely from feelings of helplessness.

Violence and crime are often attempts to escape from madness; and there can be no doubt that some mental illness is a flight from the wish to do the violence or commit the act. Is it hard for the reader to believe that suicides are sometimes committed to forestall the commiting of murder? There is no doubt of it. Nor is there any doubt that murder is sometimes committed to avert suicide.

Strange as it may sound, many murderers do not realize whom they are killing, or, to put it another way, that they are killing the wrong people. To be sure, killing anybody is reprehensible enough, but the worst of it is that the person who the killer

thinks should die (and he has reasons) is not the person he attacks. Sometimes the victim himself is partly responsible for the crime that is committed against him. It is this unconscious (perhaps sometimes conscious) participation in the crime by the victim that has long held up the very humanitarian and progressive-sounding program of giving compensation to victims. The public often judges the victim as well as the attacker.

Rape and other sexual offenses are acts of violence so repulsive to our sense of decency and order that it is easy to think of rapists in general as raging, oversexed, ruthless brutes (unless they are conquering heroes). Some rapists are. But most sex crimes are committed by undersexed rather than oversexed individuals, often undersized rather than oversized, and impelled less by lust than by a need for reassurance regarding an impaired masculinity. The unconscious fear of women goads some men with a compulsive urge to conquer, humiliate, hurt, or render powerless some available sample of womanhood. Men who are violently afraid of their repressed but nearly emergent homosexual desires, and men who are afraid of the humiliation of impotence, often try to overcome these fears by violent demonstrations.

The need to deny something in oneself is frequently an underlying motive for certain odd behavior—even up to and including crime. Bravado crimes, often done with particular brutality and ruthlessness, seem to prove *to the doer* that "I am no weakling! I am no sissy! I am no coward. I am no homosexual! I am a tough man who fears nothing." The Nazi storm troopers, many of them mere boys, were systematically trained to stifle all tender emotions and force themselves to be heartlessly brutal.

Man perennially seeks to recover the magic of his childhood days—the control of the mighty by the meek. The flick of an electric light switch, the response of an automobile throttle, the click of a camera, the touch of a match to a skyrocket—these are keys to a sudden and magical display of great power induced by the merest gesture. Is anyone already so blasé that he is no longer thrilled at the opening of a door specially for him by a a magic-eye signal? Yet for a few pennies one can purchase a far more deadly piece of magic—a stored explosive and missile encased within a shell which can be ejected from a machine at the touch of a finger so swiftly that no eye can follow. A thousand yards away something falls dead—a rabbit, a deer, a beautiful mountain sheep, a sleeping child, or the President of the United States. Magic! Magnified, projected power. "Look what I can do. I am the greatest!"

It must have come to every thoughtful person, at one time or another, in looking at the revolvers on the policemen's hips, or the guns soldiers and hunters carry so proudly, that these are instruments made for the express purpose of delivering death to someone. The easy availability of these engines of destruction, even to children, mentally disturbed people, professional criminals, gangsters, and even high school girls is something to give one pause. The National Rifle Association and its allies have been able to kill scores of bills that have been introduced into Congress and state legislatures for corrective gun control since the death of President Kennedy. Americans still spend about $2 billion on guns each year.

Fifty years ago, Winston Churchill declared that the mood and temper of the public in regard to crime and criminals is one of the unfailing tests of the civilization of any country. Judged by this standard, how civilized are we?

The chairman of the President's National Crime Commission, Nicholas de B. Katzenbach, declared . . . that organized crime flourishes in America because enough of the public wants its services, and most citizens are apathetic about its impact. It will continue uncurbed as long as Americans accept it as inevitable and, in some instances, desirable.

Are there steps that we can take which will reduce the aggressive stabs and self-destructive lurches of our less well-managing fellow men? Are there ways to prevent and control the grosser violations, other than the clumsy traditional maneuvers which we have inherited? These depend basically upon intimidation and slow-motion torture. We call it punishment, and justify it with our "feeling." We know it doesn't work.

Yes, there *are* better ways. There are steps that could be taken; some *are* taken. But we move too slowly. Much better use, it seems to me, could be made of the members of my profession and other behavioral scientists than having them deliver courtroom pronunciamentos. The consistent use of a diagnostic clinic would enable trained workers to lay what they can learn about an offender before the

judge who would know best how to implement the recommendation.

This would no doubt lead to a transformation of prisons, if not to their total disappearance in their present form and function. Temporary and permanent detention will perhaps always be necessary for a few, especially the professionals, but this could be more effectively and economically performed with new types of "facility" (that strange, awkward word for institution).

I assume it to be a matter of common and general agreement that our object in all this is to protect the community from a repetition of the offense by the most economical method consonant with our other purposes. Our "other purposes" include the desire to prevent these offenses from occurring, to reclaim offenders for social usefulness, if possible, and to detain them in protective custody, if reclamation is *not* possible. But how?

The treatment of human failure or dereliction by the infliction of pain is still used and believed in by many nonmedical people. "Spare the rod and spoil the child" is still considered wise counsel by many.

Whipping is still used by many secondary schoolmasters in England, I am informed, to stimulate study, attention, and the love of learning. Whipping was long a traditional treatment for the "crime" of disobedience on the part of children, pupils, servants, apprentices, employees. And slaves were treated for centuries by flogging for such offenses as weariness, confusion, stupidity, exhaustion, fear, grief, and even overcheerfulness. It was assumed and stoutly defended that these "treatments" cured conditions for which they were administered.

Meanwhile, scientific medicine was acquiring many new healing methods and devices. Doctors can now transplant organs and limbs; they can remove brain tumors and cure incipient cancers; they can halt pneumonia, meningitis, and other infections; they can correct deformities and repair breaks and tears and scars. But these wonderful achievements are accomplished on *willing* subjects, people who voluntarily ask for help by even heroic measures. And the reader will be wondering, no doubt, whether doctors can do anything with or for people who *do not want* to be treated at all, in any way! Can doctors cure willful aberrant behavior? Are we to believe that crime is a *disease* that can be reached by scientific measures? Isn't it merely "natural meanness" that makes all of us do wrong things at times even when we "know better"? And are not self-control, moral stamina, and will power the things needed? Surely there is no medical treatment for the lack of those!

Let me answer this carefully, for much misunderstanding accumulates here. I would say that according to the prevalent understanding of the words, crime is *not* a disease. Neither is it an illness, although I think it *should* be! It *should* be treated, and it could be; but it mostly isn't.

These enigmatic statements are simply explained. Diseases are undesired states of being which have been described and defined by doctors, usually given Greek or Latin appellations, and treated by long-established physical and pharmacological formulae. Illness, on the other hand, is best defined as a state of impaired functioning of such a nature that the public expects the sufferer to repair to the physician for help. The illness may prove to be a disease; more often it is only vague and nameless misery, but something which doctors, not lawyers, teachers, or preachers, are supposed to be able and willing to help.

When the community begins to look upon the expression of aggressive violence as the symptom of an illness or as indicative of illness, it will be because it believes doctors can do something to correct such a condition. At present, some better-informed individuals do believe and expect this. However angry at or sorry for the offender, they want him "treated" in an effective way so that he will cease to be a danger to them. And they know that the traditional punishment, "treatment-punishment," will not effect this.

What *will*? What effective treatment is there for such violence? It will surely have to begin with motivating or stimulating or arousing in a cornered individual the wish and hope and intention to change his methods of dealing with the realities of life. Can this be done by education, medication, counseling, training? I would answer *yes*. It can be done successfully in a majority of cases, if undertaken in time.

The present penal system and the existing legal philosophy do not stimulate or even expect such a change to take place in the criminal. Yet change is what medical science always aims for. The prisoner, like the doctor's other patients, should emerge from his treatment experience a different person, differ-

ently equipped, differently functioning, and headed in a different direction than when he began the treatment.

It is natural for the public to doubt that this can be accomplished with criminals. But remember that the public *used* to doubt that change could be effected in the mentally ill. No one a hundred years ago believed mental illness to be curable. Today *all* people know (or should know) that *mental illness is curable* in the great majority of instances and that the prospects and rapidity of cure are directly related to the availability and intensity of proper treatment.

The forms and techniques of psychiatric treatment used today number in the hundreds. No one patient requires or receives all forms, but each patient is studied with respect to his particular needs, his basic assets, his interests, and his special difficulties. A therapeutic team may embrace a dozen workers—as in a hospital setting—or it may narrow down to the doctor and the spouse. Clergymen, teachers, relatives, friends, and even fellow patients often participate informally but helpfully in the process of readaptation.

All of the participants in this effort to bring about a favorable change in the patient—i.e., in his vital balance and life program—are imbued with what we may call a *therapeutic attitude*. This is one in direct antithesis to attitudes of avoidance, ridicule, scorn, or punitiveness. Hostile feelings toward the subject, however justified by his unpleasant and even destructive behavior, are not in the curriculum of therapy or in the therapist. This does not mean that therapists approve of the offensive and obnoxious behavior of the patient; they distinctly disapprove of it. But they recognize it as symptomatic of continued imbalance and disorganization, which is what they are seeking to change. They distinguish between disapproval, penalty, price, and punishment.

Doctors charge fees; they impose certain "penalties" or prices, but they have long since put aside primitive attitudes of retaliation toward offensive patients. A patient may cough in the doctor's face or may vomit on the office rug; a patient may curse or scream or even struggle in the extremity of his pain. But these acts are not "punished." Doctors and nurses have no time or thought for inflicting unnecessary pain even upon patients who may be difficult, disagreeable, provocative, and even dangerous. It is their duty to care for them, to try to make them well, and to prevent them from doing themselves or others harm. This requires love, not hate. This is the deepest meaning of the therapeutic attitude. Every doctor knows this; every worker in a hospital or clinic knows it (or should).

There is another element in the therapeutic attitude. It is the quality of hopefulness. If no one believes that the patient can get well, if no one—not even the doctor—has any hope, there probably won't be any recovery. Hope is just as important as love in the therapeutic attitude.

"But you were talking about the mentally ill," readers may interject, "those poor, confused, bereft, frightened individuals who yearn for help from you doctors and nurses. Do you mean to imply that willfully perverse individuals, our criminals, can be similarly reached and rehabilitated? Do you really believe that effective treatment of the sort you visualize can be applied to people *who do not want any help*, who are so willfully vicious, so well aware of the wrongs they are doing, so lacking in penitence or even common decency that punishment seems to be the only thing left?"

Do I believe there is effective treatment for offenders, and that they *can* be changed? *Most certainly and definitely I do.* Not all cases, to be sure; there are also some physical afflictions which we cannot cure at the moment. Some provision has to be made for incurables—pending new knowledge— and these will include some offenders. But I believe the majority of them would prove to be curable. The willfulness and the viciousness of offenders are part of the thing for which they have to be treated. These must not thwart the therapeutic attitude.

It is simply not true that most of them are "fully aware" of what they are doing, nor is it true that they want no help from anyone, although some of them say so. Prisoners are individuals: some want treatment, some do not. Some don't know what treatment is. Many are utterly despairing and hopeless. Where treatment is made available in institutions, many prisoners seek it even with the full knowledge that doing so will not lessen their sentences. In some prisons, seeking treatment by prisoners is frowned upon by the officials.

Various forms of treatment are even now being tried in some progressive courts and prisons over the country—educational, social, industrial, religious, recreational, and psychological treatments. Socially

acceptable behavior, new work-play opportunities, new identity and companion patterns all help toward community reacceptance. Some parole officers and some wardens have been extremely ingenious in developing these modalities of rehabilitation and reconstruction—more than I could list here even if I knew them all. But some are trying. The secret of success in all programs, however, is the replacement of the punitive attitude with a therapeutic attitude.

Offenders with propensities for impulsive and predatory aggression should not be permitted to live among us unrestrained by some kind of social control. *But the great majority of offenders, even "criminals," should never become prisoners if we want to "cure" them.*

There are now throughout the country many citizens' action groups and programs for the prevention and control of crime and delinquency. With such attitudes of inquiry and concern, the public could acquire information (and incentive) leading to a change of feeling about crime and criminals. It will discover how unjust is much so-called "justice," how baffled and frustrated many judges are by the ossified rigidity of old-fashioned, obsolete laws and state constitutions which effectively prevent the introduction of sensible procedures to replace useless, harmful ones.

I want to proclaim to the public that things are not what it wishes them to be, and will only become so if it will take an interest in the matter and assume some responsibility for its own self-protection.

Will the public listen?

If the public does become interested, it will realize that we must have more facts, more trial projects, more checked results. It will share the dismay of the President's Commission in finding that no one knows much about even the incidence of crime with any definiteness or statistical accuracy.

The average citizen finds it difficult to see how any research would in any way change his mind about a man who brutally murders his children. But just such inconceivably awful acts most dramatically point up the need for research. Why should—how can—a man become so dreadful as that in our culture? How is such a man made? Is it comprehensible that he can be born to become so depraved?

There are thousands of questions regarding crime and public protection which deserve scientific study. What makes some individuals maintain their interior equilibrium by one kind of disturbance of the social structure rather than by another kind, one that would have landed him in a hospital? Why do some individuals specialize in certain types of crime? Why do so many young people reared in areas of delinquency and poverty and bad example never become habitual delinquents? (Perhaps this is a more important question than why some of them do.)

The public has a fascination for violence, and clings tenaciously to its yen for vengeance, blind and deaf to the expense, futility, and dangerousness of the resulting penal system. But we are bound to hope that this will yield in time to the persistent, penetrating light of intelligence and accumulating scientific knowledge. The public will grow increasingly ashamed of its cry for retaliation, its persistent demand to punish. This is its crime, *our* crime against criminals—and, incidentally, our crime against ourselves. For before we can diminish our

sufferings from the ill-controlled aggressive assaults of fellow citizens, we must renounce the philosophy of punishment, the obsolete, vengeful penal attitude. In its place we would seek a comprehensive constructive social attitude—therapeutic in some instances, restraining in some instances, but preventive in its total social impact.

In the last analysis this becomes a question of personal morals and values. No matter how glorified or how piously disguised, vengeance as a human motive must be personally repudiated by each and every one of us. This is the message of old religions and new psychiatries. Unless this message is heard, unless we, the people—the man on the street, the housewife in the home—can give up our delicious satisfactions in opportunities for vengeful retaliation on scapegoats, we cannot expect to preserve our peace, our public safety, or our mental health.

C. S. Lewis

A CRITIQUE OF THE HUMANITARIAN THEORY OF PUNISHMENT

C. S. Lewis argues that the humanitarian theory of punishment is not in the interests of the criminal. According to Lewis, this is because the humanitarian theory is concerned with the goals of reform and deterrence and not the requirements of justice. Hence the theory permits the violation of the criminal's rights as a way of promoting these goals. Moreover, Lewis claims, deciding what promotes reform and deterrence, unlike deciding what is required by justice, seems best left to experts. Yet these experts, Lewis argues, even with the best of intentions, may act "as cruelly and unjustly as the greatest tryants."

IN ENGLAND WE HAVE lately had a controversy about Capital Punishment. I do not know whether a murderer is more likely to repent and make a good end

on the gallows a few weeks after his trial or in the prison infirmary thirty years later. I do not know whether the fear of death is an indispensable deter-

From "The Humanitarian Theory of Punishment," *Res Judicatae* (1953) pp. 224–230. Reprinted by permission of the *Melbourne University Law Review* and the Trustee for the C. S. Lewis Estate.

rent. I need not, for the purpose of this article, decide whether it is a morally permissible deterrent. Those are questions which I propose to leave untouched. My subject is not Capital Punishment in particular, but that theory of punishment in general which the controversy showed to be almost universal among my fellow-countrymen. It may be called the Humanitarian theory. Those who hold it think that it is mild and merciful. In this I believe that they are seriously mistaken. I believe that the "Humanity" which it claims is a dangerous illusion and disguises the possibility of cruelty and injustice without end. I urge a return to the traditional or Retributive theory not solely, not even primarily, in the interests of society, but in the interests of the criminal.

According to the Humanitarian theory, to punish a man because he deserves it, and as much as he deserves, is mere revenge, and, therefore, barbarous and immoral. It is maintained that the only legitimate motives for punishing are the desire to deter others by example or to mend the criminal. When this theory is combined, as frequently happens, with the belief that all crime is more or less pathological, the idea of mending tails off into that of healing or curing and punishment becomes therapeutic. Thus it appears at first sight that we have passed from the harsh and self-righteous notion of giving the wicked their deserts to the charitable and enlightened one of tending the psychologically sick. What could be more amiable? One little point which is taken for granted in this theory needs, however, to be made explicit. The things done to the criminal, even if they are called cures, will be just as compulsory as they were in the old days when we called them punishments. If a tendency to steal can be cured by psychotherapy, the thief will no doubt be forced to undergo the treatment. Otherwise, society cannot continue.

My contention is that this doctrine, merciful though it appears, really means that each one of us, from the moment he breaks the law, is deprived of the rights of a human being.

The reason is this. The Humanitarian theory removes from Punishment the concept of Desert. But the concept of Desert is the only connecting link between punishment and justice. It is only as deserved or undeserved that a sentence can be just or unjust. I do not here contend that the question "Is

it deserved?" is the only one we can reasonably ask about a punishment. We may very properly ask whether it is likely to deter others and to reform the criminal. But neither of these two last questions is a question about justice. There is no sense in talking about a "just deterrent" or a "just cure". We demand of a deterrent not whether it is just but whether it will deter. We demand of a cure not whether it is just but whether is succeeds. Thus when we cease to consider what the criminal deserves and consider only what will cure him or deter others, we have tacitly removed him from the sphere of justice altogether; instead of a person, a subject of rights, we now have a mere object, a patient, a "case".

The distinction will become clearer if we ask who will be qualified to determine sentences when sentences are no longer held to derive their propriety from the criminal's deservings. On the old view the problem of fixing the right sentence was a moral problem. Accordingly, the judge who did it was a person trained in jurisprudence: trained, that is, in a science which deals with rights and duties, and which, in origin at least, was consciously accepting guidance from the Law of Nature, and from Scripture. We must admit that in the actual penal code of most countries at most times these high originals were so much modified by local custom, class interests, and utilitarian concessions, as to be very imperfectly recognizable. But the code was never in principle, and not always in fact, beyond the control of the conscience of the society. And when (say, in eighteenth-century England) actual punishments conflicted too violently with the moral sense of the community, juries refused to convict and reform was finally brought about. This was possible because, so long as we are thinking in terms of Desert, the propriety of the penal code, being a moral question, is a question on which every man has the right to an opinion, not because he follows this or that profession, but because he is simply a man, a rational animal enjoying the Natural Light. But all this is changed when we drop the concept of Desert. The only two questions we may now ask about a punishment are whether it deters and whether it cures. But these are not questions on which anyone is entitled to have an opinion simply because he is a man. He is not entitled to an opinion even if, in addition to being a man, he should happen also to be a jurist, a Christian, and a moral theologian. For they are not questions about principle but about matter of fact; and for such *cuiquam in sua arte credendum*. Only the expert "penologist" (let barbarous things have barbarous names), in the light of previous experiment, can tell us what is likely to deter: only the psychotherapist can tell us what is likely to cure. It will be in vain for the rest of us, speaking simply as men, to say, "but this punishment is hideously unjust, hideously disproportionate to the criminal's deserts". The experts with perfect logic will reply, "but nobody was talking about deserts. No one was talking about *punishment* in your archaic vindictive sense of the word. Here are the statistics proving that this treatment deters. Here are the statistics proving that this other treatment cures. What is your trouble?"

The Humanitarian theory, then, removes sentences from the hands of jurists whom the public conscience is entitled to criticize and places them in the hands of technical experts whose special sciences do not even employ such categories as rights or justice. It might be argued that since this transference results from an abandonment of the old idea of punishment, and, therefore, of all vindictive motives, it will be safe to leave our criminals in such hands. I will not pause to comment on the simple-minded view of fallen human nature which such a belief implies. Let us rather remember that the "cure" of criminals is to be compulsory; and let us then watch how the theory actually works in the mind of the Humanitarian. The immediate starting point of this article was a letter I read in one of our Leftist weeklies. The author was pleading that a certain sin, now treated by our laws as a crime, should henceforward be treated as a disease. And he complained that under the present system the offender, after a term in gaol, was simply let out to return to his original environment where he would probably relapse. What he complained of was not the shutting up but the letting out. On his remedial view of punishment the offender should, of course, be detained until he was cured. And of course the official straighteners are the only people who can say when that is. The first result of the Humanitarian theory is, therefore, to substitute for a definite sentence (reflecting to some extent the community's moral judgment on the degree of ill-desert involved) an indefinite sentence terminable only by the word of those experts—and they are not experts in moral theology nor even in

the Law of Nature—who inflict it. Which of us, if he stood in the dock, would not prefer to be tried by the old system?

It may be said that by the continued use of the word punishment and the use of the verb "inflict" I am misrepresenting Humanitarians. They are not punishing, not inflicting, only healing. But do not let us be deceived by a name. To be taken without consent from my home and friends; to lose my liberty; to undergo all those assaults on my personality which modern psychotherapy knows how to deliver; to be re-made after some pattern of "normality" hatched in a Viennese laboratory to which I never professed allegiance; to know that this process will never end until either my captors have succeeded or I grown wise enough to cheat them with apparent success—who cares whether this is called Punishment or not? That it includes most of the elements for which any punishment is feared—shame, exile, bondage, and years eaten by the locust—is obvious. Only enormous ill-desert could justify it; but ill-desert is the very conception which the Humanitarian theory has thrown overboard.

If we turn from the curative to the deterrent justification of punishment we shall find the new theory even more alarming. When you punish a man *in terrorem*, make of him an "example" to others, you are admittedly using him as a means to an end; someone else's end. This, in itself, would be a very wicked thing to do. On the classical theory of Punishment it was of course justified on the ground that the man deserved it. That was assumed to be established before any question of "making him an example" arose. You then, as the saying is, killed two birds with one stone; in the process of giving him what he deserved you set an example to others. But take away desert and the whole morality of the punishment disappears. Why, in Heaven's name, am I to be sacrificed to the good of society in this way?—unless, of course, I deserve it.

But that is not the worst. If the justification of exemplary punishment is not to be based on desert but solely on its efficacy as a deterrent, it is not absolutely necessary that the man we punish should even have committed the crime. The deterrent effect demands that the public should draw the moral, "If we do such an act we shall suffer like that man." The punishment of a man actually guilty whom the public think innocent will not have the desired effect;

the punishment of a man actually innocent will, provided the public think him guilty. But every modern State has powers which make it easy to fake a trial. When a victim is urgently needed for exemplary purposes and a guilty victim cannot be found, all the purposes of deterrence will be equally served by the punishment (call it "cure" if you prefer) of an innocent victim, provided that the public can be cheated into thinking him guilty. It is no use to ask me why I assume that our rulers will be so wicked. The punishment of an innocent, that is, an undeserving, man is wicked only if we grant the traditional view that righteous punishment means deserved punishment. Once we have abandoned that criterion, all punishments have to be justified, if at all, on other grounds that have nothing to do with desert. Where the punishment of the innocent can be justified on those grounds (and it could in some cases be justified as a deterrent) it will be no less moral than any other punishment. Any distaste for it on the part of a Humanitarian will be merely a hang-over from the Retributive theory.

It is, indeed, important to notice that my argument so far supposes no evil intentions on the part of the Humanitarian and considers only what is involved in the logic of his position. My contention is that good men (not bad men) consistently acting upon that position would act as cruelly and unjustly as the greatest tyrants. They might in some respects act even worse. Of all tyrannies a tyranny sincerely exercised for the good of its victims may be the most oppressive. It may be better to live under robber barons than under omnipotent moral busybodies. The robber baron's cruelty may sometimes sleep, his cupidity may at some point be satiated; but those who torment us for our own good will torment us without end for they do so with the approval of their own conscience. They may be more likely to go to Heaven yet at the same time likelier to make a Hell of earth. Their very kindness stings with intolerable insult. To be "cured" against one's will and cured of states which we may not regard as disease is to be put on a level with those who have not yet reached the age of reason or those who never will; to be classed with infants, imbeciles, and domestic animals. But to be punished, however severely, because we have deserved it, because we "ought to have known better", is to be treated as a human person made in God's image.

In reality, however, we must face the possibility of bad rulers armed with a Humanitarian theory of punishment. A great many popular blue prints for a Christian society are merely what the Elizabethans called "eggs in moonshine" because they assume that the whole society is Christian or that the Christians are in control. This is not so in most contemporary States. Even if it were, our rulers would still be fallen men, and, therefore, neither very wise nor very good. As it is, they will usually be unbelievers. And since wisdom and virtue are not the only or the commonest qualifications for a place in the government, they will not often be even the best unbelievers. The practical problem of Christian politics is not that of drawing up schemes for a Christian society, but that of living as innocently as we can with unbelieving fellow-subjects under unbelieving rulers who will never be perfectly wise and good and who will sometimes be very wicked and very foolish. And when they are wicked the Humanitarian theory of punishment will put in their hands a finer instrument of tyranny than wickedness ever had before. For if crime and disease are to be regarded as the same thing, it follows that any state of mind which our masters choose to call "disease" can be treated as crime; and compulsorily cured. It will be vain to plead that states of mind which displease government need not always involve moral turpitude and do not therefore always deserve forfeiture of liberty. For our masters will not be using the concepts of Desert and Punishment but those of disease and cure. We know that one school of psychology already regards religion as a neurosis. When this particular neurosis becomes inconvenient to government, what is to hinder government from proceeding to "cure" it? Such "cure" will, of course, be compulsory; but under the Humanitarian theory it will not be called by the shocking name of Persecution. No one will blame us for being Christian, no one will hate us, no one will revile us. The new Nero will approach us with the silky manners of a doctor, and though all will be in fact as compulsory as the *tunica molesta* or Smithfield or Tyburn, all will go on within the unemotional therapeutic sphere where words like "right" and "wrong" or "freedom" and "slavery" are never heard. And thus when the command is given, every prominent Christian in the land may vanish overnight into Institutions for the Treatment of the Ideologically Unsound, and it will rest with the expert gaolers to say when (if ever) they are to re-emerge. But it will not be persecution. Even if the treatment is painful, even if it is life-long, even if it is fatal, that will be only a regrettable accident; the intention was purely therapeutic. Even in ordinary medicine there were painful operations and fatal operations; so in this. But because they are "treatment", not punishment, they can be criticized only by fellow-experts and on technical grounds, never by men as men and on grounds of justice.

This is why I think it essential to oppose the Humanitarian theory of punishment, root and branch, wherever we encounter it. It carries on its front a semblance of mercy which is wholly false. That is how it can deceive men of good will. The error began, perhaps, with Shelley's statement that the distinction between mercy and justice was invented in the courts of tyrants. It sounds noble, and was indeed the error of a noble mind. But the distinction is essential. The older view was that mercy "tempered" justice, or (on the highest level of all) that mercy and justice had met and kissed. The essential act of mercy was to pardon; and pardon in its very essence involves the recognition of guilt, and ill-desert in the recipient. If crime is only a disease which needs cure, not sin which deserves punishment, it cannot be pardoned. How can you pardon a man for having a gumboil or a club foot? But the Humanitarian theory wants simply to abolish Justice and substitute Mercy for it. This means that you start being "kind" to people before you have considered their rights,

and then force upon them supposed kindnesses which they in fact had a right to refuse, and finally kindnesses which no one but you will recognize as kindnesses and which the recipient will feel as abominable cruelties. You have overshot the mark. Mercy, detached from Justice, grows unmerciful. That is the important paradox. As there are plants which will flourish only in mountain soil, so it appears that Mercy will flower only when it grows in the crannies of the rock of Justice: transplanted to the marshlands of mere Humanitarianism, it becomes a man-eating weed, all the more dangerous because it is still called by the same name as the mountain variety. But we ought long ago to have learned our lesson. We should be too old now to be deceived by those humane pretensions which have served to usher in every cruelty of the revolutionary period in which we live. These are the "precious balms" which will "break our heads."

There is a fine sentence in Bunyan: "It came burning hot into my mind, whatever he said, and however he flattered, when he got me home to his house, he would sell me for a slave." There is a fine couplet, too, in John Ball:

Be ware ere ye be woe
Know your friend from your foe.

One last word. You may ask why I sent this to an Australian periodical. The reason is simple and perhaps worth recording: I can get no hearing for it in England.

Edmund L. Pincoffs

CLASSICAL RETRIBUTIVISM

Edmund L. Pincoffs begins by setting out three principles that, he holds, express the essence of a Kantian retributive theory of punishment. He then claims that the underlying rationale for these principles is to provide a justification of the punishment to the criminal on the

From *The Rationale of Legal Punishment* (1966) pp. 2–16. Reprinted by permission of Humanities Press, Inc., Atlantic Highlands, N.J., 07716.

grounds that she has willed the punishment she now suffers. Pincoffs concludes by noting two difficulties for the retributive theory of punishment which he has not addressed: how to make punishment equal to the crime and how to distinguish punishment from revenge.

I

THE CLASSIFICATION OF KANT as a retributivist[1] is usually accompanied by a reference to some part of the following passage from the *Rechtslehre*, which is worth quoting at length.

Juridical punishment can never be administered merely as a means for promoting another good either with regard to the criminal himself or to civil society, but must in all cases be imposed only because the individual on whom it is inflicted has committed a crime. For one man ought never to be dealt with merely as a means subservient to the purpose of another, nor be mixed up with the subjects of real right. Against such treatment his inborn personality has a right to protect him, even though he may be condemned to lose his civil personality. He must first be found guilty and punishable before there can be any thought of drawing from his punishment any benefit for himself or his fellow-citizens. The penal law is a categorical imperative; and woe to him who creeps through the serpent-windings of utilitarianism to discover some advantage that may discharge him from the justice of punishment, or even from the due measure of it, according to the Pharisaic maxim: "It is better that one man should die than the whole people should perish." For if justice and righteousness perish, human life would no longer have any value in the world. . . .

But what is the mode and measure of punishment which public justice takes as its principle and standard? It is just the principle of equality, by which the pointer of the scale of justice is made to incline no more to the one side than the other. It may be rendered by saying that the undeserved evil which any one commits on another, is to be regarded as perpetrated on himself. Hence it may be said: "If you slander another, you slander yourself; if you steal from another, you steal from yourself; if you strike another, you strike yourself; if you kill another, you kill yourself." This is the Right of RETALIATION (jus talionis); and properly understood, it is the only principle which in regulating a public court, as distinguished from mere private judgment, can definitely assign both the quality and the quantity of a just penalty. All other standards are wavering and uncertain; and on account of other considerations involved in them, they contain no principle conformable to the sentence of pure and strict justice.[2]

Obviously we could mull over this passage for a long time. What, exactly, is the distinction between the Inborn and the Civil Personality? How is the Penal Law a Categorical Imperative: by derivation from one of the five formulations in the *Grundlegung*, or as a separate formulation? But we are on the trail of the traditional retributive theory of punishment and do not want to lose ourselves in niceties. There are two main points in this passage to which we should give particular attention:

i. The only acceptable reason for punishing a man is that he has committed a crime.
ii. The only acceptable reason for punishing a man in a given manner and degree is that the punishment is "equal" to the crime for which he is punished.

These propositions, I think it will be agreed, express the main points of the first and second paragraphs respectively. Before stopping over these points, let us go on to a third. It is brought out in the following passage from the *Rechtslehre*, which is also often referred to by writers on retributivism.

Even if a civil society resolved to dissolve itself with the consent of all its members—as might be supposed in the case of a people inhabiting an island resolving to separate and scatter themselves throughout the whole world—the last murderer lying in prison ought to be executed before the resolution was carried out. This ought to be done in order that every one may realize the desert of his deeds, and that bloodguiltiness may not remain upon the people; for otherwise they will all be regarded as participators in the murder as a public violation of justice.[3]

It is apparent from this passage that, so far anyway as the punishment of death for murder is concerned, the punishment awarded not only may but must be carried out. If it must be carried out "so that everyone may realize the desert of his deeds," then punishment for deeds other than murder must be carried out too. We will take it, then, that Kant holds that:

iii. Whoever commits a crime must be punished in accordance with his desert.

Whereas (i) tells us what kind of reason we must Whereas (i) tells us what kind of reason we must have *if* we punish, (iii) now tells us that we must punish *whenever* there is desert of punishment. Punishment, Kant tells us elsewhere, is "The *juridical* effect or consequence of a culpable act of Demerit."[4] Any crime is a culpable act of demerit, in that it is an "*intentional* transgression—that is, an act accompanied with the consciousness that it is a transgression."[5] This is an unusually narrow definition of crime, since crime is not ordinarily limited to intentional acts of transgression but may also include unintentional ones, such as acts done in ignorance of the law, and criminally negligent acts. However, Kant apparently leaves room for "culpable acts of demerit" outside of the category of crime. These he calls "faults," which are unintentional transgressions of duty, but "are nevertheless imputable to a person."[6] I can only suppose, though it is a difficulty in the interpretation of the *Rechtslehre*, that when Kant says that punishment must be inflicted "only because he has committed a crime," he is not including in "crime" what he would call a fault. Crime would, then, refer to any *intentional* imputable transgressions of duty; and these are what must be punished as involving ill desert. The difficulties involved in the definition of crime as the transgression of duty, as opposed to the mere violation of a legal prohibition, will be taken up later.

Taking the three propositions we have isolated as expressing the essence of the Kantian retributivistic position, we must now ask a direct and obvious question. What makes Kant hold this position? Why does he think it apparent that consequences should have *nothing to do* with the decision whether, and how, and how much to punish? There are two directions an answer to this question might follow. One would lead us into an extensive excursus on the philosophical position of Kant, the relation of this to his ethical theory, and the relation of his general theory of ethics to his philosophy of law. It would, in short, take our question as one about the consistency of Kant's position concerning the justification losophy. This would involve discussion of Kant's reasons for believing that moral laws must be universal and categorical in virtue of their form alone, and divorced from any empirical content; of his attempt to make out a moral decision-procedure based upon an "empty" categorical imperative; and, above all, of the concept of freedom as a postulate of practical reason, and as the central concept of the philosophy of law. This kind of answer, however, we must forego here; for while it would have considerable interest in its own right, it would lead us astray from our purpose, which is to understand as well as we can the retributivist position, not as a part of this or that philosophical system but for its own sake. It is a position taken by philosophers with diverse philosophical systems; we want to take another direction, then, in our answer. Is there any *general* (nonspecial, nonsystematic) reason why Kant rejects consequences in the justification of punishment?

Kant believes that consequences have nothing to do with the justification of punishment partly because of his assumptions about the *direction* of justification; and these assumptions are, I believe, also to be found underlying the thought of Hegel and Bradley. Justification is not only *of* something, it is also *to* someone: it has an addressee. Now there are important confusions in Kant's and other traditional justifications of punishment turning on the question what the "punishment" *is* which is being justified. . . . But if we are to feel the force of the retributivist position, we can no longer put off the question of the addressee of justification.

To whom is the Kantian justification of punishment directed? The question may seem a difficult one to answer, since Kant does not consider it himself as a separate issue. Indeed, it is not the kind of question likely to occur to a philosopher of Kant's formalistic leanings. A Kantian justification or rationale stands, so to speak, on its own. It is a structure which can be examined, tested, probed by any rational being. Even to speak of the addressee of justification has an uncomfortably relativistic sound, as if only persuasion of A or B or C is possible, and proof impossible. Yet, in practice, Kant does not address his proffered justification of punishment so much to any rational being (which, to put it otherwise, is to address it not at all), as to the being most affected: the criminal himself.

It is the criminal who is cautioned not to creep through the serpent-windings of utilitarianism. It is the criminal's rights which are in question in the debate with Beccaria over capital punishment. It is the criminal we are warned not to mix up with property or things: the "subjects of Real Right." In the *Kritik der Praktischen Vernunst*, the intended direction of justification becomes especially clear.

Now the notion of punishment, as such, cannot be united with that of becoming a partaker of happiness; for although he who inflicts the punishment may at the same time have the benevolent purpose of directing this punishment to this end, yet it must be justified in itself as punishment, that is, as mere harm, so that if it stopped there, and the person punished could get no glimpse of kindness hidden behind this harshness, he must yet admit that justice was done him, and that his reward was perfectly suitable to his conduct. In every punishment, as such, there must first be justice, and this constitutes the essence of the notion. Benevolence may, indeed, be united with it, but the man who has deserved punishment has not the least reason to reckon upon this.[7]

Since this matter of the direction of justification is central in our understanding of traditional retributivism, and not generally appreciated, it will be worth our while to pause over this paragraph. Kant holds here, as he later holds in the *Rechtslehre*, that once it has been decided that a given "mode and measure" of punishment is justified, then "he who inflicts punishment" may do so in such a way as to increase the long-term happiness of the criminal. This could be accomplished, for example, by using a prison term as an opportunity for reforming the criminal. But Kant's point is that reforming the criminal has nothing to do with justifying the infliction of punishment. It is not inflicted because it will give an opportunity for reform, but because it is merited. The passage does not need my gloss; it is transparently clear. Kant wants the justification of punishment to be such that the criminal "who could get no glimpse of kindness behind this harshness" would have to admit that punishment is warranted.

Suppose we tell the criminal, "We are punishing you for your own good." This is wrong, because it is then open to him to raise the question whether he deserves punishment, and what you consider good to be. If he does not deserve punishment, we have

no right to inflict it, especially in the name of some good of which the criminal may not approve. So long as we are to treat him as rational—a being with dignity—we cannot force our judgments of good upon him. This is what makes the appeal to supposedly good consequences "wavering and uncertain." They waver because the criminal has as much right as anyone to question them. They concern ends which he may reject, and means which he might rightly regard as unsuited to the ends.

In the "Supplementary Explanations of the Principles of Right" of the *Rechtslehre*, Kant distinguishes between "punitive justice (*justitia punitiva*), in which the ground of the penalty is moral (*quia peccatum est*)," and "punitive *expediency*, the foundation of which is merely pragmatic (*ne peccetur*) as being grounded upon the experience of what operates most effectively to prevent crime." Punitive justice, says Kant, has an "entirely distinct place (*locus justi*) in the topical arrangement of the juridical conceptions." It does not seem reasonable to suppose that Kant makes this distinction merely to discard punitive expediency entirely, that he has no concern at all for the *ne peccetur*. But he does hold that there is no place for it in the justification of punishment proper: for this can only be to show the criminal that the punishment is just.

How is this to be done? The difficulty is that on the one hand the criminal must be treated as a rational being, an end in himself; but on the other hand the justification we offer him cannot be allowed to appear as the opening move in a rational discussion. It cannot turn on the criminal's acceptance of some premise which, as rational being, he has a perfect right to question. If the end in question is the well-being of society, we are assuming that the criminal will not have a different view of what that well-being consists in, and we are telling him that he should sacrifice himself to that end. As a rational being, he can question whether any end we propose is a good end. And we have no right to demand that he sacrifice himself to the public well-being, even supposing he agrees with us on what that consists in. No man has a duty, on Kant's view, to be benevolent.[8]

The way out of the quandary is to show the criminal that we are not inflicting the punishment on him for some questionable purpose of our own choice, but that he, as a free agent, has exercised *his* choice in such a way as to make the punishment a necessary consequence. "His own evil deed draws the punishment upon himself."[9] "The undeserved evil which anyone commits on another, is to be regarded as perpetuated on himself."[10] But may not the criminal rationally question this asserted connection between crime and punishment? Suppose he wishes to regard the punishment *not* as "drawn upon himself" by his own "evil deed?" Suppose he argues that no good purpose will be served by punishing him? But this line of thought leads into the "serpent-windings of utilitarianism," for if it is good consequences that govern, then justice goes by the board. What may not be done to him in the name of good consequences? What proportion would remain between what he has done and what he suffers?[11]

But punishment is *inflicted*. To tell the criminal that he "draws it upon himself" is all very well, only how do we justify *to ourselves* the infliction of it? Kant's answer is found early in the *Rechtslehre*.[12] There he relates punishment to crime *via* freedom. Crime consists in compulsion or constraint of some kind: a hindrance of freedom.[13] If it is wrong that freedom should be hindered, it is right to block this hindrance. But to block the constraint of freedom it is necessary to apply constraint. Punishment is a "hindering of a hindrance of freedom." Compulsion of the criminal is, then, justified only to the extent that it hinders his compulsion of another.

But how are we to understand Kant here? Punishment comes after the crime. How can it hinder the crime? The reference cannot be to the hindrance of future crime, or Kant's doctrine reduces to a variety of utilitarianism. The picture of compulsion *vs.* compulsion is clear enough, but how are we to apply it? Our answer must be somewhat speculative, since there is no direct answer to be found in the *Rechtslehre*. The answer must begin from yet another extension of the concept of a crime. For the crime cannot consist merely in an act. What is criminal is acting in accordance with a wrong maxim: a maxim which would, if made universal, destroy freedom. The adoption of the maxim is criminal. Should we regard punishment, then, as the hindrance of a wrong maxim? But how do we hinder a maxim? We show, exhibit, its wrongness by taking it at face value. If the criminal has adopted it, he is claiming that it can be universalized. But if it is universalized

it warrants the same treatment of the criminal as he has accorded to his victim. So if he murders he must be executed; if he steals we must "steal from" him.[14] What we do to him he willed, in willing to adopt his maxim as universalizable. To justify the punishment to the criminal is to show him that the compulsion we use on him proceeds according to the same rule by which he acts. This is how he "draws the punishment upon himself." In punishing, we are not adopting his maxim but demonstrating its logical consequences if universalized: We show the criminal *what* he has willed. This is the positive side of the Kantian rationale of punishment.

II

Hegel's version of this rationale has attracted more attention, and disagreement, in recent literature. It is the Hegelian metaphysical terminology which is in part responsible for the disagreement, and which has stood in the way of an understanding of the retributivist position. The difficulty turns around the notions of "annulment of crime," and of punishment as the "right" of the criminal. Let us consider "annulment" first.

In the *Philosophie des Rechts*[15] Hegel tells us that

Abstract right is a right to coerce, because the wrong which transgresses it is an exercise of force against the existence of my freedom in an external thing. The maintenance of this existent against the exercise of force therefore itself takes the form of an external act and an exercise of force annulling the force originally brought against it.[16]

Holmes complains that by the use of his logical apparatus, involving the negation of negations (or annulment), Hegel professes to establish what is only a mystic (though generally felt) bond between wrong and punishment.[17] Hastings Rashdall asks how any rational connection can be shown between the evil of the pain of punishment, and the twin evils of the suffering of the victim and the moral evil which "pollutes the offender's soul," unless appeal is made to the probable good consequences of punishment. The notion that the "guilt" of the offense must be, in some mysterious way, wiped out by the suffering of the offender does not seem to provide it.[18] Crime, which is an evil, is apparently to be "annulled" by the addition to it of punishment, which is another evil. How can two evils yield a good?[19]

But in fact Hegel is following the *Rechtslehre* quite closely here, and his doctrine is very near to Kant's. In the notes taken at Hegel's lectures,[20] we find Hegel quoted as follows:

If crime and its annulment . . . are treated as if they were unqualified evils, it must, of course, seem quite unreasonable to will an evil merely because "another evil is there already.". . . But it is not merely a question of an evil or of this, that, or the other good; the precise point at issue is wrong, and the righting of it. . . . The various considerations which are relevant to punishment as a phenomenon and to the bearing it has on the particular consciousness, and which concern its effects (deterrent, reformative, etcetera) on the imagination, are an essential topic for examination in their place, especially in connection with modes of punishment, but all these considerations presuppose as their foundation the fact that punishment is inherently and actually just. In discussing this matter the only important things are, first, that crime is to be annulled, not because it is the producing of an evil, but because it is the infringing of the right as right, and secondly, the question of what that positive existence is which crime possesses and which must be annulled; it is this existence which is the real evil to be removed, and the essential point is the question of where it lies. So long as the concepts here at issue are not clearly apprehended, confusion must continue to reign in the theory of punishment.[21]

While this passage is not likely to dethrone confusion, it does bring us closer to the basically Kantian heart of Hegel's theory. To "annul crime" should be read "right wrong." Crime is a wrong which consists in an "infringement of the right as right."[22] It would be unjust, says Hegel, to allow crime, which is the invasion of a right, to go unrequited. For to allow this is to admit that the crime is "valid": that is, that it is not in conflict with justice. But this is what we do want to admit, and the only way of showing this is to pay back the deed to the agent: coerce the coercer. For by intentionally violating his victim's rights, the criminal in effect claims that the rights of others are not binding on him; and this is to attack *das Recht* itself: the system of justice in which there are rights which must be respected. Punishment not only keeps the system in balance, it vindicates the system itself.

Besides talking about punishment's "annulment"

of crime, Hegel has argued that it is the "right of the criminal." The obvious reaction to this is that it is a strange justification of punishment which makes it someone's right, for it is at best a strange kind of right which no one would ever want to claim! Mc-Taggart's explanation of this facet of Hegel's theory is epitomized in the following quotation:

What, then, is Hegel's theory? It is, I think, briefly this: In sin, man rejects and defies the moral law. Punishment is pain inflicted on him because he has done this, and in order that he may, by the fact of his punishment, be forced into recognizing as valid the law which he rejected in sinning, and so repent of his sin—really repent, and not merely be frightened out of doing it again.[23]

If McTaggart is right, then we are obviously not going to find in Hegel anything relevant to the justification of legal punishment, where the notions of sin and repentance are out of place. And this is the conclusion McTaggart of course reaches. "Hegel's view of punishment," he insists, "cannot properly be applied in jurisprudence, and . . . his chief mistake regarding it lay in supposing that it could."[24]

But though McTaggart may be right in emphasizing the theological aspect of Hegel's doctrine of punishment, he is wrong in denying it a jurisprudential aspect. In fact, Hegel is only saying what Kant emphasized: that to justify punishment to the criminal is to show him that *he* has chosen to be treated as he is being treated.

The injury (the penalty) which falls on the criminal is not merely implicitly *just—as just, it is* eo ipso *his implicit will, an embodiment of his freedom, his right; on the contrary, it is also a right* established *within the criminal himself, that is, in his objectively embodied will, in his action. The reason for this is that his action is the action of a rational being and this implies that it is something universal and that by doing it the criminal has laid down a law which he has explicitly recognized in his action and under which in consequence he should be brought as under his right.[25]*

To accept the retributivist position, then, is to accept a thesis about the burden of proof in the justification of punishment. Provided we make the punishment "equal" to the crime it is not up to us to justify it to the criminal, beyond pointing out to him that it is what he willed. It is not that he initiated a chain of events likely to result in his punishment, but that in willing the crime he willed that he himself should suffer in the same degree as his victim. But what if the criminal simply wanted to commit his crime and get away with it (break the window and run, take the funds and retire to Brazil, kill but live?) Suppose we explain to the criminal that *really* in willing to kill he willed to lose his life; and, unimpressed, he replies that *really* he wished to kill and save his skin. The retributivist answer is that to the extent that the criminal understands freedom and justice he will understand that his punishment was made inevitable by his own choice. No moral theory can hope to provide a justification of punishment which will seem such to the criminal merely as a nexus of passions and desires. The retributivist addresses him as a rational being, aware of the significance of his action. The burden of proof, the retributivist would argue, is on the theorist who would not start from this assumption. For to assume from the beginning that the criminal is not rational is to treat him, from the beginning, as merely a "harmful animal."

What is involved in the action of the criminal is not only the concept of crime, the rational aspect present in crime as such whether the individual wills it or not, the aspect which the state has to vindicate, but also the abstract rationality of the individual's volition. Since that is so, punishment is regarded as containing the criminal's right and hence by being punished he is honored as a rational being. He does not receive this due of honor unless the concept and measure of his punishment are derived from his own act. Still less does he receive it if he is treated as a harmful animal who has to be made harmless, or with a view to deterring and reforming him.[26]

To address the criminal as a rational being aware of the significance of his action is to address him as a person who knows that he has not committed a "bare" act; to commit an act is to commit oneself to the universalization of the rule by which one acted. For a man to complain about the death sentence for murder is as absurd as for a man to complain that when he pushed down one tray of the scales, the other tray goes up; whereas the action, rightly considered, is of pushing down *and* up. "The criminal gives his consent already by his very act."[27] "The Eu-

menides sleep, but crime awakens them, and hence it is the very act of crime which vindicates itself."[28]

F. H. Bradley's contribution to the retributive theory of punishment adds heat but not much light. The central, and best-known, passage is the following:

If there is any opinion to which the man of uncultivated morals is attached, it is the belief in the necessary connection of Punishment and guilt. Punishment is punishment, only where it is deserved. We pay the penalty because we owe it, and for no other reason; and if punishment is inflicted for any other reason whatever than because it is merited by wrong, it is a gross immorality, a crying injustice, an abominable crime, and not what it pretends to be. We may have regard for whatever considerations we please—our own convenience, the good of society, the benefit of the offender; we are fools, and worse, if we fail to do so. Having once the right to punish, we may modify the punishment according to the useful and the pleasant; but these are external to the matter, they cannot give us a right to punish, and nothing can do that but criminal desert. This is not a subject to waste words over; if the fact of the vulgar view is not palpable to the reader, we have no hope, and no wish, to make it so.[29]

Bradley's sympathy with the "vulgar view" should be apparent. And there is at least a seeming variation between the position he expresses here and that we have attributed to Kant and Hegel. For Bradley can be read here as leaving an open field for utilitarian reasoning, when the question is how and how much to punish. Ewing interprets Bradley this way, and argues at some length that Bradley is involved in an inconsistency.[30] However, it is quite possible that Bradley did not mean to allow kind and quantity of punishment to be determined by utilitarian considerations. He could mean, as Kant meant, that once punishment is awarded, then "it" (what the criminal must suffer: time in jail, for example) may be made use of for utilitarian purposes. But, it should by this time go without saying, the retributivist would then wish to insist that we not argue backward from the likelihood of attaining these good purposes to the rightness of inflicting the punishment.

Bradley's language is beyond question loose when he speaks, in the passage quoted, of our "modifying" the punishment, "having once the right to punish." But when he says that "we pay the penalty because we owe it, and for no other reason," Bradley must surely be credited with the insight that we may owe more or less according to the gravity of the crime. The popular view, he says, is "that punishment is justice; that justice implies the giving what is due."[31] And, "punishment is the complement of criminal desert; is justifiable only so far as deserved."[32] If Bradley accepts this popular view, then Ewing must be wrong in attributing to him the position that kind and degree of punishment may be determined by utilitarian considerations.[33]

III

Let us sum up traditional retributivism, as we have found it expressed in the paradigmatic passage we have examined. We have found no reason in Hegel or Bradley, to take back or qualify importantly the *three propositions* we found central in Kant's retributivism:

i. The only acceptable reason for punishing a man is that he has committed a crime.
ii. The only acceptable reason for punishing a man in a given manner and degree is that the punishment is "equal" to the crime.
iii. Whoever commits a crime must be punished in accordance with his desert.

To these propositions should be added *two underlying assumptions:*

i. An assumption about the direction of justification: to the criminal.
ii. An assumption about the nature of justification: to show the criminal that it is he who has willed what he now suffers.

Though it may have been stated in forbidding metaphysical terms, traditional retributivism cannot be dismissed as unintelligible, or absurd, or implausible.[34] There is no obvious contradiction in it; and there are no important disagreements among the philosophers we have studied over what it contends. Yet in spite of the importance of the theory, no one has yet done much more than sketch it in broad strokes. If, as I have surmised, it turns mainly on an assumption concerning the direction of justification,

then this assumption should be explained and defended.

And the key concept of "desert" is intolerably vague. What does it mean to say that punishment must be proportionate to what a man *deserves?* This seems to imply, in the theory of the traditional retributivists, that there is some way of measuring desert, or at least of balancing punishment against it. How this measuring or balancing is supposed to be done, we will discuss later. What we must recognize here is that there are alternative criteria of "desert," and that it is not always clear which of these the traditional retributivist means to imply.

When we say of a man that he "deserves severe punishment" how, if at all, may we support our position by arguments? What kind of considerations tend to show what a man does or does not deserve? There are at least two general sorts: those which tend to show that what he has done is a member of a class of action which is especially heinous; and those which tend to show that his doing of this action was, in (or because of) the circumstances, particularly wicked. The argument that a man deserves punishment may rest on the first kind of appeal alone, or on both kinds. Retributivists who rely on the first sort of consideration alone would say that anyone who would do a certain sort of thing, no matter what the circumstances may have been, deserves punishment. Whether there are such retributivists I do not know. Kant, because of his insistence on *intention* as a necessary condition of committing a crime, clearly wishes to bring in considerations of the second sort as well. It is not, on his view, merely *what* was done, but the intention of the agent which must be taken into account. No matter what the intention, a man cannot commit a crime deserving punishment if his deed is not a transgression. But if he does commit a transgression, he must do so intentionally to commit a crime; and all crime is deserving of punishment. The desert of the crime is a factor both of the seriousness of the transgression, considered by itself, and the degree to which the intention to transgress was present. If, for Kant, the essence of morality consists in knowingly acting from duty, the essence of immorality consists in knowingly acting against duty.

The retributivist can perhaps avoid the question of how we decide that one crime is morally more heinous than another by hewing to his position that no such decision is necessary so long as we make the punishment "equal" to the crime. To accomplish this, he might argue, it is not necessary to argue to the *relative* wickedness of crimes. But at best this leaves us with the problem how we *do* make punishments equal to crimes, a problem which will not stop plaguing retributivists. And there is the problem *which* transgressions, intentionally committed, the retributivist is to regard as crimes. Surely not every morally wrong action!

And how is the retributivist to fit in appeals to punitive expediency? None of our authors denies that such appeals may be made, but where and how do they tie into punitive justice? It will not do simply to say that justifying punishment to the criminal is one thing, and justifying it to society is another. Suppose we must justify in both directions at once? And who are "we" anyway—the players of which roles, at what stage of the game? And has the retributivist cleared himself of the charge, sure to arise, that the theory is but a cover for a much less commendable motive than respect for justice: elegant draping for naked revenge?

NOTES

1. . . . since in our own time there are few defenders of retributivism, the position is most often referred to by writers who are opposed to it. This does not make for clarity. In the past few years, however, there has been an upsurge of interest, and some good articles have been written. Cf. esp. J. D. Mabbott, "Punishment," *Mind*, XLVIII (1939), pp. 152–67; C. S. Lewis, "The Humanitarian Theory of Punishment," *20th Century* (Australian), March, 1949; C. W. K. Mundle, "Punishment and Desert," *The Philosophical Quarterly*, IV (1954), pp. 216–228; A. S. Kaufman, "Anthony Quinton on Punishment," *Analysis*, October, 1959; and K. G. Armstrong, "The Retributivist Hits Back," LXX (1961), pp. 471–90.

2. *Rechtslehre.* Part Second, 49, E. Hastie translation, Edinburgh, 1887, pp. 195–7.

3. *Ibid.*, p. 198. Cf. also the passage on p. 196 beginning "What, then, is to be said of such a proposal as to keep a Criminal alive who has been condemned to death . . ."

4. *Ibid.*, Prolegomena, General Divisions of the Metaphysic of Morals, IV. (Hastie, p. 38).

5. *Ibid.*, p. 32.

6. *Ibid.*, p. 32.

7. Book I, Ch. I, Sect. VIII, Theorem IV, Remark II (T. K. Abbott translation, 5th ed., revised, London, 1898, p. 127).

8. *Rechtslehre.*

9. "Supplementary Explanation of The Principles of Right," V.

10. Cf. long quote from the *Rechtslehre*, above.

11. How can the retributivist allow utilitarian considerations even in the administration of the sentence? Are we not then opportunistically imposing our conception of good on the convicted man? How did we come by this right, which we did not have when he stood before the bar awaiting sentence? Kant would refer to the loss of his "Civil Personality;" but what rights remain with the "Inborn Personality," which is not lost? How is human dignity modified by conviction of crime?

12. Introduction to The Science of Right, General Definitions and Divisions, D. Right is Joined with the Title to Compel. (Hastie, p. 47).

13. This extends the definition of crime Kant has given earlier by specifying the nature of an imputable transgression of duty.

14. There are serious difficulties in the application of the "Principle of Equality" to the "mode and measure" of punishment. This will be considered . . .

15. I shall use this short title for the work with the formidable double title of *Naturrecht und Stattswis-*

senchaft in Grundrisse; Grundlinien der Philosophie des Rechts (Natural Law and Political Science in Outline; Elements of The Philosophy of Right.) References will be to the T. M. Knox translation (*Hegel's Philosophy of Right*, Oxford, 1942).

16. *Philosophie des Rechts*, Sect. 93 (Knox, p. 67).

17. O. W. Holmes, Jr., *The Common Law*, Boston, 1881, p. 42.

18. Hastings Rashdall, *The Theory of Good and Evil*, 2nd. Edn., Oxford, 1924, vol. 1, pp. 285–6.

19. G. E. Moore holds that, consistently with his doctrine of organic wholes, they might; or at least they might yield that which is less evil than the sum of the constituent evils. This indicates for him a possible vindication of the Retributive theory of punishment. (*Principia Ethica*, Cambridge, 1903, pp. 213–214).

20. Included in the Knox translation.

21. Knox translation, pp. 69–70.

22. There is an unfortunate ambiguity in the German word *Recht*, here translated as "right." The word can mean either that which is a right or that which is in accordance with the law. So when Hegel speaks of "infringing the right as right" it is not certain whether he means a right as such or the law as such, or whether, in fact, he is aware of the ambiguity. But to say that the crime infringes the law is analytic, so we will take it that Hegel uses *Recht* here to refer to that which is right. But what the criminal does is not merely to infringe a right, but "the right *(das recht)* as right," that is, to challenge by his action the whole system of rights. (On "*Recht*," Cf. J. Austin, *The Province of Jurisprudence Determined*, London, Library of Ideas end., 1954), Note 26, pp. 285–288 esp. pp. 287–8).

23. J. M. E. McTaggart, *Studies in The Hegelian Cosmology*, Cambridge, 1901, Ch. V, p. 133.

24. *Ibid.*, p. 145.

25. *Op Cit.*, Sect. 100 (Hastie, p. 70.)

26. *Ibid.*, Lecture-notes on Sect. 100, Hastie, p. 71.

27. *Ibid.*, Addition to Sect. 100, Hastie, p. 246.

28. *Ibid.*, Addition to Sect. 101, Hastie, p. 247. There is something ineradicably *curious* about retributivism. We keep coming back to the metaphor of the balance scale. Why is the metaphor powerful and the same time strange? Why do we agree so readily that "the assassination" cannot "trammel up the consequence," that "even-handed justice comments the ingredients of our poisoned chalice to our own lips?"

29. F. H. Bradley, *Ethical Studies*, Oxford, 1952, pp. 26–7.

30. A. C. Ewing, *The Morality of Punishment*, London, 1929, pp. 41–42.

31. *Op. Cit.*, p. 29.

32. *Ibid.*, p. 30.

33. *Op. Cit.*, p. 41.

34. Or, more ingeniously, "merely logical," the "elucidation of the use of a word;" answering the question, "When (logically) *can* we punish?" as opposed to the question answered by the utilitarians, "When (morally) *may* or *ought* we to punish?" (Cf. A. M. Quinton, "On Punishment," *Analysis*, June, 1954, pp. 133–142)

Ernest van den Haag and Louis Schwartz

THE DEATH PENALTY: FOR AND AGAINST

Ernest van den Haag favors the death penalty because (1) it is the indispensable deterrent for certain crimes, (2) some evidence seems to support its deterrent value, (3) imposing the death penalty is the least risky alternative, and (4) it is a requirement of justice.

Louis B. Schwartz opposes the death penalty because (1) mistakes occur in our trial system, (2) having the death penalty makes it difficult to get convictions, (3) some evidence seems to indicate that the death penalty does not deter, (4) having the death penalty can in certain cases stimulate a criminal to kill, and (5) the process of choosing those to be executed is inevitably arbitrary.

Q Professor van den Haag, why do you favor the use of the death penalty?

A For certain kinds of crimes it is indispensable.

Thus: The federal prisons now have custody of a man sentenced to life imprisonment who, since he has been in prison, has committed three more murders on three separate occasions—both of prison guards and inmates. There is no further punishment that he can receive. In effect, he has a license to murder.

Take another case: When a man is threatened with life imprisonment for a crime he has already committed, what reason has he not to kill the arresting officer in an attempt to escape? His punishment would be the same.

In short, there are many cases where the death penalty is the only penalty available that could possibly deter.

I'll go a step further. I hold life sacred. Because I hold it sacred, I feel that anyone who takes someone else's life should know that thereby he forsakes his own and does not just suffer an inconvenience about being put into prison for some time.

Q Could the same effect be achieved by putting the criminal in prison for life?

A At present, "life imprisonment" means anything from six months—after which the parole board in Florida can release the man—to 12 years in some States. But even if it were real life imprisonment, its deterrent effect will never be as great as that of the death penalty. The death penalty is the only actually

irrevocable penalty. Because of that, it is the one that people fear most. And because it is feared most, it is the one that is most likely to deter.

Q Authorities seem to differ as to whether the death sentence really does deter crime—

A Usually the statistics quoted were compiled more than 10 years ago and seem to indicate that the absence or presence of the death penalty made no difference in murder rates.

However, in the last 10 years there have been additional investigations. The results indicate, according to Isaac Ehrlich's recent article in the *American Economic Review:* Over the period 1933 to 1969, "an additional execution per year . . . may have resulted on the average in seven or eight fewer murders."

In New York in the last six years, the murder rate went up by 60 per cent. Previous to the abolition of the death penalty, about 80 percent of all murders committed in New York were so-called crimes of passion, defined as crimes in which the victim and the murderer were in some way involved with each other. Right now, only 50 per cent of all murders in New York are crimes of passion.

Q How do you interpret those figures?

A As long as the death penalty existed, largely only people in the grip of passion could not be deterred by the threat of the death penalty. Now that there's no death penalty, people who previously were deterred—who are not in the grip of passion—are no longer deterred from committing murder for the sake of gain. Murder is no longer an irrational act,

Reprinted from *U.S. News and World Report,* (April 19, 1976) pp. 37–38. Copyright 1976, U.S. News and World Report, Inc.

least of all for juveniles for whom it means at most a few months of inconvenience.

Even if you assume the evidence for the deterrent effect of the death penalty is not clear—I make this point in my book "Punishing Criminals"—you have two risks. Risk 1: If you impose the death penalty and it doesn't have an additional deterrent effect, you have possibly lost the life of a convicted murderer without adding to deterrence and thereby sparing future victims. Risk 2: If you fail to execute the convicted murderer and execution would have had an additional deterrent effect, you have failed to spare the lives of a number of future victims.

Between the two risks, I'd much rather execute the convicted murderer than risk the lives of innocent people who could have been saved.

Q You noted that the death penalty is irrevocable once it is imposed. Does this make death such a different penalty that it should not be used?

A It makes it a different penalty. This is why it should be used when the crime is different—so heinous and socially dangerous to call for this extreme measure. When you kill a man with premeditation, you do something very different from stealing from him. I think the punishment should be appropriate. I favor the death penalty as a matter of justice and human dignity even apart from deterrence. The penalty must be appropriate to the seriousness of the crime.

"WE HAVE CHEAPENED HUMAN LIFE"

Q Can you elaborate on your statement that the penalty should match the seriousness of the crime?

A Our system of punishment is based not just on deterrence but also on what is called "justice"—namely, that we feel a man who has committed a crime must be punished in proportion to the seriousness of the crime. Since the crime that takes a life is irrevocable, so must be the punishment.

All religions that I'm aware of feel that human life is sacred and that its sacredness must be enforced by depriving of life anyone who deprives another person of life. Once we make it clear to a person that if he deprives someone else of life he will suffer only minor

inconvenience, we have cheapened human life. We are at that point today.

Q Some argue that capital punishment tends to brutalize and degrade society. Do you agree?

A Many of the same people also argue that the death penalty is legalized murder because it inflicts on the criminal the same situation that he inflicted on his victim. Yet most punishments inflict on the criminal what he inflicted on the victim. The difference between the punishment and the crime is that one is a legal measure and the other is not.

As for brutalizing, I think that people are more brutalized by their daily TV fare. At any rate, people are not so much brutalized by punishment as they are brutalized by our failure to seriously punish brutal acts.

Q Professor Schwartz, why do you oppose the death penalty?

A For a number of reasons. In the first place, mistakes do occur in our trial system. And, if the victim of a mistake has been executed, that mistake is irremediable.

For example: I myself once represented a man who had been frightened into confessing a murder. He was afraid he'd get the electric chair if he stood trial. So he pleaded guilty and got life imprisonment. Twelve years later I was able to prove he was innocent. That would have been too late if he had been executed.

In the second place—and, for me, very important—the death penalty, rarely administered as it is, distorts the whole penal system. It makes the criminal procedure so complex that it turns the public off.

Q How does it do that?

A People are so reluctant to administer the death penalty until every last doubt is eliminated that the procedural law gets encumbered with a lot of technical rules of evidence. You not only get this in the trial, but you get habeas corpus proceedings after the trial.

This highly technical procedure is applied not only to capital cases but to other criminal cases as well. So it makes it hard to convict anybody.

I believe the death penalty actually does more harm to security in this country than it does good. Without it, we would be safer from criminals than with it.

Q Do you think the death penalty is a deterrent to crime?

A The evidence is inconclusive about that.

The best studies I know, done by Thorsten Sellin, Marvin Wolfgang and their students at the University of Pennsylvania, would indicate that there is no deterrent effect. This study compared States using the death penalty with next-door States that did not use it. They also compared the homicide rates in the same State during periods when it used the death penalty and when it did not. And they found no statistical differences in homicide rates—with or without the death penalty.

I agree that there may be cases where a robber will not shoot because he doesn't want to risk "the hot seat." But, in my opinion, there are also situations where the death penalty stimulates a criminal to kill. I'm talking about cases, for instance, where a kidnaper decides to kill the only witness who could identify him, or where witnesses or informers get wiped out because the criminal says: "If I'm convicted, I'm going to get the chair anyway, and I'm safer if I kill him."

So if the death penalty is not demonstrably helpful in saving innocent lives, I don't think we ought to use it—especially considering the risk of mistakes.

Q Are there no criminals who commit crimes so heinous that they ought to be executed for society's safety?

A My view is that society is not well enough organized to make a list of those people who ought to be executed. Sometimes I think if I were permitted to make up the list of those to be executed I wouldn't mind eliminating some people. But the list that society or the Government might make would probably not be the same as my list. Who is to decide who should live and who should die?

Now we're getting to the essential basis of what the Supreme Court must decide. This is whether the processes for choosing the ones to be killed are inevitably irrational, arbitrary and capricious.

Q Do you think this element of arbitrariness or capriciousness can ever be eliminated—even by making the death-penalty mandatory for certain crimes, as many States have?

A No, I don't. No society has ever been able to make the death-penalty system operate fairly, even by making it mandatory. Look at the British system, which operated for a century with mandatory death penalties. They found juries just wouldn't convict in many cases where the conviction meant execution.

And even if the death penalty was imposed, the Home Office eventually decided who would actually be killed by granting or withholding clemency.

Taking human nature as it is, I know of no way of administering a death penalty which would be fair. Not every problem has a solution, you know—and I think this is one of those insoluble problems.

Q Have we given the death penalty a chance to prove its deterrent effect? It hasn't been applied in this country in recent years—

A Not just in recent years. Use of the death penalty has been declining for decades. In 1933, there were something like 233 people executed in the United States. Since then, the figures have been going down steadily. And, of course, there haven't been any executions since 1967 because of the litigation over the death penalty's legality. But even before that, the American public was turning against the death penalty.

If you take a poll, you find people overwhelmingly in favor of the death penalty. But when you ask a person to sit on a jury and vote to execute a defendant, you find a great reluctance—increasingly so in the modern era.

IF JUDGES AND JURIES HAD TO KILL

Q It has been suggested that jurors and judges who impose a death penalty be required to push the buttons that would carry out the execution—

A Of course, society would reject that at once. You couldn't get 12 or 13 people who would do it. They may be willing to vote for it to be done, but they don't want to be a part of it. If you really want to make execution a deterrent, make it public—put it on TV—so people can see what it can be like if they kill someone. But, of course, we won't do that. We keep it hidden away from ourselves.

Q Do you regard it as immoral to execute a criminal?

A I steer away from that question because I know people's views on the morality of it are varied—and almost unchangeable. I'm a pragmatist. I just don't think it can be made fair or workable.

GREGG V. GEORGIA

The issue before the Supreme Court of the United States was whether capital punishment violates the Eighth Amendment prohibition of cruel and unusual punishment. The majority of the Court held that it does not violate this prohibition because (1) capital punishment accords with contemporary standards of decency, (2) capital punishment may serve some deterrent or retributive purpose that is not degrading to human dignity, and (3) in the case of the Georgia law under review, capital punishment is no longer arbitrarily applied. Dissenting Justice Brennan argued that (1) through (3) do not suffice to show that capital punishment is constitutional; it would further have to be shown that capital punishment is not degrading to human dignity. Dissenting Justice Marshall objected to the majority's decision on the grounds that capital punishment is not necessary for deterrence, and that a retributive purpose for capital punishment is not consistent with human dignity. He also contended that contemporary standards of decency with respect to capital punishment are not based on informed opinion.

WE ADDRESS INITIALLY THE basic contention that the punishment of death for the crime of murder is, under all circumstances, "cruel and unusual" in violation of the Eighth and Fourteenth Amendments of the Constitution. . . .

The Court on a number of occasions has both assumed and asserted the constitutionality of capital punishment. In several cases that assumption provided a necessary foundation for the decision, as the Court was asked to decide whether a particular method of carrying out a capital sentence would be allowed to stand under the Eighth Amendment. But until *Furman* v. *Georgia*, (1972), the Court never confronted squarely the fundamental claim that the punishment of death always, regardless of the enormity of the offense or the procedure followed in imposing the sentence, is cruel and unusual punishment in violation of the Constitution. Although this issue was presented and addressed in *Furman*, it was not resolved by the Court. Four Justices would have held that capital punishment is not unconstitutional *per se*; two Justices would have reached the opposite conclusion; and three Justices, while agreeing that the statutes then before the Court were invalid as applied, left open the question whether such punishment may ever be imposed. We now hold that the punishment of death does not invariably violate the Constitution. . . .

It is clear from the foregoing precedents that the Eighth Amendment has not been regarded as a static concept. As Mr. Chief Justice Warren said, in an oft-quoted phrase, "[t]he Amendment must draw its meaning from the evolving standards of decency that mark the progress of a maturing society.". . . Thus, an assessment of contemporary values concerning the infliction of a challenged sanction is relevant to the application of the Eighth Amendment. As we develop below more fully, this assessment does not call for a subjective judgment. It requires, rather, that we look to objective indicia that reflect the public attitude toward a given sanction.

But our cases also make clear that public perceptions of standards of decency with respect to criminal sanctions are not conclusive. A penalty also must accord with "the dignity of man," which is the "basic concept underlying the Eighth Amendment." This means, at least, that the punishment not be "excessive." When a form of punishment in the abstract (in this case, whether capital punishment may ever be imposed as a sanction for murder) rather than in the particular (the propriety of death as a penalty to be applied to a specific defendant for a specific crime) is under consideration, the inquiry into "excessiveness" has two aspects. First, the punishment must not involve the unnecessary and wanton infliction of pain. Second, the punishment must not be grossly out of proportion to the severity of the crime.

Of course, the requirements of the Eighth Amendment must be applied with an awareness of the limited role to be played by the courts. This does not mean that judges have no role to play, for the Eighth Amendment is a restraint upon the exercise of legislative power. . . .

But, while we have an obligation to insure that constitutional bounds are not overreached, we may not act as judges as we might as legislators.

"Courts are not representative bodies. They are not designed to be a good reflex of a democratic society. Their judgment is best informed, and therefore most dependable, within narrow limits. Their essential quality is detachment, founded on independence. History teaches that the independence of the judiciary is jeopardized when courts become embroiled in the passions of the day and assume primary responsibility in choosing between competing political, economic and social pressures." Dennis v. United States (1951)

Therefore, in assessing a punishment selected by a democratically elected legislature against the constitutional measure, we presume its validity. We may not require the legislature to select the least severe penalty possible so long as the penalty selected is not cruelly inhumane or disproportionate to the crime involved. And a heavy burden rests on those who would attack the judgment of the representatives of the people.

This is true in part because the constitutional test is intertwined with an assessment of contemporary standards and the legislative judgment weighs heavily in ascertaining such standards. "[I]n a democratic society legislatures, not courts, are constituted to respond to the will and consequently the moral values of the people." *Furman v. Georgia.* The deference we owe to the decisions of the state legislatures under our federal system, is enhanced where the specification of punishments is concerned, for "these are peculiarly questions of legislative policy." *Gore v. United States.* . . . A decision that a given punishment is impermissible under the Eighth Amendment cannot be reversed short of a constitutional amendment. The ability of the people to express their preference through the normal democratic processes, as well as through ballot referenda, is shut off. Revisions cannot be made in the light of further experience.

. . . We now consider specifically whether the sentence of death for the crime of murder is a *per se* violation of the Eighth and Fourteenth Amendments to the Constitution. We note first that history and precedent strongly support a negative answer to this question.

The imposition of the death penalty for the crime of murder has a long history of acceptance both in the United States and in England. The common-law rule imposed a mandatory death sentence on all convicted murderers. And the penalty continued to be used into the 20th century by most American States, although the breadth of the common-law rule was diminished, initially by narrowing the class of murders to be punished by death and subsequently by widespread adoption of laws expressly granting juries the discretion to recommend mercy.

It is apparent from the text of the Constitution itself that the existence of capital punishment was accepted by the Framers. At the time the Eighth Amendment was ratified, capital punishment was a common sanction in every State. Indeed, the First Congress of the United States enacted legislation providing death as the penalty for specified crimes. . . .

For nearly two centuries, this Court, repeatedly and often expressly, has recognized that capital punishment is not invalid *per se.* . . .

Four years ago, the petitioners in *Furman* and its companion cases predicated their argument primarily upon the asserted proposition that standards of decency had evolved to the point where capital punishment no longer could be tolerated. The petitioners in those cases said, in effect, that the evolutionary process had come to an end, and that standards of decency required that the Eighth Amendment be construed finally as prohibiting capital punishment for any crime regardless of its depravity and impact on society. This view was accepted by two Justices. Three other Justices were unwilling to go so far; focusing on the procedures by which convicted defendants were selected for the death penalty rather than on the actual punishment inflicted, they joined in the conclusion that the statutes before the Court were constitutionally invalid.

The petitioners in the capital cases before the Court today renew the "standards of decency" argument, but developments during the four years since *Furman* have undercut substantially the assumptions upon which their argument rested. Despite the continuing debate, dating back to the 19th century, over the morality and utility of capital punishment, it is now evident that a large proportion of American society continues to regard it as an appropriate and necessary criminal sanction.

The most marked indication of society's endorsement of the death penalty for murder is the legislative response to *Furman*. The legislatures of at least 35 States have enacted new statutes that provide for the death penalty for at least some crimes that result in the death of another person. And the Congress of the United States, in 1974, enacted a statute providing the death penalty for aircraft piracy that results in death.[24] These recently adopted statutes have attempted to address the concerns expressed by the Court in *Furman* primarily (i) by specifying the factors to be weighed and the procedures to be followed in deciding when to impose a capital sentence, or (ii) by making the death penalty mandatory for specified crimes. But all of the post-*Furman* statutes make clear that capital punishment itself has not been rejected by the elected representatives of the people. . . .

As we have seen, however, the Eighth Amendment demands more than that a challenged punishment be acceptable to contemporary society. The Court also must ask whether it comports with the basic concept of human dignity at the core of the Amendment. Although we cannot "invalidate a category of penalties because we deem less severe penalties adequate to serve the ends of penology," the sanction imposed cannot be so totally without penological justification that it results in the gratuitous infliction of suffering.

The death penalty is said to serve two principal social purposes: retribution and deterrence of capital crimes by prospective offenders.

In part, capital punishment is an expression of society's moral outrage at particularly offensive conduct. This function may be unappealing to many, but it is essential in an ordered society that asks its citizens to rely on legal processes rather than self-help to vindicate their wrongs.

"The instinct for retribution is part of the nature of man, and channeling that instinct in the administration of criminal justice serves an important purpose in promoting the stability of a society governed by law. When people begin to believe that organized society is unwilling or unable to impose upon criminal offenders the punishment they 'deserve,'" then there are sown the seeds of an-archy—of self-help, vigilante justice, and lynch law." Furman v. Georgia.

"Retribution is no longer the dominant objective of the criminal law," but neither is it a forbidden objective nor one inconsistent with our respect for the dignity of men. Indeed, the decision that capital punishment may be the appropriate sanction in extreme cases is an expression of the community's belief that certain crimes are themselves so grievous an affront to humanity that the only adequate response may be the penalty of death.

Statistical attempts to evaluate the worth of the death penalty as a deterrent to crimes by potential offenders have occasioned a great deal of debate. The results simply have been inconclusive. As one opponent of capital punishment has said:

"[A]fter all possible inquiry, including the probing of all possible methods of inquiry, we do not know, and for systematic and easily visible reasons cannot know, what the truth about this 'deterrent' effect may be. . . .

"The inescapable flaw is . . . that social conditions in any state are not constant through time, and that social conditions are not the same in any two states. If an effect were observed (and the observed effects, one way or another, are not large) then one could not at all tell whether any of this effect is attributable to the presence or absence of capital punishment. A 'scientific'—that is to say, a soundly based—conclusion is simply impossible, and no methodological path out of this tangle suggests itself." C. Black, *Capital Punishment: The Inevitability of Caprice and Mistake* 25–26 (1974).

Although some of the studies suggest that the death penalty may not function as a significantly greater deterrent than lesser penalties, there is no convincing empirical evidence either supporting or refuting this view. We may nevertheless assume safely that there are murderers, such as those who act in passion, for whom the threat of death has little or no deterrent effect. But for many others, the death penalty undoubtedly is a significant deterrent. There are carefully contemplated murders, such as murder for hire, where the possible penalty of death may well enter into the cold calculus that precedes the decision to act. And there are some categories of murder, such as murder by a life prisoner, where other sanctions may not be adequate.

The value of capital punishment as a deterrent of

crime is a complex factual issue the resolution of which properly rests with the legislatures, which can evaluate the results of statistical studies in terms of their own local conditions and with a flexibility of approach that is not available to the courts. . . .

In sum, we cannot say that the judgment of the Georgia Legislature that capital punishment may be necessary in some cases is clearly wrong. Considerations of federalism, as well as respect for the ability of a legislature to evaluate, in terms of its particular State, the moral consensus concerning the death penalty and its social utility as a sanction, require us to conclude, in the absence of more convincing evidence, that the infliction of death as a punishment for murder is not without justification and thus is not unconstitutionally severe.

Finally, we must consider whether the punishment of death is disproportionate in relation to the crime for which it is imposed. There is no question that death as a punishment is unique in its severity and irrevocability. When a defendant's life is at stake, the Court has been particularly sensitive to insure that every safeguard is observed. But we are concerned here only with the imposition of capital punishment for the crime of murder, and when a life has been taken deliberately by the offender, we cannot say that the punishment is invariably disproportionate to the crime. It is an extreme sanction, suitable to the most extreme of crimes.

We hold that the death penalty is not a form of punishment that may never be imposed, regardless of the circumstances of the offense, regardless of the character of the offender, and regardless of the procedure followed in reaching the decision to impose it.

We now consider whether Georgia may impose the death penalty on the petitioner in this case. . . .

The basic concern of *Furman* centered on those defendants who were being condemned to death capriciously and arbitrarily. Under the procedures before the Court in that case, sentencing authorities were not directed to give attention to the nature or circumstances of the crime committed or to the character or record of the defendant. Left unguided, juries imposed the death sentence in a way that could only be called freakish. The new Georgia sentencing procedures, by contrast, focus the jury's attention on the particularized nature of the crime and the particularized characteristics of the individual defendant. While the jury is permitted to consider any aggravating or mitigating circumstances, it must find and identify at least one statutory aggravating factor before it may impose a penalty of death. In this way the jury's discretion is channeled. No longer can a jury wantonly and freakishly impose the death sentence; it is always circumscribed by the legislative guidelines. In addition, the review function of the Supreme Court of Georgia affords additional assurance that the concerns that prompted our decision in *Furman* are not present to any significant degree in the Georgia procedure applied here.

For the reasons expressed in this opinion, we hold that the statutory system under which Gregg was sentenced to death does not violate the Constitution. Accordingly, the judgment of the Georgia Supreme Court is affirmed. . . .

Mr. Justice Brennan, dissenting.[*]

The Cruel and Unusual Punishments Clause "must draw its meaning from the evolving standards of decency that mark the progress of a maturing society." The opinions of Mr. Justice Stewart, Mr. Justice Powell, and Mr. Justice Stevens today hold that "evolving standards of decency" require focus not on the essence of the death penalty itself but primarily upon the procedures employed by the State to single out persons to suffer the penalty of death. Those opinions hold further that, so viewed, the Clause invalidates the mandatory infliction of the death penalty but not its infliction under sentencing procedures that Mr. Justice Stewart, Mr. Justice Powell, and Mr. Justice Stevens conclude adequately safeguard against the risk that the death penalty was imposed in an arbitrary and capricious manner.

In *Furman* v. *Georgia*, I read "evolving standards of decency" as requiring focus upon the essence of

---

[*][This opinion applies also to No. 75–5706, *Proffitt* v. *Florida, post,* p. 242, and No. 75–5394, *Jurek* v. *Texas, post,* p. 262.]

the death penalty itself and not primarily or solely upon the procedures under which the determination to inflict the penalty upon a particular person was made. . . .

This Court inescapably has the duty, as the ultimate arbiter of the meaning of our Constitution, to say whether, when individuals condemned to death stand before our Bar, "moral concepts" require us to hold that the law has progressed to the point where we should declare that the punishment of death, like punishments on the rack, the screw, and the wheel, is no longer morally tolerable in our civilized society. My opinion in *Furman v. Georgia* concluded that our civilization and the law had progressed to this point and that therefore the punishment of death, for whatever crime and under all circumstances, is "cruel and unusual" in violation of the Eighth and Fourteenth Amendments of the Constitution. I shall not again canvass the reasons that led to that conclusion. I emphasize only that foremost among the "moral concepts" recognized in our cases and inherent in the Clause is the primary moral principle that the State, even as it punishes, must treat its citizens in a manner consistent with their intrinsic worth as human beings—a punishment must not be so severe as to be degrading to human dignity. A judicial determination whether the punishment of death comports with human dignity is therefore not only permitted but compelled by the Clause.

. . . Death for whatever crime and under all circumstances "is truly an awesome punishment. The calculated killing of a human being by the State involves, by its very nature, a denial of the executed person's humanity. . . . An executed person has indeed 'lost the right to have rights.' " Death is not only an unusually severe punishment, unusual in its pain, in its finality, and in its enormity, but it serves no penal purpose more effectively than a less severe punishment; therefore the principle inherent in the Clause that prohibits pointless infliction of excessive punishment when less severe punishment can adequately achieve the same purposes invalidates the punishment. . . .

MR. JUSTICE MARSHALL, dissenting.

. . . My sole purposes here are to consider the suggestion that my conclusion in *Furman* has been undercut by developments since then, and briefly to evaluate the basis for my Brethren's holding that the extinction of life is a permissible form of punishment under the Cruel and Unusual Punishments Clause.

In *Furman* I concluded that the death penalty is constitutionally invalid for two reasons. First, the death penalty is excessive. And second, the American people, fully informed as to the purposes of the death penalty and its liabilities, would in my view reject it as morally unacceptable.

Since the decision in *Furman*, the legislatures of 35 States have enacted new statutes authorizing the imposition of the death sentence for certain crimes, and Congress has enacted a law providing the death penalty for air piracy resulting in death. I would be less than candid if I did not acknowledge that these developments have a significant bearing on a realistic assessment of the moral acceptability of the death penalty to the American people. But if the constitutionality of the death penalty turns, as I have urged, on the opinion of an *informed* citizenry, then even the enactment of new death statutes cannot be viewed as conclusive. In *Furman*, I observed that the American people are largely unaware of the information critical to a judgment on the morality of the death penalty, and concluded that if they were better informed they would consider it shocking, unjust, and unacceptable. A recent study, conducted after the enactment of the post-*Furman* statutes, has confirmed that the American people know little about the death penalty, and that the opinions of an informed public would differ significantly from those of a public unaware of the consequences and effects of the death penalty.

Even assuming, however, that the post-*Furman* enactment of statutes authorizing the death penalty renders the prediction of the views of an informed citizenry an uncertain basis for a constitutional decision, the enactment of those statutes has no bearing whatsoever on the conclusion that the death penalty is unconstitutional because it is excessive. An excessive penalty is invalid under the Cruel and Unusual Punishments Clause "even though popular sentiment may favor" it. The inquiry here, then, is simply whether the death penalty is necessary to accomplish the legitimate legislative purposes in punishment, or whether a less severe penalty—life imprisonment—would do as well.

The two purposes that sustain the death penalty as nonexcessive in the Court's view are general deterrence and retribution. In *Furman*, I canvassed the relevant data on the deterrent effect of capital punishment. The state of knowledge at that point, after literally centuries of debate, was summarized as follows by a United Nations Committee:

"It is generally agreed between the retentionists and abolitionists, whatever their opinions about the validity of comparative studies of deterrence, that the data which now exist show no correlation between the existence of capital punishment and lower rates of capital crime."

The available evidence, I concluded in *Furman*, was convincing that "capital punishment is not necessary as a deterrent to crime in our society."

The Solicitor General in his *amicus* brief in these cases relies heavily on a study by Isaac Ehrlich, reported a year after *Furman*, to support the contention that the death penalty does not deter murder. . . .

. . . Ehrlich found a negative correlation between changes in the homicide rate and changes in execution risk. His tentative conclusion was that for the period from 1933 to 1967 each additional execution in the United States might have saved eight lives.

The methods and conclusions of the Ehrlich study have been severely criticized on a number of grounds. . . .

. . . Analysis of Ehrlich's data reveals that all empirical support for the deterrent effect of capital punishment disappears when the five most recent years are removed from his time series—that is to say, whether a decrease in the execution risk corresponds to an increase or a decrease in the murder rate depends on the ending point of the sample period. This finding has cast severe doubts on the reliability of Ehrlich's tentative conclusions. . . .

The Ehrlich study, in short, is of little, if any, assistance in assessing the deterrent impact of the death penalty. The evidence I reviewed in *Furman* remains convincing, in my view, that "capital punishment is not necessary as a deterrent to crime in our society." The justification for the death penalty must be found elsewhere.

The other principal purpose said to be served by the death penalty is retribution. The notion that retribution can serve as a moral justification for the

sanction of death finds credence in the opinion of my Brothers STEWART, POWELL, and STEVENS, and that of my Brother WHITE in *Roberts v. Louisiana*. It is this notion that I find to be the most disturbing aspect of today's unfortunate decisions.

The concept of retribution is a multifaceted one, and any discussion of its role in the criminal law must be undertaken with caution. On one level, it can be said that the notion of retribution or reprobation is the basis of our insistence that only those who have broken the law be punished, and in this sense the notion is quite obviously central to a just system of criminal sanctions. But our recognition that retribution plays a crucial role in determining who may be punished by no means requires approval of retribution as a general justification for punishment. It is the question whether retribution can provide a moral justification for punishment—in particular, capital punishment—that we must consider. . . .

The . . . contentions—that society's expression of moral outrage through the imposition of the death penalty pre-empts the citizenry from taking the law into its own hands and reinforces moral values—are not retributive in the purest sense. They are essentially utilitarian in that they portray the death penalty as valuable because of its beneficial results. These justifications for the death penalty are inadequate because the penalty is, quite clearly I think, not necessary to the accomplishment of those results.

There remains for consideration, however, what might be termed the purely retributive justification for the death penalty—that the death penalty is appropriate, not because of its beneficial effect on society, but because the taking of the murderer's life is itself morally good. . . .

The mere fact that the community demands the murderer's life in return for the evil he has done cannot sustain the death penalty, for . . . "The Eighth Amendment demands more than that a challenged punishment be acceptable to contemporary society." To be sustained under the Eighth Amendment, the death penalty must "compor[t] with the basic concept of human dignity at the core of the Amendment"; the objective in imposing it must be "[consistent] with our respect for the dignity of [other] men." Under these standards, the taking of life "because the wrongdoer deserves it" surely must fall, for such a punishment has as its very basis the total denial of the wrongdoer's dignity and worth.

The death penalty, unnecessary to promote the goal of deterrence or to further any legitimate notion of retribution, is an excessive penalty forbidden by the Eighth and Fourteenth Amendments. I respectfully dissent from the Court's judgment upholding the sentences of death imposed upon the petitioners in these cases.

SUGGESTIONS FOR FURTHER READING

Anthologies

Acton, H. B. *The Philosophy of Punishment.* London: Macmillan & Co., 1969.

Cains, Huntington. *Legal Philosophy from Plato to Hegel.* Baltimore: Johns Hopkins Press, 1967.

Ezorsky, Gertrude. *Philosophical Perspectives on Punishment.* Albany: State University of New York Press, 1972.

Feinberg, Joel, and Gross, Hyman. *Philosophy of Law.* Belmont: Wadsworth Publishing Co., 1980.

Gerber, Rudolph J., and McAnany, Patrick D. *Contemporary Punishment.* Notre Dame: University of Notre Dame Press, 1972.

Murphy, Jeffrie G. *Punishment and Rehabilitation.* Belmont: Wadsworth Publishing Co. 1973.

Basic Concepts

Golding, Martin P. *Philosophy of Law.* Englewood Cliffs: Prentice-Hall, 1975.

Richards, David A. J. *The Moral Criticism of Law.* Belmont: Dickenson Publishing Co., 1977.

The Forward-Looking and Backward-Looking Views

Andenaes, Johannes. *Punishment and Deterrence.* Ann Arbor: The University of Michigan Press, 1974.

Menninger, Karl. *The Crime of Punishment.* New York: The Viking Press, 1968.

Gross, Hyman. *A Theory of Criminal Justice.* New York: Oxford University Press, 1979.

Murphy, Jeffrie G. *Retribution, Justice and Therapy.* Boston: D. Reidel Publishing Co., 1979.

Packer, Herbert. *The Limits of the Criminal Sanction.* Stanford: Stanford University Press, 1968.

Von Hirsh, Andrew. *Doing Justice.* New York: Hill and Wang, 1976.

Practical Application

Black, Charles L., Jr. *Capital Punishment.* New York: W. W. Norton & Co., 1974.

———. "Reflections on Opposing the Penalty of Death." *St. Mary's Law Journal* (1978), pp. 1–12.

Bedau, Hugo. *The Death Penalty in America.* New York: Oxford University Press, 1982.

Van den Haag, Ernest. *Punishing Criminals.* New York: Basic Books, 1975.

WAR AND NUCLEAR DETERRENCE

BASIC CONCEPTS

The problem of war and nuclear deterrence is simply the contemporary version of the problem of determining the moral limits of military defense, which has been with us since the dawn of human history. Just war theories are attempts to specify what these moral limits are. Such theories have two components: a set of criteria which establish a right to go to war *(jus ad bellum)* and a set of criteria which determine legitimate conduct in war *(jus in bello)*. The first set of criteria can be grouped under the label "just cause," the second under the label "just means."

Consider the following specification of just cause:

There must be substantial aggression, and nonbelligerent correctives must be hopeless or too costly.

This specification of just cause implicitly contains a number of criteria, e.g., last resort, formal declaration, and reasonable hope of success, all of which are discussed by James F. Childress (pp. 292–302). It does, however, exclude the criterion of legitimate authority, which, as Childress indicates, has had a prominent place in just war theories. That criterion is excluded for the reason that it has the character of a second-order requirement: it is a requirement that must be satisfied whenever there is a question of group action with respect to any moral problem whatsoever. For example, with respect to the problem of the distribution of goods and resources in a society, we can certainly ask who has the (morally legitimate) authority to distribute or redistribute goods and resources in a society; and with respect to the problem of punishment and responsibility, we can ask who has the (morally legitimate) authority to punish offenders in a society. But before we ask such questions with respect to particular moral problems, it is important to first get clear about what are morally defensible solutions to these problems, since a standard way of identifying morally legitimate authorities is by their endorsement of such solutions. With respect to the problem of war and nuclear deterrence, therefore, it seems that we first need to determine the nature and existence of just causes before we try to identify morally legitimate authorities by their endorsement of such causes.

Now whether we define just cause independently of legitimate authority or not, pacifists will simply deny that there are any just causes that ought to be recognized. For pacifists hold that it is never morally too costly to use nonbelligerent correctives against aggression. According to pacifists, people should never defend themselves against aggression by intentionally injuring or killing other human beings.

Pacifism, however, is subject to at least two interpretations. On the one hand, pacifists might be understood as claiming that although people ought never to intentionally injure or kill other human beings, even in self-defense, doing so is not morally blameworthy provided that the criteria of just cause and just means are observed. On the other hand, pacifists might be understood as claiming that it is always morally blameworthy for people to intentionally injure or kill other human beings, even in self-defense. The problem with pacifism under this second interpretation is that the degree of self-sacrifice it requires is not something we can reasonably expect of most human beings. Assuming that "ought implies can," at least where moral blameworthiness is at issue, pacifism under this second interpretation would not be a requirement of morality. However, no comparable problem applies to pacifism under the first interpretation. Interpreted in this first way, pacifism may be the most morally defensible position to take.

Let us now consider the following specification of just means:

1. The harm inflicted on the aggressor must not be disproportionate to the aggression;
2. harm to innocents should not be directly intended as an end or as a means; and
3. harm to innocents must be minimized by accepting risks (costs) to oneself that would not doom the military venture.

The first criterion is a widely accepted requirement of just means. This criterion seems especially appropriate if one accepts Childress's view that when our prima facie duty not to injure or kill others is overridden by just war criteria, we are required to make our conduct approximate as much as possible the conduct that would have been required by that duty. Even utilitarians and forward-looking theorists generally would want to endorse (1) as the best way of maximizing good consequences. The second criterion is also widely accepted, although utilitarians (and forward-looking theorists generally) might find reason to depart from it on occasion. This criterion contains the main requirement of the doctrine of double effect (see the introduction to Section III). Many philosophers seem willing to endorse the application of the doctrine in this context, given that those to whom the doctrine applies are generally recognized to be persons with full moral status.

The doctrine of double effect, however, does not require (3), which incorporates an even stronger safeguard against harming innocents in warfare than (2). Consider the following example of what (3) would require in practice. The example is taken from Frank Richard's memoir of the First World War.

When bombing dug-outs or cellars, it was always wise to throw the bombs into them first and have a look around after. But we had to be very careful in this village as there were civilians in some of the cellars. We shouted down to them to make sure. Another man and I shouted down one cellar twice and receiving no reply were just about to pull the pins out of our bomb when we heard a woman's voice and a young lady came up the cellar steps. . . . She and the members of her family . . . had not left (the cellar) for some days. They guessed an attack was being made and when we first shouted down had been too frightened to answer. If the young lady had not cried out when she did we would have innocently murdered them all.[1]

Now the doctrine of double effect would presumably have permitted Frank Richards to throw bombs into these cellars without warning, given that only the good effects of such actions were intended and the good effects were commensurate with the evil. Only (3) appears to require what Frank Richards did. Obviously, the moral appeal of examples like this raises the serious question whether the doctrine of double effect is sufficiently restrictive. In general, it seems we should be able to morally demand not only that the good effects of an action be commensurate with the evil but also that the evil effects be minimized.

ALTERNATIVE VIEWS

As one would expect, criteria of just cause and just means have been incorporated to some degree in the military codes of different nations and adopted as international law. Yet rarely has anyone contended that the criteria ought to be met simply because they have been incorporated into military codes or adopted as international law. George I. Mavrodes, however, defends just such a view (see pp. 302–310).

Mavrodes arrives at this conclusion largely because he finds the standard attempts to specify the convention-independent basis for (2) and (3) to be so totally unsuccessful. All such attempts, Mavrodes claims, are based on an identification of innocents with noncombatants. But by any plausible standard of guilt and innocence that has moral content,

Mavrodes contends, noncombatants can be guilty and combatants innocent. For example, noncombatants who are doing everything in their power to financially support an unjust war would be morally guilty, and combatants who were forced into military service and intended never to fire their weapons at anyone would be morally innocent. Consequently, the guilt/innocence distinction will not support the combatant/noncombatant distinction.

Hoping to still support the combatant/noncombatant distinction, Mavrodes suggests that the distinction might be grounded on a convention to observe it. This would mean that our obligation to morally abide by (2) and (3) would be a convention-dependent obligation. Nevertheless, Mavrodes does not deny that we have some convention-independent obligations. Our obligation to refrain from wantonly murdering our neighbors is given as an example of a convention-independent obligation, as is our obligation to reduce the pain and death involved in combat. But to refrain from harming noncombatants when harming them would be the most effective way of pursuing a just cause is not included among our convention-independent obligations.

Yet Mavrodes does not claim that our obligation to refrain from harming noncombatants is *purely* convention-dependent. He allows that, in circumstances in which the convention of refraining from harming noncombatants does not exist, we might still have an obligation to unilaterally refrain from harming noncombatants provided that our action will help give rise to a convention prohibiting such harm, with its associated good consequences. According to Mavrodes, our primary obligation is to maximize good consequences, and this obligation requires that we refrain from harming noncombatants when that will help bring about a convention prohibiting such harm. By contrast, someone who held that our obligation to refrain from harming noncombatants was purely convention-dependent, would never recognize an obligation to unilaterally refrain from harming noncombatants. On a purely convention-dependent account, obligations can only be derived from existing conventions; the expected consequences from establishing a particular convention could never ground a purely convention-dependent obligation. But while Mavrodes does not claim that our obligation to refrain from harm-

ing noncombatants is purely convention-dependent, he does claim that this obligation generally arises only when there exists a convention prohibiting such harm. According to Mavrodes, the reason for this is that generally only when there exists a convention prohibiting harm to noncombatants will our refraining from harming them, while pursuing a just cause, actually maximize good consequences.

But is there no other way to support our obligation to refrain from harming noncombatants? Mavrodes would deny that there is. Consider, however, Mavrodes's own example of the convention-independent obligation not to wantonly kill our neighbors. There are at least two ways to understand how this obligation is supported. Some would claim that we ought not to wantonly kill our neighbors because this would not maximize good consequences. This appears to be Mavrodes's view. Others would claim that we ought not to wantonly kill our neighbors, even if doing so would maximize good consequences, simply because it is not reasonable to believe that our neighbors are engaged in an attempt upon our lives. Both these ways of understanding how the obligation is supported account for the convention-independent character of the obligation, but the second approach can also be used to show how our obligation to refrain from harming noncombatants is convention-independent. On pages 310–315, Jeffrie G. Murphy indicates how this can be done. Murphy argues that since it is not reasonable to believe that noncombatants are engaged in an attempt upon our lives, we have an obligation to refrain from harming them. So interpreted, our obligation to refrain from harming noncombatants is itself convention-independent, although it will certainly give rise to conventions.

Of course, some may argue that whenever it is not reasonable to believe that persons are engaged in an attempt upon our lives, an obligation to refrain from harming such persons will also be supported by the maximization of good consequences. Yet even if this were true, which seems doubtful, all it would show is that there exists a utilitarian or forward-looking justification for a convention-independent obligation to refrain from harming noncombatants; it would not show that such an obligation is a convention-dependent obligation, as Mavrodes claims.

Let us now consider whether the criteria of just war theories are relevant both to nuclear war and to nuclear deterrence. Obviously the most fundamental question to be asked in this context is whether either a massive or a limited use of nuclear weapons could ever be justified by the criteria of just war theories.

Consider first the massive use of nuclear weapons in a counter-city strike. It has been estimated that such a strike could result in the immediate death of as many as 165 million Americans and 100 million Russians respectively, and destroy between 70 and 80 percent of each nation's industry, in addition to running a near certain risk of a retaliatory nuclear strike by the opposing superpower.[2] Just war theories do not recognize any foreseeable end that would justify such morally horrendous consequences.

The same holds true for a massive use of nuclear weapons in a counterforce strike. It has been estimated that such a counterforce strike against ICBMs, submarine bases, and bomber bases could wipe out as many as 20 million Americans and 28 million Russians respectively, in addition to running a considerable risk of a retaliatory nuclear strike by the opposing superpower.[3] This being the case, what greater evil might foreseeably be prevented by such a use of nuclear weapons?

Of course, it should be pointed out that the above considerations do not rule out a limited use of nuclear weapons, at least in a counterforce strike.

Theoretically such a use is still possible. Yet practically it would be quite difficult for either superpower to distinguish between a limited and a massive use of nuclear weapons, especially if a full-scale conventional war is raging. In such circumstances, any use of nuclear weapons is likely to be viewed as part of a massive nuclear retaliatory strike.[4] Henry Kissinger once proposed that in a limited nuclear war a nation might announce it would not use nuclear weapons of more than 500 kilotons explosive power unless an adversary used them first. Unfortunately, however, neither the United States nor the Soviet Union has a system of instantaneous damage assessment to determine whether such a limit were being observed. In addition, war games have shown that if enough tactical nuclear weapons are employed over a limited area, such as Germany, the effect on noncombatants in that area would be much the same as in a massive nuclear attack.[5] As

Bundy, Kennan, McNamara, and Smith put the point in their recent endorsement of a doctrine of no first use of nuclear weapons:

Every serious analysis and every military exercise, for over 25 years, has demonstrated that even the most restrained battlefield use would be enormously destructive to civilian life and property. There is no way for anyone to have any confidence that such a nuclear action will not lead to further and more devastating exchanges. Any use of nuclear weapons in Europe, by the Alliance or against it, carries with it a high and inescapable risk of escalation into the general nuclear war which would bring ruin to all and victory to none.[6]

For these reasons, even a limited use of nuclear weapons would generally not be permitted by the criteria of just war theories.

But if a massive or limited use of nuclear weapons is not morally permissible by the criteria of just war theories, how could it be morally permissible to threaten to use such weapons? Such a threat would presumably imply an intention to carry out the threat if the desired response is not forthcoming. Consequently, such threats would seem to be morally permissible only if carrying them out were also morally permissible. For example, a requirement of this sort would seem to be met when punishment is justifiably threatened. But since carrying out the threat of a massive or limited use of nuclear weapons is not morally permissible, threatening such an action in order to achieve nuclear deterrence would also, it seems, not be morally permissible.

In the next selection, Michael Walzer recognizes the immorality of threatening a massive or limited use of nuclear weapons (see pp. 315–323). He contends, nevertheless, that such threats are morally defensible as a means of preventing either nuclear blackmail and foreign domination or nuclear destruction. According to Walzer, this is one place where the criteria of just war theories can be legitimately set aside in order to prevent a greater evil.

But is Walzer's defense of threatening massive or limited nuclear retaliation acceptable? Walzer claims that "any state confronted by a nuclear adversary . . . and capable of developing its own bomb, is likely to do so, seeking safety in a balance of terror." For our purposes, however, what is at issue is not the likelihood but the morality of such a response.

In determining that morality, two factors seem particularly relevant. The first is the intention of one's adversary. The second is the possibility of pursuing nuclear deterrence by means which fall short of threatening either massive or limited nuclear retaliation.

In assessing the first factor, we would do well to reflect upon the history of strategic arms control negotiations between the United States and the Soviet Union from the end of World War II to the present. For example, not many people are aware of the fact that in 1954, after the leadership of the Soviet Union accepted a U.S. backed proposal for nuclear disarmament that allowed for the on-site inspections the U.S. had always favored, the U.S. responded to this turn of events by rejecting its own proposal.[7]

With respect to the second factor, it is not generally recognized that nuclear deterrence can be effectively pursued by means that are less morally objectionable than a threat of either massive or limited nuclear retaliation. One fairly promising example of such means involves the following three elements: (1) the maintenance of a survivable nuclear force, (2) the announcement that it is in the nation's interest to threaten massive and limited nuclear retaliation, (3) yet the refusal to threaten such retaliation on the grounds that the use of such immoral means cannot be justified. Walzer, however, seems to think that such an approach is morally indistinguishable from the threat of massive or limited nuclear retaliation. Yet by refusing to threaten massive or limited nuclear retaliation while maintaining a survivable nuclear force and announcing that it is in the national interest to threaten such retaliation, a nation does achieve at least two moral objectives. First and foremost, such a refusal enables a nation to preserve the moral integrity of its citizens. For its citizens are not being asked to maintain an immoral threat of massive or limited nuclear retaliation. Second, by affirming its commitment to moral principle over national interest, a nation makes an important contribution toward motivating a political resolution of the arms race.

Of course, adopting such less morally objectionable means would involve sacrificing the additional degree of deterrence that would result from combining the possession of a survivable nuclear force with the threat to use it. Yet only by making this sacrifice can a nation preserve the moral integrity of its citi-

zens and hope to motivate a political resolution of the arms race. Jonathan Schell raises still another problem for deterrence by threat of massive nuclear retaliation. According to Schell, there is a contradiction at the heart of deterrence theory (pp. 324–330). The contradiction is that, in the hope of avoiding the extinction of the human race, we threaten a massive nuclear attack which could bring about that fate. Schell argues that this contradiction deprives deterrence theory of a credible motive for a second strike. Given that the motive of threatening a massive nuclear strike in the first place was to prevent a nuclear catastrophe, what could motivate the leaders of a country to release a second strike which is likely to guarantee such a catastrophe? Since victory is impossible, the only possible motives are an irrational commitment to retaliation or revenge.

PRACTICAL APPLICATION

But if a strategy of massive nuclear retaliation is both unbelievable and immoral, what should we do? According to George F. Kennan (see pp. 330–333), the United States should propose to the Soviet Union an immediate across-the-board 50 percent reduction of nuclear arsenals. Others today are advocating a less radical "freeze" on the development and deployment of new nuclear weapons systems (see page 334). Yet it is important to recognize that a solution to this moral problem cannot stand alone; it requires solutions to the other moral problems discussed in this anthology as well. For example, a solution to the problem of the distribution of income and wealth may show that it is morally illegitimate to purchase increased military security by sacrificing the fulfillment of the basic needs of the less advantaged members of a society instead of by sacrificing the fulfillment of the nonbasic needs of the more advantaged members of the society. Accordingly, it is impossible to solve this or any of the other practical moral problems discussed in this anthology without proposing solutions to the other moral problems as well.

NOTES

1. Quoted in Michael Walzer, *Just and Unjust Wars* (New York, 1977) p. 152.

2. *The Effects of Nuclear War*, Office of Technology Assessment (Washington, D.C., 1979) pp. 94, 100.

3. *Ibid.*, pp. 83–91.

4. Spurgeon Keeny and Wolfgang Panofsky, "MAD verse NUTS" *Foreign Affairs* (1981–2) pp. 297–298.

5. Sidney Lens, *The Day Before Doomsday*, (Boston, 1977) p. 73.

6. McGeorge Bundy, George F. Kennan, Robert S. McNamara, and Gerald Smith, "Nuclear Weapons and the Atlantic Alliance," *Foreign Affairs* (1982) p. 757.

7. See Lens, pp. 206–209.

James F. Childress

JUST-WAR THEORIES

James F. Childress claims that the general form of prima facie duties and the specific content of our prima facie duty not to injure or kill others can serve to illuminate the criteria of just war theories. According to Childress, prima facie duties by their very form embody a presumptive justification. Thus to override them we must meet a heavy burden of proof. But since prima facie duties can and do conflict, it is to be expected that some prima facie duties will be overridden in this fashion. Even when this happens, however, the overridden prima facie duties should continue to have an impact on agents' attitudes and actions. All of this holds true, Childress claims, when in accordance with the criteria of just war theories our prima facie duty not to injure or kill others is overridden. This is because only strong reasons can overcome the heavy burden of proof in favor of our duty not to injure or kill others, and the satisfaction of the criteria of just war theories requires that the conduct of war be as compatible as possible with the overridden duty. Childress concludes by discussing alternative possibilities for assigning priority and weight to the criteria of just war theories.

THERE ARE AT LEAST two useful approaches to an ethical critique of the criteria of just wars. One is to start from basic ethical principles and to ask what criteria of just wars can be derived from them. The other is to start from the just-war criteria that we have inherited and to criticize them in terms of consistency, coherence, and fidelity to fundamental ethical principles and values. Within either approach we move back and forth between our practices, including our ordinary judgments, and ethical principles and theories. . . .

I do not intend to offer a rationalist alternative to

From "Just-War Theories," *Theological Studies* (1978) pp. 427–445. Reprinted by permission of the author and *Theological Studies*.

the historicist perspective that some proponents of just-war theories have taken. Starting from our "historical deposit" of just-war criteria, now accessible in a number of fine historical studies, I try to determine what questions we need to answer in order to develop a coherent just-war theory and, indeed, to have usable criteria for policy-makers. To posit traditional criteria, without an indication of their presuppositions, grounds, interrelations, and functions, will not likely be acceptable. I shall begin with some suggestions about the way traditional just-war criteria can be explicated and defended in relation to a prima-facie duty not to injure and kill others; then I shall analyze their grounds, interrelations, priorities, and weights. Without developing a systematic just-war theory, I shall identify some of the considerations that any satisfactory theory must include.

JUST-WAR CRITERIA: THE LOGIC OF PRIMA FACIE DUTIES

The following criteria frequently appear in comprehensive just-war theories: legitimate or competent authority, just cause, right intention, announcement of intention, last resort, reasonable hope of success, proportionality, and just conduct. All these criteria taken together, with the exception of the last one, establish the *jus ad bellum*, the right to go to war, while the last criterion focuses on the *jus in bello*, right conduct within war, and includes both intention and proportionality, which are also part of the *jus ad bellum*.

"Everyone who has inquired out of prudence, piety, or pity into the propriety of the use of force," claims Ralph Potter, "has constructed an analogue of 'the just war doctrine.'"[1] Although his claim is too strong and sweeping, many analogues to traditional just-war criteria appear when people try to interpret and justify several forms of conduct including the use of force and disobedience to the state. They sometimes crop up as operative criteria even when one's ethical methodology appears to exclude them. Dietrich Bonhoeffer, a theologian who was put to death for his involvement in the July 20, 1944 plot to assassinate Hitler, justified tyrannicide by some of

the criteria of traditional just-war and just-revolution theories despite his theological-ethical methodology that appeared to exclude rules and principles. His "operative guidelines," for which his theological-ethical methodology made no provision, included: clear evidence of serious misrule; respect for the scale of political responsibility and authority (those lower in or outside the political hierarchy should act only after others have failed); reasonable assurances of successful execution; tyrannicide as a last resort; minimal necessary force. As in many justifications of revolution or tyrannicide, Bonhoeffer found a surrogate for the authority of the government in the political hierarchy; others have also appealed to the "lesser magistrates" and finally to the "people."

Some philosophers and theologians also dealt with disobedience and economic boycotts by appealing to analogous criteria. For example, James Luther Adams shows that "some of the most pertinent tests [for determining justified civil disobedience] are similar to those employed in the doctrine of the just war." And Paul Ramsey insists that the use of various forms of economic pressure "should conform to the ancient principles and limitations justifying a Christian in taking up any use of force." His discussion parallels his examination of just-war criteria.[2] While Ramsey and others account for these similarities by pointing to the presence of *force* in each of these modes of conduct, Adams thinks that the similarities between the criteria for civil disobedience and war stem from the fact that both actions deviate from normal procedures.

Actually we formulate and use criteria that are analogous to those that determine whether a war is just and justified whenever we face conflicting obligations or duties, whenever it is impossible to fulfil all the claims upon us, to respect all the rights involved, or to avoid doing evil to everyone. Sometimes we confront two or more prima-facie duties or obligations, one of which we cannot fulfil without sacrificing the other(s). In this sort of dilemma we justify sacrificing one prima-facie obligation to fulfil another only when we can answer certain questions: we need to know whether we have a just cause, proper intentions, a reasonable hope of achieving the end, a reasonable balance between probable good and evil, no other courses of action that would enable us to avoid sacrificing the obligation, etc. Thus the criteria for assessing wars and several other actions are similar because war and these other actions sacrifice some prima-facie obligation(s)—a sacrifice that must be justified along certain lines suggested by the criteria. While the fact that force is used is important, it is only one of numerous human actions that stand in need of justification because they sacrifice prima-facie obligations. Just-war criteria can be illuminated by the language of prima-facie obligations and the *content* of the particular obligations (not to injure or kill others) that the justification of war must override.

First, let us consider the notion of a prima-facie obligation or duty (which I use interchangeably in this context). W. D. Ross introduced the distinction between prima-facie and actual obligations to account for conflicts of obligations (which he thought to be "nonexistent" when fully and carefully analyzed). When two or more prima-facie obligations appear to come into conflict, we have to assess the total situation including various possible courses of actions with all their features of prima-facie rightness and wrongness to determine what we actually ought to do. The phrase "prima facie" indicates that certain features of acts that have a *tendency* to make an act right or wrong claim our attention; insofar as an act has those features, it is right or wrong. But our actual obligation depends on the act in its wholeness and entirety. For "while an act may well be *prima facie* obligatory in respect of one character and *prima facie* forbidden in virtue of another, it becomes obligatory or forbidden only in virtue of the totality of its ethically relevant characteristics." Although some prima-facie obligations are more stringent than others (e.g., nonmaleficence is more stringent than beneficence), it is not possible to provide a complete ranking or a scale of stringency of obligations.

To hold that an obligation or duty is prima-facie is to claim that it always has a strong moral reason for its performance, although this reason may not always be decisive or triumph over all other reasons. If an obligation is viewed as absolute, it cannot be overridden under any circumstances; it has priority over all other obligations with which it might come into conflict. If it is viewed as relative, the rule stating it is no more than a maxim or rule of thumb that illuminates but does not prescribe what we ought to do. If it is viewed as prima-facie, it is intrinsically

binding, but it does not necessarily determine one's actual obligation.

As individuals or members of institutions, we have a prima-facie duty not to injure others. Injury may mean an unwarranted or unjustified harm or violation of rights, or it may mean inflicting actual harm (e.g., shooting someone) which may or may not be warranted or justified. In the first sense, it is, of course, always wrong by definition; an obligation not to injure others wrongfully would be absolute rather than prima-facie. In the second sense, it is prima-facie. Insofar as an act injures another, it is prima-facie wrong and stands in need of justification. Although Joseph Fletcher and others imply that killing (which I am treating for the moment under injury) is morally neutral, William Frankena rightly insists that some kinds of action (including killing) are "intrinsically wrong." For they are

always prima facie *wrong, and they are always actually wrong when they are not justified on other moral grounds. They are not in themselves morally indifferent. They may conceivably be justified in certain situations, but they always need to be justified; and even when they are justified, there is still one moral point against them.*[3]

If the Fifth (or Sixth) Commandment means "Thou shalt not kill," it is prima-facie rather than absolute; for the Hebrews admitted killing in self-defense, capital punishment, and war. If it means "Thou shalt not commit murder," it can then be taken as absolute, but it leaves open the question which killings are to be counted as murder.

It is not necessary to defend Ross's intuitionism in order to hold that injury and killing are intrinsically prima-facie wrong. For Ross, both fall under the obligation of nonmaleficence. For Rawls, there is a "natural duty" (i.e., owed to persons generally) not to injure or harm others and not to inflict unnecessary suffering; this natural duty can be derived from the original position. Christian theologians might derive this obligation not to injure or kill others from the norm of agape. The claim that injury and killing are prima-facie wrong is thus compatible with a number of philosophical and religious frameworks.

An overridden or outweighed prima-facie obligation continues to function in the situation and the course of action one adopts. It leaves what Robert

Nozick calls "moral traces." It has "residual effects" on the agent's attitudes and actions. As A. C. Ewing suggests,

If I have a prima facie *obligation which I cannot rightly fulfill because it is overruled by another, stronger* prima facie *obligation, it does not by any means follow that my conduct ought to be unaffected by the former obligation. Even if I am morally bound to do something inconsistent with it, it should in many cases modify in some respect the way in which the act is performed and in almost all it should affect some subsequent action.*

For example, if I think that a stronger obligation requires me to break a promise, I should at least explain the situation to the promisee, ask him not to hold me to the promise, apologize for breaking it, and even try to make it up to him later. At the very least, Ewing goes on to say, the prima-facie obligation to keep the promise "should always affect our mental attitude toward the action" to the extent of evoking regret.

One important difference between many Protestant and Catholic interpretations of just war appears at this point: the appropriate attitude toward a just war that overrides the prima-facie duty not to injure or kill others. In accord with their belief in the universality of sin, many Protestant theologians such as Reinhold Niebuhr insist that the decision to wage war is always "the lesser of two evils," which they understand as "moral" as well as physical evils. Thus remorse and repentance are proper responses. With St. Augustine they stress that wars should be both just and mournful.[4] Many Catholic theologians, joined by some Protestants, most notably Paul Ramsey, insist that "an act of self-defense or an act of vindictive justice, although imposed by circumstances which are regrettable, is morally good." For them, "war is not the lesser of two evils, but the lesser of two goods (one of which [i.e., peace] appears, at the moment of choice, unattainable)."[5] Regret may be appropriate, but not remorse.

Whether a war that justly and justifiably overrides the prima-facie duty not to injure or kill others should evoke regret or remorse may be debatable, but it not only engenders certain attitudes but other obligations as well. The traces or residual effects of the overridden prima-facie duty are extremely important, as will be clear in my discussion of just-war criteria such as right intention, proportionality, and just conduct.

Before I develop those criteria, I want to summarize and amplify some implications of the prima-facie duty not to injure or kill others; they are actually presuppositions of many just-war theories that include both *jus ad bellum* and *jus in bello*.

First, because it is prima-facie wrong to injure or kill others, such acts demand justification. There is a presumption against their justification, and anyone who tries to justify them bears a heavy burden of proof.

Second, because not all duties can be fulfilled in every situation without some sacrifices (this inability may be understood as natural or as the result of sin), it is necessary and legitimate to override some prima-facie duties. Some other duties may be more stringent and thus take priority over the duty not to injure others—for instance, the prima-facie duty to uphold justice or to protect the innocent. War thus can be a moral undertaking in some circumstances.

Third, the overridden prima-facie duties should affect the actors' attitudes and what they do in waging the war. Some ways of waging war are more compatible than others with the overridden prima-facie duties not to injure or kill others. War can be more or less humane and civilized. War and politics, or peace, are not two totally separate realms or periods.[6] Both are subject to moral principles and rules, and, indeed, to many of the same principles and rules. War ought to fall within many of the boundaries that are also important in peace.

Theorists and practitioners are commonly tempted to make war merely an extension of politics, so that it requires very little to justify waging war; or they are tempted to make politics and war so discontinuous that once one enters the state of war, previously important moral, political, and legal considerations become irrelevant. Two points need to be affirmed. On the one hand, war must be justified because it violates some of our prima-facie obligations, not because it is totally immoral or amoral or utterly discontinuous with politics; on the other hand, it can be more or less humane insofar as it is conducted in accord with some standards that derive from the overridden prima-facie obligations and other obligations that endure even in war. Furthermore, however much continuity there is between peace and war, peace remains the ultimate aim of a just war.

A model of war as a rule-governed activity stands in sharp contrast to a model of war as hell, which is accepted by most pacifists and by many "realists" who recognize no restraints other than proportionality. Both models are evident in the following passage from Rolf Hochhuth's play *Soldiers:*

Bishop Bell of Chichester: "We denigrate our men if we suggest that they require directives to tell them that the burning of defenseless persons is murder."
P.M. (savagely, not looking at Bell): "War is murder. The murderer is the man who fires first. That man is Hitler."

According to one view, war is hell, murder, and there is thus only the crime of war, within which anything goes, for "all's fair. . . ." According to another view, war is a game-like (not in a frivolous sense) or a rule-governed conflict, within which one may legitimately injure, kill, and destroy, but not commit war crimes such as injuring or killing defenseless persons who are noncombatants or excombatants. For the view that war is "total" and without limits, the only critical moral factor is the decision to wage war, and moral blameworthiness may attach to the side starting the war, sometimes even to the side firing the first shot. For the view that war is a rule-governed activity, the *jus in bello* becomes very important. Any adequate theory, however, should not concede that *jus ad bellum* in unimportant because some moral principles and rules persist in war. There is an important and irreducible difference between peace and war, and for that reason the *jus ad bellum* remains indispensable. That difference, however, is not equivalent to the difference between morality and amorality or immorality.

GROUNDS OF JUST-WAR CRITERIA

Most of the criteria traditionally associated with just-war theories emerge because war involves a conflict between prima-facie obligations (when it is just and justified) and because the overridden prima-facie obligations forbid us to injure and kill others. Many

of these criteria apply in other areas, as I have suggested, because of similar conflicts between prima-facie obligations, not because the prima-facie obligations not to injure or kill others are involved at every point. Nevertheless, the content of the prima-facie obligations that are overruled in just wars certainly shapes the criteria, particularly those having to do with *jus in bello*, since the conduct of the war should be as compatible as possible with the overridden prima-facie obligations.

The first criterion of a just war is right or legitimate authority, which is really a presupposition for the rest of the criteria. In fact, it determines *who* is primarily responsible for judging whether the other criteria are met. As Quentin Quade indicates, "the principles of Just War become operative only *after* the classic political question is answered: who should do the judging?" Answering the authority question is a precondition for answering the others; it thus cannot be dismissed as a "secondary criterion." After the proper authority has determined that a war is just and justified and thus overrides the prima-facie obligation not to injure and kill others, citizens, including subject-soldiers, face a different presumption. Whereas the proper authority has to confront and rebut the presumption against war, the subject-soldier now confronts the presumption that the war is just and justified because the legitimate authority has so decided in accord with established procedures. In all political orders the subject has a moral right/duty—although not a legal right—not to fight if the war is manifestly unjust. And in a democracy the citizen is ruler as well as subject and thus has a greater responsibility to apply these criteria to war. As subject, however, his presumption ought to be that the authorities, if they are legitimate and have followed proper procedures, have decided correctly.

The requirement of a *just cause* is simply the requirement that the other competing prima-facie duty or obligation be a serious and weighty one: e.g., to protect the innocent from unjust attack, to restore rights wrongfully denied, or to reestablish a just order. Because war involves overriding important prima-facie obligations not to injure or kill others, it demands the most weighty and significant reasons.

These obligations cannot, however, be overridden if there are other ways of achieving the just aim short of war. War is the *ultima ratio*, the last resort. The requirement that war be the last resort does not mean that all possible measures have to be attempted and exhausted if there is no reasonable expectation that they will be successful. Nor does it necessarily mean that the side that first resorts to armed force should be condemned.

Insofar as a formal *declaration* is sometimes required, it stems not only from the nature of political society, but also from the requirement that war be the last resort. Ultimata or formal declarations of war "are the last measures of persuasion short of force itself." Although a formal declaration of war may not be appropriate for various reasons, the significance of this criterion, broadly understood, should not be underestimated. Conceding that the best publicists differed on the necessity of a declaration, Francis Lieber defended it because "decent regard for mankind" and "public good faith" require that a government explain and justify its departure from peace. A failure to announce the intention of and the reasons for waging war is a failure to exercise the responsibility of explaining and justifying exceptional action to those involved, including the citizens of one's own country, the enemy, and third parties who have to decide how to respond. An announcement of intentions and explanation of reasons may be more appropriate than a formal declaration of war.

The requirements of *reasonable hope of success* and *proportionality* are closely related. If war has no reasonable chance of success, it is clearly imprudent. But more than a dictate of prudence is involved in the demand for a reasonable hope of success. If none of the just and serious ends, none of the other prima-facie obligations, could be realized or fulfilled through the war, a nation should reconsider its policy, which, after all, involves overriding stringent prima-facie obligations. Nevertheless, numerous qualifications are in order. This criterion applies more clearly to offensive than to defensive wars. And in any war success may be broader than "victory." As Lieber wrote of John Brown's raid, it was irrational, but it will be historical! Success could include witnessing to values as well as achieving goals; for instance, a group might engage in resistance in order to retain self-respect even in its demise. Regarding the limited Jewish resistance in Nazi Germany, some Jewish thinkers have insisted that if the holocaust comes again, Jews must not "die like sheep."

Although Ralph Potter has derived the criterion of reasonable hope of success from the moral prohibition of suicide and from the fact that statesmen are stewards of a nation, heroic acts such as falling on a grenade to save one's comrades may be fitting for individuals and suicide itself may be justifiable in some cases, particularly if it can be noble witness to some higher values in the face of certain and imminent death. Even if a nation has good reason to think that it will be defeated anyway, its vigorous resistance may preserve significant values beyond number of lives and retention of territory or sovereignty. Furthermore, what is "reasonable" depends on the situations in which actors have to make responsible decisions; retrospective judgments by others should include only what the actors could and should have foreseen. Finally, this criterion appears only to exclude totally useless, pointless, or self-indulgent warfare which reasonable people cannot expect to achieve goals or to express values. Such warfare is excluded because it cannot override the prima-facie duties not to injure or kill others, duties as binding on states as on individuals.

Regarding *proportionality*, Ramsey writes:

It can never be right to resort to war, no matter how just the cause, unless a proportionality can be established between military/political objectives and their price, or unless one has reason to believe that in the end more good will be done than undone or a greater measure of evil prevented. But, of all the tests for judging whether to resort to or to participate in war, this one balancing an evil or good effect against another is open to the greatest uncertainty. This, therefore, establishes rather than removes the possibility of conscientious disagreement among prudent men.[7]

Here too defensive measures are less restricted than offensive ones, but this criterion includes the welfare of all countries and peoples and not merely one's own country. Certainly the weight of the cause and the probability of success enter the discussion of proportionality, but the probable negative consequences must also be considered—even beyond the negative feature of injuring or killing others.

The last major criterion of the *jus ad bellum* is right or just *intention* (which along with proportionality is very important in particular battles, engagements, and acts *within* war and not merely for the war as a whole). For the war as a whole, right intention is shaped by the pursuit of a just cause. But it also encompasses motives; for example, as St. Augustine and others have insisted, hatred is ruled out. Some would hold that the dominance, if not the mere presence, of hatred vitiates the right to wage war even if there is a just cause. For example, McKenna holds that a "war which is otherwise just becomes immoral if it is waged out of hatred." Such a contention, however, is difficult to establish; for if all the conditions of a just/justified war are met, the presence of vicious motives would not obliterate the *jus ad bellum*, although they would lead to negative judgments about the agents. Insofar as these vicious motives are expressed in disproportionate force, the infliction of unnecessary suffering, etc., one may condemn the belligerent for violating the *jus in bello*. Nevertheless, this criterion of right intention understood not merely as pursuit of a just cause but also as proper motives remains significant in part because war is conducted between public, not private, enemies. Furthermore, an attitude of regret, if not remorse, is appropriate when a prima-facie obligation is overridden.

Another interpretation of right intention focuses on *peace* as the object or end of war. It too bridges the *jus ad bellum* and *jus in bello*, and I shall emphasize its impact on the conduct of war. St. Augustine and many others have affirmed that peace is the ultimate object, end, or intention of war. In short, war as injury, killing, and destruction is not an end in itself but a means to another end—a just or better peace. Even apart from the justice that is sought, peace retains its moral claim during war and thus constitutes an ultimate or final objective. There is a duty to restore the "normal" state of affairs as quickly and surely as possible.

It may be dangerous, however, to stress that it is urgent to restore peace, especially if peace is defined as the absence of conflict rather than a specific set of relationships which may include conflict; for such an emphasis may engender support for a brutal and total war, which may undermine the limits set by the *jus in bello*. Paul Ramsey holds that unless there is a morality that intrinsically limits the conduct of war, "then we must simply admit that war has no limits—since these can hardly be derived from 'peace' as the 'final cause' of just wars."[8] But if one

does not misconstrue peace as the total absence of conflict, one can see how the prima-facie obligation not to injure or kill others persists even in the midst of war by mandating the ultimate object of peace. And through the object of peace (but not only this way) it imposes other restraints on the conduct of war. Since the aim of war is "a just peace," John Rawls contends, "the means employed must not destroy the possibility of peace or encourage a contempt for human life that puts the safety of ourselves and of mankind in jeopardy." General Orders No. 100 of 1863 held that "military necessity does not include any act of hostility which makes the return to peace unnecessarily difficult."[9]

If peace does not require mutual goodwill, it at least requires some trust and confidence. Thus perfidy, bad faith, and treachery are ruled out in part because they are destructive of the ultimate object of peace. If they are prevalent in war, to restore and maintain peace becomes very difficult short of the total subjugation of the enemy. Acceptable ruses of war, according to one commentator on the laws of war, are "those acts which the enemy would have had reason to expect, or in any event had no reason not to expect."[10] Perfidy or treachery involves the betrayal of a belligerent's confidence that is based on moral and/or legal reasons (such as the expected protection of prisoners of war). This requirement of good faith derives not only from the ultimate end of peace but also from the respect for the humanity of the enemy that is expressed in a number of prima-facie obligations.

The prima-facie obligation not to injure or kill others should also more directly affect the choice of weapons and methods to fight wars than through the ultimate object of peace. Since this prima-facie obligation is not cancelled even when it is overruled, its impact can be seen in various restrictions of the *jus in bello*.

First, the immediate object is not to kill or even to injure any particular person but to incapacitate or restrain him. The enemy soldier is not reduced to his role as combatant, and when he surrenders or is wounded, he ceases to be a combatant because he ceases to be a threat. He is now an excombatant. As a prisoner of war, he is entitled to certain protections. As a wounded person, he is entitled to medical treatment equal to that of one's own wounded comrades.

Second, directly to attack noncombatants is not legitimate. This principle is sound even if the distinction between combatant and noncombatant is contextual and thus is partially determined by the society and the type of war. In the gray areas, noncombatants include those persons whose functions in factories and elsewhere serve the needs of the person qua person rather than his or her role as military personnel. Thus, while food is essential for the soldier to function, it is indispensable for him as a human being. And chaplains and medical personnel primarily serve the soldier as human being even when their ministrations indirectly aid the war effort. Finally, indiscriminate methods of warfare are prohibited by this principle.

Third, the original prima-facie obligation not to injure others also excludes inflicting *unnecessary suffering*. Thus cruelty (inflicting suffering for the sake of suffering) and wanton destruction (destruction without a compelling reason) are wrong. Such acts are not essential to the war effort. Acts that appear to fall under these vague categories of "cruelty" and "wanton destruction" are not cruel or wanton if they are "necessary." The relation between military necessity and such categories is a serious problem area in the *jus in bello*. At any rate, certain weapons (such as dum-dum bullets and explosive or inflammable projectiles weighing less than 400 grams) are prohibited because they are calculated to cause "unnecessary suffering" or "superfluous injury." The rationale is simple. An ordinary rifle bullet or a projectile weighing less than 400 grams is designed to incapacitate only one person. To make the bullet or projectile do more damage to that one person is to inflict suffering that is unnecessary or superfluous.[11] That suffering offers no military advantage. (Of course, not all suffering that offers military advantage is necessary and justified.)

Fourth, even the indirect, incidental, or obliquely intentional effects on civilians must be justified by the principle of proportion.

I have not tried to offer an exhaustive list of the requirements of the *jus in bello*, but rather to show that some restrictions emerge from the continued pressure of the prima-facie duty not to injure or kill others even when it is overridden by the *jus ad bellum*. That duty persists and imposes restrictions indirectly through the ultimate object of peace and directly as in the protection of certain classes,

avoidance of unnecessary suffering, and care for combatants who are *hors de combat*.

APPLICATION OF CRITERIA: ORDER AND PRIORITIES

Some issues of order and priorities emerged when I examined the way some criteria derive from or relate to others and especially the overridden prima-facie duty not to injure or kill others. But there are other issues also inadequately addressed by contemporary just-war theorists. I want to identify some of them without attempting to resolve them: When public officials or citizens apply these criteria to particular wars, should they apply them in any particular order? Do some criteria have more weight than others? Is a serial ordering possible?

A good place to start is with the question, what makes a war unjust and/or unjustified? Because medieval just-war theorists were mainly interested in the question whether and when Christians could participate in war, they focused on the criteria for just wars and did "not really analyse an unjust war except as a mirror image of a just war." For different reasons, contemporary theorists also focus on just wars and neglect some of the issues that might emerge if they asked when a war is unjust and/or unjustified. How can one recognize an unjust and/or unjustified war?

Some argue that meeting each criterion is necessary for a just war; each is necessary and all are collectively sufficient. Thus the inability to meet any single criterion, such as last resort, renders a war unjust.

A second possible approach would hold that a just war must "more or less" meet or approximate the criteria. No particular criterion is absolutely necessary, but at least several must be met for a war to be just and justified. While such an approach is probably the closest to the way citizens and policymakers reason, it does not indicate what degree of approximation is sufficient to make a war just and justified.

A third approach would offer a serial or lexical ordering of the criteria, so that some must be met before others can even be considered. While the first approach requires that each criterion be met and the second one requires only that some be met, both apply the criteria *en bloc*. The third approach, however, might hold that "just cause" is an indispensable and fundamental criterion that must be satisfied before one can even consider proportionality. While this approach may have the same outcome as the first one, the order of consideration is important.

A fourth approach could consider all or some of the criteria as establishing prima-facie duties, which would then follow the logic already sketched in this essay.

A fifth approach could consider the criteria as "rules of thumb" or "maxims" that identify some morally relevant considerations. We do not start our reflection about war *de novo*, but rather begin with these traditional maxims that illuminate but do not prescribe what we ought to do. While a war is just and justified if it produces the greatest good, these maxims are useful in identifying relevant factors to put on the scale.

These five approaches obviously do not exhaust the possibilities; indeed, several combinations are possible. Nevertheless, they indicate some of the ambiguities in current just-war theories. Although it is possible to make some general points about the order of the criteria on the basis of the prima-facie obligations that are involved (as I tried to do in the order I employed in the preceding section), the order and weight of the criteria will finally be determined for any particular theory by substantive views of justice and other moral principles and values, modes of moral reasoning, etc. Many recent attempts to restate just-war criteria apparently consider them to be questions that policy-makers ought to consider. Without some substantive beliefs, they can say only "consider justice," "consider how much success is possible," "balance the benefits and costs," etc. Thus the criteria would constitute a formal framework for moral debates about the use of force. Perhaps because they are empty, they can serve to organize and orchestrate disputes in the public arena; even pacifists could and did use these criteria to condemn the war in Vietnam. While this function of the criteria should not be disparaged, it is hardly what traditional theorists expected; for they developed their criteria within substantive theories of justice and the common good.

Paul Ramsey prefers to translate *justum bellum* as "justified war" rather than "just war," in part because he does not think that a substantive theory of justice in relation to ends can be developed or that one side can legitimately claim justice while denying it to the other. Such an approach fits with a formal understanding of these criteria. When a policy-maker raises these formal questions of the *jus ad bellum* and gets affirmative answers, resort to war is "justified" although we cannot say that it is "just." A procedural justification is possible even when we lack a substantive theory of justice. Ramsey is more willing to provide content for *jus in bello* at least in terms of a principle of discrimination that rules out direct attacks on noncombatants. Indeed, he says very little about *jus ad bellum*, concentrating instead on *jus in bello*.

Many classic and contemporary theorists have construed "just cause" to include last resort, reasonable chance of success, and proportionality.[12] A nation does not have a just cause unless these other conditions are also met. Nonetheless, one way to use the just/justified distinction is to restrict the language of "justice" to war's cause or aim and then to determine whether the war is "justified" by reference to the other criteria, including last resort, reasonable chance of success, and proportionality. While a war may be "unjust," according to this approach, when its cause does not satisfy standards of justice, it is "unjustified" when it does not meet the other criteria. It is important to emphasize, as Joel Feinberg has pointed out, that one and the same act need not be both just and justified.[13] It may be *just and unjustified* (e.g., although it renders various parties their due, it violates some other moral principles or results in terrible consequences), or it may be *unjust and justified* (e.g., an unfair act is required to prevent a disaster). Only when a war is both just and justified does a state have a *jus ad bellum*.

In addition to the distinction between justice and justification, the distinction between rights and right conduct, or between rights and their exercise, may be useful, particularly in construing the relation between *jus ad bellum* and *jus in bello*. For example, perhaps one side could meet most of the conditions of *jus ad bellum* but have little chance of success without fighting the war unjustly and unfairly. We might say "You have a right to go to war, but you ought not to exercise that right." Such an approach, however, favors the established military powers. Should a theory of war make it impossible for one country (or revolutionary movement) to wage a "successful" war? Ideological bias and the tension between moral requirements and success must be confronted clearly and honestly.

Does the *jus ad bellum* establish only a right or also a duty to go to war (at least under certain circumstances)? Because the language of duty can lead to or support crusades and holy wars, it is somewhat suspect. There is no prima-facie duty to go to war (i.e., to injure and kill), but because some other prima-facie duties (e.g., to protect the innocent) may override the prima-facie duty not to injure or kill, there may be an *actual* duty to fight, especially in a situation where the language of necessity seems appropriate. To say that war stands in need of justification because it violates certain prima-facie duties is not to rule out the language of actual duty or obligation in a particular set of circumstances. To think of some wars as duties does not entail modifying or relaxing the *jus in bello*. Even a policeman who has a duty to try to stop an escaped criminal who has taken hostages still must respect certain moral and legal limits.

Finally, what degree of certitude should policymakers and citizens have about the justice/justification of a particular war? Should they be convinced that the preponderance of the evidence indicates that the war is just/justified according to the above criteria? Or should they be convinced beyond a reasonable doubt?

This essay has attempted to show how traditional just-war criteria can be interpreted and defended in relation to a prima-facie duty not to injure and kill others. Both the notion of a prima-facie duty and the content of the duty not to injure and kill others illuminate the just-war criteria which are analogous to the criteria we use whenever we cannot fulfil all the claims upon us. An overridden prima-facie duty should continue to have an impact on the actors' attitudes and actions, for example, on the *jus in bello* which also expresses other enduring duties and obligations. Finally, I identified several unresolved issues in the application of just-war criteria, particularly their order, priorities, and weight. Theorists of just wars need to pay more attention to numerous issues including the bases, interrelations, and functions of their criteria. Otherwise they will appear merely to posit traditional criteria without foundation and coherence. Of course, such issues constitute only part of the total agenda for just-war theorists in this age. Other critical issues of relevance and application also require attention, but they cannot be adequately addressed if we are not willing to face some of the ethical, philosophical, and theological questions that war raises.

NOTES

1. Ralph B. Potter, Jr., *War and Moral Discourse* (Richmond, VA: John Knox, 1969) 61. One of the best systematic examinations of just-war criteria is Potter's article "The Moral Logic of War," *McCormick Quarterly* 23 (1970) 203–33.

2. Paul Ramsey, *Christian Ethics and the Sit-in* (New York: Association, 1961), 104. Cf. Paul Ramsey, *War and the Christian Conscience* (Durham, N.C.: Duke University, 1961), and *The Just War: Force and Political Responsibility* (New York: Scribner's, 1968).

3. William K. Frankena, *Ethics* (2nd ed.; Englewood Cliffs, N.J.: Prentice-Hall, 1973) 55. Frankena holds that some kinds of acts are "intrinsically prima facie wrong" (55–6).

4. See Henry Paolucci, ed. *The Political Writings of St. Augustine* (Chicago: Regnery, 1962) 162–83, and Roland H. Bainton, *Christian Attitudes toward War and Peace* (New York: Abingdon, 1960) 98.

5. Joseph C. McKenna, S.J., "Ethics and War: A Catholic View," *American Political Science Review* 54 (1960) 658, cf. 650. For Ramsey's theoretical statement, see *Deeds and Rules in Christian Ethics* (New York: Scribner's 1967) 187–88.

6. Paul Ramsey, *The Just War*, 55, 142, 143, 475, and passim.

7. Ramsey, *The Just War* 195.

8. Ramsey, *The Just War* 152. On the dangers of an excessive emphasis on the end of peace, see Johnson, "Just War Theory" 43–44.

9. See Childress, "Francis Lieber's Interpretation of the Laws of War" 49 and 63–65.

10. Frits Kalshoven, *The Law of Warfare: A Summary of Its Recent History and Trends in Development* (Leiden: Sijthoff, 1973) 102.

11. *Weapons That May Cause Unnecessary Suffering or Have Indiscriminate Effects.* Report on the Work of Experts (Geneva: International Committee of the Red Cross, 1973).

12. See Walters, *Five Classic Just-War Theories* 316–20, and William V. O'Brien, "Morality and War: The Contribution of Paul Ramsey," *Love and Society: Essays in the Ethics of Paul Ramsey*, ed. James Johnson and David Smith (Missoula, Mont.: Scholars, 1974) 181.

13. Joel Feinberg, "On Being 'Morally Speaking a Murderer,'" in *Ethics*, ed. Judith J. Thomson and Gerald Dworkin (New York: Harper & Row, 1968) 295–97.

George I. Mavrodes

CONVENTIONS AND THE MORALITY OF WAR

George I. Mavrodes begins by criticizing the view of the "immunity theorists," those who claim that noncombatants should have immunity from being killed because they are innocent. Mavrodes contends that by any plausible standard of guilt and innocence that has moral content, noncombatants can be guilty and combatants can be innocent. Hence the guilt/innocence distinction will not support the combatant/noncombatant distinction. What does support the combatant/noncombatant distinction, Mavrodes claims, is merely a convention to observe it. Thus our obligation not to kill noncombatants, when we have one, is a convention-dependent obligation.

THE POINT OF THIS paper is to introduce a distinction into our thinking about warfare, and to explore the moral implications of this distinction. I shall make two major assumptions. First, I shall assume without discussion that under some circumstances and for some ends warfare is morally justified. These conditions I shall lump together under such terms as "justice" and "just cause," and say no more about them. I shall also assume that in warfare some means, including some killing, are morally justified. I sometimes call such means "proportionate," and in general I say rather little about them. These assumptions, incidentally, are common to all of the philosophers whom I criticize here.

The distinction which I introduce can be thought of either as dividing wars into two classes, or else as distinguishing wars from certain other international combats. I have no great preference for one of these

George I. Mavrodes, "Conventions and the Morality of War," *Philosophy & Public Affairs*, Vol. 4, no. 2 (Winter 1975). Copyright © 1975 by Princeton University Press. Reprinted by permission of Princeton University Press.

ways of speaking over the other, but I shall generally adopt the latter alternative. I am particularly interested in the moral significance of this distinction, and I shall explore in some detail its bearing on one moral question associated with warfare, that of the intentional killing of noncombatants.

My paper has two main parts. In the first I examine three closely related treatments of this moral question: the arguments of Elizabeth Anscombe, John C. Ford, and Paul Ramsey. These treatments seem to ignore the distinction which I will propose. I argue that on their own terms, and without reference to that distinction, they must be counted as unsatisfactory.

In the second part of the paper I propose and explain my distinction. I then explore what I take to be some of its moral implications, especially with reference to the alleged immunity of noncombatants, and I argue that it supplies what was missing or defective in the treatments previously criticized.

I. THE IMMUNITY THEORISTS

A number of philosophers have held that a large portion of the population of warring nations have a special moral status. This is the *noncombatant* segment of the population, and they have a moral immunity from being intentionally killed. This view seems to have been especially congenial to philosophers who have tried to apply Christian ethics to the problems of warfare. Among the philosophers who have held this view are Elizabeth Anscombe, John C. Ford, and Paul Ramsey. I shall refer to this trio of thinkers as the *immunity theorists*.

Perhaps we should indicate a little more in detail just what the immunity theorists appear to hold, specifying just what segment of the population is being discussed and just what their immunity consists in. The immunity theorists commonly admit that there is some difficulty in specifying exactly who are the noncombatants.[1] Roughly, they are those people who are not engaged in military operations and whose activity is not immediately and directly related to the war effort. Perhaps we could say that if a person is engaged only in the sort of activities which would be carried on even if the nation were

not at war (or preparing for war) then that person is a noncombatant. So generally farmers, teachers, nurses, firemen, sales people, housewives, poets, children, etc. are noncombatants.[2] There are, of course, difficult cases, ranging from the high civilian official of the government to the truck driver (either military or civilian) who hauls vegetables toward the front lines. But despite the hard cases it is held that warring nations contain large numbers of readily identifiable people who are clearly noncombatants.

What of their immunity? The writers whom I consider here make use of the "principle of double-effect."[3] This involves dividing the consequences of an act (at least the foreseeable consequences) into two classes. Into the first class go those consequences which constitute the goal or purpose of the act, what the act is done for, and also those consequences which are means to those ends. Into the other class go those consequences which are neither the sought-after ends nor the means to those ends. So, for example, the bombing of a rail yard may have among its many consequences the following: the flow of supplies toward the front is disrupted, several locomotives are damaged, and a lot of smoke, dust, etc. is discharged into the air. The disruption of transport may well be the end sought by this action, and perhaps the damage to locomotives is sought as a means of disrupting transport. If so, these consequences belong in the first class, a class which I shall generally mark by using the words "intentional" or "intended." The smoke, on the other hand, though as surely foreseeable as the other effects, may be neither means nor end in this situation. It is a side-effect, and belongs in the second class (which I shall sometimes call "unintentional" or "unintended").

Now, the moral immunity of noncombatants consists, according to these writers, in the fact that their death can never, morally, be made the intended consequence of a military operation. Or to put it another way, any military operation which seeks the death of noncombatants either as an end or a means is immoral, regardless of the total good which it might accomplish.

The *unintended* death of noncombatants, on the other hand, is not absolutely forbidden. A military operation which will foreseeably result in such deaths, neither as means nor ends but as side effects, may be morally acceptable according to these writers. It will be morally acceptable if the good end which it may be expected to attain is of sufficient weight to overbalance the evil of these noncombatant deaths (as well as any other evils involved in it). This principle, sometimes called the principle of proportionality, apparently applies to foreseen but unintended noncombatant deaths in just the same way as it applies to the intended death of combatants, the destruction of resources, and so on. In all of these cases it is held to be immoral to cause many deaths, much pain, etc., in order to achieve minor goals. Here combatant and noncombatant stand on the same moral ground, and their deaths are weighed in the same balances. But when the slaying of noncombatants is envisioned as an end or, more commonly, as a means—perhaps in order to reduce the production of foodstuffs or to damage the morale of troops—then there is an unqualified judgment that the projected operation is flatly immoral. The intentional slaying of combatants, on the other hand, faces no such prohibition. This, then, is the place where the moral status of combatant and noncombatant differ sharply.

Now, if a scheme such as this is not to appear simply arbitrary it looks as though we must find some morally relevant basis for the distinction. It is perhaps worthwhile to notice that in this context the immunity of noncombatants cannot be supported by reference to the sanctity or value of human life, nor by reference to a duty not to kill our brothers, etc. For these authors recognize the moral permissibility, even perhaps the duty, of killing under certain circumstances. What must be sought is the ground of a distinction, and not merely a consideration against killing.

Such a ground, however, seems very hard to find, perhaps unexpectedly so. The crucial argument proposed by the immunity theorists turns on the notions of guilt and innocence. Anscombe, for example, says:

Now, it is one of the most vehement and repeated teachings of the Judaeo-Christian tradition that the shedding of innocent blood is forbidden by the divine law. No man may be punished except for his own crime, and those "whose feet are swift to shed innocent blood" are always represented as God's enemies.[4]

Earlier on she says, "The principal wickedness which is a temptation to those engaged in warfare is the killing of the innocent,"[5] and she has titled one of the sections of her paper, "Innocence and the Right to Kill Intentionally." Clearly enough the notion of innocence plays a large role in her thinking on this topic. Just what that role is, or should be, will be considered shortly. Ford, in the article cited earlier, repeatedly couples the word "innocent" with "civilian" and "noncombatant." His clearest statement, however, is in another essay. There he says:

Catholic teaching has been unanimous for long centuries in declaring that it is never permitted to kill directly noncombatants in wartime. Why? Because they are innocent. That is, they are innocent of the violent and destructive action of war, or of any close participation in the violent and destructive action of war. It is such participation alone that would make them legitimate targets of violent repression themselves.[6]

Here we have explicitly a promising candidate for the basis of the moral distinction between combatants and noncombatants. It is promising because innocence itself seems to be a moral property. Hence, if we could see that noncombatants were innocent while combatants were not it would be plausible to suppose that this fact made it morally proper to treat them in different ways.

If we are to succeed along this line of thought, then we must meet at least two conditions. First, we must find some one sense of "innocence" such that all noncombatants are innocent and all combatants are guilty. Second, this sense must be morally relevant, a point of the greatest importance. We are seeking to ground a moral distinction, and the facts to which we refer must therefore be morally relevant. The use of a morally tinged word, such as "innocent," does not of itself guarantee such relevance.

Well, is there a suitable sense for "innocent"? Ford said that noncombatants "are innocent of the violent and destructive action of war." Anscombe, writing of the people who can properly be attacked with deadly force, says, "What is required, for the people attacked to be noninnocent in the relevant sense, is that they themselves be engaged in an objectively unjust proceeding which the attacker has the right to make his concern; or—the commonest case—should be unjustly attacking him." On the other hand, she speaks of "people whose mere existence and activity supporting existence by growing crops, making clothes, etc.," might contribute to the war effort, and she says, "such people are innocent and it is murderous to attack them, or make them a target for an attack which he judges will help him towards victory."[7] These passages contain, I think, the best clues we have as to the sense of "innocent" in these authors.

It is probably evident enough that this sense of "innocent" is vague in a way parallel to the vagueness of "noncombatant." It will leave us with troublesome borderline cases. In itself, that does not seem to me a crucial defect. But perhaps it is a clue to an important failing. For I suspect that there is this parallel vagueness because "innocent" here is just a synonym for "noncombatant."

What can Ford mean by saying that some people are "innocent of the violent and destructive action of war" except that those people are not engaged in the violence of war? Must not Anscombe mean essentially the same thing when she says that the non-innocent are those who are themselves "engaged in an objectively unjust proceeding"? But we need not rely wholly on these rhetorical questions. Ramsey makes this point explicitly. He first distinguishes between close and remote cooperation in military operations, and then he alludes to the distinction between the "guilty" and the "innocent." Of this distinction he says, "These are very misleading terms, since their meaning is exhaustively stated under the first contrast, and is reducible to degrees of actual participation in hostile force."[8] In this judgment Ramsey certainly seems to me to be right.

Now, we should notice carefully that a person may be an enthusiastic supporter of the unjust war and its unjust aims, he may give to it his voice and his vote, he may have done everything in his power to procure it when it was yet but a prospect, now that it is in progress he may contribute to it both his savings and the work which he knows best how to do, and he may avidly hope to share in the unjust gains which will follow if the war is successful. But such a person may clearly be a noncombatant, and (in the sense of the immunity theorists) unquestionably "innocent" of the war. On the other hand, a young man of limited mental ability and almost no education may be drafted, put into uniform, trained for a few weeks, and sent to the front as a replacement in a low-grade unit. He may have no under-

standing of what the war is about, and no heart for it. He might want nothing more than to go back to his town and the life he led before. But he is "engaged," carrying ammunition, perhaps, or stringing telephone wire or even banging away ineffectually with his rifle. He is without doubt a combatant, and "guilty," a fit subject for intentional slaughter. Is is not clear that "innocence," as used here, leaves out entirely all of the relevant moral considerations—that it has no moral content at all? Anscombe suggests that intentional killing during warfare should be construed on the model of punishing people for their crimes, and we must see to it, if we are to be moral, that we punish someone only for his own crime and not for someone else's. But if we construe the criminality involved in an unjust war in any reasonable moral sense then it must either be the case that many noncombatants are guilty of that criminality or else many combatants are innocent. In fact, it will probably be the case that *both* of these things are true. Only if we were to divest "crime" of its moral bearings could we make it fit the combatant/noncombatant distinction in modern wars.

The fact that both Anscombe and Ramsey[9] use the analogy of the criminal in discussing this topic suggests that there is an important fact about warfare which is easily overlooked. And that is that warfare, unlike ordinary criminal activity, is not an activity in which individuals engage qua individuals or as members of voluntary associations. They enter into war as members of nations. It is more proper to say that the nation is at war than that its soldiers are at war. This does not, of course, entail that individuals have no moral responsiblity for their acts in war. But it does suggest that moral responsibility may not be distributed between combatant and noncombatant in the same way as between a criminal and his children. Many of the men who are soldiers, perhaps most of them, would not be engaged in military operations at all if they did not happen to be citizens of a warring nation. But noncombatants are citizens of warring nations in exactly the same sense as are soldiers. However these facts are to be analyzed they should warn us not to rely too heavily on the analogy with ordinary criminality.

We seem, then, to be caught in a dilemma. We can perhaps find some sense for notions such as *innocence* and *criminality* which will make them fit the distinction in which we are interested. But the price of doing so seems to be that of divesting these notions of the moral significance which they require if they are to justify the moral import of the distinction itself. In the ordinary senses, on the other hand, these notions do have the required moral bearings. But in their ordinary senses they do not fit the desired distinction. In neither way, therefore, can the argument from innocence be made to work, and the alleged moral immunity of noncombatants seems to be left as an arbitrary claim.

II. CONVENTION-DEPENDENT MORALITY

Despite the failure of these arguments I have recently come to think that there may be something of importance in this distinction after all, and even that it may have an important moral bearing. How might this be?

Imagine a statesman reflecting on the costliness of war, its cost in human life and human suffering. He observes that these costs are normally very high, sometimes staggering. Furthermore, he accepts the principle of proportionality. A consequence of this is that he sometimes envisions a just war for a just cause, but nevertheless decides not to prosecute that war even though he believes it could be won. For the cost of winning would be so high as to outweigh the good which would be attained. So he must sometimes let oppression flourish and injustice hold sway. And even in those wars which can be prosecuted the costs eat very seriously into the benefits.

Then he has an idea. Suppose—just suppose—that one could replace warfare with a less costly substitute. Suppose, for example, that one could introduce a convention—and actually get it accepted and followed by the nations—a convention which replaced warfare with single combat. Under this convention, when two nations arrived at an impasse which would otherwise have resulted in war they would instead choose, each of them, a single champion (doubtless a volunteer). These two men would then meet in mortal combat, and whoever won, killing his opponent or driving him from the field, would win for his nation. To that nation would then be ceded whatever territory, influence, or other prize would have been sought in the war, and the nation whose champion was defeated would lose correspondingly.

Suppose, too, that the statesman believes that if such a convention were to come into force his own nation could expect to win and lose such combats in about the same proportion as it could now expect to win and lose ordinary wars. The same types of questions would be settled by such combats as would otherwise be settled by war (though perhaps more questions would be submitted to combat than would be submitted to war), and approximately the same resolutions would be arrived at. The costs, however—human death and suffering—would be reduced by several orders of magnitude. Would that not be an attractive prospect? I think it would.

While the prospect may seem attractive it may also strike us as hopelessly utopian, hardly to be given a serious thought. There seems to be some evidence, however, that exactly this substitution was actually attempted in ancient times. Ancient literature contains at least two references to such attempts. One is in the Bible, I Samuel 17, the combat between David and Goliath. The other is in the *Iliad*, book 3, where it is proposed to settle the siege of Troy in the very beginning by single combat between Menelaus and Paris. It may be significant that neither of these attempts appears to have been successful. The single combats were followed by bloodier and more general fighting. Perhaps this substitute for warfare is too cheap; it cannot be made practical, and nations just will not consent in the end to abide by this convention. But consider, on the one hand, warfare which is limited only by the moral requirements that the ends sought should be just and that the means used should be proportionate, and, on the other hand, the convention of single combat as a substitute for warfare. Between these extremes there lie a vast number of other possible conventions which might be canvassed in the search for a less costly substitute for war. I suggest that the long struggle, in the western world at least, to limit military operations to "counter-forces" strategies, thus sparing civilian populations, is just such an attempt.

If I am right about this, then the moral aspects of the matter must be approached in a way rather different from that of the immunity theorists. Some, but not all, of their conclusions can be accepted, and somewhat different grounds must be given for them. These thinkers have construed the immunity of noncombatants as though it were a moral fact which was independent of any actual or envisioned convention or practice. And they have consequently sought to support this immunity by argument which makes no reference to convention. I have already argued that their attempts were failures. What I suggest now is that all such attempts *must* be failures, for they mistake the sort of moral requirement which is under consideration. Let me try to make this clearer.

I find it plausible to suppose that I have a moral obligation to refrain from wantonly murdering my neighbors. And it also seems plausible to discuss this, perhaps in utilitarian terms, or in terms of the will of God, or of natural law, or in terms of a rock-bottom deontological requirement, but in any case without essential reference to the laws and customs of our nation. We might, indeed, easily imagine our laws and customs to be other than they are with respect to murder. But we would then judge the moral adequacy and value of such alternative laws and customs by reference to the moral obligation I have mentioned and not vice versa. On the other hand, I may also have a moral obligation to pay a property tax or to drive on the right side of the street. It does not seem plausible to suppose, however, that one can discuss these duties without immediately referring to our laws and customs. And it seems likely that different laws would have generated different moral duties, e.g. driving on the left. These latter are examples of "convention-dependent" moral obligations. More formally, I will say that a given moral obligation is convention-dependent if and only if (1) given that a certain convention, law, custom, etc., is actually in force one really does have an obligation to act in conformity with that convention, and (2) there is an alternative law, custom, etc. (or lack thereof) such that if that had been in force one would not have had the former obligation.

At this point, before developing the way in which it may apply to warfare, let me forestall some possible misunderstandings by a series of brief comments on this notion. I am not claiming, nor do I believe, that all laws, customs, etc., generate corresponding moral obligations. But some do. I am not

denying that one may seek, and perhaps find, some more general moral law, perhaps independent of convention, which explains why this convention generates the more specific obligation. I claim only that one cannot account for the specific obligation apart from the convention. Finally, I am not denying that one might have an obligation, perhaps independent of convention, to try to change a convention of this sort. For I think it possible that one might simultaneously have a moral obligation to conform to a certain convention and also a moral obligation to replace that convention, and thus to eliminate the first obligation.

Now, the core of my suggestion with respect to the immunity of noncombatants is this. The immunity of noncombatants is best thought of as a convention-dependent obligation related to a convention which substitutes for warfare a certain form of limited combat. How does this bear on some of the questions which we have been discussing?

To begin with, we might observe that the convention itself is presumably to be justified by its expectable results. (Perhaps we can refer to some moral rule to the effect that we should minimize social costs such as death and injury.) It seems plausible to suppose that the counter-forces convention, if followed, will reduce the pain and death involved in combat—will reduce it, that is, compared to unlimited warfare. There are surely other possible conventions which, if followed, would reduce those costs still more, e.g. the substitution of single combat. Single combat, however, is probably not a live contender because there is almost no chance that such a convention would actually be followed. It is possible, however, that there is some practical convention which is preferable to the present counter-forces convention. If so, the fact that it is preferable is a strong reason in favor of supposing that there is a moral obligation to promote its adoption.

It does not follow, however, that we now have a duty to act in conformity with this other possible convention. For the results of acting in conformity with a preferable convention which is not widely observed may be much worse than the results of acting in conformity with a less desirable convention which is widely observed. We might, for example, discover that a "left-hand" pattern of traffic flow would be preferable to the present system of "right-hand" rules, in that it would result in fewer accidents, etc. The difference might be so significant that we really would be morally derelict if we did not try to institute a change in our laws. We would be acquiescing in a very costly procedure when a more economical one was at hand. But it would be a disaster, and, I suspect, positively immoral, for a few of us to begin driving on the left before the convention was changed. In cases of convention-dependent obligations the question of what convention is actually in force is one of considerable moral import. That one is reminded to take this question seriously is one of the important differences between this approach and that of the immunity theorists.

Perhaps the counter-forces convention is not really operative now in a substantial way. I do not know. Doubtless, it suffered a severe blow in World War II, not least from British and American bombing strategies. Traffic rules are embedded in a broad, massive, comparatively stable social structure which makes their status comparatively resistant to erosion by infraction. Not so, however, for a convention of warfare. It has little status except in its actual observance, and depends greatly on the mutual trust of the belligerents; hence it is especially vulnerable to abrogation by a few contrary acts. Here arises a related difference with the immunity theorists. Taking the obligation to be convention-independent they reject argument based on the fact that "the enemy did it first," etc.[10] If the obligation were independent they would be correct in this. But for convention-dependent obligations, what one's opponent does, what "everyone is doing," etc., are facts of great moral importance. Such facts help to determine within what convention, if any, one is operating, and thus they help one to discover what his moral duties are.

If we were to decide that the counter-forces convention was dead at present, or, indeed, that no convention at all with respect to warfare was operative now, it would not follow that warfare was immoral. Nor, on the other hand, would it follow that warfare was beyond all moral rules, an area in which "anything goes." Instead, we would simply go back to warfare per se, limited only by independent moral requirements, such as those of justice and proportionality. That would, on the whole, probably be a more costly way of handling such problems. But if we live in a time when the preferable substitutes are not available, then we must either forgo the goods or bear the higher costs. If we had no traffic laws or customs, traffic would be even more dangerous and costly than it is now. Traveling, however, might still be justified, if the reason for traveling were sufficiently important.

In such a case, of course, there would be no obligation to drive on the right, or in any regular manner, nor would there be any benefit in it. Probably the best thing would be to drive in a completely ad hoc way, seeking the best maneuver in each situation as it arose. More generally, and ignoring for the moment a final consideration which will be discussed below, there is no obligation and no benefit associated with the unilateral observance of a convention. If one's cause is unjust then one ought not to kill noncombatants. But that is because of the independent moral prohibition against prosecuting such a war at all, and has nothing to do with any special immunity of noncombatants. If one's cause is just, but the slaying of noncombatants will not advance it to any marked degree, then one ought not to slay them. But this is just the requirement of proportionality, and applies equally and in the same way to combatants. If one's cause is just and the slaying of noncombatants would advance it—if, in other words, one is not prevented by considerations of justice and proportionality—this is the crucial case. If one refrains unilaterally in this situation then he seems to choose the greater of two evils (or the lesser of two goods). By hypothesis, the good achieved, i.e. the lives spared, is not as weighty as the evil which he allows in damage to the prospects for justice or in the even more costly alternative measures, e.g. the slaying of a larger number of combatants, which he must undertake. Now, if the relevant convention were operative, then his refraining from counter-population strategies here would be related to his enemy's similar restraint, and indeed it would be related to the strategies which would be used in future wars. These larger considerations might well tip the balance in the other direction. But by hypothesis we are considering the case in which there is no such convention, and so these larger considerations do not arise. One acts unilaterally. In such a situation it certainly appears that one would have chosen the worse of the two alternatives. It is hard to suppose that one is morally obligated to do so.

I said above that we were ignoring for the moment one relevant consideration. It should not be ignored forever. I have already called attention to the fact that conventions of warfare are not, like traffic rules, embedded in a more massive social structure. This makes them especially precarious, as we have noted. But it also bears on the way in which they may be adopted. One such way, perhaps a rather important way, is for one party to the hostilities to signal his willingness to abide by such a convention by undertaking some unilateral restraint on his own part. If the opponent does not reciprocate, then the offer has failed and it goes no further. If the opponent does reciprocate, however, then the area of restraint may be broadened, and a kind of mutual respect and confidence may grow up between the belligerents. Each comes to rely on the other to keep the (perhaps unspoken) agreement, and therefore each is willing to forgo the immediate advantage which might accrue to him from breaking it. If this happens, then a new convention has begun its precarious life. This may be an event well worth seeking.

Not only may it be worth seeking, it may be worth paying something for it. For a significant increase in the likelihood that a worthwhile convention will be adopted it may be worth accepting an increased risk or a higher immediate cost in lives and suffering. So there may be some justification in unilateral restraint after all, even in the absence of a convention. But this justification is prospective and finite. It envisions the possibility that such a convention may arise in the future as a result of this restraint. Consequently, the justification should be proportioned to some judgment as to the likelihood of that event, and it should be reevaluated as future events unfold.

III. CONVENTION VS. MORALITY

I began by examining some attempts to defend a certain alleged moral rule of war, the immunity of noncombatants. These defenses have in common the fact that they construe this moral rule as independent of any human law, custom, etc. I then argued that these defenses fail because they leave a certain distinction without moral support, and yet the distinction is essential to the rule. Turning then to the task of construction rather than criticism, I suggested that the immunity of noncombatants is not an independent moral rule but rather a part of a convention which sets up a morally desirable alternative to war. I argued then that some conventions, including this one, generate special moral obligations which cannot be satisfactorily explained and defended without reference to the convention. And in the final pages I explored some of the special features of the obligation at hand and of the arguments which are relevant to it.

The distinction I have drawn is that between warfare per se on the one hand, and, on the other hand, international combats which are limited by convention and custom. But the point of the distinction is to clarify our thinking about the *morality* of such wars and combats. That is where its value must be tested.

NOTES

1. Elizabeth Anscombe, "War and Murder," *War and Morality*, ed. Richard A. Wasserstrom (Belmont, Calif., 1970), p. 52; John C. Ford, "The Morality of Obliteration Bombing," ibid., pp. 19–23; Paul Ramsey, *The Just War* (New York, 1968), pp. 157, 158.

2. Ford gives a list of over 100 occupations whose practitioners he considers to be "almost without exception" noncombatants.

3. Anscombe, pp. 46, 50, 51; Ford, pp. 26–28; Ramsey, pp. 347–358.

4. Anscombe, p. 49.

5. Ibid., p. 44.

6. John C. Ford, "The Hydrogen Bombing of Cities," *Morality and Modern Warfare*, ed. William J. Nagle (Baltimore: Helicon Press, 1960), p. 98.

7. Anscombe, p. 45.

8. Ramsey, p. 153.

9. Ibid., p. 144.

10. For example, Ford, "The Morality of Obliteration Bombing," pp. 20, 33.

Jeffrie G. Murphy

THE KILLING OF THE INNOCENT

Jeffrie G. Murphy considers what it means, in the context of war, to describe someone as innocent or guilty. He claims that it usually does not refer to *legal* innocence or guilt. Nor does it refer to an overall judgment of *moral* innocence or guilt. Even the notions of moral innocence or guilt *of the war* (or of something within the war) do not straightforwardly relate to our judgment of people as innocent or guilty in war. Rather, Murphy contends, innocents in war are simply noncombatants; and noncombatants are all those of whom it is not reasonable to believe that they are engaged in an attempt to destroy you. Thus innocents in war are not necessarily morally innocent, but are persons of whom it is not reasonable to believe that they are threats to your life.

Introduction

MURDER, SOME MAY SUGGEST, is to be defined as the intentional and uncoerced killing of the innocent; and it is true by definition that murder is wrong. Yet wars, particularly modern wars, seem to require the killing of the innocent, e.g. through antimorale terror bombing. Therefore war (at least modern war) must be wrong.

The above line of argument has a certain plausibility and seems to lie behind much philosophical and theological discussion of such problems as the Just War and the nature of war crimes.[1] If accepted in full, it seems to entail the immorality of war (i.e., the position of pacifism) and the moral blameworthiness of those who participate in war (i.e. war-makers and uncoerced soldiers are all murderers). To avoid these consequences, some writers will challenge some part of the argument by maintaining (a) that there are no innocents in war or (b) that modern war does not in fact require the killing of the innocent or (c) that war involves the suspension of moral considerations and thus stands outside the domain of moral criticism entirely or (d) that contributing to the death of innocents is morally blameless so long as it is only foreseen but not intended by those involved in bringing it about (the Catholic principle of the Double Effect) or (e) that the prohibition against killing the innocent is only prima facie[2] and can be overridden by even more important moral requirements, e.g. the defense of freedom.

In this paper I want to come to terms with at least some of the important issues raised by the killing of innocents in time of war. . . .

The Concept of Innocence

The notions of innocence and guilt seem most at home in a legal context and, somewhat less comfortably, in a moral context. Legally, a man is innocent if he is not guilty, i.e. if he has not engaged in conduct explicitly prohibited by rules of the criminal law. A man may be regarded as morally innocent if his actions do not result from a mental state (e.g. malice) or a character defect (e.g. negligence) which we regard as morally blameworthy. In any civilized system of criminal law, of course, there will be a close connection between legal guilt and innocence and moral guilt and innocence, e.g. murder in the criminal law has as one of its material or defining elements the blameworthy mental state *(mens rea)* of "malice aforethought." But this close connection does not show that the legal and moral concepts are not different. The existence of strict liability criminal statutes is sufficient to show that they are different. Under a strict liability statute, a man can be guilty of a criminal offense without having, at the time of his action, any blameworthy mental state or character defect, not even negligence.[3] However, the notion of strict *moral* responsibility makes little sense; for an inquiry into moral responsibility for the most part just is an inquiry into such matters as the agent's motives, intentions, beliefs, etc.[4] Also, the issue of legal responsibility is much more easily determinable than that of moral responsibility. For example: It is noncontroversial that negligence can make one legally responsible. Anyone who doubts this may simply be given a reading assignment in any number of penal codes.[5] But whether or not negligence is a mental state or a character defect for which one is *morally* responsible is a matter about which reasonable men can disagree. No reading assignment or simple inquiry into "the facts" will lay this worry to rest.[6]

Now our reasonably comfortable ability to operate with these concepts of guilt and innocence leaves us when we attempt to apply them to the context of war. Of course, the legal notions will have application in a limited number of cases, i.e. with respect to those who are legally war criminals under inter-

national law. But this will by no means illuminate the majority of cases. For example: Those who have written on the topic of protecting innocents in war would not want to regard the killing of an enemy soldier engaged in an attack against a fortified position as a case of killing the innocent. He is surely, in the right sense (whatever that is), among the guilty (or, at least, among the noninnocent) and is thus a fitting object for violent death. But he is in no sense *legally* guilty. There are no rules of international law prohibiting what he is doing; and, even if such rules were created, they would surely not involve the setting up of a random collection of soldiers from the other side to act as judges and executioners of this law. Thus the legal notions of guilt and innocence do not serve us well here.

What, then, about moral guilt or innocence? Even to make this suggestion plausible in the context of war, we surely have to attempt to narrow it down to moral innocence or guilt *of* the war and *of* something within the war—not just moral innocence or guilt *simpliciter*. That is, we surely do not want to say that if a bomb falls (say) on a man with a self-deceiving morally impure heart who is a civilian behind the lines that this is not, in the relevant sense, a case of killing an innocent. Similarly, I think it would be odd for us to want to say that if a soldier with a morally admirable character is killed in action that this is a case of killing an innocent and is to be condemned on those grounds. If we take this line, it would seem that national leaders should attempt to make some investigation of the motives and characters of both soldiers and civilians and kill the unjust among both classes and spare the just. (Only babes in arms would be clearly protected.) Now this sort of judgment, typically thought to be reserved for God if for anyone, is surely a very disquieting thing if advocated for generals and other war leaders. Thus the notions of moral innocence and guilt *simpliciter* must be dropped in this context.

Suppose, then, we try to make use of the notions of moral innocence *of the war* or moral guilt *of the war* (or of something within the war). Even here we find serious problems. Consider the octogenarian civilian in Dresden who is an avid supporter of Hitler's war effort (pays taxes gladly, supports warmongering political rallies, etc.) and contrast his case with that of the poor, frightened, pacifist frontline soldier who is only where he is because of duress and who intends always to fire over the heads of the enemy. It seems reasonable to say that the former is much more morally guilty of the war than the latter; and yet most writers on the topic would regard killing the former, but not the latter, as a case of killing an innocent.

What all this suggests is that the classical worry about protecting the innocent is really a worry about protecting *noncombatants*. And thus the distinction between combatants and noncombatants is what needs to be illucidated. Frontline soldiers are clearly combatants; babes in arms clearly are not. And we know this without judging their respective moral and legal guilt or innocence. And thus the worry, then, is the following: Under what circumstances is an individual truly a combatant? Wars may be viewed as games (terrible ones of course) between enemies or opponents. Who, then, is an enemy or opponent?

One suggestion for defining a combatant might be the following: Only soldiers engaged in fighting are combatants. But this does not seem adequate. For if killing an enemy soldier is right, then it would also seem to be right to kill the man who *orders* him to the frontline. If anything, the case for killing (say) a general seems better, since the soldier is presumably simply acting in some sense as his agent, i.e. the general kills *through* him. Perhaps the way to put the point, then, is as follows: The enemy is represented by those who are *engaged in an attempt* to destroy you. And thus all frontline combat soldiers (though not prisoners, or soldiers on leave, or wounded soldiers, or chaplains, or medics) are enemies and all who issue orders for destruction are enemies. Thus we might try the following: Combatants are those anywhere within the *chain of command or responsibility*—from bottom to top. If this is correct, then a carefully planned attack on the seat of government, intended to destroy those civilians (and only those) directing the war effort, would not be a case of killing noncombatants or, in the relevant sense, innocents.

But what is a chain of command or responsibility? It would be wrong to regard it solely as a causal chain, though it is *at least* that. That is, the notion of responsibility has to be stronger than that expressed in the sentence "The slippery pavement was *responsible* for the accident." For to regard the chain here as solely causal in character would lead to the following consequence: If a combatant is understood solely as one who performs an action which is a causally necessary condition for the waging of war, then the following are going to be combatants: farmers, employees at a city water works, and anyone who pays taxes. Obviously a country cannot wage war if there is no food, no management of the basic affairs of its cities, and no money to pay for it. And of course the list of persons "responsible" for the war in this sense could be greatly extended. But if all these persons are in the class of combatants, then the rule "protect noncombatants" is going to amount to little more than "protect babies and the senile." But one would, I think, have more ambition for it than that, e.g. one would hope that such a rule would protect housewives even if it is true that they "help" the war effort by writing consoling letters to their soldier husbands and by feeding them and providing them with emotional and sexual relief when they are home on leave. Thus I think that it is wrong to regard the notion of chain here as merely causal in character.

What kind of chain, then, is it? Let us call it a *chain of agency*. What I mean by this is that the links of the chain (like the links between motives and actions) are held together logically and not merely causally, i.e. all held together, in this case, under the notion of who it is that is *engaged in an attempt* to destroy you. The farmer qua farmer is, like the general, performing actions which are causally necessary conditions for your destruction; but, unlike the general, he is not necessarily engaged in an attempt to destroy you. Perhaps the point can better be put in this way: The farmer's role bears a contingent connection to the war effort whereas the general's role bears a necessary connection to the war effort, i.e. his function, unlike the farmer's, is not logically separable from the waging of war. Or, following Thomas Nagel,[8] the point can perhaps be put in yet another way: The farmer is aiding the soldier qua human being whereas the general is aiding the soldier qua soldier or fighting man. And since your enemy is the soldier qua soldier, and not qua human being, we have grounds for letting the farmer off. If we think of a justified war as one of self-defense,[9] then we must ask the question "Who can be said to be *attacking* us such that we need to defend ourselves against him?" Viewed in this way, the farmer seems an unlikely candidate for combat status.

This analysis does, of course, leave us with borderline cases. But, since there *are* borderline cases, this is a virtue of the analysis so long as it captures just the right ones. Consider workers in a munitions factory. Are they or are they not combatants? At least with certain munitions factories (making only bombs, say) it is certainly going to be odd to claim that their activities bear only a contingent connection to the war effort. What they make, unlike food, certainly supports the fighting man qua fighting man and not qua human being. Thus I should be inclined to say that they are properly to be regarded as combatants and thus properly subject to attack. But what about workers in munitions factories that only in part supply the war effort, e.g. they make rifles both for soldiers and for hunters? Or workers in nonmunitions factories that do make some war products, e.g. workers in companies, like Dow Chemical, which make both Saran Wrap and Napalm? Or workers in ball bearing factories or oil refineries, some of their product going to war machines and some not? Here, I submit, we do have genuine borderline cases. And with respect to these, what should we do? I should hope that reasonable men would accept that the burden of proof lies on those claiming that a particular group of persons are combatants and properly vulnerable. I should hope that men would accept, along with the famous principle in the criminal law, the principle "noncombatant until proven otherwise" and would attempt to look at the particular facts of each case as carefully and disinterestedly as possible. I say that I hope this, not that I expect it.

Who, then, is a combatant? I shall answer this question from the point of view of one who believes that the only legitimate defense for war is self-defense.[10] It is, in this context, important to remember that one may legitimately plead self-defense even if one's belief that one's life is being threatened is false. The only requirement is that the belief be *reasonable* given the evidence that is available. If a man comes to my door with a toy pistol and says, pointing the pistol at me, "Prepare to meet your Maker for your time has come," I act in my self-defense if I kill him even if he was joking so long as my belief was reasonable, i.e. I had no way of knowing that the gun was a toy or that he was joking. Thus: combatants may be viewed as all those in the territory or allied territory of the enemy of whom it is reasonable

to believe that they are engaged in an attempt to destroy you.

What about our Dresden octogenarian? Is he a combatant on this analysis? Since he does not act *on authority*, it is at least prima facie odd to regard him as part of a chain of command literally construed— the concept of command being most at home in a context of authority. He does not, of course, have much to do with the war effort; and so we might find his claim that he is "helping to defeat the Americans" quaint on purely factual grounds. And yet none of this prevents its being true that he can properly be said to be engaged in an *attempt* to destroy the enemy. For people can attempt even the impossible so long as they do not *know* it is impossible. Thus I am prepared to say of him that he is, in fact, engaged in an attempt to destroy the enemy. But I would still say that killing him would count as a case of killing a noncombatant for the following reason: that the concept of attempt here is to be applied, not from the agent's point of view, but from the point of view of the spectator who proposes to plead self-defense in defense of his acts of killing. Combatants are all those who may *reasonably* be regarded as engaged in an attempt to destroy you. This belief is reasonable (though false) in the case of the frontline soldier who plans always to shoot over the heads of the enemy and unreasonable (even if true) in the case of our octogenarian. It would be quite unreasonable to plan a bombing raid on a nonmilitary and nonindustrial city like Dresden and say, in defense of the raid, that you are just protecting yourself or your country from all those warmongering civilians who are attempting to destroy you. For making such a judgment imposes upon you a burden of proof which, given the circumstances of war, you could not satisfy. You probably could not get *any* evidence for your claim. You certainly could not get what the law calls a "preponderance of the evidence"—much less "proof beyond a reasonable doubt."

Combatants, then, are all those of whom it is reasonable to believe that they are engaged in an attempt at your destruction. Noncombatants are all those of whom it is not reasonable to believe this. Having the distinction, we must now inquire into its moral importance. . . .

NOTES

1. "Murder," writes Miss Anscombe, "is the deliberate killing of the innocent, whether for its own sake or as a means to some further end" ("War and Murder," p. 45). Deliberate killing of the innocent (or noncombatants) is prohibited by the Just War Theory and is a crime in international law. A traditional account of the Catholic Just War Theory may be found in Chapter 35 of Austin Fagothey's *Right and Reason: Ethics in Theory and Practice* (St. Louis: C. V. Mosby Co., 1963). A useful sourcebook for inquiry into the nature of war crimes is the anthology *Crimes of War*, ed. by Richard A. Falk, Gabriel Kolko, and Robert Jay Lifton (New York: Random House, 1971).

2. By "prima facie wrong" I mean "can be overridden by other moral requirements"—*not*, as a literal translation might suggest, "only apparently wrong."

3. For example: In the criminal offense of statutory rape, the defendant is strictly liable with respect to his knowledge of the age of a girl with whom he has had sexual relations, i.e. no matter how carefully he inquired into her age, no matter how reasonable (i.e. nonnegligent) his belief that she was of legal age of consent, he is liable if his belief is in fact mistaken. For a general discussion of such offenses, see Richard Wasserstrom's "Strict Liability in the Criminal Law," *Stanford Law Review*, **12** (July, 1960).

4. In discussion, Richard Wasserstrom has expressed scepticism concerning my claim that there is something unintelligible about the concept of strict moral responsibility. One could regard the *Old Testament and Oedipus Rex* as containing a strict liability conception of morality. Now I should be inclined to argue that the primitiveness of the *Old Testament* and of *Oedipus Rex* consists in these peoples not yet being able to draw a distinction between legality and morality. However, I am prepared to admit that it might be better to weaken my claim by maintaining simply that no *civilized* or *enlightened* morality would involve strict liability.

5. In California criminal law, for example, vehicular manslaughter is defined as vehicular homicide "in the commission of an unlawful act, not amounting to felony, with gross negligence; or in the commission of a lawful act which might produce death, in an unlawful manner, and with gross negligence . . ." (*California Penal Code*, 192, 3, a).

6. For an excellent discussion of moral and legal responsibility for negligence, see H. L. A. Hart's "Negligence, *Mens Rea* and Criminal Responsibility," in his *Punishment and Responsibility: Essays in the Philosophy of Law* (Oxford: Oxford University Press, 1973).

7. I say "engaged in an attempt" rather than "attempting" for the following reason: A mortar attack on an encampment of combat soldiers who happen to be sleeping is surely not a case of killing noncombatants even though persons who are asleep cannot be attempting anything. Sleeping persons can, however, be engaged in an attempt—just as sleeping persons can be accomplices in crime and parties to a criminal conspiracy. Being engaged in an attempt, unlike attempting, is not necessarily a full time job. I am grateful to Anthony Woozley for pointing this out to me.

8. Thomas Nagel, "War and Massacre," *Philosophy and Public Affairs*, 2 (Winter, 1972). In the same issue, Richard Brandt replies to Nagel in his "Utilitarianism and the Rules of War." I am grateful to Professors Nagel and Brandt for allowing me to read their articles prior to publication.

9. For reasons of simplicity in later drawing upon important and instructive principles from the criminal law, I shall use the phrase "self-defense." (I shall later want to draw on the notion of *reasonable belief* in the law of self-defense.) However, what I really want to focus on is the concept of "defense" and not the concept of "self." For it seems to me that war can be justified, not just to defend oneself or one's nation, but also to defend others from threats that transcend nationality, e.g. genocide. If one wants to speak of self-defense even here, then it must be regarded as self-defense for the *human*, not just national, community. The phrase "self-defense" as it occurs in what follows should always be understood as carrying this qualification. And, of course, even clear cases of self-defense are not always necessarily justified. Given the morally debased character of Nazi Germany, it is by no means obvious that it acted rightly in trying to defend itself near the end of World War II (i.e. after it had ceased to be an aggressor).

10. Remember that this carries the qualification stated in note 9. For a survey of the law of self-defense, the reader may consult any reliable treatise on the criminal law, e.g. pp. 883 ff. of Rollin M. Perkins's *Criminal Law* (Brooklyn, N.Y.: Foundation Press, 1957). The criminal law is a highly moralized institution, and it is useful (though by no means always definitive) for the moral philosopher in that it provides an accumulated and systematized body of reflection on vital moral matters of our culture. For my purposes, I shall in what follows focus upon the *reasonable belief* condition in the law of self-defense. Other aspects of the law of self-defense (e.g. the so-called "retreat requirement"), have, I think, interesting implications for war that I cannot pursue here.

Michael Walzer

NUCLEAR DETERRENCE

Michael Walzer first explores whether the threat of massive nuclear destruction is morally defensible. He notes that the nature of the threat has often been misdescribed. According to Walzer, the threat is not analogous to restraining the recklessness of automobile drivers by tying innocent babies to every driver's front bumper. Rather it is analogous to attempting to prevent murder by threatening to kill the family and friends of every murderer. But even here there is a difference in the seriousness of the danger to be avoided. Nuclear deterrence is said to guard against a double danger: first, of atomic blackmail and foreign domination; and second, of nuclear destruction. Walzer concludes that "we threaten evil in order not to do it, and doing it would be so terrible that the threat seems in comparison to be morally defensible." Walzer next argues that while the threat of massive nuclear destruction may be morally defensible, nuclear war itself—even limited nuclear war—cannot be justified because (1) the collateral damage from such a war would likely be disproportionate, and in order to deter would have to be expected to be disproportionate, (2) such a war would likely lead to escalation, and (3) the collateral damage would have to be intended. Walzer concludes by criticizing Ramsey's attempt to overcome these objections to limited nuclear war.

THE PROBLEM OF IMMORAL THREATS

TRUMAN USED THE ATOMIC bomb to end a war that seemed to him limitless in its horrors. And then, for a few minutes or hours in August 1945, the people of Hiroshima endured a war that actually was limitless in its horrors. "In this last great action of the Second World War," wrote Stimson, "we were given final proof that war is death." *Final proof* is exactly the wrong phrase, for war had never been like that before. A new kind of war was born at Hiroshima, and what we were given was a first glimpse of its deadliness. Though fewer people were killed than in the fire-bombing of Tokyo, they were killed with monstrous ease. One plane, one bomb: with such a weapon the 350 planes that raided Tokyo would virtually have wiped out human life on the Japanese islands. Atomic war was death indeed, indiscriminate and total, and after Hiroshima, the first task of political leaders everywhere was to prevent its recurrence.

The means they adopted is the promise of reprisal in kind. Against the threat of an immoral attack, they have put the threat of an immoral attack, they have put the threat of an immoral response. This is the basic form of nuclear deterrence. In international as in domestic society, deterrence works by calling up dramatic images of human pain. "In the groves of *their* academy," wrote Edmund Burke of the liberal theorists of crime and punishment, "at the end of every vista, you see nothing but the gallows." The description is uncomplimentary, for Burke believed that domestic peace must rest upon some other foundation. But there is this much to be said for the gallows: in principle, at least, only guilty men need fear the death it brings. About the theorists of deterrence, however, it must be said, "In the groves of *their* academy, at the end of every vista, you see nothing but the mushroom cloud"—and the cloud symbolizes indiscriminate slaughter, the killing of the innocent (as in Hiroshima) on a massive scale. No doubt, the threat of such slaughter, if it is believed, makes nuclear attack a radically undesirable policy. Doubled by a potential enemy, the threat produces a "balance of terror." Both sides are so terrified that no further terrorism is necessary. But is the threat itself morally permissible?

The question is a difficult one. It has generated in the years since Hiroshima a significant body of literature exploring the relation between nuclear deterrence and just war. This has been the work mostly of theologians and philosophers, but some of the strategists of deterrence have also been involved; they worry about the act of terrorizing much as conventional soldiers worry about the act of killing. I cannot review this literature here, though I shall draw upon it freely. The argument against deterrence is familiar enough. Anyone committed to the distinction between combatants and noncombatants is bound to be appalled by the specter of destruction evoked, and purposely evoked, in deterrence theory. "How can a nation live with its conscience," John Bennett has asked, "and know that it is preparing to kill twenty million children in another nation if the worst should come to the worst?" And yet, we have lived with that knowledge, and with our consciences too, for several decades now. How have we managed? The reason for our acceptance of deterrent strategy, most people would say, is that preparing to kill, even threatening to kill, is not at all the same

thing as killing. Indeed it is not, but it is frighteningly close—else deterrence wouldn't "work"—and it is in the nature of that closeness that the moral problem lies.

The problem is often misdescribed—as in the following analogy for nuclear deterrence first suggested by Paul Ramsey and frequently repeated since:

Suppose that one Labor Day weekend no one was killed or maimed on the highways; and that the reason for the remarkable restraint placed on the recklessness of automobile drivers was that suddenly everyone of them discovered he was driving with a baby tied to his front bumper! That would be no way to regulate traffic even if it succeeds in regulating it perfectly, since such a system makes innocent human lives the direct object of attack and uses them as a mere means for restraining the drivers of automobiles.

No one, of course, has ever proposed regulating traffic in this ingenious way, while the strategy of deterrence was adopted with virtually no opposition at all. That contrast should alert us to what is wrong with Ramsey's analogy. Though deterrence turns American and Russian civilians into mere means for the prevention of war, it does so without restraining any of us in any way. Ramsey reproduces the strategy of the German officers during the Franco-Prussian War who forced civilians to ride on military trains in order to deter saboteurs. By contrast with those civilians, however, we are hostages who lead normal lives. It is in the nature of the new technology that we can be threatened without being held captive. That is why deterrence, while in principle so frightening, is so easy to live with. It cannot be condemned for anything it does to its hostages. It is so far from killing them that it does not even injure or confine them; it involves no direct or physical violation of their rights. Those critics of deterrence who are also committed consequentialists have had to imagine psychic injuries. Thus Erich Fromm, writing in 1960: "To live for any length of time under the constant threat of destruction creates certain psychological effects in most human beings—fright, hostility, callousness . . . and a resulting indifference to all the values we cherish. Such conditions will transform us into barbarians. . . ." But I don't know of any evidence that bears out either the assertion or the prediction; surely we are no more barbarians now than we were in 1945. In fact, for most people, the threat of destruction, though constant, is invisible and unnoticed. We have come to live with it casually—as Ramsey's babies, traumatized for life in all probability, could never do, and as hostages in conventional wars have never done.

If deterrence were more painful, we might have found other means of avoiding nuclear war—or we might not have avoided it. If we had to keep millions of people under restraint in order to maintain the balance of terror, or if we had to kill millions of people (periodically) in order to convince our adversaries of our credibility, deterrence would not be accepted for long. The strategy works because it is easy. Indeed, it is easy in a double sense: not only don't we do anything to other people, we also don't believe that we will ever have to do anything. The secret of nuclear deterrence is that it is a kind of bluff. Perhaps we are only bluffing ourselves, refusing to acknowledge the real terrors of a precarious and temporary balance. But no account of our experience is accurate which fails to recognize that, for all its ghastly potential, deterrence has so far been a bloodless strategy.

So far as consequences go, then, deterrence and mass murder are very far apart. Their closeness is a matter of moral posture and intention. Once again, Ramsey's analogy misses the point. His babies are not really the "direct object of attack," for whatever happens on that Labor Day weekend, no one will deliberately set out to kill them. But deterrence depends upon a readiness to do exactly that. It is as if the state should seek to prevent murder by threatening to kill the family and friends of every murderer—a domestic version of the policy of "massive retaliation." Surely that would be a repugnant policy. We would not admire the police officials who designed it or those pledged to carry it out, even if they never actually killed anybody. I don't want to say that such people would necessarily be transformed into barbarians; they might well have a heightened sense of how awful murder is and a heightened desire to avoid it; they might loathe the work they were pledged to do and fervently hope that they never had to do it. Nevertheless, the enterprise is immoral. The immorality lies in the threat itself, not in its present or even its likely consequences. Similarly with nuclear deterrence: it is our own intentions that we have to worry about and

the potential (since there are no actual) victims of those intentions. Here Ramsey has put the case very well: "Whatever is wrong to do is wrong to threaten, if the latter means 'mean to do' . . . If counter-population warfare is murder, then counter-population deterrent threats are murderous." No doubt, killing millions of innocent people is worse than threatening to kill them. It is also true that no one wants to kill them, and it may well be true that no one expects to do so. Nevertheless, we intend the killings under certain circumstances. That is the stated policy of our government; and thousands of men, trained in the techniques of mass destruction and drilled in instant obedience, stand ready to carry it out. And from the perspective of morality, the readiness is all. We can translate it into degrees of danger, high and low, and worry about the risks we are imposing on innocent people, but the risks depend on the readiness. What we condemn in our own government, as in the police in my domestic analogy, is the commitment to murder.[1]

But this analogy, too, can be questioned. We don't prevent murder any more than we control traffic in these bizarre and inhuman ways. But we do deter or seek to deter our nuclear adversaries. Perhaps deterrence is different because of the danger its advocates claim to avoid. Traffic deaths and occasional murders, however much we deplore them, do not threaten our common liberties or our collective survival. Deterrence, so we have been told, guards us against a double danger: first, of atomic blackmail and foreign domination; and second, of nuclear destruction. The two go together, since if we did not fear the blackmail, we might adopt a policy of appeasement or surrender and so avoid the destruction. Deterrence theory was worked out at the height of the cold war between the United States and the Soviet Union, and those who worked it out were concerned above all with the political uses of violence—which are not relevant in either the traffic or police analogies. Underlying the American doctrine, there seemed to lurk some version of the slogan "Better dead than Red" (I don't know the Russian parallel). Now that is not really a believable slogan; it is hard to imagine that a nuclear holocaust was really thought preferable to the expansion of Soviet power. What made deterrence attractive was that it seemed capable of avoiding both.

We need not dwell on the nature of the Soviet

regime in order to understand the virtues of this argument. Deterrence theory doesn't depend upon a view of Stalinism as a great evil (though that is a highly plausible view) in the same way that my argument about terror bombing depended upon an assertion about the evils of Nazism. It requires only that we see appeasement or surrender to involve a loss of values central to our existence as an independent nation-state. For it is not tolerable that advances in technology should put our nation, or any nation, at the mercy of a great power willing to menace the world or to press its authority outwards in the shadow of an implicit threat. The case here is very different from that which arises commonly in war, where *our* adherence to the war convention puts us, or would put us, at a disadvantage vis-à-vis *them*. For disadvantages of that sort are partial and relative; various counter-measures and compensating steps are always available. But in the nuclear case, the disadvantage is absolute. Against an enemy actually willing to use the bomb, self-defense is impossible, and it makes sense to say that the only compensating step is the (immoral) threat to respond in kind. No country capable of making such a threat is likely to refuse to make it. What is not tolerable won't be tolerated. Hence any state confronted by a nuclear adversary (it makes little difference what the adversary relationship is like or what ideological forms it assumes), and capable of developing its own bomb, is likely to do so, seeking safety in a balance of terror.[2] Mutual disarmament would clearly be a preferable alternative, but it is an alternative available only to the two countries working closely together, whereas deterrence is the likely choice of either one of them alone. They will worry about one another's readiness to attack; they will each assume their own commitment to resist; and they will realize that the greatest danger of such a confrontation would not be the defeat of one side or the other but the total destruction of both—and possibly of everyone else too. This in fact is the danger that has faced mankind since 1945, and our understanding of nuclear deterrence must be worked out with reference to its scope and imminence.

Supreme emergency has become a permanent condition. Deterrence is a way of coping with that condition, and though it is a bad way, there may well be no other that is practical in a world of sovereign and suspicious states. We threaten evil in order

not to do it, and the doing of it would be so terrible that the threat seems in comparison to be morally defensible.

LIMITED NUCLEAR WAR

If the bomb were ever used, deterrence would have failed. It is a feature of massive retaliation that while there is or may be some rational purpose in threatening it, there could be none in carrying it out. Were our "bluff" ever to be called and our population centers suddenly attacked, the resulting war could not (in any usual sense of the word) be *won*. We could only drag our enemies after us into the abyss. The use of our deterrent capacity would be an act of pure destructiveness. For this reason, massive retaliation, if not literally unthinkable, has always seemed undo-able, and this is a source of considerable anxiety for military strategists. Deterrence only works, they argue, if each side believes that the other might actually carry out its threat. But would we carry it out? George Kennan has recently given what must be the moral response:

Let us suppose there were to be a nuclear attack of some sort on this country and millions of people were killed and injured. Let us further suppose that we had the ability to retaliate against the urban centers of the country that had attacked us. Would you want to do that? I wouldn't . . . I have no sympathy with the man who demands an eye for an eye in a nuclear attack.

A humane position—though one that should probably be whispered, rather than published, if the balance of terror is to be sustained. But the argument might look very different if the original attack or the planned response avoided cities and people. If a limited nuclear war were possible, wouldn't it also be do-able? And might not the balance of terror then be re-established on the basis of threats that were neither immoral nor unconvincing?

Over a brief timespan, in the late 1950s and early 1960s, these questions were answered with an extraordinary outpouring of strategic arguments and speculations, overlapping in important ways with the moralizing literature I described earlier. For the debate among the strategists focused on the attempt (though this was rarely made explicit) to fit nuclear war into the structure of the war convention, to apply the argument for justice as if this sort of conflict were like any other sort. The attempt involved, first, a defense of the use of tactical nuclear weapons in deterring and, if that failed, in resisting conventional or small-scale nuclear attacks; and it involved, secondly, the development of a "counter-force" strategy directed at the enemy's military installations and also at major economic targets (but not at entire cities). These two had a similar purpose. By holding out the promise of a limited nuclear war, they made it possible to imagine actually fighting such a war—they made it possible to imagine *winning* it—and so they strengthened the intention that lay behind the deterrent threat. They transformed the "bluff" into a plausible option.

Until the late 1950s, the tendency of most people was to regard the atomic bomb and its thermonuclear successors as forbidden weapons. They were treated on analogy with poison gas, though the prohibition on their use was never legally established. "Ban the bomb" was everyone's policy, and deterrence was simply a practical way of enforcing the ban. But now the strategists suggested (rightly) that the crucial distinction in the theory and practice of war was not between prohibited and acceptable weapons but between prohibited and acceptable targets. Massive retaliation was painful and difficult to contemplate because it was modeled on Hiroshima; the people we were planning to kill were innocent, militarily uninvolved, as removed from and ignorant of the weapons with which their leaders threatened us as we were of the weapons with which our leaders threatened them. But this objection would disappear if we could deter our adversaries by threatening a limited and morally acceptable destruction. Indeed, it might disappear so entirely that we would be tempted to give up deterrence and initiate the destruction ourselves whenever it seemed to our advantage to do so. This was certainly the tendency of much strategic argument, and several writers painted rather attractive pictures of limited nuclear war. Henry Kissinger likened it to war at sea—the very best kind of war, since no one lives in the sea. "The proper analogy . . . is not traditional land warfare, but naval strategy, in which self-contained, [highly mobile] units with great fire power gradually gain the upper hand by destroying their enemy

counterparts without physically occupying territory or establishing a front line." The only difficulty is that Kissinger imagined fighting a war like that in Europe.

Tactical and counter-force warfare meets the formal requirements of *jus in bello*, and it was seized upon eagerly by certain moral theorists. That is not to say, however, that it makes moral sense. There remains the possibility that the new technology of war simply doesn't fit and cannot be made to fit within the old limits. This proposition can be defended in two different ways. The first is to argue that the collateral damage likely to be caused even by a "legitimate" use of nuclear weapons is so great that it would violate both of the proportionality limits fixed by the theory of war: the number of people killed in the war as a whole would not be warranted by the goals of the war—particularly since the dead would include many if not most of the people for whose defense the war was being fought; and the number of people killed in individual actions would be disproportionate (under the doctrine of double effect) to the value of the military targets directly attacked. "The disproportion between the cost of such hostilities and the results they could achieve," wrote Raymond Aron, thinking of a limited nuclear war in Europe, "would be colossal." It would be colossal even if the formal limits on targeting were in fact observed. But the second argument against limited nuclear war is that these limits would almost certainly not be observed.

At this point, of course, one can only guess at the possible shape and course of the battles; there is no history to study. Neither moralists nor strategists can refer to cases; instead they design scenarios. The scene is empty; one can fill it in very different ways, and it is not impossible to imagine that limits might be maintained even after nuclear weapons had been used in battle. The prospect that they would be maintained and the war extended over time is so frightening to those countries on whose soil such wars are likely to be fought that they have generally opposed the new strategies and insisted upon the threat of massive retaliation. Thus, as André Beaufre has written, "Europeans would prefer to risk general war in an attempt to avoid war altogether rather than have Europe become the theater of operations for limited war." In fact, however, the risks of escalation will be great whatever limits are adopted, simply because of the immense destructive power of the weapons involved. Or rather, there are two possibilities: either nuclear weapons will be held at such low levels that they won't be significantly different from or of greater military utility than conventional explosives, in which case there is no reason to use them at all; or their very use will obliterate the distinction between targets. Once a bomb has been aimed at a military target but has, as a side effect, destroyed a city, the logic of deterrence will require the other side to aim at a city (for the sake of its seriousness and credibility). It is not necessarily the case that every war would become a total war, but the danger of escalation is so great as to preclude the first use of nuclear weapons—except by someone willing to face their final use. "Who would even launch such hostilities," Aron has asked, "unless he was determined to persist to the bitter end?" But such a determination is not imaginable in a sane human being, let alone in a political leader responsible for the safety of his own people; it would involve nothing less than national suicide.

These two factors, the extent even of limited destruction and the dangers of escalation, seem to rule out any sort of nuclear war between the great powers. They probably rule out large-scale conventional war, too, including the particular conventional war about which the strategists of the 1950's and 1960's were most concerned: a Russian invasion of western Europe. "The spectacle a large Soviet field army crashing across the line into western Europe in the hope *and expectation* that nuclear weapons would not be used against it—thereby putting itself and the USSR totally at risk while leaving the choice of weapons to us—would seem to be hardly worth a second thought. . . ." It is important to stress that the bar lies in the totality of the risk: not in the possibility of what the strategists called a "flexible response," finely adjusted to the scope of the attack, but in the stark reality of ultimate horror should the adjustments fail. It may well be that "flexible response" enhanced the value of a counter-population deterrent by making it possible to reach that final point in "easy" stages, but it is also and more importantly true that we have never begun the staged escalation and are never likely to begin it, because of what lies at the end. Hence the persistence of counter-population deterrence, and hence also the virtual end of the strategic debate, which petered

out in the middle 1960s. At that point, I think, it became clear that given the existence of large numbers of nuclear weapons and their relative invulnerability, and barring major technological breakthroughs, *any imaginable strategy* is likely to deter a "central war" between the great powers. The strategists helped us to understand this, but once it was understood it became unnecessary to adopt any of their strategies—or at least, any particular one of them. We continue to live, then, with the paradox that pre-existed the debate: nuclear weapons are politically and militarily unusable only because and insofar as we can plausibly threaten to use them in some ultimate way. And it is immoral to make threats of that kind.

The Argument of Paul Ramsey

Before deciding (or refusing) to live with this paradox, I want to consider in some detail the work of the Protestant theologian Paul Ramsey, who has over a period of years argued that there exists a justifiable deterrent strategy. From the beginning of the moral and strategic debates, Ramsey has been a sharp opponent of the advocates of counter-city deterrence and also of those of its critics who think that it is the only form of deterrence and therefore opt for nuclear disarmament. He has condemned both these groups for the all-or-nothing character of their thinking: either total and immoral destruction or a kind of "pacifistic" inertia. He argues that these twin perspectives conform to the traditional American view of war as an all-out conflict, which must therefore be avoided whenever possible. Ramsey himself, I think, is a Protestant soldier in a different tradition; he would have Americans gird themselves for a long, continuous struggle with the forces of evil.

Now if there is to be a justified deterrent strategy, there must be a justified form of nuclear war, and Ramsey has conscientiously argued "the case for making just war possible" in the modern age. He takes a lively and well-informed interest in the strategic debates and has at various times defended the use of tactical nuclear weapons against invading armies and of strategic weapons against nuclear installations, conventional military bases, and isolated economic objectives. Even these targets are only "conditionally" permissible, since the proportionality rule would have to be applied in each case, and

Ramsey does not believe that its standards will always be met. Like everyone (or almost everyone) who writes about these matters, he has no zest for nuclear combat; his main interest is in deterrence. But he needs at least the possibility of legitimate warfare if he is to maintain a deterrent posture without making immoral threats. That is his central purpose, and the effort to achieve it involves him in a highly sophisticated application of just war theory to the problems of nuclear strategy. In the best sense of the word, Ramsey is engaged with the realities of his world. But the realities in this case are intractable, and his way around them is finally too complex and too devious to provide a plausible account of our moral judgments. He multiplies distinctions like a Ptolemaic astronomer with his epicycles and comes very close at the end to what G. E. M. Anscombe has called "double-think about double effect." But his work is important; it suggests the outer limits of the just war and the dangers of trying to extend those limits.

Ramsey's central claim is that it is possible to prevent nuclear attack without threatening to bomb cities in response. He believes that "the collateral civilian damage that would result from counterforce warfare in its maximum form" would be sufficient to deter potential aggressors. Since the civilians likely to die in such a war would be the incidental victims of legitimate military strikes, the threat of counter-force warfare plus collateral damage is also morally superior to deterrence in its present form. These are not hostages whom we intend to murder (under certain circumstances). Nor are we planning their deaths; we are only pointing out to our possible enemies the unavoidable consequences even of a war justly fought—which is, we could honestly say were we to adopt Ramsey's proposal, the only sort of war we were preparing to fight. Collateral damage is simply a fortunate feature of nuclear warfare; it serves no military purpose, and we would avoid it if we could, though it is clearly a good thing that we cannot. And since the damage is justifiable in prospect, it is also justifiable here and now to call that prospect to mind for the sake of its deterrent effects.

But there are two problems with this argument. First, the danger of collateral damage is unlikely to work as a deterrent unless the damage expected is radically disproportionate to the ends of the war or the value of this or that military target. Hence Ramsey is driven to argue that "the threat of something disproportionate is not always a disproportionate threat." What that means is this: proportionality in combat is measured, let's say, against the value of a particular missile base, while proportionality in deterrence is measured against the value of world peace. So the damage may not be justifiable in prospect (under the doctrine of double effect), and yet the threat of such damage may still be morally permitted. Perhaps that argument is right, but I should stress that its result is to void the proportionality rule. Now there is no limit on the number of people whose deaths we can threaten, so long as those deaths are to be caused "collaterally" and not by taking direct aim. As we have seen before, the idea of proportionality, once it is worked on a bit, tends to fade away. And then the entire burden of Ramsey's argument falls on the idea of death by indirection. That is indeed an important idea, central to the permissions and restraints of conventional war. But its standing is undermined here by the fact that Ramsey relies so heavily on the deaths he supposedly doesn't intend. He wants, like other deterrent theorists, to prevent nuclear attack by threatening to kill very large numbers of innocent civilians, but unlike other deterrent theorists, he expects to kill these people without aiming at them. That may be a matter of some moral significance, but it does not seem significant enough to serve as the cornerstone of a justified deterrent. If counter-force warfare had no collateral effects, or had minor and controllable effects, then it could play no part in Ramsey's strategy. Given the effects it does have and the central part it is assigned, the word "collateral" seems to have lost much of its meaning. Surely anyone designing such a strategy must accept moral responsibility for the effects on which he is so radically dependent.

But we have not yet seen the whole of Ramsey's design, for he doesn't pull back from the hardest questions. What if the likely collateral damage of a just nuclear war isn't great enough to deter a would-be aggressor? What if the aggressor threatens a counter-city strike? Surrender would be intolerable, and yet we cannot ourselves threaten mass murder in response. Fortunately (again), we don't have to. "We do not need . . . to threaten that we will use [nuclear weapons] in case of attack," Bernard Brodie has written. "We do not need to threaten anything. Their being there is quite enough." So it is, too, according to Ramsey, with counter-city strikes: the mere possession of nuclear weapons constitutes an implicit threat which no one actually has to make. If the immorality lies in uttering the threat, then it may in practice be avoided—though one may wonder at the ease of this solution. Nuclear weapons, Ramsey writes, have a certain inherent ambiguity: "they may be used either against strategic forces or against centers of population," and that means that "*apart from intention*, their capacity to deter cannot be removed from them . . . No matter how often we declare, and quite sincerely declare, that our targets are an enemy's forces, he can never be quite *certain* that in the fury or the fog of war his cities may not be destroyed." Now, the possession of conventional weapons is both innocent and ambiguous in exactly the way Ramsey suggests. The fact that I am holding a sword or a rifle doesn't mean that I am going to use it against innocent people, though it is quite effective against them; it has the same "dual use" that Ramsey has discovered in nuclear weapons. But the bomb is different. In a sense, as Beaufre has said, it isn't designed for war at all. It is designed to kill whole populations, and its deterrent value depends upon that fact (whether the killing is direct or indirect). It serves the purpose of preventing war only by virtue of the implicit threat it poses, and we possess it for the sake of that purpose. And men and women are responsible for the threats they live by, even if they don't speak them out loud.

Ramsey presses on. Perhaps the mere possession of nuclear weapons won't be enough to deter some reckless aggressor. Then, he suggests, we must distinguish "between the appearance and the actuality of being . . . committed to go to city exchanges . . . In that case, only the appearance should be cultivated." I am not sure exactly what that means, and Ramsey (for once) seems reluctant to say, but presumably it would allow us to hint at the possibility of massive retaliation without actually planning for it or intending to carry it out. Thus we are offered a continuum of increasing moral danger along which four points are marked out: the articulated prospect of collateral (and disproportionate) civilian deaths; the implicit threat of counter-city strikes; the "cultivated" appearance of a commitment to counter-city strikes; and the actual commitment. These may well be distinct points, in the sense that one can imagine

policies focused around each of them, and these would be different policies. But I am inclined to doubt that the differences make a difference. To rule out the last for moral reasons, while permitting the first three, can only make people cynical about one's moral reasons. Ramsey aims to clear our intentions without prohibiting those policies that he believes necessary (and that probably are necessary under present conditions) for the dual prevention of war and conquest. But the unavoidable truth is that all these policies rest ultimately on immoral threats. Unless we give up nuclear deterrence, we cannot give up such threats, and it is best if we straightforwardly acknowledge what it is we are doing.

The real ambiguity of nuclear deterrence lies in the fact that no one, including ourselves, can be sure that we will ever carry out the threats we make. In a sense, all we ever do is to "cultivate the appearance." We strain for credibility, but what we are putatively planning and intending remains incredible. As I have already suggested, that helps make deterrence psychologically bearable, and perhaps also it makes a deterrent posture marginally better from a moral standpoint. But at the same time, the reason for our hesitancy and self-doubt is the monstrous immorality that our policy contemplates, an immorality we can never hope to square with our understanding of justice in war. Nuclear weapons explode the theory of just war. They are the first of mankind's technological innovations that are simply not encompassable within the familiar moral world. Or rather, our familiar notions about *jus in bello* require us to condemn even the threat to use them. And yet there are other notions, also familiar, having to do with aggression and the right of self-defense, that seem to require exactly that threat. So we move uneasily beyond the limits of justice for the sake of justice (and of peace).

According to Ramsey, this is a dangerous move. For if we "become convinced," he writes, "that in the matter of deterrence a number of things are wicked which are not," then, seeing no way of avoiding wickedness, we will "set no limits on it." Once again, this argument is precisely right with reference to conventional warfare; it catches the central error of what I have called the "war is hell" doctrine. But it is persuasive in the case of nuclear warfare only if one can describe plausible and morally significant limits, and that Ramsey has not done; nor have the strategists of "flexible response" been able to do it. All their arguments depend upon the ultimate wickedness of counter-city strikes. The pretense that this is not so carries with it dangers of its own. To draw insignificant lines, to maintain the formal categories of double effect, collateral damage, noncombatant immunity, and so on, when so little moral content remains is to corrupt the argument for justice as a whole and to render it suspect even in those areas of military life to which it properly pertains. And those areas are wide. Nuclear deterrence marks their outer limits, forcing us to contemplate wars that can never be fought. Within those limits there are wars that can and will and perhaps even should be fought, and to which the old rules apply with all their force. The specter of a nuclear holocaust does not invite us to act wickedly in conventional wars. Indeed, it probably is a deterrent there, too; it is hard to imagine a repetition of Dresden or Tokyo in a conventional war between nuclear powers. For destruction on such a scale would invite a nuclear response and a drastic and unacceptable escalation of the struggle.

Nuclear war is and will remain morally unacceptable, and there is no case for its rehabilitation. Because it is unacceptable, we must seek out ways to prevent it, and because deterrence is a bad way, we must seek out others. It is not my purpose here to suggest what the alternatives might look like. I have been more concerned to acknowledge that deterrence itself, for all its criminality, falls or may fall for the moment under the standard of necessity. But as with terror bombing, so here with the threat of terrorism: supreme emergency is never a stable position. The realm of necessity is subject to historical change. And, what is more important, we are under an obligation to seize upon opportunities of escape, even to take risks for the sake of such opportunities. So the readiness to murder is balanced, or should be, by the readiness not to murder, not to threaten murder, as soon as alternative ways to peace can be found.

NOTES

1. Would it make any difference if this commitment were mechanically fixed? Suppose we set up a computer which would automatically respond to any enemy attack by releasing our missiles. Then we informed our potential enemies that if they attacked our cities, theirs would be attacked. And they would be responsible for both attacks, we might say, since in the interval between the two, no political decision, no act of the will, would be possible on our side. I don't want to comment on the possible effectiveness (or the dangers) of such an arrangement. But it is worth insisting that it would not solve the moral problem. The men and women who designed the computer program or the political leaders who ordered them to do so would be responsible for the second attack, for they would have planned it and organized it and intended that it should occur (under certain conditions).

2. This is obviously the grim logic of nuclear proliferation. So far as the moral question goes, each new balance of terror created by proliferation is exactly like the first one, justified (or not) in the same way. But the creation of regional balances may well have general effects upon the stability of the great power equilibrium, thereby introducing new moral considerations that I cannot take up here.

Jonathan Schell

THE CONTRADICTION OF NUCLEAR DETERRENCE

Jonathan Schell claims there is a contradiction at the heart of our deterrence doctrine: in the hope of avoiding the extinction of the human race, we threaten a massive nuclear attack that could bring about that fate. We both intend to do something (threatening presumably involves an intention to carry out the threat) and intend not to do it. Schell points out that deterrence doctrine differs from traditional military doctrine in that it envisions the possibility of mutual annihilation before either side exhausts its forces. Deterrence doctrine is also said to differ from traditional military doctrine in that it lacks a credible motive for a second strike. In the traditional doctrine, each side could always try for victory if deterrence failed. But in a large-scale nuclear war, victory is not possible; only irrational commitment or revenge could motivate a second strike.

THE CENTRAL PROPOSITION OF the deterrence doctrine—the piece of logic on which the world theoretically depends to see the sun rise tomorrow—is that a nuclear holocaust can best be prevented if each nuclear power, or bloc of powers, holds in readiness a nuclear force with which it "credibly" threatens to destroy the entire society of any attacker, even after suffering the worst possible "first strike" that the attacker can launch. Robert McNamara, who served as Secretary of Defense for seven years under Presidents Kennedy and Johnson, defined the policy, in his book "The Essence of Security," published in 1968, in the following terms: "Assured destruction is the very essence of the whole deterrence concept. We must possess an actual assured-destruction capability, and that capability also must be credible. The point is that a potential aggressor must believe that our assured-destruction capability is in fact actual, and that our will to use it in retaliation to an attack is in fact unwavering." Thus, deterrence "means the certainty of suicide to the aggressor, not merely to his military forces, but to his society as a whole." Let us picture what is going on here. There are two possible eventualities: success of the strategy or its failure. If it succeeds, both sides are frozen into inaction by fear of retaliation by the other side. If it fails, one side annihilates the other, and then the leaders of the second side annihilate the "society as a whole" of the attacker, and the earth as a whole suffers the consequences of a full-scale holocaust, which might include the extinction of man. In point of fact, neither the United States nor the Soviet Union has ever adopted the "mutual-assured-destruction" doctrine in pure form; other aims, such as attempting to reduce the damage of the adversary's nuclear attack and increasing the capacity for destroying the nuclear forces of the adversary, have been mixed in. Nevertheless, underlying these deviations the concept of deterring a first strike by preserving the capacity for a devastating second strike has remained constant. The strategists of deterrence have addressed the chief issue in any sane policy in a nuclear-armed world—the issue of survival—and have come up with this answer: Salvation from extinction by nuclear weapons is to be found in the nuclear weapons themselves. The possession of nuclear weapons by the great powers, it is believed, will prevent the use of nuclear weapons by those same powers. Or, to put it more accurately, the threat of their use by those powers will prevent their use. Or, in the words of Bernard Brodie, a pioneer in nuclear strategy, in "The Absolute Weapon: Atomic Power and World Order," a book published in 1946: "Thus far, the chief purpose of our military establishment has been to win wars. From now on its chief purpose must be to avert them. It can have almost no other useful purpose." Or, in the classic, broad formulation of Winston Churchill, in a speech to the House of Commons in 1955: "Safety will be the sturdy child of terror, and survival the twin brother of annihilation."

This doctrine, in its detailed as well as its more general formulations, is diagrammatic of the world's failure to come to terms with the nuclear predicament. In it, two irreconcilable purposes clash. The first purpose is to permit the survival of the species, and this is expressed in the doctrine's aim of frightening everybody into holding back from using nuclear weapons at all; the second purpose is to serve national ends, and this is expressed in the doctrine's permitting the defense of one's nation and its interests by threatening to use nuclear weapons. The strategists are pleased to call this clash of two opposing purposes in one doctrine a paradox, but in actuality it is a contradiction. We cannot both threaten ourselves with something and hope to avoid that same thing by making the threat—both intend to do something and intend not to do it. The head-on contradiction between these aims has set up a crosscurrent of tension within the policies of each superpower. The "safety" that Churchill mentions may be emphasized at one moment, and at the next moment it is the "terror" that comes to the fore. And since the deterrence doctrine pairs the safety and the terror, and makes the former depend on the latter, the world is never quite sure from day to day which one is in the ascendant—if, indeed, the distinction can be maintained in the first place. All that the world can know for certain is that at any moment the fireballs may arrive. I have said that we do not have two earths, one to blow up experimentally and the other to live on; nor do we have two souls, one for reacting to daily life and the other for reacting to the peril to all life. But neither do we have two wills, one with which we can intend to destroy our species and the other with which we can intend to save ourselves. Ultimately, we must all live together with one soul and one will on our one earth.

For all that, the adoption of the deterrence doctrine represented a partial recognition that the traditional military doctrine had become an anachronism—a doctrine that was suited well enough to the pre-nuclear world but lost all application and relevance when the first nuclear bomb flashed over the New Mexico desert. In assessing the advance made by deterrence, we must acknowledge how radically it departed from traditional military doctrine. Traditional military doctrine and nuclear doctrine are based on wholly different factual circumstances, each set of which corresponds to the technical realities of its period. Traditional military doctrine began, as I have suggested, with the premise that the amounts of force available to the belligerents were small enough to permit one side or the other to exhaust itself before both sides were annihilated. Nuclear doctrine, on the other hand, begins with the premise that the amounts of force are so great that both sides, and perhaps all mankind, will be annihilated before either side exhausts its forces. Like postulates in geometry, these two premises determine the entire systems of thought that follow, and no discussion of military strategy can make any sense unless one clearly specifies which premise one is starting from. But, as I pointed out at some length at the outset of these observations, there is no longer room for doubt that in our time the second premise is the correct one.

The chief virtue of the doctrine of nuclear deterrence is that it begins by accepting this basic fact of life in the nuclear world, and does so not only on the rhetorical plane but on the practical plane of strategic planning. Hence, it acknowledges that victory can no longer be obtained in a contest between two well-armed nuclear powers, such as the United States and the Soviet Union. Senator Barry Goldwater wrote a book, published in 1962, whose title was "Why Not Victory?" To this question the strategists of deterrence have a decisive answer: Because in the present-day, nuclear world "victory" is oblivion. From this recognition flows the conclusion, arrived at by Brodie in 1946, that the sole purpose of possessing nuclear strategic arms is not to win war but to prevent it. The adoption of the aim of preventing rather than winning war requires the adoption of other policies that fly in the face of military tradition. One is abandonment of the military defense of one's nation—of what used to be at the center of all military planning and was the most hallowed justification of the military calling. The policy of deterrence does not contemplate doing anything in defense of the homeland; it only promises that if the homeland is annihilated the aggressor's homeland will be annihilated, too. In fact, the policy goes further than this: it positively requires that each side leave its population open to attack, and make no serious effort to protect it. This requirement follows from the basic logic of deterrence, which is that safety is "the sturdy child of terror." According to this logic, the safety can be only as great as the terror is, and the terror therefore has to be kept relentless. If it were to be diminished—by, for example, building bomb shelters that protected some significant part of the population—then safety would be diminished, too, because the protected side might be tempted to launch a holocaust, in the belief that it could "win" the hostilities. That is why in nuclear strategy "destruction" must, perversely, be "assured," as though our aim were to destroy, and not to save, mankind.

In strategic terms, the requirement that the terror be perfected, and never allowed to deteriorate toward safety, translates into the requirement that the retaliatory force of both sides be guaranteed—first, by making sure that the retaliatory weapons cannot be destroyed in a first strike, and, second, by making sure that the society of the attacking power *can* be destroyed in the second strike. And since in this upside-down scheme of things the two sides will suffer equally no matter which one opens the hostilities, each side actually has an interest in maintaining its adversary's retaliatory forces as well as its own. For the most dangerous of all the configurations of forces is that in which one side appears to have the ability to destroy the nuclear forces of the other in a first strike. Then not only is the stronger side theoretically tempted to launch hostilities but—what is probably far more dangerous—the other side, fearful of completely losing its forces, might, in a crisis, feel compelled to launch the first strike itself. If on either side the population becomes relatively safe from attack or the retaliatory strike becomes vulnerable to attack, a temptation to launch a first strike is created, and "stability"—the leading virtue of any nuclear balance of power—is lost. As Thomas Schelling, the economist and noted nuclear theorist, has put it, in "The Strategy of Conflict," a book published in 1960, once instability is introduced on either side, both sides may reason as follows: "He, thinking I was about to kill him in self-defense, was about to kill me in self-defense, so I had to kill him

in self-defense." Under deterrence, military "superiority" is therefore as dangerous to the side that possesses it as it is to the side that is supposedly threatened by it. (According to this logic, the United States should have heaved a sigh of relief when the Soviet Union reached nuclear parity with it, for then stability was achieved.) All these conclusions follow from the deterrence doctrine, yet they run so consistently counter to the far simpler, more familiar, and emotionally more comprehensible logic of traditional military thinking—not to mention instinct and plain common sense, which rebel against any such notion as "assuring" our own annihilation—that we should not be surprised when we find that the deterrence doctrine is constantly under challenge from traditional doctrine, no matter how glaringly at odds with the facts traditional doctrine may be. The hard-won gains of deterrence, such as they are, are repeatedly threatened by a recrudescence of the old desire for victory, for national defense in the old sense, and for military superiority, even though every one of these goals not only would add nothing to our security but, if it should be pursued far enough, would undermine the precarious safety that the deterrence doctrine tries to provide.

If the virtue of the deterrence policy lies in its acceptance of the basic fact of life in the nuclear world—that a holocaust will bring annihilation to both sides, and possibly the extinction of man as well—its defect lies in the strategic construct that it erects on the foundation of that fact. For if we try to guarantee our safety by threatening ourselves with doom, then we have to mean the threat; but if we mean it, then we are actually planning to do, in some circumstance or other, that which we categorically must never do and are supposedly trying to prevent—namely, extinguish ourselves. This is the circularity at the core of the nuclear-deterrence doctrine; we seek to avoid our self-extinction by threatening to perform the act. According to this logic, it is almost as though if we stopped threatening ourselves with extinction, then extinction would occur. Brodie's formula can be reversed: if the aim of having nuclear forces is to avert annihilation (misnamed "war" by him), then we must cling for our lives to those same forces. Churchill's dictum can be reversed, too: If safety is the sturdy child of terror, then terror is equally the sturdy child of safety. But who is to guarantee which of the children will be born? And if survival is the twin brother of annihilation, then we must cultivate annihilation. But then we may *get* annihilation. By growing to actually rely on terror, we do more than tolerate its presence in our world: we place our trust in it. And while this is not quite to "love the bomb," as the saying goes, it decidedly is to place our faith in it, and to give it an all-important position in the very heart of our affairs. Under this doctrine, instead of getting rid of the bomb we build it ever more deeply into our lives.

The logical fault line in the doctrine runs straight through the center of its main strategic tenet—the proposition that safety is achieved by assuring that any nuclear aggressor will be annihilated in a retaliatory strike. For while the doctrine relies for its success on a nuclear-armed victim's resolve to launch the annihilating second strike, it can offer no sensible or sane justification for launching it in the event. In pre-nuclear military strategy, the deterrent effect of force was a useful by-product of the ability and willingness to wage and win wars. Deterrence was the shadow cast by force, or, in Clausewitz's metaphor, the credit that flowed from the ability to make the cash payment of the favorable decision by arms. The logic of pre-nuclear deterrence escaped circularity by each side's being frankly ready to wage war and try for victory if deterrence failed. Nuclear deterrence, however, supposedly aims solely at forestalling any use of force by either side, and has given up at the outset on a favorable decision by arms. The question, then, is: Of what object is nuclear deterrence the shadow? Of what cash payment is it the credit? The theoretical answer, of course, is: The retaliatory strike. Yet since in the nuclear-deterrence theory the whole purpose of having a retaliatory capacity is to deter a first strike, one must ask what reason would remain to launch the retaliation once the first strike had actually arrived. Nuclear deterrence requires one to prepare for armed conflict not in order to "win" it if it breaks out but in order to prevent it from breaking out in the first place. But if armed conflict breaks out anyway, what does one do with one's forces then? In pre-nuclear times, the answer would have required no second thought: it would have been to strive for the decision by arms—for victory. Yet nuclear deterrence begins by assuming, correctly, that victory is impossible. Thus, the logic of the deterrence strategy is dissolved by the very event—the first strike—that it is meant to prevent. Once the action begins, the whole doctrine is self-cancelling. In sum, the doctrine is based on a monumental logical mistake: one cannot credibly deter a first strike with a second strike whose *raison d'être* dissolves the moment the first strike arrives. It follows that, as far as deterrence theory is concerned, there is no reason for either side not to launch a first strike.

What seems to be needed to repair the doctrine is a motive for retaliation—one that is not supplied by the doctrine itself and that lies outside its premises—but the only candidates are those belonging to traditional military doctrine; namely, some variation of victory. The adherents of nuclear victory—whatever that would be—have on occasion noted the logical fallacy on which deterrence is based, and stepped forward to propose their solution: a "nuclear-war-fighting" capacity. Thus, the answer they give to the question of what to do after the first strike arrives is: Fight and "win" a "nuclear war." But victory does not suddenly become possible simply because it offers a solution to the logical contradiction on which the mutual-assured-destruction doctrine rests. The facts remain obdurately what they are: an attack of several thousand megatons will annihilate any country on earth many times over, no matter what line of argument the strategists pursue; and a "nuclear exchange" will, if it is on a large scale, threaten the life of man. Indeed, if victory were really possible there would have been no need for a deterrence strategy to begin with, and traditional military strategy would have needed no revision. This "solution" is therefore worse than the error it sets out to remedy. It resolves the contradiction in the deterrence doctrine by denying the tremendous new reality that the doctrine was framed to deal with, and that all of us now have to deal with on virtually every level of our existence. Consequently, this "solution" could lead us to commit the ultimate folly of exterminating ourselves without even knowing what we were doing. Aiming at "victory," we would wind up extinct.

In the last analysis, there can be no credible threat without credible use—no shadow without an object, no credit without cash payment. But since use is the thing above all else that we don't want, because it means the end of all of us, we are naturally at a loss to find any rationale for it. To grasp the reality of the contradiction, we have only to picture the circumstances of leaders whose country has just been annihilated in a first strike. Now their country is on its way to becoming a radioactive desert, but the retaliatory nuclear force survives in its silos, bombers, and submarines. These leaders of nobody, living in underground shelters or in "doomsday" planes that could not land, would possess the means of national defense but no nation to defend. What rational purpose could they have in launching the retaliatory strike? Since there was no longer a nation, "national security" could not be the purpose. Nor could defense of other peoples be the purpose, since the retaliatory strike might be the action that would finally break the back of the ecosphere and extinguish the species. In these circumstances, it seems to me, it is really an open question whether the leaders would decide to retaliate or not.

This conclusion is not one that is likely to be breathed aloud by anyone in or near power in either the Soviet Union or the United States. Since deterrence depends fully as much on one's adversary's perception of one's "unwavering" will to retaliate as on one's technical ability to do it, an acknowledgment that retaliation is senseless would in a way amount to unilateral disarmament by verbal means. The doctrine of nuclear deterrence thus deters debate about itself, and this incidental "deterrence" may have been no small factor in the sharp limits placed on the definition of "respectable," so-called "realistic" thinking about nuclear strategy. Nevertheless, the contradiction at the heart of the doctrine has occasioned considerable indirect intellectual twisting and turning among the nuclear theorists, and the resulting recommendations lead one into byways of the maze of strategic theory which stand out as bizarre and frightening even for the catalogues of nuclear strategic "options." The commonest solution to the problem of the missing motive for retaliation is to suggest that the policymakers try to cultivate an appearance of unreason, for if one is insane one doesn't need to supply any motive for retaliating— one might do it simply out of madness. The nuclear theorist Herman Kahn, for example, suggests that "it might best deter the attack" by an "*appearance of irrationally inexorable commitment*." Kahn first wonders whether it might not be enough merely to "pretend" to be irrationally committed, but he concludes that a pretense of unreason is not reliable,

and that one must "*really intend to do it.*" The prescription, then, which he calls the policy of "the rationality of irrationality," is to coolly resolve to be crazy. How statesmen are to go about this, Kahn does not say. Another solution, quite closely related, is to try to create either the appearance or the reality of being out of control. Uncontrol, like insanity, removes the need for a rational motive in retaliating, this time by arranging for the retaliation to occur "by accident." Thomas Schelling, addressing the general question "How can one commit himself in advance to an act that he would in fact prefer not to carry out in the event?," suggests the tactic either of pretending that the crucial decisions will be in part up to "chance" or of actually arranging things so that this is true, thus adding to Kahn's concept of reasoned insanity the planned accident. With this strategy in effect, he writes, "the brink is not . . . the sharp edge of a cliff, where one can stand firmly, look down, and decide whether or not to plunge." Rather, "the brink is a curved slope that one can stand on with some risk of slipping." Therefore, "brinkmanship involves getting onto the slope where one may fall in spite of his own best efforts to save himself, dragging his adversary with him." That these astonishing remedies are no less consequential in the real world than the doctrinal illogicality they try to remedy is testified to by, among other things, a statement in the memoirs of President Richard Nixon's chief of staff H. R. Haldeman that Nixon believed in the "Madman Theory" of the Presidency, according to which the nation's foes would bow to the President's will if they believed that he had taken leave of his senses and was ready to risk a holocaust in order to secure some limited national gain. Whether or not Nixon had read the writings of Kahn and Schelling, he was following their counsel to the letter.

The recommendation of these tactics naturally raises the question of whether, with the life of our species at stake, we want our nuclear decision-makers to be cultivating irrationality and uncontrol, and whether a slippery slope over the nuclear abyss is where we all want to be. But these questions, which I think must be answered with a resounding "no," come up only as a consequence of our reliance on "terror" to provide "safety," and on the threat of "annihilation" to provide "survival." For it is in an effort to strengthen and shore up the terror and make annihilation more certain that the strategists and statesmen are forced into these appalling postures. Their problem is to find a way of appearing "inexorably" resolved to do things that can never make any sense or ever be justified by any moral code, and irrationality and uncontrol fulfill the requirements for the very reason that they represent the abandonment of morality and sense. Adopted as policy, they lend credibility to actions that are—conveniently for strategic purposes, if not for the safety of mankind—immoral and insane.

It must be added that there is another extreme solution, which would entirely remove the defect in the doctrine of nuclear deterrence. This solution, described (but not recommended) by Kahn, would be to construct a literal doomsday machine, which would blow up the whole world as soon as an adversary engaged in some activity that had previously been defined as "unacceptable" by the machine's possessor. Kahn, who estimated in 1960 that a doomsday machine might be built for as little as ten billion dollars, points out that the machine would eliminate any doubt concerning the retaliatory strike by making it fully automatic. The retaliatory strike would still be senseless, but this senselessness would no longer cloud its "credibility," since the action would have been predetermined: the foundation would have been provided for a fully consistent policy of nuclear deterrence, under which nations would be deterred from launching nuclear attacks by the prearranged certainty that their own countries would perish in the ensuing global annihilation. But Kahn is also quick to point out a disadvantage of the doomsday machine which makes its construction immediately repugnant and intolerable to anyone who thinks about it: once it is in place, "there is no chance of human intervention, control, and final decision." And behind this objection, we may add, is an even simpler and more basic one: the chief reason we don't want a doomsday machine is that we don't want doom—not in any circumstances. Doom doesn't become any more acceptable because it comes about as someone's "final decision." And, of course, even though no enemy attack has been launched, in a moment of computer confusion the doomsday machine might make its own "final decision" to go off.

Because deterrence, on which we all now rely for whatever safety we have, is a psychological strategy, which aims at terrorizing the adversary into holding back from attacking us, it might seem that the discovery in one or the other command center of the logical absurdity of the policy would lead to the breakdown of the system—or, at least, to the abandonment of the doctrine. That this has not occurred is an indication that, even in the abstruse realm of nuclear doctrine, theory and practice, thought and reality are still different. In the real world, there are several stand-ins for the missing motive for the crucial retaliatory strike. The first stand-in is revenge, which, even though retaliation is not a rational action, might cause it to be carried out anyway. According to the emotional logic of revenge, the living act to right the wrong inflicted on the unjustly slain, who, being dead, cannot themselves realign the unbalanced scales of justice. Revenge is neither sensible nor constructive—especially not in a nuclear holocaust—but it is human, and the possibility that it would well up in the breasts of the leaders of a country that has just been effaced from the earth can by no means be ruled out by an aggressor; he has to consider that, even without any irrationality of the planned sort, a "rational" response to a nuclear attack can hardly be counted on. The second, and perhaps more important, stand-in for the missing motive is the irreducible unpredictability of events once the nuclear threshold is crossed. At this verge, with the survival of the species at stake, the human mind falters. The leaders of the nuclear powers have no choice, as they stare into McNamara's "vast unknown," but to assume that the stakes are total. Certainly there is no need for anyone to strain to appear irrational, as Kahn suggests, or out of control, as Schelling suggests: a world that has embarked on a holocaust is in its nature irrational and out of control.

Our experience of nuclear crises leads us to believe that when the leaders of nuclear powers are forced to contemplate the reality of a holocaust at close quarters they have looked on it in this light. That is, they have assumed that if limited nuclear war, or even conventional war between the superpowers, breaks out, a holocaust is the likely result. Michael Mandelbaum, in his history of nuclear strategy and experience, "The Nuclear Question," published in 1979, observes that when the Soviet and American leaders confronted one another in the Cuban missile crisis they discovered that the fearful nature of a holocaust, which during the days of the crisis partly emerged from abstraction and unreality to become almost palpable in people's emotions, strongly deterred them from inaugurating hostilities at no matter how minor a level. Brought face to face with the beast, both sides realized that "there was no way to fight a nuclear war." Thus, "in striving to avoid having to fight a nuclear war they took great care not to start a war of any kind, which they feared would become nuclear." This lesson of experience offered some complementary lessons. One was that although no one had decided to establish a doomsday machine, people had to act as though one were in place. They had to assume that one misstep could be the misstep that ended the world. The notion that there was a middle ground of "tactical" nuclear hostilities of a limited kind, or even of conventional hostilities, disappeared under the awful pressure of the crisis. The doorway to the "vast unknown" seemed always right at hand, and all the scenarios of "limited war" and the like tended to crumble.

A final "deterrent," which, although fallible, is both rational and human, but which goes unmentioned in deterrence theory, is the humanity of the leaders of the nuclear powers. History is crowded with ruthless, berserk actions, yet there are none that have attained the horror and insanity of a nuclear holocaust, and very few that have gone as far as the worst crime of which we do have experience—genocide. I believe that without indulging in wishful thinking we can grant that the present leaders of both the Soviet Union and the United States are considerably deterred from launching a nuclear holocaust by sheer aversion to the unspeakable act itself.

George F. Kennan

THE WAY OUT OF THE NUCLEAR DILEMMA

George Kennan argues that the United States should attempt to put an end to the nuclear arms race by proposing to the Soviet Union an immediate across-the-board 50 percent reduction of nuclear arsenals. Even with such a reduction, Kennan claims, there would still be plenty of overkill left. Moreover, Kennan thinks, when you weigh the risks of endorsing such a proposal against those of the current U.S. policy of continuing the arms race, there is no reasonable alternative.

WHAT CAN WE DO?

Adequate words are lacking to express the full seriousness of our present situation. It is not just that the US is for the moment on a collision course politically with the Soviet Union, and that the process of rational communication between the two governments seems to have broken down completely; it is also—and even more importantly—the fact that the ultimate sanction behind the conflicting policies of these two governments is a type and volume of weaponry which could not possibly be used without utter disaster for us all.

From "The Way Out of the Nuclear Dilemma," *Bulletin of Peace Proposals* (1981), pp. 221–224. Reprinted by permission of the *Bulletin of Peace Proposals*.

For over thirty years wise and far-seeing people have been warning us about the futility of any war fought with nuclear weapons and about the dangers involved in their cultivation. Some of the first of these voices to be raised are those of great scientists, including outstandingly that of Albert Einstein himself. But there has been no lack of others. Every president of the United States from Dwight Eisenhower to Jimmy Carter, has tried to remind us that there could be no such thing as victory in a war fought with such weapons. So have a great many other eminent persons.

When one looks back today over the history of these warnings, one has the impression that something has now been lost of the sense of urgency, the hopes, and the excitement that initially inspired them, so many years ago. One senses, even on the part of those who today most acutely perceive the problem and are inwardly most exercised about it, a certain discouragement, resignation, perhaps even despair, when it comes to the question of raising the subject again.

The danger is so obvious. So much as already been said. What is to be gained by reiteration? What good would it now do? Look at the record. Over all these years the competition in the development of nuclear weaponry has proceeded steadily, relentlessly, without the faintest regard for all these warning voices. We have gone on piling weapon upon weapon, missile upon missile, new levels of destructiveness upon old ones. We have done this helplessly, almost involuntarily: like the victims of some sort of hypnotism, like men in a dream, like lemmings heading for the sea, like the children of Hamelin marching blindly along behind their Pied Piper.

And the result is that today we have achieved, we and the Russians together, in the creation of these devices and their means of delivery, levels of redundancy of such grostesque dimensions as to defy rational understanding.

I say redundancy. I know of no better way to describe it. But actually, the word is too mild. It implies that there could be levels of these weapons that would not be redundant. Personally, I doubt that there could. I question whether these devices are really weapons at all. A true weapon is at best something with which you endeavour to affect the behaviour of another society by influencing the minds, the calculations, the intentions, of the men that control

it; it is not something with which you destroy indiscriminately the lives, the substance, the hopes, the culture, the civilisation, of another people. What a confession of intellectual poverty it would be—what a bankruptcy of intelligent statesmanship—if we had to admit that such blind, senseless acts of destruction were the best use we could make of what we have come to view as the leading elements of our military strength!

To my mind, the nuclear bomb is the most useless weapon ever invented. It can be employed to no rational purpose. It is not even an effective defence against itself. It is only something with which, in a moment of petulance or panic, you commit such fearful acts of destruction as no sane person would ever wish to have upon his conscience.

There are those who will agree, with a sigh, to much of what I have just said, but will point to the need for something called deterrence. This is, of course, a concept which attributes to others—to others, who, like ourselves, were born of women, walk on two legs, and love their children, to human beings, in short—the most fiendish and inhuman of tendencies. But all right: accepting for the sake of argument the profound iniquity of these adversaries, no one could deny, I think, that the present Soviet and American arsenals, presenting over a million times the destructive power of the Hiroshima bomb, are simply fantastically redundant to the purpose in question.

If the same relative proportions were to be preserved, something well less than twenty per cent of these stocks would surely suffice for the most sanguine concepts of deterrence, whether as between the two nuclear superpowers or with relation to any of those other governments that have been so ill-advised as to enter upon the nuclear path. Whatever their suspicions of each other there can be no excuse on the part of these two governments for holding, poised against each other and poised in a sense against the whole northern hemisphere, quantities of these weapons so vastly in excess of any rational and demonstrable requirements.

How have we got ourselves into this dangerous mess? Let us not confuse the question by blaming it all on our Soviet adversaries. They have, of course, their share of the blame, and not least in their cavalier dismissal of the Baruch Plan so many years ago. They too have made their mistakes, and I should be the last to deny it. But we must remember that it has been we Americans who, at almost every step of the road, have taken the lead in the development of this sort of weaponry. It was we who first produced and tested such a device; we who were the first to raise its destructiveness to a new level with the hydrogen bomb; we who introduced the multiple warhead; we who have declined every proposal for the renunciation of the principle of 'first use,' and we alone, so help us God, who have used the weapon in anger against others, and against tens of thousands of helpless noncombatants at that.

I know that reasons were offered for some of these things. I know that others might have taken this sort of a lead, had we not done so. But let us not, in the face of this record, so lose ourselves in self-righteousness and hypocrisy as to forget our own measure of complicity in creating the situation we face today.

What is it then, if not our own will, and if not the supposed wickedness of our opponents, that has brought us to this pass?

The answer, I think, is clear. It is primarily the inner momentum, the independent momentum, of the weapons race itself—the compulsions that arise and take charge of great powers when they enter upon a competition with each other in the building up of major armaments of any sort.

Is it possible to break out of this charmed and vicious circle? It is sobering to recognize that no one, at least to my knowledge, has yet done so. But no one, for that matter, has ever been faced with such great catastrophe, such unalterable catastrophe, at the end of the line. Others, in earlier decades, could befuddle themselves with dreams of something called 'victory.' We, perhaps fortunately, are denied this seductive prospect. We have to break out of the circle. We have no other choice.

How are we to do it?

I must confess that I see no possibility of doing this by means of discussion along the lines of the negotiations that have been in progress, off and on, over this past decade under the acronoym of SALT. I regret, to be sure, that the most recent SALT agreement has not been ratified. I regret it, because if the benefits to be expected from that agreement were slight, its disadvantages were even slighter, and it had a symbolic value which should not have been so lightly sacrificed.

But I have, I repeat, no illusion that negotiations on the SALT pattern—negotiations, that is, in which each side is obsessed with the chimera of relative advantage and strives only to retain a maximum of the weaponry for itself while putting its opponent to the maximum disadvantage—I have no illusion that such negotiations could ever be adequate to get us out of this hole. They are not a way of escape from the weapons race, they are an integral part of it.

Whoever does not understand that when it comes to nuclear weapons, the whole concept of relative advantage is illusory—whoever does not understand that when you are talking about absurd and preposterous quantities of overkill the relative sizes of arsenals have no serious meaning—whoever does not understand that the danger lies not in the possibility that someone else might have more missiles and warheads than we do but in the very existence of these unconscionable quantities of highly poisonous explosives, and their existence, above all, in hands as weak and shaky and undependable as those of ourselves or our adversaries or any other mere human beings: whoever does not understand these things is never going to guide us out of this increasingly dark and menacing forest of bewilderments into which we have all wandered.

I can see no way out of this dilemma other than by a bold and sweeping departure—a departure that would cut surgically through the exaggerated anxieties, the self-engendered nightmares, and the sophisticated mathematics of destruction, in which we have all been entangled over these recent years, and would permit us to move, with courage and decision, to the heart of the problem.

President Reagan recently said, and I think very wisely, that he would 'negotiate as long as necessary to reduce the numbers of nuclear weapons to a point where neither side threatens the survival of the other.' Now that is, of course, precisely the thought to which these present observations of mine are addressed. But I wonder whether the negotiations would really have to be at such great length?

What I would like to see the President do, after due consultation with the Congress, would be to propose to the Soviet government *an immediate across-the-boards reduction by fifty per cent of the nuclear arsenals now being maintained by the two superpowers—a reduction affecting in equal measure all forms of the weapon, strategic, medium range, and tactical, as well as all means of their delivery—all this to be implemented at once and without further wrangling among the experts, and to be subject to such national means of verification as now lie at the disposal of the two powers.*

Whether the balance of reduction would be precisely even—whether it could be construed to favour statistically one side or the other would not be the question. Once we start thinking that way, we would be back on the same old fateful track that has brought us where we are today. Whatever the precise results of such a reduction, there would still be plenty of overkill left—so much so that *if this first operation were successful, I would then like to see a second one put in hand to rid us of at least two-thirds of what would be left.*

Now I have, of course, no idea of the scientific aspects of such an operation; but I can imagine that serious problems might be presented by the task of removing, and disposing safely of, the radioactive contents of the many thousands of warheads that would have to be dismantled. Should this be the case, I would like to see the President couple his appeal for a 50 percent reduction with the proposal that *there be established a joint Soviet-American scientific committee, under the chairmanship of a distinguished neutral figure, to study jointly and in all humility the problem not only of the safe disposal of these wastes but also the question of how they could be utilised in such a way as to make a positive contribution to human life,* either in the two countries themselves—or perhaps preferably—elsewhere. In such a joint scientific venture we might both atone of some of our past follies and lay the foundation for a more constructive relationship.

It will be said: this proposal, whatever its merits, deals with only a part of the problem. This is perfectly true. Behind it there would still lurk the serious political differences that now divide us from the Soviet government. Behind it would still lie the problems recently treated, and still to be treated, in the SALT forum. Behind it would still lie the great question of the acceptability of war itself, any war, even a conventional one, as a means of solving problems among great industrial powers.

What has been suggested here would not prejudice the continued treatment of these questions just as today, in whatever forums and under whatever safe-guards the two powers find necessary. The conflict and arguments over these questions could all still proceed to the heart's content of all those who view them with such passionate commitment. The stakes would simply be smaller; and that would be a great relief to all of us.

What I have suggested is, of course, only a beginning. But a beginning has to be made somewhere; and if it has to be made, it is best that it should be made where the dangers are the greatest, and their necessity the last. If a step of this nature could be successfully taken, people might find the heart to tackle with greater confidence and determination the many problems that would still remain.

It will be argued that there would be risks involved. Possibly so. I do not see them. I do not deny the possibility. But if there are, so what? Is it possible to conceive of any dangers greater than those that lie at the end of the collision course on which we are now embarked? And if no, why choose the greater—why choose, in fact, the greatest—of all risks, in the hopes of avoiding the lesser ones?

We are confronted here with two courses. At the end of the one lies hope—faint hope, if you will—uncertain hope, hope surrounded with dangers, if you insist. At the end of the other lies, so far as I am able to see, no hope at all. Can there be—in the light of our duty not just to ourselves (for we are all going to die sooner or later) but of our duty to our own kind, our duty to the continuity of the generations, our duty to the great experiment of civilised life on this rare and rich and marvellous planet—can there be, in the light of these claims on our loyalty, any question as to which course we should adopt?

In the final week of his life, Albert Einstein signed the last of the collective appeals against the development of nuclear weapons that he was ever to sign. He was dead before it appeared. It was an appeal drafted, I gather, by Bertrand Russell. I had my differences with Russell at the time, as I do now in retrospect, but I would like to quote one sentence from the final paragraph of the statement, not only because it was the last one Einstein ever signed, but because it sums up, I think, all that I have to say on the subject. It read as follows:

'We appeal, as human beings to human beings: Remember your humanity, and forget the rest.'

THE NUCLEAR FREEZE RESOLUTION

WHEREAS THE GREATEST CHALLENGE facing the earth is to prevent the occurrence of nuclear war by accident or design;

Whereas the nuclear arms race is dangerously increasing the risk of a holocaust that would be humanity's final war; and

Whereas a freeze followed by reductions in nuclear warheads, missiles, and other delivery systems is needed to halt the nuclear arms race and to reduce the risk of nuclear war;

Resolved by the Senate and the House of Representatives of the United States of America in Congress assembled,

1. As an immediate strategic arms control objective, the United States and the Soviet Union should:

(a) pursue a complete halt to the nuclear arms race;

(b) decide when and how to achieve a mutual and verifiable freeze on the testing, production, and future deployment of nuclear warheads, missiles, and other delivery systems; and

(c) give special attention to destabilizing weapons whose deployment would make such a freeze more difficult to achieve.

2. Proceeding from this freeze, the United States and the Soviet Union should pursue major, mutual, and verifiable reductions in nuclear warheads, missiles, and other delivery systems, through annual percentages of equally effective means, in a manner that enhances stability.

SUGGESTIONS FOR FURTHER READING

Anthologies

Marrin, Albert. *War and the Christian Conscience.* Chicago: Henry Regnery Co., 1971.

Thompson, W. Scott. *From Weakness to Strength.* San Francisco: Institute for Contemporary Studies, 1980.

Wakim, Malham. *War, Morality and the Military Profession.* Boulder: Westview Press, 1979.

Wasserstrom, Richard A. *War and Morality.* Belmont: Wadsworth Publishing Co., 1970.

Basic Concepts

Walters, LeRoy. *Five Classic Just-War Theories.* Ann Arbor: University Microfilms, 1971.

Walzer, Michael. *Just and Unjust Wars.* New York: Basic Books, 1977.

Alternative Views

Allison, Graham T. *Essence of Decision.* Boston: Little, Brown & Co., 1971.

Fallows, James. *National Defense.* New York: Vintage Books, 1981.

Lens, Sidney. *The Day Before Doomsday.* Boston: Beacon Press, 1977.

Kahan, Jerome H. *Security in the Nuclear Age.* Washington, D.C.: The Brookings Institution, 1975.

Mandebaum, Michael. *The Nuclear Question.* Cambridge: Cambridge University Press, 1979.

Practical Application

Barton, John H., and Weiler, Lawrence D. *International Arms Control.* Stanford: Stanford University Press, 1976.

Ground Zero. *Nuclear War.* New York: Pocket Books, 1982.

Kennedy, Edward M., and Hatfield, Mark O. *Freeze.* New York: Bantam Books, 1982.

Senate Joint Resolution 163 and House Joint Resolution 434 (1982).